Communicate!

Communicate!

Fifteenth Edition

Kathleen S. Verderber

Northern Kentucky University

Deanna D. Sellnow

University of Central Florida

Rudolph F. Verderber

Distinguished Teaching Professor of Communication,
University of Cincinnati

CENGAGE
Learning®

Australia • Brazil • Mexico • Singapore • United Kingdom • United States

Communicate!, Fifteenth Edition
Kathleen S. Verderber, Deanna D. Sellnow,
Rudolph F. Verderber

Product Director: Monica Eckman

Product Manager: Kelli Strieby

Content Developer: Kassi Radomski

Associate Content Developer: Karolina Kiwak

Product Assistant: Colin Solan

Media Developer: Jessica Badiner

Marketing Manager: Kristin Davis

Content Project Manager: Dan Saabye

Art Director: Marissa Falco

Manufacturing Planner: Doug Bertke

IP Analyst: Ann Hoffman

IP Project Manager: Farah Fard

Production Service: MPS Limited

Compositor: MPS Limited

Text Designer: Reuter Design

Cover Designer: Red Hangar Design

Cover Image: Shutterstock/Raw Pixel

Design Image: nikkytok/Shutterstock.com

For product information and technology assistance, contact us at
Cengage Learning Customer & Sales Support, 1-800-354-9706

For permission to use material from this text or product,
submit all requests online at **www.cengage.com/permissions**.
Further permissions questions can be emailed to
permissionrequest@cengage.com.

Library of Congress Control Number: 2015940961

Student Edition:

ISBN: 978-1-305-50281-9

Loose-leaf Edition:

ISBN: 978-1-305-65513-3

Cengage Learning
20 Channel Center Street
Boston, MA 02210
USA

Cengage Learning is a leading provider of customized learning solutions
with employees residing in nearly 40 different countries and sales in
more than 125 countries around the world. Find your local representative
at **www.cengage.com**.

Cengage Learning products are represented in Canada by Nelson Education, Ltd.

To learn more about Cengage Learning Solutions, visit **www.cengage.com**.

Purchase any of our products at your local college store or at our preferred
online store **www.cengagebrain.com**.

Brief Contents

Contents

Unit II. Interpersonal Communication & Relationships 119

Preface

I am so happy to be sharing this revised version of *Communicate!* with you and hope you find the changes refreshing and relevant. As you will see, I have paid special attention to providing examples of communication as it occurs not only in face-to-face settings but also through technology-driven ones. I have also included examples of communication in a variety of contexts including friends and family, as well as across cultures and co-cultures. I hope you find this approach compelling and useful.

This edition marks the first time neither Rudy nor Kathie Verderber—the book's original authors—were actively involved in the writing and revision process. However, I have worked hard to remain true to the hallmarks of their work, while also incorporating examples that speak to the new realities of communicating today.

To Students

Congratulations! You are beginning to study communication, a subject that is important and useful to you in all parts of your life. When you want to establish or improve a relationship, when you need to work with others on a group project for class or work, or when you are asked to make a public presentation in person or online, your success will depend on how effectively you communicate in those settings.

The primary goal of this book is and always has been to equip you with the communication skills you need to be successful in your personal relationships and professional endeavors. Over the years, the Verderbers have worked to make sure that students, like you, have a book that is easy and enjoyable to read. Although both Rudy and Kathie are now enjoying retirement and are no longer playing a role in the revisions, the characteristics of their work remain. I have made sure that the information, theories, and skills discussed are relevant to the real relationships and communication situations you face. Today that means providing best practices for communicating effectively across multimodal channels and settings.

As always, *Communicate!* is written with five specific goals in mind:

1. **To explain important research-based communication concepts and theories** of human communication.

2. **To provide tools to practice and assess specific communication skills** in interpersonal, intercultural, group, and public speaking settings, as well as in both face-to-face and virtual environments.

3. **To describe and encourage you to adopt ethical communication strategies** when interacting with others.

4. **To teach you the nuances of communicating effectively in different cultures.**

5. **To stimulate critical and creative thinking** about the concepts and skills you learn as they apply to face-to-face interactions, as well as in technology-mediated ones.

To Instructors

Thank you for considering this new edition of *Communicate!* I believe the revisions will surprise and delight those of you who have used *Communicate!* in the past. I also believe that those of you looking for a new textbook will find this edition of *Communicate!* to be refreshing and engaging. In the sections that follow, I detail what's new and highlight the pre-existing features that have made *Communicate!* a perennial favorite among students and faculty alike.

New to This Edition

- **Increased emphasis on the role of technology and social media.** Because technology and social media now play such a central role in our lives, I have integrated discussions of research findings and best practices into each chapter. These discussions focus on how specific communication concepts operate both similarly and differently in technological and face-to-face environments.

- **A revised chapter on listening** (Chapter 6) that integrates contemporary research on cognitive processes being published today, as well as how technology and social media are changing the way we listen and bring new challenges to listening effectively.

- **A revised chapter on presentational aids** (Chapter 13) to honor the range of visual, audio, and audiovisual aids used so often in speechmaking today.

- A new **sample informative speech outline and transcript on** Internet identity theft.

New features:

- **Student learning outcomes** introduce each chapter to guide students to focus on main points as they read.

- Chapter summaries have been replaced with a **Reflection and Assessment** section asking students to answer key questions about the chapter before moving on to the next chapter.

- **"Apply It" boxes** in the margins encourage readers to reflect on and apply a specific communication concept or skill to their lives.

Revised features:

- **"Pop Comm!"** features have been revised and renamed as **"Communicating in the World"** to better reflect the nature of this feature, which illustrates key communication concepts and theories played out in daily life.

- **Diverse Voices** essays have been streamlined in ways that target cross-cultural communication challenges as told by real people who have experienced them.

- The **Appendix on interviewing** has been updated and revised throughout.

Chapter-by-Chapter Revisions

- **Chapter 1, "Foundations of Communication,"** continues to focus on the fundamental processes of communication and is still organized so that students see the primacy of messages and the canned plans and scripts we use to encode and decode them in different communication settings and through various channels. The chapter now also includes sections on media richness, social presence, and synchronicity as they impact communication and relationships online. The section on communication ethics has been expanded to address both the *bright side* and *dark side* of communication.

- **Chapter 2, "Perception of Self and Others,"** has been updated to reflect current research about self-concept, self-esteem, and how they influence and are influenced by communication. The chapter has also been expanded to explore more fully the role perception processes play in social media interactions.

- **Chapter 3, "Intercultural Communication,"** includes all of the foundational concepts we use to differentiate cultural perspectives from each other. In addition, the chapter focuses on how cultural identity affects communication and presents guidelines for demonstrating empathy and respect when communicating with people from cultures other than your own.

- **Chapter 4, "Verbal Messages," describes** the nature of language and how language and speech communities influence message interpretation. The chapter then explains how message meanings are derived from the words themselves (semantics), the conversational context (pragmatics), and social and cultural contexts (sociolinguistics). Special attention is also paid toward how communicating through technology-mediated channels influences semantic, pragmatic, and sociolinguistic meanings. Finally, specific guidelines for improving skills in constructing and interpreting verbal messages are proposed throughout the chapter.

- **Chapter 5, "Nonverbal Messages,"** has been updated with current research and examples of how nonverbal messages are communicated, interpreted, and misinterpreted in online environments. The chapter also describes the role proxemics (personal space, territorial space, and acoustic space) play when communicating in face-to-face and virtual settings.

- **Chapter 6, "Listening,"** has been updated to reflect what current research tells us about listening processes and challenges, particularly in light of the tendency to multitask at the expense of listening effectiveness. The chapter proposes active listening as a way to overcome these challenges.

- **Chapter 7, "Interpersonal Relationships,"** has been updated with current research and uses the friendship of Whitney and Paige to understand the stages of coming together and apart, as well as the nature of dialectical tensions in relationship.

- **Chapter 8, "Interpersonal Communication,"** has been updated with contemporary research and examples. It focuses on the role of communication in developing and maintaining a positive communication climate and a section on interpersonal conflict management styles.

- **Chapter 9, "Communicating in Groups,"** offers updated examples of types of groups and effective communication within them. It also provides an expanded discussion of virtual groups and effective virtual group communication based on current research.

Finally, the chapter offers an extended discussion about conflict in groups and how to manage it effectively when interacting in face-to-face or virtual environments.

- **Chapter 10, "Group Leadership and Problem Solving,"** focuses specifically on the nature of effective leadership and problem solving in meetings and on work group teams, which includes a comprehensive discussion about communicating group decisions in written, oral, and virtual formats.

- **Chapter 11, "Topic Selection and Development,"** continues to focus on topic selection, research, and speech development based on ongoing audience analysis and adaptation. The chapter also includes a discussion of the pros and cons of using an annotated bibliography or research cards to document information you might use in the speech.

- **Chapter 12, "Organizing Your Speech,"** includes a sample outline on the abuses of the prescription drug Adderall among college students today, as well as an expanded discussion of the rhetorical strategies one can use to gain attention in the introduction.

- **Chapter 13, "Presentational Aids,"** illustrates the role of visual, audio, and audiovisual aids in speechmaking today. In addition to choosing, preparing, and displaying presentational aids, this edition adds a section on using presentational aids during the actual speech.

- **Chapter 14, "Language and Oral Style,"** is devoted exclusively to effective formal oral language style used in public speaking as it differs from written style and casual conversational style. The chapter also highlights what is considered appropriate and inappropriate language, as well as strategies to improve clarity and vivid descriptions.

- **Chapter 15, "Delivery,"** focuses on how to practice conversational and animated delivery using your voice and body. The chapter also illustrates how to use technology to conduct effective rehearsals and to give speeches to multiple audiences when doing speeches online.

- **Chapter 16, "Informative Speaking,"** has been updated to include current examples and reflect current research. This edition also introduces a new informative speech on Internet Identity Theft.

- **Chapter 17, "Persuasive Speaking,"** has been updated with current examples and research. It continues to explain the nature of persuasion as a form of argument developed with strategies of logos, ethos, and pathos.

- The **Appendix on interviewing** has been revised to focus on the fact that many jobs are now posted and applied to online. It includes the types of questions to include in an effective interview protocol and some guidelines to follow when conducting an information-gathering interview, media interview, or employment interview as both interviewer and as interviewee. The chapter gives considerable attention to employment seekers and how to locate job openings through formal and informal networks, as well as how to prepare application materials, conduct the interview, and follow up afterward.

Hallmark Features

- **"Communication Skill" boxes** provide a step-by-step guide for each of the communication skills presented in the text. Each of these boxes includes the definition of the skill, a brief description of its use, the steps for enacting the skill, and an example that illustrates the skill.

- **"Speech Plan Action Steps"** in Chapters 11–15 guide students through a sequential speech-planning process. The activities that accompany each of these action steps guide students through an orderly process that results in better speeches.

- **Sample student speeches** appear in the text, each accompanied by an audience adaptation plan, an outline, and an annotated transcript. A new sample speech is introduced in Chapter 16: "Internet Identify Theft: Self-Protection Steps." For some of these speeches, students can use the MindTap® Speech for *Communicate!* to view videos, see the transcript and two different kinds of outlines and sample note cards, and prepare their own critiques.

- **"Communicate on Your Feet" speech assignments** in Units I and II encourage students to begin building their public-speaking skills immediately while also addressing the needs of instructors who assign prepared speeches throughout the course. In Unit IV, these assignments correspond to the speech types discussed in Chapters 16 and 17.

- **"What Would You Do? A Question of Ethics"** are short case studies that appear near the end of chapters. These cases present ethical challenges and require students to think critically, sorting through a variety of ethical dilemmas faced by communicators. Conceptual material presented in Chapter 1 lays the groundwork for the criteria on which students may base their assessments, but each case focuses on issues raised in a specific chapter.

- MindTap® Speech for *Communicate* is a fully online, highly personalized learning experience that enhances learner engagement and improves outcomes while reducing instructor workload. By combining readings, multimedia, activities, and assessments into a singular Learning Path, MindTap guides students through their course with ease and engagement. Videos are available in the Speech Video Library so that students can better comprehend the key concepts of each chapter. Activities, powered by MindApps developed specifically for this discipline, guide students through the process of analyzing sample speeches, creating topics, building outlines, and practicing and presenting their speech. Instructors personalize the Learning Path by customizing Cengage Learning resources and adding their own content via apps that integrate into the MindTap framework seamlessly with any Learning Management System.

Teaching and Learning Resources

Communicate! is accompanied by a full suite of integrated materials that will make teaching and learning more efficient and effective. **Note to faculty:** If you want your students to have access to the online resources for this book, please be sure to order them for your course. The content in these resources can be bundled with every new copy of the text or ordered separately. Contact your local Cengage Learning Consultant. *If you do not order them, your students will not have access to the online resources.*

Student Resources

- **The Speech Video Library available in MindTap** provides instructors an easy way to keyword search, review, evaluate, and assign exemplar student speeches into their classroom and online learning environment. There are more than 70 videos, including both famous historical speeches and realistic student classroom speeches. Student speech types include informative, persuasive, invitational, impromptu and group presentations. All speeches are accompanied by activities to help students refine and develop their speech preparation and critical thinking skills.

- The Speech Plan Action Steps can be completed with the **Outline Builder available in MindTap.** Outline Builder is a speech preparation resource that provides step-by-step support for students to select an appropriate topic, design balanced and organized main points and sub points, formulate citations that follow guidelines, and create succinct note cards. Students arrive well prepared and confident on speech day, with a complete and well-organized outline in hand. Outline Builder can also be customized based upon instructor preferences and expectations.

- **Practice and Present available in MindTap,** powered by YouSeeU, is a synchronous (live capture) and asynchronous speech video delivery, recording, and grading system. It compiles student video submissions in one, easy-to-access place that allows self-review, peer review, and instructor grades in one system. Instructors are able to provide feedback via rubrics and time-stamped comments so that students no longer have to wait until future class sessions to receive timely, meaningful feedback on their presentations. It can be also used to allow students to practice their speech outside of class ahead of time and get feedback, providing students with the tools to help reduce speech anxiety. It gives students the ability to synchronize visual aids to videos and also provides group presentation functionality.

- **CengageBrain.com Online Store** is a single destination for more than 15,000 new print textbooks, textbook rentals, eBooks, single eChapters, and print, digital, and audio study tools. CengageBrain.com provides the freedom to purchase Cengage Learning products à la carte—exactly what you need, when you need it. Visit **cengagebrain.com** for details.

- *A Guide to the Basic Course for ESL Students* can be bundled and is designed to assist the nonnative speaker. The *Guide* features FAQs, helpful URLs, and strategies for accent management and speech apprehension.

- *Service Learning in Communication Studies: A Handbook* is an invaluable resource for students in the basic course that integrates, or will soon integrate, a service-learning component. This handbook provides guidelines for connecting service-learning work with classroom concepts and advice for working effectively with agencies and organizations. It also provides model forms and reports and a directory of online resources.

Instructor Resources

- **Instructor's Resource Web site.** This Web site is an all-in one resource for class preparation, presentation, and testing for instructors. Accessible through Cengage.com/login with you faculty account, you will find an Instructor's Manual, Chapter-by-Chapter PowerPoint presentations, and Cengage Learning Testing files powered by Cognero.

- The **Instructor's Resource Manual** includes a sample syllabi, chapter-by-chapter outlines, summaries, vocabulary lists, suggested lecture and discussion topics, classroom exercises, assignments, and a comprehensive test bank with answer key and rejoinders. In addition, this manual includes the **"Spotlight on Scholars" boxes** that were in previous editions of the main text. These boxes feature the work of eight eminent communications scholars, putting a face on scholarship by telling each scholar's "story." These boxes can be used as discussion starters, as enrichment for students who are interested in communication scholarship, or in any other way instructors would like to integrate them into the course.

- **Special-topic instructor's manuals.** Written by Deanna Sellnow, University of Central Florida, these three brief manuals provide instructor resources for teaching public speaking online, with a service-learning approach, and with a problem-based learning approach that focuses on critical thinking and teamwork skills. Each manual includes course syllabi; icebreakers; information about learning cycles and learning styles; and public speaking basics such as coping with anxiety, outlining, and speaking ethically.

- **Cengage Learning Testing, powered by Cognero.** Accessible through Cengage.com/login with your faculty account, this test bank contains multiple choice, true/false, and essay questions for each chapter. Cognero is a flexible, online system that allows you to author, edit, and manage test bank content. Create multiple test versions instantly and deliver through your LMS platform from wherever you may be. Cognero is compatible with Blackboard, Angel, Moodle, and Canvas LMS platforms.

- *The Teaching Assistant's Guide to the Basic Course,* based on leading communication teacher training programs, covers general teaching and course management topics as well as specific strategies for communication instruction—for example, providing effective feedback on performance, managing sensitive class discussions, and conducting mock interviews.

- The *Media Guide for Interpersonal Communication* provides faculty with media resource listings focused on general interpersonal communication topics. Each listing provides compelling examples of how interpersonal communication concepts are illustrated in particular films, books, plays, Web sites, or journal articles. Discussion questions are provided.

- **CourseCare training and support.** Get trained, get connected, and get the support you need for the seamless integration of digital resources into your course. This unparalleled technology service and training program provides robust online resources, peer-to-peer instruction, personalized training, and a customizable program you can count on. Visit **cengage.com** to sign up for online seminars, first days of class services, technical support, or personalized, face-to-face training. Our online and onsite trainings are frequently led by one of our Lead Teachers, faculty members who are experts in using Wadsworth Cengage Learning technology and can provide best practices and teaching tips.

- **Flex-text customization program.** With this program you can create a text as unique as your course: quickly, simply, and affordably. As part of our flex-text program, you can add your personal touch to *Communicate!* with a course-specific cover and up to 32 pages of your own content—at no additional cost. The Media and Media Literacy bonus chapter can also be added.

- **A single chapter on public speaking** is available through Cengage Custom Publishing for survey courses in which developing public speaking skills is not an emphasis. This chapter, written by the *Communicate!* authors, presents a concise overview of public speaking and the speech-making process. It is designed to substitute for Chapters 11–17 of *Communicate!* and to provide an overview, rather than a comprehensive guide to the speech-making process.

Acknowledgments

This fifteenth edition of *Communicate!* has benefitted from the work of many people I would like to recognize. First, the instructors who provided their feedback, which helped shape this new edition: Eric Batson, Community College of Baltimore County; Kimberly Batty-Herbert, South Florida State College; Glen Beck, Dowling College; Susan Cain, Southwestern Community College; Shera Carter, San Jacinto College; Keith Corso, Westminster College; Steven Epstein-Ferrero, Suffolk Community College; Diane Ferrero-Paluzzi, Iona College; Joseph Ganakos, Lee College; Khalil Islam-Zwart, Spokane Falls Community College; Doreen Kutufam, Carroll College; Amy Lenoce, Naugatuck Valley Community College; Jennifer McCullough, Kent State University; Virginia McDermott, High Point University; Laurie Metcalf, Blinn College; John Parrish, Tarrant County College; Chris Sawyer, Texas Christian University; Christy Takamure, Leeward Community College; Charlotte Toguchi, Kapiolani Community College; Joseph Velasco, Sul Ross State University; Chaffey College; Jim Wilson, Shelton State Community College; Carleen Yokotake, Leeward Community College.

Second, thanks to the great editorial team that has been instrumental in getting this edition launched: Monica Eckman, product director; Nicole Morinon and Kelli Strieby, product managers; Jessica Badiner, senior content developer; Karolina Kiwak, associate content developer; Colin Solan, product assistant; Sarah Seymour, marketing manager; Dan Saabye, content project manager; Marissa Falco, senior art director; Ed Dionne, project manager at MPS Limited; Maura Brown, copy editor; Ann Hoffman, intellectual property analyst; Farah Ford, intellectual property project manager; Nazveena Syed, image researcher; and Manjula Subramanian, text permission researcher. Most important, however, huge thanks go to Kassi Radomski, content developer. She is an amazing champion for this project. Thanks, Kassi. You are the best! Finally, thanks be to God who undergirds everything I do.

Deanna D. Sellnow

Communicate!

Foundations of Communication

In the words of educational philosopher, Robert M. Hutchins, former dean of the Yale Law School and former president and chancellor of the University of Chicago,

> *A world community can only exist with world communication, which means something more than extensive software facilities scattered about the globe. It means common understanding, a common tradition, common ideas and common ideals.*

The title of the book you are about to read is *Communicate!* and from it you will gain skills designed to help you achieve what Hutchins describes. Before we embark on our journey, however, we ought to begin with a common understanding of what *communication* means. We know that communication has to do with things like reading, writing, talking, and listening. What people sometimes fail to realize, however, is that communication is something we can learn to do more effectively through study and practice.

At its core, communication stems from the desire to share our thoughts, feelings, and ideas with others. We do this through the messages we send and receive every day. Messages are made up of a combination of verbal symbols (words), nonverbal cues (behaviors), and perhaps visual images. Through reflection and analysis, we interpret the messages of others—sometimes accurately and sometimes not.

New technologies provide new channels for communicating and new challenges. For example, e-mailing, texting, tweeting, blogging, Facebook messaging, Skyping, and Snapchatting are expanding our ability to stay in touch with distant others. With these opportunities, however, comes an intensified need to improve our communication competence as we tailor our messages to be appropriate for these different communication channels. So this book focuses on effective communication (1) in various settings such as interpersonal encounters, small groups, and public forums, as well as (2) using a variety of channels ranging from flat print to face-to-face to mediated and technology-driven ones.

This first unit consists of six chapters devoted to the fundamental elements of effective communication. In Chapter 1, we discuss the nature of communication and the communication process. Chapter 2 focuses on perceptions of self and perceptions of others. Chapter 3 examines how cultural norms affect communication. Chapter 4 is devoted to verbal messages and Chapter 5 to nonverbal messages. Finally, Chapter 6 examines the listening process and offers specific suggestions for improving listening skills when communicating in both face-to-face and virtual settings. By the time you finish this introductory unit, you will be ready—and we hope excited—to study how to apply these basic concepts in interpersonal, group, and public communication contexts.

Foundations of Communication

When you've finished this chapter, you will be able to:

- Describe the nature of communication.

- Define key components in the communication process.

- Explain the characteristics of communication.

- Assess messages using the principles of ethical communication.

- Develop a personal communication improvement plan.

MindTap®

Start with a quick warm-up activity.

Jennifer was running late. She stood at the kitchen counter eating a piece of toast while preparing a grocery list she would use on her way home from work. She noticed that the Weather Channel was forecasting heavy rain and wondered where she left her umbrella. She added "get umbrella" to her shopping list. Jennifer quickly texted Greta, a coworker she was driving with to work today, to ask if Greta had an extra one she could borrow.

As she was texting Greta, Jennifer's 16-year-old daughter, Hailey, bounded into the kitchen and asked, "Mom, can I get a tattoo? Kayla and Whitney are both getting them and we want to match."

"Not now, Hailey. I'm late for work. We can talk about it tonight."

"But mom. . . ."

"Yes, Hailey, yes, alright. We'll talk more tonight. . . ." Jennifer exclaimed as she headed to the door. Just then she heard her computer signal an incoming e-mail message. Jennifer thought, "I'd better just get going. I can check it on my phone on the way to pick up Greta."

As Hailey waited for the school bus, she quickly texted her friends, "Awesome! My mom said YES!"

2

Terry Vine/Getty Images

APPLY IT

Consider a time when someone started reading or sending texts on their smart phone while you were talking to them. How did that influence your opinion of them? Of their interest in you? Of the value they place on your relationship?

MindTap®

Photo 1.1 What are your career goals? How might effective communication help you achieve them?

Can you relate to Jennifer? We live in an era when multitasking has become a norm. Part of that multitasking includes communicating both with ourselves and with others. Like Jennifer, we get ready for work or school while checking voice messages and Facebook pages, answering texts and e-mails, as well as eating breakfast, monitoring the forecast, and getting dressed.

Some argue that the same technology that was supposed to simplify life has actually made it more complex. In fact, communication today extends across interpersonal, group, and public communication settings through flat print, face-to-face, and mediated technology-enhanced channels. Jennifer, for example, composed her grocery list on *a piece of paper* while learning about the weather forecast on *television* and texting Greta on her *smart phone*. Then, when Hailey tried to talk to her *face to face*, Jennifer was so distracted that her communication signals implied to Hailey that she had granted Hailey permission to get a tattoo.

Unfortunately, one of the negative consequences of having so many modes through which we can communicate is the false sense of competence it gives us about our ability to have several conversations at once. This chapter and the ones that follow focus on *why* it's important to improve our communication skills and *how* to do so. As a result, we can avoid the negative consequences of ineffective communication that can hurt our personal and professional relationships.

At its core, communication is the attempt to satisfy the innate human desire to share our thoughts, feelings, and ideas with others. We do this through the messages we send and receive every day. Messages are made up of a combination of verbal symbols (words), nonverbal cues (behaviors), and visual images.

New technologies provide new channels and new challenges for communicating. For example, e-mailing, texting, tweeting, blogging, Skyping, and Facebooking are expanding our ability to communicate with distant others around the world. With these opportunities, however, comes an intensified need to tailor our messages for the different channels we use and the different audiences those channels might address.

What this book intends to help you learn, then, is how to communicate effectively (1) in various settings such as interpersonal encounters, small groups, and public forums, as well as (2) using a variety of channels ranging from flat print to face-to-face to technology-driven ones.

Our ability to make and keep friends, to be good members of our families, to have satisfying intimate relationships, to participate in or lead groups, and to prepare and present formal speeches and presentations depends on our communication skills. Time and time again, surveys and studies conclude that employers of college graduates seek oral communication, teamwork, and interpersonal skills (College Learning for the New Global Century, 2008; Darling & Dannels, 2003; Hansen & Hansen, 2007; Hart, 2006; Young, 2003). Unfortunately, these same employers also say communication skills are the ones many new graduates lack (Hart, 2010). Thus, what you learn from this book can not only improve your personal relationships, but also increase your ability to get a job and be successful in your chosen career (Photo 1.1).

© monkey Business Images/Shutterstock.com

We begin this chapter by describing the nature of communication and the communication process followed by several characteristics of communication and ethical considerations. Finally, we explain how to become a more competent communicator by developing and following your own personal communication improvement plan.

The Nature of Communication

Communication is a complex process through which we express, interpret, and coordinate messages with others. We do so to create shared meaning, to meet social goals, to manage personal identity, and to carry out our relationships. At its core, then, communication is about messages.

Messages are the verbal utterances, visual images, and nonverbal behaviors used to convey thoughts and feelings. We refer to the process of creating messages as **encoding** and the process of interpreting them as **decoding**. So when a toddler points to her bottle and cries out "Ba-ba," her message (comprised of a nonverbal gesture—pointing—and a verbal utterance—"Ba-ba") expresses her desire for her caregiver to give her the bottle of milk. How the caregiver responds, however, depends on how he or she decodes the message. The caregiver might respond by handing her the bottle or by saying, "Sorry, cutie, the bottle is empty." Either response is also a message. **Feedback** is a response message that indicates how the initial message was interpreted.

Canned Plans and Scripts

But how do we actually go about encoding (or forming) and decoding (or interpreting) messages? We begin based on our canned plans and scripts. A **canned plan** is a "mental library" of scripts each of us draws from to create messages based on what worked for us or others in the past (Berger, 1997). A **script** is an actual text of what to say and do in a specific situation. We have canned plans and scripts for a wide variety of interactions like greeting people, making small talk, giving advice, complimenting or criticizing someone, and persuading others. Each canned plan may contain many scripts tailored to different people and occasions. For example, we may have a "canned greeting plan" that contains a different script for greeting a friend, family member, co-worker, or supervisor. It may also include tailored scripts for doing so in person, over e-mail, or on social media. Patricia, for example, typically begins e-mail messages to her friends by greeting them with their first name. However, when she writes to her professors, she always begins with "Dear Professor." Doing so helps convey respect for their authority.

Suppose you spot a good friend sitting at a table across the room from you at a restaurant. How might you say hello? How might you tailor your greeting if that person is a romantic partner, work supervisor, co-worker, or classmate?

We develop canned plans and scripts from our own previous experiences and by observing what appears to work or not work for other people, even fictitious people we see on TV or in movies (Frank, Prestin, Chen, & Nabi, 2009) (Photo 1.2). When our canned plan doesn't appear to include a good script for a specific situation, we search for scripts that are *similar to* the current situation and customize an appropriate message. For example, if you have never met a celebrity, you probably don't have a greeting script for doing so in your canned plan mental library. Suppose you are waiting to board a plane and spot a famous athlete, singer, or actor also waiting to board. What would you say?

---

communication
the process through which we express, interpret, and coordinate messages with others

messages
the verbal utterances, visual images, and nonverbal behaviors used to convey thoughts and feelings

encoding
the process of putting our thoughts and feelings into words and nonverbal behaviors

decoding
the process of interpreting another's message

feedback
responses to messages

canned plan
a "mental library" of scripts each of us draws from to create messages based on what worked in the past

script
an actual text of what to say and do in a specific situation

APPLY IT

What do you say when you greet (a) a stranger you pass on the sidewalk, (b) a casual friend or classmate, (c) a romantic partner, or (d) a family member? In what ways are your scripts similar and different? Why?

AP Images/Rob Bennett

Photo 1.2 Sometimes we develop canned plans and scripts by observing fictional characters or people on TV. What television programs might have influenced your canned plans and scripts? Why and how?

communication context
the physical, social, historical, psychological, and cultural situations that surround a communication event

physical situation
location, environmental conditions (temperature, lighting, noise level), distance between communicators, seating arrangements, and time of day

social presence
a sense of "being there" with another person virtually

social situation
the nature of the relationship that exists between participants

historical situation
the background provided by previous communication between the participants

As you figure that out, you are likely to draw from similar scripts and customize them for the person and occasion.

The point here is that we don't usually start from scratch to form messages. Instead we recognize what type of message we want to form, search our mental canned plan library for an appropriate script, and then customize it to fit the unique parts of the current situation. All of this mental choosing typically happens in nanoseconds. We also use our canned plans and scripts to interpret messages from others. Obviously, the larger your canned plan library is, the more likely you will be to form appropriate and effective messages, as well as understand and respond appropriately to the messages of others.

Communication Context

According to noted German philosopher Jürgen Habermas, the ideal communication situation is impossible to achieve, but considering context as we communicate can move us closer to that goal (Littlejohn & Foss, 2010). The **communication context** is made up of the physical, social, historical, psychological, and cultural situations that surround a communication event.

The **physical situation** includes the location, the environmental conditions (temperature, lighting, noise level), and the physical proximity of participants to each other. The physical situation may also be virtual as we interact with others via social media on our computers, tablets, and smart phones. The physical situation can influence how we interpret the messages we send and receive. We are likely to be most successful when we are present with those with whom we are interacting, either literally, as in face-to-face situations, or virtually. The term we use for creating a sense of "being there" with another person virtually is **social presence**. One technology-enhanced communication channel that does not lend itself to conveying social presence is e-mail. As a result, e-mail messages can often be misinterpreted, cause hurt feelings, or damage relationships. Jonas, for instance, gasped when he read the e-mail from his professor that seemed to be accusing him of cheating. He began to fire off a reply but stopped and made an appointment to speak in person so as to avoid the misinterpretation that can come from the lack of social presence provided via e-mail.

The **social situation** is the nature of the relationship that already exists between the participants. The better you know someone and the better relationship you have with them, the more likely you are to accurately interpret their messages and to give them the benefit of the doubt when a message seems negative.

The **historical situation** is the background provided by previous communication between the participants. For instance, suppose Chas texts Anna to tell her he will pick up the draft of the report they had left for their manager. When Anna sees Chas at lunch later that day, she says, "Did you get it?" Another person listening to the conversation would have no idea what the "it" is to which Anna is referring. Yet Chas may well reply, "It's on my desk." Anna and Chas understand one another because of their earlier exchange.

The **psychological situation** includes the moods and feelings each person brings to the encounter. For instance, suppose Corinne is under a great deal of stress. While studying for an exam, a friend stops by and asks her to take a break to go to the gym. Corinne, who is normally good-natured, may respond with an irritated tone of voice, which her friend may misinterpret as Corinne being mad at him.

psychological situation
the moods and feelings each person brings to a conversation

The **cultural situation** includes the beliefs, values, orientations, underlying assumptions, and rituals that belong to a specific culture (Samovar, Porter, & McDaniel, 2009). Everyone is part of one or more cultural group (e.g., race, ethnicity, religion, age, sex, gender, sexual orientation, physical ability). When two people from different cultures interact, misunderstandings may occur because of their different cultural values, beliefs, orientations, and rituals. The *Communicating in the World* section in this chapter describes how the cultural ritual of mourning is changing in the United States today.

cultural situation
the beliefs, values, orientations, underlying assumptions, and rituals that belong to a specific culture

COMMUNICATING IN THE WORLD

Mourning in the United States, 21st-Century Style

Mourning is a universal human communication process of celebrating the life of someone while grieving his or her death. Mourning rituals and traditions vary by culture and religion and change over time. So it is not surprising that mourning in the United States in the 21st century is adapting past practices to modern life.

Today in the United States, for instance, many of the rituals traditionally associated with funerals and memorial services often take place online. Increasingly, one or more family member may prepare a commemorative Web page that memorializes the life of the departed. For example, an article in the *Boston Globe* recounted the story of Shawn Kelley, who created a "moving tribute" to his brother Michael, a National Guardsman killed in Afghanistan. The 60-second video features a slide show of images of Michael growing up while quiet classical music plays softly and a voice-over recounts Michael's attributes and interests. Shawn reported that it made him feel good to be able to "talk" about his brother, and over a year later he was still visiting the site to watch the video and to view the messages that continue to be left by family members and friends (Plumb, 2006). The popularity of such Web sites can be summarized in the fact that Legacy.com, the most popular site for posting online memorials, boasts of more than 24 million unique visitors each month (http://www.legacy.com/ns/about/).

How did you/do you mourn when someone you care about dies? How do you share messages with others in the process?

MindTap®

Communication Settings

The communication setting also affects how we form and interpret messages. **Communication settings** differ based on the number of participants and the level of formality in the interactions (Littlejohn & Foss, 2008, pp. 52–53). These settings are intrapersonal, interpersonal, small group, public, and mass.

Intrapersonal communication refers to the interactions that occur in our minds when we are talking to ourselves (Photo 1.3). We usually don't verbalize our intrapersonal communication. When you sit in class and think about what you'll do later that day or when you send yourself a reminder note as an e-mail or text message, you are communicating intrapersonally. A lot of our intrapersonal communication occurs subconsciously (Kellerman, 1992). When we drive into the driveway "without thinking," we are communicating intrapersonally on a subconscious level. The study of intrapersonal communication often focuses on its role in shaping self-perceptions and in managing communication apprehension, that is, the fear associated with communicating with others (Richmond & McCroskey, 1997). Our study of intrapersonal communication focuses on self-talk as a means to improve self-concept and self-esteem and, ultimately, communication competence in a variety of situations.

Interpersonal communication is characterized by informal interaction between two people who have an identifiable relationship with each other (Knapp & Daly, 2002). Talking to a friend between classes, visiting on the phone with your mother, and texting or chatting online with your brother are all examples of interpersonal communication. In Part II of this book, our study of interpersonal communication includes the exploration of how we develop, maintain, improve, and end interpersonal relationships.

Small-group communication typically involves three to 20 people who come together to communicate with one another (Beebe & Masterson, 2006; Hirokawa, Cathcart, Samovar, & Henman, 2003). Examples of small groups include a family, a group of friends, a group of classmates working on a project, and a workplace management team. Small-group communication can occur in face-to-face settings, as well as online through electronic mailing lists, discussion boards, virtual meetings, and blogs. In Part III, our study of small groups focuses on the characteristics of effective groups, ethical and effective communication in groups, leadership, problem-solving, conflict, and group presentations.

Public communication is delivered to audiences of more than 20 people. Examples include public speeches, presentations, and forums we may experience in person or via mediated or technology-driven channels. For example, when a president delivers the State of the Union address, some people may be in attendance on location, others watch on TV or the Internet, and still others view it later in the form of televised broadcast snippets, digital recordings, or Internet videos. The Internet is also becoming the medium of choice for posting job ads and résumés, for advertising and buying products, and for political activism. In Part IV, our study of public communication focuses on preparing, practicing, and delivering effective oral presentations in both face-to-face and virtual environments.

---

communication setting
the different communication environments within which people interact

intrapersonal communication
the interactions that occur in a person's mind when he or she is talking with himself or herself

interpersonal communication
informal interaction between two people who have an identifiable relationship with each other

small-group communication
three to 20 people who come together for the specific purpose of solving a problem or arriving at a decision

public communication
one participant, the speaker, delivers a message to a group of more than 20 people

---

Photo 1.3 We communicate intrapersonally when we talk to ourselves, reflect about people and events, and write in a journal. What are some examples of your own intrapersonal communication activities today?

AmpH/istockphoto.com

Mass communication is delivered by individuals and entities through mass media to large segments of the population at the same time. Some examples include newspaper and magazine articles and advertisements, as well as radio and television programs and advertisements. The bonus chapter on mass communication and media literacy focuses specifically on effective mass communication in both flat print and digital modalities.

The Communication Process

The **communication process** is a complex set of three different and interrelated activities intended to result in shared meaning (Burleson, 2009). These activities are message production, message interpretation, and interaction coordination. They are affected by the channels used and by interference/noise.

Message Production

Message production is what we do when we *encode* a message. We begin by forming goals based on our understanding of the situation and our values, ethics, and needs. Based on these goals, we recall an effective canned plan script and adapt it to the current situation.

Message Interpretation

Message interpretation is what we do when we *decode* a message. We read or listen to someone's words, observe their nonverbal behavior, and take note of other visuals. Then we interpret the message based on the canned plan scripts we remember that seem similar. Based on this interpretation, we prepare a feedback message.

Interaction Coordination

Interaction coordination consists of the behavioral adjustments each participant makes in an attempt to create shared meaning (Burgoon, 1998) (Photo 1.4). Shared meaning occurs when the receiver's interpretation is similar to what the speaker intended. We can usually gauge the extent to which shared meaning is achieved by the sender's response to the feedback message. For example, Sarah says to Nick, "I dropped my phone and it broke." Nick replies, "Cool, now you can get a Droid™." To which Sarah responds, "No, you don't understand, I can't afford to buy a new phone." Sarah's response to Nick's feedback message lets Nick know he misunderstood her. The extent to which we achieve shared meaning can be affected by the channels we use and by the interference/noise that compete with our messages.

Channels

Channels are both the route traveled by the message and the means of transportation. Face-to-face communication has three basic channels: verbal symbols,

Hero Images/Getty Images

emoticons
textual images that symbolize the sender's mood, emotion, or facial expressions

acronyms
abbreviations that stand in for common phrases

media richness
how much and what kinds of information can be transmitted via a particular channel

synchronicity
the extent to which a channel allows for immediate feedback

interference/noise
any stimulus that interferes with the process of achieving sharing meaning

physical noise
any external sight or sound that distracts us from the message

psychological noise
thoughts and feelings that compete with the sender's message for our attention

nonverbal cues, and visual images. Technologically mediated communication uses these same channels, though nonverbal cues such as movements, touch, and gestures are represented by visual symbols like **emoticons** (textual images that symbolize the sender's mood, emotion, or facial expressions) and **acronyms** (abbreviations that stand in for common phrases) (Photo 1.5). For example, in a face-to-face interaction, Barry might express his frustration about a poor grade verbally by noting why he thought the grade was unfair, visually by showing the assignment along with the grading criteria for it, and nonverbally by raising his voice and shaking his fist. In an online interaction, however, he might need to insert a frowning-face emoticon (☹) or the acronym "POed" to represent those emotions and nonverbal behaviors.

With so many technology-driven channels available for communicating today, we must now thoughtfully select the best channel for our purpose, audience, and situation. We can do so by considering media richness and synchronicity.

Media richness refers to how much and what kinds of information can be transmitted via a particular channel. Face-to-face is the richest channel because we can hear the verbal message content and observe the nonverbal cues to interpret its meaning. Sometimes, however, communicating face-to-face is either impossible or not a good use of time. The less information offered via a given channel, the leaner it is. The leaner the channel, the greater the chances are for misunderstanding. For example, texts and "tweets" are lean because they use as few characters as possible whereas videoconferencing channels such as Skype and FaceTime are richer because we can observe nonverbal cues almost as much as in a face-to-face setting.

Synchronicity is the extent to which a channel allows for immediate feedback. Synchronous channels allow communication to occur in "real time" and asynchronous channels allow for "lag time." Synchronous channels allow for immediate feedback to clarify potential misunderstandings whereas asynchronous channels provide time to careful craft and revise our messages (Condon & Cech, 2010). Generally, you should use a rich channel if your message is complicated, difficult, or controversial. It is also usually a good idea to use a synchronous channel in these cases. You might choose an asynchronous channel, however, if you could benefit from having extra time to carefully organize and word your message. On the other hand, use a lean channel when you merely want to convey simple and emotionally neutral information. Figure 1.1 illustrates the continuum of communication channels available today.

Interference/Noise

Interference, also referred to as **noise,** is any stimulus that interferes with the process of achieving shared meaning. Noise can be physical or psychological. **Physical noise** is any external sight or sound that distracts us from the message. For example, when someone enters the room, a cell phone goes off, or someone near us is texting while a speaker is talking, we might be distracted from the message. Or, when communicating online, we might be distracted when we get a Facebook or Twitter notification. **Psychological noise** refers to the thoughts and feelings we experience that compete with the sender's message for our attention. So when we daydream about what we have to do at work or feel offended when a

Photo 1.5 What emoticons and acronyms do you use in text messages and why?

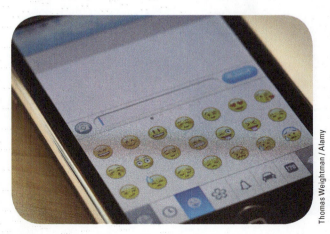

Thomas Weightman / Alamy

ASYNCHRONOUS					SYNCHRONOUS	
Bulk Letters	Posted Letters	Facebook	Interactive	Telephone	Skype	Face-to-Face
Posters	E-mail	My Space	Chat		iChat	
E-mail Spam	Text	Other social			Other video	
	Messages	media Web sites			conferencing	
LEAN						**RICH**
LOW SOCIAL PRESENCE						**HIGH SOCIAL PRESENCE**

© Cengage Learning

Figure 1.1

Continuum of communication channels

speaker uses foul language, we are being distracted by psychological noise. Recall how Jennifer in the opening vignette was distracted by both physical and psychological noise while attempting to multitask getting herself ready for work. That's why it is a good practice to close social media sites and power off smart phones while engaged in important face-to-face or online conferences, meetings, or classroom discussions.

A Model of the Communication Process

In summary, let's look at a graphic model of a message exchange between two people presented in Figure 1.2. The process begins when one person who we will call Andy is motivated to share his thoughts with another person, Taylor. Andy reviews the communication situation, including the communication context, and sorts through the scripts in his canned plan library to find one he thinks will be appropriate. Based on this script, he encodes a customized message and shares it with Taylor.

Taylor decodes the message using her understanding of the situation and matching it to scripts in her canned plan library. She might misinterpret Andy's intended meaning because she is distracted by physical or psychological interference/noise, or because her scripts don't match Andy's. Taylor encodes a feedback message using a script from her canned plan library as a guide. She then shares her feedback message and Andy decodes it. If Taylor understood what Andy was saying, he will extend the conversation. If, on the other hand, Andy believes Taylor misunderstood his meaning, he will try to clarify what he meant before extending the conversation. Finally, the communication process is not linear. In other words, both Andy and Taylor simultaneously encode and decode verbal and nonverbal messages throughout the message exchange.

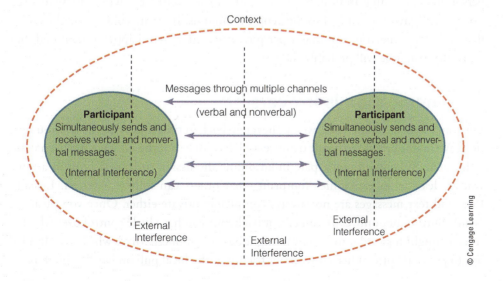

Figure 1.2

Model of communication

Characteristics of Communication

Just as we learn to walk, so do we learn to communicate. Because communication is learned, we can always improve our ability to communicate. Several communication characteristics provide a foundation for practicing and improving our communication skills.

Communication Has Purpose

Whenever we communicate, we have a purpose for doing so. The purpose may be serious or trivial, and we may or may not be aware of it at the time. Here we list five basic purposes we'll be addressing throughout the book.

1. **We communicate to develop and maintain our sense of self.** Through our interactions, we learn who we are and what we are good at.

2. **We communicate to meet our social needs.** Just as we need food, water, and shelter, so too do we need contact with other people. Two people may converse happily for hours about inconsequential matters that neither one remembers later. Still, their communication functions to meet this important human need.

3. **We communicate to develop and maintain relationships.** For example, when Beth calls Leah to ask whether she'd like to join her for lunch to discuss a class project, her purpose actually may be to resolve a recent misunderstanding, because she wants to maintain a positive relationship with Leah.

4. **We communicate to exchange information.** Whether trying to decide how warmly to dress or whom to vote for in the next election, we all communicate to exchange information. We do so through observation, reading, and direct communication with others both face-to-face and virtually.

5. **We communicate to influence others.** We may communicate to try to convince friends to go to a particular restaurant or to see a certain movie, a supervisor to alter the work schedule, or an instructor to change a grade.

Communication Is Continuous

We are always sending and interpreting messages. Even silence communicates if another person infers meaning from it. Why? Because our nonverbal behavior represents reactions to our environment and to the people around us. If we are cold, we might shiver; if we are hot or nervous, we might perspire; if we are bored, happy, or confused, our nonverbal language will probably show it.

Communication Is Irreversible

Once an exchange takes place, we can never go back in time and erase the communication. We might be able to repair damage we have done, but the message has been communicated. When you participate in an online discussion or leave a post on a blog, you are leaving an electronic "footprint" that others can follow and read. E-mails, IMs, and text messages are not always completely private either. Once you push the "send" button, not only can't you take it back, but you have little control over who the receiver might forward it to or how it might be used publicly. That's why Sarah decided not to post a picture of herself with her friends at the local pub on her Facebook page.

Even though she could limit which of her "friends" could see it, she also knew that any of them could also then share it with others, as well. She didn't want a photo like this to hurt her professional image.

Communication Is Situated

Communication occurs within a specific setting that affects how the messages are produced, interpreted, and coordinated (Burleson, 2009). Do you swear when you talk? For most of us the answer to that is "it depends." While we may occasionally use curse words when we are with friends or peers, many of us wouldn't consider swearing in front of our supervisors, teachers, grand-

Photo 1.6 How might you signal trust and intimacy during a conversation?

mothers, or religious leaders. Similarly, the interpretation of the statement "I love you" varies depending on the setting. During a candlelit anniversary dinner, it may be interpreted as a statement of romantic feelings. If a mother says it as she greets her daughter, it may be interpreted as motherly love. If it is made in response to a joke delivered by someone in a group of friends gathered to watch a football game, it may be interpreted as a complement for being clever.

Communication Is Indexical

How we communicate is also an **index** or measure of the emotional temperature of our relationship at the time. For instance, when they are getting in the car to leave for a holiday, Laura says to Darryl, "I remembered to bring the map." She is not just reporting information. Through her tone of voice and other nonverbal cues, she is also communicating something about the relationship, such as, "You can always depend on me," or "You never remember to think of these things." More specifically, communication may signal the level of trust; who has control; and the degree of intimacy in a relationship (Millar & Rogers, 1987).

Trust is the extent to which partners believe they can rely on, depend on, and have faith in their partners (Photo 1.6). For instance, Mark says, "I'll do the final edits and turn in the paper." Sandy replies, "Never mind, I'll do it so that it won't be late," which may signal that she doesn't trust Mark to get the group's paper in on time.

Control is the extent to which partners believe themselves to be "in charge" in the relationship. When Tom says to Sue, "I know you're concerned about the budget, but I'll see to it that we have enough money to cover everything," through his words, tone of voice, and nonverbal behavior, he is signaling that he is "in charge" of the finances. In turn, Sue may respond by either verbally responding or nonverbally showing she agrees with him or by challenging him and asserting her desire to control the budget. In other words, control is communicated with either complementary or symmetrical feedback. **Complementary feedback** signals agreement about who is in control, whereas **symmetrical feedback** signals disagreement. If Sue says, "Great, I'm glad you're looking after it," her feedback complements his message. But if Sue responds, "Wait a minute, you're

index
measure of the emotional temperature of our relationship at the time

trust
the extent to which partners have faith that their partners will not intentionally do anything to harm them

control
the degree to which one participant is perceived to be more dominant or powerful

complementary feedback
a message that signals agreement about who is in control

symmetrical feedback
a message that signals disagreement about who is in control

the one who overdrew our checking account last month," she is challenging his control with a symmetrical response. Relational control is not negotiated in a single exchange, but through many message exchanges over time. The point, however, is that control is negotiated through communication.

intimacy
the degree of emotional closeness, in a relationship

Intimacy is the degree of emotional closeness in a relationship. When Cody asks Madison what she is thinking about, and Madison begins to pour out her problems, she is revealing a high level of intimacy in the relationship. If she replies, "Oh I'm not really thinking about anything important. Did you hear the news this morning about . . . ," her subject change may signal that the relationship is not intimate enough to share her problems.

Communication Messages Vary in Conscious Thought

Recall that creating shared meaning involves encoding and decoding verbal messages, nonverbal cues, and even visual images. Our messages may (1) occur spontaneously, (2) be based on a "script," or (3) be carefully constructed.

spontaneous expressions
spoken without much conscious thought

constructed messages
formed carefully and thoughtfully when our known scripts are inadequate for the situation

Many messages are **spontaneous expressions**, spoken without much conscious thought. For example, when you burn your finger, you may blurt out, "Ouch!" When something goes right, you may break into a broad smile. Some messages are *scripted* and drawn from our canned plan libraries. Finally, some are **constructed messages** that are formed carefully and thoughtfully when our known scripts are inadequate for the situation.

Communication Is Guided by Cultural Norms

culture
a system of shared beliefs, values, symbols, and behaviors

Culture may be defined as a system of shared beliefs, values, symbols, and behaviors. How messages are formed and interpreted depends on the cultural background of the participants. We need to be mindful of our communication behavior as we interact with others whose cultural backgrounds differ from our own, so we don't unintentionally communicate in ways that are culturally inappropriate or insensitive.

According to Samovar, Porter, and McDaniel (2007) "a number of cultural components are particularly relevant to effective communication. These include (1) perception, (2) patterns of cognition, (3) verbal behaviors, (4) nonverbal behaviors, and (5) the influence of context" (p. 13). Because cultural concerns permeate all of communication, each chapter of this book points out when certain concepts and skills may be viewed differently by members of various cultural groups. The authors of the *Diverse Voices* feature found in many chapters in this text explain how they or their culture views a concept presented in the text.

Communication Ethics

ethics
a set of moral principles held by a society, group, or individual

Ethics are moral principles held by a society, group, or individual that differentiate right from wrong. In other words, ethics reflect what we believe we "ought to" and "ought not to" think and do. Every field of study—from psychology and biology to sociology and history—has a set of ethical principles designed to guide the practice of that field. Communication is no exception. Every time we communicate, we make choices with ethical implications. The general principles that guide ethical communication include:

1. **Ethical communicators are honest.** "An honest person is widely regarded as a moral person, and honesty is a central concept to ethics as the foundation for a moral life" (Terkel & Duval, 1999, p. 122). In other words, we should not intentionally try to deceive others.

2. **Ethical communicators act with integrity.** In other words, ethical communicators "practice what they preach." The person who says, "Do what I say, not what I do," lacks integrity. We often refer to such individuals as hypocrites. The person who "practices what he or she preaches" acts with integrity.

3. **Ethical communicators behave fairly.** A fair person attempts to be impartial. To be fair to someone is to gather all of the relevant facts, consider only circumstances relevant to the situation at hand, and not be swayed by prejudice. For example, if two siblings are fighting, their mother exercises fairness if she allows both children to explain "their side" before she decides what to do.

4. **Ethical communicators demonstrate respect.** Behaving respectfully means showing regard for others, including their point of view, their rights, and their feelings, even when they differ from ours.

5. **Ethical communicators are responsible.** Responsible communicators recognize the power of words. Our messages can hurt others and their reputations. So we act responsibly when we refrain from gossiping, spreading rumors, bullying, and so forth.

Bright Side and Dark Side Messages

Interpersonal communication scholars, Spitzberg and Cupach (2011) came up with metaphors to characterize the differences between ethical/appropriate and unethical/inappropriate communication. They label messages that are both ethical and appropriate as **bright side messages**. In contrast, **dark side messages** are unethical and/or inappropriate. "Hard dark side" messages are somewhat ethical and unethical because they are honest, but also potentially damaging to the relationship. "Easy dark side" messages are somewhat ethical and unethical because they are dishonest in order to maintain a good relationship. Finally, "evil dark side" messages are both disrespectful and damaging to the relationship (see Figure 1.3).

bright side messages
both ethical and appropriate

dark side messages
not ethical and/or appropriate

Let's use Liz as an example. She just spent a fortune having her hair cut and colored and asks her good friend, Pat, "Do you like my new hairstyle?" Pat, who doesn't really like the new look, could respond to Liz as follows:

Bright side response: "Liz, it doesn't matter what I think. I can see that you really like how it looks and that makes me happy." (This response is ethical and appropriate. It is both honest and respectful.)

Hard dark side response: "Wow Liz, it's a dramatic change. I liked your hair long and I'd always admired the red highlights you had. But I'm sure it will grow on me." (This response is honest but could hurt Liz's feelings and damage the relationship.)

Easy dark side response: "It looks great." (This response is dishonest but doesn't hurt Liz's feelings.)

Evil dark side response: "It doesn't matter what you do to your hair, you're still fat and ugly." (This response is unethical and inappropriate. It is hurtful and damaging to Liz's feelings and the relationship.)

As you can see, relationships may benefit from bright, hard, and easy side responses depending on the situation. But dark side responses damage people and relationships.

	Ethical	
	Bright Side	**Hard Side**
Appropriate		**Inappropriate**
	Easy Side	**Evil Dark Side**
	Unethical	

Figure 1.3

Understanding dark-side messages

© Cengage Learning

We often face ethical dilemmas and must sort out what is more or less right or wrong. In making these decisions, we reveal our ethical communication standards. Each chapter in this book features "A Question of Ethics" case related to material in that chapter. Consider each case and the questions we pose based on these ethical communication principles.

Communication Competence

communication competence
the impression that communicative behavior is both appropriate and effective in a given situation

Communication competence is the impression that communicative behavior is appropriate and effective in a given situation (Spitzberg, 2000, p. 375). Communication is *effective* when it achieves its goals and *appropriate* when it conforms to what is expected in a situation. Our goal is to communicate in ways that increase the likelihood that others will judge us as competent.

Communication competence is achieved through personal motivation, knowledge acquisition, and skills practice (Spitzberg, 2000, p. 377). First, we have to be *motivated*—that is, we must want to improve. Second, we must know what to do. Third, to improve, we must practice communication skills we learn.

credibility
a perception of a speaker's knowledge, trustworthiness, and warmth

social ease
communicating without appearing to be anxious or nervous

Credibility and social ease also influence whether others perceive us to be competent communicators. **Credibility** is a perception of a speaker's knowledge, trustworthiness, and warmth. Listeners are more likely to be attentive to and influenced by speakers they perceive as credible. **Social ease** means managing communication apprehension so we do not appear nervous or anxious. Communicators that appear apprehensive are not likely to be regarded as competent, despite their motivation or knowledge.

Communication Apprehension

communication apprehension
fear or anxiety associated with real or anticipated communication with others

Photo 1.7 Does public speaking make you nervous? If so, you are like 75% of the population. Did you know that speaking effectively requires some nervousness?

Communication apprehension is "the fear or anxiety associated with real or anticipated communication with others" (McCroskey, 1977, p. 78). Although most people think of public speaking anxiety when they hear the term *communication apprehension* (CA), there are actually four different types of CA (Photo 1.7). People who experience *traitlike communication apprehension* feel anxious in most speaking situations. About 20 percent of all people experience traitlike CA (Richmond & McCroskey, 2000). People who experience *audience-based communication apprehension* feel anxious about speaking only with a certain person or group of people. *Situational communication apprehension* is a short-lived feeling of anxiety that occurs during a specific encounter, for example, during a job interview. Finally, *context-based communication apprehension* is anxiety only in a particular situation, for example, when speaking to a large group of people. All these forms of communication anxiety can be managed effectively in ways that help convey social ease. Throughout this book, we offer strategies for managing communication apprehension in various settings.

Dennis MacDonald / PhotoEdit

The combination of motivation, knowledge, skills, perceived credibility, and social ease make up competent communication. The goal of this book is to help you become a competent communicator in interpersonal, group, and public speaking situations.

COMMUNICATE ON YOUR FEET

Speech Assignment

Introduce a Classmate

The Assignment

Following your instructor's directions, partner with someone in the class. Spend some time getting to know him or her and then prepare a short 2-minute speech introducing your partner to the rest of the class.

Questions to Ask

1. What is your background? (Where were you born and raised? What is the makeup of your family? What else do you want to share about your personal background?)
2. What are you majoring in and why?
3. What are some of your personal and professional goals after college?
4. What are two personal goals you have for this class and why?
5. What is something unique about you that most people probably don't know?

Speeches of Introduction

A speech of introduction is given to acquaint a group with someone they have not met. We make short "speeches" of introduction all the time. When a friend from high school comes to visit for a weekend, you may introduce her to your friends. Not only will you tell them her name, but you will probably mention other things about her that will make it easy for your friends to talk with her. Likewise, a store manager may call the sales associates together in order to introduce a new employee. The manager might mention the new team member's previous experience, interests, and expertise that will encourage the others to respect, help, and become acquainted with the new employee.

Speeches of introduction also often precede formal addresses. The goal of the introducer is to establish the credibility of the main speaker by sharing the speaker's education, background, and expertise related to the topic and to build audience interest.

Speech to Introduce a Classmate

Because your classmate will not be giving a formal address after you introduce him or her, we suggest you organize your speech as follows:

1. **The introduction:** Start with an attention catcher—a statement, story, or question tied to something about the speaker that will pique audience curiosity. Then offer a thesis and preview of main points, which can be as simple as "I'm here today to introduce [name of person] to you by sharing something about his personal background, personal and professional goals, and something unique about him."

2. **The body:** Group the information you plan to share under two to four main points. For example, your first main point might be "personal background," your second main point "personal and professional goals," and your third main point "something unique." Then offer two or three examples or stories to illustrate what you learned regarding each main point. Create a transition statement to lead from the first main point to the second main point, as well as from the second main point to the third main point. These statements should remind listeners of the main point you are concluding and introduce the upcoming main point. For example, "Now that you know a little bit about [name of person]'s personal background, let's talk about his personal and professional goals."

3. **The conclusion:** Remind listeners of the name of the classmate you introduced and the two to four main points you discussed about him or her. Then, end with a clincher—a short sentence that wraps the speech up by referring to something you said in the speech (usually in the introduction) that will encourage listeners to want to know him or her better.

WHAT WOULD YOU DO?

A Question of Ethics

Molly has just been accepted to Stanford Law School and calls her friend Terri to tell her the good news.

MOLLY: Hi Terri! Guess what? I just got accepted to Stanford Law!

TERRI: [*Surprised and disappointed*]: Oh, cool.

MOLLY: [*Sarcastic*]: Thanks—you sound so enthusiastic!

TERRI: Oh, I am. Listen, I have to go—I'm late for class.

MOLLY: Oh, OK. See you.

The women hang up, and Terri immediately calls her friend Monica.

TERRI: Monica, it's Terri.

MONICA: Hey, Terri. What's up?

TERRI: I just got some terrible news—Molly got into Stanford!

MONICA: So, what's wrong with that? I think it's great. Aren't you happy for her?

TERRI: No, not at all. I didn't get in, and I have better grades and a higher LSAT score.

MONICA: Maybe Molly had a better application.

TERRI: Or maybe it was what was on her application.

MONICA: What do you mean?

TERRI: You know what I mean. Molly's black.

MONICA: Yes, and . . . ?

TERRI: Don't you see? It's called affirmative action.

MONICA: Terri, give it a rest!

TERRI: Oh, please. You know it and I know it. She only got in because of her race and because she's poor. Her GPA is low and so is her LSAT score.

MONICA: Did you ever stop to think that maybe she wrote an outstanding essay? Or that they thought the time she spent volunteering in that free legal clinic in her neighborhood was good background?

TERRI: Yes, but we've both read some of her papers, and we know she can't write. Listen, Monica, if you're black, Asian, American Indian, Latino, or any other minority and poor, you've got it made. You can be as stupid as Jessica Simpson and get into any law school you want. It's just not fair at all.

MONICA [**Angrily**]: No, you know what isn't fair? I'm sitting here listening to my so-called friend insult my intelligence and my ethnic background. How dare you tell me that the only reason I'll ever get into a good medical school is because I'm Latino. Listen, honey, I'll get into medical school just the same way that Molly got into law school—because of my brains, my accomplishments, and my ethical standards. And based on this conversation, it's clear that Molly and I are way ahead of you.

Describe how well each of these women followed the ethical standards for communication discussed in this chapter.

MindTap®

Communication Improvement Plans

You can use a personal communication improvement plan to hone your skills and become a more competent communicator. As you read each chapter, select one or two skills to work on. Then write down your plan in four steps.

1. **Identify the problem:** "Even though some of the members of my class project group have not produced the work they promised, I haven't spoken up because I'm not very good at describing my feelings."

2. **State the specific goal:** "To describe my disappointment to other group members about their failure to meet deadlines." Hint: Be sure to identify a measurable outcome.

3. **Outline a specific procedure for reaching the goal:** "I will practice the steps of describing feelings. (1) I will identify the specific feeling I am experiencing. (2) I will encode the emotion I am feeling accurately. (3) I will include what has triggered the feeling. (4) I will own the feeling as mine. (5) I will then put that procedure into operation when I am talking with my group members."

4. **Devise a method for measuring progress:** "I will have made progress each time I describe my feelings to my group members about missed deadlines."

Figure 1.4 provides another example of a communication improvement plan, this one relating to a public speaking problem.

Figure 1.4

Sample communication improvement plan

> **Problem:** When I speak in class or in the student senate, I often find myself burying my head in my notes or looking at the ceiling or walls.
>
> **Goal:** To look at people more directly when I'm giving a speech.
>
> **Procedure:** I will take the time to practice oral presentations aloud in my room. (1) I will stand up just as I do in class. (2) I will pretend various objects in the room are people, and I will consciously attempt to look at those objects as I am talking. (3) When giving a speech, I will try to be aware of when I am looking at my audience and when I am not.
>
> **Test for Achieving Goal:** I will have achieved this goal when I am maintaining eye contact with my audience most of the time.

© Cengage Learning

Reflection and Assessment

At its core, communication is the process of creating shared meaning whether in informal conversations, group interactions, or public speeches via flat print, face-to-face, or technology-enhanced channels. To assess how well you've learned what we addressed in these pages, answer the following questions. If you have trouble answering any of them, go back and review that material. Once you can answer each question accurately, you are ready to move ahead to read the next chapter.

1. What is the nature of communication and the role of canned plans and scripts in it?

2. Describe the process of communication and how interference may impact it.

3. What are the key characteristics of communication?

4. What does it mean to be an ethical communicator as related to bright side and dark side messages?

5. What is a competent communicator and what steps can you take to improve your communication competence?

COMMUNICATE!

RESOURCE AND ASSESSMENT CENTER

MindTap®

Now that you have read Chapter 1, go to your MindTap for *Communicate!* for quick access to the electronic resources that accompany this text.

Applying What You've Learned

Impromptu Speech Activity

Identify one of your "heroes." Your hero may or may not be famous. Identify one of the five ethical principles of communication this hero's life adheres to and why. In your two to three minute impromptu speech, provide at least two incidents that serve as evidence regarding how this person demonstrates/demonstrated the principle.

Assessment Activities

1. Visit your Facebook page. If you don't have an account, you might make one to observe while completing this course or ask a friend if you can look at theirs. Find one example of ethical communiation, and describe the principles of ethical communication that it follows.

2. Find an example of unethical communication on Facebook and describe the principles that it doesn't follow.

Skill-Building Activities

1. Identifying Elements of the Communication Process For the following interaction, identify the message, channels, contexts, interference (noise), and feedback:

Maria and Damien are meandering through the park, talking and drinking bottled water. Damien finishes his bottle, replaces the lid, and tosses the bottle into the bushes at the side of the path. Maria, who has been listening to Damien talk, comes to a stop, stares at Damien, and says, "I can't believe what you just did!" Damien blushes, averts his gaze, and mumbles, "Sorry, I'll get it—I just wasn't thinking." As the tension drains from Maria's face, she smiles and says, "Well, just see that it doesn't happen again."

1. Message
2. Channels

3. Contexts
   a. Physical
   b. Social
   c. Historical
   d. Psychological
4. Interference (noise)
5. Feedback

Complete this activity, and see the author's answers on MindTap for *Communicate!*.

2. Communicating Over the Internet Consider the advantages and disadvantages of communicating via the following Internet-based mediums: e-mail, newsgroups, Blogs, iChat, Facebook, Twitter, and Skype. Enter your thoughts into a two-column table, with advantages in the first column and disadvantages in the second. Did your analysis produce any discoveries that surprised you?

MindTap®

Perception of Self and Others

MindTap®

Start with a quick warm-up activity.

Donna approached her friend Camille and said, "David and I are having a really tough time. I think he's going to break up with me."

"I'm sorry to hear that, Donna," replied Camille. "What's up?"

"Well, did you notice how quiet he was at the restaurant last night? And, on top of that, he hasn't responded to any of my texts today. He must be really mad at me."

"Yeah, he was quiet, but I just thought he was tired from the all-nighter he pulled finishing his history paper. And didn't he have to go to work really early today? You know he's not allowed to respond to texts at work."

"Yeah."

"So, if his quietness at dinner is the only thing you noticed, I think you may be jumping to a wrong conclusion," Camille said.

"Really? Do you think so? I just can't figure out what he's thinking. What do you think I should do?"

2

Two different women had two different interpretations of the same man's behavior. Who's right? Is David about to break up with Donna or is he just tired? **Social perception**—who we believe ourselves and others to be—influences how we communicate. To explain how, we begin this chapter by reviewing the basics of sensory perception. Then we explore the role communication plays in forming self-perceptions. From there, we discuss how we form perceptions of others and offer communication strategies for improving them. Ultimately, what you learn in this chapter will equip you to make conscious choices to promote a positive self-concept and self-esteem, as well as foster positive interactions and relationships with others.

The Perception Process

Perception is the process of selectively attending and assigning meaning to information (Gibson, 1966). At times, our perceptions of the world, other people, and ourselves agree with the perceptions of others. At other times, our perceptions differ significantly from those of others. For each person, however, perception becomes our reality. What one person sees, hears, and interprets is real and considered true to that person. When our perceptions differ from those with whom we interact, sharing meaning becomes more challenging. So how does perception work? Essentially, the brain selects some of the information it receives from the senses (sensory stimuli), organizes the information, and then interprets it.

Attention and Selection

Although we are constantly exposed to a barrage of sensory stimuli, we focus our attention on relatively little of it. Just think about how many TV channels you watch regularly compared to the number of channels offered. Or consider how many Web sites pop up when you do an Internet search. Can you imagine visiting all of them? Because we cannot focus on everything we see and hear all the time, we choose what stimuli to concentrate on based on our needs, interests, and expectations.

Needs We choose to pay attention to information that meets our biological and psychological needs. When we go to class, attend a workshop, or participate in a meeting, how well we pay attention usually depends on whether we believe the information is relevant. Our brains communicate intrapersonally by asking such questions as, "Will what I learn here help me in school, in the work world, and/or in my personal life?"

Interests We are likely to pay attention to information that piques our interests. Our interests are piqued when we see its relevance to us or those we care about (Sellnow, et al., 2014). For instance, when we hear or see a news story about a crisis event or natural disaster, we are more likely to pay attention when it is happening in our local community.

Expectations Finally, we are likely to see what we expect to see and miss what violates our expectations. Take a quick look at the phrases in the triangles in Figure 2.1. If you have never seen these triangles, you probably read "Paris in the springtime," "Once in a lifetime," and "Bird in the hand." Now take a closer look. Do you see the repeated words? They are easy to miss because we don't *expect* to see the word repeated.

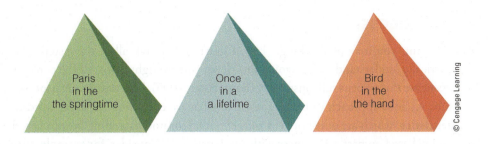

Figure 2.1

Expectations and perception

© Cengage Learning

Organization

Through the process of attention and selection we reduce the number of stimuli our brains must process. Still, the number of stimuli we attend to at any moment is substantial. So our brains organize these stimuli using the principles of simplicity and pattern.

Simplicity If the stimuli we attend to are complex, our brains simplify them into some commonly recognized form. We simplify both the nonverbal and verbal messages we receive. Based on a quick look at what someone is wearing, how she is standing, and the expression on her face, we may perceive her as a business executive, a doctor, or a soccer mom. Similarly, after Tony's boss described four major strengths and two minor areas for improvement during a performance review, Tony simplified the message by saying to his coworker, Jerry, "Well, I'd better shape up or I'm going to get fired!"

Pattern The brain also makes sense of complex stimuli by relating them to things it already recognizes. For example, when we see a crowd of people, instead of perceiving each individual, we may focus on sex and "see" men and women or on age and "see" children, teens, and adults.

Interpretation

As the brain selects and organizes information, it also assigns meaning to it (Photo 2.1). Look at these three sets of numbers. What are they?

A. 631 7348

B. 285 37 5632

C. 4632 7364 2596 2174

If you are used to seeing similar sets of numbers every day, you might interpret A as a telephone number, B as a Social Security number, and C as a credit card number. But your ability to interpret these numbers depends on your familiarity with the patterns. A French person may not recognize *631 7348* as a phone number since the pattern for phone numbers in France is: *0x xx xx xx xx*.

Throughout this chapter, we apply this basic information about perception to the study of social perceptions of self and others as they influence and are influenced by communication.

Photo 2.1 What assumptions do you make about this person based on how you organize and interpret what you see? Why?

Kayte Deioma/PhotoEdit

Dual Processing

At this point, you may be thinking, "Hey, I don't go through all of these steps. I just automatically 'understand' what's going on." If so, you are right. Most of the perceptual processing we do happens subconsciously (Baumeister, 2005). This **automatic processing** is a subconscious approach to making sense of what we encounter. In other words, we use **heuristics**, which are our short-cut *rules of thumb* for understanding how to perceive something based on past experiences with similar stimuli. Consider, for example, sitting at a red light. When it turns green, you go. You probably don't consciously think about taking your foot off the brake and applying it to the gas pedal.

But what happens when we encounter things that are out of the realm of our normal experiences or expectations? Then we must exert conscious effort to make sense of what is going on. **Conscious processing** is a slow deliberative process of examining and reflecting about the stimuli. Remember when you were first learning to drive? It took a lot of concentration to figure out what was happening on the road and how you were supposed to react. You probably thought carefully about doing things like taking your foot off the brake and applying it to the gas pedal when the light turned green.

Whether we engage in automatic or conscious processing, perception influences and is influenced by communication in a number of ways. The rest of this chapter is devoted to how we form perceptions of ourselves and others and the role communication plays in each.

Perception of Self

Self-perception is the overall view we have of ourselves, which includes both self-concept and self-esteem. **Self-concept** is the perception we have of our skills, abilities, knowledge, competencies, and personality (Weiten, Dunn, & Hammer, 2012). **Self-esteem** is the evaluation we make about our personal worthiness based on our self-concept (Hewitt, 2009; Smith & Mackie, 2007). In this section, we explain how self-concept and self-esteem are formed.

Self-Concept

How do we decide what our skills, abilities, competencies, and personality traits are? We do so based on the interpretations we make about our personal experiences and how others react and respond to us.

Our personal experiences are critical to forming our self-concept. We cannot know if we are competent at something until we've tried doing it, and we cannot discover our personality traits until we uncover them through experience. We place a great deal of emphasis on our first experiences with particular phenomena (Bee & Boyd, 2011). When we have a positive first experience, we are likely to believe we possess the competencies and personality traits associated with that experience. So if Sonya discovers at an early age that she does well on math problems and exams, she is likely to incorporate "competent mathematician" into her self-concept. If Sonya continues to excel at math throughout her life, that part of self-concept will be reinforced and maintained.

Similarly, when our first experience is negative, we are likely to conclude we do not possess that particular skill or trait. For instance, if you get anxious and draw a blank while giving a speech for the first time, you might conclude that you are a poor public speaker. Unfortunately, once we've had a negative first experience, it will likely take more several

automatic processing
a subconscious approach to making sense of what we encounter

heuristics
short-cut rules of thumb for understanding how to perceive something based on past experience with similar stimuli

conscious processing
a slow deliberative process of examining and reflecting about the stimuli

self-perception
the overall view we have of ourselves, which includes both our self-concept and self-esteem

self-concept
the perception we have of our skills, abilities, knowledge, competencies, and personality

self-esteem
the evaluation we make about our personal worthiness based on our self-concept

APPLY IT

Identify a skill you believe you are good at and one you believe you are not good at (e.g., "I am a good piano player. I am a terrible cook."). Now describe some personal experiences you've had that helped reinforce these beliefs.

MindTap

positive experiences to change our negative self-concept. So even if you succeed the second time you give a speech, it will probably take several more positive public speaking experiences for you to change your original conclusion about not being a good public speaker.

Our self-concept is also shaped by how others react and respond to us in two important ways (Weiten, Dunn, & Hammer, 2012). First, we use other people's comments to validate, reinforce, or alter our perceptions of who we think we are. For example, if during a brainstorming session, one of your co-workers says, "You're really a creative thinker," you may decide this comment fits your image of who you are, thus reinforcing your self-concept as someone who can think "outside the box."

Second, the feedback we receive from others may reveal abilities and personality characteristics we had never before associated with ourselves. For example, on the way back to campus after volunteering at the local Head Start Center, Janet commented to her friend Michael, "Gee, you're a natural with kids, they just flock to you." Michael thought about Janet's comment and similar ones he had received from others and decided to explore careers in early childhood education. Today he owns his own day care center and credits Janet with helping him recognize his natural ability to connect with preschoolers.

Not all reactions and responses have the same effect on our self-concept. For instance, reactions and responses coming from someone we respect or someone we are close to tend to be more powerful (Berk, 2012). This is especially important in families. Since self-concept begins to form early in life, information we receive from our family deeply shapes our self-concept (Photo 2.2) (Bee & Boyd, 2011). Thus, one major ethical responsibility of family members is to notice and comment on traits and abilities that help develop accurate and positive self-concepts in other family members. When Jeff's dad compliments him for keeping his bedroom clean because he is "so organized" or Carla's brother tells her she did a great job on her science project because she is "really smart," they are encouraging positive self-concepts.

As we interact with others, we also form an **ideal self-concept**, which is what we would like to be (Abel, Buff, & O'Neill, 2013). For example, although Jim may know he is not naturally athletic, in his ideal self-concept he wants to be. So he plays on an intramural basketball team, works out at the gym daily, and runs in local 5k and 10k races regularly.

ideal self-concept
what we would like to be

Photo 2.2 Our family members shape our self-concept. Can you recall a time when someone in your family praised you for something you did? Is that something you still consider yourself to be good at?

Self-Esteem

Self-concept and self-esteem are two different but related components of self-perception. Whereas self-concept is our perception of our competencies and personality traits, self-esteem is the positive or negative evaluation we attach to them. So self-esteem is not just our perception of how well or poorly we do things (self-concept), but also the importance we place on what we do well or poorly (Argyle, 2008). For instance, Mitchell believes he is an excellent piano player, a faithful friend, and good with kids. But if he doesn't value these competencies

© Blend Images/Shutterstock.com

and traits, then he will have low self-esteem. It takes both the perception of having a competency or trait and a belief that it is valuable to produce high self-esteem.

As is the case with self-concept, self-esteem depends not only on what each individual views as worthwhile but also on the ideas, morals, and values of the family and cultural group(s) to which the individual belongs. So if Mitchell comes from a family where athletic success is valued but artistic talents are not, if he hangs out with friends who don't appreciate his piano playing, and if he lives in a society where rock guitarists (not piano players) are the superstars, then his piano-playing ability may not raise his self-esteem.

We've already noted that families are critically important to developing one's self-concept, but they are even more central to developing positive self-esteem. For example, when Jeff's dad pointed out that Jeff's room is always tidy, he also said he was proud of Jeff, which raised Jeff's self-esteem about being organized. And when Carla's brother said she did a great job on her science project, he reinforced the value their family places on being smart, which raised her self-esteem about that attribute of her self-concept. Unfortunately, in some families, negative messages repeatedly sent can create an inaccurate self-concept and damage self-esteem. Communicating blame, name-calling, and constantly pointing out shortcomings are particularly damaging to self-esteem and some people never fully overcome the damage done to them by members of their families.

Our self-esteem can affect the types of relationships we form and with whom. Individuals with high self-esteem tend to form relationships with others who reinforce their positive self-perception, and similarly, individuals with low self-esteem tend to form relationships with those who reinforce their negative self-perception (Fiore, 2011). This phenomenon plays out in unfortunate ways when a person (very often a woman) perpetually goes from one abusive relationship to another (Engel, 2005).

Bullying also damages self-esteem. Children who are just forming their self-concepts and self-esteem, and adolescents whose self-concepts and self-esteem are in transition are particularly sensitive to bullying messages. Unfortunately, **cyberbullying**—the use of technology and particularly social media to harass others in a deliberate, repeated, and hostile manner—is becoming increasingly common especially among teenagers (U.S. Department of Health and Human Services, www.stopbullying.gov/cyberbullying /what-is-it/). Cyberbullying is extremely devastating to self-esteem. The effects of bullying can have long-lasting effects on self-esteem. In fact, many years after bullying incidents that occurred during childhood, people may still have inaccurate self-perceptions (Hinduja & Patchin, 2010).

Cultural Norms and Self-Perceptions

Cultural norms play a critical role in shaping both self-concept and self-esteem (Becker, et al., 2014). Two important ways they do so are in terms of independence/interdependence and masculinity/femininity.

In some cultures, such as the dominant American culture in the United States, people form and value independent self-perceptions. In other cultures, like the collectivist cultures of Japan and China, people form and value interdependent self-perceptions (Becker et al., 2014). **Independent self-perceptions** are based on the belief that traits and abilities are internal to the person and are universally applicable to all situations. The goal for someone with an independent self-perception is to demonstrate their abilities, competencies, characteristics, and personalities during interactions with others.

cyberbullying
the use of technology and social media to harass others in a deliberate, repeated, and hostile manner

independent self-perceptions
based on the belief that traits and abilities are internal to the person and are universally applicable to all situations

For example, if you have an independent self-concept and believe that one of your competencies is your ability to persuade others, you gain self-esteem by demonstrating your skill, convincing others, and having others praise you for it.

Interdependent self-perceptions are based on the belief that traits and abilities are specific to a particular context or relationship. The goal of people with interdependent self-perceptions is to maintain or enhance the relationship by demonstrating the appropriate abilities and personality characteristics for the situation. People with interdependent self-perceptions don't think, "I'm really persuasive," but rather, "When I am with my friends I am able to convince them to do what is good for all of us. When I am with my father I do what he believes is best for the good of our family." High self-esteem comes from knowing when to be persuasive and when to be compliant.

Cultural norms also play a role in shaping self-perception around masculinity and femininity. In the dominant culture of the United States, for instance, many people continue to expect boys to behave in "masculine" ways and girls to behave in "feminine" ways (Wood, 2007). In the past, boys in the United States were taught to base their self-esteem on their achievements, status, and income, and girls learned that their culture valued their appearance and their relationship skills. So boys and girls developed high or low self-esteem based on how well they met these criteria (Wood, 2007).

Today these cultural norms about "appropriate" characteristics and behaviors for males and females are becoming less rigid, but they do still exist and are promoted incessantly in popular culture and entertainment media. Consider just about any television sitcom. Most of them continue to portray women as the "natural" caregivers for the family, and when men attempt to perform a caregiver behavior, they often make a mess of the situation (Photo 2.3). Think about your family experiences growing up. How do they compare? Similarly, in terms of appearance, you only need to flip through the pages of any popular magazine to see the narrowly defined perceptions of what is valued as "ideal" for women and men.

Some people are intimately involved in more than one cultural group. If one of the cultures encourages interdependent and/or gendered self-perceptions and the other encourages independent and/or gender neutral self-perceptions, these people may develop both types of self-perception and actually switch between them based on the cultural group they are interacting within at a given time. They are more likely to do this well when they see themselves as part of and appreciate the strengths of both cultures (Benet-Martínez & Haritatos, 2005).

Accuracy and Distortion of Self-Perceptions

The accuracy of our self-concept and self-esteem depends on the accuracy of our perceptions of our own experiences and observations, as well as how we interpret others' reactions and responses to us. All of us experience successes and failures, and all of us hear praise and criticism. Since our perceptions are more likely than our true abilities to influence our behavior, accurate self-perception is critical to competent communication. Self-perception may suffer from **incongruence** when there is a

interdependent self-perceptions
based on the belief that traits and abilities are specific to a particular context or relationship

incongruence
a gap between self-perception and reality

Photo 2.3 Can you think of television programs that depict men, rather than women, as competent caregivers for a family?

AP Images/Mario Perez

Fuse/Getty Images

Photo 2.4 Who have you known that seems to have an over-inflated self-perception? Did you or do you enjoy interacting with him or her? Why or why not?

self-fulfilling prophecy
an inaccurate perception of a skill, characteristic, or situation that leads to behaviors that perpetuate that false perception as true

Photo 2.5 Have you known someone who seems to have a deflated perception of self? Did you or do you enjoy interacting with him or her? Why or why not?

© Goodluz/Shutterstock.com

gap between self-perception and reality. For example, Sean may actually possess all of the competencies and personality traits needed for effective leadership, but if he doesn't perceive himself to have these skills and characteristics, he won't step forward when leadership is needed. Likewise, Yuri is ashamed to be too assertive at work. So she doesn't voice her opinion even when the problem is in her area of expertise and could help solve a serious problem. Unfortunately, individuals tend to reinforce these incongruent self-perceptions by behaving in ways that conform to them rather than attempting to break free from them.

If we are overly attentive to successful experiences and positive responses, our self-perception may become inflated (Photo 2.4). We tend to describe such individuals as "arrogant," "pompous," "haughty," or "snobbish." On the other hand, if we dwell on our failures and not our successes, remember only the criticism we receive, or focus on how we don't measure up to our ideal self-concept, we may have a deflated self-perception (Photo 2.5). Winnie the Pooh's friend Eeyore, the donkey who is always "having a bad day," is an example of someone with a deflated sense of self. We tend to describe such individuals as "depressed," "despondent," "sullen," or "gloomy." Neither the person with the inflated or deflated perception of self accurately reflects who they are. These incongruent and distorted self-perceptions are magnified through self-fulfilling prophecies, filtering messages, and media images.

Self-fulfilling prophecies A **self-fulfilling prophecy** is an inaccurate perception of a skill, characteristic, or situation that leads to behaviors that perpetuate that false perception as true (Merton, 1968). Self-fulfilling prophesies may be self-created or other-imposed.

Self-created prophecies are predictions we make about ourselves. We often talk ourselves into success or failure. For example, when people expect rejection, they are more likely to behave in ways that lead others to reject them (Downey, Freitas, Michaelis, & Khouri, 2004). So Aaron, who sees himself as unskilled in establishing new relationships, says to himself, "I doubt I'll know anyone at the party—I'm going to have a miserable time." Because he believes he'll have trouble interacting with others, he doesn't introduce himself to anyone, and just as he predicted, spends much of his time standing around alone thinking about when he can leave. In contrast, Stefan sees himself as quite social and able to get to know people easily. As a result, he looks forward to the party, and just as he predicted, makes several new acquaintances and enjoys himself.

Sometimes a self-fulfilling prophecy is other-imposed and based on what others say about us. When teachers act as if their students are bright, students buy into this expectation and learn more as a result. Likewise, when teachers act as if students are not bright, students may "live down" to these imposed prophecies and fail to achieve. A good example takes place in the popular book *Harry Potter and the Order of the Phoenix*. A prophecy was made that suggested Harry Potter would vanquish the Dark Lord (Voldemort). So the Dark Lord sets out to kill Harry Potter. Dumbledore explains to Harry that the prophecy is only true because the Dark Lord believes it. Still, because the Dark Lord will not rest until he kills Harry, it becomes inevitable that Harry will, in fact, have to kill Voldemort (or vice versa).

Filtering messages Our self-perceptions can also become distorted through the way we filter what others say to us. We tend to pay attention to messages that reinforce our self-perception, and downplay or ignore messages that contradict this image. For example, suppose you prepare an agenda for your study group. Someone comments that you're a good organizer. If you spent your childhood hearing how disorganized you were, you may downplay or even ignore this comment. If, however, you think you are good at organizing, you will pay attention to the compliment and may even reinforce it by responding, "Thanks, I AM a pretty organized person. I learned it from my mom."

Helen Sloan/HBO/Everett Collection

Photo 2.6 How might media portrayals of "ideal" male and female figures distort self-perception?

Media images Another way self-perception can become distorted is through our interpretation of what we see on television, in the movies, and in popular magazines (Photo 2.6). Social cognitive learning theory suggests that we strive to copy the characteristics and behaviors of the characters portrayed as perfect examples or "ideal types" (Bandura, 1977). Persistent media messages of violence, promiscuity, use of profanity, bulked-up males, and pencil-thin females have all been linked to distorted self-perceptions among viewers. One particularly disturbing study found that before TV was widely introduced on the Pacific island of Fiji, only 3 percent of girls reported vomiting to lose weight or being unhappy with their body image. Three years after the introduction of TV, that percentage had risen to 15 percent, and an alarming 74 percent reported being too big or too fat (Becker, 2004). Unfortunately, distorted body image perceptions lead to low self-esteem and, sometimes, to self-destructive behaviors such as anorexia and bulimia.

APPLY IT

Identify an actor and an actress that society portrays as beautiful. Why? How might that influence the self-perception of viewers that don't "measure up" to this ideal?

MindTap®

Communication and Self-Perception

Self-perception influences how we talk to ourselves, how we talk about ourselves with others, how we talk about others to ourselves, the self we present to others, and our ability to communicate with others. Knowing how it does so may provide us with strategies for changing negative self-perceptions into positive ones.

Self-talk (a.k.a. intrapersonal communication) is the internal conversations we have with ourselves in our thoughts. People who have a positive self-perception are more likely to engage in positive self-talk, such as "I know I can do it" or "I did a really good job." People who have a negative self-perception are more likely to engage in negative self-talk, such as "There's no way I can do that" or "I really blew it." Not surprisingly, a high level of speech anxiety (the fear of public speaking) is often rooted in negative self-talk.

Self-perception also influences how we talk about ourselves with others. If we have a positive self-perception, we are likely to convey a positive attitude and take credit for our successes. If we have a negative self-perception, we are likely to convey a negative attitude and downplay our accomplishments. Why do some people put themselves down regardless of what they have done? Perhaps people with a negative self-perception find it less painful to put themselves down than to hear criticism from others. Thus, to preempt the possibility that others will comment on their unworthiness, they often do it first.

self-talk
the internal conversations we have with ourselves in our thoughts

Some research suggests that the Internet can influence how we communicate about ourselves with others in unique ways (Graham & Durron, 2014). Some Internet discussion groups, for example, are designed to be online journals where the user engages in reflection and introspection. These users are actually communicating with themselves while imagining a reader. Other research points to relationships between messages exchanged via e-mail, Twitter, Facebook, and other social networks and deception, disclosure, identity, influence, perception, privacy, sexual fidelity, and social support (Wright & Webb, 2010).

Self-perception also influences how we talk about others to ourselves. First, the more accurate our self-perception, the more likely we are to perceive others accurately. Second, the more positive our self-perception is, the more likely we are to see others favorably. Studies show that people who accept themselves as they are tend to be more accepting of others; similarly, those with a negative self-perception are more likely to be critical of others. Third, our own personal characteristics influence the types of characteristics we are likely to perceive in others. For example, people who are secure tend to see others as equally secure. If you recall that we respond to the world as we perceive it to be (and not necessarily as it is), you can readily see how negative self-perception can account for misunderstandings and communication breakdowns.

Our self-perceptions are the complete picture of how we view ourselves. When we communicate with others, however, most of us share only the parts we believe are appropriate to the situation. Research calls this phenomenon the **social construction of self**. For example, Damon presents his "manager self" at work where he is a serious task-oriented leader. When he is with his good friends, however, he is laid back, jovial, and more than happy to follow what the group wants to do. Which is the "real" Damon? Both are.

Do you have a Facebook page? Think of the time and effort you spend creating that "self." Does it accurately reflect all aspects of who you are? Do you pick and choose what to post on your page? Do you sometimes choose to "friend" certain people or not to "confirm" a friend request from others because of how you have constructed yourself on your Facebook page? These choices are based on the different aspects of ourselves we choose to highlight with different people. In fact, many people actually have two Facebook pages, one they share with personal friends and another they use to portray their professional selves. Others use a LinkedIn page for such connections. Social networking sites like these add another twist to the social construction of self because once we have posted information, others can co-opt our identity and actually reconstruct us in ways we never intended to do.

How effective we are at constructing different social selves depends on how actively we self-monitor. **Self-monitoring** is the internal process of being aware how we are coming across to others and adjusting our behavior accordingly. It involves being sensitive to other people's feedback and using that information to determine how we will respond (Rose & Kim, 2011). If you have ever been in a situation where you made a remark and did not get the response you expected, you may have thought to yourself, "Ooh, I wish I hadn't said that. I wonder how to fix it." This is an example of self-monitoring. Some people are naturally high self-monitors, constantly aware of how they are coming across to others. But even low self-monitors are likely to self-monitor when they are in a new situation or relationship.

We all use self-monitoring to determine which "self" we choose to display in different situations and with different people. Celebrities use self-monitoring to decide which

---

social construction of self
phenomenon of presenting different aspects of our self-concept based on the situation and people involved

APPLY IT

How do you act or portray yourself differently with the various people you interact with (e.g., siblings, parents or grandparents, close friends, teachers, bosses)?

MindTap®

self-monitoring
the internal process of being aware how we are coming across to others and adjusting our behavior accordingly

COMMUNICATING IN THE WORLD

Self-Monitoring and Celebrity Culture

Eduardo Munoz/Reuters

When she burst onto the pop music scene in 2009, Lady Gaga became known for outrageous performances and heavily stylized celebrity personas. In 2010, she wore a dress made of raw meat to the MTV Video Awards and in 2011 she showed up at the Grammys in a giant egg. Gaga has built her celebrity image not just on her musical talent but on her ability to draw public attention to herself.

We all socially construct the selves we present in certain situations. Is that the same thing as the person who was born Stefani Germonotta turning herself into Lady Gaga? Who is the real person beneath the celebrity image? For Gaga, as with all celebrities, being in the public eye means negotiating perceptions of who she is outside of her public image as a pop singer. Lady Gaga readily admits that such self-monitoring is a necessary part of her celebrity image. "[P]art of my mastering of the 'art of fame' is getting people to pay attention to what you want them to, and not pay attention to the things you don't want them to pay attention to," she explained in a *60 Minutes* interview.

Like all personas, Gaga's physical appearance and how she behaves in public is carefully constructed, but it is not necessarily fake or inauthentic.

Do you think Lady Gaga goes too far in creating her different social constructions of self? Why or why not?

MindTap®

"self" to portray in public, which may be very different from the "self" they are in their private lives. The *Communicating in the World* feature in this chapter highlights how and why Lady Gaga does so.

Self-concept and self-esteem are fairly enduring characteristics, but they can be changed. Comments that contradict your current self-perception may lead you to slowly change it. Certain situations expedite this process, for example, when you experience a profound change in your social environment. When children begin school or go to sleep-away camp; when teens start part-time jobs; when young adults go to college; or when people begin or end jobs or relationships, become parents, or grieve the loss of someone they love, they are more likely to absorb messages that contradict their current self-perceptions.

Therapy and self-help techniques can help alter our self-concept and improve our self-esteem. In fact, noted psychologist, Christopher Mruk (2013) points out that anyone can improve their negative self-concept and self-esteem through hard work and practice.

So why is this important to communication? Because our self-perception affects who we choose to form relationships with, how we interact with others, and how comfortable we feel when we are called on to share our opinions or present a speech. Essentially, improving self-perception improves how we interact with others, and improving how we interact with others improves self-perception. Emina's *Diverse Voices* story offers one example of how self-perception can change as a result of a profound change in one's social environment; in her case, in moving from Bosnia to the United States.

Who Am I? The Self-Perception Struggles of a Bosnian American

by Emina Herovic

It was not until my 22nd year of life that I began identifying myself as more American than Bosnian. I spent most of my childhood, adolescence, and young adulthood struggling with my cultural self-concept.

Born in the Balkan region of Bosnia, I was not yet three years old when war broke out. To escape the tragedies of war, my parents moved our family to Turkey where we lived for the next two and a half years. When our temporary settlement in Turkey expired, my father boldly moved us again, this time to the United States. By the time I was five years-old, I had lived in three different countries on three different continents and experienced three different cultures and languages.

Can you imagine my confusion and frustration? Just when I began speaking fluent Bosnian, we moved to Turkey. Then, just when I was becoming fluent in Turkish, I was thrown into a totally different cultural environment that used yet another language I didn't understand or speak. I remember walking into my kindergarten classroom on the first day of school in the United States. After observing the other kids for a few minutes, I remember turning to my mother saying, "These kids don't know how to talk!" I learned later that I was actually the oddball.

There was very little diversity among the people at the school I attended in the States. I was obviously the only "foreign" girl. I was surrounded by English-speaking teachers and peers and was exposed to American society at full force. When I was home, however, I was once again immersed in my native Bosnian cultural tradition and language: My parents would speak Serbo-Croatian around me; I ate Bosnian food; and I celebrated Bosnian traditions and customs. My religious practices also differed from those of my peers. Raised a Muslim, my family and I celebrated Islamic holidays. I remember as a little girl, when it was the month of Ramadan, I would go to the library at school during lunchtime to avoid the bombardment of questions from my peers as to why I was fasting. When I explained that it was a religious practice, some of them did not understand. Experiences such as these differentiated me from my peers and created a greater divide between my bi-cultural identities.

As a young girl and adolescent I did not perceive myself to be American at all. However, my strong Bosnian self-concept diminished as I got older. As I spoke, studied, and wrote in English every day at school and was exposed to Bosnian language only at home, I started to speak Bosnian less fluently. I also began to understand the American way of life, humor, and culture more. Year by year, I began to see myself as a bit more American.

However, my experiences as an immigrant child defined me in many ways that were vastly different from my peers. My peers could not fathom many of the hardships, circumstances, and events I had experienced growing up. In this sense, my self-perception actually became more unclear as I got older.

When I started feeling less Bosnian, I also felt guilty about losing the part of me that my parents had tried so hard to maintain after we immigrated to the United States.

By the time I was 22, I accepted my self-perception based on my dual identification with Bosnia and the United States. I also accepted that my American identity is now stronger than my Bosnian one. I have lived in the United States for most of my life. It is my home. I choose to acknowledge that being Bosnian will always be a part of me, and I would never want to change that. My experiences have educated me and I look on the world more broadly. I understand that everyone in the world has their own culture and customs. I know that other foreign-born Americans struggle with this aspect of self-perception. And that's why I have chosen to study this phenomenon in order to help others like me make successful self-perception transitions that honor their roots in more than one culture.

Source: Reprinted by permission of Emina Herovic.

COMMUNICATE ON YOUR FEET

Speech Assignment

Presenting Your Self-Concept

The Assignment

Jot down ten terms that describe your self-concept. Then create a short poem, rap, cheer, or song using those terms to present *who you see yourself as*. Perform it for the class. The presentation should take less than 2 minutes to perform.

Perception of Others

Now that we have discussed self-perception and the role of communication in it, let's look at how we perceive others and the role of communication in that process. When we meet others for the first time, questions might arise such as: "What is this person like?" and "What is this person likely to do, and why?" We might wonder whether we have anything in common, whether they like us, whether we will get along, and whether we'll enjoy the experience or feel uncomfortable. Our natural reaction to such feelings is to say and do things that will reduce these uncertainties (Littlejohn & Foss, 2011).

Speedbump.com. Creators Syndicate. Nov. 28 2011

Uncertainty Reduction

Uncertainty reduction, first conceptualized by Charles Berger and Richard Calabrese in 1975, is a communication theory that explains how individuals monitor their social environment in order to know more about themselves and others (Littlejohn & Foss, 2010). When people interact, they look for information to help them understand who their partner is and predict what their partner is likely to do. As we reduce uncertainty, we usually become more comfortable communicating (Guerrero, Andersen, & Afifi, 2007). To reduce uncertainty, we form impressions and make judgments about others as we interact with them.

uncertainty reduction
explains how individuals monitor their social environment to know more about themselves and others

Forming Impressions We engage in a variety of processes to form our perceptions about others. Researchers call these processes **impression formation**. Three of the most important ways we form impressions are based on physical appearance, perceived personality, and assumed similarity.

impression formation
processes we use to form perceptions of others

- **Physical Appearance.** The first thing we notice about other people is how they look. Although it may seem superficial, we form these first impressions very quickly. In fact, one study found that we assess how attractive, likeable, trustworthy, competent, and aggressive we think people are after looking at their faces for only 100 milliseconds (Willis & Todorov, 2006).

- **Implicit Personality Theory.** We also form impressions based on assumptions we make about another's personality. **Implicit personality theory** is our tendency to assume that two or more personality characteristics go together. So if we see someone displaying one trait, we assume they have the others we associate with it. For example, if you meet someone who is multilingual you might assume she is also intelligent. Or if you meet someone who volunteers at a homeless shelter, you might assume that he is compassionate.

implicit personality theory
tendency to assume that two or more personality characteristics go together

assumed similarity
assuming someone is similar to us in a variety of ways until we get information that contradicts this assumption

- **Assumed Similarity.** We also form impressions about others by thinking that others who share one characteristic with us also share others. Researchers call this **assumed similarity**. We assume someone is similar to us in a variety of ways until we get information that contradicts this assumption. For instance, when Sam attended a campaign event for a city council candidate who belonged to the same political party, he expected the candidate's views on locating a new prison in the city to be the same as his. Sam was pleased to hear that the candidate agreed with his viewpoint, but he was shocked to hear the candidate's racist reasoning.

Making Attributions At the center of our quest to reduce uncertainty is the need to predict how others will behave. By its nature, predicting something depends on understanding the cause and effect relationship between two things. So when we see someone acting a certain way we try to figure out why. Then we use this explanation to predict how that person will act in similar situations in the future. **Attributions** are reasons we give for others and our own behavior. For instance, suppose a co-worker with whom you had a noon lunch date has not arrived by 12:30. How do you explain her tardiness? One way you might explain it is to make a **situational attribution**, a reason that is beyond the control of the person. So you might assume that your co-worker must have had an accident on the way to the restaurant. On the other hand you may have made a **dispositional attribution**, attributing behavior to some cause that is under the control of the person. So you may perceive that your co-worker is forgetful, self-absorbed, or insensitive to others. In any case, your attribution reduces your uncertainty by answering the question, "Why is my co-worker late?" But the type of attribution you make influences how you interact with your co-worker once she shows up. If you believe it is not her fault, you are likely to be concerned, understanding, and supportive. On the other hand, if you made a dispositional attribution, you are likely to be annoyed or hurt.

attributions
reasons we give for others and our own behavior

situational attribution
a reason that is beyond the control of the person

dispositional attribution
attributing behavior to some cause that is under the control of the person

Inaccurate and Distorted Perceptions of Others

As we work to reduce uncertainty, we must be careful to reduce perceptual inaccuracies. Because perception is a complex process, we use shortcuts to help focus attention, interpret information, and make predictions about others. Selective perceptions, faulty attributions, forced consistency, and prejudice can lead to perceptual inaccuracies.

Selective perception is the perceptual distortion that arises from paying attention only to what we expect to see or hear and ignoring what we don't expect. For instance, if Donna sees Nick as a man with whom she would like to develop a strong relationship, she may choose to see the positive side of Nick's personality and ignore the negative side. Similarly, if Dean thinks his landlord is mean and unfair, he may ignore any acts of kindness or generosity offered by the landlord.

Forced consistency is the inaccurate attempt to make several perceptions about another person agree with each other. It arises from our need to eliminate contradictions. Imagine that Leah does not like her co-worker, Jill. If Jill supplies some information Leah missed on a form, Leah is likely to perceive Jill's behavior as interference, even if Jill's intention was to be helpful. If Leah likes Jill, however, she might perceive the very same behavior as helpful—even if Jill's intention was to interfere. In each case, the perception of "supplying missing information" is shaped by the need for consistency. It is consistent to regard someone we like as doing favors for us. It is inconsistent to regard people we don't like as doing favors for us. However, consistent perceptions of others are not necessarily accurate.

selective perception
the perceptual distortion that arises from paying attention only to what we expect to see or hear and ignoring what we don't expect

forced consistency
the inaccurate attempt to make several perceptions about another person agree with each other

Prejudice is judging a person based on the characteristics of a group to which the person belongs without regard to how the person may vary from the group (Dovidio & Gaertner, 2010). Prejudices are based on **stereotypes**, which are exaggerated or oversimplified generalizations used to describe a group. A professor may see a student's spiked purple hair and numerous tattoos and assume the student is a rebel who will defy authority, slack off on classroom assignments, and seek attention. In reality, this person may be a polite, quiet, serious honor student who aspires to go to graduate school. Prejudice can lead to **discrimination**, which is acting differently toward a person based on prejudice (Dovidio & Gaertner, 2010). Prejudice deals with perception and attitudes, while discrimination involves actions. For instance, when Laura meets Wasif and learns that he is Muslim, she may use her knowledge of women's roles in Islamic countries to inform her perception of Wasif and conclude that he is a chauvinist without really talking to him. This is prejudice. If based on this prejudice she refuses to be in a class project group with him she would be discriminating. Although he is an Iraqi American, Wasif may be a feminist, but Laura's use of the perceptual shortcut may prevent her from getting to know Wasif for the person he really is, and she may have cost herself the opportunity of working with the best student in class.

Racism, ethnocentrism, sexism, heterosexism, ageism, and **ableism** are various form of prejudice, in which members of one group believe that the behaviors and characteristics of their group are inherently superior to those of another group. All people can be prejudiced and act on their prejudices by discriminating against others. Nevertheless, "prejudices of groups with power are farther reaching in their consequences than others" (Sampson, 1999, p. 131). Because such attitudes can be deeply ingrained and are often subtle, it is easy to overlook behaviors we engage in that in some way meet this definition. Prejudicial perceptions may be unintentional, or they may seem insignificant or innocuous, but even seemingly unimportant prejudices rob others of their humanity and severely impede competent communication.

prejudice
judging a person based on the characteristics of a group to which the person belongs without regard to how the person may vary from the group

stereotypes
exaggerated or oversimplified generalizations used to describe a group

discrimination
acting differently toward a person based on prejudice

racism, ethnocentrism, sexism, heterosexism, ageism, and ableism
various form of prejudice in which members of one group believe that the behaviors and characteristics of their group are inherently superior to those of another group

Communication and Perceptions of Others

Because perceptions of others influence how we communicate, improving perceptual accuracy is an important element of competent communication. We offer the following guidelines to improve your perceptions of others and their messages.

1. **Question the accuracy of your perceptions.** Questioning accuracy begins by saying, "I know what I think I saw, heard, tasted, smelled, or felt, but I could be wrong. What other information should I be aware of?" By accepting the possibility that you have overlooked something, you will stop automatic processing and begin to consciously search out information that should increase your accuracy.

2. **Choose to use conscious processing as you get to know people.** When you mindfully pay attention to someone, you are more likely to understand the uniqueness of him or her. Doing so can increase the accuracy of your perceptions.

3. **Seek more information to verify perceptions.** If your perception is based on only one or two pieces of information, try to collect additional information. Note that your perception is tentative—that is, subject to change. The best way to get additional information about people is to talk with them. It's OK to be unsure about how to treat someone from another group. But rather than letting your uncertainty cause you to make mistakes, talk with the person and tell them you want to be

respectful. Then ask them for the information you need to become more comfortable about interacting appropriately and respectfully with them.

4. **Realize that your perceptions of a person will change over time.** People often base their opinions, assumptions, and behaviors on perceptions that are outdated. So when you encounter someone you haven't seen for a while, let the person's current behavior rather than their past actions or reputation inform your perceptions. For example, a former classmate who was wild in high school may well have changed and become a mature, responsible adult.

5. **Seek clarification respectfully by perception checking.** One way to assess the accuracy of a perception is to verbalize it and see whether others agree with what you see, hear, and interpret. A **perception check** is a verbal statement that reflects your understanding of another's behavior. It is a process of describing what you have seen and heard and then asking for feedback. A perception check statement consists of three parts. First, describe what you observed in a non-evaluative way. Second, offer two possible interpretations. Third, ask for clarification.

Recall Donna's predicament in the opening scenario of this chapter. She jumped to the conclusion that David was going to break up with her because he had been so quiet the night before and wasn't responding to any of her texts. Rather than jump to a conclusion and cause a defensive reaction when she does talk to David, she could employ a perception-checking message—something like this:

> *"When you didn't respond to my texts today"* (nonjudgmental description of the observed behavior), *"I thought you were mad at me"* (first interpretation), *"or maybe you were really busy at work"* (second interpretation). *"Is everything ok? Is it something else?"* (request for clarification).

Basically, perception checking is a tool to respectfully check for understanding of another's behavior without assuming your interpretation is correct.

---

perception check
a message that reflects your understanding of the meaning of another person's behavior and seeks clarification

---

COMMUNICATION SKILL

Perception Checking

Skill	Use	Procedure	Example
Making a verbal statement that reflects your understanding of another person's behavior.	To enable you to test the accuracy of your perceptions.	1. Offer a nonjudgmental description of the behavior that led to your perception. 2. Offer your interpretation of the behavior. 3. Offer a second possible interpretation. 4. Request clarification.	After taking a phone call, Shimika comes into the room with a completely blank expression and neither speaks to Donnell nor acknowledges that he is in the room. Donnell says, "Shimika, from your blank look, I get the feeling that you're in a state of shock. Or perhaps you are just tired. Has something happened? Is it something else?"

WHAT WOULD YOU DO?

A Question of Ethics

"There," exclaimed Ryan, "my résumé is done and ready to post on LinkedIn. Will you take a look at it and tell me what you think?"

"Sure," Shara replied. As she began to read, Shara gasped, "Ryan, it says here you have a degree in chemical engineering. But you don't."

"Well, that's my major. I'll have a degree in it eventually. Besides, everybody stretches the truth a little on their résumés."

"And what about this statement about your job responsibilities while working at LexCo," Shara continued. "I know you were a receptionist for two summers. You make it sound like you were a supervisor and that you actually worked there for two years."

"Well," Ryan replied, "remember how Professor Jarman said we need to sell ourselves if we want to get selected for the interview? I'm trying to make myself stand out as a leader."

"I'm not sure that's what he meant, Ryan. You need to be honest," Shara responded.

"Yeah, well, I can clarify the details in the interview. I just want to make sure I actually get an interview."

What, if any, ethical principles is Ryan violating and how?

MindTap

Reflection and Assessment

The way we perceive ourselves and others influences how we communicate and the kinds of relationships we form. To assess how well you've learned what we addressed in these pages, answer the following questions. If you have trouble answering any of them, go back and review that material. Once you can answer each question accurately, you are ready to move ahead to read the next chapter.

1. What is involved in the perception process and why?
2. How do we form and maintain our self-concept and self-esteem?
3. What strategies can we employ to improve our self-perceptions?
4. How do we form perceptions of others?
5. What can we do to improve the accuracy of our perceptions of others and their messages?

COMMUNICATE!

RESOURCE AND ASSESSMENT CENTER

MindTap®

Now that you have read Chapter 2, go to your MindTap for *Communicate!* for quick access to the electronic resources that accompany this text.

Applying What You've Learned

Impromptu Speech Activity

Self-Concept Speech Prepare a 2- to 3-minute speech discussing how your initial impression of a friend has evolved over time.

Assessment Activities

1. Your Socially Constructed Selves Consider your roles in various situations in the last three days such as "lunch with a friend" or "grocery store shopper at the checkout" or "meeting with a professor about an assignment." Describe the social construction of self you portray in each setting. Then, prepare a 1- to 2-page paper and/or 2- to 3-minute speech answering the following questions:

- To what extent did your "self" change across situations?
- What factors contributed to these differences?
- Are there certain roles you take on more than others?
- Are there roles you would like to modify?
- How satisfied are you with the "selves" you have enacted and why?

2. Who Am I? Complete this journal activity to assess how your self-concept aligns with how others see you.

First ask: *How do I see myself?* List the skills, abilities, knowledge, competencies, and personality characteristics that describe how you see yourself. To generate this list, try completing these sentences: "I am skilled at . . ."; I have the ability to . . ."; "I know things about . . ."; I am competent at doing . . . "; and "One part of my personality is that I am . . .". List as many characteristics in each category as you can think of. What you have developed is an inventory of your self-concept.

Second ask: *How do others see me?* List the skills, abilities, and so on that describe how you think others see you by completing these sentences: "Other people believe I am skilled at . . ."; "Other people believe I have the ability to . . ."; "Other people believe I know things about . . ."; "Other people believe I am competent at doing . . ."; and "One part of my personality is that other people believe I am . . .".

Compare your two lists. How are they similar? Where are they different? Do you understand why they differ? After you have thought about each, write a paragraph titled "Who I Am, and How I Know This."

3. Stereotypes and Media For a few days, catalog the stereotypes you come across as portrayed in mass media. Enter your research into a log broken down into the following categories: (1) medium of communication (TV, radio, magazines, newspapers, the Internet, signage/posters); (2) source (general content or advertising); (3) target (race, ethnicity/culture, religion, gender, sexual orientation, age, income, profession, hobby, appearance); and (4) connotation (positive or negative).

After you have completed your research, analyze the results. What target was most frequently stereotyped in your findings? Did some mediums of communication indulge in more stereotyping the others? Did regular programming or advertising employ more stereotyping than the other? Were the majority of the stereotypes positive or negative in connotation? Did anything in your research surprise you? Write a paragraph explaining what you learned in this activity.

4. Internet Impression Formation and Management Do an Internet vanity search of yourself online. Search for content and images using multiple search engines. What image does the search suggest about you? Do the same thing for a person whom you respect. What surprised you about what you found. What image does the Internet portray about you? About the person whom you respect? How might you adjust the story being told of you? How might you check the perception the Internet story gives you of the other person. Write up a 400-500 word reflection essay you can share with your instructor and/or classmates.

Skill-Building Activities

1. Perception Checking Practice As an individual or with a partner, prepare a perception-checking response to each of the following scenarios. Be ready to share your response aloud if called upon by your instructor.

   a. Your neighbor Bill usually responds in kind to your "good morning" as you head out for the day. He hasn't responded for the last three days. What would you say to him?

   b. You and your roommate have a deal: Whoever makes the evening meal also does the dishes. He made the meal last night. When you wake up in the morning, you see the dirty dishes still in the sink. When you see your roommate, what might you say?

   c. You haven't received a phone call from your mom in over a month. The last time you talked with her, you had an argument because you are not planning to go home for the holidays this year. What would you say to her when you call her?

   d. When you see your advisor in the hallway, you ask if you can make an appointment to talk about internship possibilities. He says, "Of course. I don't have my calendar with me. Let's set a date and time over e-mail." You haven't heard from him in two weeks, so you decide to e-mail him yourself. What do you say?

2. Practicing Perception Checking Sentences For each of the following situations, write a well-phrased perception check.

   a. When Franco comes home from the doctor's office, you notice he looks pale, and his shoulders are slumped. Glancing at you with a sad look, he shrugs his shoulders. You say:

   b. As you return the basketball you borrowed from Liam, you smile and say, "Thanks, here's your ball." You notice Liam stiffen, grab the ball, and, turning abruptly, walk away. You say:

   c. You see your advisor in the hall and ask her if she can meet with you on Wednesday afternoon to discuss your schedule of classes for next term. You notice that she pauses, frowns, sighs, turns slowly, and says, "I guess so." You say:

Compare your written responses to the guidelines for effective perception checking discussed earlier. Edit your responses where necessary to improve them. Now say them aloud. Do they sound "natural"? If not, revise them until they do.

Intercultural Communication

MindTap®

Start with a quick warm-up activity.

"Wow," Martina exclaimed, "the mall is packed today! It's going to be tough to find a parking spot."

"Just take that one over there. It's really close to the main entrance," Gloria responded as she pointed to the spot.

Just as Martina began to pull in, she noticed the reserved parking sign.

"Bummer, we can't park there."

"Why not? We're only going to be here for a couple of minutes and there are several other empty spots reserved for people with disabilities," remarked Gloria. "Besides, my uncle says most people that have handicapped parking stickers aren't really disabled. See," she said as she pointed, "just look at that guy getting out of his car. He doesn't look disabled to me."

Martina replied, "Hey Gloria, not all people living with disabilities are in wheelchairs, you know."

culture
the system of shared values, beliefs, attitudes, and norms that guide what is considered appropriate among an identifiable group of people

values
commonly accepted standards of what is considered right and wrong, good and evil, fair and unfair, and so on

ideal values
values members profess to hold

real values
values that guide members actual behavior

intercultural communication
the interactions that occur between people of different cultures

culture shock
psychological discomfort one feels when engaging in a new cultural situation

How could we evaluate Gloria's assumptions? Are Martina's assumptions more accurate? In both cases, their judgments are based on perceptions of people that are culturally different from themselves.

Because culture has a profound impact on perception and communication, this chapter focuses on the relationship between culture and communication. We begin by explaining some basic concepts of culture and several ways cultures are unique. We end by offering strategies for improving intercultural communication competence.

Culture and Communication

Culture is the system of shared values, beliefs, attitudes, and norms that guide what is considered appropriate among an identifiable group of people (Samovar, Porter, & McDaniel, 2012). In a real sense, culture is a way of life. It's the taken-for-granted *rules* for how and why we believe and behave as we do.

At the heart of any culture are its values. **Values** are the commonly accepted standards of what is considered right and wrong, good and evil, fair and unfair, just and unjust, and so on. Cultures have both ideal and real values. **Ideal values** are the ones that members profess to hold, whereas **real values** are the ones that guide their actual behavior. For example, the United States Constitution professes equal rights and opportunities for all (ideal value), yet some people are treated unfairly based on sex, race, ethnicity, age, disability, or sexual orientation (real value in action).

Intercultural communication refers to the interactions that occur between people whose cultures are so different that the communication between them is altered (Samovar, Porter, & McDaniel, 2012). To become effective intercultural communicators, we must begin by understanding what a culture is, then identifying how cultures differ from one another, and finally realizing how those differences influence communication.

We do not have to journey to other countries to meet people of different cultures. The United States population, for example, includes not only recent immigrants from other countries, but also descendents of earlier immigrants and of native peoples. So understanding how communication varies among cultural groups can help us as we interact with the people we encounter every day right here in the United States.

Because each of us is so familiar with our own customs, norms, and values, we may feel anxious when they are disrupted. We call this psychological discomfort when engaging in a new cultural situation **culture shock** (Klyukanov, 2005, p. 33). We are likely to feel culture shock most profoundly when thrust into an unfamiliar culture through travel, business, or studying abroad. In the film *Lost in Translation*, for example, Bill Murray's character struggles with culture shock while filming a commercial on location in Japan.

Culture shock can also occur when interacting with others within one's own country (Photo 3.1). For example, Brittney, who is from a small town in Minnesota, experienced culture shock when she visited Miami, Florida, for the first time. She was overwhelmed as she noted the distinct Latin flavor of the city, heard Spanish spoken on the street, and saw billboards written in Spanish. Brittney was disoriented because what she witnessed seemed foreign to her. Likewise, if Maria, who lives in Miami, were to visit the small Minnesota town where Brittney grew up, she might also experience culture shock. She might feel uncomfortable because Brittney's hometown might seem a bit like the rural Minnesota towns whose values and customs are humorously highlighted on Garrison Keillor's public radio program *A Prairie Home Companion*.

Culture is both transmitted and modified through communication. In Western cultures, for example, most people eat using forks, knives, spoons, individual plates, and bowls. In some cultures, people may eat with chopsticks, use bread as a utensil, or use their fingers and share a common bowl. All of these dining rituals are culturally based and taught by one generation to the next through communication.

Communication is also the mechanism through which culture is modified. For example, several generations ago, most American children were taught to show respect by addressing adult family friends using a title and last name (e.g., Mr. Jones, Miss Smith). Today, children often address adult family friends by their first names. How did this cultural norm change? In earlier generations, adults corrected young children who addressed an adult by his or her first name. But toward the end of the 20th century, adults began giving children permission to use first names and, over time, the norm changed. So communication is both the means by which culture is transmitted and the way a culture is changed.

Photo 3.1 Culture shock can occur when visiting other countries, and even places in one's own country. When and where have you experienced culture shock?

Dominant Cultures, Co-Cultures, and Cultural Identity

Dominant culture refers to the learned system of norms held by the majority group of empowered people in a society. The dominant culture of the United States has evolved over time. It once strictly reflected and privileged the values of white, western European, English-speaking, Protestant, heterosexual men. Before the 1960s, people immigrating to the United States were expected to adapt to this dominant culture in place of the culture of their native country. Immigrants even changed their names to sound more American. They were expected to learn English quickly and use it instead of other languages. Since the 1960s, however, the United States has begun to experience a gradual modification of the dominant culture to demonstrate respect for the diverse cultures that co-exist here.

In addition to embracing the dominant American culture, then, many people also identify with one or more co-cultures. A **co-culture** is a group comprised of a smaller number of people who hold common values, beliefs, attitudes, and customs that differ from those of the dominant culture.

Co-culture also influences communication behavior. For example, co-cultural group members sometimes **code switch**, altering their linguistic and nonverbal patterns to conform to the dominant or co-culture depending on the topic and participants involved in a conversation (MacSwan, 2013) (Photo 3.2). So Linh may speak Vietnamese and defer to her older relatives while conversing at the dinner table. She may speak English and question her teachers openly during class discussions at school. And she may speak a mixture of Vietnamese and English (as well as slang and other accepted *in-group* jargon) when hanging out with friends. If you are familiar with the movie *Windtalkers,* you might know that the film is based on the real-life role Navajo code

dominant culture
the learned system of norms held by the majority group of empowered people in a society

co-culture
a group comprised of a smaller number of people who hold common values, beliefs, attitudes, and customs that differ from those of the dominant culture

code switch
altering one's linguistic and nonverbal patterns to conform to the dominant of co-culture depending on the topic and participants involved

Hemis/Alamy

Photo 3.2 Code switchers vary their language to communicate with the dominant culture and to members of their co-culture. Do you ever code switch when conversing with members of a particular group to which you belong?

cultural identity
part of the self-concept that is based on how closely one associates with the dominant culture and various co-cultures

ethnicity
a shared cultural heritage that is learned

native (or first) language
language of one's ethnic heritage

APPLY IT

Because so many U.S. citizens speak Spanish as a first or second language and because it is so widely spoken around the world, there is considerable debate about whether it should be adopted as a second official language of the United States. Where do you stand on this issue and why?

MindTap®

switchers played in Saipan during World War II (Jackson, 2004). You can see a short story about these Navajo code switchers on the Navajo Code Talkers Web site.

Cultural identity is the part of our self-concept that is based on how closely we associate with both the dominant culture and various co-cultures (Ting-Toomey & Chung, 2012). For example, you may be proud to be a third-generation Polish American who embraces the co-culture of your heritage through communication patterns, religion, food choices, and so on. Or you might identify more with the dominant American culture and rarely think about being Polish. If the dominant culture stigmatizes your co-culture, you might downplay this part of your identity to fit into the dominant culture or identify even more closely with the co-culture and become a vocal activist for it. For example, Cindy is a Polish American who hid that fact while growing up because her classmates often told jokes that stigmatized Polish Americans as foolish and unintelligent.

Some of the co-cultures that exist in the United States today are formed around shared beliefs and values related to, for example, race, ethnicity, sex and gender, sexual orientation, religion, socioeconomic status, age or generation, and disability.

Race Traditionally, the term "race" was used to classify people based on physical, biological characteristics (e.g., skin and eye color, hair texture, body shape). However, today the use of the word "race" has become problematic and some scholars prefer to use the term "populations" instead (Waples & Gaggiotti, 2006). Nevertheless, people do experience the social effects of *perceived race* and form co-cultures based on similar experiences with respect to it (Rhodes, Lie, Ewing, Evangelista, & Tanaka, 2010). For example, the dominant American culture respects police officers as protectors. However, based on collective experiences of unjust treatment by some police officers, some African American co-cultures may not respect police officers as protectors, but instead view them with suspicion.

Ethnicity Whereas race is related to biological characteristics, **ethnicity** refers to a shared cultural heritage that is learned rather than inherited. The degree to which people identify with their ethnicity can vary greatly. For example, Maria and Juan are both Mexican Americans. Juan, who immigrated to the United States recently, continues to identify strongly with his ethnicity in terms of the foods he eats and the way he dresses. Maria, who is a fourth-generation Mexican American, identifies more as an American than a Mexican American.

Native (or first) language is the language of one's ethnic heritage and is typically the language a person learns from birth. Native language obviously influences communication. Even after learning English, many immigrants choose to speak their native language at home and to live in close proximity to others from their home country. Although the United States is considered an English-speaking country, Spanish is the second most common language spoken here and is the primary language spoken at home by 38.3 million people in the United States (U.S. Census Bureau, 2010). Not only that, Spanish is the third most common language used on the Internet (Global Internet Usage, 2014). So today, most toll-free telephone numbers offer the option of conversing in English or Spanish; most cable and satellite television packages include Spanish-language channels; and Spanish radio stations can be heard across the country.

Sex and Gender In the dominant American culture, **sex** (which consists of biologically determined physical traits) and **gender** (which consists of the learned roles and communication patterns deemed "appropriate" for males and females) tend to be inter-

Lance King/Getty Images Sport/Getty Images

Photo 3.3 Many schools used to offer cheerleading as a girls'-only sport. Today, both females and males compete in all kinds of sports, including cheer teams. What sports do or did you and your family members compete in? In what ways might gendered norms have influenced the decisions made?

twined. In other words, the dominant American culture expects men to communicate in masculine ways and women to communicate in feminine ways. If you have ever heard someone tell an outspoken young girl to "hush up and act like a lady," or a weeping boy to "buck up and act like a man," you have witnessed young people *learning gender* based on their sex. Generally, women who identify with the feminine gender co-culture may tend to speak more about their personal relationships, more easily describe their feelings, be more likely to include others in conversation, and actively respond to others (e.g., head nods, smiles). On the other hand, men who identify with masculine gender co-culture may focus more on tasks and outcomes, as well as emphasize control, competition, and status (Wood, 2010). Obviously, people differ in the extent to which they identify with these gendered co-cultures, and those who do not strongly identify with them may not behave in accord with these expectations at all (Photo 3.3).

Sexual Orientation The dominant American culture has historically valued and privileged heterosexuality. People who deviated from the heterosexual norm were severely mistreated (Photo 3.4). Although laws that reflect a change in attitude toward sexuality are gaining popularity, people who are not heterosexual still face discrimination, as well as legal and physical threats. Thus, co-cultures exist across the country based on the collective experiences of those who embrace a sexual orientation that is not heterosexual. Although many people are working hard to modify the dominant American culture with regard to sexual orientation, and some progress has been made, much remains to be done.

Religion A **religion** is a belief system with a set of rituals and ethical standards based on a common perception of what is sacred or holy. Although the dominant culture in the United States values religious freedom, historically it has privileged monotheistic Judeo-Christian values and practices. However, many religious co-cultures exist harmoniously across the country today. Unfortunately, some people in the United States have become prejudiced against Muslims based on a misunderstanding that inaccurately equates all Muslims with Al-Qaeda, the militant group responsible for the 9/11 terrorist attacks and, more recently, ISIS, the Islamic State of Iraq and Syria, which promotes extreme violence and mass killings in the name of its extremist religious ideology. These terrorist groups, however, are not representative of Muslim religious views. About 23 percent (1.6 billion people) of the

sex
biologically determined physical traits

gender
learned roles and communication patterns deemed "appropriate" for males and females

religion
a belief system with a set of rituals and ethical standards based on a common perception of what is sacred or holy

Focus Features/The Kobal Collection/Picture Desk

Photo 3.4 In the 1970s, Harvey Milk became the mayor of San Francisco, and by proxy, the first openly gay politician in America. This spurred a movement for others to stand up for their human rights as gay Americans. Milk was assassinated at the height of his popularity. Do you have friends or family members who are gay? How might this fact make their lives different from yours?

socioeconomic status
the position of a person or family in the power hierarchy of a society based on income, education, and occupation

world's population is Muslim, and among the core values of this religion are peace, mercy, and forgiveness (DeSilver, 2013; Faruqi, 2007).

Socioeconomic Status (SES)
Socioeconomic status (SES) is the position of a person or family in the power hierarchy of a society based on income, education, and occupation. SES is typically divided into three categories: high, middle, and low. Most Americans identify with the middle class even though they may really be members of a higher or lower class (U.S. Department of Commerce, 2010). People develop co-cultures that reinforce distinct values, rituals, and communication practices based on SES. Although not true in all cases, parents in low SES groups tend to emphasize obedience, acceptance of what others think, and hesitancy in expressing desires to authority figures. Middle-class parents tend to emphasize intellectual curiosity. Such differences based on SES may lead those from middle-class backgrounds to speak more directly and assertively than people from lower-class backgrounds. And, in terms of nonverbal communication, people of high SES backgrounds tend to perform more disengagement cues (e.g., doodling) and fewer engagement cues (e.g., head nods, laughs) than people from low SES backgrounds (Bornstein & Bradley, 2003; Kraus & Keltner, 2009). Finally, SES is at the heart of the American dream. Unfortunately, however, recent reports suggest that "the widening gap between the rich and poor is eroding the American dream" (Lynch, 2013).

Age/Generation People born and raised in the same generation may identify with a co-culture distinct to it. Although not all people identify with their generational co-culture, generally speaking, people who grew up during the Great Depression tend to be frugal and those who grew up during World War II tend to value sacrifice of self for cause and country. Baby Boomers who came of age during the turbulent 1960s are likely to question authority. Many Generation Xers, who grew up as *latch-key kids* (with parents at jobs outside the home when they got home from school), are likely to be self-sufficient and adaptable. Millennials (a.k.a. Generation Y and Generation NeXt), who grew up during the 1990s and came of age after 9/11, have never known life without computers, became aware of the realities of school and world violence at an early age, and experienced globalization. They tend to be adept at using technology to multitask, be cautious about issues of safety, and appreciate diversity (Pew Research Center, 2007). Finally, Generation Z (a.k.a. the Internet Generation or Digital Natives) were born after the Cold War era and the fall of the Soviet Union. They have never known a world without instant access to information via Internet searches on computers and smart phones, nor access to others via text messaging and social media sites like Facebook. They are adept at multitasking, as well as learning and using new technologies such as gaming (Prensky, 2001; Wallice, 2006).

When people from different generations interact, their co-cultural orientations can cause communication challenges (Photo 3.5). For example, when people who came of age after the

1960s interact with people from earlier generations, different expectations about how to demonstrate respect might cause misunderstandings and even conflict.

Disability A **disability** is any physical, emotional, mental, or cognitive impairment that impacts how a person functions in society. A disability co-culture is a group of people who share a distinct set of shared values, beliefs, and attitudes based on their common experiences of being differently abled (Brown, 2002).

Recently, a number of feature films and documentaries have been produced to help people who do not live with a disability to both understand and respect various differently-abled co-cultures. For example, HBO came out with a film about the real life of Temple Grandin (2010), a professor of animal science who improved the ethical treatment of animals, and who is also autistic. *Music Within* tells the story of what two Vietnam veterans did to help get the Americans with Disabilities Act passed, and *Front of the Class* focuses on the true story of a boy with Tourette syndrome who grew up to become a gifted teacher. Such films help break through misinformed stereotypes and prejudiced thinking about the value and human potential of people that are differently-abled (a.k.a. living with a disability).

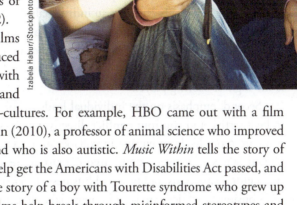

Izabela Habur/iStockphoto.com

Photo 3.5 Many young people today prefer to text rather than call friends and family. How might that preference influence communication with people of earlier generations who might prefer conversing on the phone or in person?

disability
any physical, emotional, mental, or cognitive impairment that impacts how a person functions in society

How Cultures Differ

We may be able to speculate as to which cultural groups people identify with based on their language, attire, or personal artifacts (e.g., religious markers worn as jewelry or placed in the home). Usually, however, such signs don't really tell us much beyond surface assumptions.

The early work of Edward T. Hall and more recently Gerard Henrik (Geert) Hofstede give us ways to understand how cultures are similar to and different from one another and how these cultural variations may affect communication. Based on their work, we offer several dimensions for consideration: (1) individualism/collectivism, (2) context, (3) chronemics, (4) uncertainty avoidance, (5) power distance, (6) masculinity/femininity, and (7) long-term/short-term orientation.

Individualism/Collectivism

Cultures differ in the extent to which individualism or collectivism is valued. Highly **individualistic cultures** value personal rights and responsibilities, privacy, voicing one's opinion, freedom, innovation, and self-expression (Andersen, Hecht, Hoobler, & Smallwood, 2003). People in highly individualistic cultures place primary value on the self and personal achievement. Competition is both desirable and useful, and the interests of others are considered primarily as they affect personal interests. Cultures in the United States, Australia, Great Britain, Canada, and Northern and Eastern European countries are considered to be highly individualistic.

In contrast, highly **collectivist cultures** value community, collaboration, shared interests, harmony, the public good, and avoiding embarrassment (Andersen, Hecht, Hoobler,

individualistic cultures
value personal rights and responsibilities, privacy, freedom, innovation, and self-expression

collectivist cultures
value community, collaboration, shared interests, harmony, the public good, and avoiding embarrassment

& Smallwood, 2003). Highly collectivist cultures place primary value on the interests of the group and group harmony. Decisions are shaped by what is best for the group, regardless of whether they serve an individual's personal interests. Maintaining harmony and cooperation is valued over competition and personal achievement. A variety of cultures throughout South and Central America, East and Southeast Asia, and Africa are considered to be highly collectivist.

Individualism and collectivism influence many aspects of communication (Samovar, Porter, & McDaniel, 2012). First, individualism and collectivism affect self-concept and self-esteem. People in individualist cultures form independent self-concepts and base their self-esteem on individual accomplishments. People in collectivist cultures form interdependent self-concepts and base their self-esteem on how well they work in a group. So, if LuAnne is raised in an individualistic culture and she is the highest-scoring player on her basketball team, she will probably identify herself as "winner," even if her team has a losing season. But if LuAnne is from a collectivist culture, the fact that her team had a losing season is more likely to influence her self-esteem than the fact that she is the highest-scoring player.

Second, emphasis on the individual leads members of highly individualistic cultures to be assertive and confront conflict directly, whereas members of highly collectivist cultures are more likely to engage in collaboration or to avoid conflict (Photo 3.6). In the United States, assertiveness and argumentation are skills used in personal relationships, small group situations, politics, and business. In Japan, a highly collectivist culture, common business practices are based on an elaborate process called *nemawashii* (a term that also means "binding the roots of a plant before pulling it out"). To maintain harmony and avoid confrontational argument, any subject that might cause conflict should be discussed among individuals before the group meets to ensure that interactions during the meeting will not seem rude or impolite (Samovar, Porter, & McDaniel, 2012).

Finally, individualism and collectivism influence how people make group decisions. In highly collectivist cultures, group members strive for consensus and may sacrifice optimal outcomes for the sake of group harmony. In highly individualistic cultures, optimal outcomes are paramount, even at the expense of disharmony. Groups comprised of members that come from both highly individualistic and highly collectivist cultures may experience difficulties because of these different cultural values related to individualism and collectivism.

low-context cultures
people rely mainly on words to convey meaning

Photo 3.6 As you can imagine, conducting a business meeting with professionals from both individualistic and collectivist cultures can prove quite challenging. Have you ever found yourself in such a situation? If so, how did communication work among members?

© VGstockstudio/Shutterstock.com

Context

Another cultural distinction that affects communication is the extent to which members rely on contextual cues to convey the meaning of a message (Hall, 1976; Schein, 2010). In **low-context cultures**, speakers use words to convey most of the meaning. In low-context cultures like those of the United States, Germany, and Scandinavia, verbal messages are direct, specific, and detailed. Speakers are expected to say exactly what they mean and get to the point. In **high-context cultures**, much of the speaker's message is understood from the context. Much of the meaning is conveyed indirectly and can only be accurately interpreted by referring to unwritten cultural rules and subtle nonverbal behaviors. So in high-context cultures such as those of American Indian, Latin American, and Asian communities, verbal messages are ambiguous and understood by "reading between the lines" (Chen & Starosta, 1998).

high-context cultures
speaker's message is understood mainly based on context

Effective communication between members of high- and low-context cultures can be challenging. When low-context communicators interact with high-context communicators, they should be mindful that building a good relationship first is important for long-term effectiveness. Also, nonverbal messages and gestures will probably be more important than what is actually said. When high-context communicators interact with low-context communicators, they should recognize that the verbal message should be taken at face value and direct questions, assertions, and observations are not meant to be offensive. Finally, they need to recognize that low-context communicators might not notice or understand indirect contextual cues.

Chronemics

Chronemics is the study of how the perception of time differs among cultures (Hall, 1976). **Monochronic cultures** view time as a series of small units that occur sequentially. Monochronic cultures value punctuality, uninterrupted task completion, meeting deadlines, following plans, and doing things one at a time. For instance, when Margarite (who values a monochronic time orientation) is interrupted by her roommate, who wants to share some good news about her day, Margarite may respond, "I can't talk now. It's my study time!" The dominant culture of the United States values a monochronic orientation to time.

chronemics
perception of time

monochronic cultures
view time as a series of small units that occur sequentially

Polychronic cultures, for example, Latin American, Arab, and Southern European cultures, view time as a continuous flow. Thus, appointment times and schedules are perceived as approximate and fluid. People who abide by polychronic orientation to time are comfortable doing several things at once, having a flexible schedule or none at all, and disregarding deadlines to satisfy other needs (Chen & Starosta, 1998). Interruptions are not perceived as annoying but as natural occurrences.

polychronic cultures
view time as a continuous flow

Differences in time orientation can make intercultural communication challenging. In polychronic cultures, relationships are more important than schedules. So when Dante, who is polychronic, shows up for a noon lunch with Sean at 12:47 because a coworker had needed some help, he doesn't perceive this as a problem. But Sean, who is monochronic, is annoyed because Dante arrived so "late," and quickly moves the discussion to the business they need to complete. Sean's attitude and immediate discussion of business seems rude to Dante.

Uncertainty Avoidance

Cultures differ in their attitudes toward **uncertainty avoidance**, which is the extent to which people desire to predict what is going to happen. **Low uncertainty-avoidance cultures** such as those of the United States, Sweden, and Denmark tolerate uncertainty and are less driven to control unpredictable people, relationships, or events. People tend to accept unpredictability, tolerate the unusual, prize creative initiative, take risks, and think there should be as few rules as possible.

uncertainty avoidance
the extent to which people desire to predict what is going to happen

low uncertainty-avoidance cultures
tend to have a high tolerance for uncertainty

high uncertainty-avoidance cultures
tend to have a low tolerance for uncertainty

High uncertainty-avoidance cultures such as those of Germany, Portugal, Greece, Peru, and Belgium have a low tolerance for uncertainty and a high need to control unpredictable people, relationships, or events. These cultures often create systems of formal rules as a way to provide more security and reduce risk. They also tend to be less tolerant of people or groups with deviant ideas or behaviors. They often experience anxiety when confronted with unpredictable people, relationships, or situations (Samovar, Porter, & McDaniel, 2012).

How we view uncertainty impacts communication. People from high uncertainty-avoidance cultures tend to value and use precise language to be more certain of what a person's message means. Imagine a teacher declaring to a class, "The paper must be well-researched with evidence cited appropriately and must look professional in format and appearance." Students from high uncertainty-avoidance cultures might ask a lot of questions about what kind of research is appropriate, how much evidence is needed, what writing style to use, and how long the paper should be. These students would probably welcome a specific checklist of the exact criteria by which the paper would be graded. By contrast, students from low uncertainty-avoidance cultures might be annoyed if given such a specific list of rules, viewing them as a barrier to creativity. As you can imagine, a teacher with students from both cultural orientations would face a difficult challenge when trying to explain an assignment.

Uncertainty avoidance also influences how people communicate in new and developing relationships. People from high uncertainty-avoidance cultures tend to be wary of strangers and may not seek out new relationships with people they perceive as different, and thus, unpredictable. They might prefer meeting people through friends and family. And in the early stages of a developing relationship, they might guard their privacy and refrain from self-disclosure. People from low uncertainty-avoidance cultures, on the other hand, are likely to initiate new relationships with people who seem unusual and unique, and might enjoy the excitement of disclosing personal information as a way to get to know one another earlier in the relationship. Zixou and Grant are good examples. Both are planning to graduate this year and are hoping to meet the "right girl" and marry soon. Zixue who comes from China, a low-uncertainty culture, enlists help from family and friends to meet potential partners. Grant, who grew up in the United States, a high-uncertainty culture, decides to post his profile on several dating Web sites to see what possible "matches" show up.

Power Distance

power distance
degree to which power is equally or unequally shared

high power-distance cultures
accept unequal power distribution is accepted

Power distance is the extent to which members of a culture expect and accept that power will be equally or unequally shared. In a **high power-distance culture**, unequal distribution of power is accepted by both high and low power holders. Although no culture distributes power equally, people in high power-distance cultures (like many countries in the Middle East, Malaysia, Guatemala, Venezuela, and Singapore) view unequal power distribution as normal.

low power-distance cultures
prefer power to be equally distributed

In a **low power-distance culture**, members prefer power to be more equally distributed. In the cultures of Austria, Finland, Denmark, Norway, and the United States, inequalities in power and status are muted. People know that some individuals have more clout, authority, and influence, but lower-ranking people are not in awe of or more respectful toward people in higher positions of power. Even though power differences exist, people value democracy and egalitarian behavior (Photo 3.7).

Our cultural beliefs about power distance naturally affect how we interact with others in authority positions. If you are a student or employee living in a high power-distance culture, you are not likely to argue with your teacher, supervisor, or boss. Rather, you will probably do what is ordered without question. In contrast, if you come from a low power-distance culture where status differences are muted, you might be more comfortable questioning or even arguing with those in authority.

Masculinity/Femininity

Cultures may also differ in how strongly they value traditional gender role distinctions. In a highly **masculine culture**, men and women are expected to adhere to traditional gender roles and behaviors. These cultures also value masculine roles more highly than feminine ones. If you come from a highly masculine culture (like those of Mexico, Italy, and Japan), you are likely to expect men to act in assertive and dominant ways and to expect women to be nurturing, caring, and service-oriented. You are likely to feel uncomfortable when you encounter people who don't meet these expectations. You are also likely to view masculine behaviors as more valuable, regardless of your sex. As a result, even though women are not supposed to enact such behaviors, you are likely to value the traditionally masculine characteristics of performance, ambition, assertiveness, competitiveness, and material success enacted by men more than you value traditionally feminine traits such as service, nurturing, relationships, and helping behaviors enacted by women embracing traditional gender roles and behaviors (Hofstede, 2000).

In a highly **feminine culture**, people assume a variety of roles and are valued for doing so regardless of sex. In feminine cultures (like those of Sweden, Norway, and Denmark), both men and women are accustomed to being nurturing, caring, and service oriented and value those traits as much as performance, ambition, and competitiveness depending on the circumstances of a situation (Hofstede, 1998).

Whether you come from a highly masculine or feminine culture influences how you communicate with others. People from masculine cultures have strict definitions of what are appropriate behaviors for males and females and are rewarded for adhering to them. Men in these cultures tend to be unprepared to engage in nurturing and caring behaviors and women tend to be unprepared to be assertive or to argue persuasively. Both women and men in feminine cultures learn to nurture, empathize, assert, and argue, and are rewarded for doing so. The Nordic countries (e.g., Sweden, Norway, and the Netherlands) have been identified as the most feminine countries in this regard (Hofstede, 2010).

Long-Term/Short-Term Orientation

Long-term and short-term orientations deal with how a culture values patience in arriving at rewards in the future or immediately in the here and now. A **short-term oriented** culture tends to value rewards in the here and now and, thus, emphasizes quick results, fulfilling social obligations, and getting to the bottom line efficiently. Cultures with a short-term orientation such as those found in the United States, Pakistan, Russia,

Photo 3.7 In the United States, a low power-distance culture, employers and employees often interact informally in many work settings. How have you interacted with your bosses? Has it varied from workplace to workplace?

masculine culture
adhere to traditional gender roles and behaviors

feminine culture
people assume a variety of roles regardless of sex

short-term orientation
value rewards in the here and now

© Denis Simonov/Shutterstock.com

Canada, Norway, and the United Kingdom tend to determine what result is desired at the outset of an experience and then do whatever it takes to achieve it. People in short-term oriented cultures also value keeping leisure time distinctly separate from working time. **Long-term oriented** cultures, such as those of China, Japan, Hong Kong, and Taiwan, emphasize potential future rewards that will be realized after slow and steady perseverance toward achieving a mutually acceptable result. Adaptability and honoring relationships are more important than quickly achieving the bottom line. And leisure time is not expected to be separate from working time.

> **long-term orientation**
> *value rewards that will be realized in the future*

Misunderstandings may arise when people from cultures with a long-term orientation interact with people from cultures with a short-term orientation. One of your authors experienced this on a business trip to Shanghai, China. Coming from a short-term oriented culture, when her hosts began discussing business ideas at dinner, she lightheartedly said, "No talking business at the dinner table." While this remark would have been quite appropriate in the United States, where a short-term orientation values leisure time as separate from working time, her hosts politely reminded her that they always talk business at the dinner table.

Cross-Cultural Adaptation Understanding how cultures differ becomes critical when we interact with people whose cultural norms differ from ours, because it helps us empathize and adapt our communication patterns accordingly (Kim, 2001; 2005; Kim & McKay-Semmler, 2013). Consequently, we end up demonstrating the ethical principles of respect and integrity. Perhaps one of the most illuminating ways to explain the **cross-cultural adaptation** process is through a personal narrative of someone who experienced it first-hand. Read Min Liu's story about moving from China to the United States in the *Diverse Voices* feature that follows.

> **cross-cultural adaptation**
> *empathizing with and adapting communication patterns based on cultural differences*

DIVERSE VOICES

My Story of Cross-Cultural Adaptation

by Min Liu

Associate Professor of Communication Southern Illinois University at Edwardsville

I was born and raised in China, which is a collectivist country. China also rates high on context (we prefer indirect face-saving communication over direct verbal language), chronemics (we value nurturing relationships over deadlines and schedules), uncertainty avoidance (we like rules and predictability), power distance (we respect hierarchical authority), and long-term orientation (we value perseverance over quick problem-solving). So I was raised very differently from people in the dominant American culture of the United States.

I arrived in the United States for the first time in August of 2002 to begin the Ph.D. program at North Dakota State University (NDSU) in Fargo, North Dakota. I chose NDSU for a number of reasons, but one that really stands out in my mind is the fact that Fargo was listed as one of the safest cities in the United States at the time. You see, my family was concerned about sending their daughter to study in the most individualistic country in the world. They felt a bit more at ease knowing I would be studying in one of its safest cities. Even my decision to attend NDSU was influenced by my family and our collectivist ideals. Little did I know how much culture shock I would experience once I set foot on campus.

When I arrived, I felt prepared to study in the United States because I had been trained to be a college English instructor back in China. I had also aced the English proficiency test (TOEFL) required of international students. I remember feeling pretty confident about communicating with my American colleagues. As I walked across campus for my first day of orientation, I thought to myself, "Worst-case scenario, I'll forget how to say something in English and that's what my digital Chinese–English dictionary is for."

I would soon learn, however, that the issue of translating vocabulary was not the worst-case scenario. I could not find an answer for most of my communication struggles in the dictionary. For example, in one of my first graduate classes, the professor asked everyone to call her by her first name (Deanna). Without hesitation, all my American classmates began doing so. Calling a professor by her first name was unheard of for Chinese students like me! As a sign of respect for their power and authority, we always call our teachers by their titles—Dr. Sellnow, Professor Sellnow, or Teacher Sellnow. Wherever you are on a college campus in China, it's clear who is the teacher and who are the students. I thought, "How am I to call a professor by her first name?"

For a long time, I felt torn as to what to do—continuing to call her Dr. Sellnow may seem too distant and she might correct me. I want to honor her request out of respect for her authority. But everything in my Chinese norms and values suggested that calling her Deanna was disrespectful. So I simply avoided calling her anything. This solution worked fairly well in face-to-face communication situations—I would walk up to her, smile, and then start the conversation. This approach was working fairly well for me until the day came when I needed to e-mail her. I remember sitting in front of my computer for almost an hour trying to fine-tune a one-paragraph e-mail. Soon I realized the message was fine. The reason I couldn't bring myself to press "Send" was because I had begun with "Hello Deanna." I finally changed it to "Dr. Sellnow,"

followed by an apologetic explanation asking her to understand my dilemma and why I addressed her in this way. To my surprise, she responded by saying there was nothing wrong in addressing her as "Dr. Sellnow" and that I should continue to do so if that is what feels most appropriate to me.

Another culture shock experience I had to reconcile had to do with disagreeing with my professor. In the United States, students learn to form opinions and defend their viewpoints and are rewarded for doing so in classroom presentations and debates. Professors perceive students who challenge viewpoints with evidence and reasoning as intelligent and motivated. Students who do so are perceived very differently in the Chinese culture, where public disagreement with an authority figure is not only rare, but also inappropriate. Doing so, it seemed to me, would be extremely disrespectful. Yet I observed classmates being lauded for such comments. Eventually, I found the courage to write my comments to the professor in e-mails. In the online environment, I found I could be honest and explain my disagreement with respect. Fortunately, many of my professors soon realized my cultural-values dilemma and adapted their communication styles to accept my approach. Still today, I prefer to present my viewpoints concerning controversial issues in a paper, a letter, an e-mail message, or an online post rather than in a meeting or other face-to-face discussion.

Although I have been living in the United States for several years now, I continue to learn new things about how to communicate best in this individualistic, low-uncertainty avoidance, low power distance, and short-term orientation culture as compared to my home in China. Based on my experiences, I would have to say the most important thing to remember when interacting with people who come from different cultures is for all of us to always be mindful of those differences so we can both perceive communication by others correctly and acknowledge and adapt our own styles accordingly.

Potential Barriers to Intercultural Communication Competence

Several of the most common barriers to effective intercultural communication include anxiety, assuming similarity or difference, ethnocentrism, stereotyping, incompatible communication codes, and incompatible norms and values.

1. **Anxiety.** It is normal to feel some level of discomfort when entering a cultural setting whose norms and customs are unfamiliar to us. Most people experience fear, dislike, and distrust when first interacting with someone from a different culture (Luckmann, 1999).

2. **Assumed Similarity or Difference.** When we cross into an unfamiliar cultural environment, we might assume that the norms that apply to our culture will also apply in the new one. When traveling internationally from the United States, for example, many people expect to eat their familiar hamburgers and fries and to be provided with rapid service when ordering. Likewise, they may be annoyed when shops and restaurants close during the early afternoon in countries that observe the custom of a siesta.

    It can be just as great a mistake to assume that everything about an unfamiliar culture will be different. For example, Marissa, a Mexican-American student from California who is studying at a small private college in Vermont, may feel that no one understands her and her experiences. As she makes friends, however, she may learn that while Rachel, who is Jewish, didn't have a *quinceañera* party, she did have a bat mitzvah celebration, and Kate, who is Irish Catholic, had a big confirmation party. While these occasions are different, each rite celebrates a coming of age. As Marissa makes these and other connections, she will become more comfortable in her new environment.

ethnocentrism
the belief that one's own culture is superior to others

stereotyping
assuming everyone in a cultural group is the same

Photo 3.8 Prejudice and stereotypes can negatively impact not only our relationships with people we know personally but also with our larger communities. How do you suppose this protester's sign affects the young girls in the photo?

3. **Ethnocentrism. Ethnocentrism** is the belief that one's own culture is superior to others. The stereotype of the tourist in the host country, loudly complaining about how much better everything is back home, is the classic example of ethnocentrism. Ethnocentrism exists in every culture to some degree (Haviland, 1993) and can occur in co-cultures, as well. An ethnocentric view of the world leads to attitudes of superiority and messages that are condescending in content and tone.

4. **Stereotyping.** Recall that **stereotyping** is a perceptual shortcut in which people assume that everyone in a cultural group is the same. When we interact based on stereotypes, we risk engaging in inaccurate and even unethical communication that is likely to damage our relationships (Photo 3.8). The *Communicating in the World* feature focuses on the debate that arose about race and stereotypes in the critically acclaimed film, *The Help,* based on the bestselling book by Kathryn Stockett.

5. **Incompatible Communication Codes.** When others speak a different language than we do, it is easy to see that we have incompatible communication codes. But even when people speak the same language, cultural variations can result from belonging to different co-cultures. For example, people from Great Britain take a "lift" to reach a higher floor and eat "chips" with their fish. Americans ride an "elevator" and eat "french fries" with their burgers. Within the United States, many Midwesterners drink "pop" rather than "soda." Co-cultural groups

Joe Raedle/Getty Images

COMMUNICATING IN THE WORLD

The Help: Race and Stereotypes in Popular Culture

Moviestore collection Ltd/Alamy

One of the most successful movies of the summer of 2011 was also one of the most controversial. Set in the South during the pre–Civil Rights era, *The Help*, based on Kathryn Stockett's 2009 best seller, depicts the relationships between upper-middle-class white women and the working-class black women who took care of their homes and families. On the surface, the film seems to challenge racism and offer a richer view of the lives of the black domestic workers. However, it sparked debate among film critics and audiences about its representation of race, questioning whether or not the black maids and their co-cultural experiences within a dominant white culture were accurately depicted or if the film relied too heavily on stereotypes about race and racism that have long permeated popular culture.

The narrative of this film centers on the daily struggles of two black domestic workers, Aibileen (Viola Davis) and Minny (Octavia Spencer), employed in white households in Jackson, Mississippi, during the early 1960s. Their struggles as domestics are brought to light when Skeeter (Emma Stone), the white daughter of Aibileen's employer, writes a book based on interviews with Aibileen, Minny, and other black maids.

For many African Americans in particular, *The Help* resurrected negative stereotypes about black culture. Prior to the release of the film, a statement issued by the Association of Black Women Historians challenged *The Help* on many levels, including its reliance on the "Mammy" stereotype that frames black women as "asexual, loyal, and contented caretakers of whites" who support the physical and emotional development of white children to the detriment of their own families. This stereotype, they argue, fails to recognize the economic realities that historically forced black women into such low-paying and often exploitative domestic work, as well as racist political and social discourses that framed relationships between black domestic workers and white families. By framing the film as "a progressive story of triumph over racial injustice," they argue, "*The Help* distorts, ignores, and trivializes the experiences of black domestic workers."

This is not to say that all black audiences rejected *The Help*'s representation of race relations in the United States. Patricia Turner, African American studies professor and vice provost for undergraduate studies at the University of California–Davis, suggests that because the film in fact tackled the complex issue of race in America, it does indeed represent an important step toward successful intercultural dialogue in this country. As a black woman raised in the era of Civil Rights by a mother who, like the women in the film, worked as a maid, Turner argues that *The Help* creates the opportunity for an important public dialogue about race ("Dangerous White Stereotypes"). She challenges audiences to recognize the underlying messages about race and racism called up by the film and compare its fictionalized representation of black and white relationships to historical realities. Similarly, *Entertainment Weekly* film critic Owen Gleiberman calls on audiences to engage with the film and its problems rather than simply condemning it as "racist." He "envision[s] audiences, black *and* white, watching *The Help*, all sharing a greater understanding of our past" ("Is 'The Help' a condescending movie for white liberals?"). He hopes that instead of simply rejecting the film as "racist," audiences will use the potential problems of the film as a starting point for discussion about how this depiction of race in America's past speaks to our understanding of race in the present.

Do you think films like *The Help* offer audiences a way to challenge our own co-culturally ingrained stereotypes or do they simply reinforce them in the name of entertainment?

MindTap

will often purposefully develop "in-group" codes that are easily understood by co-culture members but are unintelligible to those from the outside. Just try having a conversation about a computer problem with your friend, Sam, who is a "tech geek." If you are not a "tech geek" yourself, Sam's vocabulary is likely to be as foreign to you as if he were speaking Icelandic.

6. **Incompatible Norms and Values.** Sometimes what is considered normal in one culture is offensive in another. To the Vietnamese, dog meat is considered a delicacy. Many Americans might find the practice of eating dog meat disgusting but think nothing of eating beef. However, practicing Hindus may not eat beef because the cow is sacred to their religion. Different norms and values can cause serious problems when communicating unless we are aware of and respect differences.

Developing Competent Intercultural Communication Strategies

Unfortunately, there is no "silver bullet" strategy for communicating effectively across cultures. However, competent intercultural communicators work to overcome potential cultural barriers by acquiring accurate information about other cultures' values and practices, adopting an appropriate attitude, and developing culture-centered skills.

Acquire Accurate Knowledge

The more we know about other cultures before we attempt to interact with people in them, the more likely we are to be competent intercultural communicators (Neuliep, 2006). There are several ways to learn about other cultures.

1. **Formal study.** You can learn about other cultures by reading books, periodicals, and Web sites about them. You can read personal accounts and ethnographic research studies, take courses, and interview members of the group. Rick, for example, was planning to study abroad in China. He began his formal study by Googling each of cities he would visit and read about the cultural norms and practices he could expect to see when he arrived.

nonparticipant observation
learning about a culture or group by watching members interact

2. **Observation.** You can learn about a culture or co-culture by watching members interact with each other. We call this form of watching **nonparticipant observation**. As you watch, you can notice how certain values, rituals, and communication styles are similar to and different from your own.

participant observation
learning about a culture or group by actively participating in it

3. **Immersion.** You can learn a great deal about another culture by actively participating in it. When you live or work with people whose cultural assumptions are different from yours, you not only acquire obvious cultural information, but you also learn nuances that escape passive observers and are not accessible through formal study alone. We call this form of immersion **participant observation**. One reason study-abroad programs often include home stays is to ensure that students become immersed in the culture of the host country.

Adopt an Appropriate Attitude

We must have a genuine desire to succeed when communicating across cultures (Neuliep, 2006). We must be willing to adapt rather than expect the other person to adjust to our communication style. We must go into the experience following the motto of "assuming the best first" so as not to jump to wrong conclusions based on preconceived assumptions. We can begin to adopt an appropriate attitude by tolerating ambiguity, being open-minded, and acting altruistically.

1. **Tolerate ambiguity.** Communicating with strangers creates uncertainty, and when the stranger also comes from a different culture, we can become anxious about what he or she will expect of us. When communicating, we must be prepared to tolerate a high degree of uncertainty about the other person and to tolerate it for a long time. If you enter an intercultural interaction believing that it is OK to be unsure about how to proceed, you are likely to pay closer attention to the feedback you receive. You can then work to adjust your communication to demonstrate respect and to achieve mutual understanding.

When Jerome read the Partner Assignment List posted outside the lab, he discovered that his lab partner, Meena, was an exchange student from Mumbai. Over the semester, Jerome worked hard to attune his ear to Meena's accent and Meena worked hard to understand him. As it turned out, Jerome was really happy to have Meena as a partner. She really had a much better grasp of chemistry than he did, and tutored him as they worked on assignments. Meena didn't mind tutoring Jerome because he demonstrated genuine respect for both her cultural values and her intelligence.

2. **Be open-minded.** Open-minded people are aware of their own cultural norms and values and recognize that other people's norms and values may be different, but not wrong. Resist the impulse to judge the values of other cultures in terms of your own culture. Also, avoid jumping to conclusions about what you think others mean by something they say or do. Instead, seek to learn from those you interact with by assuming their intentions are honorable and asking sincere questions about what they say and do differently and why.

COMMUNICATE ON YOUR FEET

Acquiring Cultural Knowledge

The Assignment

Choose a culture you're not familiar with but are curious about. Prepare a 3- to 5-minute speech to deliver in class by gathering materials from (a) reviewing an online encyclopedia entry, (b) researching two or three academic sources about the culture, and (c) interviewing someone from that culture either face-to-face or online. Use what you learn from the encyclopedia and the academic sources to shape the questions you ask in the interview. In your speech, discuss what you learned from each source by answering the following questions:

1. What did you know about the culture before you began your research?

2. What did you learn from the encyclopedia article that changed or deepened your knowledge?

Speech Assignment

3. How was your understanding enriched from the additional academic sources you read?

4. What did you learn from your interviewee, and how did the interview compare to your other sources?

Use Diverse Resources

When researching your topic, consult a variety of information sources. Whether online or in print, encyclopedias are a good jumping-off point. Specialized sources like books and articles by experts provide additional details. Finally, personal interviews with experts add another dimension or level of specificity. For example, in this assignment, when you interview someone from another culture, you can ask for specific examples about his or her experiences and about whether what you read in other sources is accurate.

altruism
a display of genuine unselfish concern for the welfare of others

egocentricity
a selfish interest in one's own needs

3. **Be altruistic. Altruism** is a display of genuine and unselfish concern for the welfare of others. The opposite of altruism is **egocentricity**, a selfish interest in one's own needs to the exclusion of everything else. Egocentric people are focused on themselves, whereas altruistic people are focused on others. Altruistic communicators do not neglect their own needs, but they recognize that for a conversation to be successful, both parties must be able to contribute what they want and take what they need from the exchange. One way to demonstrate this is to learn some basic phrases in the language of your peer's culture and try to use them when possible. When people hear you say "please" and "thank you" in their native language, even if your pronunciation is imperfect, they are likely to perceive you as respectful and are likely to engage more openly with you as a result.

Develop Culture-Centered Skills

To be effective in intercultural situations, you may need to adapt the basic communication skills you learn in this course to a particular culture. Three very useful skills are listening, empathy, and flexibility.

1. **Practice listening.** There are cultural differences in how people value and engage in listening. In the dominant culture of the United States, people listen closely for concrete facts and information and often ask questions while listening. In other cultures, such as those in Japan, Finland, and Sweden, listeners tend to be more reserved

WHAT WOULD YOU DO?

A Question of Ethics

Tyler, Jeannie, Margeaux, and Max were sitting around Margeaux's dining room table working on a group marketing project. It was 2:00 A.M. They had been working since 6:00 P.M. and still had several hours of work remaining.

"Oh, the agony," groaned Tyler, "If I never see another photo of a veggie burger it will be too soon. Why didn't we choose a more 'appetizing' product to base our project on?"

"I think it had something to do with someone wanting to promote a healthy alternative to greasy hamburgers," Jeannie replied.

"Right," Tyler answered. "I don't know what I could have been thinking. Speaking of greasy hamburgers, is anyone else starving? Anyone up for ordering a pizza or something?"

"Sorry, but no one will deliver up here so late," Margeaux apologized. "But I have a quiche that I could heat up."

"Oh, oui, oui," Tyler quipped.

"You wish," Margeaux said. "It came out of a box."

"Sure, it sounds great, thanks," Jeannie said. "I'm hungry too."

"It doesn't have any meat in it, does it?" asked Max. "I don't eat meat."

"Nope, it's a cheese and spinach quiche," Margeaux answered.

Tyler and Margeaux went off to the kitchen to prepare the food. Tyler took the quiche, which was still in its box, from the refrigerator. "Uh-oh," he said. "My roommate is a vegetarian, and he won't buy this brand because it has lard in the crust. Better warn Max."

"Shhh!" said Margeaux. "I don't have anything else to offer him, and he'll know the difference anyway. Just pretend you didn't notice."

What ethical principles are involved in this case?

MindTap

and do not ask as many questions (Samovar, Porter, & McDaniel, 2012). Many cultures in East Asian countries value listening more than speaking.

As you practice, remember to check your understanding about what you see and hear. One way you can do so is to ask them their name and then try to say it back as accurately as possible. One of your authors did this when visiting with college students at Shanghai University. Although each student first introduced himself or herself with an "English" name, your author also asked them to offer their Chinese name. Then she repeated it back to them. When the students heard her make this genuine attempt to honor them and their given Chinese names, they began to trust her and opened up more during the classroom discussion. People who make a sincere effort to listen attentively and respond in an other-centered way find the most success when interacting with people from cultures that differ from their own.

2. **Practice intercultural empathy. Intercultural empathy** means imaginatively placing yourself in the other person's cultural world and attempting to experience what he or she is experiencing (Ting-Toomey, 1999). The saying "Don't judge a person until you have walked a mile in his or her shoes" captures this idea. Conveying intercultural empathy demonstrates that we sincerely respect the other person and their cultural norms even though those norms may not be ones upheld in our culture. Try to honor the practices of the host culture. If you are in an East Asian country, try to use the chopsticks rather than asking for a knife and fork. Similarly, learn whether shaking hands is appropriate when greeting others. Did you know, for instance, that Chinese people find it disrespectful to exchange business cards with one hand (rather than two) and extremely disrespectful to put the cards in your back pocket? Because business cards are considered an extension of the self, placing a person's business card in your back pocket is interpreted as something akin to sitting on their face.

    intercultural empathy
    imagining oneself in the other person's cultural world

3. **Develop flexibility. Flexibility** is the ability to adjust your communication to fit the other person and the situation. With flexibility, you can use a wide variety of communication skills during an interaction and modify your behavior within and across situations. Being flexible means analyzing a situation, making good decisions about how to communicate in that situation, and then modifying your communication when necessary as you go along.

    flexibility
    the ability to adjust one's communication to fit the other person and situation

Reflection and Assessment

Becoming a competent intercultural communicator requires genuine effort. To assess how well you've learned what we addressed in these pages, answer the following questions. If you have trouble answering any of them, go back and review that material. Once you can answer each question accurately, you are ready to move ahead to read the next chapter.

1. How is cultural identity formed, maintained, and reformed?

2. What are some ways in which cultural norms and values differ?

3. What are some barriers to effective intercultural communication you can personally work on to overcome?

4. What are some specific strategies you can employ to improve your intercultural communication competence?

COMMUNICATE!

RESOURCE AND ASSESSMENT CENTER

MindTap®

Now that you have read Chapter 3, go to your MindTap for *Communicate!* for quick access to the electronic resources that accompany this text.

Applying What You've Learned

Impromptu Speech Activity

Select a photograph of a person or people from a magazine advertisement provided by your instructor. Prepare an impromptu speech about the assumptions you make about their cultural norms and values based on what you see in the photograph. Close by explaining what you would do to check the accuracy of your assumptions.

Assessment Activities

1. Consider your family as a co-cultural group. First, describe the scope of your family unit. Are you considering your nuclear family, extended family, etc? Who are the people who make up your family group? Now describe some generally held stories that everyone knows. What do these stories tell you about your family co-culture's norms and values? What sorts of beliefs and behaviors does your family group consider normal/not normal, desirable/undesirable, appropriate/inappropriate? How do you know? Describe events/interactions and the consequences of them that have helped shape your family's set of norms and values. Finally, describe your family along the five dimensions of Hofstede's cultural dimensions theory. Explain why you have assessed your family this way.

2. Visit the toys section of an online retailer and see if you can identify what are being promoted as "toys for boys" and "toys for girls," as well as how the categories of "toys for boys" and "toys for girls" are different if at all. What do your observations suggest about what and how children are being taught gender? Prepare a one-page paper to share your observations and analysis.

Skill Building Activity

Acquiring Accurate Cultural Knowledge For the next week, conduct research into a distinct culture with which you have little or no familiarity. This can be a co-culture based on race, religion, ethnicity, sex and gender, socioeconomic status, sexual orientation, age/generation, or some combination. Be sure you can access it locally. First, arrange to observe members of the culture engaged in a typical activity and note as many of their individual communication behaviors as you can. Take your notes respectfully, being careful not to offend those you observe. Second, spend some time formally researching publications about the culture and its communication behaviors. Finally, observe members of the culture once more and then write a paragraph in which you answer these questions: What were your impressions of the culture's communication behaviors the first time you observed its members? How were these first impressions altered, if at all, by your formal research into the culture? How did your formal research affect your second observation of the culture?

To help you complete this activity, look for the Chapter 3 Skill Building activities on MindTap for *Communicate!*

MindTap®

Verbal Messages

When you've finished this chapter, you'll be able to:

- Explain the nature and characteristics of language.

- Compose effective verbal messages based on semantic, pragmatic, and sociolinquistic meanings.

MindTap®

Start with a quick warm-up activity.

As Anthony, Lauren, and Carla began to settle in for their work session, Anthony noticed that Bethney hadn't arrived yet and said: "Hey, maybe we should wait a few minutes for Bethney before we get started."

Lauren responded, "No, I don't think she's coming. She texted me this afternoon. Here, look at this."

Lauren showed the text message chain to Anthony and Carla:

LAUREN:	"U coming to study?"
BETHNEY:	"In 2 hrs, right?"
LAUREN:	"Yep, Union coffee shop at 5."
BETHNEY:	"Argh . . . gotta go to the store. . . . Forgot to make cupcakes. . . . Addie's turn to bring snacks."
LAUREN:	"Hang in there. I ♥ U!"

Carla said, "I really don't know how Bethney does it all, I mean school and kids and work. I know I couldn't do it."

"Yeah, I know," Lauren responded, "but I'm sure you understand now why she's not coming tonight."

"Absolutely," Carla replied.

4

MindTap®

Read, highlight, and take notes online.

utterance
complete unit of talk bounded by the speaker's literal or figurative silence

turn-taking
utterance exchanges

language
a system of symbols used by people to communicate

lexicon
collection of words and expressions

phonology
sounds used to pronounce words

Photo 4.1 In what ways do we use language to compare or judge?

poweroffforever/iStockphoto.com

Anthony jumped in, "Hey, wait a minute. Bethney never said she wasn't going to make it, just that she had a lot to do first."

"You think so, Anthony?" Lauren remarked. "I thought she was letting us know why she wouldn't be joining us."

Just then Bethney hurried over to the table and said, "Sorry I'm late. Thanks for waiting. What a day! Oh well. Hey, I can't wait to show you the research I found last night for our project. Check this out!"

What just happened? Why did Lauren, Carla, and Anthony interpret Bethney's texts differently? After all, each of them read the very same words. As you'll learn in this chapter, there are many reasons for such different interpretations, which can lead to serious misunderstandings that affect our relationships.

We begin by explaining the nature of language. Then we describe the relationship between language and meaning and offer suggestions for improving how you can craft verbal messages to communicate both face-to-face and online.

Language

Although many different languages are used throughout the world, the fundamentals of it are the same. All languages are based on exchanging utterances. An **utterance** is a complete unit of talk bounded by the speaker's silence (Arnoff & Rees-Miller, 2001). "Silence" can be literal, as during a face-to-face or telephone conversation, or it can be figurative as when waiting for a response to a text message. Exchanging utterances is known as **turn-taking**. We use language to label, compare, and define. For example, we label some music as hip hop to differentiate it from other musical genres. We also use language to compare and judge things as better or worse (Photo 4.1). Television programs like *What Not to Wear* and *American Idol* are based on this very principle. We also use language to learn from the experiences of others. We might do so by taking a course, attending a lecture, visiting with a friend, watching a TV program, or surfing the Internet. For example, although Karlie had never been to Panama, she learned a lot about the country and its customs by reading her friend's study abroad blog and Facebook page. With these fundamentals and purposes in mind, let's turn now to a more specific discussion about what a language is and what its characteristics are.

What Is a Language?

A **language** is a system of symbols used by people to communicate. They are comprised of a **lexicon**, a collection of words and expressions; a **phonology**, sounds used to pronounce words; as well as **syntax** and **grammar,** rules for combining words to form sentences.

All people who understand a particular language are part of a **language community.** For example, most of the people who live in Australia, England, Scotland, Ireland, and the United States belong to the same language community because they speak English. The five largest language communities in the world, are Chinese, Spanish, English, Arabic, and Hindi (Lewis, 2009).

If all people in a particular language community knew all the words (lexicon), pronounced them the same way (phonology), and used the same rules of grammar and syntax, communication would be easy. Unfortunately, however, this is not the case. The English spoken in England is not the same as the English spoken in the United States. And the English spoken in Boston is not the same as the English spoken in Biloxi, Mississippi, or in Fargo, North Dakota (Baker, Eddington, & Nay, 2009).

Languages are really collections of dialects. A **dialect** is a unique form of a more general language spoken by a specific culture or co-culture (O'Grady, et al., 2001). These smaller groups that speak a common dialect are known as **speech communities**. Dialects exist on a continuum. The more commonalities shared by two dialects, the closer they are on the continuum. This is why Americans can generally understand Canadians more easily than they can understand Scots or Aussies.

No one dialect is better or worse than another. Each just uses different lexicons, phonology, grammar, and syntax. However, some dialects are *perceived* to be "better" than others because they are spoken by the power elite of a language community. This dialect tends to be promoted as the "proper" form.

As is demonstrated in the cases of the former Yugoslavia and China, what is called a *language* and what is called a *dialect* are usually rooted in politics. When Yugoslavia was a country, its official language (Serbian-Croatian) was comprised of many similar dialects among various regions. Since the collapse of Yugoslavia in the 1990s, however, each region is now a separate country and many of these regional dialects are also considered the official languages of each country. Serbian is spoken in Serbia, Croatian in Croatia, Bosnian in Bosnia, and Montenegrin in Montenegro (Cvetkovic, 2009).

On the other hand, the official language of China is Chinese and all literate people use this same written symbol system. Thus, people from one part of the country can easily read compositions written by someone in other parts of the country. But the written symbols do not have commonly shared pronunciations. So although the regional tongues of Mandarin, Wu, Cantonese, and Min are dialects of Chinese, speakers of one dialect often can't understand someone speaking another (Wright, 2010). In the *Diverse Voices* feature that follows, Raj shares his story about how Indian English differs from American English spoken in the United States.

In addition to language and dialect, each of us uses our own personal symbol system called an **idiolect**, which includes our active vocabularies and our unique pronunciations, grammar, and syntax (Higginbotham, 2006). We may have words in our personal lexicon that are understood by very few people as well as words understood by large numbers of people. Likewise, we may pronounce some words or use grammar or syntax in idiosyncratic ways. Those who talk with us most understand our idiolect best.

Why Does Raj Talk Funny?

Raj Gaur, Ph.D.
University of Kentucky

I grew up in India. In my home we spoke Hindi, but from the time I began school at five years old, I was also taught English. By the time I was fourteen years old I was fluent in English—at least what I thought of at the time as English. Ten years ago, I came to the United States and have since learned that the English I speak is somewhat different from the English spoken here in the United States. You see, the English I learned as a child is a *nativization* of English that might more accurately be called "Indian English." What is nativization?

Nativization is the unconscious process of adapting a foreign language so it conforms to the linguistic style and rhetorical patterns of the native language spoken in a particular culture. You are familiar with the ways American English differs between regions and among groups within the United States, as well as differences between British English and American English. If there are differences among native English speakers, imagine what happens when a cultural group like Indians, whose native language is Hindi, adopts English as a second language! As you would probably expect, they adapt English to include some of the grammar, syntax, and pronunciation rules that characterize their first language, as well as by adopting some of the rhetorical and idiomatic expressions that they use in their mother tongue. It's not that Indians consciously decide to make these changes. Rather, the changes simply occur as the new language, in this case English, is used in everyday conversations with other Indians.

Prior to coming to the United States, most of the people I knew spoke English just like I did, and I had no problem understanding them or being understood by them. So imagine my consternation when after arriving in the United States some of my American colleagues, professors, and students had trouble understanding me when I spoke. What made this particularly interesting was that they didn't seem to have trouble understanding what I wrote. It was only when I spoke that I got quizzical looks and requests to repeat myself.

What I now understand is that there are major differences between the way certain words are pronounced by those speaking American English and those speaking Indian English. Some of these differences are due to the rules each type uses for accenting syllables. In American English, words with more than one syllable alternate between accented and unaccented syllables. So if the first syllable is accented the second is not and vice versa. But in Hindi, some sounds always receive an accent and others do not regardless of their position in a word. So in Indian English, "pho" is pronounced the same whether the speaker is using the word *photo* or *photography*. If you speak American English, you are used to hearing "pho·TOG·gra·phy," but when I pronounce it in Indian English, I say "PHO·to·GRAPH·y." If you're an American English speaker and you hear me say this, you may not understand me or may think, "Oh he just mispronounced that word." But to me, your pronunciation sounds just as strange because in India, that is how we pronounce the word.

There are also syntactic differences between Indian and American English. The syntactic issue that I have struggled most with is the use of articles (a, an, the, etc.). In Hindi, we may or may not use articles, and this practice also guides our Indian English. So an Indian English student may say, "I go to university in city of Mumbai," rather than "I go to *the* university in *the* city of Mumbai. Indian English speakers also form questions without using an auxiliary verb (do, should, can, must, etc.). In Hindi, auxiliary verbs are not required when forming an interrogatory sentence. So in Indian English I may ask: "I know you?" Rather than "*Do* I know you?" or "I finish it?" rather than "*Should*" or "*can*" or "*must* I finish it?"

Nativization of English can also be perceived at the idiomatic level when I attempt to express Indian

continued

sensibilities and Indian realities to my American friends. To clarify, as a speaker of Indian English, I sometimes exploit the syntactic structures of the language by directly translating Hindi idioms to English. For example, I might say "wheatish complexion" in Indian English to mean "not dark skinned, tending toward light." Or I might use the phrase "out of station" to mean "out of town," which has its origins to denote army officers posted to far-off places during the British rule. Indians also commonly substitute "hotel" for "restaurant," "this side" and "that side" for "here" and "there," "cent per cent" for "100 percent," and "reduce weight" for "lose weight."

Any one of these English adaptations might not pose problems, but taken together they make the brand of English I speak very different from that of my American friends. Indian English is integrated into much of Indian culture. English is taught in schools, business is conducted in English, and English is used in government dealings. Nonetheless, the English of Delhi is not the English of London, or Berlin, or New York, or Lexington, Kentucky. And I find it ironic that after living in the United States for nearly ten years now and struggling to be understood by Americans, my friends in India now complain about my English too. They say it's too American!

References

Don't care for Nano or No-No: Mamta. (2009, March 23). Hindustan Times. http://www .hindustantimes.com; Kachru, B.B. (1992). The other tongue: English across cultures. Urbana, IL: University of Illinois Press; Kachru, B. B. (1986). The alchemy of English: The spread, functions, and models of non-native Englishes. Oxford: Pergamon Press; Guj riots a national shame, not IPL going abroad: PC. (2009, March 23). The Financial Express. Retrieved from http://www .expressindia.com; Patrolling intensified in sea, on shores in Tamil Nadu. (2009, March 23). Press Trust of India. Retrieved from http://www.ptinews.com; Wiltshire, C., & Moon, R. (2003). Phonetic stress in Indian English vs. American English. World Englishes, 22(3), 291–303; Zardari is 5th biggest loser in world: Foreign policy magazine. (2009, March 23). NDTV. Retrieved from http://www.ndtv.com.

Characteristics of Language

Sharing meaning can be difficult because we speak different languages and use different dialects and idiolects than those with whom we are communicating. Sharing meaning can also be difficult because language is arbitrary, abstract, and constantly changing.

1. **Language is arbitrary.** The **words** used to represent things in any language are arbitrary symbols. There is not necessarily any literal connection between a word and the thing it represents. For a word to have meaning, it must be recognized by members of the language or speech community as standing for a particular object, idea, or feeling. The word D-O-G is nothing more than three letters used together unless members of a community agree that it stands for a certain four-legged animal. Different language communities use different word symbols to represent the same phenomenon. In Spanish, for instance, *el perro* stands for the same thing as *dog* does in English. Different speech communities within a language community may also use different words to represent the same phenomenon. For example, the storage compartment of an automobile is called a "trunk" in the United States and called a "boot" in England.

2. **Language is abstract.** For example, in the United States, the word "pet" is commonly understood as an animal kept for companionship. Still, if Rema refers

words
arbitrarily chosen symbols used to represent thoughts and feelings

Ursula Alter/iStockphoto.com

Photo 4.2 Depending on where you live, you might call a knitted hat like this one a tuque, a bobble hat, a burglar beanie, a stocking cap, or a toboggan. What do you call it? Did you know of these other names for it?

dialect leveling
the process of melding dialects

simply to her "pet," Margi may think of a dog, cat, snake, bird, or hamster. Even if Rema specifically mentions her cat, Margi still might think of cats of various breeds, sizes, colors, and temperaments.

3. **Language changes over time.** New words are constantly being invented and existing words abandoned or assigned new meanings. Just think, for example, of the words that have been invented to represent new technologies, such as *texting, Googling, cyberbullying, sexting, tweeting, retweeting, netiquette, webinar, emoticon,* and *blogging.* Some of the new words most recently added to English dictionaries include *vanity sizing* (the deliberate undersizing of clothes), *twirt* (flirt via Twitter), *mankle* (the male ankle), and *cougar* (an older woman in a romantic relationship with a younger man). Did you know that the *Oxford English Dictionary* now also includes *OMG, LOL,* and *<3* as actual words?

Some words become obsolete because the thing they represent is no longer used. For example, today we use *photocopiers* and *computers* to make multiple copies of print documents rather than *mimeographs* (low-cost printing presses) and *stencils.* We record audio and video data using *smartphones* rather than using *tape recorders, cassette tapes,* and *videotapes.* We send documents as e-mail attachments and Web links rather than through postal mail. And we take notes on *iPads* and *laptops* rather than on paper that we organize in a *Trapper Keeper* (a loose-leaf binder used by school children in the United States during the 1970s and 1980s).

Sometimes the meanings of existing words change. For example, in the United States, *gay* once meant *happy* and only that. Today, its more common usage references one's sexual orientation. In some communities, *bad* might mean *not good,* in others it might mean *naughty,* and in others it might mean *really great* (e.g., "That movie was really bad."). And, language can change as a result of melding aspects of multiple languages (Photo 4.2). This process of borrowing blending words among langauges is known as calque and the melding of dialects as **dialect leveling** (Hinskins, 1996). *Tex-Mex* and *Spanglish* for instance, both blend English and Spanish and we don't think twice about the fact that children go to *kindergarten,* a word absorbed by the United States from German immigrants.

The Relationship Between Language and Meaning

Because words are arbitrary and abstract, and the meanings of them can change over time, we must consider not only the words themselves, but also how they are used in conversational, social, and cultural contexts. In this section, we focus specifically on the relationship between language and meaning in terms of semantics (meanings derived

COMMUNICATING IN THE WORLD

Blurring the Lines: The Pragmatics of Celebrity Gossip and Mainstream Journalism

Lya_Cattel/iStockphoto.com

The celebrity gossip magazines that line the checkout aisles entice shoppers to find out the latest juicy details about the private lives of their favorite celebrities. Headlines pasted over photos of famous women like Angelina Jolie, Jennifer Aniston, Beyoncé, and Taylor Swift often proclaim: "I'm having a baby!" "Yes, I'm pregnant!" or "Breaking up for Good!" We're usually not surprised, however, when the actual story turns out to be very different from what aroused our curiosity on the cover.

On the other hand, when we read or listen to a mainstream news story, we assume the facts are accurate, unbiased, and trustworthy. So when a mainstream headline proclaims that Jennifer Aniston is pregnant, we have a context that prompts us to assume the story will contain facts verifying that the actress is, in fact, "with child."

Celebrity gossip magazines and blogs rely on language and pragmatic context more than facts to shape the meaning behind their stories. A candid photo of Jennifer Aniston touching her stomach does not necessarily provide any proof that she is pregnant. But when captioned with the words "a baby at last?" or "is that a baby bump?" the magazine encourages audiences to believe that Aniston may be pregnant. The fun of these gossip magazines is the invitation to negotiate meaning and "truth" by judging the facts promised by the headlines against the information within the text of the articles rather than accepting them at face value.

However, there is increasing concern about the tabloidization of the mainstream press. Tabloidization is a word coined in the 1980s to represent the ongoing "decline in traditional journalistic standards" (Bird, 2008, p. 4947). As news media try to stay viable, "tabloid-style news" is becoming more commonplace in mainstream outlets, as well (Uberti, 2014). Considering this trend toward blurring the lines between celebrity gossip news and real mainstream news reporting, consider the following questions.

Given these changes, how should we approach mainstream media stories?

MindTap®

---

from the words themselves), pragmatics (meanings derived from the conversational context), and sociolinguistics (meanings derived from social and cultural contexts).

Semantics

Semantic meaning is derived from the words themselves and how they are arranged into sentences. Because *words* are arbitrarily chosen symbols used to represent thoughts and feelings, our ability to express ourselves and understand others is limited by the size and accuracy of our vocabulary. Identifying the meaning of a word is tricky because words actually have two types of meanings.

semantic meaning
derived from the words themselves and how they are arranged into sentences

Photo 4.3 Our connotative definitions are influenced by previous experiences. How might your experiences with a family pet, an attack dog, or a hunting dog influence your connotative feelings about dogs?

denotation
explicit meaning found in the dictionary of a language community

connotation
implicit meaning associated with a word

Denotation is the explicit meaning found in the dictionary of a language community. However, different dictionaries may define words in slightly different ways and many words have multiple denotative definitions. For instance, the *Random House Dictionary of the English Language* lists 23 definitions for the word *great*. Not only that, the lexicon of our personal idiolect rarely corresponds precisely to the definitions found in formal dictionary definitions. Thus, your definition of a word may be different from mine. So when your friend says your performance was *great*, he might mean it was very good, exceptional, powerful, or that it lasted a long time. All are denotative dictionary definitions of *great*.

Connotation is the implicit additional meaning we associate with a word. For example, think of the different meanings people might associate with the word "family," based on their experiences growing up. To one person, a "family" may connote a safe place where one is loved unconditionally. To another, it might connote a dangerous place where people must fend for and protect themselves. Word denotation and connotation are important because the only message that counts is the message that is understood, regardless of whether it is the one you intended (Photo 4.3).

Semantic meaning is based on both the words themselves and how they are combined into meaningful phrases, sentences, and larger units of expression. For example, you might communicate the same message by saying:

"When he went to the pound he adopted a 3-pound puppy."

"He went to the pound and adopted a 3-pound puppy."

"Upon arriving at the pound, he adopted a 3-pound puppy."

These three sentences use slightly different syntax and grammar to convey the same semantic meaning. But notice how the semantic meaning can change by deleting one word:

"He, the 3 pound adopted puppy, went to the pound."

Now the semantic meaning is that an adopted 3-pound premature canine went to the place where unclaimed animals are kept. Next consider how the semantic meaning can change based on its position in a sentence. The word *pound* is used twice in each sentence but in one instance it signifies a unit of weight and in the other it signifies a place. We knew which meaning to apply based on syntax. With this in mind, let's consider several semantics guidelines for forming effective verbal messages.

Guidelines for Improving Semantics

To improve semantics, choose words and arrange them in ways that both improve clarity and demonstrate respect. You can do so by using specific, concrete, and familiar words, by embellishing them with descriptive details and examples, and by demonstrating linguistic sensitivity. In terms of clarity, compare the language used in the following two descriptions of the same incident:

"Some nut almost got me a while ago."

"About 1:00 p.m. last Saturday afternoon, an older man in a banged-up Honda Civic ran through the red light at Calhoun and Clifton and came within inches of hitting my car while I was in the intersection waiting to turn left."

In the second description, the speaker used specific, concrete language, as well as descriptive details and examples, to improve semantic clarity. Let's look closer at each one.

1. **Use specific language. Specific language** refers to precise words that clarify by narrowing what is understood from a general category to a particular item or group within that category. For example, saying "a banged-up Honda Civic" is more specific than saying "a car."

2. **Use concrete language. Concrete language** clarifies semantic meaning by appealing to the senses (e.g., seeing, hearing, feeling, tasting, smelling). Instead of saying Jill "speaks in a weird way," we might say, Jill *mumbles, whispers, blusters,* or *drones.*

3. **Use familiar language.** We also need to use words our receivers will understand. We should only use jargon or slang we are certain the meaning will be clear or by defining it clearly the first time we use it. Overusing and misusing abbreviations and acronyms can also hinder understanding.

4. **Use descriptive details and examples.** Sometimes semantic meaning can be improved by using descriptive details or examples. Suppose Lucy says, "Rashad is very *loyal.*" Since the meaning of *loyal* (faithful to an idea, person, company, and so on) is an abstract word, Lucy might add, "I mean, he never criticizes friends behind their backs." By following up the abstract concept of loyalty with an example, Lucy clarifies what she means as it applies to Rashad.

5. **Demonstrate linguistic sensitivity. Linguistic sensitivity** is achieved by using language that is inclusive and demonstrates respect for others.

Inclusive language does not use words that apply only to one sex, race, or other group as though they represent everyone. In the past, English speakers used the masculine pronoun *he* to represent all humans regardless of sex. This approach is not inclusive because it excludes half of the population. Instead, use plurals or both male and female pronouns. So rather than saying, "When *a person* shops, *he* should have a clear idea of what *he* wants to buy," say "When *people* shop, *they* should have a clear idea of what *they* want to buy."

To be inclusive, we also need to avoid words that indicate a sex, race, age, or other group distinction (Photo 4.4).

specific language
precise words that clarify by narrowing from a general category to a particular item or group within it

concrete language
words that clarify semantic meaning by appealing to the senses

linguistic sensitivity
inclusive word choices that demonstrate respect for others

inclusive language
use of words that do not apply only to one sex, race, or other group

Photo 4.4 Why does referring to these people as policemen fail to demonstrate linguistic sensitivity?

anouchka/iStockphoto.com

COMMUNICATE ON YOUR FEET

Speech Assignment

What Does It Mean?

The Assignment

Following your instructor's instructions, work alone, partner with someone in the class, or form a small group. Make up a nonsensical word and then develop a short speech clarifying its meaning using the tools you have learned in this chapter. If you work with a partner or in a small group, identify a representative to present the speech to the class. After each speech has been presented, ask a volunteer from the audience to paraphrase the meaning of the word.

Guidelines

1. Be sure to follow the speech organization directions provided by your instructor.

2. Be sure to incorporate the concepts for clarifying semantic meaning in ways that are specific, concrete, descriptive, and linguistically sensitive.

For example, rather than saying *fireman, mailman, waitress,* and *stewardess,* say *firefighter, postal carrier, server,* and *flight attendant.*

Demonstrating linguistic sensitivity also means avoiding potential offensive humor, profanity, and vulgarity. Dirty jokes and racist, sexist, or other "-ist" remarks may not be intended to be offensive, but if someone perceives them to be offensive, then that person will likely lose sight of your intended meaning and focus on the offensive remark instead. The same thing can happen when you pepper your message with profanity and vulgar expressions. Listeners may be offended and focus on those words rather than on the semantic meaning of your intended message.

Pragmatics

pragmatic meaning
interpreting a message related to the conversational context of it

Pragmatic meaning comes from interpreting a message related to the conversational context of it. Whereas semantic meaning focuses on what *words* mean (Korta & Perry, 2008), pragmatic meaning focuses on what *people* mean. So, pragmatic meaning changes across speakers and situations (Photo 4.5).

speech act
utterance of a verbal message by a speaker and what it implies about how the listener should respond

A **speech act** is the utterance of a verbal message by a speaker and what it implies about how the listener should respond. In other words, when we *speak*, we *do*. Although the words we speak are usually explicit, what we are doing is often implied. In other words, we consider "What is the speaker *doing* (i.e., implying) by saying these words to me right now?" For example, if I say, "Karen, pass me the bowl of potatoes," I have directly ordered Karen to pick up the bowl of potatoes and hand them to me. Instead, suppose I ask, "Karen, would you mind passing me the potatoes?" At the semantic level, this question appears to give Karen a choice to pass the potatoes or not. At the pragmatic level, however, what I am doing is the same. I am directing her to pass the bowl of potatoes to me. So, we can accomplish the same pragmatic goal with either a direct/explicit or indirect/implicit speech act.

What is meant by a speech act also depends on the context. Let's look at a simple example. When Harry's car wouldn't start one morning, he made three phone calls:

Phone Call 1:

HARRY: The car won't start.

KATIE: Sorry about that. I'll just take the bus.

Phone Call 2:

HARRY: The car won't start.

AAA CUSTOMER SERVICE REPRESENTATIVE: Where is the car, sir? I'll send a tow truck right away.

Phone Call 3:

HARRY: The car won't start.

PREVIOUS OWNER WHO RECENTLY SOLD THE CAR TO HARRY: Wow, that never happened to me. But I told you I was selling the car "as is."

In all three cases, the verbal utterance and the semantic meaning of Harry's message is the same. In terms of pragmatic meaning, however, Harry performed three different speech acts. What he was *doing* when he was talking to Katie was different from what he was *doing* when he was talking with the customer service representative at AAA and different still from what he was *doing* when he made the statement to the person who sold him the car. He expressed his feelings by apologizing to Katie and implied that Katie should understand and release him from his obligation to take her to school. With the AAA representative, Harry's speech act was a demand for assistance. When Harry called the previous owner of the car, he was complaining and implying that the previous owner should accept responsibility. In each case, Harry used the same words and syntax, but three different speech acts.

The feedback from each person illustrates that each had understood Harry's pragmatic meaning. Katie's response showed that she understood and would need to find another way to get to school. The AAA representative expected the call to be about car trouble so she responded by asking where the car was located. The previous owner also understood Harry's speech act when he responded by refusing to accept responsibility for the problem.

Sometimes the media use the principles of pragmatics to get the attention of and even mislead us about what the facts are in a given situation. The *Communicating in the World* feature on page 71 illustrates how celebrity gossip magazines do so to entice potential readers to buy magazines and how the practice is being adopted by mainstream media outlets today.

Guidelines for Improving Pragmatics

We understand pragmatic meaning based on an assumption that both partners want to achieve mutual understanding (Grice, 1975). With this in mind, we suggest the following guidelines.

1. **Tell the truth.** This guideline seems pretty self-explanatory. Say only what you believe to be true based on evidence to support your position. Sometimes we tell partial truths and rationalize that we are "protecting" our listeners or ourselves. For example,

AP Images/Toby Talbot

Photo 4.5 What indirect or implied meanings are being communicated in this advertisement?

APPLY IT

How can examining implied meanings in speech acts help you detect attempts at being influenced in biased media reporting or advertisements?

MindTap

Donna Day/Getty Images

Photo 4.6 Have you ever witnessed someone going on and on about something unrelated to the question you asked? How did that influence your judgment of their ethical communication behavior?

when your friend asks you what you think of her new boyfriend you may offer a noncommittal response that masks your immediate dislike for the guy. You might say, "Well, he certainly appears to like you." Your friend may interpret your remark as approval rather than as your attempt to spare her feelings. Obviously, this makes it more difficult to correctly understand what you truly believe. You can tell the truth by adding a comment about something you don't particularly like about him.

2. **Provide the right amount of information.** Include all the information needed to fully answer the question and refrain from adding irrelevant information (Photo 4.6). For instance, when Sam is getting ready to leave for work, he asks Randy where he parked the car. Randy answers "down the street." In this case, Randy does not provide enough information because Sam needs to know exactly where to find the car. If Randy responds with, "You just wouldn't believe the trouble I had finding a parking space . . ." followed by a five-minute monologue about trying to find a parking space after midnight, he would be providing too much irrelevant information.

3. **Relate what you say to the topic being discussed.** Link your messages to the purpose of the conversation and interpret the messages of others in line with the topic at hand. For example, Barry asks, "Who's going to pick up Mom from work today?" His brother answers, "I've got a big test tomorrow." Barry assumes that his brother's remark is relevant to the topic at hand and interprets it as, "I can't; I have to study." Barry was able to correctly understand the pragmatic meaning of his brother's answer because he assumed that it was relevant to figuring out how to get their mother home.

4. **Acknowledge when your message violates a guideline.** When you violate one of these guidelines, you should tell your partner that you are breaking it. Doing so will help your partner interpret what you are saying accurately. For example:

   - If you violate guideline #1, you might say "I don't know if this is true, but my sister said . . .,"

   - If you violate guideline #2, you might say "If I told you, I'd have to kill you . . .,"

   - If you violate guideline #3, you might say "This may be beside the point, but . . .,"

5. **Assume the best first.** At times, you or your partner may intentionally break one of these guidelines and not signal it beforehand. In these instances, employ perception-checking in an attempt to come to mutual understanding.

Sociolinguistics

sociolinguistic meaning
varies according to the norms of a particular culture or co-culture

Sociolinguistic meaning varies according to the norms of a particular culture or co-culture. Sociolinguistic misunderstandings occur when we interact with someone who operates using different norms regarding how words are combined, how to say what to whom and when, and verbal style.

1. Cultures and co-cultures may assign meaning to specific words and combinations of words that differs from their semantic meaning. For example, in English we associate the word "pretty" with women and "handsome" with men, even though both refer to physical beauty. So choosing to say "She is a pretty woman" sends a different message than saying, "She is a handsome woman" (Chaika, 2008). Cultures also use **idioms**, which are expressions whose meaning is different from the literal meanings associated with the words used in them. So imagine how confusing it is to someone learning English when we say, "That test was *a piece of cake*" or "that test was *a real killer.*"

idioms
expressions whose meanings are different from the literal meanings associated with the words used in them

2. Cultures and co-cultures may have different norms about what is appropriate to say to whom, by whom, when, and about what. For example, the "appropriate" way to compliment others and accept compliments can vary from culture to culture. In the dominant culture of the United States, you might compliment your Japanese friend by saying, "Miki, this is the *best* miso soup I have ever tasted." To Miki, however, your compliment might sound insincere because in Japanese culture the language of compliments is more humble. So she might reply, "Oh, it's nice of you to say that, but I am sure that you have had better miso soup at sushi restaurants in the city." Similarly, Midwesterners often smile and say "Hi" to strangers on the street as a sign of being friendly. In China, acknowledging a stranger in this way typically assumes an unwarranted familiarity and is likely to be considered rude.

3. Preferred verbal style differs from culture to culture, particularly in terms of how direct or indirect a person ought to be (Ting-Toomey & Chung, 2005). A **direct verbal style** is characterized by language that openly states the speaker's intention in a straightforward and unambiguous way. An **indirect verbal style** is characterized by language that masks the speaker's true intentions in a roundabout and ambiguous way. Consider the following example of how these different styles can create communication challenges.

direct verbal style
language that openly states the speaker's intention in a straightforward and unambiguous way

indirect verbal style
language that masks the speaker's true intentions in a roundabout and ambiguous way

Jorge and Kevin are college roommates who come from the same hometown as Sam, who lives across the hall and has a car. Thanksgiving is fast approaching and both men need to find a ride home. One night while watching a football game in Sam's room, the following conversation occurs:

JORGE SAYS TO SAM:	"Are you driving home for Thanksgiving?" [Maybe he'll give me a ride.]
SAM:	"Yep." [If he wanted a ride he'd ask.]
KEVIN:	"Well I'd like a ride home."
SAM:	"Sure, no problem."
JORGE:	"Are you taking anyone else?" [I wonder if he still has room for me.]
SAM:	"Nope. I'm leaving early, after my last class on Tuesday and not coming back until late Sunday evening." [I guess Jorge already has a ride home.]
JORGE:	"Well, enjoy Thanksgiving!" [If he wanted to give me a ride I gave him plenty of opportunities to offer. I guess I'll take the bus.]

APPLY IT

Do you usually communicate using a direct or indirect verbal style? Identify a time when misunderstandings or even hurt feelings came about as a result of you and your partner using different verbal styles.

MindTap

WHAT WOULD YOU DO?

A Question of Ethics

Abbie was adding sweetener to her latte when she spied her friends Ethan and Nate sitting at a table in a corner of the coffee shop. She popped a top on her drink and strolled over to join them.

"Hi guys. What are you doing?" Abbie asked.

"Not much. Ethan and I were just comparing our biology notes. How about you?"

"I'm just heading over to my philosophy class," Abbie replied. "But, I've got to say I don't know why I even bother going."

"Why not? What's up?" asked Nate.

"Well," responded Abbie, "Professor Miller is so mean. The other day, I offered my opinion and she told me I was wrong. Can you believe it? I mean, she could have praised me for offering my opinion. What makes her opinion so 'right' anyway? She is so narrow-minded and *obviously* doesn't care about her students."

Ethan asked, "Well, were you?"

"Was I what?" Abbie asked.

"Wrong."

"Well, I guess so. But that's not the point," Abbie contested.

"Actually, I think it *is*," Ethan replied. "Maybe she said you were wrong because she *does* care about her students and wants you to learn. Maybe she sets high standards and wants to help you achieve them."

"Whatever. That's *your* opinion. I bet you'd feel differently if she embarrassed *you* in front of the other students," Abbie retorted.

"Maybe you should go talk to her about it during her office hours," suggested Nate. "She probably doesn't even realize she embarrassed you."

"Oh, she knows," replied Abbie. "And there is *no way* am I going to talk to her about it. I'm just going to get through the semester and then tell her *exactly* what I think on the end-of-semester evaluations. See you later!"

What ethical principles if any are at issue in this case?

MindTap®

In this conversation, Jorge used an indirect style he learned growing up in Nicaragua. His questions were meant to prompt Sam to offer him a ride home. But Sam, who grew up in New York, used a direct style and completely missed Jorge's intent. As a result, Jorge rode the bus even though Sam would have gladly given him a ride if their preferred verbal styles had not gotten in the way of mutual understanding.

Guidelines for Improving Sociolinguistic Understanding

1. **Develop intercultural competence.** The more you learn about other cultures, the better you will be able to convey and interpret messages when communicating with those whose sociolinguistic verbal styles differ from yours.

mindfulness
paying attention to what is happening at any given moment during a conversation

2. **Practice mindfulness. Mindfulness** is the practice of paying attention to what is happening at any given moment (Kabat-Zinn, 2009). If we are mindful when interacting with others, we will constantly attend to how our cultural norms, idioms, scripts, and verbal styles are similar to and different from our conversational partners.

3. **Respect and adapt to the sociolinguistic practices of others.** The old saying, "When in Rome, do as the Romans do" captures the essence of this guideline.

For example, if you are invited to your Indonesian American friend's home for the weekend, you should adapt your verbal style to that of your hosts. Or if you are from a low-context culture and are talking with someone from a high-context culture, be sensitive to the indirect meanings in their verbal messages. If you are fluent in more than one language or dialect, you can even codeswitch and converse in the language or dialect of your conversational partner.

Reflection and Assessment

Although many different languages are spoken throughout the world, all of them share the same purposes and are based on the same fundamental principles. Sharing meaning can be challenging, however, because language is arbitrary, abstract, and constantly changing. To assess how well you've learned what we addressed in these pages, answer the following questions. If you have trouble answering any of them, go back and review that material. Once you can answer each question accurately, you are ready to move ahead to read the next chapter.

1. What are the fundamental purposes of language?

2. Why is sharing meaning through verbal messages so challenging?

3. What is semantic meaning and how can we improve semantics?

4. What is pragmatic meaning and how can we improve pragmatics?

5. What is sociolinguistic meaning and how can we improve sociolinguistic understanding?

RESOURCE AND ASSESSMENT CENTER

MindTap

Now that you have read Chapter 4, go to your MindTap for *Communicate!* for quick access to the electronic resources that accompany this text.

Applying What You've Learned

Impromptu Speech Activity

Draw a slip of paper from a container provided by your instructor. On it, you will find the name of a superhero, cartoon character, or comic strip character. Prepare and deliver a 2–3 minute impromptu speech making a case for him or her as either a positive or negative example of effective verbal communication. Be sure to draw on the principles offered in this chapter to make your case.

Assessment Activities

1. Pick an article from a favorite magazine. Read through it, highlighting instances in which the writer uses specific language, concrete language, and familiar language, and identify passages in which the writer might improve in each area. Then look for examples of the writer's linguistic sensitivity and find places where the writer might have done a better job. Write a 400–500-word essay identifying strengths and suggestions for improvement based on your assessment.

2. Select one of these popular TV sitcoms: *Modern Family, The Big Bang Theory, Family Man,* or *Parks & Recreation.* Watch an episode and record the following for each of the main characters: (a) use of profanity and vulgarity, (b) use of biased (not inclusive) language, and (c) use of offensive humor. Based on your analysis, would you consider each of them a model of ethical or unethical communication behavior? Why or why not?

Skill-Building Activities

1. Reword the following messages using more specific, concrete, and familiar words:

   a. You know that I really love baseball. Well, I'm practicing a lot because I'm hoping to get a tryout with the pros.

   b. I'm really bummed out. Everything with Corey is going down the tubes. We just don't connect anymore.

   c. She's just a pain. She's always doing stuff to tick me off. And then just acting like, you know.

   d. My neighbor has a lot of animals in her yard.

   e. My sister works for a large newspaper.

2. Reword the following sentences to demonstrate linguistic sensitivity:

   a. Margaret is a fantastic waitress.

   b. Mark, a Jewish fireman, is going to the Bahamas next week.

   c. I believe in equal rights and opportunities for all of mankind.

   d. I can't figure out why Mrs. B makes us learn how to calculate these damned math problems by hand.

   e. Geez. It really bugs me when Erin acts like such a dumb blonde. She's actually a pretty smart girl.

Nonverbal Messages

When you've finished this chapter, you'll be able to:

- Describe the major characteristics of nonverbal messages.

- Identify the types of nonverbal messages we use to communicate.

- Employ strategies to improve your nonverbal communication as both a sender and receiver.

MindTap®

Take I: The Verbal Exchange

Amber enters the apartment.

Amber: "I'm home. Are we going to dinner soon?"

Louisa: "Uh huh."

Amber: "Good, because I'm starving. I worked so long in the Chem lab that I completely missed lunch and had to make do with a stale granola bar I found at the bottom of my backpack. "

Louisa: "Uh huh."

Amber: "Hey, I've been thinking about spring break. What would you think about doing an alternative spring break? Student government is sponsoring three different trips and one is to Haiti. I thought we could do some good and get some sun. What do you think?"

Louisa: "Whatever."

[**Amber thinks:** *Wow. What'd I do wrong this time? Sometimes I just don't understand her.*]

5

What just happened? From the verbal transcript alone it's hard to tell. Now let's look at another account of the conversation; one that includes both the verbal and nonverbal messages involved.

Take II: The Nonverbal and Verbal Exchange

Amber enters the apartment to find Louisa sitting at the kitchen table typing furiously on her laptop. Books and papers are piled all around her.

"I'm home. Are we going to dinner soon?" Amber asks, smiling brightly as she drops her backpack on the floor and flops down on the futon across the room and turns on the TV.

"Uh huh," mumbles Louisa as she furrows her eyebrows, hunches closer to the computer screen, and continues typing furiously.

"Good, because I'm starving," Amber says. "I worked so long in the Chem lab that I completely missed lunch. All I've had to eat today is a stale granola bar I found at the bottom of my backpack."

"Uh huh," Louisa mutters as she takes a deep breath, sighs loudly, and continues typing with her eyes focused intently on the screen.

Noticing the commercial for a three-day cruise to the Bahamas, Amber recalls an idea and exclaims, "Hey Louisa, I've been thinking about doing an alternative spring break. Student Government is sponsoring a service trip to Haiti. I thought we could do some good and get some sun. What do you think? Want to go?" Amber gets up from the futon and plops down next to Louisa, sending books and papers flying.

"Whatever," Louisa shouts as she bangs her laptop closed, gathers her papers, and storms out of the room.

["*Wow*," Amber wonders with astonishment as she stares wide-eyed at the door Louisa just slammed shut. "*What'd I do wrong this time? Sometimes I just don't understand her.*"]

Amber had completely ignored the nonverbal messages Louisa was sending and that lead to misunderstandings and hurt feelings. The last chapter focused on the verbal messages we send to communicate thoughts and feelings. This chapter is dedicated to **nonverbal communication**, which consists of all the messages we send in ways that transcend spoken or written words (Knapp, Hall, & Horgan 2014). More specifically, **nonverbal messages** are cues we send with our body, voice, space, time, and appearance to support, modify, contradict, or even replace a verbal message.

Nonverbal messages play an important role in communication. In fact, research suggests that 65–90 percent of meaning comes from the nonverbal messages we use to communicate in face-to-face interactions (Burgoon & Bacue, 2003: Littlejohn & Foss, 2009; Mehrabian, 1972). In fact, it is difficult to separate verbal and nonverbal messages since they operate simultaneously as we communication (Knapp, Hall, & Horgan, 2014). As we can see from Amber's and Louisa's conversation, interpreting nonverbal messages accurately is critical to understanding and responding appropriately to what others are "saying."

The widespread use of social media and smart phone technology to communicate today (e.g., e-mail, Facebook, Twitter, Instagram, texting) emphasizes the important role of nonverbal messages. Because these modes force us to rely only on words, we often use emoticons, all capital letters and acronyms like LOL to represent the nonverbal messages

MindTap®

Read, highlight, and take notes online.

nonverbal communication
all the messages we send in ways that transcend spoken or written words

nonverbal messages
cues we send with our body, voice, space, time, and appearance to communicate

APPLY IT

Identify a time when someone misinterpreted the meaning of a text or e-mail message you sent. In hindsight, what emoticons, acronyms, or other techniques might you have used to represent nonverbal cues to clarify meaning?

MindTap®

we would employ in face-to-face communication (Yuasa, Saito, & Mukawa, 2011) (Photo 5.1).

We begin this chapter by briefly describing the characteristics of nonverbal communication. Next, we identify the types of nonverbal messages we use to communicate with others, including use of body (kinesics), use of voice (paralanguage), use of space (proxemics), use of time (chronemics), and appearance (including clothing and grooming). Finally, we offer suggestions for improving nonverbal messages as both senders and receivers.

Photo 5.1 Nonverbal communication is so important that we have developed emoticons, acronyms, and avatars to represent it in computer-mediated and text messages. What emoticons and acronyms do you use when communicating online?

Characteristics of Nonverbal Communication

We use nonverbal messages to emphasize, substitute for, or contradict verbal messages. We also use nonverbal messages to cue a sender to continue, repeat, elaborate, or finish up what he or she is saying. And, whether we do so intentionally or not, our nonverbal messages give people an impression of who we are. The challenge of conveying and interpreting nonverbal messages accurately is rooted in four fundamental characteristics.

1. **Nonverbal communication is *inevitable*.** The phrase "We cannot NOT communicate" (Watzlawick, Bavelas, & Jackson, 1967) captures the essence of this characteristic. If you are in the presence of someone else, your nonverbal messages (whether intentional or not) are communicating. When Austin yawns and stares off into the distance during class, one classmate might interpret this nonverbal message as a sign of boredom, another might see it as a sign of fatigue, and yet another may view it as a message of disrespect. Meanwhile, Austin may be oblivious to all of the messages his behavior is sending.

2. **Nonverbal communication is the primary conveyer of emotions.** We interpret how others feel based almost entirely on their nonverbal messages. In fact, some research suggests that an overwhelming 93 percent of a message's emotional meaning is conveyed nonverbally (Mehrabian, 1972). So, when Janelle frowns, clenches her fists, and forcefully says, "I am NOT angry!" her sister is likely to ignore the verbal message and believe the contradicting nonverbal messages, which communicate that Janelle is actually very angry.

3. **Nonverbal communication is *multi-channeled*.** We perceive meaning from a combination of nonverbal behaviors including, for example, posture, gestures, facial expressions, vocal pitch and rate, and appearance. So, when Anna observes her daughter Mimi's failure to sustain eye contact, her bowed head, and her repetitive toe-stubbing in the dirt, she may decide that Mimi is lying when she says she did not hit her brother. The fact that nonverbal communication is multi-channeled is one reason people are more likely to believe nonverbal communication when nonverbal messages contradict the verbal message (Burgoon, Blair, & Strom, 2008).

APPLY IT

List all the situations in which you text, check e-mail, or use Snapchat, Instagram, or Facebook. For example, when you're hanging out with your friends, having dinner with parents or grandparents, at the movies, during a lecture at school, etc. How might your nonverbal behaviors be interpreted by others in each of these situations?

MindTap

4. **Nonverbal communication is *ambiguous*.** Very few nonverbal messages mean the same thing to everyone. The meaning of one nonverbal behavior can vary based on culture, sex, gender, and even context or situation. For example, in the dominant American culture, direct eye contact tends to be understood as a sign of respect. That's why parents often tell their children, "Look at me when I'm talking to you." In some cultures, however, direct eye contact might be interpreted as disrespectful. Not only can the meaning of nonverbal messages vary among different cultures, but the meaning of the same nonverbal message also can differ based on the situation. For example, a furrowed brow might convey Byron's confusion when he did not understand his professor's explanation of the assignment, or Monica's anger when she discovered she did not get the internship she had worked so hard for, or Max's disgust when he was dissecting a frog during biology lab.

Types of Nonverbal Communication

We use various types of nonverbal messages to communicate. These include the use of body (kinesics), voice (vocalics/paralanguage), space (proxemics), time (chronemics), and appearance.

Use of Body: Kinesics

Kinesics is the technical name for what and how the body communicates (Birdwhistell, 1970). We may use gestures, eye contact, facial expression, posture, and touch.

Gestures **Gestures** are the movements of our hands, arms, and fingers. We use **emblems** to substitute entirely for a word or words. For example, when we raise a finger and place it vertically across our lips, it signifies "Be quiet." We use **illustrators** to clarify the verbal message. When we say "about this high" or "nearly this round," we are likely to use a gesture to clarify what we mean. We also often use gestures to emphasize our emotional stance. For example, when expressing anger or frustration, we might also clench our fists. Particularly when giving formal speeches, we may use gestures to signal moving from one main point to the next, as well as to make reference to a presentational aid. Some gestures, called **adaptors**, are unconscious responses to physical or psychological needs. For example, we may scratch an itch, adjust our glasses, or jingle the keys in our pocket. In these cases, we probably don't intend to communicate, but others may notice and attach meaning to them (Lakin, 2006).

The use and meaning of gestures can vary greatly across cultures. For example, the American hand sign for "OK" has an obscene sexual meaning in some European countries, means "worthless" in France, is a symbol for money in Japan, and stands for "I'll kill you" in Tunisia (Axtell, 1998). Similarly, in the dominant American culture, people nod their heads to communicate "I am listening to you." In some parts of India, however, they shift their heads from side to side to demonstrate they are listening. When communicating with people coming from different cultures, be especially careful about the gestures you use; their meaning is not necessarily universal (Photo 5.2).

Eye Contact The technical term for **eye contact** is oculesics. It has to do with how and how much we look at others when communicating.

What is considered appropriate eye contact varies across cultures. Studies show that in Western cultures, talkers hold eye contact about 40 percent of the time and listeners nearly

---

kinesics
what and how body motions communicate

gestures
movements of our hands, arms, and fingers to communicate

emblems
gestures that substitute entirely for a word or words

illustrators
gestures that clarify the verbal message

adaptors
unconscious responses to physical or psychological needs

eye contact (oculesics)
how and how much we look at others when communicating

APPLY IT

Name someone you know who uses a lot of gestures when talking. Does it enhance the message or distract from it? Why?

70 percent of the time (Knapp, Hall, & Horgan, 2014). In Western cultures people also generally maintain more eye contact when discussing topics they are comfortable with, when they are genuinely interested in what another person is saying, and when they are trying to persuade others. Conversely, they tend to avoid eye contact when discussing topics that make them feel uncomfortable, when they aren't interested in the topic or the person talking, or when they are embarrassed, ashamed, or trying to hide something.

In the dominant American culture, people tend to expect those with whom they are communicating to "look them in the eye." It tends to signal respect and that we are paying attention. But direct eye contact is not universally considered appropriate (Samovar, Porter, McDaniel, & Roy, 2012). For instance, in Japan, prolonged eye contact is considered rude, disrespectful, and threatening. Similarly, in China and Indonesia, too much direct eye contact is a sign of bad manners. In many Middle Eastern countries, people tend to use continuous and direct eye contact with others to demonstrate keen interest.

Various co-cultural groups within the United States use eye contact differently, as well. For instance, African Americans tend to use more continuous eye contact than European Americans when they are speaking, but less when they are listening (Samovar, Porter, McDaniel, & Roy, 2012). Native Americans tend to avoid eye contact when communicating with superiors as a sign of respect for their authority. And women tend to use more eye contact during conversations than men do (Santilli & Miller, 2011; Wood, 2007).

Facial Expression **Facial expression** is using facial muscles to convey emotions (Photo 5.3). For example, we may furrow our brows and squint our eyes when we are confused, or purse our lips and raise one eyebrow to convey skepticism. Facial expressions are so important for communicating emotions that we often use smiley face ☺, sad face ☹, and winking face emoticons ;) to represent emotions when texting, sending e-mail, or using other forms of social media. Emoticons have actually been in use since 1982 when Scott Fahlman, a computer science professor at

Christian Steinhausen/Taxi/Getty Images

Photo 5.2 The same nonverbal cue can mean very different things in different cultures. What does this gesture mean to you?

facial expression
using facial muscles to communicate emotions

Jason LaVeris/FilmMagic/Getty Images

Photo 5.3 Comedic actors often use a lot of facial expressions to convey emotions. What is being communicated here?

Carnegie Melon University, first combined a colon, hyphen, and parenthesis to represent a smiley face (Walther & Parks, 2002).

Unlike gestures and eye contact, many facial expressions mean something similar across cultures (Samovar, Porter, McDaniel, & Roy 2012). For instance, a slight raising of the eyebrow communicates recognition and wrinkling one's nose conveys repulsion (Martin & Nakayama, 2006). However, whether or not doing so is appropriate may vary across cultures and co-cultures. For instance, in some cultures, people downplay facial expressions like frowning and smiling; whereas members of other cultures amplify emotional meaning through facial expressions.

posture
how we position and move our body

body orientation
how we position our body in relation to other people

body movement
changing body position

Posture **Posture** is how we position and move our body. Posture can communicate attentiveness, respect, and dominance. **Body orientation** refers to how we position our body in relation to other people. *Direct body orientation* is when two people face each other squarely and *indirect body orientation* is when two people sit or stand side-by-side. Direct body orientation tends to signal attentiveness and respect. In a job interview, for example, we are likely to sit up straight and face the interviewer directly. **Body movement** is changing body position. It can be motivated (movement that helps clarify meaning) or unmotivated (movement that distracts listeners from the point being made). When making a speech, an upright stance and squared shoulders communicates poise and confidence. Taking a few steps to the left or right can signal a transition from one main point to the next, but pacing may actually distract listeners from the message.

haptics
what and how touch communicates

Touch **Haptics** is the technical term for what and how touch communicates. We may pat, hug, slap, kiss, pinch, stroke, or embrace others.

There are three types of touch: spontaneous touch, ritualized touch, and task-related touch. *Spontaneous touch* is automatic and subconscious. Patting someone on the back after learning that he or she won an award is an example of spontaneous touch. *Ritualized touch* is scripted rather than spontaneous. Handshakes, high-fives, and fist bumps are examples of ritualized touch. *Task-related touch* is used to perform a certain unemotional function. For instance, a doctor may touch a patient during a physical examination or a personal trainer may touch a client during a gym workout.

Some people like to touch and be touched and others do not. Touching behavior that seems innocuous to one person may be perceived as overly intimate or threatening to another. Moreover, touch that is considered appropriate in a private situation may be perceived as inappropriate in public contexts (Knapp, Hall, & Horgan, 2014).

Touching behavior is also highly correlated with culture (Gudykunst & Kim, 1997). Frequent touching is considered normal in some cultures and inappropriate in others. Some countries in South and Central America, as well as southern Europe may engage in frequent touching (Neuliep, 2006). Many Eastern cultures, on the other hand, do not engage in touching behavior, particularly in public contexts. Because the United States is a country of immigrants, the degree of touching behavior considered appropriate varies widely from individual to individual based on family heritage and norms.

APPLY IT

Did you grow up in a household where people frequently hugged to say hello and goodbye? How does that norm translate when you meet people with a different hugging norm? Explain.

Use of Voice: Paralanguage

paralanguage (vocalics)
the voiced part of a spoken message that goes beyond the actual words

Paralanguage (also known as *vocalics*) is the voiced part of a spoken message that goes beyond the actual words. Six characteristics of paralanguage are pitch, volume, rate, quality, intonation, and vocalized pauses.

Pitch Pitch is the highness or lowness of vocal tone. We raise and lower our pitch to signal a question, to emphasize ideas, and to convey emotions. We may raise our pitch when feeling nervous or afraid. We may lower our pitch to convey sadness (as in a speech given at a funeral) or force (as when a parent scolds a child for misbehaving).

pitch
highness or lowness of vocal tone

Volume Volume is the loudness or softness of vocal tone. Some people have booming voices that carry long distances and others are soft-spoken. Regardless of our normal volume level, however, we also tend to vary our volume depending on the situation, the topic of discussion, and emotional intent. For example, we might talk louder when we wish to be heard in noisy settings and when we are angry. We might speak softer when we are being reflective or romantic. There are also some cultural variations in the meanings attached to volume. For example, some Middle Easterners tend to speak with a great deal of volume to convey strength and sincerity; whereas soft voices tend to be preferred in Britain, Japan, and Thailand (Samovar, Porter, McDaniel, & Roy, 2012).

volume
loudness or softness of vocal tone

Rate Rate is the speed at which a person speaks. Most people in the United States naturally speak between 100 and 200 words per minute. People tend to talk more rapidly when they are happy, frightened, nervous, or excited and more slowly when they are problem-solving out loud, emphasizing an important idea, or sad. People who speak too slowly run the risk of boring listeners, and those who speak too quickly may not be understood.

rate
the speed at which a person speaks

Quality (Timbre) Quality is the sound of a person's voice that distinguishes it from others. Voice quality may be breathy (Marilyn Monroe), strident (Joan Rivers or Marge Simpson), throaty (Morgan Freeman or Jack Nicholson), or nasal (Fran Drescher in *The Nanny*). Although each person's voice has a distinct quality, too much breathiness can make people sound frail, too much stridence can make them seem hypertense, too much throatiness can make them seem cold and unsympathetic, and too much nasality can make them sound immature or unintelligent.

quality
the sound of a person's voice that distinguishes it from others

Intonation Intonation is the variety and inflection in one's voice. Voices that use very little or no intonation are described as monotone and tend to bore listeners. If you've ever seen the movie *Ferris Bueller's Day Off*, you may recall the teacher (played by Ben Stein) who is portrayed as boring via a monotone voice as he questions the class: "Anyone? Anyone? Bueller? Bueller?" Voices that use a lot of intonation may be perceived as ditzy, sing-songy, or childish. People prefer to listen to voices that use a moderate amount of intonation.

intonation
the variety and inflection in one's voice

In the United States, there are stereotypes about masculine and feminine voices. Masculine voices are expected to be low-pitched and loud, with moderate to low intonation; feminine voices are expected to be higher-pitched, softer in volume, and more expressive. Although both sexes have the option to portray a range of masculine and feminine paralanguage, most people usually conform to the expectations for their sex (Wood, 2007).

Vocalized Pauses Vocalized Pauses are extraneous sounds or words that interrupt fluent speech. They are essentially "place markers" designed to fill in momentary gaps while we search for the right word or idea. The most common vocalized pauses are "uh," "er," "well," "OK," "you know," and "like." We all use some vocalized pause words and phrases. However, when used excessively, vocalized pauses can give others the impression that we are unsure of ourselves. Sometimes speakers use so many vocalized pauses that listeners are distracted by them to the point of not being able to concentrate on the meaning of the message.

vocalized pauses
extraneous sounds or words that interrupt fluent speech

APPLY IT

How do your pitch, volume, rate, and intonation change when expressing anger with a friend or family member? When expressing excitement? When expressing disappointment?

Photo 5.4 Why might these men find it rude if you backed away?

proxemics
how space and distance communicate

personal space
the distance we try to maintain when interacting with others

territorial space
the physical space over which we claim ownership

artifacts
objects we use to mark our territory

Use of Space: Proxemics

Proxemics refers to how space and distance communicate (Hall, 1968). We communicate through our use of personal space, territorial space, and acoustic space.

Personal space **Personal space** is the distance we try to maintain when interacting with others. How much space we perceive as appropriate depends on our individual preference, the nature of the relationship, and cultural norms (Photo 5.4). With these variations in mind, the amount of personal space we view as appropriate generally decreases as the intimacy of our relationship increases. For example, in the dominant American culture, four distinct distances are generally perceived as appropriate based on the context and relationship. *Intimate distance* is defined as up to 18 inches and is appropriate for private conversations between close friends. *Personal distance*, from 18 inches to 4 feet, is the space in which casual conversation occurs. *Social distance*, from 4 to 12 feet, is where impersonal business such as a job interview is conducted. *Public distance* is anything more than 12 feet (Hall, 1968).

When "outsiders" violate our personal space, we tend to become uncomfortable. For instance, in a sparsely populated movie theater, people tend to leave one or more seats empty between themselves and others they do not know. If a stranger sits right next to us in such a setting, we are likely to feel uncomfortable and may even move to another seat. We will accept intrusions into our personal space only in certain settings and then only when all involved follow the unwritten rules. For example, we tend to tolerate being packed into a crowded elevator or subway by following unwritten rules, such as standing rigidly, looking at the floor or above the door, and not making eye contact with others.

Territorial Space **Territorial space** is the physical space over which we claim ownership. As with personal space, we expect others to respect our territory and may feel annoyed or even violated when they do not. Sometimes we do not realize how we are claiming or "marking" our territory. For example, Graham may have subconsciously marked "his chair" in the family room and others just know not to sit in it when Graham is around. Other times we mark our territory quite consciously, for example, by using locks, signs, and fences. Territorial space can also communicate status. To clarify, higher-status people generally claim larger and more prestigious territory (Knapp, Hall, & Horgan, 2014). In business, for example, the supervisor is likely to have the largest and nicest office in the unit.

We often use **artifacts**—or objects—to mark our territory. We display things on our desks and in our offices and homes, not just for their function but also because they communicate about our territory in some way. For example, we use artifacts to signal what we expect to happen in the space. The chairs and couch in your living room may approximate a circle that invites people to sit down and talk. Classroom seating may be arranged in auditorium style to discourage conversation. A manager's office with a chair facing the manager across the desk encourages formal conversation and signals status.

It says, "Let's talk business—I'm the boss and you're the employee." A manager's office with a chair placed at the side of her desk encourages more informal conversation. It says, "Don't be nervous—let's just chat."

Acoustic space **Acoustic space** is the area over which our voice can be comfortably heard. Competent communicators protect acoustic space by adjusting the volume of our voices to be easily heard by our conversational partners and not overheard by others. Loud cell phone conversations occurring in public places violate acoustic space. With the invention of Bluetooth technology, this problem has become even more pronounced. This is why some communities have ordinances prohibiting cell phone use in restaurants, hospitals, and theaters.

Use of Time: Chronemics

Recall that **chronemics** is how we interpret the use of time and it is largely based on cultural norms. Just as cultures tend to be more monochronic or polychronic, so too are individuals. If your approach to time is different from those with whom you are interacting, your behavior could be viewed as inappropriate and put strains on your relationship. When Carlos, who is polychronic, regularly arrives late to meetings with his monochromic teammates, they might resent his tardiness and perceive him to be full of himself, disrespectful, or perhaps as a slacker. In this chapter's *Diverse Voices*, Charles Okigbo offers his personal example of moving from what he calls "African time" to "American time."

acoustic space
the area over which our voice can be comfortably heard

chronemics
how we interpret the use of time

DIVERSE VOICES

Changing Times

by Charles Okigbo

Professor of Communication, North Dakota State University and Head, Policy Engagement & Communication African Population and Health Research Center Nairobi, Kenya

It is ironic that time is universal in the sense that every society understands the passage of time as it is connected to growth, aging, and transitions from one life stage to another. And yet, the concept of time also varies from one society to another. I have experienced this similar, yet varying sense of time in my own life, as I grew up in Nigeria, came to the United States for higher education, and have traveled between the United States and different African countries. In much of Africa, there are two time modes—cultural time, which is imprecise, and Western, or as we call it in Nigeria, "English" time. In Nigeria, we call this precise clock-based accounting for time "English time" because the British colonized us.

Other African countries that had different colonists might call it by a different name.

Time in much of traditional Africa is seen as an inexhaustible resource that flows endlessly and is hardly in short supply. Growing up in my Igbo village in southeastern Nigeria, the setting for Chinua Achebe's novel *Things Fall Apart,* I saw my people mark time with the rising and setting of the sun. Longer periods were marked by the rainy and dry seasons, and people's ages were gauged by historic events such as the world wars, the invasion of locusts, or the British colonialists' confiscation of all guns. Such loose characterization meant that precision was not possible. I vividly remember my people saying that a morning meeting would start "after sunrise" or "at the first cockcrow" or "after the morning market." Whereas this might appear confusing to Western time observers, to us, it presented no problems at all.

My first experience with Western (a.k.a. "English") time was when I went to kindergarten and later

continued

elementary school. We were taught to be punctual, and tardiness exacted strict sanctions, usually severe flogging. The severity of the punishment depended on how late one came to school.

When I came to the United States for graduate studies at Ohio University, I was already comfortable with Western time and never had any problem with punctuality. In fact, many Africans in the United States are often hypersensitive about punctuality issues and tend to be too punctual. This may be a case of over-compensating to avoid relapsing to cultural time. The adjustment to Western time can present some challenges, especially in situations when we have exclusive African events in the United States. For example, I remember as an African student and teacher in the United States, many meetings organized by Nigerian or other African students hardly ever started "on time" by Western standards because we often relapsed to our cultural time for exclusively African events.

So, we seem capable of successfully weaving in and out of cultural time depending on our expectation of whether the occasion is for Africans only or for Africans and "others." When the "others" are people with Western time orientation, we make every effort to be punctual. But when they are people who seem to share our sense of time, we respond accordingly. This represents a chronemics co-orientation, by which I mean that unconsciously we size up the other to know where to position them on the continuum of "cultural" and "Western" time. If they are closer to the former, we expect them to have a more relaxed approach to time, but if they are closer to the latter, we try to be punctual and seriously time conscious in dealing with them.

The tendency is for people to adjust their sense of time depending on the situation or the expectation of the audience. Professional meetings, conferences, even appointments with doctors or lawyers are loosely treated depending on one's expectations of how the other side sees time.

I must say that we Africans are not the only ones who could benefit from engaging in chronemics co-orientation. People who are usually Western in their approach to keeping appointments may decide not to be so punctual if they expect the other party will keep them waiting. For example, sometimes Africans may need to adjust to the precision of Western time, and at other times, Europeans and Americans who are dealing with exclusive African groups should consider adjusting to cultural time.

I have noticed that many African Americans in the United States are similar to Africans from the continent with respect to time consciousness, and many Native Americans in North Dakota and Minnesota share a similar cultural time orientation. So when African Americans host a party where most of the guests are also African American, the invitation may state that the party starts at 7:00 p.m., but most guests may not arrive until after 9:30 p.m.

While both cultural time and Western time continue to guide human behavior, increasing globalization and the information technological revolution are dictating a global approach to time that runs by the precision of the clock rather than by the natural rhythms of the rising or setting of the sun or the beginning or ending of seasons. Whether this move is ultimately in the best interest of humankind remains to be seen.

Source: By Charles Okigbo, Professor of Communication, North Dakota State University. Used with permission.

Physical Appearance

physical appearance
how we look to others

Physical appearance is how we look to others and is one of the first things others notice and judge. The dominant American culture places so much emphasis on physical appearance that entire industries are devoted to it. Options for changing our physical appearance range from surgical procedures to weight loss programs and products to cosmetics and clothing lines.

Today, more than ever, people use clothing choices, body art, and other personal grooming to communicate who they are and what they stand for (Insert Photo 5.5). Likewise, when we meet someone, we are likely to form our first impression of them based on how they are dressed and groomed. Thus, we can influence how others are likely to perceive us by our clothing and grooming choices. For example, Marcus, a successful sales representative, typically wears dress slacks and a collared shirt to the office, a suit and tie when giving a formal presentation, and a graphic T-shirt and jeans when hanging out with friends. Body art (such as piercings and tattoos) is quite popular in the United States today. Although body art can be an important means of self-expression, we often make choices about how much of it to display based on the situation and how others are likely to judge us based on it. For example, when Tiffany is at work she dresses

Photo 5.5 People use appearance to communicate about themselves and groups they identify with. What are some things this hipster may be saying about him/herself through clothing and personal grooming?

conservatively and covers the tattoo on her arm by wearing long-sleeved blouses. But on evenings and weekends, she does not. The *Communicating in the World* feature that follows points out some important considerations regarding body art and how it communicates.

COMMUNICATING IN THE WORLD

Body Art and Nonverbal Communication

Since ancient times, people have been painting, piercing, tattooing, and shaping their bodies. In fact, there is no culture that didn't or doesn't use body art to signal people's place in society, mark a special occasion, or just make a fashion statement (American Museum of Natural History, 1999). Body art is also a poignant form of nonverbal communication.

For centuries, Eastern cultures have used henna to dye hands and other body parts to communicate rites of passage such as marriages. Similarly, traditional Indian women may wear a *bindi* (a red spot or a piece of jewelry between their eyebrows) to indicate they are married. Women often use cosmetics, sports fans paint their faces and bodies, and some people

choose to pierce body parts or get tattoos to communicate an aspect of who they are or what they believe.

Tattooing is actually the oldest form of body art and tattooed mummies have been found in various parts of the world. Celebrities, soccer moms, corporate executives, star athletes, and high school students may sport tattoos as statements of individuality or group solidarity. Some people have tattoos strategically placed so that they can choose to display them or hide them from view depending on the self image they want to portray in different settings. Certainly, body art is very often not only art, but a powerful form of nonverbal communication.

When you see someone who has taken body art to an extreme, what do you think? How does this affect your interaction with this person?

MindTap

Guidelines for Improving Nonverbal Communication

Because nonverbal messages are inevitable, multi-channeled, ambiguous, and sometimes unintentional, interpreting them accurately can be tricky. Add to this the fact that the meaning of any nonverbal behavior can vary by situation and culture, and the reasons we so often misinterpret the nonverbal communication of others becomes clear. The following guidelines can help improve the likelihood that your nonverbal messages will be perceived accurately and that you will accurately interpret the nonverbal messages of others.

Sending Nonverbal Messages

1. **Consciously monitor your nonverbal messages.** Try to be more consciously aware of the nonverbal messages you send through your use of body, voice, space, time, and appearance. If you have difficulty doing this, ask a friend to point them out to you.

2. **Intentionally align your nonverbal messages with your purpose.** When nonverbal messages contradict verbal messages, people are more likely to believe the nonverbal messages, so it is important align your nonverbal messages with your purpose. If you want to be persuasive, use direct eye contact, a serious facial expression, an upright posture, a commanding vocal tone with no vocalized pauses, and professional clothing and grooming. If you want to be supportive and convey empathy, you might use less direct eye contact, a more relaxed facial expression, a softer voice, a nonthreatening touch, and a lean inward toward your partner.

3. **Adapt your nonverbal messages to the situation.** Just as you make language choices to suit different situations, so should you do so with nonverbal messages. Assess what the situation calls for in terms of use of body, voice, space, time, and appearance. For example, you would not dress the same way for a wedding as you would for a workout.

4. **Reduce or eliminate distracting nonverbal messages.** Fidgeting, tapping your fingers on a table, pacing, mumbling, using lots of pauses, and checking your phone often for texts and e-mails can distract others from the message you are trying to convey (Photo 5.6). Make a conscious effort to learn what distracting nonverbal messages have become habitual for you and work to eliminate them from your communication with others.

Photo 5.6 Be mindful of the distracting nonverbal messages you display. What might this person's nonverbal messages be saying?

GoGo Images/Jupiter Images

Interpreting Nonverbal Messages

1. **Remember that the same nonverbal message may mean different things to different people.** Most nonverbal messages have multiple meanings that vary from person to person, culture to culture, and even situation to situation. Just because you fidget when you are bored, doesn't mean that others are bored when they fidget. What you perceive as an angry vocal tone might not be intended as such by the person talking. So always try to consider multiple interpretations of the nonverbal messages you receive and seek clarification, particularly when your first interpretation is negative. This guideline becomes even more important when interpreting messages sent via social media and technology. For example, when Larissa read her brother's text, "CALL ME!", rather than jump to any conclusions, she interpreted his meaning as urgent and stepped into the hallway to call him right away to seek clarification rather than waiting until later.

2. **Consider each nonverbal message in context.** Because any one nonverbal message can mean different things in different contexts, take the time to consider how it is intended in a given situation. Also realize that you might not understand all the details of the situation. For example, if you see a classmate sleeping during

COMMUNICATE ON YOUR FEET

Speech Assignment

Communicating Emotions Nonverbally: Encoding and Decoding Skill and Practice

The Assignment

Your instructor will display a simple sentence for you to recite to your classmates while attempting to convey a particular emotion nonverbally. First, you will use only your voice; then you will use your voice and face; and finally you will use your voice, face, and body. The sentence could be as simple as "I had bacon and eggs for breakfast this morning."

1. Draw a card from a stack offered by your instructor. Without letting your classmates see, turn the card over to read what emotion is written on the front. Some possible emotions include *anger, excitement, fear, joy, worry,* and *sadness*. Consider how you will use vocalics and kinesics to convey that emotion.

2. When your instructor calls on you, go to the front of the classroom and shield your face with a piece of paper (so that your classmates cannot

see your face). Try to convey that emotion with only your voice while saying the sentence with your back to the class.

3. The class might make some guesses about the emotion you are conveying and give some reasons for their guesses. You should not tell them whether they are correct at this point.

4. Turn around to face your classmates and say the sentence again, this time trying to reinforce the emotion with your face and eyes.

5. The class might again make some guesses.

6. Repeat the sentence once more, this time using your voice, face, and body to convey the emotion.

7. The class might again make some guesses.

8. Tell them the emotion that was on the card and what you did with your voice, face, and body to convey it.

9. Your instructor may lead a discussion about what worked and didn't, as well as how you could have made the emotional message more clear.

WHAT WOULD YOU DO?

A Question of Ethics

After finishing their grueling mixed-doubles volleyball game, Bengt and Lisa joined their competitors, Brad and Eleni, for burgers at the local bar and grill. Brad and Eleni, who had been dating for about a year, had won the games thanks to Eleni's killer spikes.

After some general conversation about the game, Bengt said, "Eleni, your spikes tonight were awesome!"

"Yeah, I was really impressed. You rocked!" Lisa added.

"Thanks, guys," Eleni said in a tone of gratitude, "I've really been working on them."

"Careful guys. We don't want too many compliments to go to Eleni's head," Brad said jokingly. Then after a pause, he said, "Oh, Eleni, would you get my sweater? I left it on that chair by the other table."

"You're kidding, right Brad? The chair is right next to you," Eleni replied.

Brad said nothing as he focused his gaze directly at Eleni.

Eleni quickly said, "OK, Brad. It's cool," and got the sweater for him.

"Isn't she sweet?" Brad said as Eleni gave him the sweater.

Lisa smiled, glanced at Bengt, and said, "Well, I'm out of here. I've got a lot to do this evening."

"Me too," Bengt said as he quickly stood up to join Lisa.

"See you next week," they said in unison as they hurried out the door, leaving Brad and Eleni alone at the table.

What do you think Brad's nonverbal messages were attempting to communicate?

MindTap®

---

your speech, you might interpret the nonverbal message as boredom or disrespect. What it might be communicating, however, is utter exhaustion because your classmate just finished back-to-back 12-hour shifts at work while trying to keep up with homework for a full load of courses.

3. **Pay attention to the multiple nonverbal messages being sent and their relationship to the verbal message.** In any one interaction, you are likely to get simultaneous messages from a person's appearance, eye contact, facial expressions, gestures, posture, voice, as well as use of space and touch. By taking all nonverbal messages into consideration in conjunction with the verbal message, you are more likely to interpret their messages accurately.

4. **Use perception checking.** Perception checking lets you see if your interpretation of another person's message is accurate. By describing the nonverbal message you notice, sharing two possible interpretations of it, and asking for clarification, you can get confirmation or correction of your interpretation.

Reflection and Assessment

Nonverbal communication consists of all the messages that transcend spoken or written words. Nonverbal messages may emphasize, substitute for, or contradict a verbal message. They can regulate our conversations and project an image about who we are to others. It is also the primary way we convey our emotions. To assess how well you've learned what we addressed in these pages, answer the following questions. If you have trouble answering any of them, go back and review that material. Once you can answer each question accurately, you are ready to move ahead to read the next chapter.

1. What are the key characteristics of nonverbal communication and why is it critical to effective communication?

2. What are some examples of the different types of nonverbal messages we use to communicate?

3. What are some specific strategies you can employ to improve your nonverbal communication as both a sender and receiver of these messages?

COMMUNICATE!

RESOURCE AND ASSESSMENT CENTER

MindTap®

Now that you have read Chapter 5, go to your MindTap for *Communicate!* for quick access to the electronic resources that accompany this text.

Applying What You've Learned

Impromptu Speech Activity

Select a card from a stack provided by your instructor. Each card identifies a different emotion. Using no words, go to the front of the room and attempt to convey the emotion using only your body (including your hands and eyes). Ask the class to identify the emotion you are conveying and then discuss what you did to try to convey it.

Assessment Activities

1. Read this scenario and answer the questions that follow by applying the concepts of nonverbal communication we discussed in this chapter:

> Jesa and Madison were lounging on a blanket in the park one spring afternoon, enjoying the sunshine as they reviewed for an upcoming test. Jesa looked into the distance, then jerked her head around, bolted upright, quickly gathered her things, and quietly said, "See you back at the apartment." With that she took off at a fast clip.
>
> Madison quickly glanced in the direction that Jesa had been looking just before she took off, then shouted, "Wait a sec, I'm coming too."
>
> Once they were back in their apartment Madison sighed and said, "Okay, Jesa, what's really going on with you? Who was that guy you saw in the park? And why are you acting so scared?"
>
> "What guy? I don't know what you're talking about," Jesa mumbled, looking down at her feet. "And I'm not scared," she added as she turned to the window pulled back the corner of the curtain and peeked outside.

- How is each of the characteristics of nonverbal communication exemplified in this scene?
- Do you think Jesa was telling the truth? What about her nonverbal communication led you to this conclusion?

2. Go to a public place (for example, a restaurant or coffee shop) where you can observe two people having a conversation. You should be close enough so that you can observe their eye contact, facial expression, and gestures, but not close enough to hear what they are saying.

Carefully observe the interaction, with the goal of answering the following questions: What is their relationship? What seems to be the nature of the conversation (social chitchat, plan making, problem solving, argument, intimate discussion)? How does each person feel about the conversation? Do feelings change over the course of the conversation? Is one person more dominant? Take note of the specific nonverbal behaviors that led you to each conclusion, and write a paragraph describing this experience and what you have learned.

3. Enter a crowded elevator and face the back. Make direct eye contact with the person you are standing in front of. When you disembark, record the person's reactions. On the return trip, introduce yourself to the person who is standing next to you and engage in an animated conversation. Record the reaction of the person and others around you. Then get on an empty elevator and stand in the exact center. Do not move when others board. Record their reactions. Be prepared to share what you have observed with your classmates.

Skill-Building Activity

Perception Check Provide a perception check for each of the following nonverbal messages:

a. Larry walks into the cubicle, throws his report across the desk, smiles, and loudly proclaims, "Well, that's that!"

   Perception Check:

b. Christie, dressed in her team uniform, with her hair going every which way, charges into the room and announces in a loud voice, "I'm here, and I'm ready."

   Perception Check:

c. It was dinnertime and Anthony was due home from work at any minute. Suddenly the door flew open, banging against its hinges and Anthony stomped in, crossing the room in three long strides, plopped onto the sofa, crossed his arms, and with a sour expression stared straight ahead.

   Perception Check:

To help you complete this activity, look for the Chapter 5 Skill Building activities on MindTap for *Communicate!*

MindTap®

Listening

When you've finished this chapter, you'll be able to:

- Describe what listening is and why it is so important to effective communication.

- Explain why effective listening is such a challenge.

- Employ strategies to improve your listening skills.

- Employ strategies to respond effectively to what you've heard based on the audience and occasion.

MindTap®

Start with a quick warm-up activity.

As Beth pours another cup of coffee, Bart storms into the kitchen and blurts out, "Beth, do you have my car keys? I can't find them and I have to take the car or I'll be late for class."

"No," Beth replies, "but it doesn't matter because . . ."

Before Beth can finish, Bart interrupts, "I can't believe it. I was sure I left them here on the counter last night. It figures. Just because I'm in a hurry, I can't find them!" Bart starts shuffling through the papers on the counter and digging through the drawers.

"Bart, I . . ."

"I swear I put them here on the counter," Bart continues, growing noticeably more agitated. "Are you sure you didn't stuff them in a drawer when you were cleaning the kitchen or something?"

"Bart, chill out."

"Chill out?! If I'm late, I won't be able to do my presentation and it's worth 50 percent of the course grade! I won't pass the class and I need at least a B to declare my major. Beth, this is a very big deal."

"Bart, I've been trying to tell you . . ."

6

"Oh, sure—I'll just go into Professor Harrington's office and say, 'By the way, the reason I wasn't in class was that I couldn't find my car keys. Can I please do my presentation tomorrow?' I'll sound like a slacker who wasn't ready. There's no way he'll buy that argument even if it is true."

Beth takes Bart's hands in hers, looks him in the eye, and says calmly but firmly, "Bart, listen. I've been trying to tell you—I went out to get milk this morning and knew you would be leaving soon, so I left the keys in the car for you."

"Gee whiz, Beth, why didn't you tell me?"

MindTap®

Read, highlight, and take notes online.

Does this conversation sound familiar? Do you ever find yourself jumping to conclusions like Bart, especially when you're under pressure? We shouldn't underestimate the importance of listening; it can provide clarification, help us understand and remember material, improve our personal and professional relationships, and increase our ability to evaluate information effectively (e.g., Donoghue & Siegel, 2005; Gearhart, Denham, & Bodie, 2014; Weger, Jr., Bell, Minel, & Robinson, 2014). In fact, survey after survey reports that listening is one of the most important skills employers seek in job candidates and also one of the skills they are least effective at performing (e.g., Galagan, 2013; Mumford, 2007; National Association of Colleges and Employers, 2012; Pomeroy, 2007). So the skills you learn and apply from this chapter will set you apart in ways that will benefit you both personally and professionally.

We begin with a discussion of what listening is and some of the challenges we must overcome to listen effectively. Then, we offer several specific strategies to improve listening related to each of the steps in the active listening process. Finally, we suggest strategies for responding appropriately in different listening situations.

What Is Listening?

hearing
physiological process

listening
cognitive process of receiving, attending to, constructing meaning from, and responding to messages

People sometimes make the mistake of thinking that hearing and listening are the same, but they're not. **Hearing** is a physiological process. **Listening**, on the other hand, consists of complex affective, cognitive, and behavioral processes. Affective processes are those that motivate us to attend to a message. Cognitive processes include understanding and interpreting its meaning (Imhof, 2010) and behavioral processes are those related to responding with verbal and nonverbal feedback (Bodie, et al., 2012). Listening is important because studies show that, even when we factor in the use of technology such as social media and e-mail, as well as cell phone texting, listening is still "the most widely used daily communication activity" (Janusik & Wolvin, 2009, p. 115). Not only that, even when we try to listen carefully, most of us remember only about half of what we heard shortly after and less than 25 percent two days later (International Listening Association, 2003).

We choose to listen for various reasons depending on the situation. For example, when we listen to music for enjoyment and to speakers because we like their style, we engage in *appreciative listening*. When we listen to infer what more a speaker might mean beyond the actual words being spoken, we engage in *discriminative listening*. For instance, when a doctor is explaining test results, we might also try to discern whether the results are routine or cause for concern. When our goal is to recall information—for example, material a professor shares during a lecture—we engage in *comprehensive listening*. Finally, when we want to really understand and critically evaluate the worth of a message, we engage in *critical listening*. Because we need to hear, understand, evaluate, and assign worth to the message, as well as remember it, critical listening requires more psychological processing than the others.

Listening Challenges

To become effective listeners in any situation, we need to first overcome three key challenges. These challenges are rooted in our listening apprehension, preferred listening style, and approach we take to processing what we hear.

Listening Apprehension

Listening apprehension is the anxiety we feel about listening (Photo 6.1). Listening apprehension may increase when we worry about misinterpreting the message, or when we are concerned about how the message may affect us psychologically (Brownell, 2006). For example, if you are in an important meeting or job training session, you may worry about trying to absorb all the important technical information needed to do your job well. Or you might feel anxiety when the material you need to absorb is difficult or confusing. Likewise, your anxiety may increase when you feel ill, tired, or stressed about something else going on in your life. Listening apprehension makes it difficult to focus on the message. In the *Diverse Voices* selection, "How I Learned to Shut Up and Listen," Eileen describes how her apprehension actually taught her the value of listening.

> **listening apprehension**
> *the anxiety we feel about listening*

Listening Style

Listening style is our favored and usually unconscious approach to listening (Watson, Barker, & Weaver, 1995). Each of us tends to favor one of four listening styles. However, we also may change our listening style based on the situation and our goals for the interaction (Gearhart, Denham, & Bodie, 2014).

> **listening style**
> *our favored and usually unconscious approach to listening*

Content-oriented listeners focus on and evaluate the facts and evidence. Content-oriented listeners appreciate details and enjoy processing complex messages that may include a good deal of technical information. Content-oriented listeners are also likely to ask questions to get even more information.

> **content-oriented listeners**
> *focus on and evaluate the facts and evidence*

People-oriented listeners focus on the feelings their conversational partners may have about what they are saying. For example, people-oriented listeners tend to notice whether their partners are pleased or upset and will encourage them to continue by using nonverbal cues like head nods, eye contact, and smiles.

> **people-oriented listeners**
> *focus on the feelings the speaker may have about what they're saying*

Action-oriented listeners focus on the ultimate point the speaker is trying to make. Action-oriented listeners tend to get frustrated when ideas are disorganized and when people ramble. Action-oriented listeners also often anticipate what the speaker is going to say and may even finish the speaker's sentence for them.

> **action-oriented listeners**
> *focus on the ultimate point the speaker is trying to make*

Finally, **time-oriented listeners** prefer brief and hurried conversations and often use nonverbal and verbal cues to signal that their partner needs to be more concise. Time-oriented listeners may tell others exactly how much time they have to listen, interrupt when feeling time pressures, regularly check the time on smart phones, watches, or clocks, and may even nod their heads rapidly to encourage others to pick up the pace.

> **time-oriented listeners**
> *prefer brief and hurried conversations and use nonverbal and verbal cues to signal that their partner needs to be more concise*

Each of these styles has advantages and disadvantages. Content-oriented listeners are likely to understand and remember details, but may miss the overall point of the message and be unaware of the speaker's feelings. People-oriented listeners are likely to understand how the speaker feels, empathize, and offer comfort and support. However, they

Photo 6.1 Have you ever felt your anxiety increase because you really wanted to understand an explanation of difficult information or directions?

might become so focused on the speaker's feelings that they miss important details or fail to evaluate the facts offered as evidence. Action-oriented listeners may notice inconsistencies but, because they tend to anticipate what will be said rather than hearing the speaker out, may miss important details. Finally, time-oriented listeners are prone to only partially listen to messages while also thinking about their time constraints; thus, they might miss important details and be insensitive to their partner's emotional needs. In our opening scenario, Bart fell victim to the consequences of being too action-oriented and time-oriented when listening to Beth. With these challenges in mind, let's turn now to some specific techniques we can employ to improve our active listening skills in both face-to-face and virtual settings.

Preferred listening style may also be influenced by cultural and co-cultural identity (Gonzalez, Houston, & Chen, 2011). For example, women who identify with the feminine co-culture are more likely to describe themselves as person-oriented. Similarly, men who identify with the masculine co-culture are more likely to be time-oriented (Salisbury & Chen, 2007). People in collectivist cultures, where maintaining group harmony is highly valued, are more likely to have a people-oriented listening style; people from individualistic cultures are more likely to have an action-oriented listening style (Carbaugh, Nuciforo, Salto, & Shin, 2011). People from high-context cultures tend to favor a person-oriented listening style and people from low-context cultures tend to prefer an action-oriented style (Harris, 2003).

APPLY IT

Identify two or three close friends or family members. Which listening style do you think each one prefers? Provide an example to support your opinion.

MindTap®

DIVERSE VOICES

How I Learned to Shut Up and Listen

By Eileen Smith

Bearshapedsphere.com

Living in the "wrong" country for nearly seven years, Eileen calls Chile home now. She bikes, photographs, writes, eats, and talks about language. She was raised in Brooklyn, New York.

I sat at a table of no fewer than fifteen people on the street Pio Nono, entry to Bellavista, the down-home party section of Santiago, Chile. I'd been invited to go out for a beer after the monthly critical mass bike ride. We sat at a long series of card tables extending down the street, serving ourselves beer from the liter bottles of Escudo on the center of the tables. Some drinkers mixed theirs with Fanta. I drank mine plain and listened.

I arrived to Chile in 2004, with way more than a passing knowledge of Spanish. Between high school and a couple of travel and study stints in the *mundo hispanohablante* (Spanish-speaking world), I could express myself fairly well, if not cleverly. Hadn't I explained the electoral college to a group of teachers in Antigua, Guatemala, in the 1990s? Wasn't it me who grabbed other travelers by the hand to take them to the post office, the bus station, or to get their hair cut? I enjoyed helping, expressing, being in charge. I could get you a seat on the bus, a doorstop, tape to fix a book—you name it. I could ask for it directly or circumlocute it. I spoke, and people understood. At the time, I felt that this was the only

continued

necessary linguistic accomplishment. You, listen to me. And then it was over.

While output was the feather in my linguistic cap, my listening wouldn't have won any awards. Still, I was skilled enough (or so I thought). Ask a predictable question while travelling, and get a predictable answer. "Where" questions should lead to a location. "When" questions should yield a time or day. "I don't know" might come up at any time, so be prepared. Other times you might get a "probably," or "No, we're out of that (on the menu), what about this?" These little sayings are repetitive, predictable, often accompanied by hand and head motions, and occasional pointing. Understandable.

But what happens when you get out of the predictable, and put fifteen of your new closest friends on a loud sidewalk, add an unfamiliar accent, country-specific slang, and not just a touch of cheap beer? As an ESL teacher I'd seen students reduced to frustration, to squinching their eyes shut against visual input while they leaned their heads closer to the audio, hoping that the problem wasn't their ear for English, but their hearing. Try as I might there on the sidewalk, no matter of eye squinching or head leaning was going to fix the fact that I was simply not up to the task. My Chilean friends could understand me, but of the reading/writing/listening/speaking quadrifecta that make up second-language learning, clearly my listening was the weakest. I'm loquacious at the best of times, grate-on-your-nerves chatty when it's worse. But here, on the street in Santiago, 5,000 miles from a place where I could understand easily (and foolishly had taken this for granted), I was relegated to good listener status. I could understand enough to follow, kind of, but not fast enough to say anything relevant to the conversation while the topic was still hot.

I was also in Chile, which, with the exception of not letting people off the metro before getting on, is one of the most polite places I'd ever been. What this means is that any time I so much as appeared to want to say anything, a hush would fall over the string of tables. People knew they might not understand me easily, so they wanted to give me their complete attention.

Between the hot topic issue and the *plancha* (embarrassment) I felt at having all eyes on me,

the venerable communicator, I simply had to take a different tact. No longer was I Eileen, wordsmith extraordinaire. I was Aylín, the good listener. I was polite and people described me as quiet.

Not being able to participate in a conversation is like being in disguise. For the first time in my life I was getting to know the patient people, the ones that reach out to quiet ones. I'd never met them before because I was so busy with my soundtrack. It made people want to take me into their confidence, their inner circle. I was not a person who repeated private information. As far as they could tell, I didn't even speak.

After several months of more listening than speaking, I took it up as a new challenge: To follow every conversation with surgical precision, and say nothing, or nearly nothing. I could feel the cloud of wonder and panic lifting, and still I chose to stay quiet. I learned about body language and turn-taking, Chilean social niceties, and watched the other quiet people to see what they were doing. They weren't bland, just quiet. It was a revelation.

Nearly five years later, I don't have to just listen any more. I can exchange jokes and fling around slang with abandon. But what I've found is that I often don't want to. I'm often happy to let events take place without interrupting them, just listening to people say what they have to, what they want to. I don't interrupt as much and I've discovered this whole new world, even among my very own family, the self-professed masters of interrupting and simultaneous yammering (I blame Brooklyn). Sometimes I just try to let them talk themselves out before chiming in. Because when people are talking, they tend not to be great listeners. I'd rather have their attention before saying something.

I'm often told I've changed quite a bit since being in Chile. Years have passed, and in that time we've all changed. But what I learned there is that you don't have to be on your game at every possible second. You can watch from the sidelines and participate at the same time. Sometimes the story we tell when we're not saying a word is the most important story of all.

Originally posted April 2, 2009, at Travelblogs.com.

Source: Reprinted by permission of Eileen Smith.

Photo 6.2 When we listen passively, we usually miss important information. How will you try to keep focused on important messages in the future?

passive listening
the habitual and unconscious process of receiving messages

active listening
the deliberate and conscious process of attending to, understanding, remembering, evaluating, and responding to messages

attending
intentionally perceiving and focusing on a message

Processing Approach

You may recall from Chapter 2 that we process information in two ways—passively or actively. **Passive listening** is the habitual and unconscious process of receiving messages. When we listen passively, we are on automatic pilot. We may attend only to certain parts of a message and assume the rest. We tend to listen passively when we aren't really interested or when we are multitasking (Photo 6.2). By contrast, **active listening** is the deliberate and conscious process of attending to, understanding, remembering, evaluating, and responding to messages. Active listening requires practice. The rest of this chapter focuses on helping you become a better active listener.

Active Listening Strategies

Active listening is a complex process made up of five steps. These steps are (a) attending, (b) understanding, (c) remembering, (d) evaluating, and (e) responding to the messages we receive. In this section, we offer specific strategies to improve listening related to each step.

Attending

Effective active listening begins with attending. **Attending** is the process of intentionally perceiving and focusing on a message (O'Shaughnessey, 2003). Poor listeners have difficulty exercising control over what they attend to, often letting their minds drift to thoughts unrelated to the topic. One reason for this stems from the fact that people typically speak at a rate of about 120 to 150 words per minute, but our brains can process between 400 and 800 words per minute (Wolvin & Coakley, 1996). This means we usually assume we know what a speaker is going to say before he or she finishes saying it. So our minds have lots of time to wander from the message. In the opening vignette, Bart seemed to have trouble attending to Beth, in part because he thought he knew what she was going to say before she said it.

Not only does the gap between speaking and processing create opportunities for inattention, but research suggests that, thanks in part to the Internet, smart phones, and other technologies, our attention spans continue to get shorter and shorter (Dukette & Cornish, 2009). Consider your own experiences. Do you ever find yourself daydreaming or checking Facebook during class or when participating in an online conference or meeting?

The first step to becoming a good active listener, then, is to train ourselves to focus on or attend to what people are saying regardless of potential distractions. Let's consider four techniques for doing so.

1. **Get physically ready to listen.** Good listeners create a physical environment that reduces potential distractions and adopt a listening posture. For example, you might turn off background music, your cell phone, and irrelevant Web sites on your computer so you won't be tempted to turn your attention to them when you are trying to listen. You can also adopt a listening posture by sitting upright in your chair, leaning slightly forward, and looking directly at the person speaking in the room or on the computer screen.

2. **Resist mental distractions.** Work consciously to block out wandering thoughts that might come from a visual distraction (e.g., a classmate who enters the room

while the professor is lecturing), an auditory distraction (e.g., coworkers chatting beside you while your supervisor is giving instructions), or a physical distraction (e.g., wondering what you'll eat for lunch because your stomach is growling).

3. **Hear the person out.** Far too often, we stop listening because we disagree with something the speaker says, we assume we know what they are going to say, or we become offended by an example or word used. To be effective at attending, we need to train ourselves not to mentally argue with the speaker and stay focused on the message. When Beth realized Bart was not hearing her out, she helped him regain focus by taking his hands in hers and looking him in the eye. The *Communicating in the World* feature in this chapter highlights noted author Dale Carnegie's tips for winning friends and influencing people by engaging in effective active listening.

COMMUNICATING IN THE WORLD

Dale Carnegie's Tips for Talking and Listening

Everett Collection Inc/Alamy

Dale Carnegie's best-selling book, *How to Win Friends and Influence People*, was first published in 1936. During its more than 75 years on the market, it has sold over 15 million copies, and it remains one of the most influential self-help communication guides available today. Dale Carnegie Training, a communication leadership program Carnegie founded in 1912, also continues to flourish worldwide with offices in over 80 countries. Carnegie's advice on public speaking, leadership, teambuilding, interpersonal communication, and human relations has trained more than 8 million people worldwide and includes over 400 *Fortune* 500 companies on its client list.

Carnegie's advice for winning friends and influencing people can be summarized in the form of six key principles:

1. *Become genuinely interested in other people.*

2. *Smile.*

3. *Remember that a person's name is to that person the sweetest and most important sound in any language.*

4. *Be a good listener. Encourage others to talk about themselves.*

5. *Talk in terms of the other person's interests.*

6. *Make the other person feel important—and do it sincerely.*

(Carnegie, 1936, pp. 110–111)

He elaborates on principle number 4—be a good listener—in this way:

> *If you want to know how to make people shun you and laugh at you behind your back and even despise you, here is the recipe: Never listen to anyone for long. Talk incessantly about yourself. If you have an idea while the other person is talking, don't wait for him or her to finish: bust right in and interrupt in the middle of a sentence.*
>
> *If you aspire to be a good conversationalist, be an attentive listener. Ask questions that other persons will enjoy answering. Encourage them to talk about themselves and their accomplishments.*
>
> *Remember that the people you are talking to are a hundred times more interested in themselves and their wants and problems than they are in you and your problems. . . . Think of that the next time you start a conversation.* (pp. 95–96)

Do you think—as some do—that effective listening as described by Carnegie is becoming a "lost art"? Why or why not?

MindTap®

Understanding

Understanding is accurately interpreting a message. Let's discuss four strategies to improve listening to understand.

1. **Identify the main point.** As you listen, ask yourself, "What does the speaker want me to understand?" and "What is the point being made?" In addition to the surface message, you might also need to consider the pragmatic meaning couched within it. For example, when Marlee, who is running for city council, asks Joanna what she thinks about the plans for the new arts center and begins to talk about some of its pros and cons, Joanna understands that, beneath the surface, Marlee is also attempting to persuade Joanna to vote for her.

2. **Ask questions.** A **question** is a statement designed to clarify information or get additional details. Suppose Chris says, "I am totally frustrated. Would you stop at the store on the way home and buy me some more paper?" You may be a bit confused by his request and need more information to understand. Yet if you simply respond, "What do you mean?" Chris, who is already frustrated, may become defensive. Instead, you might ask one of three types of questions to increase your understanding:

   - *To get details*: "What kind of paper and how much should I get?"

   - *To clarify word meanings*: "What you mean by *frustrated*?"

   - *To clarify feelings*: "What's frustrating you?"

3. **Paraphrase. Paraphrasing** is putting a message into your own words. For example, during an argument with her sister, Karen paraphrased what she thought she heard her sister saying: "I think I hear you saying that I'm trying to act like I'm better than you when I talk about my work so much." Paraphrases may focus on content or feelings. A **content paraphrase** focuses on the denotative meaning of the message. In the example, "when I talk about my work so much" is a content paraphrase. A **feelings paraphrase** focuses on the emotions attached to the message. The second part of the example ("you feel that I'm trying to act like I'm better than you") is a feelings paraphrase.

   By paraphrasing, you give the speaker a chance to verify your understanding. The longer and more complex the message, the more important it is to paraphrase. When the speaker appears to be emotional or when the speaker is not using his or her native language, paraphrasing is essential to understanding.

   To paraphrase effectively, (1) listen carefully to the message, (2) notice what images and feelings you experience from the message, (3) determine what the message means to you, and (4) create a message that conveys these images or feelings.

4. **Empathize. Empathy** is intellectually identifying with the feelings or attitudes of another. Three approaches are empathic responsiveness, perspective taking, and sympathetic responsiveness (Gearhart, et al., 2014).

   - **Empathic responsiveness** occurs when you experience an emotional response parallel to another person's actual or anticipated display of emotion (Photo 6.3). For instance, when Jackson tells Janis that he is in real trouble financially, and

Janis senses the stress and anxiety that Jackson is feeling, we would say that Janis has demonstrated empathic responsiveness.

- **Perspective taking** occurs when we use everything we know about the sender and his or her circumstances to understand their feelings. For example, suppose Jackson tells Janis that he is in serious financial trouble. Janis, who has known Jackson since grade school, understands that Jackson was raised by parents who were very frugal and paid their bills on time. Because of what she knows about Jackson, Janis understands that Jackson must be very worried about his rising debts.

- **Sympathetic responsiveness** is feeling concern, compassion, or sorrow for another's situation. Sympathy differs from the other two approaches. Rather than attempting to experience the feelings of the other, we translate our intellectual understanding of what the speaker has experienced into feelings of concern, compassion, and sorrow for that person. In our previous example, Janis has sympathy for Jackson when she understands that Jackson is embarrassed and worried, but instead of trying to feel those same emotions herself, she feels concern and compassion for her friend.

How well we empathize also depends on how observant we are of others' behavior and how clearly we read their nonverbal messages. To improve these skills, develop the habit of silently posing two questions to yourself: "What emotions do I believe the person is experiencing right now?" and "On what cues from that person am I basing this conclusion?"

To further increase the accuracy of reading emotions, you can also use perception checking. This is especially helpful when the other person's culture is different from yours. Let's consider an example. Atsuko, who was raised in rural Japan and is now studying at a university in Rhode Island, may feel embarrassed when her professor publicly compliments her work. Her friend Meredith might notice Atsuko's reddened cheeks and downcast eyes and comment, "Atsuko, I noticed that you looked down when Professor Shank praised you. Did the compliment embarrass you, make you feel uncomfortable, or was it something else?"

Bruce Ayres/Riser/Getty Images

Photo 6.3 Sometimes effective listening means demonstrating empathy for someone who is obviously distressed. Who do you typically go to for empathy and support when you feel stressed, and why?

perspective taking
using everything we know about sender and his or her circumstances to understand their feelings

sympathetic responsiveness
feeling concern, compassion, or sorrow for another's situation

"Cheer up, Nicole! What does Princeton know? Say, you got any plans for that last bit of cobbler?"

COMMUNICATION SKILL

Paraphrasing

Skill	Use	Procedure	Example
A response that conveys your understanding of another person's message.	To increase listening efficiency; to avoid message confusion; to discover the speaker's motivation.	1. Listen carefully to the message. 2. Notice what images and feelings you have experienced from this message. 3. Determine what the message means to you. 4. Create a message that conveys these images or feelings.	Grace says, "At two minutes to five, the boss gave me three letters that had to be in the mail that evening!" Bonita replies, "If I understand, you were really resentful that your boss dumped important work on you right before quitting time when she knows you have to pick up the baby at day care."

remembering
being able to retain and recall information later

repetition
saying something aloud or mentally rehearsing it two, three, or more times

mnemonic device
a technique that associates a special word or very short statement with new and longer information

Photo 6.4 Some people remember the color spectrum using the mnemonic device "Roy G. Biv" for red, orange, yellow, green, blue, indigo, and violet. What mnemonics have you used to remember information?

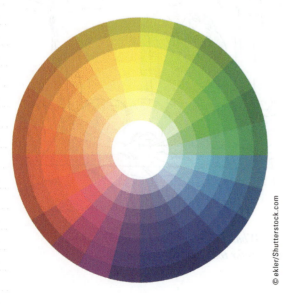

© ekler/Shutterstock.com

Remembering

Remembering is being able to retain and recall information later. We may find remembering difficult, for instance, because we filter out information that doesn't fit our learning style, our listening anxiety prevents us from recalling what we have heard, we engage in passive listening, we practice selective listening and remember only what supports our position, and we fall victim to the primacy–recency effect of remembering only what is said at the beginning and end of a message. Let's look at three strategies to improve our ability to remember information.

1. **Repeat the information. Repetition**—saying something aloud or mentally rehearsing it two, three, or more times—helps store information in long-term memory. So when you are introduced to a stranger named Jon McNeil, if you mentally think, "Jon McNeil, Jon McNeil, Jon McNeil," you increase the chances that you will remember his name. Likewise, when a person gives you directions to "go two blocks east, turn left, turn right at the next light, and it's the second apartment building on the right," you should immediately repeat the directions to yourself to help remember them.

2. **Construct mnemonics.** A **mnemonic device** associates a special word or very short statement with new and longer information (Photo 6.4). One of the most common mnemonic techniques is to form a word with the first letters of a list of items you are trying to remember. For example, a popular mnemonic for the five Great Lakes is HOMES (*H*uron, *O*ntario, *M*ichigan, *E*rie, *S*uperior). Most beginning music students learn the mnemonic "*every good boy does fine*" for the notes on the lines of the treble clef (E, G, B, D, F) and the word *face* (F, A, C, E) for the notes on the spaces.

3. **Take notes.** Although note taking may not be an appropriate way to remember information when engaged in casual interpersonal

encounters, it is a powerful tool for increasing recall during lectures, business meetings, and briefing sessions. Note taking provides a written record that you can go back to later. It also allows you to take an active role in the listening process (Dunkel & Pialorski, 2005; Kobayashi, 2006; Titsworth, 2004).

What constitutes good notes varies depending on the situation. Useful notes may consist of a brief list of main points or key ideas plus a few of the most significant details. Or they may be a short summary of the entire concept (a type of paraphrase). For lengthy and detailed information, however, good notes are likely to consist of a brief outline, including the overall idea, the main points, and key supporting material.

Evaluating

Evaluating is the process of critically analyzing a message to determine its truthfulness, utility, and trustworthiness. This may involve ascertaining the accuracy of facts, the amount and type of evidence used, and how a position relates to your personal values. Here are some strategies for evaluating messages effectively.

evaluating
critically analyzing what you hear

1. **Separate facts from inferences. Facts** are statements whose accuracy can be verified as true. If a statement is offered as a fact, you need to determine if it is true. Doing so often requires asking questions that probe the evidence. For example, if Raoul says, "It's going to rain tomorrow," you might ask, "Oh, did you see the weather report this morning?" **Inferences** are assertions based on the facts presented. When a speaker makes an inference, you need to determine whether the inference is valid. You can ask: (1) What are the facts that support this inference? (2) Is this information really central to the inference? (3) Is there other information that would contradict this inference? For example, if someone says, "Better watch it—Katie's in a really bad mood today. Did you catch the look on her face?" you should stop and think, is Katie really in a bad mood? The support for this inference is her facial expression. Is this inference accurate? Is Katie's expression one of anger, or unhappiness, or something else? Is the look on her face enough to conclude that she's in a bad mood? Is there anything else about Katie's behavior that could lead us to believe she's not in a bad mood? Separating facts from inferences is important because inferences may be false, even if they are based on verifiable facts.

facts
statements whose accuracy can be verified as true

inferences
assertions based on the facts presented

2. **Probe for information.** Sometimes we need to encourage the speaker to delve deeper into the topic in order to truly evaluate the message critically (Photo 6.5). For example, suppose that Jerrod's prospective landlord asked him to sign a lease. Before signing it, Jerrod should probe for more information. He might ask about the term of the lease and the consequences for breaking the lease early. He might also ask about a deposit and what he will need to do to get the deposit back when the lease is up. He may have noticed inconsistencies between the rental ad on Craigslist and something the landlord says. In that case he might say, "Your ad said that utilities would be paid by the landlord, but just now you said the tenant pays the utility bill. Which one is correct?" With questions like these, Jerrod is probing to accurately evaluate the message.

Photo 6.5 Effective managers understand the value of making notes about problems that employees point out. How can you use note taking at work to improve your performance?

Dana White/PhotoEdit

COMMUNICATE ON YOUR FEET

Active Listening to and Evaluating a Speech

Attend a formal public presentation on campus or in your community. Your goal is to listen actively to understand, remember, and critically evaluate what you hear. Be sure to take notes as you listen. Afterward, analyze what you heard using the following questions to guide your thinking:

- What was the purpose of the speech? What was the speaker trying to explain to you or convince you about?
- Was it easy or difficult to identify the speaker's main ideas? What did you notice about how the speaker developed each point she or he made?
- Did the speaker use examples or tell stories to develop a point? If so, were these typical

examples, or did the speaker choose examples that were unusual but seemed to prove the point?

- Did the speaker use statistics to back up what was said? If so, did the speaker tell you where the statistics came from? Did the statistics surprise you? If so, what would you have needed to hear that would have helped you to accept them as accurate?
- Do you think the speaker did a good job? If so, why? If not, what should the speaker have done to be more effective?

When you have finished your analysis, follow your instructor's directions. You may be asked to deliver a short speech about what you learned.

---

responding
providing feedback

nonverbal feedback cues
nonverbal signals that we are attending to and understanding the message

supportive responses
create an environment that encourages the other person to talk about and make sense of a distressing situation

Photo 6.6 It is especially challenging to hear a speaker out when engaged in a heated argument. What might you do to keep from interrupting another person on these occasions?

Responding

Responding is providing feedback. When we respond to a friend or family member who appears emotionally upset to a colleague's ideas, or to a public speech, we need to do so in ways that demonstrate respect for the speaker even when we disagree with him or her. Because how we respond is so critical to effective communication in different situations, we devote the next section to it.

Listening Response Strategies

Regardless of the situation, we want to respond in ways that demonstrate respect, as well as clarity. We can do so by providing appropriate nonverbal feedback cues while the speaker is talking and verbal feedback only after the speaker has finished (Photo 6.6). **Nonverbal feedback cues** are the signals we use to illustrate that we are attending to and understanding the message. Nodding, smiling, laughing, head cocking, frowning, and eyebrow furrowing are examples. Next we offer some specific strategies when our goal in responding is to provide emotional support, constructive criticism, and formal constructive speech critiques.

1. **Emotional support response strategies.** Sometimes the appropriate response is to reassure, encourage, soothe, console, or cheer up (Photo 6.7). **Supportive responses** create an environment that encourages the other person to talk about and make sense of a distressing

© Dragon Images/Shutterstock.com

Figure 6.1

Guidelines for supportive responses.

Guidelines	Examples
1. Clearly state that your aim is to help.	*I'd like to help you, what can I do?*
2. Express acceptance or affection; do not condemn or criticize.	*I understand that you just can't seem to accept this.*
3. Demonstrate care, concern, and interest in the other's situation; do not give a lengthy recount of a similar situation.	*What are you planning to do now? OR tell me more; what happened then?*
4. Indicate that you are available to listen and support the other without intruding.	*I know that we've not been that close, but sometimes it helps to have someone to listen and I'd like to do that for you.*
5. State that you are an ally.	*I'm with you on this OR Well, I'm on your side; this isn't right.*
6. Acknowledge the other's feelings and situation, and express your sincere sympathy.	*I'm so sorry to see you feeling so bad; I can see that you're devastated by what has happened.*
7. Assure the other that their feelings are legitimate; do not tell the other how to feel or to ignore those feelings.	*Hey, get it. With all that has happened to you, you have a right to be angry.*
8. Use prompting comments to encourage elaboration.	*Uh-huh, Yeah, OR I see. How did you feel about that? OR Tell me more.*

© Cengage Learning

situation. Supporting does not mean making false statements or telling someone only what he or she wants to hear. Figure 6.1 summarizes research-based guidelines for forming supportive messages (Burleson, 2010).

2. **Constructive Criticism Response Strategies.** When we simply cannot agree with what a speaker says, our messages will be most effective if they clearly demonstrate respect. Figure 6.2 provides some guidelines to help demonstrate respect when disagreeing with or critiquing others.

3. **Formal Constructive Speech Critique Strategies.** The goals when providing a formal constructive speech critique are to be respectful, honest, and helpful. To do so, you need to use "I" language, be specific, and identify what the speaker did well before offering suggestions for improvement. Good speech critiques address content, structure, and delivery, as well as presentational aids if used.

- When critiquing content, comment on the appropriateness of the speech for that particular audience, the use of facts and inferences, the logic of the arguments, and the evidence used to support ideas.

- When critiquing structure, focus on the introduction (attention catcher, thesis statement, main point preview), organization pattern of the main points, transitions, and concluding remarks.

Photo 6.7 Effective supportive messages provide emotional encouragement. Who do you typically go to for support and encouragement and why?

David Frazier/Science Source

Figure 6.2

Guidelines for demonstrating respect when disagreeing with or critiquing others

Guidelines	Examples
1. Use "I" language to clearly own the comments you make. Do not ascribe them to others.	*Carla, I really like the way you cited the references for your opening quotation.*
2. Use specific language and specific examples to point out areas of disagreement and areas for improvement.	*I can't agree to this plan because I cannot afford a 15% reduction in my personnel budget. I could probably live with a 10% decrease.*
3. Find a point to agree with or something positive to say before expressing your disagreement or offering a negative critique.	*I really appreciate what you have to say on this topic and agree that we need to support our co-workers who need after school care for their children. I wonder, though, if we should brainstorm more potential solutions before settling on one.*

© Cengage Learning

WHAT WOULD YOU DO?

A Question of Ethics

Janeen always disliked talking on the phone. So she usually let her incoming calls go to voice mail and then text the caller back.

One day while studying for final exams, Janeen got a call from a number she didn't recognize. So she answered it. The caller was Barbara, a home town friend she hadn't talked to in a few years. When she answered, she found herself bombarded with information about old high school friends and their whereabouts. Not wanting to disappoint Barbara, who seemed eager to talk, Janeen put her phone on speaker, set it down, and returned to studying her notes. She answered Barbara with the occasional "uh-huh," "hmm," or "wow, that's cool!" After a few minutes, she realized Barbara was no longer talking. Suddenly very ashamed, she said, "I'm sorry, what did you say? The phone . . . uh, there was just a lot of static."

Barbara replied with obvious hurt in her voice, "I'm sorry I bothered you. You must be terribly busy."

Embarrassed, Janeen muttered, "I'm just really stressed, you know, with exams coming up and everything. I guess I wasn't listening very well; you didn't seem to be saying anything really important. I'm sorry. What were you saying?"

"Nothing 'important,'" Barbara answered. "I was just trying to figure out a way to tell you. I know you are friends with my brother Billy, and you see, we just found out yesterday that he's terminally ill with a rare form of leukemia. But you're right; it obviously isn't really important." With that, she hung up.

Which principles of effective listening did Janeen violate by how she listened to Barbara? Explain how each of these principles apply specifically to active listening.

MindTap®

	Ineffective critique	Effective critique
Content	"The sources you cited are old and no longer represent current thinking on the topic."	"I noticed you relied heavily on Johnson's 1969 essay about global warming. For me, your argument would be more compelling if you were to cite research that has been published in the last five years."
Structure	"You were really hard to follow."	"I really appreciate what you had to say on this topic. I would have been able to follow your main points better if I had heard clear transitions between each one. Transitions would have helped me notice the switch from one topic to the next."
Delivery	"You talk too fast!'	"I was fascinated by the evidence you offered to support the first main point. It would have been even more compelling for me if you were to slow down while explaining that information. That would give me time to understand the material more fully before we moved on to the next main point."

© Cengage Learning

Figure 6.3

Examples of effective and ineffective speech critiques

- When critiquing delivery, comment on use of voice (intelligible, conversational, expressive) and use of body (attire, poise, eye contact, facial expressions, gestures).

- When critiquing presentational aids, talk about construction (large, neat colorful, visual symbol system) and integration (concealed, revealed, and referenced during the speech).

Figure 6.3 provides examples of ineffective and effective speech critique statements.

Reflection and Assessment

Listening is the process of receiving, attending to, constructing meaning from, and responding to messages. It is critical to communication in both personal and professional relationships. To assess how well you've learned what we addressed in these pages, answer the following questions. If you have trouble answering any of them, go back and review that material. Once you can answer each question accurately, you are ready to move ahead to read the next chapter.

1. What is listening and why is it so important to effective communication?

2. What are some challenges we must overcome to listen effectively?

3. What are some strategies you can employ to (a) attend to, (b) understand, and (c) remember information?

4. What are some key strategies to employ when your goal is to (a) provide emotional support, (b) give constructive criticism, or (c) prepare a formal constructive speech critique?

COMMUNICATE!

RESOURCE AND ASSESSMENT CENTER

MindTap®

Now that you have read Chapter 6, go to your MindTap for *Communicate!* for quick access to the electronic resources that accompany this text.

Applying What You've Learned

Impromptu Speech Activity

Draw a slip of paper from a stack provided by your instructor. Read the scenario and formulate an appropriate response based on the information provided in the chapter. Deliver a short impromptu speech where you (a) read the scenario aloud, (b) identify which response you think is most appropriate (emotional support, critique, speech evaluation) and why, and (c) articulate the response based on the guidelines for it from this chapter. Be sure to structure your message using a thesis, preview, transitions, summary, and clincher.

Assessment Activities

1. Personal Listening Style Profile Go to MindTap for *Communicate!* for the Personal Listening Style Profile. Then write a short essay in which you report how you scored on this profile, whether you agree with the styles that the profile indicates are your dominant ones, and explain how your style helps and hinders your ability to actively listen. Then, based on what you have learned in this chapter, describe two or three steps you can take to improve your listening.

2. Conversation and Analysis: Damien and Chris. Go to MindTap for *Communicate!* and access the Damien and Chris dialogue in the Chapter 6 materials. Watch the video of this conversation between Damien and Chris and note examples of the participants using the active listening process. Be sure to note which specific skills and guidelines each follows, as well as any challenges or problems you see in their listening behavior. How is this conversation affected by the use of active listening?

Skill-Building Activities

1. Writing Questions and Paraphrases Provide an appropriate question and paraphrase for each of the following statements. To get you started, the first prompt has been completed for you.

a. **Luis:** "It's Dionne's birthday, and I've planned a *big* evening. Sometimes, I think Dionne believes I take her for granted—well, I think after tonight she'll know I think she's something special!"

Question: What specific things do you have planned?

Content paraphrase: If I'm understanding you, you're planning a night that's going to cost a lot more than what Dionne expects on her birthday.

Feelings paraphrase: From the way you're talking, I get the feeling you're really proud of yourself for making plans like these.

b. **Angie:** "Brother! Another nothing class. I keep thinking one of these days he'll get excited about something. Professor Romero is a real bore!"

Question:

Content paraphrase:

Feelings paraphrase:

c. **Jerry:** "Everyone seems to be talking about that movie on FX last night, but I didn't see it. You know, I don't watch the 'idiot box' very often."

Question:

Content paraphrase:

Feelings paraphrase:

d. **Kaelin:** "I don't know if it's something to do with me or with Mom, but lately we just aren't getting along."

Question:

Content paraphrase:

Feelings paraphrase:

e. **Aileen:** "I've got a report due at work and a paper due in management class. On top of that, it's my sister's birthday, and so far I haven't even had time to get her anything. Today's going to be a disaster."

Question:

Content paraphrase:

Feelings paraphrase:

2. Creating Mnemonics Practice remembering the four personal listening styles and the steps in the active listening process by creating a mnemonic for each. Record your mnemonics. Tomorrow morning while you are dressing see whether you can recall the mnemonics you created. Then see how many of the personal listening styles and active learning steps you can recall using the cues in your mnemonics.

3. Listening to Remember On your MindTap for *Communicate!* practice remembering the four personal listening styles and the steps in the active listening process by creating a mnemonic for each. Record your mnemonics. Tomorrow morning while you are dressing see whether you can recall the mnemonics you created. Then see how many of the personal listening styles and active learning steps you can recall using the cues in your mnemonics. Complete this exercise on MindTap for *Communicate!*

To help you complete this activity, look for the Chapter 6 Skill Building activities on MindTap for Communicate!

MindTap®

UNIT TWO
Interpersonal Communication & Relationships

II

President Franklin Delano Roosevelt once said:

> *If civilization is to survive, we must cultivate the science of human relationships . . .*
> *the ability of all peoples, of all kinds, to live together, in the same world, at peace.*

This unit focuses on that very thing: how to use communication to cultivate positive human relationships. In other words, we discuss the nature of interpersonal relationships, how they are formed and maintained, and what role communication plays in them.

Although communicating to form and maintain personal relationships is as old as humankind itself, the formal study of interpersonal communication did not emerge until the 1960s. One of the most significant scholarly books grounding the formal study of interpersonal communication is *Pragmatics of Human Communication* written by Paul Watzlawick, Janet Beavin Bavelas, and Don D. Jackson and published in 1967. In it, the authors present five principles that continue to influence our understanding of interpersonal communication today.

- We cannot *not* communicate. In other words, everything we say and do, including silence, communicates something to others.

- Every communication interaction has both a content and relational aspect to it. When we communicate, we do more than share information by *what* we say. We also indicate how we feel about the relationship by *how* we say it.

- The nature of a relationship depends on how participants *punctuate* the interactions between them. In other words, each participant believes our communication is a reaction to (or *caused by*) the other's behavior.

- Human communication is both digital (spoken words) and analogic (nonverbal behaviors).

- All communication exchanges are *symmetrical* (based on *equal power* between participants) or *complementary* (based on *power differences*).

These five principles have been reinforced, challenged, and expanded upon by interpersonal scholars since they were first coined over forty years ago.

The next two chapters expand on these themes. Chapter 7 focuses on the different types of interpersonal relationships and how they are formed, maintained, and ended or redefined. Chapter 8 turns specifically to interpersonal communication and how we use messages in our interpersonal encounters.

Interpersonal Relationships

When you've finished this chapter, you'll be able to:

- Employ communication best practices in different types of interpersonal relationships.

- Describe how disclosure functions in interpersonal relationships.

- Explain the stages of interpersonal relationship life cycles.

- Evaluate the role of technology in relationship development, maintenance, and dissolution.

- Manage dialectical tensions effectively in your interpersonal relationships.

MindTap®

Start with a quick warm-up activity.

Whitney was headed to the Student Center to grab a quick lunch before her next class. On the way, she spotted Paige, a classmate in her calculus course.

"Hey, Paige. How are you doing?"

"Ok," Paige replied. "What did you think of that calc test we took yesterday?"

"Argh. Not good. It was so hard! I definitely didn't study right for it," Whitney responded with a nervous laugh.

"I know what you mean," said Paige. "I hope we get them back tomorrow so I can see what it will take to bounce back from that one. Well, I'd better get going or I'll be late to biology. See you tomorrow."

Whitney watched Paige cross the street. She was still thinking about the test, so she was startled when she heard, "Hey, pretty lady!"

"Zach!" Whitney said to her boyfriend with a big smile on her face. "What are you doing on campus? I thought you had to work today."

"Yeah, I was supposed to, but I got a text this morning saying I didn't have to come in," Zach replied. "So, I figured I'd go to the library to work on my philosophy paper where it's quiet, but I need to grab some lunch first. Want to join me?"

"Of course!" Whitney exclaimed. "I'm famished."

7

PeopleImages/Istockphoto.com

MindTap®

interpersonal communication
all those interactions that occur between two people to help start, build, maintain, and sometimes end or redefine the relationship

interpersonal relationship
defined by sets of expectations two people have for each other based on their previous interactions

healthy relationship
ones that are satisfying and beneficial to all those involved

acquaintances
people we know by name, but with whom our interactions are largely impersonal

impersonal communication
interchangeable chitchat involving no or very little self-disclosure

saving face
the process of attempting to maintain a positive self-image in a relational situation

Photo 7.1 Which of your online "friends" would you describe as acquaintances and why?

Interpersonal communication is all those interactions that occur between two people to help start, build, maintain, and sometimes end or redefine our interpersonal relationships. We may communicate interpersonally in face-to-face settings, as well as through social media. **Interpersonal relationships** are defined by the sets of expectations two people have for each other based on their previous interactions (Littlejohn & Foss, 2011). Interpersonal relationships help satisfy our innate human need to feel connected with others and run the gamut from impersonal acquaintances (like Whitney and Paige) to intimate friends (like Zach and Whitney). We want to be involved in **healthy relationships** that are satisfying and beneficial to all those involved. How we communicate is central to achieving that goal.

We begin this chapter by describing three types of interpersonal relationships and offering guidelines for healthy communication in each of them. Next, we explain the role of disclosure in the stages of relationship life cycles. Finally, we propose guidelines for managing the dialectical tensions that exist in any interpersonal relationship.

Types of Relationships

How we communicate varies based on relationship type. Moving on a continuum from impersonal to personal, we can classify our relationships as acquaintances, friends, and intimates.

Acquaintances

Acquaintances are people we know by name, but with whom our interactions are largely impersonal. For example, we may be acquaintances with those living in the same neighborhood, apartment building, or residence hall. We may also be acquaintances with classmates or co-workers. Whitney and Paige, who meet in calculus class for example, may talk with each other about class-related issues but make no effort to share personal information or to see each other outside of class. Most conversations with acquaintances can be defined as **impersonal communication**, which is essentially interchangeable chit-chat (Beebe, Beebe, & Ivy, 2007). In other words, we may talk about the same thing—for instance, the weather—with a grocery clerk, sales associate, bank teller, and restaurant server. If you have an online social networking profile on *Facebook, Twitter*, or *LinkedIn*, many of your online "friends" are probably acquaintances if your conversations with them are primarily surface-level ones.

Our goals when communicating with acquaintances are usually to reduce uncertainty and maintain face. We attempt to reduce uncertainty by seeking information that may reveal similar beliefs, attitudes, and values (Berger, 1987). We may do so in person or online through social media (Gibbs, Ellison, & Lai, 2011). In doing so, however, we may say or do something that offends the other person or is taken the wrong way. So, our second goal is to help one another save face. **Saving face** is the process of attempting to maintain a positive self-image in a relational situation (Ting-Toomey, 2004, 2005).

Acquaintanceship guidelines To meet other people and develop acquaintance relationships, it helps to be good at initiating and facilitating conversations (Photo 7.1).

David J. Green - lifestyle 2/Alamy

The following guidelines can help you develop scripts to become more competent in doing so:

- **Initiate a conversation** by introducing yourself, referring to the physical context, referring to your shared experience or observation, or making a joke. For example:

    WHITNEY: "Do you think it's hot in here, or is it just me? By the way, I'm Whitney."

- **Make your comments relevant** to what has been said before changing subjects:

    PAIGE: "My name's Paige. Yes, I'm burning up. I think the air conditioner is broken. Hey, do you know if this class meets for 75 or 90 minutes today?"

- **Develop an other-centered focus** by asking questions, listening carefully, and following up on what has been said. For example:

    WHITNEY: "I'm pretty sure it's only a 75-minute session. Have you ever taken a class from this professor?"

    PAIGE: "Yeah, I took algebra from her."

    WHITNEY: "What is she like?"

    PAIGE: "She's pretty good. Her tests are hard, but fair. I learned a lot."

    WHITNEY: "Did she offer study guides?"

    PAIGE: "Yes, and we had what she called 'algebra *Jeopardy*' review sessions. That worked well for me."

    WHITNEY: "Sounds like I'm going to like this class and this instructor!"

- **Engage in appropriate turn-taking** by balancing talking with listening and not interrupting. In his best-selling book, *How to Win Friends and Influence People,* Dale Carnegie (1936) put it this way: "Listen first and let them finish. Do not resist, defend or debate. This only raises barriers. . . . Remember that the people you are talking to are a hundred times more interested in themselves and their wants and problems than they are in you and your problems" (pp. 98, 127).

- **Be polite.** Consider how your conversational partner will feel about what you say and work to phrase your comments in a way that allows your partner to save face. For example:

    WHITNEY: "I wish I wouldn't have signed up for this section that meets right at noon. I'm famished. Here, do you want some M&Ms?"

    PAIGE: "No thanks."

    WHITNEY: "Are you sure? I don't mind sharing. A little sugar never hurt anyone."

    PAIGE: "I'm diabetic."

    WHITNEY: "Oh, I'm so sorry. I'll save these for later."

APPLY IT

Have you ever been in a conversation with someone who made it difficult for you to get a word in? How did that make you feel about that person and your relationship with them? Why?

APPLY IT

Identify four or five of your "high school friends." How many of them do you still interact with regularly either face-to-face or online? How have the topics you discuss with them changed and why?

MindTap®

friends
people with whom we have voluntarily negotiated more personal relationships

Friends

Friends are people with whom we have voluntarily negotiated more personal relationships (Canary, Cody, & Manusov, 2008). For example, Whitney and Paige may decide to get together after class to work out at the gym. If they find that they enjoy each other's company, they may continue to meet outside of class and eventually become friends.

We often refer to friends according to the context in which we interact with them. For example, we may have tennis friends, work friends, or neighborhood friends. These context friendships may fade if the context changes. For instance, our friendship with a co-worker may fade if one of us takes a job with a different company.

Friendship guidelines Several guidelines may help you maintain friendships whether you live close to one another or are separated by a distance and can only communicate via social media (Walther, 2011).

- **Initiation.** Be proactive about setting up times to spend together. A friendship is not likely to form or endure when people rarely interact. For example, because Charles values his relationship with his brother, who is serving in the Peace Corps and stationed in Mumbai, India, he initiated a regularly weekly Skype session on Friday afternoons.

- **Responsiveness.** Ask questions and then focus on listening and responding to what they say.

- **Self-disclosure.** Although acquaintances can be maintained by conversations that discuss surface issues, friendships are based on the exchange of more personal information, opinions, and feelings. For example, after Paige and Whitney start to spend more time together, they might have this conversation:

PAIGE:	"Can I tell you something and trust you to keep it between us?"
WHITNEY:	"Of course."
PAIGE:	"Well, you know I've been seeing David for a while now."
WHITNEY:	"Yeah, he seems like a nice guy."
PAIGE:	"Well, the other night we got into a little fight and he pushed me onto the couch. I actually have a bruise here on my arm from it."

- **Emotional support.** Provide comfort and support when needed. When our friends are hurting, they need us to support them by clarifying our supportive intentions, confirming their feelings, helping them make sense of what has happened, and giving advice (Burleson, 2009).

WHITNEY:	"Oh, no. I'm here to help in any way I can."
PAIGE:	"He said he was sorry and I believe him, but I just don't feel comfortable around him now."
WHITNEY:	"I understand. I'm not sure I would feel comfortable either. Is there anything I can do?"
PAIGE:	"No, not really. I guess I just wanted someone to confirm that I'm not overreacting."

WHITNEY: "Well, I don't think you're overreacting at all. Please let me know what I can do to help, OK?"

PAIGE: "OK. I'm so lucky to have you for a friend."

- **Conflict management.** Friends will sometimes disagree about ideas or behaviors. Healthy friendships handle these disagreements effectively through conversation.

WHITNEY: "Maybe you should talk to a campus counselor about this."

PAIGE: "No, I don't want to make a big deal out of it."

WHITNEY: "Paige, you got a bruise. That seems like a big deal to me."

PAIGE: "Actually, I bruise really easily. I don't want to see a counselor. Maybe I shouldn't have even told you about it."

WHITNEY: "Oh, Paige. I'm so glad you did and I totally respect your decision. If anything like this happens again, though, will you please talk to someone?"

PAIGE: "OK, if something happens again, I promise I will."

"Jerkins and I worked it out. He can have the office with the window."

Intimates

Intimates are people with whom we share a high degree of interdependence, commitment, disclosure, understanding, affection, and trust. We may have countless acquaintances and many friends, but we are likely to have only a few truly intimate relationships (Photo 7.2). Unfortunately, the percentage of Americans who identify having even just one intimate relationship beyond family members declined from 80 percent in 1985 to 57 percent in 2006 (McPherson, Smith-Lovin, & Beshears, 2006). Today, most Americans report having no more than two intimate friends, including family members (Bryner, 2011). In fact, according to a recent University of Oxford study, even though we may have hundreds of "Facebook friends," the number of truly close friends is still very small (Saramaki, et al., 2014). This dramatic decline is particularly troubling given that intimate relationships are the most important predictor of life satisfaction and emotional well-being (Gilbert & Lindzey, 2010; Moore, 2003; Peterson, 2006).

Intimate relationships can be platonic or romantic (Photo 7.2). A **platonic relationship** is one in which the partners are not sexually attracted to each other or do not act on an attraction they feel. If you're familiar with the television series *Parks and Recreation*, the relationship between Leslie and Ron is platonic, but they are also intimate friends. Conversely, a **romantic relationship** is one in which the partners acknowledge their sexual attraction toward one another. Today, many people use matchmaking sites to find romantic relationship partners. In fact,

intimates
people with whom we share a high degree of interdependence, commitment, disclosure, understanding, affection, and trust

platonic relationship
an intimate relationship where partners are not sexually attracted to each other or do not act on an attraction they feel

romantic relationship
an intimate relationship where the partners openly acknowledge and possibly act on their sexual attraction

Photo 7.2 We have intimate relationships with romantic partners and platonic friends. Who would you identify as your close intimate friends and why?

trust
*placing confidence in another
in a way that almost always
involves some risk*

some research suggests that as many as 1 in 5 romantic relationships today begin online. Sometimes people also use ghostwriters to help create their matchmaking profile. The *Communicating in the World* feature in this chapter raises some ethical decisions to consider when doing so.

In both platonic and romantic intimate relationships, partners must trust each other. **Trust** is placing confidence in another in a way that almost always involves some risk. As we share private information and feelings, we monitor how well our partner keeps our confidence. If our partner keeps our confidence, we share more and the relationship becomes more intimate. If our partner proves untrustworthy, we share less and intimacy decreases. When there is a severe breach of trust, we may even abruptly end the relationship altogether.

Cultural and Co-cultural Influences on Intimacy Research suggests that intimate relationships are based on four types of interactions. The first comes from physical touch (e.g., holding hands, hugging, kissing, engaging in sexual relations). The second comes from sharing thoughts and opinions and the third from sharing feelings. The final type comes from participating in shared activities.

Our cultural identity may influence which type of interactions we are most likely to engage in. For example, women who identify with the feminine co-culture may be comfortable sharing their thoughts and feelings (Dindia, 2009). Men who identify with the masculine co-culture may prefer participating in shared activities (Dindia & Canary, 2006). Of course, since masculine and feminine co-cultural norms are socialized, these generalizations are not true for all men or for all women. Frankly, recent research suggests that such differences are increasingly becoming less prominent in the United States.

Intimacy development norms also vary across cultures (Lustig & Koester, 2013). In collectivist cultures such as China, Taiwan, and Japan, for example, people may not typically reach out to acquaintances until properly introduced and then take care to keep private information about close friends and family to themselves. In individualistic cultures such as the United States, people may be more likely to share private information and personal feelings with acquaintances. As with gender, however, such differences are becoming increasingly less pronounced as the world becomes more connected through travel, media, and technology (Hatfield & Rapson, 2006).

Intimacy guidelines The following guidelines can help you establish and maintain affection, understanding, trust, and commitment in your intimate relationships:

- **Be dependable** so your partner learns that he or she can rely on you. Of course, nobody is perfect. But striving to be dependable will provide a foundation for understanding when something does come up.

- **Be responsive** in meeting your partner's needs. At times, this will require you to put their needs before your own.

- **Be collaborative** in managing conflict. Doing so includes saying you're sorry for something you've done or said, agreeing to disagree, and letting go of the need to be "right."

- **Be faithful** by maintaining your partner's confidential information and by abiding by sexual or other exclusivity agreements between you and your partner.

- **Be transparent** by honestly sharing your ideas and feelings with your partner.

- **Be willing** to put your relationship first. This is not to say you should give up all other activities and relationships. However, you should strive for a balance between doing things together and doing things apart (Baxter & Montgomery, 1996).

COMMUNICATING IN THE WORLD

David J. Green/lifestyle themes/Alamy

Throughout history—in life, literature, and the media—people hoping to find love have solicited help from others. In Henry Wadsworth Longfellow's poem "The Courtship of Miles Standish," the shy Miles asks his friend John Alden to plead his case with the beautiful Priscilla Mullins. John complies, but in a classic love triangle scenario, Priscilla asks John, "Why don't you speak for yourself, John?" And most of us remember at least one occasion in junior high when we asked a friend to find out if a cute classmate was interested in us.

Today we've expanded our search for love to online dating services, but advanced technologies don't eliminate the need some of us have to seek outside help in expressing ourselves. There are multiple books on the topic, such as *Data: A Love Story. How I Cracked the Online Dating Code to Meet My Match* by Amy Webb or *Online Dating: Effective Strategies from Profiles to Lifelong Relationships* by Abby Olivia Collins.

Personal coaching for online dating is also on the rise. Online services such as Dating-Profile.com, ProfileHelper.com, and E-Cyrano.com help singles write their profiles for a fee.

Laurie Davis, founder and CEO of eFlirt Expert, suggests online dating should be approached as "the same thing as a personal branding campaign" and encourages clients to use her site to help make "the ultimate virtual first impression and transition their digital selves into meaningful, in-person dating experiences" (Wang, 2011; eFlirt homepage). Her site helps clients create and manage profiles for online dating sites as well as for other social networking platforms, like Facebook and Twitter.

Opinions vary on the ethics of using such ghostwriting services on dating profile sites. Jenny Cargile, a Match.com user, says hiring someone to help write her profile would obscure who she truly is. "I'm not a person who is put together or always knows the right thing to say," she says. "I would feel like if I went out on a date with someone, I would have to be what they read instead of myself" (Alsever, 2007).

However, online dater Jim West sings the praises of ProfileHelper.com, where he learned to be more specific and inquisitive when communicating on online dating sites (Alsever, 2007). In his case, a profile-writing coach stressed basic communication principles that helped West more accurately convey the kind of person he was, pinpointed the types of things he enjoyed, and what he was looking for in a potential partner. Likewise, eFlirt client Monica Astley says, "I only use [the ghostwriter's] stuff for the initial contact. After that, it's all me. . . . [S]omeone else just writes it up for you, and you approve it" (Ianotti, 2010).

Whether you are in favor of or opposed to profile-writing coaches, most would agree that communication on online dating sites is tricky. An article in *Skeptic* explores the pros and cons of self-disclosing when dating online (King, Austin-Oden, & Lohr, 2009): On one hand, information presented online is easy to manipulate and control, so people can present themselves in any way they like—even if what they present isn't 100 percent accurate. On the other hand, the relative anonymity of online communication "accelerates intimacy through increased openness about aspects of the self." When what we disclose about ourselves is true, self-disclosure is an important step in making a successful relationship.

What do you think—is true self-disclosure encouraged or obscured by online dating?

COMMUNICATE ON YOUR FEET

Speech Assignment

Relationships Speech

The Assignment

Prepare a 3- to 5-minute speech about your friends. Identify one person you have known for some time that you would consider an acquaintance, one that you would consider a friend, and one that you would consider an intimate or best friend. Describe each person and your relationship, as well as why you placed them in the category you did. Identify the kinds of topics you typically discuss with them and the kinds you would not be likely to talk about with them. Be sure to follow the Speech Organization Guidelines as you prepare. At your instructor's request, deliver your speech for your classmates.

Speech Organization Guidelines

Introduction

1. Catch attention
2. Provide listener relevance and speaker credibility
3. State thesis with preview of main points

Body

1. Acquaintance

Transition

2. Friend

Transition

3. Best friend

Conclusion

1. Restate thesis with summary of main points
2. Clincher

---

relationship life cycle
moving back and forth among the relationship phases

disclosure
the process of revealing confidential information

feedback
the verbal and nonverbal responses we make to messages we receive

self-disclosure
sharing thoughts and feelings that are unknown to the other person

other-disclosure
confidential information shared about someone by a third party

social penetration theory
describes the different kinds of self-disclosure used in relationships

Johari window
a tool for examining the relationship between disclosure and feedback in relationships

Disclosure in Relationship Life Cycles

Relationships are not something we *have,* but rather are something we *make* as we communicate with others (Parks, 2006). Even though no two relationships develop in exactly the same way, all relationships tend to move through identifiable and overlapping phases of coming together and coming apart (Knapp & Vangelisti, 2005). This moving back and forth among the phases is known as the **relationship life cycle**.

How we move among the phases depends on how we communicate with one another (Duck, 2007). We do so through **disclosure**, which is the process of revealing confidential information, and **feedback**, which includes the verbal and nonverbal responses to such information. Disclosure can come in the form of **self-disclosure**, which is the confidential information we deliberately choose to share about ourselves, and **other-disclosure**, which is confidential information shared about someone by a third party (Petronio, 2002). **Social penetration theory** describes the different kinds of self-disclosure we use in our relationships and the **Johari window** explains how these various forms of disclosure and feedback operate in them. Knowing these processes can help us make wise disclosure decisions depending on relationship type and life cycle stage.

Social Penetration

Not all self-disclosure is equally revealing. Some messages reveal more about our thoughts and feelings than others. Irwin Altman and Dalmas Taylor (1973; 1987) conceptualized a model of self-disclosure based on breadth and depth of information shared. *Breadth* has to do with the range of different subjects you discuss with your partner. *Depth* has to do with the quality of information shared, which can range from relatively impersonal and "safe" to very confidential and "risky." For example, when Whitney and Paige first met, the breadth of subjects they discussed focused on their families, hometowns, and things they were learning in class. As their relationship became more intimate they added subjects about career ambitions, feelings about people they were dating, and feelings about their own relationship. The depth of disclosure also deepened. For example, in addition to sharing impersonal information, such as how many siblings they each have, they also disclosed characteristics they liked and did not like about their brothers and sisters. Discussions about their hometowns became deeper as they shared personal stories about positive and negative experiences they had growing up. And discussions about class grew to include opinions each had about whether what they were learning would help them achieve their career goals. Paige and Whitney's social penetration model is illustrated in Figure 7.1.

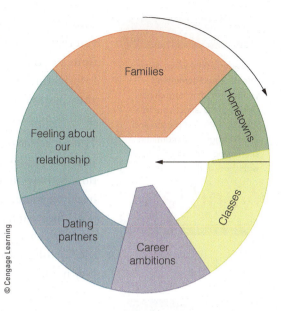

Figure 7.1

Social penetration model

The Johari Window

Relational closeness depends on appropriate self-disclosure along with appropriate feedback and other-disclosure. One way to understand the nature of disclosure and feedback in interpersonal relationships is through the Johari window. The Johari window, named after its two originators, Joe Luft and Harry Ingham (1970), consists of four panes that comprise all information about you. You and your partner each know some (but not all) of this information (see Figure 7.2).

The Open Pane The "open" pane represents the information about you that both you and your partner know. It might include mundane information that you share with most people, such as your college major, but may also include information that you disclose to relatively few people. It may also include benign observations your partner has made, such as how you doodle when you're bored, or more serious ones such as how you behave when you're angry.

Figure 7.2

The Johari window

The Secret Pane The "secret" pane contains everything you know about yourself, but your partner does not yet know. As you share secret information through self-disclosure, it moves into the open pane. For example, suppose you were once engaged to be married, but backed out just weeks before the wedding day. You may not want to share this with casual acquaintances or friends, so it will be in the secret pane in those relationships. But when you disclose this fact to an intimate friend, it moves into the open pane with this person. As you disclose more information, the secret pane becomes smaller and the open pane larger.

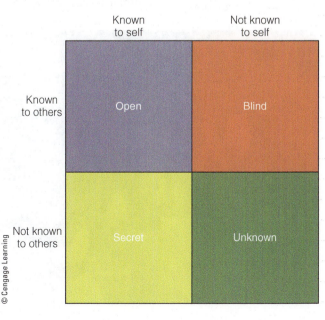

The Blind Pane The "blind" pane contains information your partner knows about you that you don't realize about yourself. They may have discovered it from observations of you or from other-disclosure shared by a mutual friend or acquaintance. Information moves from the blind pane to the open pane through feedback. When your partner shares this information with you, it moves from the blind pane into open pane.

The Unknown Pane The "unknown" pane contains information that neither you nor your partner knows about you. Obviously, you cannot develop a list of this information. So how do we know that it exists? Well, because periodically we discover it. If, for instance, you have never tried zip lining, then nobody knows whether you will like it or not. Once you try it, you gain information about yourself that becomes part of the secret pane, which you can move to the open pane through disclosure. Also, once you have tried it, others who observe you will have information about your performance that you may not know unless they give you feedback.

Stages of Relationships

Every relationship develops and changes with time. We can describe these changes as coming together, staying together, and coming apart (Dindia, 2003; Knapp & Vangelisti, 2005). Our relationships move among these stages based on the *information* we share and our *interpretation* of it (Duck, 2007).

Coming Together: Beginning and Developing Relationships

The stages of coming together focus on beginning and developing relationships. Communication concentrates on reducing uncertainty as we try to understand how our partner sees the world. Noted interpersonal communication scholar Steve Duck (1999) conceived the *Relationship Filtering Model* to explain the process relationships go through in the beginning stages. When we first meet someone, we assume they are similar to us until what they say or do tells us otherwise. We begin by communicating very generally about noncontroversial topics and asking questions about surface information such as where they grew up and if they have any hobbies (Photo 7.3). Then we make inferences about their general attitudes, values, and ways of thinking. If we decide we have enough in common, we will choose to develop the relationship by disclosing more.

Let's look again at Whitney and Paige. They decided to become college roommates and are a bit nervous about it. To reduce uncertainty, they get to know each other better through disclosure and feedback. They talk about favorite hobbies, foods, movies, and music. They discover

Photo 7.3 One exciting thing about the college experience is the opportunity to meet new people and form new friendships. What new relationships have you begun since you arrived on campus?

© Tyler Olson/Shutterstock.com

that although Whitney is majoring in fine arts and Paige is pre-med, both are passionate environmentalists and vegetarians. As they learn more, they begin to relax and find that although they have many differences, they like and respect each other. Over the semester, life in the room they share begins to take on a predictable pattern. When one of them is stressing over a class project, the other often goes to the library or to the lounge to give her space.

Relationships can begin in face-to-face or online environments. Online communication may present a potentially less difficult way to meet others than traditional face-to-face interactions (Photo 7.4). The initial interaction can occur in the comfort of your own home and at your own pace. You need not be concerned about physical aspects of the self or the other, and you can more precisely select what you are going to say (Ward & Tracy, 2004).

Michael Kemp/Alamy

Photo 7.4 If you have ever initiated a relationship with someone online, what did you say and do to reduce uncertainty and what were the results?

As a relationship develops, we continue coming together by disclosing more and engaging in more physical contact (Duck & McMahan, 2012). Through disclosure and feedback, we identify and capitalize on our similarities and tolerate or negotiate our differences. Physical contact may involve sitting closer together, leaning toward each other, and engaging in more eye contact and touch. Physical contact may or may not involve romantic feelings. Even platonic friends increase physical contact with each other as the relationship develops, for example, through hugs, high-fives, and fist bumps. Let's say the relationship between Whitney and Paige is working out well. They spend time together, get to know each other well, and consider themselves to be intimate friends. By second semester, they hug each other when they return from spring break, share clothes, and help fix each other's hair.

Of course, cultural norms also affect how people engage in physical contact in relationships (Photo 7.5). Take a moment to read the *Diverse Voices* article by Saba Ali on page 132–133 to learn how holding hands with a man she considered marrying influenced her decision.

As a relationship develops, partners will feel psychologically closer as well (Duck, 1999). If we share no common interests, attitudes, or ways of interpreting the world, we are not likely to develop a deeper relationship. Think about the people you met during your first weeks on campus. Which ones did not become your friends and why? Most likely, you gathered information during your initial encounters that reduced uncertainty about them, but what you learned was that they did not share enough common interests or attitudes to warrant developing a relationship. Finally, many people engage in coming together via social media and some report achieving more closeness in their online relationships than in equivalent face-to-face ones (Brooks, 2011).

Photo 7.5 What forms of physical contact do you engage in with acquaintances, friends, and intimates?

Jupiterimages/Getty Images

Staying Together: Maintaining Relationships

relationship maintenance
communication strategies used to keep a relationship operating smoothly and satisfactorily

Once a relationship has developed, we employ communication strategies to maintain it. **Relational maintenance** consists of those communication strategies used to keep a relationship operating smoothly and satisfactorily (Dindia, 2009). Researchers have catalogued many relational maintenance strategies. Some of them include prosocial behaviors like being friendly and polite, observing ceremonial occasions (e.g., birthdays, anniversaries, regular "date nights"), thanking, praising, and expressing appreciation. For example, Paige and Whitney celebrate one another's birthdays by going out to a movie and dinner. Paige also tries not to be overtly critical when Whitney strews papers around while working on a big project, knowing that Whitney will tidy things up when she is finished. Instead, Paige admires Whitney for having such a serious work ethic.

Other strategies include spending time together (both with one another and with mutual friends), communicating honestly and frequently about both deep and everyday topics, and offering words and actions that demonstrate affection and respect for one another. Whitney and Paige, for example, gave each other "best friend" status on their *Facebook* pages, decided to join some of the same clubs and, even visited each other's hometowns to meet each other's families and high school friends.

sacrifice
putting one's needs or desires on hold to attend to the needs of one's partner or the relationship

Partners also **sacrifice** by putting their needs or desires on hold to attend to the needs of their partner or the relationship. For example, when Whitney was ill, Paige sacrificed a date in order to stay home and take care of her sick roommate. Because all relationships involve give and take, being willing to do what is best for the other person or for the relationship itself can help maintain it.

Finally, because conflict is inevitable in developed relationships, we may do or say things that hurt our partner. If not handled properly, such transgressions can harm the relationship and move it to a less intimate level. By forgiving minor transgressions, we can keep a relationship at the desired level of closeness. For example, Whitney and Paige each have little habits that annoy the other, but they choose not to let these annoyances get in the way of a good friendship.

DIVERSE VOICES

Close Enough to Touch Was Too Far Apart

by Saba Ali

Saba Ali lives in upstate New York.

Who knew that holding hands, the very act that signals the start of so many relationships, would be the end of mine? For scarf-wearing Muslims like me, premarital interaction between the sexes (touching, talking, even looking) is strictly controlled. Men and women pray, eat, and congregate separately.

Boys sit on one side of the hall, girls on the other, and married couples in the middle.

My friends and I had high expectations for marriage, which was supposed to quickly follow graduation from college.

There were no tips from our mothers or anyone else on how to meet the right man or to talk to him. It's simply expected that our lives will consist of two phases: unmarried and in the

continued

company of women, and then married and in the company of a man.

It's all supposed to start with a conversation, but not a private one. My friends and I call them "meetings." The woman comes with her chaperone, a family member, and the man comes with his. Talking points include such questions as "What do you expect from your husband?" and "Would you mind if my parents were to move in with us after the reception?"

Yet now, at 29, despite all of my "meetings," I remain unmarried.

My interest was piqued last year when a friend from college told me about a radiologist in his early 30s who was also Muslim and unmarried. Our first get-together was for brunch at a little French café near Central Park. I listened as he talked about his past relationships. Not the most appropriate topic for a first date, perhaps, but more comfortable for me than the typical pressurized questions: "Do you cook?" and "How many children do you want?" As he talked about the girls who either broke his heart, or whose hearts he had broken, I watched his hands, wondering what they would feel like to touch.

We kept getting to know each other by phone, often talking for hours at a time. Our lingering problem, however, was the difference in how religious we each were; he hadn't planned on marrying someone who wore the traditional head scarf. But I reveled in the recognition. Covering was a choice I had made in high school. To me, the scarf is more than a piece of fabric—it's a way of life. On my wedding night, going topless would mean unpinning my scarf and letting it fall down.

In order to get him over his hesitation, I planned our dates to take place in very public places. We played miniature golf, ate out at restaurants, and went blueberry picking. I looked at his objection as a challenge, a project. I wanted to convince him that even though I did stand out with my hijab, it didn't matter because no one really took notice of the scarf after the first glance.

One evening he called to tell me he had gone to a lounge with a few of his buddies. "I visualized what it would feel like to have you sitting next to me," he told me.

"And how did it feel?" I asked.

"Pretty good," he said. "Manageable."

And then came the night of the movie, his idea. I'm a movie fanatic and remember the details of almost every movie I've ever seen. I can't remember the title of the one we saw that night. I looked over at him and smiled, convincing myself that the weightiness I felt was because I was in uncharted territory. We were moving forward, talking about meeting each other's families. So when he leaned over and asked, "Can I hold your hand?" I didn't feel I could say no. I liked him for taking the risk.

Nearly 30 years old, I had thought about holding hands with a boy since I was a teenager. But it was always in the context of my wedding day. Walking into our reception as husband and wife, holding hands, basking in that moment of knowing this was forever.

A lifetime's worth of expectations culminated in this single gesture in a dark theater over a sticky armrest. I'm not sure it's possible to hold hands wrong, but we were not doing it right. It felt awkward with my hand under his, so we changed positions: my arm on top, his hand cradling mine. It was still uncomfortable, and soon my hand fell asleep, which was not the tingling sensation I was hoping for. Finally, I took it away.

But the damage had been done. We had broken the no-contact rule, and in doing so, I realized I wasn't willing to be the kind of girl he wanted. I believe in my religion, the rules, the reasons, and even the restrictions. At the same time, I've always wanted to be married, and the thought of never knowing that side of myself, as a wife and a mother, scares me. Being with him made me compromise my faith, and my fear of being alone pushed me to ignore my doubts about the relationship.

When we took it too far, I shut down. It wasn't supposed to happen that way. So after the date, I split us up. And I never saw him again.

Coming Apart: Declining and Dissolving Relationships

When one or both partners fail to engage actively in relational maintenance strategies, the relationship may begin to come apart and could eventually even end altogether. Relationships between acquaintances, casual friends, coworkers, and neighbors are more likely to end than highly developed ones (Parks, 2007). The communication in declining relationships is marked by four stages: circumscribing, stagnating, avoiding, and terminating.

circumscribing
communication decreases in both quantity and quality

Circumscribing This is the first sign that a relationship is coming apart. During this stage, communication decreases in both quantity and quality. Rather than discuss a disagreement, for example, both parties ignore it outwardly even when it troubles them inside. Although Whitney and Paige were close during their first two years of college, they drifted apart as they each met people with more aligned personal and professional interests. They found they had less and less to talk about when they were together, so they started spending less time with each other.

stagnating
partners just go through the motions of interacting without enthusiasm or emotion

Stagnating If circumscribing continues, it may eventually lead to **stagnating**, which is when partners just go through the motions of interacting without enthusiasm or emotion. When employees reach this stage, we say they have "job burnout." Because Whitney and Paige share a dorm room, they continue to engage in the routines they had developed for eating, cleaning, and studying. But they now do so in silence, neither of them wanting to make the effort to initiate a conversation about meaningless topics.

avoiding
creating physical distance and making excuses not to do things together

Avoiding When a relationship that has stagnated becomes too painful, partners begin **avoiding** one another by creating physical distance between them and by making excuses not to do things together. The overriding tone is usually not marked by hostility but by indifference. When Whitney tells Paige she is moving into an apartment with other friends, Paige responds with "Whatever."

grave-dressing
explanations about why the relationship failed

Terminating Of course, not all relationships end. However, when partners decide the relationship is no longer worth trying to maintain, it will end. People give many reasons for terminating relationships, including poor communication, lack of fulfillment, differing lifestyles and interests, rejection, outside interference, absence of rewards, and boredom. Research calls these attempts to explain why the relationship failed **grave-dressing** (Duck & McMahan, 2012).

Unfortunately, partners sometimes look for reasons to blame each other rather than trying to find equitable ways of bringing the relationship to an acceptable conclusion. They do so by using strategies of manipulation, withdrawal, and avoidance. Manipulation involves being indirect and failing to take any responsibility for ending the relationship. Manipulators may purposely sabotage the relationship hoping that the other person will break it off. Withdrawal and avoidance, also less than competent ways to terminate a relationship typically lead to a slow and often painful death of the relationship.

The most competent way to end a relationship is to be direct, open, and honest. If two people have had a satisfying and close relationship, they owe it to themselves and to each other to be forthright and fair about terminating it. Although some people terminate their romantic relationships via text message, it is more respectful to do so in person. For example, when DeMarcus decided to break up with his girlfriend, Larissa, he thought about just ignoring her e-mails and texts hoping she would "get the hint." Instead he invited her to coffee and explained his feelings honestly and respectfully. To his surprise, she thanked him for telling her in person rather than via text like her last boyfriend.

Even when partners agree that their relationship in its current form is over, they may continue to interact through a different type of relationship. This is called **relationship transformation**. Romantic relationships may transform into friendships, best friends may become casual friends, and even marriages may continue on friendly terms or as a type of business relationship where child-rearing practices and expenses are coordinated (Photo 7.6) (Parks, 2006). After Whitney and Paige graduate, for example, their friendship may be transformed into one of acquaintances that enjoy seeing each other at reunions.

Klaus Vedfelt/Iconica/Getty Images

Photo 7.6 How relationships end depends on the interpersonal competence of both people. Do you know people who are amicably divorced? How do they differ from people with hostile divorces?

relationship transformation
the process of changing a relationship from one type to another

The Role of Technology in Interpersonal Relationship Formation, Development, and Dissolution

The use of Internet technology is changing how we build and maintain relationships today. For example, people can begin friendships and even meet romantic partners online. We also strategically manage what others know about us. Joe Walther (1996), a noted communication scholar who studies computer mediated communication coined the term **hyperpersonal communication** to describe this phenomenon of "putting our best foot forward" and assuming our online conversational partner is similar to us as in the beginning stages of relationship formation.

hyperpersonal communication
interacting online based on the assumption that our online partner is similar to us

Not only do we use technology to form relationships, but social media also makes it easy to stay connected and maintain existing relationships that were once bound by time and space. When my daughter was living in Panama, for instance, I often Skyped with her and when my son was living in Japan, I sent him e-mail messages in my early afternoon, which he would read when he woke up in the morning. Our use of many different mediums to maintain our relationships is known as **media multiplexity** and some research suggests that we use more media channels to communicate with close friends than casual ones (e.g., Gilbert, et al., 2008; Haythornthwaite, 2005).

media multiplexity
the use of many different mediums to maintain relationships

Finally, we also often use technology to disengage from relationships. Just as we distance ourselves physically in face-to-face relationships, we also disengage by exchanging fewer texts, e-mails, and phone calls. We may stop following people on Twitter or even block friends on Facebook as a signal of coming apart. For example, Brian began letting phone calls from Ruth go to voice mail rather than picking up. He also stopped responding to her e-mails and texts. Ruth, who was not ready to let go of the relationship, began checking Brian's Facebook page more frequently to figure out why he wasn't responding. This scenario is not uncommon. In fact, research suggests that young adults today choose to "break up" using technology rather than by having a face-to-face conversation even though they believe it is an inappropriate way to end a relationship (Gershon, 2010).

Internet technology and social media are certainly providing new channels for communicating and continue to become increasingly popular among people of all ages. We are only just beginning to learn how using them influences interpersonal communication and relationships.

Dialectics in Interpersonal Relationships

Have you ever felt ambivalent about a relationship? On the one hand, you really wanted to be close but at the same time you wanted your "space." Or have you met someone who seemed a bit too nosy even though you did want to get to know them? Have you ever enjoyed the stability of a long-term relationship, but at the same time longed for the same excitement as when you first met? If so, you were experiencing what scholars call a relational dialectic. A **dialectic** is a tension between conflicting forces. **Relational dialectics** are the competing psychological tensions that exist in relationships. Let's take a look at some specific relational dialectics and how to manage these inevitable tensions effectively.

Relational Dialectics

Three dialectics common to most relationships are the tugs between autonomy and connection, openness and closedness, and novelty and predictability (Baxter & Montgomery, 1996; Baxter 7 Braithwaite, 2009; Baxter, 2011). How these tensions are dealt with can alter the stage and life cycle of a relationship.

Autonomy/Connection **Autonomy** is the desire to do things independent of your partner. **Connection** is the desire to link your actions and decisions with your partner. Joel and Shelly have been dating for about a year. At this point in their relationship, Shelly wants to spend most of her free time with Joel and enjoys making decisions together, but Joel has begun to feel stifled. For example, he wants to go out with the guys without having to clear it first with Shelly. Still, he doesn't want to hurt Shelly's feelings or ruin their relationship. Shelly is happy and doesn't even realize there is any tension. If Joel begins to act autonomously, he may relieve his own tension but at the same time create new tension in the relationship.

Openness/Closedness **Openness** is the desire to share intimate ideas and feelings whereas **closedness** is the desire to keep them to yourself. Suppose Joel believes it is important to disclose his intimate feelings to Shelly, and he expects her to do the same. Shelly is a more private person and does disclose to Joel, but not as much as he would like. These differences in preferred levels of self-disclosure are a dialectical tension in their relationship.

Novelty/Predictability **Novelty** is the desire for originality, freshness, and uniqueness in your behavior, your partner's behavior, or the relationship. **Predictability** is

dialectic
a tension between conflicting forces

relational dialectics
the competing psychological tensions in a relationship

autonomy
the desire to make decisions and do things independent of one's partner

connection
the desire to make decisions and do things with one's partner

openness
the desire to share intimate ideas and feelings with one's partner

closedness
the desire to keep intimate ideas and feelings to oneself

novelty
originality, freshness, and uniqueness in one's behaviors or in the relationship

predictability
consistency, reliability, and dependability in a relationship

the desire for consistency, reliability, and dependability. Because Shelly and Joel have been dating for over a year, much of the uncertainty is gone from their relationship. But they do not want to eliminate uncertainty altogether. With no uncertainty at all, a relationship becomes so predictable and so routine that it is boring. Although Shelly and Joel know each other well, can predict much about each other, and have quite a few routines in their relationship, they also want to be surprised and have new experiences together. Shelly may shock Joel by spontaneously breaking into their favorite song in the middle of the mall. Joel might surprise Shelly by taking her on a "mystery date."

Although this example of Shelly and Joel is an intimate relationship, dialectical tensions exist in all relationships—and they are always in flux. Sometimes these dialectical tensions are active and in the foreground and other times they are in the background. Nevertheless, when we experience them, they influence the nature of our relationship.

Managing Dialectical Tensions

How do people satisfy opposing needs at the same time? Four strategies for doing so include temporal selection, topical segmentation, neutralization, and reframing.

Temporal selection is the strategy of choosing one desire while ignoring the other for the time being. Perhaps you and a friend realize that you have spent too much time apart lately (autonomy), so you make a conscious decision to pursue connection. You plan several activities together for a few weeks and then begin to feel that you are spending too much time together. As a result, you start cancelling dates. Seesawing back and forth like this is one way to temporarily manage a relational dialectic.

temporal selection
choosing one dialectical tension and ignoring its opposite for a while

Topical segmentation is the strategy of choosing certain topics to satisfy one desire and other topics to satisfy the opposing desire. You and your mom may practice openness by sharing your opinions and feelings about certain topics such as school, work, and politics, but maintain your privacy concerning your sex lives. This segmentation satisfies your relationship needs for balance in the openness/closedness dialectic.

topical segmentation
choosing certain topics to satisfy one dialectical tension and other topics to satisfy its opposite

Neutralization is the strategy of compromising between the desires of one person and the desires of the other. Neutralization partially meets the needs of both people but does not fully meet the needs of either. A couple might pursue a moderate level of novelty and spontaneity in their lives, which satisfies both of them. The amount of novelty in the relationship may be less than what one person would ideally want and more than what the other would normally desire, but they have reached a middle point comfortable to both.

neutralization
compromising between the desires of the two partners

Reframing is the strategy of changing your perception about the opposing desires so they no longer seem quite so contradictory. Maybe you are tense because you perceive that you are more open and your partner is more closed. You might decide to discuss this issue and in doing so begin to realize the times you have also held back (closedness) and you partner was open. After the conversation, you see yourselves as more similar than different on this dialectic. You have reframed your perception of the tension.

reframing
changing one's perspective about the level of tension

WHAT WOULD YOU DO?

A Question of Ethics

Jeff and Magda, seniors at a small rural college, had been dating each other since they were freshmen. Jeff loved Magda, and he planned to propose to her after they graduated in the spring. At the same time, though, he reluctantly recognized that their relationship had fallen into a bit of a rut over the previous six months, and he missed the excitement and romance of their first year together. Although he was troubled by these conflicting feelings, Jeff was unsure what to do about them.

One day Jeff decided, on a whim, to create a fake Facebook profile for the person he wanted to be in his fantasies. He spent quite a bit of time researching and designing the profile of his imaginary persona, a rap singer/flamenco guitarist/snowboarder/kung fu expert who went by the user name "MoonDog13." Jeff inserted photos of an obscure young Romanian actor he found online into MoonDog13's user profile. He posted lyrics to rap songs he wrote on MoonDog13's page and joined online user groups for those interested in flamenco guitar, snowboarding, and kung fu. In very little time, MoonDog13 had made a number of online friends, many of whom were admiring young women. MoonDog13 loved to flirt with them.

Jeff told Magda nothing about MoonDog13, even when the time he spent online began to interfere with their relationship. He justified this decision with the belief that MoonDog13 was an imaginary figure who existed only in cyberspace. As long as fantasy didn't cross into reality, there was no reason Jeff had to feel guilty about anything MoonDog13 said online.

How is Jeff acting ethically or unethically in this situation?

MindTap®

In most cases whether you are coming together, maintaining, or coming apart, it helps to talk openly and honestly about these dialectical tensions and come to an agreement about how to manage them going forward. Sometimes, however, partners are unable to resolve the tensions. In these instances, the relationship may deteriorate or end.

Reflection and Assessment

Healthy interpersonal relationships are mutually satisfying and beneficial to both parties. Relationships move through a series of stages based on communication disclosure and feedback. To assess how well you've learned what we addressed in these pages, answer the following questions. If you have trouble answering any of them, go back and review that material. Once you can answer each question accurately, you are ready to move ahead to read the next chapter.

1. What are some guidelines for communicating effectively with acquaintances, friends, and intimate partners?

2. How does disclosure and feedback operate in interpersonal relationships?

3. What are some examples of a relationship coming together and coming apart?

4. How do use of different technologies impact relationship development, maintanence, and dissolution?

5. What dialectical tensions might you experience in your interpersonal relationships with a close friend, a family member, and a romantic partner?

COMMUNICATE!

RESOURCE AND ASSESSMENT CENTER

MindTap

Now that you have read Chapter 7, go to your MindTap for *Communicate!* for quick access to the electronic resources that accompany this text.

Applying What You've Learned

Impromptu Speech Activities

1. Select a scenario from a stack of options provided by your instructor. Each one will describe a relationship that is experiencing a dialectical tension. Together with a classmate, create a role-play where you effectively manage the tension. If called upon to do so, enact the scenario and your solution in front of the class.

2. Draw a slip of paper from a stack provided by your instructor. The paper will identify one of the relationship types or stages we have discussed in this chapter. Together with a partner, enact a script in the form of a role-play in front of your classmates that demonstrates this relationship type or stage. Then see if the class can identify which one you and your partner were displaying and why.

Assessment Activities

1. Dialectics in Your Relationships Choose one of your current close friendships or intimate relationships. It can be with a friend or family member. Briefly explain this assignment and ask your relationship partner if she or he is willing to help you with this assignment and to have what you discuss become part of a short paper you are doing for this class. Only if your partner consents should you proceed; otherwise, find another friend or intimate.

- Briefly explain the concept of relationship dialectics to your partner. You may want to have them read the section of this chapter that explains these.
- Once your partner understands the concepts, have a conversation about how each of you has experienced each of these tensions over the course of your relationship. Can you each think of specific instances when you were "out of sync"? How did this play out in the relationship? Be specific and be sure to talk about each of the three dialectical tensions.
- Based on your conversation, write a short paper/journal entry in which you describe what you learned. How has hearing your partner talk about how he or she experienced these changed your understanding?
- Given what you have learned in this conversation, how can you use this to improve this relationship going forward.

2. Distinguishing between Relationship Types

- List three people you have known for some time that you consider to be acquaintances. Why do you consider these people to be acquaintances rather than friends? What do you talk about with each of these people? What subjects do you avoid? Do any of these relationships have the potential to become friendships? If so, what would you have to do to make that transition?

- List three people you have known for some time whom you consider to be friends. Why do you consider each of these people to be a friend? How does your relationship with each differ from your relationships with your acquaintances? What do you talk about with each of these people? What subjects do you avoid? Do any of these relationships have the potential to become best friendships or intimate relationships? If so, what would you have to do to make the transition?

- List one to three people you have known for some time whom you consider to be your best friends or intimates. Why do you consider each of these people to be best friends or intimates? What do you talk about with each of these people? What subjects do you avoid? How does each of these relationships differ from those you have with your friends?

- Write a short essay in which you describe what you have learned about your relationships.

3. Johari Window Select five or six adjectives from the Johari Window grid provided on p. 129, which you feel accurately describe yourself. Enter your name (or an alias if you'd prefer) and save your grid. Then ask a few of your friends, relatives, or colleagues to access your grid and pick out five or six adjectives from that grid that they feel describe you. When you have finished, write a paragraph discussing what you have learned.

- Did the adjectives other people picked to describe you match the adjectives you picked for yourself?
- How does this information explain your experiences in developing and sustaining relationships?
- Does this suggest any changes you need to make to improve your relationships?

4. Conversation and Analysis: Trevor and Meg After you have watched the video of Trevor and Meg on MindTap answer the following questions.

- How do Trevor and Meg disclose their feelings and offer feedback?
- What stage of their relationship life cycle do they seem to be in and why?
- What dialectical tensions are they dealing with and what strategies are they, or should they be, using to manage them?
- What is Meg's real fear?

Interpersonal Communication

MindTap®

Start with a quick warm-up activity.

"Chuck," Susan said, "when that interviewer at the movie theatre asked whether you'd rather see a comedy or a thriller, you said 'thriller'! We've been together for four years, and I'm just now learning that you'd rather see a thriller? We've *never* gone to a thriller in all the time we've been dating."

Chuck responded, "I'm sorry, Susan. I didn't think you liked thrillers and so I never suggested seeing one with you. If I do want to see one, I just go with Larry."

"Chuck, it's not that I don't like them. In fact, I really wanted to see *Gone Girl*." Susan asks, "Are there other things you like or don't like that you haven't told me about?"

"Well, I don't know. Probably, I guess ."

"Probably? Why haven't you been honest with me?"

"Well, I don't think I'm being dishonest. I guess I just some things are all that important."

"Not important? Chuck, I thought we trusted each other enough to be honest. Now I find out you keep things from me. I just don't know what to think!"

"Sue, why didn't you tell me you wanted to see *Gone Girl*?" Chuck asked.

"Well I, uh, uh. . . ."

8

Poor Chuck, poor Susan! In the last chapter, we talked about how we form, maintain, and end relationships and the dialectical tensions inherent in them. As we interact, we create the **communication climate**—the overall emotional tone of the relationship—through the messages we exchange (Cissna, 2011). A **positive communication climate** is one where partners feel valued and supported. We use **confirming communication messages** to convey that we care about our partner. We say "you're important to me" through our verbal and nonverbal messages. At the same time, we avoid **disconfirming communication messages**, which signal a lack of regard for our partner. In this chapter, we look at how to create confirming messages when we want to: (1) respond to a partner who is experiencing emotional distress, (2) share or keep private some of our personal information, (3) express a personal desire or expectation, and (4) resolve conflict.

Providing Emotional Support

Can you recall a time when you were emotionally distraught? Perhaps someone close to you died unexpectedly, or a romantic partner dumped you, or someone you trusted betrayed you, or a supervisor treated you unfairly. If so, you probably appreciated the emotional support you received from some friends and family members (Photo 8.1). You can also probably recall times when you've comforted others when they were feeling distressed. **Comforting** is helping others feel better about themselves, their behavior, or their situation by creating a safe space to express their thoughts and feelings. Comforting also helps those doing the comforting by improving self-esteem and their relationship with the person being comforted (Burleson, 2002).

Many people believe that women expect, need, and provide more emotional support than men. However, a growing body of research suggests that both men and women value emotional support from their partners in a variety of relationships, including same-sex friendships, opposite-sex friendships, romantic relationships, and sibling relationships (Burleson, 2003). Providing emotional support is also generally valued across cultural and co-cultural groups (p. 574).

Comforting Guidelines

The following guidelines can help you succeed when providing emotional support.

1. **Clarify supportive intentions.** When people are experiencing emotional turmoil, they may have trouble trusting the motives of those wanting to help. You can clarify your supportive intentions by openly stating that your goal is to help. Notice how David does this:

   DAVID: *(noticing Paul sitting in his cubicle with his head in his lap and his hands over his head)* Paul, is everything OK?

   PAUL: *(sitting up and looking miserable)* Yeah, I'm fine.

   DAVID: Paul, we've been working together for five years and I care about you. You're one of the best technicians in this company. If something is going on, I'd like to help, even if all I can do is listen. So, what's up?

2. **Buffer potential face threats. Face** is the perception we want others to have of our worth (Ting-Toomey & Chung, 2012). **Positive face needs** are the desires we have to be appreciated, liked, and valued. **Negative face needs** are the desires we have to be independent and self-sufficient. The very act of providing comfort can threaten your partner's face needs. So effective comforting messages must be *buffered* to address the other person's positive and negative face needs. When David says to Paul, "You're one of the best technicians in this company," he attends to Paul's positive face need to be valued. When David says, all he "can do is listen," he attends to Paul's negative face need for independence.

3. **Use other-centered messages. Other-centered messages** encourage those feeling emotional distress to talk about what happened and how they feel about it. These messages can come in the form of questions or prods (e.g., uh-huh, wow, I see, go on, tell me more) encouraging others to elaborate. Other-centered messages are the most highly valued type of comforting message among most cultural and co-cultural groups (Burleson, 2003).

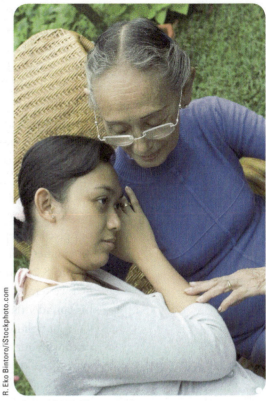

Photo 8.1 Can you recall a time when you were upset and someone comforted you? Did you feel closer to this person as a result?

4. **Reframe the situation.** We might **reframe the situation** by offering ideas, observations, information, or explanations that help our partner understand the situation in a different light. For example, imagine that Travis returns from class and tells his friend Abe, "Well, I'm flunking calculus. It doesn't matter how much I study. I just can't get it. I might as well just drop out of school before I flunk out completely. I can ask for a full-time schedule at work and not torture myself with school anymore." To reframe the situation, Abe might remind Travis that he has been putting in many hours of overtime at work and ask Travis if he thinks the heavy work schedule might be cutting into his study time. Or he might suggest that Travis seek help at the tutoring center, a resource many of their mutual friends found helpful. In each case, Abe has provided new observations and information to help Travis reframe the situation.

5. **Give advice.** In some cases, we may comfort by **giving advice**—presenting relevant suggestions for resolving a problem or situation. We should only give advice, however, after our supportive intentions have been understood, we have attended to our partner's face needs, and we have sustained an other-centered conversation for some time. Even then, we should ask permission before offering advice and acknowledge that this advice is only one suggestion and it's OK if they choose not to follow it.

face
the perception we want others to have of our worth

positive face needs
the desire to be appreciated, liked, and honored

negative face needs
the desire to be independent and self-sufficient

other-centered messages
encourage partners to talk about and elaborate on what happened and how they feel about it

reframe the situation
offering messages that help a partner understand a situation in a different light

giving advice
presenting relevant suggestions to resolve a problem or situation

Managing Privacy and Disclosure

As we discussed in Chapter 7, people in relationships experience dialectical tensions, one of which is the tension between openness and closedness. When we want more openness, we disclose confidential information and feelings. When we want more closedness, we manage privacy to limit what others know about us.

communication privacy management theory
the decision-making process regarding whether or not to disclose confidential information about oneself or others

Communication privacy management theory describes the decision-making process we go through as we choose whether or not to disclose confidential information about ourselves (self-disclosure) or about others (other-disclosure) (Petronio, 2013). Suppose Jim tells Mark that he wet the bed until he was 12 years old (self-disclosure), but had never told anyone because he didn't want to be teased. If Mark later tells a friend that Jim was once a bed wetter, Mark is also disclosing, but he is disclosing Jim's private information, not his own (other-disclosure). Like Jim, you can choose whether to reveal or conceal personal information to your partner. Then either of you can choose to reveal that sensitive information to others or maintain it within the privacy of your relationship.

If your partner has your permission to share some of your personal information, then disclosing it to others is unlikely to affect your relationship. However, if you have not given your partner permission to disclose certain information and you expect it to remain between the two of you, then **disclosure** is likely to damage your relationship (Photo 8.2). So when Jim hears that Mark told a mutual friend that Jim is a former bed wetter, he may feel embarrassed, hurt, and betrayed if he believes Mark breached his confidentiality.

disclosure
revealing confidential information about yourself or others

Controlling who has access to your personal information is becoming more complicated with our ever-increasing use of technology and social media. For example, Web providers like Google routinely track our searches. And, according to a recent article published in the *New York Times,* a "bug" in Apple software allowed people to access photos stored on personal cell phones (Bilton, 2012). Similarly, when we post something to a Facebook page, that comment or image can quickly become viral when a friend decides to comment on it or tag it for another network of friends to see. For example, Darius posted an album of New Year's Eve party photos to Facebook. Gretchen then tagged a photo of Ellen and Darius dancing on a table at the party. When Ellen saw it, she sent a private message asking Darius to remove it because she was on the job market and knows that potential employers look at what people post on their social networking sites. In addition, information posted on the Web has no expiration date. So before you post, you should consider whether the information is something you are comfortable sharing not only with your friends and your friends' friends, but also to potential employers and strangers today and in the future.

APPLY IT

Do a Google search of yourself (including Google Images). What comes up? Are there any images or information you would rather not have posted for others to see? If so, why?

MindTap®

Effective communicators choose to disclose or withhold information and feelings based on their relational motive, the situation, and a careful risk–benefit analysis. One of the most important criteria we use to decide whether to disclose information or keep it private is the risk–benefit analysis. That is, we weigh the advantages we might gain by disclosing or maintaining private information against the disadvantages of doing so. Common benefits of disclosing include building the relationship, coping with stress, and emotional or psychological catharsis. Common benefits of maintaining privacy include control and independence. The risks of disclosing include loss of control, vulnerability, and embarrassment. Risks of maintaining privacy include social isolation and being misunderstood.

Photo 8.2 Gossip is a form of disclosing somebody else's private information, which may or may not be true, without permission. Have you ever been the victim of gossip? What were the consequences for you? For others?

In the *Diverse Voices* feature, "Long Overdue," Naomi Shihab Nye describes her experiences with anti-Arab prejudice. As you read this excerpt, consider her courage in disclosing information about herself and her feelings.

DIVERSE VOICES

Long Overdue

by Naomi Shihab Nye

Poets like Naomi Shihab Nye devote their lives to using words to communicate their feelings and ideas, yet when Shihab Nye, who is of Palestinian descent, encountered anti-Arab prejudice, she was unable to disclose her Arab roots and to respond.

The words we didn't say. How many times? Stones stuck in the throat. Endlessly revised silence. What was wrong with me? How could I, a person whose entire vocation has been dedicated one way or another to the use of words, lose words completely when I needed them? Where does vocal paralysis come from? Why does regret have such a long life span? My favorite poet, William Stafford, used to say, "Think of something you said. Now write what you *wish* you had said."

But I am always thinking of the times I said nothing.

In England, attending a play by myself, I was happy when the elderly woman next to me began speaking at intermission.

"Smashingly talented," she said of Ben Kingsley, whose brilliant monologue we'd been watching. "I don't know how he does it—transporting us so effortlessly; he's a genius. Not many in the world like him." I agreed. But then she sighed and made an odd turn. "You know what's wrong with the world today? It's Arabs. I blame it all on the Arabs. Most world problems can really be traced to them."

My blood froze. Why was she saying this? The play wasn't about Arabs. Ben Kingsley was hardly your blue-blooded Englishman, either, so what brought it up? Nothing terrible about Arabs had happened lately in the news. I wasn't wearing a keffiyeh [traditional Arab headdress] around my neck.

But my mouth would not open.

"Why *did* so many of them come to England?" she continued, muttering as if she were sharing a confidence. "A ruination, that's what it is."

It struck me that she might be a landlady having trouble with tenants. I tried and tried to part my lips. She chatted on about something less consequential, never seeming to mind our utterly one-sided conversation, till the lights went down. Of course, I couldn't concentrate on the rest of the play. My precious ticket felt wasted. I twisted my icy hands together while my cheeks burned.

Even worse, she and I rode the same train afterwards. I had plenty of time to respond, to find a vocabulary for prejudice and fear. The dark night buildings flew by. I could have said, "Madam, I am half Arab. I pray your heart grows larger someday." I could have sent her off, stunned and embarrassed, into the dark.

Years later, my son and I were sitting on an American island with a dear friend, the only African American living among 80 or so residents. A brilliant artist and poet in his seventies, he has made a beautiful lifetime of painting picture books, celebrating expression, encouraging the human spirit, reciting poems of other African American heroes, delighting children and adults alike.

We had spent a peaceful day riding bicycles, visiting the few students at the schoolhouse, picking up rounded stones on the beach, digging peat moss in the woods.

Our friend had purchased a live lobster down at the dock for supper. My son and I were sad when it seemed to be knocking on the lid of the pot of boiling water. "Let me out." We vowed quietly to one another never to eat a lobster again.

After dinner, a friend of our friend dropped in, returned to the island from her traveling life as an anthropologist. We asked if she had heard anything

continued

about the elections in Israel—that was the day Shimon Peres and Benjamin Netanyahu vied for prime minister and we had been unable to pick up a final tally on the radio.

She thought Netanyahu had won. The election was very close. But then she said, "Good thing! He'll put those Arabs in their places. Arabs want more than they deserve."

My face froze. Was it possible I had heard correctly? I didn't speak another word during her visit. I wanted to. I should have, but I couldn't. My plate littered with red shells.

After she left, my friend put his gentle hand on my shoulder. He said simply, "Now you know a little more what it feels like to be black."

So what happens to my words when the going gets rough? In a world where certain equalities for human beings seem long, long, long, overdue, where is the magic sentence to act as a tool?

Where is the hoe, the tiller, the rake?

Pontificating, proving, proselytizing leave me cold. So do endless political debates over coffee after dinner. I can't listen to talk radio, drowning in jabber.

But then the headlines take the power. "Problem is, we can't hear the voices of the moderates," said the Israeli man, who claimed his house was built on a spot where Arabs had never lived. "Where are *they*? Why don't they speak *louder*?"

(They don't like to raise their voices.)

(Maybe they can't hear you either.)

Excerpt from Naomi Shihab Nye, "Long Overdue," Post Gibran: An Anthology of New Arab American Writing (Syracuse University Press, 2000), p. 127. Reprinted by permission of the author.

APPLY IT

Describe a conversation you experienced in which too much information was disclosed. What happened and why?

MindTap®

APPLY IT

Identify a time when you shared private information with someone. Did you expect them to reciprocate right away? Did they?

MindTap®

Effects of Disclosure and Privacy on Relationships

Privacy and disclosure decisions affect relationships in three major ways. They affect intimacy level, reciprocity expectations, and information co-ownership.

Intimacy Because disclosure is the mechanism for increasing intimacy, you might think people move in a clear-cut way toward deeper disclosure as relationships develop. However, people actually move back and forth between periods of choosing to disclose and choosing to maintain privacy (Altman, 1993). We may choose privacy over disclosure to protect the other person's feelings, avoid unnecessary conflict, protect the relationship, or re-establish a boundary of independence (Petronio, 2013). For example, disclosing an infidelity to a romantic partner may do irreparable damage to the relationship and opting for privacy may actually preserve intimacy (Hendrick, 1981) and avoid conflict (Roloff & Ifert, 2000).

Reciprocity Whether your disclosure is matched by similar disclosure from your partner also can affect your relationship. Although you may expect immediate reciprocity, research suggests there can also be some lag time after one person discloses before the other reciprocates (Dindia, 2000b).

Information Co-ownership A third way disclosure and privacy can affect relationships has to do with how partners treat the private information they know about one another. When we disclose private information, the person with whom we share it becomes a co-owner of it. When a partner shares confidential information without permission, it is likely to damage our relationship at least temporarily.

As we rely more and more on technology to develop and maintain relationships, the lines between what is public and what is private are blurring (Photo 8.3) (Kleinman, 2007). For example, we use cell phones and Bluetooth technology to carry on even the most private conversations in public spaces. Similarly, when we e-mail a friend, we can't be sure that friend won't forward the message to others. The same problem exists on social networking sites.

Once we post information, it is there for others to take and share with anyone. The *Communicating in the World* feature, "Our Right to Privacy in a Mediated Society," describes some of the ethical issues we must confront in our brave new mediated world.

Disclosure Guidelines

Follow these guidelines when sharing personal information, sharing feelings, and providing feedback.

Sharing personal information

1. **Self-disclose the kind of information you want others to disclose to you.** How do you determine whether certain information is appropriate to disclose? You can do so by asking yourself whether you would feel comfortable if the other person were to share similar information with you.

2. **Self-disclose private information only when doing so represents an acceptable risk.** Some risk is inherent in any self-disclosure. The better you know your partner, the more likely a difficult self-disclosure will be well received.

3. **Move gradually to deeper levels of self-disclosure.** Because receiving self-disclosure can be almost as threatening as giving it, most people become uncomfortable when the level of disclosure exceeds their expectations. So we should disclose surface information early in a relationship and more personal information after it has become more intimate (Petronio, 2013).

4. **Continue self-disclosing only if it is reciprocated.** When disclosure is clearly not being returned, consider limiting the amount of additional self-disclosure you make. Failure to reciprocate suggests that your partner does not feel comfortable with that level of intimacy.

Photo 8.3 Information co-ownership is increasingly prevalent on online social networking sites. How do you try to manage your privacy online?

Sharing personal feelings At the heart of intimate self-disclosure is sharing personal feelings. Doing so demonstrates a bond of trust. Effective communicators share by **describing feelings**. Doing so teaches others how to treat us by describing how what has happened affects us emotionally without judging. For example, if you tell Paul that you enjoy it when he visits you, this description of your feelings should encourage him to visit you again. Likewise, when you tell Gloria that it bothers you when she borrows your iPad without asking, she may be more likely to ask the next time. To practice describing feelings, follow these three guidelines:

describing feelings
naming the emotions you are feeling without judging them

1. **Identify what *triggered* the feeling.** What did someone specifically say or do?

2. **Identify the *specific emotion* you feel as a result.** If what you are feeling is similar to anger, try to be more specific. Are you annoyed, betrayed, cheated, crushed, disturbed, furious, outraged, or shocked?

COMMUNICATING IN THE WORLD

The Right to Privacy in a Mediated Society

For over a century, celebrities have complained that the media invades their privacy. The death of Princess Diana in 1997 focused worldwide attention on the extent to which some public figures are denied any right to privacy. Certainly, public figures expect to be scrutinized regarding their professional lives and should be held accountable for misconduct, but the current cult of celebrity has created a situation in which the media also pries into their private lives for reasons that often have little or nothing to do with their professional careers. The debate over invasive media coverage was particularly relevant in September of 2014 when a video emerged of NFL football player, Ray Rice, punching his then fiancé, Janay, in the face and dragging her limp body out of the elevator. Do celebrities have a right to privacy even in a case of public domestic violence, such as this one? Janay Rice posted an Instagram message saying "No one knows the pain that the media and unwanted opinion from the public has caused my family . . . THIS IS OUR LIFE! What don't you all get?"

What about Janay's right to privacy? Where should the line be drawn? In this age of new media, celebrities are not the only ones who have to worry about such issues of privacy. Social networking sites have made it easier and faster to communicate with others, but they also open some important questions about how we control our identities, protect our privacy, and manage relationships online. One controversy arose regarding the Web site IsAnyoneUp.com, launched in 2010, which features thousands of explicit photos submitted by users. These amateur nude photos often began as private photos exchanged between partners, but are submitted to the site as a form of "revenge" by jilted exes or former friends without the consent of those pictured (Chen, 2011). The pictures are accompanied by the subjects' real names and screenshots of their Facebook profiles and Twitter feeds, further exposing the private lives of those pictured across the Internet. Even though they did not submit the photos nor consent to having them posted, under current communication law, those pictured have little recourse. Site founder Hunter Moore defends his posting of the pictures by suggesting it teaches people a valuable lesson about privacy. "[I]t might sound rough, but how else are you going to learn not to do this again?" Moore says. "It's like you're playing Russian roulette like, oh, let's hope this doesn't get out" (Gold, 2011).

Is the media justified in exposing the private moments of celebrities' lives, no matter how personal or painful, if doing so raises public awareness?

MindTap®

3. **Frame your response as an "I" statement.** "I" statements help neutralize the impact of an emotional description because they do not imply blame. For example, "I feel happy/sad/irritated/excited/vibrant." Be careful, however, not to couch a blaming statement as an "I" statement. For example, "I feel like you don't respect me" is actually a blaming statement because it doesn't let the other person know how you feel (e.g., hurt, angry, betrayed) about what happened. The following two examples describe feelings effectively:

"Thank you for the compliment [trigger]; I [the person having the feeling] feel gratified [the specific feeling] that you noticed my efforts."

"I [the person having the feeling] feel hurt [the specific feeling] when you criticize my cooking after I've worked all afternoon to prepare it [trigger]."

Providing personal feedback

Follow these guidelines when providing feedback:

Jetta Productions/Iconica/Getty Images

1. **Describe the specific behavior.** As when sharing feelings, be descriptive when **describing behavior** and specific rather than vague. A statement like "You're so mean" is ineffective because it is both evaluative and vague. Instead, describe the specific behavior(s) without commenting on appropriateness. What led you to conclude someone was *mean*? Was it something the person said or did? If so, what? Once you identify the specific behaviors, actions, or messages that led to your conclusion, you can share that information as feedback. For example, rather than saying, "You're so mean," you could be more specific by saying, "You called me a liar in front of the team knowing I have no way to prove that I told the truth."

2. **Praise positive behavior. Praise** is not the same as flattery. When we flatter someone, we use insincere compliments to ingratiate ourselves to that person. Praise compliments are sincere. To praise effectively, identify the specific behavior you

Photo 8.4 Describing feelings is difficult for many people because it makes them feel vulnerable. Can you recall a time when you masked your feelings because you didn't trust the other person? Was your fear justified?

describing behavior
recounting specific behaviors of another without commenting on their appropriateness

praise
describing the specific positive behaviors or accomplishments and the effect of them on others

COMMUNICATION SKILL

Describing Feelings

Skill	Use	Procedure	Example
Naming the emotions you are feeling without judging them.	For self-disclosure; to teach people how to treat you.	1. Identify the behavior that has triggered the feeling. 2. Identify the specific emotion you are experiencing as a result of the behavior. Anger? Joy? Be specific. 3. Frame your response as an "I" statement. "I feel _____." 4. Verbalize the specific feeling.	"I just heard I didn't get the job, and I feel cheated " or "Because of the way you defended me when I was being belittled by Leah, I feel both grateful and humbled."

want to reinforce and then describe any positive feelings you or others experienced as a result. So if your sister, who tends to be forgetful, remembers your birthday, saying something like "Thanks for the birthday card; I really appreciate that you remembered my birthday" describes the specific behavior you want to reinforce and the effect it had on you.

constructive criticism
describing specific behaviors that hurt the person or that person's relationships with others

3. **Give constructive criticism.** Although the word *criticize* can mean judgment, **constructive criticism** does not condemn but instead is based on empathy and a sincere desire to help someone understand the impact of his or her behavior (Photo 8.5). Use the following guidelines when providing constructive criticism:

   - *Ask for permission.* A person who has agreed to hear constructive criticism is more likely to be receptive to it than someone who was not accorded the respect of being asked beforehand.

   - *Describe the behavior and its consequences precisely.* Your objective description allows the other to maintain face while receiving accurate feedback about the damaging behavior. For example, DeShawn asks, "What did you think of the visuals I used when I delivered my report?" If you reply, "They weren't very effective," you would be too general and evaluative to be helpful. In contrast, you might say, "Well, the small font size on the first two made it hard for me to read." Notice this constructive criticism does not attack DeShawn's competence. Instead, it describes the font size and its consequences, and in so doing, enables DeShawn to see how to improve.

   - *Preface constructive criticism with an affirming statement.* Remember, even constructive criticism threatens the innate human need to be liked and admired. So, preface constructive criticism with statements that validate your respect for the other person. You could begin your feedback to DeShawn by saying, "First, the chart showing how much energy we waste helped me see just how much we could improve. And the bold colors you used really helped me focus on the main problems. I think using a larger font size on the first two PowerPoint slides would have made it easier for me to see from the back of the room."

   - *When appropriate, suggest how the person can change the behavior.* Because the goal of constructive criticism is to help, you can do so by providing suggestions that might lead to positive change. In responding to DeShawn's request for feedback, you might also add, "In my communication class, I learned that most people in a small audience should be able to read 18-point font or larger. You might want to give that a try." By including a positive suggestion, you not only help the person by providing useful information, you also show that your intentions are respectful.

Privacy Management Guidelines

Because reciprocity is a way to develop a relationship, maintaining privacy without damaging the relationship can be difficult. We offer three indirect strategies and one direct strategy to use when being pressed to disclose something you do not want to share.

Indirect strategies You may choose to maintain privacy by changing the subject, masking your feelings, or practicing strategic ambiguity.

- **Change the subject.** Observant partners will recognize changing the subject as a signal that you don't want to disclose. For example, as Pat and Eric leave economics class, Pat says to Eric, "I got an 83 on the test, how about you?" If Eric doesn't want to share his grade, he might redirect the conversation by saying, "Hey, that's a B. Good going. Did you finish the homework for calculus?"

- **Mask feelings.** If you decide that sharing your personal feelings is too risky, you might mask your emotions. For example, Alita masks her feelings of betrayal and embarrassment by laughing along with the others as Manny makes fun of something she said or did. On occasion, masking feelings can be an effective strategy. If we make it a regular habit, however, we might experience health problems as a result. We also run the risk of damaging our relationships because our partners won't really know or understand us.

Photo 8.5 Why might learning how to give constructive criticism help you maintain positive relationships with those you care about?

- **Practice strategic ambiguity.** You can sometimes be intentionally ambiguous to avoid embarrassment to you or your partner. So when Pat asks Eric about his grade on the test, Eric might respond, "I'm not sure. I got a few tests back this week."

Direct strategy Changing the subject, masking feelings, and using strategic ambiguity are indirect ways to maintain privacy and generally work in one-time situations. But these strategies will eventually damage your relationships if used repeatedly. So you might decide to use a more direct approach. **Establishing a personal boundary** is a direct approach for responding to people who expect you to disclose information or feelings you prefer to keep private.

To do so, begin by recognizing why you choose not to share the information. For example, when Pat asks Eric about the grade he received on a history paper, Eric may tell Pat he feels uncomfortable doing so. Then identify your privacy policy that guided this decision. Eric, who has been teased for getting good grades, has developed a rule that he does not disclose the grades he receives. Next, preface your personal boundary statement with an apology or other face-saving statement. Eric might tell Pat that he values the fact that Pat is interested in Eric's achievement. Finally, form an "I"-centered message that briefly establishes a boundary (Figure 8.1). For example, Eric might say:

> *"I'm sorry. I know that everyone's different, and I don't mean to be rude, but I'm not comfortable sharing my grades. It's been my policy not to ask other people about their grades or to discuss my own ever since getting teased about grades when I was a kid. I value you and our friendship and hope my policy doesn't offend you."*

establishing a personal boundary
a direct approach for responding to people who expect you to disclose something you would rather keep private

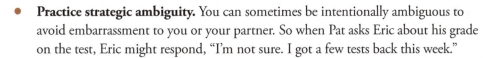

1. Recognize why you choose not to share the information.
2. Identify your privacy policy that guided the decision.
3. Preface your personal boundary statement with an apology or other face-saving statement.
4. Form an "I" centered statement that briefly establishes the boundary.

Figure 8.1

Setting boundaries

© 2017 Cengage Learning

COMMUNICATE ON YOUR FEET   **Speech Assignment**

Personal Narrative

The Assignment

Prepare a 3- to 5-minute speech that is a story about something that happened to you and is not generally known by others. Your story might be humorous, serious, or somewhere in between. It might be about something that happened recently or about an event from your past.

Begin by making a list of stories you might tell. As you think about the stories on your list, use the privacy and disclosure guidelines in this chapter to determine whether the story is appropriate for a classroom setting. Remember to consider not only your own privacy, but also the privacy of others who are part of the story.

As you prepare your speech, think about how to tell the story so that your audience can easily follow what you are saying. We tell most stories in chronological order, introducing people in the story as they make their appearance in the events. You can help your audience follow your story if you divide it into two, three, or four sequential parts, similar to the chapters of a book. For example, if you are going to tell a story about a cake-baking disaster, you could divide your story into three parts: problems with ingredients, problems with mixing, and problems with baking.

Briefly introduce your story in a way that piques the interest of your audience members. End your story by summarizing what you learned from the experience.

Phrasing his response this way lets Pat know that Eric's decision is based on a personal boundary rule rather than an indication of his trust in Pat or their relationship.

Expressing Desires and Expectations

Even two people in a mutually satisfying, intimate relationship have different needs, desires, and expectations (Alberti & Emmons, 2008). How they choose to express them to their partner will affect the relationship's communication climate. Let's look at four such communication styles and how each can affect the climate of a relationship.

Passive Communication Style

passive communication style
submitting to another's demands while concealing one's own desires and expectations

A **passive communication style** is submitting to another's demands while concealing one's own desires and expectations. For example, Aaron and Katie routinely go to the gym at 10 a.m. on Saturday mornings. Aaron's Friday work schedule changed recently and now he doesn't get home until 3 a.m. on Saturdays. Aaron behaves passively if he doesn't say anything to Katie and drags himself out of bed even though he'd much rather sleep. We tend to choose a passive approach when we value our relationship with the other person more than we value asserting our own particular need. If used habitually, however, passive communication will eventually damage the relationship because we will begin to resent our partner as we continually ignore our own needs, desires, and expectations.

Aggressive Communication Style

aggressive communication style
belligerently or violently confronting another with little or no regard for the others

An **aggressive communication style** is attacking another person's self-concept and/or expressing personal hostility in order to inflict psychological pain (Rancer & Avtgis, 2006).

Verbally aggressive messages disregard a partner's right to be treated with dignity and respect. Examples of aggressive communication range from yelling, badgering, and name calling to sarcasm, put-downs, and taunting. Suppose Aaron continues to meet Katie at the gym on Saturdays at 10 a.m. without telling her about his work schedule change. If Katie suggests they meet even earlier next week, Aaron may explode and aggressively reply, "No way! We always do what you want when you want. I'm sick of it. You are so selfish and inconsid-

erate. In fact, I don't care if I ever work out on Saturday again!" Katie, who has no context for understanding this aggressive outburst, may be startled, hurt, and confused. People may use verbal aggression when they perceive themselves to be powerful, do not value the other person, lack emotional control, or feel defensive (Photo 8.6). Verbally aggressive communication can lead to less satisfying relationships, family violence, divorce, and loss of credibility (Hample, 2003). Unfortunately, the fact that some people today use technology to convey verbally aggressive messages has become so prevalent that we coined the term cyberbullying to describe it (Kleinman, 2007).

Photo 8.6 Have you ever engaged in or been the victim of aggressive road rage? Was it effective in achieving its goal? Were there any unanticipated consequences?

Passive-Aggressive Communication Style

A **passive-aggressive communication style** is expressing hostility indirectly. For example, you may say yes when you want to say no or complain about others behind their backs. Suppose Aaron apologizes for his outburst and then tells Katie about his work schedule change. Although Katie claims to accept the apology and tells Aaron "It's no big deal," the next week she doesn't call him and instead goes alone to the gym. When Aaron shows up and asks for an explanation, Katie shrugs her shoulders and says, "Well, I thought you said you were sick of always doing things 'my way.'" Over time, passive-aggressive behavior damages relationships because it undercuts mutual respect.

passive-aggressive communication style
expressing hostility indirectly

Assertive Communication Style

An **assertive communication style** uses messages that describe personal needs, rights, desires, and expectations honestly and directly in ways that also demonstrate respect and value for you, your partner, and the relationship. An effective assertive message (1) describes the behavior or event as objectively as possible, (2) proposes your interpretation of it, (3) names the feeling you have as a result, (4) identifies potential consequences for you, your partner, or others, and (5) suggests your intentions regarding how you will act and/or what you expect in the future. For example,

assertive communication style
expressing personal desires and expectations while respecting those of others

Aaron could have responded to Katie's suggestion to go to the gym at 8 a.m. assertively in this way:

> *"I understand that you want to work out at 8 a.m. starting next week (description). I am guessing you want more time to run errands, do chores, or study (interpretation). The thought of working out at 8 a.m. frustrates me (feeling) because my work schedule changed and I don't even get home until 3 a.m. on Saturdays now. I can't imagine having the energy to exercise at 8 a.m. (consequence). But I really like working out together and would like to keep doing so. So maybe we could start at 9 a.m. instead, or you could start earlier and I could join you at 9 a.m. (intention)."*

Notice how Aaron honestly and directly communicates his desires in confirming ways that demonstrate respect for Katie and his relationship with her.

Cultural and Co-cultural Considerations

Assertiveness is typically valued in individualistic cultures, such as in the United States where direct communication is preferred. This style is not necessarily the norm across the world (Holt & DeVore, 2005). For example, collectivist cultures such as China and Japan that value accord and harmony may tend to prefer passive behavior (Samovar, Porter, & McDaniel, 2012). In fact, those who abide by traditional collectivist norms may even find what North Americans interpret as appropriate assertive communication to be rude and insensitive (Alberti & Emmons, 2008).

Co-cultural groups within the United States may also prefer different communication styles. For example, females who have been socialized to embrace feminine gender norms are likely to use passive or passive-aggressive communication styles

COMMUNICATION SKILL

Assertive Communication Style

Skill	Use	Procedure	Example
Messages that describe your needs, rights, desires, and expectations in an honest and direct way that demonstrates respect and value for both you and your partner.	To stand up for yourself and express legitimate concerns without denying the worth of your partner.	1. Describe the behavior or event as objectively as possible. 2. Propose your interpretation of it. 3. Name the feeling(s) you have as a result. 4. Identify potential consequences for you, your partner, or others. 5. Suggest your intentions regarding how you will act and/or what you expect of them in the future.	When you refer to us as "girls" after I explained we want to be called "women" (behavior), I feel disrespected (feeling) because it seems like you don't appreciate how important the difference is to me (interpretation). Even though you may not mean to hurt me, because this really bothers me, it is hurting the intimacy I feel for our relationship (consequences). I'll keep bringing it up if you keep using "girls" to refer to us (intention).

(Hess & Hagen, 2006). In fact, numerous books and workshops exist today to help women learn to replace passive and passive-aggressive communication styles with assertive ones. Similarly, males who embrace masculine gender norms tend to use aggressive communication styles and similarly benefit from learning to replace them with assertive messages, as well.

Although differences exist across cultures and co-cultures, the distinctions are becoming less dramatic. Still, when talking with people whose cultural or co-cultural norms differ from your own, you may need to observe their behavior and their responses to your statements before you can be sure about how best to communicate your needs, rights, desires, and expectations.

Managing Interpersonal Conflict

Interpersonal conflict is an expressed struggle between two interdependent people who perceive incompatible goals, scarce resources, and interference from the other in achieving their goals (Wilmot & Hocker, 2010). Let's untangle this definition. To be an *expressed struggle,* both people must be aware of the disagreement. To be *interdependent,* achieving a satisfactory outcome for each person depends on the actions of the other. By *perceived incompatible goals* we mean both people believe they have something to lose if the other person gets their way. *Perceived scarce resources* assumes there isn't enough of something to go around and *perceived interference* is the belief that the other person is forcing us to do or not to do something. For example, when sixteen-year-old Darla's mother (interdependence) told her she would not waste money (scarce resources) on a tattoo (perceived interference), she claimed Darla would regret it when she grew up (perceived incompatible goals), and they argued (expressed struggle). In conflict situations such as this one, participants have choices about how they communicate with each other to manage, and hopefully, to resolve it.

Conflict is not necessarily a bad thing. In fact, conflict is a natural part of interpersonal relationships, and when managed effectively, can actually strengthen them (Wilmont & Hocker, 2010). When not managed effectively, however, conflict can hurt people and relationships. The consequences of poorly managed conflict can be particularly devastating when communicating across cultures (Ting-Toomey & Chung, 2012). In this section, we discuss five conflict management styles and how to skillfully initiate and respond to conflict situations that arise in your relationships (see Figure 8.2). These five styles are avoiding, accommodating, competing, compromising, and collaborating (Thomas & Kilmann, 1978).

interpersonal conflict
an expressed struggle between two interdependent people who perceive incompatible goals, scarce resources, and interference from the other in achieving their goals

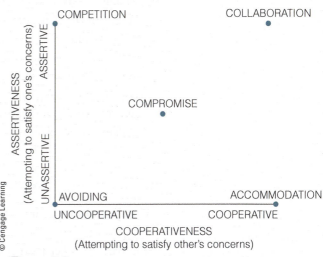

Figure 8.2

Conflict management style taxonomy

Avoiding (Lose–Lose)

Avoiding involves physically or psychologically removing yourself from the conflict. It is typically characterized as a lose–lose approach. Avoiding may be appropriate when hot tempers need to cool down or when either the issue or the relationship isn't

avoiding
physically or psychologically removing yourself from the conflict

important to us. For instance, imagine Eduardo and Justina get into an argument about their financial situation. Eduardo may say, "I don't want to talk about this" and physically walk out the door. Or he may psychologically withdraw by simply ignoring Justina. Similarly, when Karna finished reading Jeremy's text, she could tell he was upset but just needed to vent and the issue wasn't really that important to her. So she chose not to respond right away and let him cool down. We risk damaging our relationships when avoiding becomes a habit because doing so doesn't deal with or resolve the conflict and usually makes it more difficult to deal with later on.

Accommodating (Lose–Win)

accommodating
satisfying others' needs or accepting others' opinions while neglecting our own

Accommodating is satisfying the needs or accepting the opinions of our partner while neglecting our own needs or opinions. It is typically characterized as a lose–win approach. Accommodating may be appropriate when the issue is not important to us, but the relationship is. For instance, Anthony doesn't particularly enjoy romantic movies but he knows Marianne has her heart set on seeing *The Vow*. He suggests going to see it because he doesn't really care which movie they see and wants to please her because he values his relationship with her.

Competing (Win–Lose)

competing
satisfying our own needs or desires with little or no concern for the needs of the other or the relationship

Competing is satisfying our own needs or desires with little or no concern for the needs or desires of our partner or the relationship. It is typically characterized as a win–lose approach. It may be appropriate when quick and decisive action must be taken to ensure your own or another's welfare or safety. For example, David knows that, statistically speaking, the likelihood of death or serious injury increases dramatically if one does not wear a helmet when riding a motorcycle. So he insists that his sister wear one when she rides with him.

If one partner uses competing and the other responds by avoiding or accommodating, the conflict may seem to have resolved even though it has not. And if both partners engage in competing, the conflict is likely to escalate. Finally, although competing may result in getting your way, when you use it repeatedly, it will usually hurt your partner and damage the relationship.

Compromising (Partial Lose–Lose)

compromising
giving up part of what you want to provide at least some satisfaction for both parties

Compromising occurs when each partner gives up part of what they desire to satisfy part of what their partner wants. It is typically characterized as a partial lose–lose approach. Neither partner is completely satisfied, but it seems to be the best solution either can hope for.

Compromising may be appropriate when the issue is moderately important, when there are time constraints, when doing so will buy credits for future negotiations, and when attempts at collaborating have not been successful. For example, if Heather and Paul need to meet outside of class to complete a class project but both have busy schedules, they may compromise to meet at a time that isn't ideal for either of them.

1995 Baby Blues Partnership. Reprinted by permission of King Features Syndicate, Inc

Collaborating (Win–Win)

Collaborating is when people work through the problem together to discover a mutually acceptable solution. It is typically characterized as a win–win approach. Collaborating may be appropriate when the issue is too important for a compromise, when the relationship is important, and when we want to come up with a creative solution to a problem. We collaborate by discussing the issues, describing feelings, and identifying the characteristics of a solution that will satisfy everyone. For example, Fadi really wants to vacation alone with Aliana and Alaina wants to invite their friends, Greg and Shelly. Aliana may explain how she thinks that vacationing with friends would lower the cost of the trip. Fadi may describe his desire to have "alone time" with Aliana. As they discuss their vacation goals, they arrive at a plan that meets both of their needs. For example, they may decide to vacation alone, but camp rather than stay in hotels to lower their expenses. Or they may share a condo with their friends, but schedule alone time each day.

collaborating
working together to discover a mutually satisfying solution

APPLY IT

Think about the last time you experienced conflict with a friend or family member. How did you deal with it? Did you try to avoid it, give in, win, compromise, or collaborate? Looking back, how satisfied are you with your actions? Your partner's actions? Why?

Collaboration Guidelines

Follow these guidelines when using collaboration to resolve a conflict:

- **Identify the problem and own it as your own:** "Hi, I'm trying to study and I need your help."

- **Describe the problem in terms of behavior, consequences, and feelings:** "When I hear your music, I listen to it instead of studying, and then I get frustrated and behind schedule."

- **Refrain from blaming or accusing:** "I know you aren't trying to ruin my studying and are just enjoying your music."

- **Find common ground:** "I would guess that you have had times when you became distracted from something you needed to do, so I'm hoping that you can help me out by lowering the volume a bit."

- **Mentally rehearse so that you can state your request briefly.**

It is more difficult to collaborate when you have to respond to a conflict that someone else initiates in a confrontational manner. But you can shape the conversation toward collaboration by following these guidelines:

- **Disengage:** Avoid a defensive response by emotionally disengaging. Remember your partner has a problem and you want to help.

WHAT WOULD YOU DO?

A Question of Ethics

Ronaldo sat in the study hall cramming for a final examination when two of his classmates, Chauncey and Doug, walked up to his table.

"Studying hard?" Chauncey asked.

"Yeah. I'm really stressing over this final," said Ronaldo. "What about you guys?"

"Hardly studying," said Chauncey.

Doug laughed.

Ronaldo looked at the two and saw that they both seemed relaxed and confident. "Something's not right with this picture," he said. "You're not going to tell me you guys are ready for this thing, are you?"

"Yep," said Chauncey.

Doug nodded.

"I don't get it," said Ronaldo. "You mean you've already gone back and studied everything we've covered this semester?"

"Hey, you only need to study what's actually on the test," said Chauncey.

"And how would you know that when McAllister didn't even give us a study guide?"

asked Ronaldo. He was beginning to put the puzzle together.

Doug placed his hand on Chauncey's arm and said, "Don't tell him anything else, man."

"No, it's all right. Ronaldo's cool," said Chauncey. "He knows how to keep a secret. Don't you?"

"I guess," Ronaldo said uneasily.

"It's like this," said Chauncey. "Doug's little brother hacked into McAllister's system and downloaded a copy of the final exam. You interested in getting a head start?"

Assuming that Ronaldo declines Chauncey's offer to cheat, what other ethical issues must he grapple with? Which would be more ethically compromising: letting Chauncey and Doug get away with cheating, or betraying their trust by notifying the professor?

MindTap®

- **Respond with genuine concern:** Sometimes your partner needs to vent before being ready to problem solve: "I can see that you're angry. Tell me about it."

- **Paraphrase and ask questions:** "Is it the volume of my music or the type of music that is making it difficult for you to study?"

- **Seek common ground:** "I can understand that you would be upset about losing precious study time."

- **Ask for alternative solutions:** "Can you give me a couple of ideas about how we could resolve this so your study is more effective?"

Reflection and Assessment

We develop and maintain interpersonal relationships through communication. We do so by: (1) providing emotional support, (2) dealing with competing needs for privacy and disclosure, (3) expressing different desires and expectations, and (4) managing conflict. To assess how well you've learned what we addressed in these pages, answer the following questions. If you have trouble answering any of them, go back and review that material. Once you can answer each question accurately, you are ready to move ahead to read the next chapter.

1. What strategies will you employ when attempting to comfort someone that appears to be emotionally distressed?

2. How will you manage disclosure and privacy in your relationships in both face-to-face and online settings?

3. What are some ways to express your desires and expectations and possible consequences for doing so?

4. What guidelines will you follow when seeking to resolve a conflict through collaboration?

COMMUNICATE!

RESOURCE AND ASSESSMENT CENTER

MindTap

Now that you have read Chapter 8, go to your MindTap for *Communicate!* for quick access to the electronic resources that accompany this text.

Applying What You've Learned

Impromptu Speech Activity

Communication Negotiation Styles Identify a recent incident in which you behaved either passively, aggressively, or passive aggressively. Now analyze the situation. What type of situation was it? Did someone make a request? Did you need to express a preference or right? What type of relationship did you have with the person (stranger, acquaintance, friendship, intimate)? How did you feel about how you behaved? If you had used an assertive message, what might you have said? Prepare a short, well-organized speech (2–3 minutes) describing your analysis and be prepared to deliver it to the class if called upon by your instructor.

Assessment Activities

1. Self-Disclosure and Popular Media American popular culture has a reputation for promoting self-disclosure that probably exceeds that of any other culture in the world. Yet clearly, as the phrase "TMI" (too much information) indicates, inappropriate self-disclosure still happens. Of course, what may be inappropriate for one person can be appropriate for another. Find three instances of self-disclosure in popular media (film, television, radio, magazines, newspapers, or the Internet) and write a paragraph on each, explaining why you think the particular instance of self-disclosure is appropriate or inappropriate.

2. Your Conflict Profile Go to the MindTap for *Communicate!* at cengagebrain. com to access and print out your conflict profile, which is the article "How Do You Manage Conflict?" by Dawn M. Baskerville. Fill out and score the self-assessment questionnaire and graph your results. Read the description of each pattern. Study these results. Do they seem to capture your perception of your conflict profile accurately? Which are your dominant styles? Are your scores close together, or are there one or two styles that seem to dominate and other styles you prefer not to use? How does this pattern equip you to handle the conflicts you have experienced? Based on the information from this self-assessment, what do you need to do to become better able to handle conflict in your relationships? Write a paragraph in which you describe what you have learned about your conflict profile.

3. Conversation and Analysis: Jan and Ken After you've watched the video of Jan and Ken on MindTap for *Communicate!* answer the following questions.

- How does each person handle this conflict?
- How well does each person listen to the other?
- Are Jan and Ken appropriately assertive?
- Comment on how well each provides feedback and describes feelings?

When you're done with this activity, compare your answers to the authors' on Mind-Tap for *Communicate*!

Skill-Building Activities

1. Describing Feelings and Communicating Boundaries Each of the following statements expresses feelings. Rephrase each to describe feelings or where appropriate to communicate a boundary.

a. Expressed: *"I can't believe you told that story without my permission!"*

Described: It makes me unhappy when you tell somebody else a story I told you in private. I'm going to have to think about what I tell you in the future.

b. Expressed: *"Growing up without a dad was hard. But it's really none of your business."*

Described:

c. Expressed: *"It's not fair to expect me to share our dorm room with your boyfriend."*

Described:

d. Expressed: *"All you've done this whole lunch is text. I don't know why I bothered to come!"*

Described:

2. Describing Behavior Rephrase each statement so that it describes the behavior(s) that might have led you to this generalization.

a. *"You're a really good friend."*

Described:

b. *"You're always picking on me."*

Described:

c. *"I can't believe that you stabbed me in the back."*

Described:

d. *"One of the things I admire about you is that you are so thoughtful."*

Described:

3. Disclosing Personal Feedback For each of the following situations, write an appropriate feedback message.

a. You have been car pooling to school for about three weeks now with a fellow student referred by the school transportation office. Everything about the situation is great (e.g., he's on time, your schedules match, and you enjoy your conversations), except he drives ten to fifteen miles per hour faster than the speed limit, and this scares you.

Feedback:

b. A good friend has a habit of saying "like" and "you know" more than once every sentence. Although she is an "A" student, you believe this habit makes her sound uneducated. She is about to graduate and has been doing on-campus job interviews. So far every potential employer she has interviewed with has rejected her. She asks why you think she is having such a hard time.

Feedback:

c. Your professor has asked you for feedback on his or her teaching style. Based on your experience in this class, write a message of praise and one of constructive criticism.

Feedback:

4. Assertive Messages Write an assertive message for each of the following situations. Indicate what type of assertion you are making: a complaint, a personal request, or a refusal.

a. You come back to your dorm, apartment, or house to finish a paper that is due tomorrow, only to find that someone else is using your computer.

Assertive response:

b. You work part-time at a clothing store. Just as your shift is ending, your manager says to you, "I'd like you to work overtime, if you would. Martin's supposed to replace you, but he just called and can't get here for at least an hour." You have tickets to a concert that starts in an hour.

Assertive response:

c. You and your friend made a date to go dancing, an activity you really enjoy. When you meet, your friend says, "I don't feel like dancing tonight. Let's go to Joey's party instead."

Assertive response:

d. You're riding in a car with a group of friends on the way to a party when the driver begins to clown around by swerving the car back and forth, speeding up to tailgate the car in front, and honking his horn. You believe this driving is dangerous, and you're becoming scared.

Assertive response:

5. Initiating a Conflict Prepare a message that would effectively initiate a conflict for each of the following situations.

a. Situation: *You observed your long-time romantic partner flirting with another person. Your partner's arm was around this person's waist and they were quietly talking, laughing together, and periodically whispering in each other's ear.*

Initiating Message:

b. Situation: *Your roommate borrowed your iPod and returned it late last night. You put it on your desk without really looking at it. This morning when you grabbed it to use at the gym, you noticed that the display was cracked. You are certain it was not damaged before your roommate borrowed it.*

Initiating Message:

c. Situation: *Halfway through your shift, your manager called you into her office and told you that someone had called in sick and that you would have to stay until closing. You have a test tomorrow and need to study.*

Initiating Message:

6. Responding to Conflict Prepare a response that would move the conflict toward a collaboration for each of the following situations.

    a.   Initiating Message: *"I saw you yesterday and, boy, were you enjoying yourself. So I hope you really had fun because, it's over between you and me. You can't cheat on me and expect me to take it."*

        Your Response:

    b.   Initiating Message: *"I can't believe that you broke my iPod and then didn't have the guts to tell me."*

        Your Response:

    c.   Initiating Message: *"There's no way I'm staying late again to close the store. You never even consider the fact that some of us have other things to do besides cover your ass."*

        Your Response:

To help you complete this activity, look for the Chapter 8 Skill Building activities on MindTap for *Communicate!*

MindTap°

UNIT THREE

Group Communication

In the words of famous American cultural anthropologist Margaret Mead:

> *Never doubt that a small group of thoughtful, committed people can change the world. Indeed, it is the only thing that ever has.*

When groups of people work together effectively to achieve a common goal, the results of their collective efforts can be profound. On the other hand, when groups of people function ineffectively, the results can range from meaningless to disastrous.

Although we participate in many different types of groups (e.g., families, friends, teams) every day, formal group communication research did not emerge until the 20th century (Forsyth & Burnette, 2005). In fact, most of the research on groups conducted in the first half of the 20th century came from analysts working in business and industry, rather than academics (Cartwright & Zander, 1968).

It wasn't until about 1950 that the formal study of groups and group communication found its home in colleges and universities across the country. Today, new technologies are generating renewed interest in group communication research and practice as it occurs in both face-to-face and virtual environments.

Although we cannot provide you with all that is known about the nature of groups and group communication in two chapters, we can introduce you to some major themes, fundamental theories and principals, and practical guidelines to make your group communication interactions both effective and rewarding. Chapter 9 introduces you to the nature and types of groups and the role of communication in them. We also discuss the characteristics of healthy groups as a rationale for working with others rather than alone. Chapter 10 focuses specifically on communication, leadership, and problem-solving processes when participating in workgroup teams.

We believe the best practices provided in these chapters will improve your group experiences in a variety of settings. We also hope these principles and strategies will encourage you to learn more about the nature of groups and group communication as a rich, fascinating, and practical field of study. In doing so, perhaps you will help accomplish what Margaret Mead suggests you can: *change the world.*

Communicating in Groups

MindTap®

Start with a quick warm-up activity.

"Hi, Mom. I'm just calling to tell you that I'm not going to make it home for the family dinner you're having tonight. The gang at work really needs me to close because Jennifer just called in sick."

"I can't believe it! Tonight is Sarah's last night at home before she deploys, and you know that your Grandma, Grandpa, Uncle Bill, and Aunt Vivien are all coming over for a big family dinner. What's wrong with you, Darla? Two nights ago you weren't home because you were playing softball with your friends; last night you begged off, claiming you had some team meeting for a class project; and now you're going to miss your sister's going-away family dinner? I just don't understand you. Isn't your family important to you at all? I mean, where do we fall in your priorities? It seems to me that you have a lot of commitments to other groups of people and we are always last."

"But, Mom. . . ."

Like Darla, we all belong to many different formal and informal groups. Although each of them has a distinct purpose, one thing they all have in common is that their effectiveness depends on communication. In fact, year after year, surveys conducted by the National Association of Colleges and Employers report "the ability to work well in groups" is one of the top ten skills sought in college graduates. Unfortunately, however, very few students actually graduate having had any formal training in how to communicate effectively in groups.

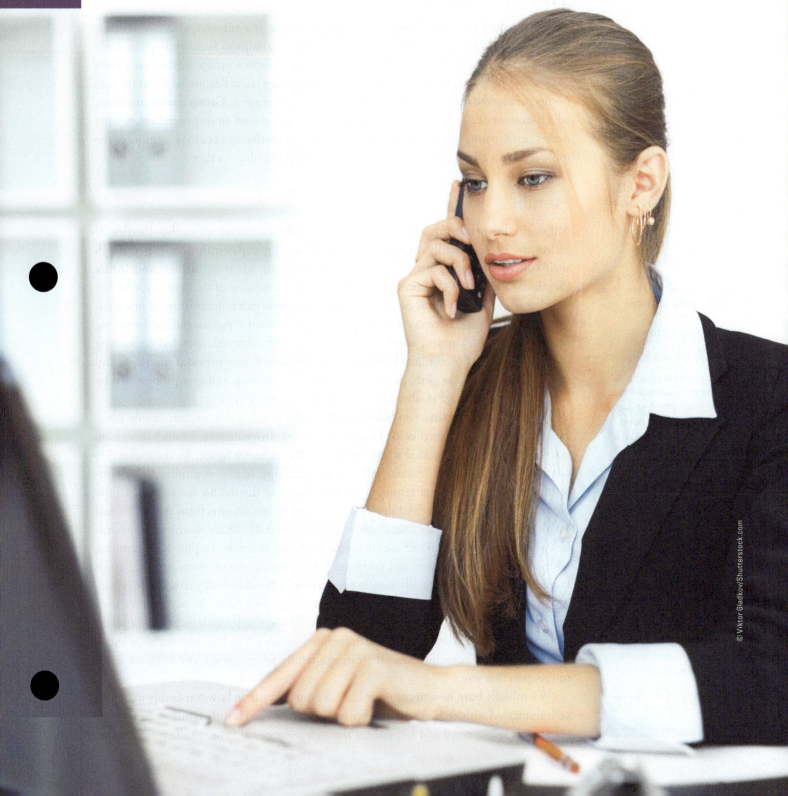

9

Thus, this chapter and the one that follows are devoted to how groups function and how to communicate most effectively within them. We begin this chapter by defining the nature and types of different groups, as well as some of the communication challenges we face when interacting in them. Then we describe key characteristics of healthy groups and the stages of group formation and development. We end this chapter by providing guidelines for managing group conflict effectively.

The Nature and Types of Groups

Take a moment to think about the groups of people you interact with consistently. Examples may range from student clubs to friendship groups to family groups to study groups to social network groups. What makes each of them a group rather than a mere assembly of people? Scholars generally agree that a **group** is a collection of about three to twenty people who feel a sense of belonging and common purpose. **Group communication,** which consists of all the verbal and nonverbal messages shared among members, is what makes participating in groups a positive or negative experience. Let's look at some of the most common group types and the role communication plays in them.

Families

Although the nature of what constitutes a family continues to evolve (Settles & Steinmetz, 2013), a **family** can generally be defined as a group of intimates who, through their communication, generate a sense of home, group identity, history, and future (Segrin & Flora, 2014). Families can be nuclear (consisting of two parents who live together with their biological or adopted children), single parent (consisting of one adult living with his or her children), extended (consisting of a parent or parents and children living with grandparents, cousins, aunts and uncles, or other relatives), blended (consisting of committed or married adults living with the children of their previous marriages and relationships, as well as perhaps the children of their union), and groups unrelated by either blood or marriage (Galvin, Braithwaite, & Bylund, 2015).

Research suggests that families typically function using one of four family communication patterns (Koerner & Fitzpatrick, 2006). In protective families, issues are not discussed and are decided solely by the family authority figure. In the movie *The Sound of Music,* prior to Maria's arrival, the Von Trapp family exemplified this family dynamic. In consensual families, all members may discuss an issue but a family authority figure makes the final decision. Many television sitcoms from the 1950s and 1960s such as *Father Knows Best, Leave It to Beaver*, and *The Brady Bunch* portray families with a benevolent and self-sacrificing father filling this role. In pluralistic families, all members discuss an issue and everyone participates in the decision making. These families may have formal family meetings to decide important family issues. The household portrayed in the popular 1980s television sitcom *Full House,* in which three men raised children together, operated as a pluralistic family. Finally, in laissez-faire families, members may discuss an issue, but each member makes his or her own decision and is responsible for its consequences. The cartoon family portrayed on *The Simpsons* tends to function this way.

We initially learn how to communicate in groups based on how our family members communicated with each other while we were growing up. Healthy family communication builds self-concept and self-esteem through messages of (1) praise (e.g., "awesome

group
a collection of about three to 20 people who interact and attempt to influence each other in order to accomplish a common purpose

group communication
all the verbal and nonverbal messages shared among group members

family
comprised of intimates who, through their communication, generate a sense of home, group identity, history, and future

APPLY IT

Identify several groups you belong to or belonged to at some point. Which ones do/did you most enjoy being a part of and which ones do/did you least enjoy? Why?

MindTap®

APPLY IT

What family communication pattern best describes your experiences growing up? Is it the same or different today? How and why?

MindTap®

job on that painting"), (2) acceptance (e.g., "whether you decide to go to college or get a full time job, just know that we support you"), and (3) love (e.g., "I love you no matter what"). Unfortunately, however, not all families engage in healthy communication (Segrin & Flora, 2014).

Social Groups

A **social group** is composed of people who genuinely care about each other and enjoy spending time together (Platow, Grace, & Smithson, 2011). Most of us belong to more than one social group. You may have had a group of friends you hung out with

CBS Photo Archive/Getty Images

Photo 9.1 In what ways might this social group be similar to and different from a family?

social group
comprised of friends who have a genuine concern about each other's welfare and enjoy spending time together

in high school and now another group of friends in college. You may have a group of friends you play softball, tennis, trivia, or video games with regularly. Sometimes people who work together evolve into a social group when they begin to get together for activities outside of the workplace. Popular TV programs such as *New Girl, How I Met Your Mother*, and *Big Bang Theory* provide examples of social groups (Photo 9.1).

Because social groups fulfill our need to belong, communication in them should (1) encourage quieter members to participate in conversations ("Hey, Jules, you haven't had a chance to catch us up on how your Dad is doing"); (2) protect members from playful harassment ("Hey Jenna, cool it, you've been picking on Pam all evening"); and (3) provide opportunities for friends to disclose problems and receive support ("Hey, Zach, I heard your sister was in a bad accident. How's she doing?").

Support Groups

A **support group** is composed of people who come together to provide encouragement, honest feedback, and a safe environment for expressing deeply personal feelings about a problem common to the members. Support groups include, for example, addiction recovery groups like AA (Alcoholics Anonymous), grief counseling support groups, caregiver support groups, and abuse recovery support groups. Until recently, support groups only met face-to-face, but today thousands of online support groups also connect people who have never met face-to-face.

Support group members need to feel safe disclosing highly personal information. So members need to communicate by following the guidelines for comforting we discussed in Chapter 8. These include clarifying supportive intentions, buffering face threats, using other-centered language, framing, and selectively offering advice.

support group
comprised of people who come together to provide encouragement, honest feedback, and a safe environment for expressing deeply personal feelings about a problem common to the members

Interest Groups

An **interest group** is composed of individuals who come together because they share a common interest, hobby, or activity. These groups may be formal such as a 4-H club or community theater troupe or informal like a neighborhood book or gardening club. Some interest groups are externally focused on a common political or social issue and

interest group
comprised of individuals who come together because they share a common concern, hobby, or activity

adopt an agenda to achieve change. MADD (Mothers Against Drunk Driving) is an example. Other interest groups are internally focused on increasing skills or knowledge of their members. Toastmasters, for instance, is focused on helping its members improve their public speaking skills. As is the case with support groups, many interest groups meet regularly online. Meetup.com is an Internet site that helps people find others who share their interests.

Because interest group members share a common passion, members ought to (1) encourage others to share their success stories ("I'm really glad that Brian was able to get Ace Hardware to donate the camp stove supplies for our hiking trip. Brian, can you tell us what you said and did?"), and (2) encourage all members to highlight what they know without demeaning the knowledge or opinions of others ("I really liked hearing Brian's story and I'd like to know how other people approach getting donations.").

Service Groups

service group
comprised of individuals who come together to perform hands-on charitable works or to raise money to help organizations that perform such work

A **service group** is composed of individuals who come together to perform hands-on charitable works or to raise money to help organizations that perform such work. Service groups may be local affiliates of larger secular or religious service organizations like Lions Club International, the Red Cross, the Salvation Army, and Habitat for Humanity. Other service groups are local and function independently. Examples include small soup kitchens and community beautification groups.

Because service groups are both voluntary and task-oriented, members need to be dedicated to the task, as well as sensitive to the emotional needs of others. So communication should (1) be clear about individual tasks, roles, and responsibilities ("Jim, as I recall, you agreed to work on patching the roof"); (2) praise member accomplishments ("I was really impressed with how compassionate you were when you helped Mrs. Smith put on her jacket"); and (3) be polite ("Mary, thank you so much for pitching in to stuff envelopes today. I could not have finished the job without your help.")

Work Groups and Teams

work group
comprised of three or more people formed to solve a problem or complete a task

work group team
a subset of a work group where members also hold themselves mutually accountable

A **work group** is a collection of three or more people formed to work together to complete a specific task. A **work group team** is a subset of a work group where members also hold themselves mutually accountable (Katzenbach & Smith, 2003). Examples of work group teams include class project groups (established to create a joint presentation, paper, or other learning project) and workplace teams (established as needed to perform specific activities in the workplace). Effective work group teams have an appropriate number of members with diverse skills and viewpoints, clearly defined goals, and explicit roles and rules for members (Katzenbach & Smith, 2003).

What is the best size for a work group team? In general, the ideal size for most work group teams is five to seven members (Myers & Anderson, 2008). However, the best size is the smallest number of people capable of effectively achieving the goal (Beebe & Masterson, 2014). As the size of the group increases, the time spent discussing also increases. Smaller groups can make decisions more quickly than larger ones. However, if the goals and issues are complex, a group with more members is more likely to have the breadth of information, knowledge, and skills needed to make high-quality decisions.

heterogeneous group
comprised of individuals with diverse knowledge, perspectives, values, and interests.

Effective work group teams are also composed of people who offer different but relevant knowledge and skills (Beebe & Masterson, 2014). A **heterogeneous group** is usually better than a **homogeneous group**. In homogeneous groups, members are likely to know the same things, come at the problem from the same perspective, and consequently, may overlook some important information or take shortcuts in the problem-solving process. In contrast, members in heterogeneous groups are more likely to have diverse information, perspectives, and values, and consequently, may discuss issues more thoroughly before reaching a decision. For example, a medical group composed of seven nurses might be considered a homogeneous group compared to a group composed of nurses, doctors, nutritionists, and physical therapists. The heterogeneous medical group would probably make a more comprehensive decision about a patient's care than the homogeneous group of nurses.

What are the elements of an effective work group team goal? An effective **work group team goal** is a clearly stated objective desired by enough members to motivate the group to work toward achieving it (Beebe & Masterson, 2014). Effective work group team goals meet four important criteria.

1. **Effective goals are specific.** For example, the crew at a local fast-food restaurant that began with the goal of "increasing profitability" made it more specific in this way: "During the next quarter, the crew will increase profitability by reducing food costs by 1 percent. They will do so by throwing away less food due to precooking."

2. **Effective goals serve a common purpose.** Achieving one goal must not prevent achieving another. For the fast-food crew, all members must believe that reducing the amount of precooked food on hand will not hinder their current level of service.

3. **Effective goals are challenging.** Achieving them will require hard work and team effort.

4. **Effective goals are shared.** People tend to support things they help create. So group members who participate in setting the goals are likely to exert high effort to achieve them as well.

Finally, effective work group teams develop explicit member roles and rules (Belbin, 2010). Because the goals of work group teams are typically quite challenging, all members must understand and perform their specific roles for the group to succeed (Belbin, 2010). These roles and rules are always discussed and sometimes even written down in a formal or informal contract.

Most work group team communication focuses on task-related issues and should (1) update other members on the status of individual efforts ("I want to let you know that I will be about two days late with that feasibility report because the person providing me with the cost data is on vacation"); (2) appropriately credit the contributions of other team members ("Although I am presenting the conclusions today, Len did the initial research and Mavis did the quantitative analysis that led to them"); (3) keep the discussion focused on the task ("Since we've only got 30 minutes together today, let's try to stick to the agenda, ok everyone?"); and (4) seek collaboration to solve problems ("Felicia, I'm stuck and I really need your help.").

Virtual Groups

Until recently, group communication occurred almost exclusively in face-to-face settings. A **virtual group** is one whose members are separated geographically but come together to "meet" through various forms of electronic media. Today we can interact with our

---

homogeneous group
comprised of individuals that share similar knowledge, perspectives, values, and interests

work group team goal
a clearly stated objective desired by enough members to motivate the group to work toward its achievement

virtual group
comprised of members that "meet" via technological media

families, social groups, support groups, interest groups, service groups, and work group teams from different physical locations through e-mail, teleconferences and videoconferences, and online social networks such as LinkedIn, Instagram, Facebook, and Twitter (Timmerman & Scott, 2006). We can even form these virtual groups without ever meeting the other members in person.

virtual group communication
communication that occurs in virtual groups

Since these technologies continue to evolve, research about how communication functions in them is also only just beginning. We do know, however, that effective **virtual group communication** follows the same fundamental principles as effective communication in face-to-face groups but is also unique in several ways (Berry, 2011). Technology makes virtual group communication possible (1) at the same time and location, (2) at the same time but from different locations, (3) at different times but from the same location, and (4) at different times and from different locations. Teleconferences and videoconferences are examples of virtual group communication taking place in **real time**, which means at the same time. Communication in videoconferences most closely resembles group communication in face-to-face settings because participants can interact using both verbal and nonverbal messages. Social networking sites, blogs, and Web sites are examples of virtual group communication that occurs at the same location (on a particular Web page), but not necessarily at the same time. E-mail and threaded discussion boards are examples of virtual group communication that typically occurs at different times. A group member can send a message and wait hours or days before getting a reply.

real time
at the same time

Virtual groups are becoming popular for a number of reasons. First, members can participate across space. That is, the members can participate while in different cities, states, and countries. Second, **asynchronous virtual groups**—those whose members can post and respond to messages at any time—allow members to participate across time. Busy people often struggle to find a meeting time that works for everyone. So a group can "meet" via a threaded discussion instead. Third, virtual meetings can save money members may have spent traveling to a specific meeting site, as well as paying for accommodations, meals, and parking.

asynchronous virtual groups
virtual groups where members interact across time

These benefits can also come with potential costs. For example, communication problems can impact both task and relational outcomes. Face-to-face groups are often more dedicated to accomplishing a goal, to fostering positive relationships, and to building cohesion than virtual groups (Kimble, 2011). Thus, we offer a few guidelines to overcome these challenges and foster effective communication when participating in virtual groups.

1. **Use the richest form of technology available.** While e-mails and threaded discussions allow people the freedom to communicate at their own convenience, these technologies also convey the fewest social nonverbal cues. When possible, try to meet via videoconference to both see and hear the other group members.

2. **Make sure all members are both equipped and trained to use the technology.** Don't assume that all members know how to use the technology or are aware of all of its capabilities. Although this is crucial for virtual work groups and teams, it is equally important for any group that chooses to meet online.

3. **Create opportunities for group members to become acquainted, develop and maintain social bonds, and build trust.** Just as members of face-to-face groups take time to socialize and get to know one another, so is doing so important when meeting virtually.

4. **Develop ground rules.** Because mis-understandings can abound when communicating via technology, virtual groups will operate most effectively when rules for communicating are set up at the outset (Photo 9.2). These rules are often referred to as **netiquette**. They may include, for example, being courteous and respectful, being attentive and focused (e.g., not checking e-mail during the meeting), using emoticons and imogees, keeping messages short, and being patient with new users (Shoemaker-Galloway, 2007).

5. **Create regular opportunities to evaluate the technology and use of it.** Regularly scheduled surveys of group members can identify emerging problems some members may be experiencing in order to correct them before they undermine the group's goals.

Now that we have illustrated some different types of groups and the role communication plays in them, let's turn to a discussion of the similarities among healthy groups regardless of type.

Photo 9.2 What are some specific communication strategies you should follow when meeting virtually?

netiquette
rules for communicating respectfully and effectively in virtual groups

Characteristics of Healthy Groups

Healthy groups are formed around a constructive purpose and are characterized by ethical goals, interdependence, cohesiveness, productive norms, accountability, and synergy.

healthy group
formed based on a constructive purpose and characterized by ethical goals, interdependence, cohesiveness, productive norms, accountability, and synergy

Healthy Groups Have Ethical Goals

The goals of healthy groups are ethical. That is, they are honest, upright, and honorable. Sometimes a group's goal is unethical and other times fulfilling the goal would require some or all group members to behave in unethical ways. For example, criminal gangs can be highly effective but unethical groups. They may make lots of money, but do so at the expense of society at large and often by risking the welfare of members. In this chapter's *Communicating in the World* feature, "The Dark Side of Online Social Groups," you can read about online groups with unethical goals. By contrast, healthy groups have goals that benefit the members and the larger society. Fulfilling these goals may require sacrifice and hard work, but accomplishing them does not depend on illegal, harmful, or unethical behavior.

Healthy Groups Are Interdependent

In **interdependent groups**, members rely on each other's skills and knowledge to accomplish the ultimate group goal(s). One concrete way to understand interdependence is to observe a musical group, for instance, a symphony orchestra. One reason the music we hear is so beautiful has to do with the fact that the violins, violas, cellos, and basses not only sound different but each performs a different part made up of different notes. If any of the musicians did not perform their part well, the beautiful sound would be compromised.

interdependent group
members rely on each other's skills and knowledge to accomplish the group goals

The Dark Side of Online Social Groups

Christopher LaMarca/Redux

Imogen D'Arcy was only 13 years old when she hanged herself in her bathroom, because despite being described as fit and well-liked, she felt fat and ugly (Stokes, 2008). Laura Dunnegan developed an eating disorder at age seven. Sixteen years later, she sees her disorder as a "lifestyle option" rather than as a disease that may kill her (Croucher, 2008). What do these girls have in common? Both regularly visited Web sites where they received encouragement and reinforcement of their distorted self-images.

The Internet provides a space for individuals to form social groups with others who share interests or concerns. However, not all of these virtual group spaces demonstrate the characteristics of healthy groups. For example, the "pro-ana" (promoting anorexia nervosa) sites, such as the types D'Arcy visited before she died and that Dunnegan frequently visits, are online spaces where people with eating disorders can find support and share their experiences without judgment. On the surface, these sites may seem to provide a positive environment, however, they often encourage people to develop and continue dangerous behaviors. For example, pro-ana sites often feature advice on how to starve yourself effectively or photos of extremely underweight women as "thinspiration" for members.

C. J. Pascoe (2008), a sociologist who studies teenagers and digital media at the University of California, Berkeley, explains that, before the Internet, anorexics had to check into a psychiatric hospital to find others like themselves. Now, they can find community without seeking treatment. In the *British Journal of Social Psychology*, David Giles (2006) suggests that "The Internet offers a perfect sanctuary for people with interests that are unacceptable to the general public. By serving as a counter-culture to official discourse around health and illness, the Web may serve to undermine the professionals so that more and more people find ways of opting out of conventional society (e.g., health care) if they can locate supportive communities online" (p. 2).

On the other hand, online outlets for social groups can also be a good thing. One example is the *It Gets Better* project. The Web site was originally created in 2010 by syndicated columnist and author Dan Savage in response to a rash of bullying-related suicides among lesbian, gay, bisexual, and transgendered (LGBT) youth. Today, the site features over 50,000 user-created videos of support for LGBT teens facing harassment to illustrate that it WILL get better once they get through the teen years. Ultimately online social groups can be "a double-edged sword. For better or for worse, kids who are marginalized can find community online" (Pascoe, 2008, p. 2).

Do you think the pros of online social groups outweigh the cons? Why or why not?

MindTap®

Likewise, in any group, if one person tries to do all the "work," or if anyone performs their work poorly, or if everyone does the same piece of "work" while other pieces are left unattended, that group is not interdependent and also not as effective as it could be.

Healthy Groups Are Cohesive

cohesiveness
the force that brings group members closer together

Cohesiveness is the force that brings group members closer together (Eisenberg, 2007). In a highly cohesive group, members genuinely respect each other and work cooperatively to reach the group's goals. Because cohesiveness is such an important characteristic of healthy groups, many newly formed groups often engage in **team-building activities** designed to build rapport and develop trust among members (Midura & Glover, 2005). Five factors help foster cohesiveness in groups. First, members are attracted to its purpose. Daniel, for example, joined the local Lions Club because he was attracted to its community service mission. Second, groups are generally more cohesive when membership is voluntary. If Daniel had joined the Lions Club because he felt obligated to do so, cohesiveness would have

Steve Debenport/Getty Images

suffered. Third, members feel safe expressing themselves even when they disagree with others. Fourth, members support, encourage, and provide positive feedback to each other. Finally, members perceive the group to be achieving its goals and celebrate their accomplishments. For example, when the local chapter of the Lions Club surpassed its previous fundraising record for the annual Journey for Sight 5K Community Run, the group celebrated the accomplishment with a picnic in the park.

Photo 9.3 Most clubs follow a set of norms to keep meetings on track. What norms might this group follow and why?

team-building activities
activities designed to build rapport and develop trust among members

Healthy Groups Develop and Abide by Productive Norms

Norms are expectations about the way group members are to behave. Healthy groups develop norms that help them achieve their goals and foster cohesiveness (Levine, 2013). Norms can be developed through formal discussions or informal group processes. Some groups choose to formulate explicit **ground rules**, prescribed behaviors designed to help the group meet its goals and conduct its conversations. These may include sticking to the agenda, refraining from interrupting others, keeping comments brief, expecting everyone to participate, focusing on issues rather than personalities, and sharing decision making.

In most groups, however, norms evolve informally. When we join a new group, we act in ways that were considered appropriate in the groups we participated in previously. When members of our new group respond positively to our actions, an informal norm is established. For example, suppose Daniel and two others show up late for a Lions Club meeting. If the latecomers are greeted with disapproving glares, then Daniel and the others will learn that this group has an on-time norm. A group may never actually discuss informal norms, but members understand what they are, behave in line with them, and educate new members about them.

We sometimes find ourselves struggling to act appropriately in different groups because each seems to have different norms. This can be especially true for people who move from one country to another, as was the case for Dr. Mina Tsay, an assistant professor at Boston University who emigrated from Taiwan to the United States and maintains strong ties with groups in both countries. She describes her experiences in this chapter's *Diverse Voices* feature.

norms
expectations for the way group members are to behave

ground rules
prescribed behaviors designed to help the group meet its goals and conduct its conversations

APPLY IT

What were your family ground rules growing up (e.g., rules about eating meals together, curfews, playing video games)?

DIVERSE VOICES

Managing Competing Group Norms

by Mina Tsay, Ph.D.
Assistant Professor of Communication, Boston University

Although I emigrated from Taiwan to the United States when I was only two years old, my memories are still surprisingly vivid. What I remember most is clinging to my mother as we faced our first blustery winter in Boston, Massachusetts. As a naturalized Chinese American growing up in Boston, I faced numerous challenges in managing competing group norms.

The first conflicting norm I remember struggling with was whether to speak English or Mandarin, which is my native language. I always spoke Mandarin at home but was expected to speak English at school. My parents made it very clear that they did not want me to forget how to speak Mandarin. In fact, this norm was so important to them that they enrolled my sister and me in a Chinese school in a Boston suburb when I was in third grade.

I must admit I did not fully appreciate the heavy workload at Chinese school. But, I gradually came to enjoy learning calligraphy, diabolo, literature, and dance. Learning these customs was exceptionally rewarding, but being enrolled in both schools made it difficult for me to shift from the norms of one school to those of another. I often felt conflicted. In Chinese school, I became grounded in and celebrated my cultural roots. Then, when I went to American school, I found myself compromising some of my Chinese cultural norms to be accepted by my American peers.

Adjusting to competing norms at Chinese and American schools here in the United States was demanding, but I also faced a similar challenge when I traveled to Taiwan to visit relatives. In Taiwan, I would often sense a strong pull to adhere to norms in the other direction. On one hand, it was comforting to know that my extended family held similar politeness, spiritual, and collectivist norms. On the other hand, my relatives would sometimes say that I was acting more American than Chinese. At times like these, I again felt the struggle of trying to adhere to competing norms.

Back in the United States as a college student at the University of Michigan and then at Pennsylvania State University, I also recall feeling torn between competing norms when Chinese international students would make remarks that I had become "Westernized." Those comments made me feel apprehensive about whether I was losing aspects of my cultural identity. Such realizations encouraged me to seek ways to consciously integrate the norms of two worlds in order to maintain my unique sense of self. As a result, I have negotiated standards and customs to both preserve my own Chinese norms and assimilate to American norms with regard to independence, discipline, religion, group identification, and life goals.

As a Chinese American, I continue to negotiate between competing norms, trying my best to integrate norms of both cultural worlds. When I meet new people and encounter new situations, I consciously try to adapt my behavioral norms in order to "fit in." Although these cultural negotiations are challenges, I choose to view them as opportunities to develop and cultivate a more refined sense of self. After all, I am a Chinese American, which means I honor and value both sets of norms, those grounded in my Chinese roots and those I have acquired as an American naturalized citizen.

Used with permission.

Healthy Groups Are Accountable

Accountability means all group members are held responsible for adhering to the group norms and working toward the group's goal. This means a group will sanction a member who violates a group norm. The severity of the sanction depends on the importance of the norm, the extent of the violation, and the status of the person who violated it. Violating a norm that is central to a group's performance or cohesiveness will generally receive a harsher sanction than violating a norm that is less central. Violations by a newcomer also generally receive more lenient sanctions. As a new Lions Club member, for example, Daniel's sanction for arriving late was merely a stern look from the others. Group members who have achieved higher status in the group also tend to receive more lenient sanctions or even escape sanctioning altogether.

Being accountable can also mean changing counterproductive norms. For example, suppose a few folks tell jokes, stories, and generally ignore attempts by others to begin more serious discussion about community service issues at the Lions Club meetings. If the group does not effectively sanction this behavior, then it could become a counterproductive group norm. As a result, work toward the group's goals could be delayed, set aside, or perhaps even forgotten. If counterproductive behavior continues for several meetings and becomes a norm, it will be very difficult (though not impossible) to change.

What can a group member do to try to change a norm? We can help change a counterproductive norm by (1) observing the norm and its outcome, (2) describing the results of the norm to the group, and (3) soliciting opinions of other members of the group. For instance, Daniel observed that every Lions Club meeting began 15–20 minutes late and that this was making it necessary to schedule additional meetings. When members became frustrated about holding extra meetings, he could bring up his observations and the consequences and ask the group for their reaction.

Photo 9.4 Have you ever been on an underdog team that went on to win a big game or championship? Do you think synergy played a role? Why or why not?

accountability
being held responsible for adhering to the group norms and working toward the group's goal

Healthy Groups Are Synergetic

The old saying "two heads are better than one" captures an important characteristic of healthy groups. **Synergy** is the multiplying force of a group of individuals working together, which results in a combined effort greater than any of the parts (Photo 9.4) (Goffey & Jones, 2013). For instance, the sports record books are filled with "no-name teams" that have won major championships over opponents with more talented players. A healthy group can develop a collective intelligence and dynamic energy that translates into an outcome that exceeds what even a highly talented individual could produce. When a group has ethical goals and is interdependent, cohesive, and held accountable to productive norms, the group is well on its way toward achieving synergy.

synergy
the multiplying force of a group working together that results in a combined effort greater than any of the parts

Photo and Co/The Image Bank/Getty Images

Stages of Group Formation and Development

Just as interpersonal relationships go through identifiable life cycles, so too do groups move through overlapping stages of development. Although numerous models have been proposed to describe these stages, Tuckman's (1965) model remains the most widely accepted because it identifies central issues facing a group at each stage. In this section, we describe each of these stages and the nature of communication during each one.

Forming

Forming Stage
characterized by orientation, testing, and dependence

Storming Stage
characterized by conflict and power plays as members seek to have their ideas accepted and to find their place within the group's power structure

groupthink
a deterioration of mental efficiency, reality testing, and moral judgment that results from in-group pressure to conform

Norming Stage
the stage during which the group solidifies its rules for behavior, resulting in greater trust and motivation to achieve the group goal

The **Forming Stage** is characterized by orientation, testing, and dependence. Members try to understand precisely what the goal is, what role they will play in reaching it, and what the other members are like. As the goal becomes clearer, members assess how their skills, talents, and abilities might be used in accomplishing it. Group interactions are typically polite and tentative because members want to be perceived as flexible and likable. During the Forming Stage, you should communicate a positive attitude; refrain from making abrasive or disagreeable comments; self-disclose appropriately benign information and feelings; and demonstrate open-minded and genuine interest in others (White, 2008).

Storming

As members figure out the goal and become comfortable with each other, they begin to express their honest opinions and vie for power and position. This **Storming Stage** is characterized by conflict and power plays as members seek to have their ideas accepted and to find their place within the group's power structure (Photo 9.5). The politeness exhibited during forming may be replaced by pointedly aggressive exchanges between some members. Members may also take sides and form coalitions. Although storming occurs in all groups, some groups manage it better than others. When storming is severe, it can threaten the group's survival. However, if a group does not storm, it may experience **groupthink**, a deterioration of mental efficiency, reality testing, and moral judgment that results from in-group pressure to conform (Janis, 1982). To avoid groupthink, encourage constructive disagreement, avoid name-calling and inflammatory language, and use active listening skills with an emphasis on paraphrasing and honest questioning (White, 2009).

Photo 9.5 Why is storming an important stage of group development?

Troels Graugaard/iStockphoto.com

Norming

The **Norming Stage** is characterized by increased cohesion, collaboration, and motivation to achieve the group goal. Having expressed honest opinions, resolved major differences, and sorted out specific roles, members become loyal to each other and to the group goal. During this stage, members come to appreciate their differences, strengthen their relationships, and freely express their ideas and opinions. Members accept the norms established by the group and provide positive and constructive feedback to each other.

Performing

The **Performing Stage** is characterized by harmony, productivity, problem solving, and shared leadership. During this stage, the group capitalizes on the skills, knowledge, and abilities of all members to work toward achieving its goal. Groups cannot achieve their full potential in this stage unless they have successfully resolved storming conflicts and developed productive norms.

Adjourning and Transforming

The **Adjourning Stage** is characterized by celebrating goal accomplishment and each member's role in achieving it, reflecting on what they learned, and disengaging. Sometimes a group will formally disband but a few members will continue to interact interpersonally with one another. A group that stays together and also establishes a new goal is in the **Transforming Stage.** The new goal will inevitably cause the members to revisit the earlier stages of group development, but the cohesion, trust, and norms developed earlier are likely to help the group move quickly and more smoothly through them.

Conflict in Groups

Just as conflict is inevitable in interpersonal relationships, so is it to be expected in groups (Bradley, Postlethwaite, Klotz, Hamdani, & Brown, 2012). Groups that experience no conflict are likely to engage in groupthink. Groups that experience conflict but fail to manage it effectively are unlikely to ever achieve their goal. Conflict can be directed toward other members (interpersonal conflict) or ideas (issues) or both (Li & Hambrick, 2005; Wilmot & Hocker, 2007). The key is to manage conflict effectively. Let's look at three types of group conflict and some communication strategies to manage them effectively.

Pseudo-Conflict

Pseudo-conflict occurs when group members who actually agree about something believe they disagree due to poor communication. Since *pseudo* means *fake,* the perceived conflict is essentially a misperception. So, to manage or resolve pseudo-conflict, employ the effective listening, perception-checking, and paraphrasing skills we discussed in Chapters 6, 7, and 8. Doing so will reveal misinterpretations and result in a moment of revelation that you are actually on the same page after all.

Issue-Related Group Conflict

Issue-related group conflict occurs when two or more group members' goals, ideas, or opinions about the topic are incompatible. One major advantage of collaboration is the synergy that occurs as a result of expressing diverse points of view. So issue-related conflict can be good when handled appropriately. To manage issue-related conflict effectively, begin by clarifying your position and the position of the other group member(s) using perception-checking and paraphrasing skills. Then, as we discussed in Chapter 8, express your position using assertive communication supported with facts rather than opinions or feelings. Finally, make the conflict a group discussion by asking others for input regarding it, and if possible, postpone making a final decision until a later date.

Performing Stage
the stage during which the skills, knowledge, and abilities of all members are combined to overcome obstacles and meet goals successfully

Adjourning Stage
the stage during which members assign meaning to what they have done and determine how to end or maintain interpersonal relations they have developed

Transforming Stage
when a group continues to exist with a new goal

APPLY IT

Identify a group you've recently joined. What stage is the group in and why do you think so?

MindTap®

pseudo-conflict
when group members who actually agree about something believe they disagree due to poor communication

issue-related group conflict
when two or more group members' goals, ideas, or opinions about the topic are incompatible

Doing so provides time for doing additional research to make an informed decision and for tensions among members to lessen.

Personality-Related Group Conflict

Personality-related group conflict occurs when two or more group members become defensive because they feel like they are being attacked. Typically, personality-related conflicts are rooted in a power struggle (Sell, Lovaglia, Mannix, Samuelson, & Wilson, 2004).

Personality-related conflicts sometimes emerge from poorly managed issue-related conflict. For example, Jack thought the group should do something fun to celebrate the end of finals. Jill thought they should do a service project to give something back to the community before everyone headed home for the summer. What began as an issue-related conflict turned sour as Jill exclaimed, "Jack, all you ever think about is yourself. You are so self-centered!" and Jack retorted with, "You are such a dork, Jill. You don't even know HOW to have fun. That's why you end up sitting alone in your room so much!" Factions emerged and, ultimately, some group members sided with Jill and others with Jack. The group ended up doing nothing to mark the successful completion of the semester. Had the group handled the issue-related conflict effectively, they could probably have done both. Instead, they did neither and departed feeling frustrated and dissatisfied.

To manage personality-related conflict effectively, try to turn the conflict into an issue-related problem to be solved rather than a conflict someone has to win and someone has to lose. Develop rules that allow for differences of opinion. Be descriptive rather than evaluative. Use "I" language and perception-checking. Finally, if the conflict isn't central to the group's goal, agree to disagree and move on.

Culture and Conflict

People belonging to different cultural and co-cultural groups tend to abide by unique communication norms. Keep in mind that cultural differences may exist when managing conflict in groups, as well. For instance, people who identify with individualistic cultural norms tend to use direct verbal methods to manage conflict whereas those who identify with collectivist norms tend to use indirect nonverbal methods for doing so (Ting-Toomey & Chung, 2012). Knowing that cultural differences may exist can help you select communication strategies for managing group conflict effectively and for interpreting the messages of others accurately, as well.

Virtual Groups and Conflict

Managing conflict effectively in virtual groups poses an additional set of challenges because it can be more difficult to catch the subtle meanings of group members' messages. This is due, in part, to the fact that most technology channels reduce our ability to send and receive nonverbal messages, particularly emotional and relational cues. Most of us use emoticons and acronyms to represent missing nonverbal cues; however, a smiley face can be offered sincerely or sarcastically and it can be difficult for the receiver to ascertain the difference. Unfortunately, conflict goes unresolved more often in virtual groups than in face-to-face groups because in most virtual settings we cannot see the nonverbal reactions of frustration that are visible when interacting in person (Walther, 2013). However, when communication is effective, the bonds among members of virtual groups can be even stronger than those in face-to-face ones (Jiang, Bazarova, & Hancock, 2011; Wang, Walther, & Hancock, 2009).

So, to manage potential conflict effectively in virtual groups, work to overcome its limitations by making a conscious effort to communicate both what you *think* and

WHAT WOULD YOU DO?

A Question of Ethics

The community service and outreach committee of Students in Communication was meeting to determine what cause should benefit from their annual fund-raiser, a talent contest.

"So," said Mark, "does anyone have any ideas about whose cause we should sponsor?"

"Well," replied Glenna, "I think we should give it to a group that's doing literacy work."

"Sounds good to me," replied Mark.

"My aunt works at the Boardman Center as the literacy coordinator, so why don't we just adopt them?" asked Glenna.

"Gee, I don't know much about the group," said Reed.

"Come on, you know, they help people learn how to read," replied Glenna sarcastically.

"Well, I was kind of hoping we'd take a look at sponsoring the local teen runaway center," offered Angelo.

"Listen, if your aunt works at the Boardman Center," commented Leticia, "let's go with it."

"Right," said Pablo, "that's good enough for me."

"Yeah," replied Heather, "let's do it and get out of here."

"I hear what you're saying, Heather," Mark responded, "I've got plenty of other stuff to do."

"No disrespect meant to Glenna, but wasn't the Boardman Center in the news because of questionable use of funds?" countered Angelo. "Do we really know enough about them?"

"OK," said Mark, "enough discussion. I've got to get to class. All in favor of the literacy program at the Boardman Center indicate by saying 'aye.' I think we've got a majority. Sorry, Angelo—you can't win them all."

"I wish all meetings went this smoothly," Heather said to Glenna as they left the room. "I mean, that was really a good meeting."

Regardless of whether the meeting went smoothly, is there any ethical problem with this process? Explain.

MindTap®

---

how you *feel* about a topic. You can do so most clearly in your verbal messages although emoticons and acronyms can also help when used deliberately for such purposes.

Reflection and Assessment

A group is more than a mere assembly of people. A group is a collection of three or more people who share a common purpose or goal. We all interact in many different types of groups including families, social groups, support groups, interest groups, service groups, as well as work groups and teams. We may participate in any of these groups in person or virtually through the use of a variety of technologies. To assess how well you've learned what we addressed in this chapter, answer the following questions. If you have trouble answering any of them, go back and review that material. Once you can answer each question accurately, you are ready to move ahead to read the next chapter.

1. How are family, social, support, interest, and service groups both similar and different?

2. What are work groups and work group teams?

3. What are the characteristics of healthy groups?

4. How do groups develop over time?

5. Why is conflict important in groups and how can you manage it effectively?

COMMUNICATE!

RESOURCE AND ASSESSMENT CENTER

MindTap®

Now that you have read Chapter 9, go to your MindTap for *Communicate!* for quick access to the electronic resources that accompany this text.

Applying What You've Learned

Impromptu Speech Activity

Identify a group you enjoy being a part of. Prepare and present a 2- to 3-minute speech describing the group and why you enjoy being part of it based on the characteristics of healthy groups discussed in this chapter.

Assessment Activities

1. Group Membership Identify two groups (for example, a sports team, study group, community group, or work group team) to which you belong; one should have a homogeneous membership and the other a heterogeneous membership.

Analyze the demographic differences in each group. When you have completed this analysis, write a paragraph that discusses cohesiveness in each group. How cohesive is each group? Are both groups equally cohesive? Was it easier to establish cohesiveness in one of the groups? What real or potential pitfalls result from the level of cohesiveness in each group? Prepare a short 400- to 500-word essay explaining what you discovered.

2. Group Formation and Development Think of a group to which you have belonged for less than three months. If you have an assigned group in this course, you may use it. Now, write a 400- to 500-word essay that begins by identifying the stage of development the group is currently in and then describe how this group transitioned through each of the previous stages of group development. What event(s) do you recall as turning points, marking the group's movement from one stage to another? Has the group become stuck in a stage, or has it developed smoothly? What factors contributed to that? What can you do to help this group succeed in the stage it is in and to transition to the next stage?

Skill-Building Activities

1. Classroom Norms Identify 4 to 5 communication norms for this class. They may be verbal or nonverbal, as well as explicit or implicit. Then on a scale of 1 through 5 (with 5 being "excellent"), rate yourself on each. For ratings lower than "5," write down a specific strategy you will employ to improve your rating.

2. Nonverbal Cues This activity is designed to help you make conscious decisions about nonverbal cues in face-to-face groups and virtual groups. For each emotion or message listed, identify how you will demonstrate it when communicating with a group in a face-to-face setting and in a virtual setting.

Emotion/Message	Face-To-Face Group	Virtual Group
Agreement		
Disagreement		
Frustration		
Pleasure		
Excitement		
Boredom		
Hurt feelings		

Group Leadership and Problem Solving

MindTap®

Start with a quick warm-up activity.

Members of the campus chapter of the Public Relations Student Society of America (PRSSA) chatted while Dolores, the chapter president, distributed the agenda. The recession had taken its toll on the chapter's membership, and the original budget was now unrealistic. They would have to cut corners somewhere to make ends meet. Dolores began, "Well, we all know why we're here this evening. We've got to decide what to do to balance our budget. It's not going to be fun, but let's get started." After a few seconds of silence, Dolores asked, "Drew, what ideas do you have?"

"Well, I don't know," Drew replied, "I haven't really given it much thought." (*There were nods of agreement.*)

"Well to be honest," Jeremy said, "I'm not sure I even remember what our projected expenses are."

"But when I sent you the e-mail reminder about the meeting, I attached the agenda and a detailed spreadsheet and some questions to think about before this meeting," Dolores replied.

"Oh, I'm so sorry, Dolores," Bethany said. "I read the part about the meeting, but I guess I didn't get a chance to look at the attachments."

10

Hill Street Studios/Blend Images/Getty Images

Dolores responded, "We've got some tough decisions to make. Do we cut our donations to the food pantry? Do we cut travel support for those planning to attend the annual convention? Do we stop printing our monthly newsletter and just offer the online version? Do we raise our dues? Do we add another fundraising project?"

"Anything you think would be appropriate is OK with me," Mina replied.

"Well, I'm not comfortable making these decisions alone. Let's each of us plan to review the materials I sent and meet again tomorrow night with some ideas, okay?" Dolores suggested. (*There were nods of agreement.*) "Meeting adjourned."

As the group dispersed, Dolores overheard Drew whisper to Mina, "These meetings sure are a waste of time, aren't they?"

Perhaps you have attended a meeting like this one and felt just as frustrated. When group meetings are ineffective, it is easy to point the finger at the leader. But as was the case with this group, the responsibility for the "waste of time" lies not with one person; instead, it is part of the complex nature of making decisions in groups. Although working in groups can have its disadvantages, it is the preferred approach in business and industry today (Levi, 2013; Williams, 2013). Business leaders realize that when groups work effectively to solve problems, they generate greater breadth and depth of ideas, promote positive group morale, and increase productivity. For these reasons, you can expect to work in groups many times throughout your life.

This chapter focuses on effective leadership and problem solving in groups. We begin by discussing what effective leadership means and the responsibilities of every group member in achieving it. Then we illustrate how shared leadership and effective communication plays out before, during, and after group meetings. From there we teach you a systematic problem-solving process that leads to good decision-making. Finally, we propose methods for communicating your results with others and evaluating group effectiveness.

Leadership

leadership
a process whereby an individual influences a group of individuals to achieve a common goal

formal leader
a person designated or elected to facilitate the group process

informal emergent leaders
members who help lead the group to achieve different leadership functions

shared leadership functions
the sets of roles that group members perform to facilitate the work of the group and help maintain harmonious relationships between members

role
a specific communication behavior that group members perform

Leadership is a process "whereby an individual influences a group of individuals to achieve a common goal" (Northouse, 2012, p. 5). When we think of leadership, we typically think of a person who is in charge (Gardner, 2011). In fact, scholars once thought that leaders were "born"—that some people inherited traits that made them naturally suited to be leaders. This trait theory approach was called "The Great Man Theory of Leadership" (Kippenberger, 2002). Later, scholars believed that different leadership styles were more or less effective based on the goal and situation. These classic theories suggest that *leadership* is enacted by one *person*. Today, however, we understand leadership as a set of communication functions performed by any group member at various times based on each one's unique strengths and expertise (Fairhurst, 2011; Frey & Sunwulf, 2005). So although a group may have a **formal leader**, a person designated or elected to oversee the group process, a series of **informal emergent leaders**, members who help lead the group to achieve different leadership functions, make for the most effective leadership in groups.

Shared leadership functions are the sets of roles you and other members perform to facilitate the work of the group and help maintain harmonious relationships among members (Photo 10.1). A **role** is a specific communication behavior group members perform to address the needs of the group at any given point in time. When these roles are performed effectively, the group functions smoothly. Shared leadership functions may be categorized as task, maintenance, or procedural roles.

Task Roles

Task leadership roles help the group acquire, process, or apply information that contributes directly to completing a task or goal.

- Information and opinion givers provide content for the discussion. People who perform this role are well informed and share what they know with the group. "Well, the articles I read all conclude that . . ." and "Based on how much money our club raised for the Ronald McDonald House doing the dance-a-thon last year, we could . . ." are statements typical of information and opinion givers.

- Information and opinion seekers probe others for their ideas and opinions. Typical comments by those performing this role include "Before going further, what information do we have about how raising fees is likely to affect membership?" or "How do other members feel about the idea of doing another dance-a-thon?"

- Information and opinion analyzers help the group scrutinize the content and reasoning, and help members understand the hidden assumptions in their statements. Information and opinion analyzers make statements such as "Drew, that's one good example. Can you give us some others?"

Maintenance Roles

Maintenance leadership roles help the group to develop and maintain cohesion, commitment, and positive working relationships.

- Supporters encourage others. When someone comments, supporters may smile, nod, or vigorously shake their heads. They might also say things like "Good point, Mina," "I really like that idea, Drew," or "Wow, Dolores, you've really done your homework."

- Interpreters use their knowledge about the social and cultural diversity in the group to help members understand each other (Jackson & Joshi, 2011). For example, an interpreter might say privately to Drew, "Since Mina is Chinese, when she says she will think about the dance-a-thon idea, she might actually not support it but doesn't want to embarrass you in front of the others." When there is no interpreter and members come from different cultures, effective group process can suffer. This was the case for Lily Herakova when she came to the United States from Bulgaria to study. You can read Lily's story in the *Diverse Voices* feature in this chapter.

- Harmonizers help resolve conflicts. Harmonizers are likely to make statements such as "Cool it, everybody. We're coming up with some really great ideas. Let's not criticize any of them until after we thoughtfully consider them."

- Mediators help the group find a mutually acceptable (win–win) resolution. Mediators do this by maintaining neutrality,

task leadership roles
help a group acquire, process, or apply information that contributes directly to completing a task or goal

APPLY IT

Which task roles do you believe yourself to be good at and not-so-good at? Why?

MindTap

maintenance leadership roles
help a group develop and maintain cohesion, commitment, and positive working relationships

Photo 10.1 Some group members provide information to the group, others help maintain harmonious relations among the group members, and still others help the group stay on track. Which roles do you usually assume?

Pressmaster/Shutterstock.com

keeping the discussion focused, and identifying areas of common ground. As a mediator, Bethany might say, "So, we've been talking about balancing our budget by holding a dance-a-thon, a 5K fun run, and a raffle. It looks like we all agree that we should do a fundraiser to help balance our budget."

- Tension relievers help relieve stress among members through humor. We know that humor "facilitates communication, builds relationships, reduces stress, provides perspective, and promotes attending and energizes" (Sultanoff, 1993, para 2). *Fortune* 500 companies such as General Electric, AT&T, Lockheed, and IBM all emphasize the value of workplace humor in their training programs. A tension reliever might tell a joke, kid around, or tell a lighthearted story. Although the tension reliever momentarily distracts the group from its task, this action helps the group remain cohesive.

DIVERSE VOICES

The Effects of Cultural Diversity When Problem Solving in Groups

by Lily Herakova

I'll never forget the day—it must have been early October—in the rural Minnesota town where I had arrived from Bulgaria to pursue my dreams of attaining a diverse and challenging education was still holding on to the warm traces of summer. In history class that day, the professor assigned us to work in what he called "problem-solving groups." We were to review each other's papers and offer suggestions for improvement. He said, "Use this not only as an editing exercise, but as a problem-solving activity. I want you to rely on your group partners' responses to move toward solutions of problems you might be having in your papers."

The bright sunshine outside the classroom window carried me away and, in my mind, I was back in my parents' bedroom in Bulgaria. That was where our family computer was and where, consequently, I did a lot of my paper writing and editing. Although I hadn't ever been asked to do so in a class with my peers before, I thought to myself: "I know how to do this. I've done it plenty of times. In fact, it's kind of cool that professors here in the United States allow us time in class to 'problem-solve' and learn from each other." Confident in my understanding, I began reading my classmates' papers. I was going to help "solve problems" and help my group mates improve their papers.

I was fairly confident because back home in Bulgaria my friends and I often reviewed each others' papers and offered suggestions for improvement. Although I had never heard of the concept of "problem solving in groups," it seemed to me I actually had experience in doing so. You see, in Bulgaria computers and printers were scarce and it cost a lot of money to hire someone to type and print your term paper. So my parents agreed to let my friends use our computer to type and print their papers. Because classes in Bulgaria were usually large lectures where we rarely knew our professors, our insecurities about expectations abounded. Our collaborative paper writing was our way of checking perceptions in terms of identifying and defining the goals (e.g., problem) of the assignment, getting information from each other (e.g., analyzing the problem), and developing papers that met the assignment guidelines (e.g., solution). So, we did actually solve problems in groups. It was just something my friends and I did informally as opposed to as an in-class activity.

In our informal problem-solving sessions, my Bulgarian classmates and I would offer conflicting opinions, argue, and laugh about our "mistakes." We straightforwardly pointed out when we thought something in the text was wrong, and quietly

continued

swallowed our pride as the others made candid comments and offered constructive criticism. For example, members might say, "This sentence doesn't make any sense," "It's grammatically weird," "It's completely missing a verb," or "How is this even relevant?" Responses to this feedback ranged from anger—"I give up! No one seems to get me!"—to much quieter resignation—"Fine, I'll just do it your way. . . ." Most of the time, though, reactions fell somewhere in between. We often dove into long conversations about what someone actually wanted to say and why it wasn't coming through that way on paper.

Though sometimes painful to hear, more often than not, these group sessions helped me. Comments sometimes hurt my pride but often deepened the analysis and always clarified my writing. Ultimately, we all benefitted because we produced papers that usually met and often exceeded the expectations of the instructor.

So, in history class that day in rural Minnesota, I felt I had the proper experience to participate effectively in what he called "problem-solving" groups! I proceeded confidently to read the papers. When I read one of the papers and it was mostly composed of incomplete sentences, I said to the author, "This will make so much more sense if you would write in complete sentences. It's kind of hard to get what you mean when you're missing verbs." In retrospect, I only remember what I said because of the reaction that followed. She immediately raised her hand to call the instructor over to our group and said, "I don't know why you let her respond to our papers. She's not even a native English speaker, and she's telling me I don't know how to write! I want someone else to read my paper." I believed I was acting appropriately in my role as an information analyzer, which was what our instructor expected us to do. My group member, however, was unwilling to listen (regardless of whether I may have been correct) because English was not my first language.

To this day, I don't know for certain if her reaction was due to cultural differences (perhaps ethnocentrism), an inability to accept feedback (especially accepting constructive criticism), or some other issue. Throughout the years, however, this experience has stayed with me as an unresolved confusion—why did my nationality matter in terms of functioning as an analyzer in the group? Did it somehow automatically disqualify me from having a good command of the English language or a good understanding of history? I could have taken her response personally and been hurt by it, but, interestingly, this was not my reaction. Instead, I keep this question in the forefront of my mind when asked to work in a group to solve problems: How can we problem solve together without creating new problems out of our good-natured attempts to "help," especially when cultural diversity might play a role?

Used with permission of author.

Procedural Roles

Procedural leadership roles provide logistical support and record the group's accomplishments and decisions.

procedural leadership roles *provide logistical support and record the group's accomplishments and decisions*

- Logistics coordinators arrange for appropriate spaces for group meetings, procure the supplies and equipment needed, and manage other details to meet the group's physical needs (Photo 10.2). The logistics coordinator's leadership role is usually carried out behind the scenes, but is crucial to a group's success.

- Expediters keep track of the group's objectives and help move the group through the agenda. When the group strays, expediters make statements like "Let's see, aren't we still trying to find out whether these are the only ideas we should be considering?"

Photo 10.2 A good logistics coordinator leads by providing for the physical needs of the group and its members. Can you think of a group experience you have had in which no one provided this type of leadership?

minutes
a public written record of the group's activities

APPLY IT

What procedural roles do you believe yourself to be good at and not-so-good at? Why?

MindTap

- Gatekeepers make sure all members have an opportunity to participate. If one or two members begin to dominate the conversation, the gatekeeper invites others to share. Gatekeepers also notice nonverbal signals that a member wants to share. As a gatekeeper, Jeremy might notice that Bethany is on the edge of her chair and appears eager to say something. He might interrupt the others to say, "Bethany, what are you thinking about?"

- Recorders take careful notes of group discussions and decisions. Recorders usually distribute edited copies of their notes prior to the next meeting. Sometimes these notes are published as **minutes**, which are a public written record of the group's activities.

When work group teams work well, the product is better than what any one member could have accomplished alone. This synergy occurs when all members adhere to five critical shared leadership responsibilities (see Figure 10.1).

1. **Be committed to the group goal.** Being committed means finding a way to align your expertise with the agreed-upon goal of the group. In addition to demonstrating responsibility, doing so also conveys both integrity and respect. So, for a class project, this might mean working together on a topic that wasn't your first choice and not dredging up old issues that have already been settled. Although Drew had wanted to do a dance-a-thon, once the group agreed to do a raffle instead, he offered to ask the bookstore manager about donating some prizes.

2. **Keep discussions on track.** It is every member's responsibility to keep the discussion on track by offering only relevant comments and by gently reminding others to stay focused if the discussion starts to get off track. It is unproductive to talk about personal issues during the team's work time. Moreover, it is unethical to try to get the discussion off track because you disagree with what is being said.

3. **Complete individual assignments on time.** One potential advantage of group work is that tasks can be divided among members. However, each member is responsible for completing his or her tasks thoroughly and on time.

4. **Encourage input from all members.** All too often, extroverts overshadow quiet members. Sometimes, outspoken members interpret this silence as having nothing to contribute or not wanting to contribute. If you are an extrovert, you have a special responsibility to refrain from dominating the discussion and to ask others for their opinions. Likewise, if you tend to be an introvert, make a conscious effort to express yourself. You might write down what you want to share or even raise your hand to get the attention of other members in an unobtrusive way.

5. **Manage conflict among members.** As you learned in Chapter 9, all small groups experience some *conflict*—disagreement or clash among ideas, principles, or people. If managed appropriately, conflict can actually be beneficial to the group goal by stimulating thinking, fostering open communication, encouraging diverse opinions, and enlarging members' understanding of the issues (de Wit, Greer, & Jehn, 2012). Doing your part to manage pseudo-conflict, issue-related conflict, and personality-related conflict effectively demonstrates ethical principles of responsibility and respect for others.

Now that we have a clear understanding of effective leadership in groups, let's turn our attention to one of the most common group communication workplace events—meetings.

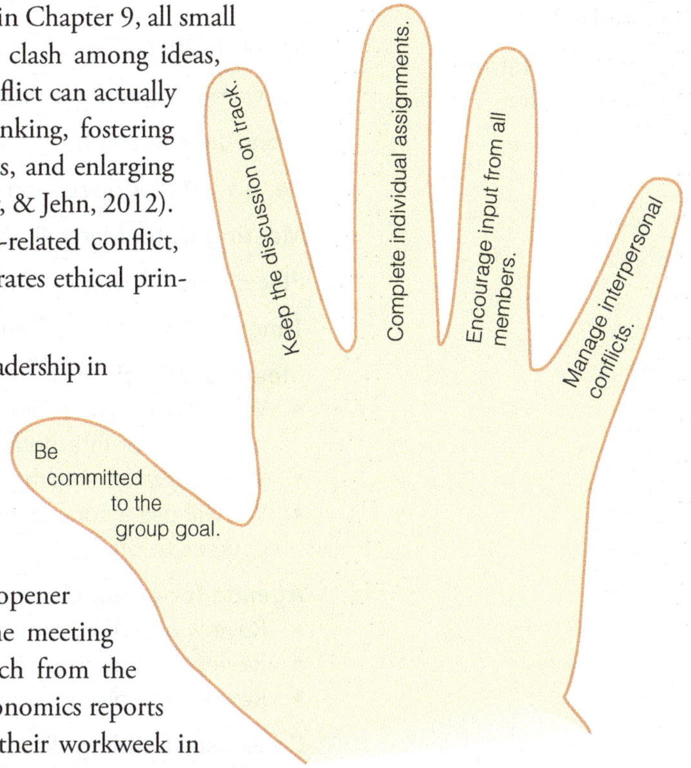

Meetings

The disastrous meeting experience in the chapter opener stemmed from poor communication skills by both the meeting facilitator and the participants. In fact, recent research from the Harvard Business School and the London School of Economics reports that business managers spend more than 18 hours of their workweek in meetings. What is particularly troubling, however, is that they say 25–50% of these meetings are waste of time (Bailey, 2013). To ensure that your meetings are not a waste of time, let's look at several guidelines for meeting leaders and meeting participants.

Guidelines for Meeting Leaders/Conveners

Most of us will be responsible for convening a group meeting at some point in our lives. Whether you are the designated formal leader for a class project, a task force at work, or substituting for your manager at the monthly department meeting, knowing how to effectively plan for, facilitate, and follow up after meetings are useful skills.

Before the Meeting

1. **Prepare and distribute an agenda.** An **agenda** is an organized outline of the information and decision items to be covered during a meeting. It is a road map that lets the members know the purpose of the meeting and what they are expected to accomplish as a result of attending. Agenda items should move the group toward its goals. You can identify the items for your agenda by:

   - reviewing your notes and the formal minutes of the previous meeting;
   - clarifying what the group decided to accomplish between meetings; and
   - identifying what decisions the group expected to make in this next session.

   Then you can structure the agenda into information items and decision items. In other words, you can have members report on their assignments (information items), then make decisions and determine next steps.

   The agenda should be distributed at least 24 hours before the meeting so members have time to prepare. You can e-mail the agenda, post it to the group's Web page, or

© Cengage Learning

Figure 10.1

Shared leadership responsibilities of all group members: Which of these do you find most challenging to perform and why?

(Hand illustration labels: Keep the discussion on track. / Complete individual assignments. / Encourage input from all members. / Manage interpersonal conflicts. / Be committed to the group goal.)

agenda
an organized outline of the information and decision items to be covered during a meeting

Figure 10.2

Agenda for the Internet course committee

March 1, 2016

To: Campus computer discussion group

From: Janelle Smith

Re: Agenda for discussion group meeting

Meeting Date: March 8, 2016

Place: Student Union, Conference Room A

Time: 3:00 p.m. to 4:30 p.m.

Meeting objectives
- We will familiarize ourselves with each of three courses that have been proposed for Internet-based delivery next semester.
- We will evaluate each course against the criteria we developed last month.
- We will use a consensus decision process to determine which of the three courses to offer.

Agenda for group discussion
- Review and discussion of Philosophy 141 (Report by Justin)
- Review and discussion of Art History 336 (Report by Marique)
- Review and discussion of Communication 235 (Report by Kathryn)

Consensus building discussion and decision
- Which proposals fit the criteria?
- Are there non-criteria-related factors to consider?
- Which proposal is more acceptable to all members?

Discussion of next steps and task assignments

Set date of next meeting

© Cengage Learning

---

hand-deliver it. None of us likes to come to a meeting and be embarrassed because we forgot to complete an assignment or be called on to make decisions about something we have not had time to think about. As the meeting leader/convener, you are responsible for providing the information members need to come prepared. Figure 10.2 shows an agenda for a group meeting to decide which one of three courses to offer over the Internet next semester.

2. **Decide who should attend the meeting.** In most cases, all group members will attend meetings. Today, very often some or all members might meet virtually via teleconferencing or videoconferencing platforms.

3. **Manage meeting logistics.** You may choose to enact this role or ask another group member to do so. But even if you delegate, it remains your responsibility to confirm that the meeting arrangements are made and appropriate. If the group is meeting face to face, make sure the room is appropriate and any equipment needed is available and operational. The room should be configured to encourage interaction. This usually means sitting around a table with plenty of space for writing and laptops or tablets. If the entire group or some group members are attending the meeting from remote locations, you will need to make sure the technology needed is available and in working order. Because groups become less effective in long meetings, a meeting should last no longer than 90 minutes.

4. **Speak with each participant prior to the meeting.** As the leader, you need to understand members' positions and personal goals. Time spent discussing issues in advance allows you to anticipate conflicts that might emerge during the meeting and plan how to manage them effectively if they do.

During the Meeting

1. **Review and modify the agenda.** Begin the meeting by reviewing the agenda and modifying it based on members' suggestions. Reviewing the agenda ensures that the group will be working on items that are still relevant and gives members a chance to provide input into what will be discussed.

2. **Monitor member interaction.** If other group members are assuming the task-related, maintenance, and procedural leadership functions, you need do nothing. But when there is a need for a particular role and no one is assuming it, it is the leader's charge to do so. For example, if you notice that some people are talking more than their fair share and no one is trying to draw out quieter members, you should assume the gatekeeper role and invite reluctant members to comment. Similarly, if a discussion becomes too heated, you may need to take on the role of harmonizer or tension reliever.

3. **Monitor the time.** Although another group member may serve as expediter, it is ultimately your responsibility to make sure the group stays on schedule.

4. **Praise in public and reprimand in private.** Meetings provide an excellent opportunity to praise individuals or the entire group for jobs well done. Being recognized among one's peers often boosts self-esteem and group morale. Conversely, criticizing individuals or the entire group during a meeting has the opposite effect. The humiliation of public criticism can deflate self-esteem, group morale, and motivation.

5. **Check periodically to see if the group is ready to make a decision.** You should listen carefully for agreement among members and move the group into its formal decision-making process when the discussion is no longer adding insight.

6. **Implement the group's decision rules.** You are responsible for executing the decision-making rule the group has agreed to use. If the group is deciding by consensus, for example, you must make sure all members feel they can support the chosen alternative. If the group is deciding by majority rule, you call for the vote and tally the results.

7. **Summarize decisions and assignments.** You should summarize what has been and is left to accomplish, as well as assignments tasked to various members.

8. **Set the next meeting.** Clarify when future meetings will take place if necessary.

Following Up

1. **Review the meeting outcomes and process.** A good leader learns how to be more effective by reflecting on how well the meeting went. Did the meeting accomplish its goals? Was group cohesion improved or damaged in the process? What will you do differently next time to improve the experience?

2. **Prepare and distribute a meeting summary or minutes.** Although some groups have a designated recorder, many groups rely on their leader to

© 2002 Ted Goff

"At 10:01, Mr. Holtz fell asleep. At 10:17, Ms. Sommer fell asleep. At 10:31, everyone else fell asleep. Those are the minutes of our last meeting."

2002 Ted Goff www.tedgoff.com

do so. If your group has a designated recorder, be sure to review the minutes and compare them to your notes before they are distributed. Summaries are most useful when they are distributed within two or three days of the meeting when everyone's memories are still fresh.

3. **Repair damaged relationships.** If any heated debate occurred during the meeting, some members may have left angry or hurt. You should help repair relationships by seeking out these participants and talking with them. Through empathic listening, you can soothe hurt feelings and spark a recommitment to the group.

4. **Conduct informal progress reports.** When participants have been assigned specific task responsibilities, you should periodically check to see if they have encountered any problems in completing those tasks and how you might help them.

Guidelines for Meeting Participants

Just as there are guidelines for effective conveners/formal leaders to follow before, during, and after meetings, there are also guidelines for meeting participants.

Before the Meeting As the chapter opener illustrated, too often people think of group meetings as a "happening" that requires attendance but no preparation. Countless times we have observed people arriving at a meeting unprepared even though they come carrying packets of material they received in advance (Photo 10.3). Here are some important preparation guidelines for meeting participants.

1. **Study the agenda.** Consider the meeting's purpose and determine what you need to do to be prepared. If you had an assignment, make sure you are ready to report on it.

2. **Study the minutes.** If this is one in a series of meetings, read the minutes and your own notes from the previous meeting. Doing so should provide the basis for what you need to prepare for the next one.

3. **Do your homework.** Read the material distributed prior to the meeting and do what is necessary to be informed about each agenda item. Bring with you any materials that may help the group accomplish its objectives.

Photo 10.3 Some people wait until the last minute to prepare for meetings. Do you find it annoying to attend meetings at which people arrive unprepared to participate?

Tony Freeman/PhotoEdit

4. **List questions.** Make a list of questions related to any agenda items that you would like to have answered during the meeting.

5. **Plan to play a leadership role.** Consider which leadership functions and roles you are best at and decide what you will do to enact them during the meeting.

During the Meeting Go into the meeting planning to be a full participant.

1. **Listen attentively.** Concentrate on what others say so you can make a meaningful contribution to the discussion.

2. **Stay focused.** Keep your comments focused on the specific agenda item under discussion. If others get off the subject, do what you can to get the discussion back on track.

3. **Ask questions.** Honest questions, whose answers you do not already know, help stimulate discussion and build ideas.

4. **Take notes.** Even if someone else is responsible for providing the official minutes, you'll need notes to remember what occurred and any tasks you agreed to take on after the meeting.

5. **Play devil's advocate.** When you think an idea has not been fully discussed or tested, be willing to voice disagreement or encourage further discussion.

6. **Monitor your contributions.** Especially when people are well prepared, they have a tendency to dominate discussion. Make sure that you are neither dominating the discussion nor abdicating your responsibility to share insights and opinions.

Following Up When meetings end, too often people leave and forget about what took place until they arrive at the next meeting. Instead:

1. **Review and summarize your notes.** Do this soon after the meeting while the discussion is still fresh in your mind. Make sure your notes include what you need to do before the next meeting.

2. **Evaluate your effectiveness.** How effective were you in helping the group move toward achieving its goals? Where were you strong? Where were you weak? What should you do next time to improve and how? For example, if you didn't speak up as much as you would have liked to, you might write down questions or topics when they come to you and use them as notes to encourage you to speak up next time.

3. **Review decisions.** Make notes about what your role was in making decisions. Did you do all that you could have done? If not, what will you do differently next time, why, and how?

4. **Communicate progress.** Inform others who need to know about information conveyed and decisions made in the meeting.

5. **Complete your tasks.** Make sure you complete all assignments you agreed to take on.

6. **Review minutes.** Compare the official meeting minutes to your own notes and report any discrepancies to the member who prepared them.

Sometimes the goal of a workplace meeting is to regroup and refocus as we perform the regular duties assigned to us. Other times, however, we will meet as part of a work group team charged with a specific problem-solving challenge. In these situations, we will be most successful if we work through the problem or issue using a systematic problem-solving process.

Systematic Problem Solving

When a work group team is charged with tackling a problem together, they may use an orderly series of steps or a less-structured spiral pattern in which they refine, accept, reject, modify, combine ideas, and circle back to previous discussion as they go along.

Whether the deliberations are linear or spiral, groups that arrive at high-quality decisions accomplish the six tasks that make up what is known as the Systematic Problem-Solving Process. This process, first described by John Dewey in 1933 and since revised by others, remains a tried and true approach to individual or group problem solving (Duch, Groh, & Allen, 2001; Edens, 2000; Levin, 2001; Weiten, Dunn, & Hammer, 2011).

Step One: Identify and Define the Problem

The first step is to identify the problem and define it in a way that all group members understand. Even when a group is commissioned by an outside agency that provides a description of the problem, the group still needs to understand precisely what is at issue and needs to be resolved. Many times what appears to be a problem is only a symptom of a problem, and if the group focuses on solutions that eliminate only a symptom, the underlying problem will remain. For example, in the opening vignette, the group's budget crisis was described as stemming from a recession-related membership drop. How does the group know that the inability to fund the budget is the problem and not just a symptom of the problem? What if their membership drop has some other cause? If that is the case, then cutting the budget may be a temporary fix but will not solve the problem. One way to see if you have uncovered the root cause or real problem is to ask, "If we solve this problem, are we confident that the consequences of the problem will not reoccur?" In other words: If you cut the budget, are you confident that you won't have to cut it further? If not, then you probably need to look further for the root problem. You will need to look more closely at causes for the drop in membership and other ways besides dues for funding the budget. The real problem may be how to fund the budget.

Once your group agrees about the nature of the root problem, you will want to draft a **problem definition**, which is a formal written statement describing the problem. An effective problem definition is stated as a question of fact, value, or policy; it contains only one central idea; and it uses specific, precise, and concrete language. **Questions of fact** ask the group to determine what is true or to what extent something is true. "What percentage of our projected expenses can be covered with our existing revenue?" is a question of fact. **Questions of value** ask the group to determine or judge whether something is right, moral, good, or just. Questions of value often contain words such as *good, reliable, effective, or worthy*—for instance, "What is the most effective way to recruit new members?" **Questions of policy** concern what course of action should be taken or what rules should be adopted to solve a problem—for example, "Should we sponsor an annual fund-raising event with the local Public Relations Society of America (PRSA) chapter in order to help fund our budget?" After some discussion, the student chapter decided that the problem they needed to solve was a policy question that could be best stated: "How can we increase our revenues in order to meet our budget in the current economic conditions?"

problem definition
a formal written statement describing a problem

question of fact
asked to determine what is true or to what extent something is true

question of value
asked to determine or judge whether something is right, moral, good, or just

question of policy
asked to determine what course of action should be taken or what rules should be adopted to solve a problem

Step Two: Analyze the Problem

To analyze a problem, you need to find out as much as possible about it. Most groups begin this process with each member sharing information he or she already knows about the problem. Then the group needs to determine what additional questions they need to answer and search for additional information to answer them. The information gathered

- What are the symptoms of this problem?
- What are the causes of this problem?
- Can this problem be subdivided into several smaller problems that each may have individual solutions?
- What have others who have faced this problem done?
- How successful have they been with the solutions they attempted?
- How is our situation similar and different from theirs?
- Does this problem consist of several smaller problems? If so, what are their symptoms, causes, previously tried solutions, and so forth?
- What would be the consequences of doing nothing?
- What would be the consequences of trying something and having it fail?

Figure 10.3

Questions to guide problem analysis

© Cengage Learning

should help the group answer key questions about the nature of the problem such as those listed in Figure 10.3.

The PRSSA chapter, for example, might interview the Dean of Student Affairs to understand how other campus groups increased their revenues and to learn of any campus policies that govern fundraising by student groups. Some group members might network with other student groups on campus and PRSSA chapters at other schools. Finally, the group could survey former members to understand why they dropped out of the group and what might entice them to rejoin, as well as survey eligible students who are not members to find out what would entice them to join.

During the information gathering and analysis step, it is important to consciously encourage members to share information that is either new or contradicts the sentiments or preferences expressed in the group. A group that is willing to consider new and unexpected information will more deeply analyze the problem and, therefore, will likely come to a more effective solution.

Step Three: Determine Criteria for Judging Solutions

Criteria are standards used for judging the merits of proposed solutions—a blueprint for evaluating them. Research suggests that when groups develop criteria before they think about specific solutions, they are more likely to come to a decision that all members can accept (Young, Wood, Phillips, & Pedersen, 2007). Without clear criteria, group members may argue for their preferred solution without regard to whether it will adequately address the problem or whether it is truly feasible. Figure 10.4 poses questions that can help a group think about the types of criteria a solution might need to meet.

criteria
standards used for judging the merits of proposed solutions

- What are the quantitative and qualitative measures of success that a solution must be able to demonstrate?
- Are there resource constraints that a good solution must meet (costs, time, manpower)?
- Is solution simplicity a factor?
- What risks are unacceptable?
- Is ease of implementation a consideration?
- Is it important that no constituency be unfairly harmed or advantaged by a solution?

Figure 10.4

Questions to guide discussion of solution criteria.

© Cengage Learning

Once you've agreed on the list of solution criteria, the group needs to prioritize the list and agree about which criteria are major (must meet) and which are minor (would like to meet). The PRSSA chapter agreed on three major criteria and one minor criterion. A good plan must comply with the university's policy on fundraising by student groups. It must cost less than $500 to implement. It must raise at least $4,000. And ideally (minor criterion), it should not require more than 20 hours of work from each member.

Step Four: Generate a Host of Solutions

Arriving at a good solution depends on having a wide variety of possible solutions to choose from. Many groups fail at generating a variety of possible solutions because they criticize the first ideas expressed; which discourages members from taking the risk to put their ideas out for the group to consider. One way to encourage everyone's ideas is to use the brainstorming technique. **Brainstorming** is an uncritical, non-evaluative process of generating possible solutions by being creative, suspending judgment, and combining or adapting ideas. It involves verbalizing and recording all ideas that come to mind without stopping to evaluate their merits. To ensure creativity is not stifled, no solution should be ignored, and members should build on the ideas shared by others. You might come up with twenty or more solutions. At a minimum, you should come up with at least eight to ten.

The PRSSA chapter brainstormed and came up with these ideas for balancing their budget:

brainstorming
an uncritical, non-evaluative process of generating possible solutions by being creative, suspending judgment, and combining or adapting ideas

- Place an ad on the Communication Department's Web site to recruit members.

- Place an ad on the college Web site to recruit members.

- Ask faculty to allow PRSSA members to do 2-minute "testimonials" in classes as a way of recruiting members.

- Text-message and tweet all the people we know about upcoming PRSSA events.

- Run a monthly raffle at the PRSA meetings. The winning ticket would get 4 hours of work from a PRSSA member.

- Find PRSA chapter members whose businesses would sponsor student scholarships to the national convention.

- Do a dance-a-thon fundraising event.

- Do a 5K fun run fundraising event.

- Set up a consulting program to provide public relations help to other student groups for a fee.

- Set up a consulting program to provide public relations help to small businesses for a fee.

- Do a virtual newsletter instead of a printed one.

- Double membership dues.

- Cosponsor a golf outing with the local PRSA chapter.

- Raffle off a spring break getaway for six to the island of St. Thomas.

Step Five: Evaluate Solutions and Decide

Here you need to evaluate the merits of each potential solution based on the criteria established by the group. Consider each solution as it meets the criteria and eliminate solutions that do not meet them adequately. Once each potential solution has been thoroughly evaluated based on the criteria, the group must select the best one(s).

Decision making is the process of choosing among alternatives. Sometimes your group will make the decision. Other times, your group may present the results of your work to someone else who will then make the final decision. Five methods are commonly used to reach a group decision.

decision making
the process of choosing among alternatives

1. **The expert opinion method.** Once the group has eliminated those alternatives that do not meet the criteria, the group asks the member who has the most expertise to make the final choice. Obviously, this method is quick and useful if one member is much more knowledgeable about the issues or has a greater stake in the implementation of the decision. The PRSSA chapter, for instance, might ask its president to make the final choice among the two or three solutions that best met the criteria.

2. **The average group opinion method.** In this approach, each group member ranks each of the possible solutions that meet all the criteria. Their rankings are then averaged, and the solution receiving the highest average becomes the choice. This method is useful for routine decisions or when a decision needs to be made quickly. It can also be used as an intermediate straw poll so the group can eliminate low-scoring alternatives before moving to a different process for making the final decision.

3. **The majority rule method.** Here the group votes on each alternative, and the one that receives a majority of votes (a minimum of 50 percent + 1) is selected. Although this method is considered democratic, it can create problems. If the solution wins by a slight majority, then nearly as many members oppose the choice as support it. If these minority members strongly object, they could sabotage implementation of the solution either actively or passively.

4. **The unanimous decision method.** In this method, the group must continue deliberating until every member believes that the same solution is the best. Achieving a unanimous decision takes a lot of time; however, each member is likely to be committed to helping implement it in the end.

5. **The consensus method.** In consensus, the group continues deliberation until all members find an acceptable solution they can support and be committed to helping implement. It may not be the first choice of all members, but all feel they can live with it. Although reaching consensus is easier than reaching unanimity, is still difficult. The consensus method is a wise investment if the group needs everyone's support to implement the decision successfully.

Sometimes a group will choose only one solution. But frequently a group will decide on a multi-pronged approach that combines two or three of the acceptable solutions. The PRSSA chapter, for instance, reached consensus on a plan to place ads on both the college and department Web sites and to launch a text-message and Twitter campaign 24 hours before their next meeting. They also decided to approach PRSA chapter members and ask them to sponsor student members to the national convention. Finally, they decided to conduct a raffle fundraising event.

Step Six: Implement the Agreed-Upon Solution and Assess It

Finally, the group implements the agreed-upon solution or, if the group is presenting the solution to others for implementation, makes recommendations for how it should be implemented. The group has already considered implementation in terms of selecting a solution, but now must fill in the details. What tasks are required by the solution(s)? Who will carry out these tasks? What is a reasonable time frame for implementation generally and for each of the tasks specifically? Because the agreed-upon solution may or may not prove effective, the group should determine a point at which they will revisit and assess its success. Doing so builds in an opportunity to revise or replace the solution if warranted.

We discussed unique communication challenges when interacting in a virtual group in Chapter 9. The *Communicating in the World* feature in this chapter, "Problem Solving in Cyberspace: *Dungeons & Dragons* and *World of Warcraft*," points to some unique opportunities in online gaming virtual group communication.

Communicating Group Solutions

deliverables
products of work that must be provided to someone else

Once a group has completed its deliberations, it is usually expected to communicate its results. **Deliverables** are products of group work that is provided to someone else. Although some deliverables are objects, typically the deliverables from problem-solving groups come in the form of communicating the information, analyses, decisions, and recommendations of the group. These deliverables can be communicated in written formats, oral formats, or virtual formats.

Written Formats

written brief
a very short document that describes a problem, background, process, decision, and rationale so that a reader can quickly understand and evaluate a group's product

1. A **written brief** is a very short document that describes the problem, background, process, decision, and rationale so that the reader can quickly understand and evaluate the group's product. Most briefs are one or two pages long. When preparing a brief, begin by describing your group's task. What problem were you attempting to solve and why? Then briefly provide the background information the reader will need to evaluate whether the group adequately studied the problem. Present solution steps and timelines for implementation as bullet points so the reader can quickly understand what is being proposed. Close with a sentence or very short paragraph that describes how the recommendation will solve the problem, as well as any potential side effects.

comprehensive report
a written document that provides a detailed review of the problem-solving process used to arrive at a recommendation

2. A **comprehensive report** is a written document that provides a detailed review of the problem-solving process used to arrive at the recommendation. A comprehensive report is usually organized into sections that parallel the problem-solving process.

executive summary
a one-page synopsis of a comprehensive report

Because comprehensive reports can be very long, they usually include an executive summary. An **executive summary** is a one-page synopsis of the report. This summary contains enough information to acquaint readers with the highlights of the full document without reading it. Usually, it contains a statement of the problem, some background information, a description of any alternatives, and the major conclusions.

COMMUNICATING IN THE WORLD

Problem Solving in Cyberspace:
Dungeons & Dragons and *World of Warcraft*

AP Images/Eckehard Schulz

For some, mention of games like *Dungeons & Dragons* and *World of Warcraft* might conjure up the stereotypical image of a teenage boy typing away at his computer, alone. But role-playing games are actually social interactions that encourage successful group problem solving, incorporating the six steps we discuss in this chapter: identifying and defining the problem, analyzing the problem, developing criteria for evaluation solutions, brainstorming possible solutions, selecting one, and implementing it.

Dungeons & Dragons, the first modern role-playing game of its kind (Williams, Hendricks, & Winkler, 2006), is typically played among a group of friends at a table, without a computer. A Dungeon Master narrates and creates rules for a fantasy story, and people at the table act as the story's characters. Together, the players work to defeat monsters, find treasure, gain experience, and face other challenges. One of the creators of *Dungeons & Dragons*, Gary Gygax, said in a 2006 telephone interview, "The essence of a role-playing game is that it is a group, cooperative experience. There is no winning or losing" (Schiesel, 2008). *Newsweek's* Patrick Enright remembers his own *Dungeons & Dragons* experiences as a boy (Ebeling, 2008):

> If you suddenly wanted to attack your traveling companions with a broadsword or a Finger of Death spell, there was nothing stopping you. The amazing thing is how rarely that happened. Unless the neighborhood bully joined in (and almost never did those tanned, skinned-kneed fellas venture into our dank lairs), we

all helped each other and together defeated whatever dragon or monster we were battling. Yes, I'll say it: *Dungeons & Dragons* taught me everything I need to know about teamwork.

Dungeons & Dragons inspired *World of Warcraft*, a popular MMORPG (massively multiplayer online role-playing game). *World of Warcraft* differs from *Dungeons & Dragons* in that it is played online, and the game, regulates the story and the rules. To advance, players must still work with others to defeat monsters, find treasure, and gain experience, but they communicate with one another using text or voice chat programs (Newman, 2007).

In a *Business Week* online article, researcher John Seely Brown and business consultant John Hagel (2009) argue that many aspects of *World of Warcraft* encourage group problem solving and can even be applied as innovative workplace strategies. These aspects include

- Creating opportunities for teams to self-organize around challenging performance targets.
- Providing opportunities to develop tacit knowledge without neglecting the exchange of broader knowledge.
- Encouraging frequent and rigorous performance feedback.

Based on these benefits, some MMORPGs are actually being developed for a range of "real-life" applications. For example, the Bill and Melinda Gates Foundation recently awarded a $3 million grant to the MIT Education Arcade to develop games that help high school students learn math and biology. Professor Eric Klopfer, director of the Education Arcade, says, "This genre of games is uniquely suited to teaching the nature of science inquiry because they provide collaborative, self-directed learning situations. Players take on the roles of scientists, engineers, and mathematicians to explore and explain a robust virtual world" (MIT's Education Arcade Uses Online Gaming to Teach Science, 2012).

Do you think online gaming is a good teaching method? Why or why not?

Oral Formats

oral brief
a summary of a written brief delivered to an audience by a group member

1. An **oral brief** is essentially a summary of a written brief delivered verbally by a group member to an audience. Typically, an oral brief can be delivered in less than 10 minutes.

oral report
a detailed review of a group's problem-solving process delivered to an audience by one or more group members

2. An **oral report** is similar to a comprehensive report. It provides a more detailed review of a group's problem-solving process. Oral reports can range from 30 to 60 minutes.

panel discussion
a structured problem-solving discussion held by a group in front of an audience

3. A **panel discussion** is a structured problem-solving discussion held by a group in front of an audience. One member serves as moderator, introducing the topic and providing structure by asking a series of planned questions that panelists answer. Their answers and the interaction among them provide the supporting evidence. A well-planned panel discussion seems spontaneous and interactive but requires careful planning and rehearsal to ensure that all relevant information is presented and that all speakers are afforded equal speaking time. After the formal discussion, the audience is often encouraged to question the participants. Perhaps you've seen or heard a panel of experts discuss a topic on a radio or television talk show like *Sports Center, Meet the Press,* or *The Doctors.*

symposium
a set of prepared oral reports delivered sequentially by group members before a gathering of people who are interested in the work of the group

4. A **symposium** is a set of prepared oral reports delivered sequentially by group members before a gathering of people who are interested in the work of the group. A symposium may be organized so that each person's speech focuses on one step of the problem-solving process, or it may be organized so that each speaker covers all of the steps in the problem-solving process as they relate to one of several issues or recommendations that the group worked on or made. In a symposium, the speakers usually sit together at the front of the room. One member acts as moderator, offering the introductory and concluding remarks and providing transitions between speakers. When introduced by the moderator, each speaker may stand and walk to a central spot, usually a lectern. Speakers who use a computerized slideshow should coordinate their slides so that there are seamless transitions between speakers. Symposiums often conclude with a question-and-answer session facilitated by the moderator, who directs one or more of the members to answer based on their expertise. Questions can be directed to individuals or to the group as a whole.

Virtual Formats

remote access report (RAR)
a computer-mediated audiovisual presentation of a group's process and outcome

1. A **remote access report (RAR)** is a computer-mediated audiovisual presentation of the group's process and outcome that others can receive through e-mail, Web posting, and so forth. Prepared by one or more members of the group, the RAR is prepared using computer slideshow software (e.g., PowerPoint, Prezi) and provides a visual overview of the group's process, decisions, and recommendations. Effective RARs typically consist of no more than 15 to 20 slides. Slides are titled and content is presented in outline or bullet-point phrases or key words (rather than complete sentences or paragraphs), as well as through visual representations of important information. For example, a budget task force might have a slide with a pie chart depicting the portions

of the proposed budget that are allocated to operating expenses, salaries, fundraising, and travel (see Figure 10.5). RARs may be self-running so that the slides automatically forward after a certain number of seconds, but it is better to let the viewer choose the pace and control when the next slide appears. RARs can be silent or narrated. When narrated, a voice-over accompanies each slide, providing additional or explanatory information.

2. A **streaming video** is a recording that is sent in compressed form over the Internet. You are probably familiar with streaming video from popular Web sites such as *YouTube*. Streaming videos are a great way to distribute oral briefs, but they also can be used to distribute recordings of oral reports, symposiums, or panel presentations. Streaming videos are useful when it is inconvenient for some or all the people who need to know the results of the group's work to meet at one time or in one place.

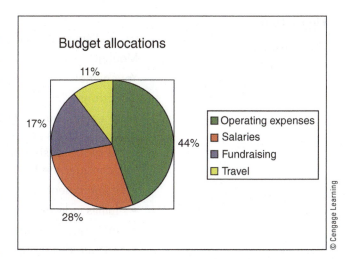

Figure 10.5

Example of a slide in a remote access report

streaming video
a recording that is sent in compressed form over the Internet

Evaluating Group Effectiveness

As with any communication skill, group communication can improve over time based on practice, reflective assessment, and revision. In this section, we offer some guidelines for evaluating the group communication process and a group presentation.

Group Dynamics

To be effective, group members must work together as they define and analyze a problem, generate solutions, and select a course of action. They also need to work together as they prepare their written report, as well as prepare and practice their oral presentation. These communication interactions among members to achieve a goal are known as **group dynamics**.

Effective groups periodically stop and evaluate how their interactions are affecting what they are accomplishing and how members perceive themselves and others. At times you may be asked to provide a formal evaluation of the group dynamics of a class project group or other work team. You can do so by considering what each person did well and could improve on regarding each of the five key responsibilities of group members we discussed earlier. Figure 10.6 is one example of a form you can use for evaluating group member participation. Alternatively, you could prepare a "reflective thinking process paper," which details in paragraph form what each member did well and could improve upon, as well as a self-analysis of your own contributions and what you could do to improve.

Like the performance evaluations business managers make of employees, these evaluations serve to document the efforts of group members. They can be submitted to the instructor, just as they would be submitted to a supervisor. In business, these documents provide a basis for determining promotion, merit pay, and salary

group dynamics
the way a group interacts to achieve its goal

Figure 10.6

Group dynamics
evaluation form

Group Dynamics Evaluation Form

Meeting date: _____

Your name: _____

Directions

After each required group meeting, provide ethical critiques for both your group members and yourself. Rate each individual on his or her performance in the group. Justify the rating with specific examples. As you rate each member, consider the following:

- commitment to the group goal
- fulfills individual assignments
- manages interpersonal conflicts
- encourages group participation
- helps keep the discussion on track

Yourself _____

Circle overall individual rating

0	1	2	3	4	5	6	7

(poor)   (met requirements)   (excellent)

Tasks accomplished:

Tasks assigned:

Ethical critique:

Group member _____

Circle overall individual rating

0	1	2	3	4	5	6	7

(poor)   (met requirements)   (excellent)

Tasks accomplished:

Tasks assigned:

Ethical critique:

Group member _____

Circle overall individual rating

0	1	2	3	4	5	6	7

(poor)   (met requirements)   (excellent)

Tasks accomplished:

Tasks assigned:

Ethical critique:

Group member _____

Circle overall individual rating

0	1	2	3	4	5	6	7

(poor)   (met requirements)   (excellent)

Tasks accomplished:

Tasks assigned:

(Continued)

Ethical critique:
Group member —————————————————————————
Circle overall individual rating

| 0 | 1 | 2 | 3 | 4 | 5 | 6 | 7 |

(poor)   (met requirements)   (excellent)

Tasks accomplished:
Tasks assigned:
Ethical critique:

Figure 10.6
(Continued)

adjustments. In the classroom, they can provide a basis for determining a portion of each member's grade.

Group Presentations

Effective group presentations depend on quality individual presentations as well as overall group performance. So evaluations of group presentations should consist of both an individual and a group component (see Figure 10.7). And, if you are serious about improving your individual presentation skills, you will also evaluate yourself to discover areas where you can improve (see Figure 10.8).

COMMUNICATE ON YOUR FEET

Speech Assignment

Panel Discussion

The Assignment

Form a small group with three to five classmates. As a group, decide on a social issue or problem you would like to study in depth. Then select one group member to serve as moderator and the others as expert panelists. Each member should do research to find out all they can about the issue, why it is a problem, how it affects people and to what degree, as well as potential ideas for solving it. The moderator's role is to come up with four to six good questions to ask the panelists. The panelists should prepare notes about the research they discovered.

On the day determined by the instructor, engage in a 15- to 20-minute panel discussion in front of your classmates. The moderator will guide the discussion by asking questions of the panelists, as well as asking for questions from the class.

Suggested Format

1. Moderator thanks the audience for coming and introduces the panelists and the topic.
2. Moderator asks panelists a series of questions, letting a different panelist respond first each time.
3. Moderator asks follow-up questions when appropriate.
4. Moderator asks for questions from the audience.
5. Moderator thanks the panelists and the audience members for participating.

Figure 10.7

Sample evaluation form for group presentations

Group Member Name: _____

Critic (your name): _____

Directions: Evaluate the effectiveness of each group member according to each of the following criteria for effective presentations individually and as a group.

Rating Scale:

1	2	3	4	5	6	7
(poor)						(excellent)

INDIVIDUAL PERFORMANCE CRITIQUE

_____ **Content** (Breadth and depth and listener relevance)
(rating) Critique (Provide a rationale for the rating you gave):
_____ **Structure** (Macrostructure and microstructure/language)
(rating) Critique (Provide a rationale for the rating you gave):
_____ **Delivery** (Use of voice and use of body)
(rating) Critique (Provide a rationale for the rating you gave):

GROUP PERFORMANCE CRITIQUE

_____ **Content** (Thematic? Focused? Thorough? Construction of presentational aids?)
(rating) Critique (Provide a rationale for the rating you gave):
_____ **Structure** (Balanced? Transitions? Flow? Attn/Clincher?)
(rating) Critique (Provide a rationale for the rating you gave):
_____ **Delivery** (Teamwork? Cooperation? Fluency? Use of aids?)
(rating) Critique (Provide a rationale for the rating you gave):

Overall Comments: _____

© Cengage Learning

Directions: Complete the items below with regard to your presentation in the group symposium.

1. If I could do my portion of the oral presentation over again, I would do the following things differently:
   a.
   b.
2. In terms of content, I did the following things well in my oral presentation:
   a.
   b.
3. In terms of structure, I did the following things well in my oral presentation:
   a.
   b.
4. In terms of delivery, I did the following things well in my oral presentation:
   a.
   b.
   c.
5. In terms of my role as a group member, I am most proud of how I:
6. In terms of my role as a group member, I am least proud of how I:
7. Overall, I would give myself a grade of _____ for the group speech because:

© Cengage Learning

Figure 10.8

Sample self-critique form for group presentations

WHAT WOULD YOU DO?

A Question of Ethics

"You know, Sue, we're going to be in big trouble if the group doesn't support McGowan's resolution about dues reform."

"Well, we'll just have to see to it that all the arguments in favor of that resolution are heard, but in the end it's the group's decision."

"That's very democratic of you, Sue, but you know if it doesn't pass, you're likely to be out on your tail."

"That may be, Heather, but I don't see what I can do about it."

"You don't want to see. First, right now the group respects you. If you would just apply a little pressure on a couple of the members, you'd get what you want."

"What do you mean?"

"Look, this is a good cause. You've got something on just about every member of the group. Take a couple of members aside and let them know that this is payoff time. I think you'll see that some key folks will see it your way."

Is it appropriate to use personal influence to affect the outcome of group decisions? Why or why not?

MindTap®

Reflection and Assessment

Effective work group teams rely on shared leadership and problem-solving skills among all members. This chapter provided communication guidelines to help you function most successfully in groups. To assess how well you've learned what we addressed in these pages, answer the following questions. If you have trouble answering any of them, go back and review that material. Once you can answer each question accurately, you are ready to move ahead to read the next chapter.

1. What is meant by shared leadership and what are your responsibilities as a group member?

2. What are several things you should and should not do to participate effectively in a meeting?

3. What are the steps in the systematic problem-solving process?

4. What options might you choose from to communicate group solutions to others?

5. How do you evaluate group dynamics and presentations?

COMMUNICATE!

RESOURCE AND ASSESSMENT CENTER

MindTap

Now that you have read Chapter 10, go to your MindTap for *Communicate!* for quick access to the electronic resources that accompany this text.

Applying What You've Learned

Impromptu Speech Activity

Draw a slip of paper from a pile provided by your instructor. The paper will have the name of a famous real-life person (e.g., Taylor Swift, Justin Bieber, Jennifer Lawrence, Jimmy Kimmel, NFL quarterback Tom Brady) or fictional character (e.g., Bugs Bunny, Scooby-Doo, Homer Simpson, Harry Potter) on it. Prepare a 2- to 3-minute speech about why you think the person or character would or would not be an effective work group team leader.

Assessment Activities

1. Group Problem Solving Analyze a situation in which a group to which you belong attempted to solve a problem. Write a paragraph answering the following questions. Did the group use all six of the problem-solving steps listed in this chapter? If not, which steps did the group overlook? Were there any steps the group should have placed more emphasis on? Was the group successful in its efforts to solve the problem? Prepare a 400- to 500-word essay explaining why you think this was or was not the case.

2. Leadership on *Survivor* Watch a recent episode of one of the popular CBS series *Survivor*. Select one tribe and identify the dominant roles each member of the group seems to play in that episode. Who is vying for informal leadership? How are they trying to gain or maintain their leadership? What do you think will happen to each leader candidate? Write a short 400- to 500-word essay explaining your answers.

Skill-Building Activity

Identifying Roles Match the typical comment to the role of which it is most characteristic.

Roles

a. aggressor

b. analyzer

c. expediter

d. gatekeeper

e. harmonizer

f. information or opinion giver

g. information or opinion seeker

h. interpreter

i. supporter

j. tension reliever

Comments

1. "Did anyone discover if we have to recommend only one company?"

2. "I think Rick has an excellent idea."

3. "Stupid idea, Katie. Why don't you stop and think before you open your mouth?"

4. "Kwitabe doesn't necessarily agree with you, but he would consider it rude to openly disagree with someone who is older."

5. "Josiah, in your plan, weren't you assuming that we'd only need two days rest for rehearsal?"

6. "Lisa, I understand your point. What do you think about it, Paul?"

7. "Okay, so we've all agreed that we should begin keeping time logs. Now shouldn't we be thinking about what information needs to be on them?"

8. "Wow, it's getting tense in here. If we don't chill out soon, we're likely to spontaneously combust. And, hello, that'll be a problem because we're the only engine company in this area of town, right?"

9. "Barb, I don't think that your position is really that different from Saul's. Let me see if I can explain how they relate."

10. "I've visited that home before, and I found that both the mom and dad are trying very hard to help their son."

UNIT FOUR
Public Speaking

Unlike interpersonal and group communication, which didn't emerge as areas of study in the communication field until the middle of the twentieth century, the study and practice of public speaking has a long and rich history dating back more than 2000 years to ancient Greek (e.g., Aristotle and Plato) and Roman (e.g., Cicero and Isocrates) philosophers. They coined the terms *rhetoric* and *oratory* to describe the processes of preparing and delivering effective public speeches.

Public speaking was the primary means by which to conduct business, debate public issues, make public decisions, and gain and maintain power. Fundamental to effective public speaking then and now is *audience*. The ancient Greek philosopher and teacher Aristotle is often credited with saying, "The audience is the end and object of the speech." Whether conveyed in written, oral, or visual form, or some combination of them, a message is only effective if it is understood and internalized by the people being addressed. So understanding our audience and tailoring the message accordingly is key to effective public speaking.

These ancient orators also conceptualized the process of speechmaking based on five rhetorical canons. These canons—(1) invention, (2) arrangement, (3) style, (4) delivery, and (5) memory—have also withstood the test of time. The chapters comprising this unit take you through a five-step speech preparation process based on these canons. These speechmaking "action steps" are covered in detail in Chapters 11 through 15.

If you read these chapters thoughtfully and apply the guidelines offered in them diligently as you prepare, practice, and present your public speeches, you will be a successful public speaker. Not only that, you will discover that effective public speaking skills will catapult you into leadership roles in both your personal and professional life.

Topic Selection and Development

When you've finished this chapter, you'll be able to:

- Determine a speech topic and goal appropriate to the rhetorical situation.

- Evaluate information sources for validity, accuracy, and reliability.

- Choose different types of evidence such as statistics, examples, expert opinions, and elaborations.

- Show appropriate methods for recording information and sources.

- Demonstrate ways to effectively cite sources effectively in your speeches.

MindTap®

Start with a quick warm-up activity.

Chen Chen was awarded "server of the month" three times since she started working at the restaurant. Customers really liked her and several had begun to request that they be seated in her section. Her manager asked her to give a pep talk to the managers and other servers about "how she does it" at the next company-wide meeting.

Jediah landed an interview for his dream job as an electrical engineer. The interview is going to be conducted via videoconference. To prepare for the interview, Jediah was asked to create a 10- to 15-minute webinar explaining why he is the best candidate for the position.

Romeo has been invited to speak to a student assembly at the inner-city middle school he attended years ago. He really wants the students to understand what they need to do *now* to have a shot at going to college *later*. He wonders where to look for information that will help them realize how relevant the topic is for them today.

Alyssa is taking an online public speaking class and is scheduled to give a speech in two weeks. She volunteers regularly at the local homeless shelter and wants to focus on the value of doing community service as college students. She doesn't have the foggiest idea where to find good information beyond her own personal experiences and opinions.

Kameron decided to enter an upcoming speech contest. He was stumped about what would be a good topic. He wondered where to begin. . . .

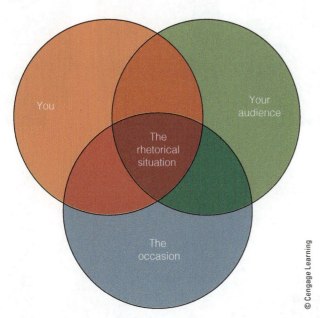

Figure 11.1

The rhetorical situation

Although you may not realize it, each of these is an example of public speaking. **Public speaking** is simply a sustained formal presentation by a speaker to an audience. Public speaking today might occur in a face-to-face setting as it will for Chen Chen, Romeo, and Kameron; or in an online environment as it will for Alyssa and Jediah. Whether giving a "job talk" speech during an interview, presenting oral reports and proposals, responding to questions, or training other workers, you will spend a good portion of your work life in activities that require effective public speaking skills. This chapter focuses on the first steps in effective speechmaking: (1) selecting a specific speech goal that is adapted to the rhetorical situation and (2) gathering and evaluating information to develop your speech.

Sometimes we are provided with a topic and goal like Chen Chen and Jediah. Other times, we are left to come up with the topic and goal on our own like Romeo, Alyssa, and Kameron. When this is the case, we do so by determining a speech goal that is appropriate to the rhetorical situation.

Determine an Appropriate Speech Topic and Goal

rhetorical situation
a state in which you, the audience, and the occasion overlap

exigence
the reason the speech needs to be given

audience analysis
the study of the intended audience for your speech

audience adaptation
the process of tailoring your speech to the needs, interests, and expectations of your audience

uncertainty reduction theory
explains the processes we go through to get to know strangers

As Figure 11.1 illustrates, the **rhetorical situation** is the composite of you (and your knowledge and intentions), the audience (and their knowledge and expectations), and the occasion (setting, purpose, and constraints). Effective speakers address all three throughout the speech preparation and presentation process. Lloyd Bitzer (1968, 1995), the rhetorician who introduced the concept of the rhetorical situation, believed that the particular speech given by an individual to an audience on a specific occasion is the result of some real or perceived need that the speech might help address. He referred to this *reason the speech needs to be given* as "**exigence**" (Exigence, 2009). Because audience is a crucial component of the rhetorical situation, effective speech goals are based on **audience analysis**, the study of the intended audience, and **audience adaptation**, the process of tailoring the speech to address their unique needs, interests, and expectations. Audience analysis and adaptation are rooted in what communication scholars refer to as **uncertainty reduction theory** (Berger & Calabrese, 1975; Knobloch & mcAninch, 2014). Although effective speakers adapt their speech to the audience throughout the speech preparation and presentation process, they begin doing so at the point of determining a specific speech goal.

To determine a specific speech goal adapted to the rhetorical situation, begin by identifying lots of subjects and topics that interest you. Then, based on your analysis of both the audience and the occasion, narrow your list down to include only those that (a) interest you and you know something about, (b) can be adapted to address

ACTION STEP 1

Determine a Specific Speech Goal Adapted to the Rhetorical Situation

the needs, interests, and expectations of the audience, and (c) are appropriate for the occasion.

Identify Potential Topics

Good speech topics come from subjects we have some knowledge about and interest in. A **subject** is a broad area of knowledge, such as contemporary cinema, renewable energy, computer technology, or the Middle East. A **topic** is a narrower aspect of a subject. So, if your broad subject area is contemporary cinema, you might feel qualified to speak on a variety of topics such as how the Academy Awards nomination process works; the relationships between movie producers, directors, and distributors; or how technology is changing movie production. Let's look at how you can identify subject areas and potential speech topics.

Photo 11.1 Brainstorm for potential speech topics from broad subject areas that interest you. What subject areas interest you?

Subjects You can identify subjects by listing those that (1) are important to you and (2) you know something about. Subjects may be related to careers that interest you, your major area of study, special skills or competencies you have or admire, your hobbies, as well as your social, economic, or political interests. So if your major is marketing, favorite hobbies are skateboarding and snowboarding, and issues that concern you include illiteracy, substance abuse, and obesity, then these are *subjects* from which you can identify potential speech topics.

At this point, you might be thinking, "What if my audience isn't interested in the subjects that interest me?" In reality, topics in any subject area can be of interest when they are adapted to address the needs and expectations of the audience. Figure 11.2 contains a list of subjects that Kameron came up with for the speech contest.

Brainstorm and Concept Map Because a topic is a specific aspect of a subject, you can identify many topics related to one subject. Two methods for identifying topics are brainstorming and concept mapping.

Brainstorming is an uncritical, nonevaluative process of generating associated ideas. When you brainstorm, you list as many ideas as you can think of without evaluating them (Photo 11.1). One subject Kameron identified, for example, was civil rights. By brainstorming, he came up with a list of potential topics that included: the role of suffragists in gaining women's right to vote; the rise and fall of Jim Crow in the American South; gun control; and same-sex marriage.

Concept mapping is a visual means of exploring connections between a subject and related ideas (Moon, Hoffman, Novak, & Canas, 2011). To generate connections, you might ask yourself questions about your subject, focusing on who, what, where, when, and how. In Figure 11.3, you can see Kameron's concept map on the subject of gun control.

APPLY IT

Identify 3 or 4 topics that have interested you enough to learn about them and gain some expertise. Do you think any of them would make a good speech topic? Why?

MindTap®

subject
a broad area of knowledge

topic
some specific aspect of a subject

brainstorming
an uncritical, nonevaluative process of generating associated ideas

concept mapping
a visual means of exploring connections between a subject and related ideas

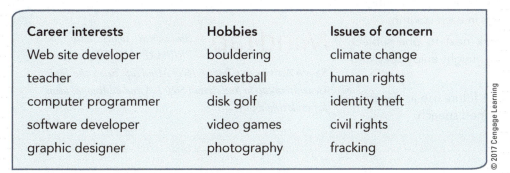

Career interests	Hobbies	Issues of concern
Web site developer	bouldering	climate change
teacher	basketball	human rights
computer programmer	disk golf	identity theft
software developer	video games	civil rights
graphic designer	photography	fracking

Figure 11.2

Kameron's subject list

Figure 11.3

Kameron's concept map

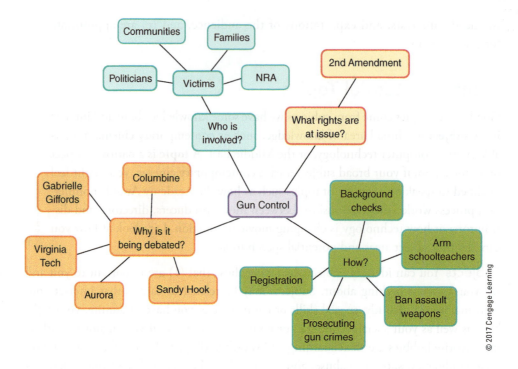

Analyze the Audience Because addressing the specific needs and expectations of your intended audience is integral to the rhetorical situation, you need to examine who they are by collecting both demographic and subject-related data. This information will help you select and tailor your topic and goal to meet their needs, interests, and expectations.

Demographic Data Helpful demographic information includes, for example, each person's approximate age, education level, sex, income, occupation, socioeconomic status,

ACTION STEP 1.A

Brainstorm and Concept Map for Topics

1. Develop a subject list.

   a. Divide a sheet of paper into three columns. Label column 1 "career interests," column 2 "hobbies," and column 3 "issues of concern."

   b. Working on one column at a time, identify subjects that interest you. Try to identify at least three subjects in each column.

   c. Place a check mark next to one subject in each column you might enjoy speaking about.

   d. Keep these lists for future use in choosing a topic for an assigned speech.

2. For each subject you checked, brainstorm a list of potential speech topics related to it.

3. Then, for each subject you checked, develop a concept map to identify potential speech topics.

MindTap® *Brainstorm topics with the PREPARE Your Informative Speech Activity in Chapter 16 of MindTap. Select the Topic Generation tab to find Action Step 1.A and additional ideas for exploring topics.*

Age: What is the average age range of your audience members?

Educational Level: What percentage of your audience has a high school, college, or postgraduate education?

Sex: What percentage of your audience is male? Female?

Occupation: Is a majority of your audience from a single occupational group, industry, or major? Or do they come from a variety of occupations, industries, or majors?

Socioeconomic Status: What percentage of your audience comes from high-, middle-, or low-income families?

Race: Are most members of your audience of the same race, or is there a mixture of races represented?

Ethnicity: What cultural and co-cultural groups do your audience members identify with?

Religion: What religious traditions are represented?

Geographic Uniqueness: Are audience members from the same state, city, or neighborhood?

Language: What language (if any) is spoken by all audience members? What are the most common primary languages?

© Cengage Learning

Figure 11.4

Demographic and subject-specific audience analysis questions

race, ethnicity, religion, geographic uniqueness, and first language. Figure 11.4 presents a list of questions that will help you uncover important demographic information.

Subject-Related Data You also want to collect subject-related audience disposition data, including: their level of knowledge, initial level of interest in, and attitude toward the potential topics you are considering. Once you know this information, you can use a process of elimination to choose a topic and goal that will offer some new information, insight, or perspective for them.

In our opening scenario, for example, Alyssa wants to give her speech on the value of doing community service as college students. If she is not sure what the audience understands about community service, she could infer what they know by examining demographic data. Since most of her classmates are majoring in sociology, communications, and social work, she infers they know the basics about what community service is. However, they may not know what organizations exist in their communities or how to go about locating one to serve in. Since some of her classmates are in other majors, she decided to also collect subject-related data to learn what they know about community service and whether they are interested in getting involved.

Data-Gathering Methods You can use several different methods to gather data about your audience.

1. **Conduct a survey.** Although it is not always possible, the most direct way to collect audience data is to survey them. A **survey** is a direct examination of people to gather information about their ideas and opinions. Some surveys are done as interviews; others as written questionnaires. Darius, who wanted to know what his classmates thought about social networking sites like Facebook, Twitter, and LinkedIn, created

APPLY IT

Based on the process of elimination, select a potential topic you identified in your brainstorming or concept-mapping. How might you adapt it to your audience based on the results of the demographic and subject-related analysis you did?

survey
a direct examination of people to gather information about their ideas and opinions

Figure 11.5

Sample survey questions

Two-sided question

Are you _____ a man _____ a woman?

Question with multiple responses

Which is the highest educational level you have completed? _____ less than

high school _____ high school _____ attended college _____ associate's degree

_____ bachelor's degree _____ master's degree _____ doctorate degree _____

postdoctorate

Scaled items

How much do you know about Islam? _____ not much _____ a little _____ some

_____ quite a lot _____ detailed knowledge

Open-ended item

What do you think about labor unions?

© Cengage Learning

an online survey in Qualtrics and posted it on the class Web site. Four common items used in a survey are two-sided, multiple-response, scaled, and open-ended. *Two-sided items* force respondents to choose between two answers (e.g., yes/no, for/against). *Multiple-response items* give respondents several alternatives from which to choose. *Scaled items* measure the direction of intensity of respondents' feelings or attitudes toward something (e.g., on a scale from 1 to 5, with 5 being "very likely," . . .). *Open-ended items* encourage respondents to elaborate on their opinions without forcing them to answer in a predetermined way. Figure 11.5 gives some examples of each type.

2. **Observe informally.** If you are familiar with audience members, you can learn a lot through informal observation (Photo 11.2). For instance, after being in class for even a couple of sessions, you should be able to estimate the approximate age or age range and the ratio of men to women. As you listen to your classmates talk, you will learn more about their interest in, knowledge of, and attitudes about many issues.

Photo 11.2 You can learn a lot about an audience through informal observation. What are some things you've observed about the classmates that will make up your audience?

3. **Question a representative.** When you are invited to speak to a group you are unfamiliar with, ask your contact person for demographic and subject-related audience data related to your topic. Romeo, from our opening scenario, visited with the Principal in advance to learn about student attitudes about attending college.

4. **Make educated guesses.** If you can't get information in any other way, you can make educated guesses based on indirect data such as the general makeup of the people who live in a certain community, belong to a certain organization, or are likely to attend the speech event.

iStockphoto.com/CEFutcher

Ethical Use of Audience Data Once you have collected audience data you can use it to tailor your speech to their interests, needs, and expectations. To demonstrate respect for everyone, you will want to avoid making inappropriate or inaccurate assumptions based on the data you've collected. Two potential pitfalls to avoid are marginalizing and stereotyping.

Marginalizing is the practice of ignoring the values, needs, and interests of some audience members, leaving them to feel excluded. For example, if you discover that most of your audience members have played adult video games, you will want to avoid marginalizing the few members who have never done so. So you might show a brief demonstration of one during the introduction of your speech on violence in adult video games.

Stereotyping is assuming all members of a group have similar knowledge, behaviors, or beliefs simply because they belong to that group. If, for instance, you find out that the average age of your audience is 65, you might stereotype and assume that most of them know nothing about video games when, in fact, many of them have either played them or observed family members doing so, To avoid stereotyping based on demographic data, you need to collect subject-related data from them, as well.

You also can reduce your chances of marginalizing or stereotyping by identifying and acknowledging the diversity represented in your audience. **Audience diversity** is the range of demographic and subject specific differences represented in an audience. So while the average age of your audience may be 65, there may also be some in the audience who are much younger. This chapter's *Diverse Voices* feature, "Considering Cultural Differences When Speaking," serves as a reminder of the diversity that might be represented in your audiences and to avoid making potentially inaccurate assumptions about them.

marginalizing
ignoring the values, needs, interests, and subject specific knowledge of some audience members

stereotyping
assuming all members of a group have similar knowledge levels, behaviors, or beliefs simply because they belong to that group

audience diversity
the range of demographic characteristics and subject specific differences represented in an audience

DIVERSE VOICES

Considering Cultural Differences When Speaking

by Sheila Wray Gregoire

So often we assume that those to whom we're speaking are just like us, but they're not.

We need to be really sensitive about our audiences. Let me give you an example. I think the biggest difference [between] Canadian and American audiences is that Canadians don't see it as a plus to sell yourself. We don't brag about ourselves; we tend to brag about others. Saying good things about yourself sounds odd.

That comes off as bragging and that's a huge no-no. I see American speakers—even [best-]selling authors—do this all the time up here in Canada and

they lose the whole audience. Perhaps that sounds like I'm being mean to Americans, and I don't mean to be, but in general Canadians are much more low-key about sharing our own successes. And it's important to know this about your audience if you're going to communicate effectively.

Another big difference: we're not as dramatic. Twice I have seen American speakers actually get down on the floor and act out a horrible experience from their past, thrashing around down there and everything. Canadians would NEVER do this. (Note: both these speakers were speaking before audiences of thousands, and were headlining large events up here.)

continued

When we tell our sad or difficult stories, we tell them quietly. We never act them out. It looks fake.

Speaking is a form of communication. You are saying something that you want others to hear. But communication is a two-way street: you put it out there, but your listeners have to take a hold of it. And that means understanding and researching your niche.

Whenever I speak, I ask who is going to be in the audience. Are they married? Single? A blend? What [are] their ages? Do they work outside the home? Is it multicultural? Are they mostly Christians, or not? You have to know these things, or your talk may go right over their heads. If I find out, for instance, that many in the audience aren't married, I will always

choose at least one anecdote that has nothing to do with marriage or children, and focuses more on one's workplace or something.

So know your audience. Don't assume they are just like you. Make sure you communicate in a way that they understand. And then your message is much more likely to get through!

Source: Adapted from Gregoire, S. W. (2009, December 8). Considering cultural differences when speaking. Becoming a Christian Woman's Speaker: With author and speaker Sheila Wray Gregoire. Retrieved April 7, 2012, from http://christianwomensspeaker.wordpress.com/2009/12/08/considering-cultural-differences-when-speaking/

ACTION STEP 1.B

Analyze Your Audience

1. Decide on the audience characteristics (demographic and subject-related data) you want to research in order to adapt your topic and speech effectively.
2. Choose a method for gathering audience information.
3. Collect the data.

MindTap *Analyze your audience with the PREPARE Your Informative Speech Activity in Chapter 16 of the MindTap. Select the Topic Generation tab to find Action Step 1.B and additional ideas for audience analysis.*

APPLY IT

What are some examples of audience diversity among your classmates and how will you adapt your speech to be inclusive and respectful?

MindTap

occasion
the expected purpose and setting for the speech

Examine the Occasion The **occasion** is made up of the expected purpose and setting (location) for the speech. Answers to several questions about the occasion should guide you when selecting your topic and throughout the speech-making process (Photo 11.3).

1. **What is the intended purpose (exigence) of the speech?** In other words, why does the audience think this speech is being given? At a religious service, for example, the congregation expects the leader's message to have a religious theme. At a national sales meeting, the field representatives expect to hear about new products. For your classroom speeches, a major expectation is that your speech will meet the assignment criteria.

2. **What is the expected length?** Time limits for classroom speeches are usually quite short, so choose a topic that is narrow enough to be accomplished in the brief time allotted. For example, "Three Major Causes of the Declining Honeybee population"

could probably be covered in a 5-minute speech; however, "A History of Human Impact on the Environment" could not. Speakers who speak for more or less time than allotted can seriously interfere with event programming and lose the respect of both their hosts and their audience.

3. **Where will the speech be given?** Rooms vary in size, shape, lighting, and seating arrangements. Some are a single level, some have stages or platforms, and some have tiered seating. The space affects the speech. For example, in a long, narrow room, you may have to speak loudly to be heard in the back row. If you are speaking in an auditorium to a large group of people, you may need to use a microphone. You will also need to use large gestures and presentational aids that can be seen and heard easily in all parts of the room. The brightness of the room and the availability of shades may affect what kinds of presentational aids you can use. So you will want to know and consider the layout of the room as you plan your speech. If possible, visit the room in advance either physically or virtually via online photo galleries or virtual tours posted on the venue's Web site.

4. **When will the speech be given?** A speech given early in the morning requires a different approach from one given right after lunch or in the evening. If a speech is scheduled after a meal, for example, the audience may be lethargic, mellow, or even on the verge of sleep. So you may want to plan more material that gains and regains their interest throughout the speech. Similarly, where you are placed on the schedule of events should influence your speech planning. For example, if you are first, you may need to "warm up" the audience and be prepared to deal with the distraction of latecomers entering the room while you are speaking. If you speak later in the program, you may need to integrate attention-catching material to keep the interest of a weary audience.

5. **What equipment is necessary and available?** Would you like to use a microphone, lectern, flip chart, smart board, or computer, LCD projector, and speakers to display visuals and audiovisuals? If so, does the room have adequate means for displaying visuals and projecting audio? Do you plan to use the Internet and, if so, is the room wired for Internet or Wi-Fi? It is your responsibility to check with your host to make sure the equipment can be made available or make alternative arrangements. Regardless of the arrangements made, however, experienced speakers realize that something may go wrong and always prepare a backup plan. So if you are planning to use a computerized slide show, you might also prepare handouts of key slides in case the equipment fails.

Photo 11.3 How does the setting and the occasion dictate what a speaker will talk about?

Select a Topic

As you review your topic list, compare each to your audience profile. Are any topics too simple or too difficult for this audience's knowledge base? If so, eliminate those topics. Are some topics likely to bore the audience and you can't think of any way to pique their interest with new information or a new perspective on them? Eliminate those, as well. How might the audience's age range, ethnicity, and other demographic characteristics mesh with each topic? By asking these and similar questions, you will be able to identify topics and perspectives on topics that are appropriate for the audience.

APPLY IT

Consider a time when an instructor kept you beyond the allotted class time. How did that influence your attitude about your instructor and their opinion of you?

MindTap

ACTION STEP 1.C

Analyze the Occasion

Hold a conversation with the person who arranged for you to speak and get answers to the following questions:

1. What is the intended purpose of the speech?

2. What is the expected length for the speech?

3. Where will the speech be given and to how many people?

4. When will the speech be given?

5. What equipment is necessary to give the speech?

Write a short paragraph discussing which aspects of the occasion are most important to consider for your speech and why.

MindTap® *Analyze the occasion with the PREPARE Your Informative Speech Activity in Chapter 16 of the MindTap. Select the Topic Generation tab to find Action Step 1.C.*

Next, consider the occasion. Are some topics inappropriate for the intended purpose? Are some too broad to cover adequately in the time allotted? Would any require equipment that cannot be made available where you will be speaking? Answers to these kinds of questions will help you identify topics appropriate to the occasion.

ACTION STEP 1.D

Select a Topic

Use your responses to Action Steps 1.A, 1.B, and 1.C to complete this step.

1. Write each of the topics that you checked in Action Step 1.A. on the lines below:

2. Using the information you compiled in Action Step 1.B (audience analysis), compare each topic to your audience profile. Draw a line through topics that seem less appropriate for your audience.

3. Using the information you compiled in Action Step 1.C (analysis of the occasion), compare the remaining topics to the expectations of the occasion. Draw a line through topics that seem less suited to the occasion.

4. From the remaining topics, choose one that you would find enjoyable preparing and sharing in your speech.

MindTap® *Select your topic with the PREPARE Your Informative Speech Activity in Chapter 16 of the MindTap. Select the Topic Generation tab to find Action Step 1.D and to evaluate your selected topic.*

Write a Speech Goal Statement

Once you have chosen a topic, you are ready to identify the general goal of your speech and then to write your specific goal statement tailored to the audience and occasion.

General and Specific Speech Goals The **general goal** is the overall intent of the speech. Most speeches intend to entertain, inform, or persuade, even though each type can include elements of the others. Consider the following examples. Seth Meyers opening monologue on *Late Night with Seth Meyers* is generally intended to entertain, even though it may include persuasive material (Photo 11.4). Presidential campaign speeches are intended to persuade, even though they also include informative material. The general goal is usually dictated by the occasion. (In this course, your instructor is likely to specify it.)

Whereas the general goal is typically determined by the occasion, the **specific speech goal** (or specific purpose) is a single statement that identifies the desired response a speaker wants from the audience. For a speech about "vanishing honeybees," you might state a specific goal as, "I want my audience to understand the four reasons honeybees are vanishing" if your general goal is to inform. If your general goal is to persuade, you might say, "I want my audience to donate money to *Honeybee Advocacy International,* a group trying to solve the problem and stop the crisis." Figure 11.6 offers additional examples of informative and persuasive speech goals.

Photo 11.4 Although the general goal of Seth Meyers' opening monologues is to entertain, he may also include informational and persuasive material in them.

general goal
the overall intent of the speech

specific speech goal
a single statement that identifies the desired response a speaker wants from the audience

Phrasing a Specific Goal Statement A specific speech goal statement must be carefully crafted because it lays the foundation for organizing your speech. The following guidelines can help you do so.

1. **Write a first draft of your specific speech goal statement.** Julia, who has been concerned with and is knowledgeable about the subject of illiteracy, drafts the following: "I want my audience to understand the effects of illiteracy." Julia's draft is a complete sentence, and it specifies the response she wants from the audience: *to understand* the effects of illiteracy. Thus, she is planning to give an informative speech.

2. **Make sure the goal statement contains only one central idea.** Suppose Julia had written: "I want the audience to understand the nature of illiteracy and innumeracy." This would need to be revised because it includes two distinct ideas: illiteracy and innumeracy. It would be difficult to adequately address both within one speech. If your goal statement includes the word *and*, you probably have more than one idea and need to narrow your focus.

Figure 11.6

Informative and persuasive
speech goals

© Cengage Learning

Informative Goals

Increasing understanding: I want my audience to understand the three basic forms of a mystery story.

Increasing knowledge: I want my audience to learn how to light a fire without a match.

Increasing appreciation: I want my audience to appreciate the intricacies of spider-web designs.

Persuasive Goals

Reinforce belief: I want my audience to maintain its belief in drug-free sports.

Change belief: I want my audience to believe that SUVs are environmentally destructive.

Motivation to act: I want my audience to join Amnesty International.

---

3. **Revise the statement until it clearly articulates the desired audience response.** The draft "I want my audience to understand illiteracy" is a good start, but it is fairly broad. Julia narrows the statement to: "I want my audience to understand three effects of illiteracy." This version is more specific, but still does not clearly capture her intention, so she revises it again to: "I would like the audience to understand three effects of illiteracy in the workplace." Now the goal is limited by Julia's focus not only on the specific number of effects but also on a specific situation.

ACTION STEP   1.E

Write a Specific Speech Goal Statement

General speech goal

1. Write a draft of your specific speech goal, using a complete sentence that specifies the type of response you want from the audience: (e.g., to learn about, to understand, to take action)

2. Review the specific goal statement. If it contains more than one idea, select one and redraft your specific goal statement.

Write out your revised specific speech goal statement:

_____

_____

_____

MindTap® *Write your specific speech goal with the PREPARE Your Informative Speech Activity in Chapter 16 of the MindTap. Select the Outline tab to find Action Step 1.E and additional ideas for developing your specific goal.*

COMMUNICATION SKILL

Crafting an Effective Specific Speech Goal Statement

Skill	Use	Procedure	Example
The process of identifying a speech purpose that draws on the speaker's knowledge and interests and is adapted to the audience and occasion.	To identify a specific goal that matches speaker interest and expertise with audience and occasion.	1. Identify topics within subject areas in which you have interest and expertise. 2. Analyze audience demographics, interests, and attitudes toward your subject. 3. Understand the expectations and location for the speech. 4. Select a topic that meets the interests and expectations of the audience and occasion. 5. Write a specific speech goal that clearly states the desired response you want from your audience.	Ken first writes, "I want my audience to know what to look for in adopting a dog." As he revises, he writes, "I want my audience to understand four important considerations in adopting the perfect dog." Once Ken has a goal with a single focus and a clearly specified, desired audience reaction, he tests his first version by writing two differently worded versions.

ACTION STEP 2

Gather and Evaluate Information to Develop Your Speech

To use the most effective information to support your speech goal, you must be able to locate and evaluate appropriate sources, identify and select relevant information, and cite information and sources appropriately during your speech.

Locate and Evaluate Information Sources

How can you quickly find the best information related to your specific speech goal? You can start by assessing your own knowledge and experience. Then you can move to **secondary research**, which is the process of locating information discovered by other people. This includes doing Internet and library searches for relevant books, articles, general references, and Web sites. If the information you find from secondary sources doesn't answer all your questions, you may need to conduct **primary research**, which is the process of collecting data about your topic directly from the real world.

secondary research
the process of locating information about your topic discovered by other people

primary research
the process of collecting data about your topic directly from the real world

Personal Knowledge and Experience

Because you will be speaking on a topic you know something about, you can include examples from your personal experiences. For instance, a saxophone player knows how to select

Christopher Futcher/iStockphoto.com

and care for a reed. Likewise, entrepreneurs know the key features of a business plan, and dieticians have a wealth of information about healthy diets. So Diane, a skilled long-distance runner, can draw from her own knowledge and experience to develop her speech on "How to Train for a Marathon." (See Photo 11.5.) If you have personal knowledge and experience about the topic, however, you should also share your **credentials**—your experiences or education that qualifies you to speak with authority on a subject. For Diane, establishing her credentials means briefly mentioning her training and expertise as a long-distance runner before she launches into her speech about training for a marathon.

Secondary Research

Even if you are an expert on your topic, you may need to do secondary research as you adapt the information for your intended audience. To conduct secondary research, you'll need to know how to locate sources, what types of sources you can draw from, as well as how to skim and evaluate them.

Internet Sources Thanks to the major advances in computer technology that have occurred in recent years—including laptops, tablets, and smart phones, as well as wireless and personal hot spot accessibility—we literally have instant access to a plethora of information about any topic. The challenge comes in sifting through all this information to select the best information for our speech. We typically begin online searches by typing key words into a general search engine such as Google, Bing, or Ask. These searches will reveal "hits" (links to all sorts of Web pages, images, videos, articles, etc.) that include material about the key words. When Alyssa typed in "benefits of volunteering," for example, she came up with 41,700,000 hits.

Many times one of the hits will be to an online encyclopedia entry in Wikipedia. These entries can be a good starting point for learning general information and for locating additional references about a given topic. There is some controversy today about whether or not to use Wikipedia. The *Communicating in the World* feature "To Wikipedia or Not to Wikipedia? That's a Good Question" discusses some of the issues surrounding its use. Justin read the Wikipedia entry that came up from his "vanishing honey bees" search and learned that the official name for the phenomenon is colony collapse disorder. He also perused the Reference List and Further Reading list where he found articles published by the *New York Times, Science News* and *The Proceedings of the National Academies of Sciences*. And he discovered several helpful Web sites listed under External Links from organizations such as the United States Department of Agriculture (USDA) and the National Honeybee Board. There is nothing wrong with starting the research process by reading a Wikipedia entry. In fact, doing so can be quite helpful.

Other hits may include commercial web sites, which are created and maintained by for-profit organizations. Commercial Web site URLs typically end in .com. Commercial Web sites can be helpful for locating information about a company such as the National Honey Bee Board, for finding current or popular culture material, and for finding presentational aids. Justin found a short audiovisual clip to use in the speech about the vanishing honey bee phenomenon this way.

Nonprofit organization Web sites can be distinguished from commercial ones because their URLs will usually end in .org. These organizations are dedicated to issues or causes and

COMMUNICATING IN THE WORLD

To Wikipedia or Not to Wikipedia?: That's a Good Question

Wikipedia

Since its creation in 2001, Wikipedia has grown into one of the top ten Web sites used worldwide, offering over 30 million articles in 285 different languages. According to the Wikimedia Foundation (2015), the English language section alone features over 4.5 million articles. Because it is [. . .] edited collaboratively mainly by anonymous volunteers, many educators discourage their students from using it as a research tool.

But some educators argue that to simply dismiss Wikipedia as a "bad" source misses the opportunity for students to think critically about how to do authoritative research. A study of Wikipedia conducted by Roy Rosenzweig for *The Journal of American History* actually found that many Wikipedia entries were "as accurate or more accurate than more traditional encyclopedias" (Jaschik, 2007). Moreover, Mesgari, Okoli, Mehdi, Nielson, and Lanamaki (2014) call it the "best-developed attempt thus far of the enduring quest to gather all human knowledge in one place." But even Wikipedia supporters caution that, like any

encyclopedia, it, should be a regarded only as a starting point for research and not a primary source.

Many university librarians suggest that instead of simply banning its use, today's college students need to be taught to develop information literacy skills that will help them navigate an increasingly complex information environment. Steven Bell, associate librarian for research and instructional services at Temple University, says students should be taught "how to 'triangulate' a source like Wikipedia, so they could use other sources to tell whether a given entry could be trusted" (Jaschik, 2007). For example, instead of simply accepting the Wikipedia entry as "fact," students should, at the very least, verify the information by clicking on the sources in the "Notes" section at the end of an entry to see if it comes from a primary and trusted source, such as books, magazine, newspaper, and journal articles, original interviews, and court decisions. Darren Crovitz and W. Scott Smoot (2009) write, "Talking with [students] about how the site operates is essential in helping them move from passive acceptors of information to practicing analyzers and evaluators." So rather than summarily dismissing Wikipedia, perhaps educators should be teaching students how to use it as a starting point and how to evaluate the information and sources provided in its entries.

Why should Wikipedia be used only as a starting point for research rather than a primary source?

MindTap®

can often provide emotional appeals examples. Justin found some startling statistics about $15 billion in crops the United States would lose without the bees' pollination of plants.

Blogs are Web sites that provide personal viewpoints of their author. They can be created and maintained by an individual or an organization. They might focus on a particular subject and include images, audios, and audiovisuals. Because they are often biased toward the opinion of the blogger, information on them may have to be verified with other sources. However, they can be a good source for finding public opinion examples and for humanizing the topic. The most efficient way to find blogs is to use a blog search engine such as Google Blog Search or Blogarama. Justin found some interesting opinions on Dady Cherie's *News Junkie Post* blog. Because blogs can be written by anyone, you will need to determine whether the author is a credible source by locating his or her credentials. If you cannot determine their credentials, you should not use the information in your speech.

blogs
Web sites that provide personal viewpoints of their author

Online social networks are Web sites where communities of people interact with one another. Some popular examples include Facebook, LinkedIn, Twitter, and Instagram. Like blogs, postings on these sites can be used to find supporting material to humanize a topic, appeal to emotions, and serve as presentational aids.

Other Types of Sources You can also find pertinent information in sources that can be found online or in a local library (Photo 11.6). These include, for example, encyclopedias, books, articles in academic journals and magazines, newspapers, statistical sources, biographies, quotation books and Web sites, and government documents.

Photo 11.6 Have you ever taken a course in online research, perhaps at your library? If not, consider doing so. You will save yourself a lot of time, and it will help you locate great sources of useful information.

online social networks
Web sites where communities of people interact with one another

periodicals
magazines and journals that appear at regular intervals

1. ***Encyclopedias*** Encyclopedia entries (including Wikipedia) can serve as a good starting point by providing an overview of the basic terminology associated with a topic. But because encyclopedias provide only overviews, they should never be the only source you rely on. General encyclopedias contain short articles about a wide variety of subjects. In addition, specialized encyclopedias focus on areas such as art, history, religion, philosophy, and science. For instance, a college library is likely to have the *African American Encyclopedia, Latino Encyclopedia, Asian American Encyclopedia, Encyclopaedia Britannica, Encyclopedia Americana, World Book Encyclopedia, Encyclopedia of Computer Science, Encyclopedia of Women, Encyclopedia of Women in American Politics*, and many more.

2. ***Books*** If your topic has been around for awhile, there are likely to be books written about it. Although books are excellent sources of in-depth material about a topic, keep in mind that most of the information in a book is likely to be at least two years old by the time it is published. So books are not a good resource if you're looking for the most current information on a topic.

3. ***Articles*** Articles, which may contain more current or highly specialized information on your topic than a book would, are published in **periodicals**—magazines and journals that appear at regular intervals. The information in periodical articles is often more current than that published in books because many periodicals are published weekly, biweekly, or monthly. So a periodical article is likely to be a better source if a topic is one that's "in the news."

4. ***News Media*** News media articles can provide facts about and interpretations of both contemporary and historical issues and provide information about local issues and perspectives. Keep in mind, however, that most authors of newspaper articles are journalists who are not experts themselves on the topics they write about. So, it is best not to rely solely on news media articles for your speech. Today, most traditional news media publications are available online (*New York Times, Wall Street Journal*), which makes them very accessible. You might also find good information in new media online-only sources such as the Huffington Post and the Drudge Report.

5. ***Statistical Sources*** Statistical sources present numerical information on a wide variety of subjects. When you need facts about demography, continents, heads of state, weather, or similar subjects, access one of the many single-volume sources that report such data.

6. ***Biographies*** When you need an account of a person's life, from thumbnail sketches to reasonably complete essays, you can use a biographical reference source. Some examples include *Who's Who in America* and *International Who's Who, Contemporary Black Biography, Dictionary of Hispanic Biography, Native American Women, Who's Who of American Women, Who's Who Among Asian Americans,* and many more.

7. ***Quotation Books and Web Sites*** A good quotation can be especially provocative as well as informative, and there are times you want to use a quotation from a respected person. *Bartlett's Familiar Quotations* is a popular source of quotes from historical as well as contemporary figures. But many other collections of quotations are also available. Some others include *The International Thesaurus of Quotations; Harper Book of American Quotations; My Soul Looks Back, 'Less I Forget: A Collection of Quotations by People of Color; The New Quotable Woman;* and *The Oxford Dictionary of Quotations.* Some popular quotation Web sites include *The Quotations Page* and *Quoteland.com.*

8. ***Government Documents*** If your topic is related to public policy, government documents may provide useful information. The *Federal Register* publishes daily regulations and legal notices issued by the executive branch of the United States and all federal agencies. It is divided into sections, such as rules and regulations and Sunshine Act meetings. Of special interest are announcements of hearings and investigations, committee meetings, and agency decisions and rulings. The *Monthly Catalog of United States Government Publications* covers publications of all branches of the federal government.

Skim Sources Because your search of secondary sources is likely to uncover far more information than you can use, you will want to skim sources to determine whether or not to read them in full. **Skimming** is a method of rapidly viewing a work to determine what is covered and how (Photo 11.7).

As you skim an article, think about whether it really presents information on the area of the topic you are exploring and whether it contains any documented statistics, examples, meaningful visuals, or quotable opinions. You can start by reading the **abstract**—a short paragraph summarizing the research findings. As you skim a book, read the table of contents carefully, look at the index, and review the headings and visuals in pertinent chapters, asking the same questions as you would for a magazine article. A few minutes spent skimming will save hours of time.

Evaluate Sources The validity, accuracy, and reliability of sources vary. **Valid sources** report factual information that can be counted on to be true. Tabloid magazines and tabloid newspapers are generally considered less valid sources for information on celebrities than mainline news organizations that use "fact-checkers" before publishing an article. **Accurate sources** present unbiased information that often includes a balanced discussion of controversial ideas. For example, the *Congressional Record* provides an accurate account of what each member of U.S. Congress has said on the House or

skimming
rapidly viewing a work to determine what is covered and how

abstract
a short paragraph summarizing the research findings

valid sources
report factual information that can be counted on to be true

accurate sources
present unbiased information that includes a balanced discussion of controversial ideas

Photo 11.7 Surfing the Internet is actually a form of skimming that you can also use with articles and books. How do you take notes while skimming online?

© Yuri Arcurs/Shutterstock.com

reliable sources
sources with a history of presenting accurate information

Senate floor. **Reliable sources** are those with a history of presenting accurate information. Four criteria can help you assess the validity, accuracy, and reliability of sources.

1. **Authority.** The first test of a source is the expertise of its author and/or the reputation of the publishing or sponsoring organization. When an author is listed, you can check the author's credentials through biographical references or by seeing if the author has a home page listing professional qualifications. Use the electronic periodical indexes or check the Library of Congress to see what else the author has published in the field.

    On the Internet, you will sometimes find information that is anonymous or credited to someone whose background is not clear. In these cases, your ability to trust the information depends on evaluating the qualifications of the sponsoring organization. URLs ending in ".gov" (governmental), ".edu" (educational), and ".org" are noncommercial sites with institutional publishers. The URL ".com" indicates that the sponsor is a for-profit organization. If you do not know whether you can trust the sources, do not use the information.

stance
an attitude, perspective, or viewpoint on a topic

2. **Objectivity.** Although all authors have a **stance**—an attitude, perspective, or viewpoint on a topic—be wary of information that seems excessively slanted. Documents that have been published by business, government, or public interest groups should be carefully scrutinized for obvious biases or good public relations fronts. To evaluate the potential biases in articles and books, read the preface or identify the thesis statement. These often reveal the author's point of view. When evaluating a Web site, look for its purpose. Most home pages contain a purpose or mission statement (sometimes in a link called "About"). Armed with this information, you are in a better position to recognize potential biases regarding the topic.

3. **Currency.** In general, more recent information is preferred (unless, for example, you are documenting a historical event). Be sure to consult the latest information you can find. One of the reasons for using Web-based sources is that they can provide more up-to-date information than printed sources. But just because a source is found online does not mean the information is timely. To determine how current the information is, you will need to find out when the book was published, the article was written, the study was conducted, or the article was placed on the Web or revised. Web page dates are usually listed at the end of the article. If there are no dates listed, you have no way of judging how current the information is.

4. **Relevance.** During your research, you will likely come across a great deal of interesting information. Whether that information is appropriate for your speech is another matter. Relevant information is directly related to your topic and supports your main points, making your speech easier to follow and understand. Irrelevant information will only confuse listeners, so you should avoid using it no matter how interesting it is.

Primary Research

When there is little secondary research available on your topic or on a main idea you want to develop in your speech, or when you wonder whether what you are reading about is true in a particular setting, consider doing primary research. Recall that *primary research* is conducting your own study in the real world. But keep in mind that primary research is much more labor intensive and time consuming than secondary research—and, in the professional world, much more costly. You can conduct fieldwork observations, surveys, interviews, original artifact or document examinations, or experiments.

Fieldwork Observations You might choose to learn about a group of people and their practices by conducting **fieldwork observations**, which is a method also known as **ethnography**. You can conduct fieldwork as a *participant observer* by engaging in interactions and activities with the people you are studying or a *nonparticipant observer* by observing but not engaging with them. If, for instance, you are planning to talk about how social service agencies help the homeless find shelter and job training, or the process involved in adopting a pet, you can learn more by visiting or even volunteering for a period of time at a homeless shelter or humane society. By focusing on specific behaviors and taking notes on your observations, you will have a record of specifics to use in your speech.

fieldwork observations
a research method focused on careful observations of people or groups of people while immersed in their community

ethnography
collecting data by acting as a participant or non-participant observer

Surveys Recall that a survey is an examination to get information about peoples' ideas and opinions. Surveys may be conducted in person, over the phone, via the Internet, or in writing.

Interviews Like media reporters, you may get some of your best information from an **interview**—a planned, structured conversation where one person asks questions and another answers them. Appendix A provides information and guidelines for conducting effective interviews.

interview
a planned, structured conversation where one person asks questions and another answers them

Original Artifact or Document Examinations Sometimes the information you need has not been published. Rather, it may exist in an original unpublished source, such as an ancient manuscript, a diary, personal correspondence, or company files. Or you may need to view an object to get the information you need, such as a geographic feature, a building, a monument, or an artifact in a museum.

Experiments You can design an experiment to test a **hypothesis**, which is an educated guess about a cause-and-effect relationship between two or more things. Then you can report the results of your experiment in your speech. Keep in mind that experiments take time, and you must understand the principles of the scientific process to be able to trust the results of a formal experiment. However, sometimes you can conduct an informal experiment to test the results of a study you learn about elsewhere.

hypothesis
an educated guess about a cause and effect relationship between two or more things

ACTION STEP 2.A

Locate and Evaluate Information Sources

The goal of this activity is to help you compile a list of potential sources for your speech.

1. Brainstorm a list of key words related to your speech goal.

2. Identify gaps in your knowledge that you would like to fill.

3. Using a search engine like *Google*, identify Internet-sponsored and personal Web sites that may be information sources for your speech.

4. Search electronic databases to identify library resources.

5. Gather and skim the resources you have found to identify potentially useful information.

6. Evaluate the validity, accuracy, and reliability of each source.

7. If needed, conduct primary research to find answers to questions you couldn't find from your secondary research.

MindTap® *Locate and evaluate information sources with the PRE-PARE Your Informative Speech Activity in Chapter 16 of the MindTap. Select the Research tab to find Action Step 2.A and additional help with research.*

Identify and Evaluate a Variety of Information

Once you have collected a variety of sources, you need to identify different types of information or evidence to use in your speech. These include factual statements, expert opinions, and elaborations. You may find the information written in narrative form or presented as a graphic in visual form.

Factual Statements

factual statements
statements that can be verified

Factual statements are those that can be verified. *A recent study confirmed that preschoolers watch an average of 28 hours of television a week* and *The microprocessor, which was invented by Ted Hoff at Intel in 1971, made the creation of personal computers possible* are both statements of fact that can be verified. One way to verify whether a statement is accurate is to check it against other sources on the same subject. Never use any information that is not carefully documented unless you have corroborating sources. Factual statements may come in the form of statistics or real examples.

statistics
numerical facts

1. **Statistics. Statistics** are numerical facts. *Only five of every ten local citizens voted in the last election* or *The national unemployment rate for March 2010 was 9.7 percent* can provide impressive support for a point, but when statistics are poorly used in a speech, they may be boring and, in some instances, downright deceiving. Here are some ethical guidelines for using statistics:

   - Use only statistics you can verify to be reliable and valid. Taking statistics from only the most reliable sources and double-checking any startling statistics with another source will guard against the use of faulty statistics.

   - Use only recent statistics so that your audience will not be misled.

   - Use statistics comparatively. You can show growth, decline, gain, or loss by comparing two numbers. For example, according to the U.S. Department of Labor, the national unemployment rate for February 2015 was 5.5 percent. This statistic is more meaningful when you compare it to 6.7 percent in February 2014, 7.7 percent in February 2013, and 8.3 percent in February 2012.

   - Use statistics sparingly. A few pertinent numbers are far more effective than a battery of statistics.

   - Remember that statistics can be biased. Mark Twain once said there are three kinds of lies: "lies, damned lies, and statistics." Not all statistics are lies, of course, but consider the source of statistics you'd like to use, what that source may have been trying to prove with these data, and how the data were collected and interpreted. So statistics, like other types of information, must be thoughtfully evaluated and cross-checked for validity, accuracy, and reliability.

examples
specific instances that illustrate a general factual statement

2. **Examples. Examples** are specific instances that illustrate a general factual statement. One or two short examples like the following ones provide concrete detail that makes a general statement more meaningful to the audience:

   "One way a company increases its power is to buy out another company. Recently, Delta bought out Northwest and thereby became the world's largest airline company."

   "Professional figure skaters practice many long hours every day. Adam Rippon, 2010 Olympic Gold medalist, practices 20 to 25 hours per week."

Expert Opinions

Expert opinions are interpretations and judgments made by an expert in a subject area. They can help explain what facts mean or put them into perspective. *Watching 28 hours of television a week is far too much for young children, but may be OK for adults* and *Having a firewire port on your computer is absolutely necessary* are opinions. Whether they are expert opinions depends on who made the statements. An **expert** is a person who has mastered a specific subject, usually through long-term study, and who is recognized by other people in the field as being a knowledgeable and trustworthy authority. When you use expert opinions in your speech, remember to cite their credentials.

expert opinions
interpretations and judgments made by authorities in a particular subject area

expert
a person who has mastered a specific subject, usually through long-term study

Elaborations

Both factual information and expert opinions can be elaborated upon through anecdotes and narratives, comparisons and contrasts, or quotable explanations and opinions.

1. **Anecdotes and narratives. Anecdotes** are brief, often amusing stories; **narratives** are accounts, personal experiences, tales, or lengthier stories. Because holding audience interest is important and because audience attention is likely to be captured by a story, anecdotes and narratives are worth looking for or creating. The key to using them is to be sure the point of the story directly addresses the point you are making in your speech. Good stories and narratives may be humorous, sentimental, suspenseful, or dramatic. You can often find anecdotes and brief narrative on social media sites such as YouTube.

anecdotes
brief, often amusing stories

narratives
accounts, personal experiences, tales, or lengthier stories

2. **Comparisons and contrasts.** One of the best ways to give meaning to new ideas or facts is through comparison and contrast. **Comparisons** illuminate a point by showing similarities, whereas **contrasts** highlight differences. Although comparisons and contrasts may be literal, like comparing and contrasting the murder rates in different countries, they may also be figurative.

   - *Figurative comparison:* "In short, living without health insurance is as much of a risk as having uncontrolled diabetes or driving without a safety belt" (Nelson, 2006, p. 24).

   - *Figurative contrast:* "If this morning you had bacon and eggs for breakfast, I think it illustrates the difference. The eggs represented 'participation' on the part of the chicken. The bacon presented 'total commitment' on the part of the pig!" (Durst, 1989, p. 325).

comparisons
illuminate a point by showing similarities

contrasts
illuminate a point by highlighting differences

3. **Quotations.** At times, information you find will be so well stated that you want to quote it directly in your speech. Because the audience is interested in listening to your ideas and arguments, you should avoid using quotations that are too long or too numerous. But when you find that an author or expert has worded an idea especially well, quote it directly and then verbally acknowledge the person who said or wrote it. Using quotations or close paraphrases without acknowledging their source is **plagiarism**, the unethical act of presenting another person's work as your own.

plagiarism
the unethical act of presenting another person's work as your own

Diverse Cultural Perspectives

When identifying supporting material, be sure to include a variety of cultural perspectives. For example, when Carrie was preparing her speech on proficiency testing in grade schools, she purposefully searched for articles written by noted Hispanic, Asian

American, African American, and European American authors. In addition, she interviewed two local school superintendents—one from an urban and another from a suburban district. Doing so boosted Carrie's confidence that her speech would accurately reflect multiple sides of the debate on proficiency testing.

Record Information and Sources

As you find information, you need to record it accurately and keep a careful account of your sources so you can cite them appropriately during your speech. How should you keep track of the information you plan to use? One way to do so is to compile an annotated bibliography of the sources you believe are relevant and create a research card for each individual item of information you plan to cite in the speech.

Annotated Bibliography

annotated bibliography
a preliminary record of the relevant sources you find as you conduct your research

An **annotated bibliography** is a preliminary record of the relevant sources you find as you conduct your research. It includes a short summary of information in that source and how it might be used in your speech. A good annotated bibliography includes:

- A complete bibliographic citation for each source using an appropriate style (e.g., APA or MLA);

- Two or three sentences summarizing the pertinent information;

- Two or three sentences explaining how the information might support your speech; and

- Any direct quotations you might want to include verbatim in your speech.

Research Cards

research cards
individual cards or electronic facsimiles that record one piece of relevant information for your speech

Research cards are individual 3 × 5- or 4 × 6-inch index cards or electronic facsimiles that record one piece of information relevant to your speech along with a key word or main idea and the bibliographic information identifying where you found it. Recording each piece of information using a key word or main idea identifier on a unique research card allows you to easily find, arrange, and rearrange individual pieces of information as you prepare your speech.

As your stack of research cards grows, you can sort the material and place each item under the heading to which it is related. Figure 11.7 provides a sample research card.

Figure 11.7

A sample research card

Topic: Fracking

Key Term/Main idea: Health Issues

Theo Colborn, president of The Endocrine Disruption Exchange in Paonia, Colorado, believes that some drilling and fracking additives that can end up in produced water are neurotoxic; among these are 2-butoxyethanol. "If you compare [such chemicals] with the health problems the people have," Colborn says, "they match up."

Brown, Valerie J. (February 2007). "Industry Issues: Putting the Heat on Gas". Environmental Health Perspectives (US National Institute of Environmental Health Sciences),115, 2.

ACTION STEP 2.B

Prepare Research Cards: Record Facts, Opinions, and Elaborations

The goal of this step is to review the source material you identified in Action Step 2.A and to record specific items of information that you might wish to use in your speech.

1. Carefully read all print and electronic sources (including Web site material) you have identified and evaluated as appropriate sources for your speech. Review your notes and any recordings from interviews and observations.

2. As you read an item (fact, opinion, example, illustration, statistic, anecdote, narrative, comparison/contrast, quotation, definition, or description) that you think might be useful in your speech, record it on a research card.

MindTap® *Prepare Research Cards with the PREPARE Your Informative Speech Activity in Chapter 16 of the MindTap. Select the Research tab to find Action Step 2.B.*

Cite Sources

In your speeches, as in any communication in which you use information that is not your own, you need to acknowledge the sources of it. Specifically mentioning your sources not only helps the audience evaluate them but also enhances your credibility. Frankly, failure to cite sources constitutes plagiarism. Just as you would provide internal citations or footnotes in a written document, you must provide oral footnotes during your speech. **Oral footnotes** are references to an original source, made at the point in the speech where information from that source is presented. The key to preparing oral footnotes is to include enough information for listeners to access the sources themselves and to offer enough credentials to enhance the credibility of the information you are citing. Examples or oral footnotes are provided in Figure 11.8.

oral footnote
references to an original source, made at the point in the speech where information from that source is presented

"Thomas Friedman, noted columnist for *The New York Times*, stated in his book *The World Is Flat . . .*"

"In an interview with *New Republic* magazine, Governor Chris Christie stated . . ."

"According to an article on the *U.S. News & World Report* Web site, the average college graduate . . ."

"In the latest Gallup poll cited in the February 10 issue of *The New York Times Online . . . .*"

"But to get a complete picture, we have to look at the statistics. According to the 2015 *Statistical Abstracts*, the level of production for the European Economic Community fell from . . ."

"During the U.S.–Pakistan Strategic Dialogue in 2015, Secretary of State John Kerry stated . . ."

© Cengage Learning

Figure 11.8

Sample oral footnotes

ACTION STEP   2.C

Citing Sources

On the back of each research card, write a short phrase that you can use in your speech as an oral footnote.

MindTap *Prepare your source citations with the PREPARE Your Informative Speech Activity in Chapter 16 of the MindTap. Select the Research Generation tab to find Action Step 2.C and more help citing sources.*

WHAT WOULD YOU DO?

A Question of Ethics

Alessandra decided to do her speech on the limited educational opportunities for women in the developing world. This topic was close to her heart, as her mother had struggled for years to improve education for women in her native country of Eritrea before immigrating to the United States. Moreover, Alessandra had already done quite a bit of reading on the topic.

As chance would have it, Alessandra came down with the flu the week before her speech was due and was flat on her back for four days so she didn't begin working on her speech until the afternoon before it was due. Still, by midnight, she had completed what she felt was a strong draft.

The next morning she cleaned up a few typos and errors in her outline and then practiced delivering it for the next two hours. Just before leaving for school, she read the instructions one last time to double-check that she had done everything correctly. Were her eyes playing tricks on her? The speech needed to be supported by no fewer than five published sources, yet she had cited only four. How could she have overlooked this detail? Alessandra thought frantically. She could ask for an extension, but she had too much other schoolwork to do in the coming days and needed to complete this project now. She could leave her speech as it was, but Mr. Allen was a stickler for little details and he'd certainly lower her grade over the missing source.

Alessandra had, of course, read other books on her topic in the past, even if she hadn't cited them in her speech. Although she couldn't remember the specific details of these books, she recalled their general message well enough. That was the solution! She would write a few quotations from one of the books based on her memory, drop them into her speech—she knew just the spot—and then update her references with credit information pulled from the Internet.

In less than a half hour, Alessandra completed her emergency revisions and was on her way to class.

What ethical obligations does Alessandra have to her sources?

MindTap

COMMUNICATE ON YOUR FEET

Speech Assignment

Citing Oral Footnotes

The Assignment

Do secondary research on a topic assigned to the class by your instructor. For that topic, create research cards and oral footnotes for the following kinds of sources:

- One newspaper article
- One journal or magazine article

- One book
- One Web site or Blog

Be prepared when called on in class to present the information on your research card with an appropriate oral footnote. You should be equally prepared to critique the oral footnotes your classmates present and to hear critiques of yours.

Reflection and Assessment

This chapter focused on the first two action steps in the speechmaking process: selecting a specific speech goal that is adapted to the rhetorical situation, and gathering and evaluating information to develop speech content. To assess how well you've learned what we addressed in these pages, answer the following questions. If you have trouble answering any of them, go back and review that material. Once you can answer each question accurately, you are ready to move ahead to read the next chapter.

1. How do you tailor a speech topic to make it appropriate for the rhetorical situation?
2. Where can you go to locate appropriate information sources?
3. What are the criteria you can use to evaluate different types of evidence?
4. How can you record information and sources for your speech?
5. What should you include in an oral footnote and why?

COMMUNICATE!

RESOURCE AND ASSESSMENT CENTER

MindTap

Now that you have read Chapter 11, go to your MindTap for *Communicate!* for quick access to the electronic resources that accompany this text.

Applying What You've Learned

Impromptu Speech Activity

Draw an information source from a box in the front of the room. It might be a book, a magazine or academic journal article, or a printout from a discussion board or blog or Web site. Read or skim the source. Then prepare a proper APA reference citation. Go to the front of the room and write the citation on the board. Then present a 2- to 3-minute informative speech on how well the source meets each of the four evaluation criteria for a speech on a related topic. Provide evidence for your assessments. Be sure to quote something from the information source using a proper oral footnote during the speech.

Assessment Activities

1. Evaluating Information and Sources in a Demo Reel Go to the VS Video Productions Web site at www.vsvideoproductions.com and click on the "demo reels" link. What kinds of information and information sources are used to compel viewers to use this company's services?

Which are most compelling to you and why?

2. Audience Analysis of a Public Speech Attend a public speech delivered outside your school. If your schedule makes going to a live speech difficult, you may watch a speech delivered on TV or cable (try C-SPAN). When watching the speech, give close consideration to the audience and occasion and evaluate how they might have influenced the speaker. Was the speech pitched directly at the immediate interests of the audience?

If not, did the speaker attempt to draw connections between his or her topic and the audience's interests?

Did the speaker use any particular words or gestures to connect better with the audience?

What about the manner in which the speaker was dressed; how might this have played with the audience?

Can you discern any influence the setting might have played on the speaker?

3. Recognizing a Specific Goal Find a speech online about a topic that interests you. (Try sites such as AmericanRhetoric.com or www.whitehouse.gov/briefing_room.) Then read that speech to identify the speaker's goal. Was the goal clearly stated in the introduction? Was it implied but nevertheless clear? Was it unclear? Note how this analysis can help you clarify your own speech goal. Write a paragraph explaining what you have learned.

4. Evaluating Sources Compare the definitions of *fracking* presented on these two Web pages:

(a) http://www.bbc.com/news/uk-14432401

(b) http://www.foodandwaterwatch.org/water/fracking/

Note the specific wording of each definition. Use the concept of source bias to explain this difference. Locate a third source that defines fracking that is less biased than the two provided. On what basis did you decide it was less biased?

Organizing
Your Speech

When you finish this chapter, you'll be able to:

- Develop your speech body into two to four main points using an appropriate main point pattern.

- Construct an introduction to get attention, convey listener relevance, establish speaker credibility, and identify the thesis statement.

- Create a conclusion that summarizes the main ideas and leaves the audience with a vivid impression.

- Compile the reference list and formal speech outline.

MindTap®

Start with quick warm-up activity.

Katie and Alyssa are taking a public speaking course online over the summer. That way, they can still make progress toward graduation while living at home where they both have great summer jobs. Most of the class is conducted asynchronously; but every Monday afternoon from 1:00 to 3:00 p.m., all students are required to "attend class virtually" using MindTap. That's when students deliver their formal speeches. Matt just finished his speech when Alyssa got a text from Katie:

"Matt's speech was awesome! So many powerful stories!"

Alyssa replied, "Great stories but hard to follow. What were his main points?"

Katie responded, "Hmm . . . not sure ☺. I hope mine will be easier to follow."

"Mine too," Alyssa exclaimed. "Uh oh. Late for work. CU."

12

Katie's and Alyssa's experiences are not that unusual. Even well-known speakers sometimes give speeches that are hard to follow. Yet, when your speech is well organized, you are far more likely to achieve your goal. A well-organized speech has three identifiable parts: an introduction, a body, and a conclusion. In this chapter, we describe the third of the five speech plan action steps: organizing ideas into a well-structured outline.

ACTION STEP   3

Organize Ideas Into a Well-Structured Outline

organizing
the process of arranging your speech material

Organizing, the process of arranging your speech material, is guided by what you learned from your audience analysis. The *Communicating in the World* feature "Raise a Glass: Giving a Toast," illustrates the negative consequences of a poorly organized speech. To turn your ideas into a well-organized outline, begin by developing the body, then the introduction, and finally, the conclusion.

COMMUNICATING IN THE WORLD

Raise a Glass: Giving a Toast

Purestock/GettyImages

Public speaking is not just something you do in the classroom. People are often asked to give short speeches at a variety of social events, including weddings, funerals, and even birthday parties. The wedding toast is one of the most common "real-life" examples of public speaking. It's also a speech where a person's *lack* of public speaking skills really shows. Many Hollywood films play off the awkward situations that arise from poorly delivered wedding toasts. While it is fun to chuckle at Alan's (Zach Galifianakis's) ridiculous "wolf pack" speech from *The Hangover,* cringe at the awkward one-upmanship between Annie (Kristen Wiig) and Helen (Rose Byrne) during the engagement party in *Bridesmaids,* or laugh at Steve Buscemi's drunken rant in *The Wedding Singer,* chances are you don't want to follow these models should you

ever be called upon to give a toast. But how do you make sure this doesn't happen to you?

It may seem like this is not the place for a prepared and structured speech, but most experts agree that it's best to prepare and organize your remarks ahead of time. Practicing aloud in advance also helps you sound more natural and conversational. But that doesn't mean you need to prepare something lengthy. Renowned etiquette expert Emily Post says "[Y]ou can never go wrong if you keep it short and sweet" ("Vermont Vows: The Toast!," 2010). The fundamental goal of the wedding toast is to honor the bride and groom, and some of the best toasts accomplish this goal in just one or two minutes.

When considering how to structure your toast, About.com Weddings writer Nina Calloway suggests beginning by introducing yourself and indicating how you know the couple. Humorous or heartfelt anecdotes about the couple can be a great way to personalize the speech and keep your audience interested. In fact, including a joke or a poignant memory about the bride or groom can be an effective way to start your toast and set the tone for the entire speech. Remember to keep such personal anecdotes positive

continued

rather than embarrassing. Lisa B. Marshall and Trent Armstrong (2010) say, "[T]his is not the time to bring up past relationships or the time she got drunk and lost her lunch in your backseat. That is a sure-fire way to lose a friend and sour a nice moment." Be mindful of your audience, too, as it's unlikely that Grandma wants to hear a raunchy story about either the bride's or groom's single days. You can end with your own words or turn again to popular quotations for traditional wedding blessings that exemplify the positive emotions you've expressed during your toast.

Weddings are meant to be joyous occasions, and your toast should ultimately be celebratory and focused on the couple, not on you. Slate.com writer Troy Patterson (2011) offers succinct and humorous advice: "[K]eep it brief. Stand up straight. In a wedding toast—unlike in marriage itself—love is all you need."

What are some things you will be sure to do (and *not* do) if you ever find yourself responsible for giving a toast, and why?

MindTap®

Develop the Body

Once you have completed the first two Action Steps (identified your general and specific speech goal and assembled a body of information on your topic), you are ready to develop the body of your speech by (a) identifying and arranging the main points; (b) crafting them into a well-phrased thesis statement; (c) developing each main point with appropriate supporting material (evidence and reasoning); and (d) creating transitions to move smoothly from one main point to the next.

Identify Main Points

Begin by identifying two to four main point ideas that will help you achieve your speech goal. Then develop each main idea with supporting material. In fact, the difference between a 5-minute speech and a 25-minute speech with the same speech goal is not the number of main points, but the extent to which each one is developed with supporting material.

For some goals, determining the main points is easy. For example, if your goal is to teach your audience how to create a Web site, your main points will likely be the steps involved in developing a very basic one. Most times, however, identifying main points is more complex. How can you identify the main ideas when they aren't obvious? First, list the ideas you believe relate to your specific goal. You will probably find it easy to list as many as nine or more. Second, eliminate ideas that you believe this audience already understands. Third, eliminate any ideas that might be too complicated or too broad for this audience to comprehend in the time allotted. Fourth, check to see if some of the ideas can be grouped together under a broader theme. Finally, from the ideas that remain, choose two to four that will help you accomplish your specific speech goal (Photo 12.1).

Let's look at how Katie used these steps to identify the main points for her speech about the growing problem of Adderall use among college students. To begin, Katie listed ideas she had discovered while doing her research.

What is a prescription drug?

What is Adderall?

What are the ingredients in Adderall?

Photo 12.1 Why is it important to limit your speech to two to four main points?

Tetra Images/Getty Images

How is Adderall made?

What is the history of Adderall?

Who takes Adderall?

Why is it prescribed?

What are its benefits?

What are its risks?

How many college students take Adderall without a prescription?

What are the demographics of college students who take Adderall without a prescription?

Why do college students who don't have a prescription take it (perceived benefits)?

What are the benefit myths?

What are actual results and/or consequences of taking Adderall without a prescription?

Second, Katie eliminated the idea "what is a prescription drug" because she knew her audience already understood this. Third, Katie noticed that several ideas seemed to be related. What Adderall is, why it is prescribed, who takes it, and the risks and benefits seemed to go together. How many people take it, demographics, and perceived benefits of college students who take Adderall without a prescription also seemed to related. And benefit myths and actual results/consequences could be grouped together. Fourth, Katie decided the ingredients, history, and how Adderall is made were too broad to cover adequately in the time she was allotted for the speech and were not directly related to her goal. Finally, Katie decided her main points would be: (1) understanding the nature and purpose of Adderall as a prescription drug; (2) its growing popularity as a study aid among college students; and (3) problems involved with using Adderall without a prescription. These main points became the framework for the body of Katie's speech. When she finished her analysis and synthesis, Katie's list looked like this:

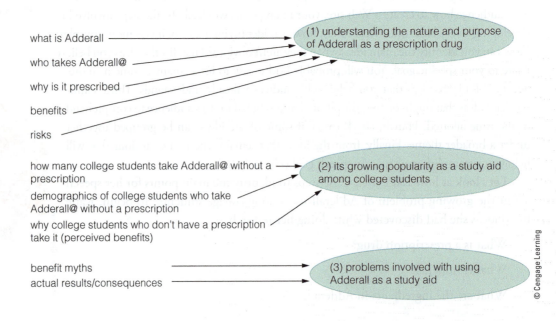

what is Adderall ⟶ (1) understanding the nature and purpose of Adderall as a prescription drug

who takes Adderall@ ⟶

why is it prescribed ⟶

benefits ⟶

risks ⟶

how many college students take Adderall@ without a prescription ⟶ (2) its growing popularity as a study aid among college students

demographics of college students who take Adderall@ without a prescription ⟶

why college students who don't have a prescription take it (perceived benefits) ⟶

benefit myths ⟶ (3) problems involved with using Adderall as a study aid

actual results/consequences ⟶

© Cengage Learning

ACTION STEP 3.A

Choose Main Points

The goal of this activity is to help you identify two to four main points you can use as the framework for your speech.

1. List all the ideas you have found that relate to the specific goal of your speech.
2. If you have trouble limiting the number, do the following:
   a. Draw a line through each idea that you believe the audience already understands, that you have no supporting information for, or that just seems too complicated.

b. Combine ideas that can be grouped together under a single heading.
3. From the ideas that remain, choose the two to four you will use as main points in your speech.

MindTap *Work on your main points using the PREPARE Your Informative Speech Activity in Chapter 16 of the MindTap. Open the Outline Tab and then "Add Point" to find Action Step 3.A and more help choosing main points.*

Word Main Points

Once you have identified your two to four main points, you can begin to shape each into a clear sentence. Let's look at how Katie did this.

Katie wrote her first draft of main points as follows:

   I. What exactly is Adderall, and why is it prescribed?
   II. College student use
III. Risks

Some people refer to this first version of wording main points as a **preparation outline**. It provides a draft of main points but doesn't do so in the form of a complete sentence. Katie might clarify her main points like this:

   I. What exactly is Adderall?
   II. An increasing number of American college students are using Adderall.
   III. Abusing Adderall is risky.

preparation outline
a draft of main points not formed into complete sentences

Study these statements. Do they seem a bit vague? Let's consider Katie's draft statements more carefully. Her three main points are complete sentences, which is good. To assure herself that she has achieved the best wording, Katie next applies two test questions to them.

1. **Is the relationship between each main point and the speech goal clearly specified?**
   Katie's first main point statement doesn't indicate what purposes Adderall serves as a prescription medicine. So she could improve this statement by saying:

   What exactly is Adderall prescribed for?

Similarly, she can improve the second main point statement by saying:

   Adderall abuse is becoming increasingly popular among American college students.

The third point might be redrafted to state:

   Abusing Adderall as a study aid is dangerous.

2. **Are the main points parallel in structure?** **Parallel structure** means the main points all follow the same structural pattern. Parallel structure is not a requirement, but it can help the audience recognize main points when you deliver your speech. So, Katie made one more small adjustment:

   I. First, what exactly is Adderall prescribed for?

   II. Second, a growing number of American college students are using Adderall.

   III. Third, abusing Adderall as a study aid is dangerous.

Parallelism can be achieved in many ways. Katie used numbering: "first . . . second . . . third." Another way is to start each sentence with an active verb. Suppose Adam wants his audience to understand the steps involved in writing an effective job application cover letter. He wrote the following first draft of his main points:

   I. Format the heading elements correctly.

   II. The body of the letter should be three paragraphs long.

   III. When concluding, use "sincerely" or "regards."

   IV. Then you need to proofread the letter carefully.

Adam then revised his main points to make them parallel in structure by using active verbs (italicized):

   I. *Format* the heading elements correctly.

   II. *Organize* the body into three paragraphs.

   III. *Conclude* the letter with "sincerely" or "regards."

   IV. *Proofread* the letter carefully.

Select a Main Point Pattern

A speech can be organized in many different ways. Although speeches may use many different **organizational patterns**, four fundamental patterns are **time (a.k.a. sequential or chronological) order**, narrative order, topical order, and logical reasons order.

1. **Time order**, sometimes called *sequential order* or *chronological order,* arranges main points in sequence or by steps in a process. When you explain how to do something, how to make something, how something works, or how something happened, you use time order (Photo 12.2). Adam's speech on the steps in writing a job application and cover letter followed a time order pattern. Let's look at another example.

Specific Goal: I want the audience to understand the four steps involved in developing a personal network.

   I. First, analyze your current networking potential.

   II. Second, position yourself in places for opportunity.

   III. Third, advertise yourself.

   IV. Fourth, follow up on contacts.

2. **Narrative order** conveys ideas through a story or series of stories. Narrative order is rooted in narrative theory, which suggests that one important way people communicate is through storytelling (Photo 12.3). We use stories to teach and learn, to entertain, and to make sense of the world around us (Fisher, 1987). While a narrative may be presented in chronological order, it may also use a series of flashbacks or flash forwards to increase the

Linda Kennedy/Alamy

dramatic effect. Each main point may be an event in a single story or each main point may be a different story that illustrates the thesis. Lonna shared her story about having anorexia to help listeners understand the impact of the condition on someone's life.

Specific Speech Goal: I want my audience to understand how anorexia nervosa affects the lives of its victims and their loved ones.

I. First, let's talk about a typical day for me as a recovering anorexic.

II. Second, let's focus on a historical account about how I became anorexic.

III. Finally, let's discuss an inspirational story about two people who basically saved my life.

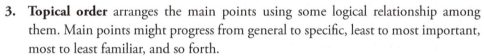

Photo 12.3 Narrative order is a way to organize your ideas as a story or series of stories. Who do you know that is a really good story teller and why?

3. **Topical order** arranges the main points using some logical relationship among them. Main points might progress from general to specific, least to most important, most to least familiar, and so forth.

Specific Goal: I want the audience to understand three proven methods of ridding our bodies of harmful toxins.

I. One proven method for ridding our bodies of harmful toxins is reducing our intake of animal products.

II. A second proven method for ridding our bodies of harmful toxins is eating more natural whole foods.

III. A third proven method for ridding our bodies of harmful toxins is keeping well hydrated.

topical order
structures the main points using some logical relationship among them

logical reasons order
structures the main points as reasons for accepting the thesis as desirable or true

4. **Logical reasons order** structures the main points according to reasons for accepting the thesis as desirable or true. Logical reasons order is usually used when your goal is to persuade.

Specific goal: I want the audience to donate money to the United Way.

I. When you donate to the United Way, your one donation can be divided among many charities.

II. When you donate to the United Way, you can stipulate which charities you wish to support.

III. When you donate to the United Way, you know that a high percentage of your donation will go directly to the charities you've selected.

Photo 12.4 If you were giving a speech on the phenomenon of soldiers creating blogs about their combat experiences, what organizational pattern do you think would best suit your speech?

These four organizational patterns are the most basic ones (Photo 12.4). In Chapters 16 and 17, introduce several additional patterns for structuring main points of informative and persuasive speeches.

Write the Thesis Statement

A **thesis statement** is a one- or two-sentence summary that incorporates your general and specific goals and previews the main points of your speech. Katie crafted the following thesis statement for her speech on Adderall: "Off-label Adderall use by college students is growing in popularity among college students. To clarify, let's discuss the nature and purpose of Adderall as a prescription drug, its growing popularity as a study aid among college students, and problems associated with using Adderall as a study aid." Figure 12.1 illustrates several additional examples.

Outline the Speech Body

Once you have identified each main point, ordered them according to an appropriate main point pattern, and constructed your thesis statement, you are ready to develop the speech body. A good way to do so is to construct an outline. An **outline** is a written framework of the sequential and hierarchical relationships among ideas in the speech. In most speeches, three levels of hierarchy are all you need: main points (numbered with Roman numerals), subpoints that support a main point (ordered under each main point with capital letters), and sometimes sub-subpoints (numbered under the relevant subpoint with Arabic numbers). Figure 12.2 shows the general form of most speech outlines. Notice that it proposes between two and four main points and offers at least two subpoints under each main point.

> **General goal:** I want to inform my audience.
>
> **Specific goal:** I want my audience to understand how to improve their grades in college.
>
> **Thesis statement:** Three proven techniques for improving test scores in college are to attend classes regularly, develop a positive attitude, and study efficiently.
>
> **General goal:** I want to inform my audience.
>
> **Specific goal:** I want the audience to understand the benefits of volunteering.
>
> **Thesis statement:** Some important benefits of volunteering include helping underprivileged populations, supporting nonprofit organizations, and improving your own self-esteem.
>
> **General goal:** I want to persuade my audience.
>
> **Specific goal:** I want my audience to believe that parents should limit the time their children spend viewing television.
>
> **Thesis statement:** Parents should limit the time their children spend viewing television because heavy television viewing desensitizes children to violence and increases violent tendencies in children.
>
> **General goal:** I want to persuade my audience.
>
> **Specific goal:** I want my audience to believe that they should learn to speak Spanish.
>
> **Thesis statement:** You should learn to speak Spanish because it will benefit you personally, economically, and practically.

Figure 12.1

Goal and thesis statement examples

© Cengage Learning

ACTION STEP 3.B

Write a Thesis Statement

The goal of this activity is to develop a well-worded thesis statement for your speech.

1. Write the general and specific goals you developed in Chapter 11 with Action Step 1.E.

2. List the main points you determined in Action Step 3.A.

3. Now write a complete sentence that combines your specific goal with your main point ideas.

MindTap *Complete your thesis statement with PREPARE Your Informative Speech Activity in Chapter 16 of the MindTap. Access the Outline Tab, and click on the Thesis box to find Action Step 3.B and more help developing your thesis statement.*

Limit your speech to two, three, or four main points.
Use at least two subpoints to support each main point.
If you support any subpoints with a sub-subpoint, be sure to offer at least two.

I. Main point one

  A. Subpoint A for main point one

    1. Sub-subpoint one (optional)

    2. Sub-subpoint two (optional)

  B. Subpoint B for main point one

II. Main point two

  A. Subpoint A for main point two

    1. Sub-subpoint one (optional)

    2. Sub-subpoint two (optional)

  B. Subpoint B of main point two

  C. Subpoint C of main point two

    1. Sub-subpoint one (optional)

    2. Sub-subpoint two (optional)

    3. Sub-subpoint three (optional)

III. Main point three

  A. Subpoint A for main point three

    1. Sub-subpoint one (optional)

    2. Sub-subpoint two (optional)

  B. Subpoint B of main point three

    . . . and so on.

© Cengage Learning

Figure 12.2

General form for a speech outline

ACTION STEP 3.C

Outline the Main Points

The goal of this activity is to help you phrase and order your main points.

1. Write your thesis statement (Action Step 3.B).

2. Using the thesis statement you wrote in Action Step 3.B, underline the two to four main points for your speech.

3. Review the main points as a group.

   a. Is the relationship of each main point statement to the goal statement clearly specified? If not, revise.

   b. Are the main points parallel in structure? If not, revise.

4. Choose an organizational pattern for your main points.

5. Write your main points down in this order. Place a "I." before the main point you will make first, a "II." before your second point, and so on.

MindTap *Organize your main points using PREPARE Your Informative Speech Activity in Chapter 16 of the MindTap. Access the Outline tab, and click on "Add point" to find Action Step 3.C and more help developing main points.*

Develop Main Points

subpoints
statements that elaborate on a main point

supporting material
developmental material gathered through secondary and primary research

You develop each main point with subpoints and supporting material. **Subpoints** are statements that elaborate on a main point. A main point may have two, three, or even more subpoints depending on the complexity of it. Subpoints are developed further with **supporting material**—evidence you gathered through secondary and primary

ACTION STEP 3.D

Identify and Outline Subpoints

The goal of this activity is to develop and outline your subpoints. Complete the following steps for each of your main points.

1. List the main point.

2. Using your research cards or annotated bibliography, list the key information related to that main point.

3. Analyze that information and cross out items that seem less relevant or don't fit.

4. Look for items that seem related and can be grouped under a broader heading.

5. Try to group information until you have between two and four supporting points for the main point.

6. Write those supporting subpoints in full sentences.

7. Repeat this process for all main points.

8. Write an outline using Roman numerals for main points, capital letters for supporting points, and Arabic numbers for material related to supporting points.

MindTap *Develop your subpoints using PREPARE Your Informative Speech Activity in Chapter 16. In the Outline tab, create a subpoint to find Action Step 3.D and more help with subpoints.*

research along with reasoning you use to link it to the main point is supports. You can identify subpoints by sorting through the research you compiled in your annotated bibliography and/or on research cards to find evidence (e.g., definitions, examples, facts statistics, stories). Then, look for relationships between and among ideas. As you analyze, you can draw lines connecting items of information that fit together logically, cross out information that seems less important or doesn't really fit, and combine similar ideas using different language. One subpoint in each main point should be a **listener relevance link**, a piece of information that alerts listeners to why the main point is relevant to them.

listener relevance link
a piece of information that informs listeners why the topic or main point is relevant to them

Create Transitions

Transitions are words, phrases, or sentences that show the relationship between and bridge two ideas. Good transitions are certainly important in writing, but they are crucial in public speaking. If listeners get lost or think they have missed something, they cannot go back and check as they can when reading. Transitions can come in the form of section transitions or signposts.

transitions
words, phrases, or sentences that show the relationship between and bridge ideas

Section Transitions **Section transitions** are complete sentences that show the relationship between and bridge major parts of the speech. They typically summarize what has just been said in one main point and preview the one coming up next. Essentially, section transitions are the "glue" that links the main points of your speech together.

section transition
complete sentence that shows the relationship between and bridges major parts of the speech

For example, suppose Adam just finished his introduction on creating a cover letter and is now ready to launch into his main points. Before stating his first main point, he might say, "Creating a good cover letter is a process that has four steps. Now, let's consider the first one." When his listeners hear this transition, they are signaled to listen to and remember the first main point. When he finishes his first main point, he uses another section transition to signal that he is finished speaking about the first main point and is moving on to the second main point: "Now that we understand what is involved in creating the heading elements, let's move on to discuss what to include in the body of the letter."

signposts
words or short phrases that connect pieces of supporting material to the main point or subpoint they address

Photo 12.5 Sometimes signposts are used to highlight numerical order. How might you emphasize them with nonverbal cues?

Section transitions are important for two reasons. First, they help the audience follow the organization of ideas in the speech. Second, they help audience members remember information.

Signposts **Signposts** are words or short phrases that connect pieces of supporting material to the main point or subpoint they address. Sometimes signposts number ideas: *first, second, third,* and *fourth* (Photo 12.5). Sometimes they help the audience focus on a key idea: *foremost, most important,* or *above all.* Signposts can also be used to introduce an explanation: *to illustrate, for example, in other words, essentially,* or *to clarify.* Signposts can also signal that a lengthy anecdote, or even the speech itself, is coming to an end: *in short, finally, in conclusion,* or *to summarize.* Just as section transitions serve as the glue that holds your big-picture main points together, signposts connect subpoints and supporting material together within each main point.

ZUMA Press, Inc./Alamy

ACTION STEP 3.E

Prepare Section Transitions

The goal of this exercise is to prepare section transitions. Section transitions appear as parenthetical statements before or after each main point. Using complete sentences:

1. Write a transition from your first main point to your second.

2. Write a transition from each remaining main point to the one after it.

3. Add these transitional statements to your outline.

MindTap *Write transitions using PRE-PARE Your Informative Speech Activity in Chapter 16. In the Outline tab, click "Add Transitions" to find Action Step 3.E and more help on preparing transitions.*

Develop the Introduction

Once you have developed the speech body, you need to decide how to introduce it. Because the introduction is so important to success, you should develop two or three different introductions and then select the one that seems best for the audience you will be addressing. An introduction is generally about 10 percent of the length of the entire speech, so for a five-minute speech (approximately 750 words), an introduction of about 30 seconds (approximately 60–85 words) is appropriate.

An effective introduction achieves four primary goals: to get attention, convey listener relevance, establish speaker credibility, and identify the thesis statement (speech goal and main point preview).

Get Attention

An audience's physical presence does not guarantee people will actually listen to your speech. Your first goal, then, is to create an opening that will arouse curiosity and motivate your audience to want to know more about your topic. Some rhetorical strategies for doing so include: startling statements, questions, stories, jokes, personal references, quotations, action, and suspense.

Startling Statements A **startling statement** is a shocking expression or example. Chris used this startling statement to get his listeners' attention for his speech about how automobile emissions contribute to global warming:

> *Look around. Each one of you is sitting next to a killer. That's right. You are sitting next to a cold-blooded killer. Before you think about jumping up and running out of*

startling statement
a shocking expression or example

this room, let me explain. Every-one who drives an automobile is a killer of the environment. Every time you turn the key to your ignition, you are helping to destroy our precious surroundings.

Questions Questions are requests for information that encourage the audience to think about something related to your topic. Questions can be *rhetorical* or *direct*. A **rhetorical question** doesn't require an overt response. Notice how a student began her speech on counterfeiting with three short, rhetorical questions:

What would you do with this $20 bill if I gave it to you? Would you take your friend to a movie? Or would you treat yourself to pizza and drinks? Well, if you did either of these things, you could get in big trouble—this bill is counterfeit!

Unlike a rhetorical question, a **direct question** seeks an overt response from the audience. It might be a "yea" or "nay" or a show of hands. For example, here's how author and motivational speaker, Harvey MacKay, started his commencement address at the University of Southern California:

Let me start by asking all of you in the audience this question: How many people talk to themselves? Please raise your hands. I count approximately 50 percent. To the other 50 percent who didn't raise your hands, I can just hear you now, saying to yourself: "Who me? I don't talk to myself!"

Well I think all of you will be talking to yourself about the day's events on your way home this evening. This is an unforgettable moment among many fine hours you will have in your career and life. (Mackay, 2009)

Direct questions get audience attention because they require a physical response (Photo 12.8). However, getting listeners to actually comply with your request can also pose a challenge.

Stories A **story** is an account of something that has happened (actual) or could happen (hypothetical). Most people enjoy a well-told story, so it makes a good attention getter. One drawback is that stories can sometimes take more time to tell than is appropriate for the length of your speech. Use a story only if it is short or if you can abbreviate it. Yash Gupta, dean of the Carey Business School at Johns Hopkins University, used a story to get attention about assumptions, prejudices, and policies about older people:

Imagine this.

You are boarding a routine business flight. As you get on the plane you notice the pilot looks perhaps a bit . . . grandfatherly. In fact, he is only two years away from his FAA-mandated retirement age.

You sit and open a magazine. You know, in advertisements flight attendants always look like the champagne they are pouring: fresh and bubbly. But looking around the

Photo 12.6 Why might a speaker choose *not* to use a direct question to get attention?

questions
requests for information that encourage the audience to think about something related to your topic

rhetorical question
a question that doesn't require an overt response

direct question
a question that seeks an overt response from the audience

story
an account of something that has happened or could happen

APPLY IT

Would you ever try to get attention by asking a direct question? Why or why not?

cabin at the flight crew the words that instead come to mind are mature and no-nonsense. All three flight attendants are in their 50s.

You are belted comfortably, your seat is in the upright position, and you have just felt the wheels lift off the runway from LaGuardia Airport.

Only a couple minutes into your flight there is a loud bang, followed by another loud bang. Flames shoot out from the plane's two jet engines, and then they both go silent. Less than three minutes later, the pilot makes one terse announcement: prepare for impact.

The next thing you know you're floating on the Hudson River and the flight crew is quickly and efficiently moving you onto the wings of the aircraft. They know their jobs.

Flight attendant Doreen Welsh is 58. She's been flying since 1970—almost 40 years' experience. Sheila Daily is 57. She's been flying since 1980, and the other flight attendant, 51-year-old Donna Dent, has been flying since 1982.

As you watch the rescue boats approach, one thought goes through your mind: At moments like this, who needs fresh and bubbly?

The story of Flight 1549 suggests that, in our society, perhaps we have been too quick to praise youth, too ready to underestimate the value of age, wisdom, and experience. One thing is certain: As we look forward to the middle years of the 21st century, we are going to have ample opportunity to discover if our assumptions, our prejudices, and our policies about older people are valid—or if perhaps we have some serious reconsidering to do. (Gupta, 2010)

joke
anecdote or a piece of wordplay designed to make people laugh

personal reference
a brief account of something that happened to you or a hypothetical situation that listeners can imagine themselves in

Photo 12.7 Which stand-up comedians do you know that follow the 3 R's rule?

Jokes A **joke** is an anecdote or a piece of wordplay designed to make people laugh. A joke can be used to get attention when it meets the *three R's test*: It must be realistic, relevant, and repeatable (Humes, 1988). In other words, the joke can't be too far-fetched, unrelated to the speech purpose, or potentially offensive to some listeners (Photo 12.7). In his speech about being a person of integrity, for example, Joel Osteen offered this joke to get attention:

A kindergarten teacher asked one of her students what she was drawing a picture of. The little girl said, "I'm drawing a picture of God." The teacher replied, "Oh honey, nobody knows what God looks like." Without missing a beat, the little girl replied, "They will in a minute . . .". (Osteen, 2012)

Personal References A **personal reference** is a brief account of something that happened to you or a hypothetical situation that listeners can imagine themselves in. A personal reference like the one that follows is suitable for a speech of any length:

Were you panting when you got to the top of those four flights of stairs this morning? I'll bet there were a few of you who vowed you're never going to take a class on the top floor of this building again.

ZUMA Press, Inc./Alamy

But did you ever stop to think that maybe the problem isn't that this class is on the top floor? It just might be that you are not getting enough exercise.

Quotations A **quotation** is a comment made by and attributed to someone other than the speaker. A particularly vivid or thought-provoking quotation can make an excellent attention getter as long as it relates to your topic. For instance, notice how Sally Mason, provost at Purdue University, used a quotation to get the attention of her audience:

> *There is an ancient saying, "May you live in interesting times." It is actually an ancient curse. It might sound great to live in interesting times. But interesting times are times of change and even turmoil. They are times of struggle. They are exciting. But, at the same time, they are difficult. People of my generation have certainly lived through interesting times and they continue today. (Mason, 2007, p. 159)*

quotation
a comment made by and attributed to someone other than the speaker

Action An **action** is an attention-getting act designed to highlight and arouse interest in your topic. You can perform an action yourself, just as Juan did when he split a stack of boards with his hand to get attention for his speech on karate. Or you can ask volunteers from the audience to perform the action. For example, Cindria used three audience members to participate in breaking a piñata to create interest in her speech on the history of the piñata. If you choose to use audience members, consider soliciting participants ahead of time to avoid the possibility of having no volunteers when you ask during your speech. Finally, you can ask your entire audience to perform some action related to your speech topic. If you'd like to ask your whole audience to perform an action, realistically assess whether what you are asking is something your audience is likely to comply with.

action
an act designed to highlight and arouse interest in a topic

Suspense To create **suspense**, you word your attention-getter so that what is described generates uncertainty or mystery and excites the audience. When your audience wonders, "What is she leading up to?" you have created suspense. A suspenseful opening is especially valuable when your audience is not particularly interested in hearing about your topic. Consider this suspenseful statement:

suspense
wording your attention-getter so that it generates uncertainty and excites the audience

> *It costs the United States more than $116 billion per year. It has cost the loss of more jobs than a recession. It accounts for nearly 100,000 deaths a year. I'm not talking about drug abuse—the problem is alcoholism. Today I want to show you how we can avoid this inhumane killer by abstaining from it.*

By putting the problem, alcoholism, at the end, the speaker encourages the audience to try to anticipate the answer. And because the audience may well be thinking the problem is drugs, the revelation that the answer is alcoholism is likely to be that much more effective.

Establish Relevance

Even if you successfully get the attention of your listeners, to *keep* their attention you need to motivate them to listen to your speech. You can do this by offering a clear listener relevance link in the introduction, a statement of how and why your speech relates to or might affect your audience. Sometimes your attention-getting statement will also serve this function, but if it doesn't, you need to provide a personal connection between your topic and your audience. Notice how Tiffany created a listener relevance link for her speech about being a vegetarian:

> *Although a diet rich in eggs and meat was once the norm in this country, more and more of us are choosing a vegetarian lifestyle to help lower blood pressure, reduce cholesterol, and even help prevent the onset of some diseases.*

When creating a listener relevance link, answer these questions: Why should my listeners care about what I'm saying? In what way(s) might they benefit from hearing about it? How might my speech address my listeners' needs or desires for such things as health, wealth, well-being, self-esteem, success, and so forth?

Establish Credibility

credibility
the perception your audience has about your competence and character

If someone hasn't formally introduced you, audience members are going to wonder who you are and why they should pay attention to what you say. So, another goal of the introduction is to begin to build your credibility. **Credibility** is the perception your audience has about your competence and character. Your goal is to highlight that you are a credible speaker on this topic, one who respects the audience and occasion, not that you are *the* or even *a* final authority on the subject. Carmen Mariano, president of Archbishop Williams High School, established credibility and goodwill in a "welcome back, students" speech this way:

> *Ladies and gentlemen, you will hear one word many times this morning. That word is welcome. Please know how much we mean that word. Please know how much I mean that word.*
>
> *Why will we mean that word so much?*
>
> *Because without you, this is just a building on 80 Independence Avenue. And with you, this is Archbishop Williams High School. That's right. When you walked through those doors this morning, you made this building a school again.*
>
> *So welcome back.*
>
> *And welcome to your school.*

State the Thesis

Because audiences want to know what the speech is going to be about, it's important to state your thesis. After Miguel gained the audience's attention and established relevance and credibility, he introduced his thesis, "In the next five minutes, let's discuss the three elements of romantic love: passion, intimacy, and commitment."

ACTION STEP 3.F

Write Speech Introductions

The goal of this activity is to create choices for how you will begin your speech.

1. For the speech body you outlined earlier, write three different introductions that you believe meet the goals of effective introductions and that you believe would set an appropriate tone for your speech goal and audience.

2. Of the three you drafted, which do you believe is the best? Why?

3. Write that introduction in outline form.

MindTap *Write your Introduction with the PREPARE Your Informative Speech Activity in Chapter 16 of the MindTap. In the Outline tab, click "Introduction" to find Action Step 3.F and more help on transitions.*

In a commencement address at Stanford University, Steve Jobs stated the main points in his introduction in this way: "Today I want to tell you three stories from my life. That's it. No big deal. Just three stories" (Jobs, 2005).

Image100/Alamy

Develop the Conclusion

Shakespeare once said, "All's well that ends well." Effective conclusions heighten the impact of a good speech by summarizing the main ideas and leaving the audience with a vivid impression (Photo 12.8). Even though the conclusion is a relatively short part of the speech—seldom more than 5 percent (35 to 40 words for a 5-minute speech)—your conclusion should be carefully planned. As with your speech introduction, you should prepare two or three conclusions and then choose the one you believe will be the most effective with your audience.

Photo 12.8 How might you conclude your speech to make a lasting impression?

Summarize Goal and Main Points

An effective speech conclusion includes an abbreviated restatement of your goal and main points. An appropriate summary for an informative speech on how to improve your grades might be "So I hope you now understand [informative goal] that three techniques to help you improve your grades are to attend classes regularly, to develop a positive attitude toward the course, and to study systematically [main points]." A short ending for a persuasive speech on why you should exercise might be "So you should exercise for at least 30 minutes each day [persuasive goal] to improve your appearance, as well as your physical and mental health [main points]."

Clinch

Although a good summary helps the audience remember your main points, a good clincher leaves the audience with a vivid impression. A **clincher** is a short statement that provides a sense of closure by driving home the importance of your speech in a memorable way. If you can, try to devise a clincher that refers back to the introductory comments in some way. Two effective strategies for clinching are using vivid imagery and appealing to action.

clincher
a short statement that provides a sense of closure by driving home the importance of your speech in a memorable way

Vivid Imagery To develop vivid imagery, you can use any of the devices we discussed for getting attention (startling statement, question, story, joke, personal reference, quotation, action, or suspense). For example, in Tiffany's speech about being a vegetarian, she referred back to the personal reference she made in her introduction about a vegetarian Thanksgiving meal:

> So now you know why I made the choice to become a vegetarian and how this choice
> affects my life today. As a vegetarian, I've discovered a world of food I never knew
> existed. Believe me, I am salivating just thinking about the meal I have planned for

ACTION STEP 3.G

Create Speech Conclusions

The goal of this activity is to help you create choices for how you will conclude your speech.

1. For the speech body you outlined earlier, write three different conclusions that review important points you want the audience to remember and that are intended to leave the audience with a vivid impression.

2. Which do you believe is the best? Why?

3. Write that conclusion in outline form.

MindTap *Create your conclusion with the PREPARE Your Informative Speech Activity in Chapter 16 of the MindTap. In the Outline tab, click "Conclusion" to find Action Step 3.G and more help with conclusions.*

APPLY IT

Identify a speech that made a lasting impression on you. How did the speaker conclude?

MindTap

appeal to action
describes the behavior you want your listeners to follow after they have heard your arguments

this Thanksgiving: fennel and blood orange salad; followed by baked polenta layered with tomato, Fontina, and Gorgonzola cheeses; an acorn squash tart; marinated tofu; and with what else but pumpkin pie for dessert!*

Sounds good, doesn't it? Clinchers with vivid imagery are effective because they leave listeners with a picture imprinted in their minds.

Appeal to Action The appeal to action is a common clincher for persuasive speeches. The **appeal to action** describes the behavior you want your listeners to follow after they have heard your arguments. Notice how Matthew Cossolott, president and founder of Study Abroad Alumni International, concluded his speech on global awareness and responsibility with a strong appeal to action:

So, yes, you should have this re-entry program. Yes, you should network and explore international career opportunities. That's all good.

COMMUNICATE ON YOUR FEET

Speech Assignment

The Assignment

1. Identify a favorite toy, game, food, or hobby you had as a child.

2. Come up with a thesis statement and three main points you could talk about for that toy, game, food, or hobby.

3. Prepare an introduction, section transitions, and conclusion for a "speech" about that toy, game,

food, or hobby. But do not prepare any supporting material.

4. At your instructor's request, come to the front of the room and deliver the introduction, section transitions, and conclusion for a speech on that topic.

5. Be prepared to hear critiques from your classmates and to offer suggestions on theirs as well.

But I also encourage you to Globalize Your Locality. I urge you to Think Global. . . . Act Global. . . . Be Global.

This is an urgent call to action . . . for you and other study abroad alumni . . . to help us reduce the global awareness deficit.

You can do so by becoming involved with SAAI . . . and other organizations such as the National Council for International Visitors, Sister Cities, or Rotary International.

You can speak to local schools and community organizations about your study abroad experience and the need for more global awareness.

When you studied abroad, I'm sure you were told many times that you would be serving as unofficial ambassadors of the United States . . . your campus . . . and even your community back home.

Now that you're home again, I hope you'll become ambassadors for the value of the study abroad experience and for the need for greater international awareness.

In wrapping up . . . I'd like to leave you with this image . . . just picture in your mind's eye that iconic photograph of planet earth. I'm sure you've seen it. Taken over four decades ago . . . in December 1968 . . . on the Apollo 8 mission to the moon.

The photograph—dubbed Earthrise—shows our small, blue planet rising above a desolate lunar landscape. This photo was a true watershed in human history . . . marking the first time earthlings, . . . fellow global citizens, had traveled outside earth's orbit and looked back on our lonely planet.

The widespread publication of Earthrise had a lot to do with launching the worldwide environmental movement. It's no accident that the first Earth Day— on April 22, 1970—took place so soon after the publication of this remarkable photograph.

We're all privileged to inhabit this same planet—truly an island in space. And voices to the contrary notwithstanding . . . whether we want to admit it or not . . . we are all, undeniably and by definition, citizens of the worlds.

The only question is: will we accept the responsibilities of global citizenship?

Your future . . . and perhaps the survival of the planet . . . just may depend on how many of us answer yes to that question. (Cossolotto, 2009)

Compile the Reference List and Formal Outline

Regardless of the type or length of your speech, you'll want to prepare a list of the sources you use in it. This list will allow you to direct audience members to the specific source of any information you used and to quickly find the information at a later date. The two standard methods of organizing source lists are (1) alphabetically by author's last name or (2) by content category, with items listed alphabetically by author within each category.

Many formal style formats can be used (e.g., MLA, APA, Chicago, CBE). The "correct" style differs by professional or academic discipline. Check to see if your instructor has a preference about which style you use for this class. Figure 12.3 gives examples of Modern Language Association (MLA) and American Psychological Association (APA) citations for the most commonly used sources.

Figure 12.3

Examples of MLA and APA citation forms for speech sources

	MLA style	APA style
Book	Thebarge, Sarah. *The Invisible Girls: A Memoir*. New York: Jericho Books, 2013.	Thebarge, S. (2013). *The invisible girls: A memoir*. New York: Jericho Books.
Academic Journal	Milford, Mike. "Kenneth Burke's punitive priests and the redeeming prophets: The NCAA, the college sports media, and the University of Miami scandal." *Communication Studies*, 66.1(2015): 45–62.	Milford, M. (2015). Kenneth Burke's punitive priests and the redeeming prophets: The NCAA, the college sports media, and the University of Miami. *Communication Studies, 66*(1,) 45–62.
Magazine	O'Leary, Kevin. "Kris in Denial." *US Weekly*, 16 February, 2015: 38–43.	O'Leary, K. (2015, February 16). Kris in denial. *US Weekly, 1044*, 38–43.
Web Site	"Supplier Responsibility at Apple." Apple.com. n.d. Web. 01 June 2012.	Apple. (n.d.). Supplier responsibility at Apple. Retrieved from http://www.apple.com /supplierresponsibility/
Blog Post	Ramsey, G. "Forget the wins, Calipari still pushing improvement." Cat Scratches: The Official Blog of UK Athletics. ukathletics.com. 20 February 2015. Web. 20 February 2015.	Ramsey, G. (2015, February 20). Forget the wins, Calipari still pushing improvement [Web log post]. Retrieved from http://www.ukathletics. com/blog/mens-basketball/
Movie	*American Sniper*. Dir. Clint Eastwood. Prod. Bradley Cooper. Warner Brothers, 2014. DVD.	Cooper, B. (Producer), & Eastwood, C. (Director). (2014). *American Sniper* [Motion picture]. United States: Warner Brothers.
Online Video	"Angelo Vermeulen: How to go to space, without having to go to space." TEDtalks. *YouTube*. 2015. Web. 19 February 2015.	TEDtalksDirector. (2015, February 19). *Angelo Vermeulen: How to go to space, without having to go to space* [Video file]. Retrieved from https://www.youtube.com /watch?v=S2H_8lfxzT4

© Cengage Learning

ACTION STEP 3.H

Compile a Reference List

The goal of this activity is to help you record the list of sources you used in the speech.

1. Review your research cards and/or annotated bibliography, separating those with information you used in your speech from those you did not use.

2. List the sources of information used in the speech by copying the bibliographic information recorded into a "references" or "works cited" list using the format required by your instructor.

3. Arrange your entries alphabetically by the last name of the first author.

MindTap® *Compile your research with the PREPARE Your Informative Speech Activity in Chapter 16 of the MindTap. In the Research tab, complete Action Step 3.H and find more help with research.*

COMMUNICATION SKILL

Organizing the Speech

Skill	Use	Procedure	Example
The process of identifying main points, constructing a thesis statement, outlining the body of the speech, creating an introduction, crafting a conclusion, and cataloguing a list of sources.	To create a hierarchy and sequence of ideas that help a particular audience to easily understand the speaker's goal and main ideas in the speech.	1. Identify your main ideas. 2. Write a thesis statement. 3. Outline the body of the speech by carefully wording main points, selecting an organizational pattern, selecting and organizing subpoints, and preparing transitions. 4. Create three introductions and select the best one. 5. Create three conclusions and select the best one. 6. List sources.	The **three aspects** of romantic love are passion, intimacy, and commitment. I. Passion is the first aspect of romantic love to develop. II. Intimacy is the second. III. Commitment is the third. **Example** for "passion": A. Passion is a compelling feeling of love. B. (Focus on function.) C. (Discuss maintenance.) **Transition from I to II:** Although passion is essential to a relationship, passion without intimacy is just sex. **Possible attention-getter:** What does it mean to say "I'm in love"? And how can you know whether what you are experiencing is not just a crush? **Possible main point summary:** Developing romantic love involves passion, intimacy, and commitment. **Sample entry:** Sternberg, Robert J., and Michael L. Barnes, eds. *The Psychology of Love.* New Haven, CT: Yale University Press, 1988.

Figure 12.4

Reviewing the formal outline

Answer these key questions when reviewing your formal outline and reference list:

1. **Have I used a standard set of symbols to indicate structure?** Main points are indicated by Roman numerals, major subpoints by capital letters, sub-subpoints by Arabic numerals, and further subdivisions by lowercase letters.

2. **Have I written my main points as complete sentences?**

3. **Do my main points each contain only one single idea?**

4. **Does each major subpoint relate to (support) its major point?**

5. **Have I included potential subpoint elaborations?** Because you don't know how long it might take you to discuss each elaboration, you should include more than you are likely to use. While giving your speech, monitor the time to determine whether to include or skip over them.

© Cengage Learning

formal speech outline

a full sentence outline of your speech that includes internal references and a complete reference list

At this point, you will want to compile and review your formal outline. A **formal speech outline** is a full sentence outline of your speech that includes internal references and a complete reference list. Figure 12.4 poses some questions you can use to guide you as you review it. Finally, Figure 12.5 is Katie's formal outline for her speech on Adderall.

Figure 12.5

Sample complete formal outline

Using and Abusing Adderall: What's the Big Deal?
by Katie Anthony University of Kentucky
General goal: I want to inform my audience.
Specific goal: I would like the audience to understand the uses and abuses of Adderall by college students.
Thesis statement: I want to inform you about the growing problem of off-label Adderall usage by college students, explaining the nature and legal uses of Adderall, its growing popularity as a study aid for college students, and the problems associated with abusing Adderall.
Introduction

I. *Attention getter:* Raise your hand if anyone you know has taken the drug Adderall. Keep your hand raised if the person you know to be taking Adderall is doing so without a prescription for the drug.

II. *Listener relevance:* The illegal use of stimulants like Adderall among college students has increased dramatically over the past decade. The latest National Study on Drug Use and Health found that nearly 7 percent of full-time college students reported using Adderall without a prescription. So if you know ten people who are in college, it is likely that you know someone who is abusing Adderall.

III. *Speaker credibility:* I became interested in this topic my freshman year when my roommate received a call from her mother telling her that her best friend, who was a sophomore at a different college, had died suddenly from an Adderall-induced heart attack. Because I had several friends who were also using Adderall without a prescription but who thought it was safe to do so, I began to read all I could about the drug, its use, and its risks. Not only have I become versed in the written information on Adderall, but I have also interviewed several faculty here who are studying the problem, and I have become an undergraduate research assistant

© Cengage Learning

helping one faculty member to collect data on this problem. Today, I want to share with you some of what I have learned.

IV. ***Thesis statement:*** Specifically, I want to inform you about the growing problem of off-label Adderall usage by college students, explaining the nature and legal uses of Adderall, its growing popularity as a study aid for college students, and the problems associated with abusing Adderall.

Body

I. Adderall is a psychostimulant prescribed to treat three conditions.

   Listener relevance link: Understanding the intended medical uses of the drug Adderall may help you understand why the drug is so widely abused by collegians.

   A. Adderall, the brand name for amphetamikne-dextroamphetamine, is a psychostimulant, one of a class of drugs intended to promote concentration, suppress hyperactivity, and promote healthy social experiences for patients (Willis, 2001).

      1. Adderall stimulates the central nervous system by increasing the amount of dopamine and norepinephrine in the brain. These chemicals are neurotransmitters that help the brain send signals between nerve cells (Faraone, Biederman, Weiffenbach, et al., 2014).

      2. Mentally, Adderall brings about a temporary improvement in alertness, wakefulness, endurance, and motivation.

      3. Physically, it can increase heart rate and blood pressure and decrease perceived need for food or sleep.

   B. Adderall is prescribed for the medical treatment of attention deficit hyperactivity disorder (ADHD) in children and adults as well as for narcolepsy and clinical depression.

      1. ADHD is a neurobehavioral developmental disorder characterized by problems of attention coupled with hyperactivity.

         a. According to the Centers for Disease Control and Prevention, since the mid-1990s, there has been a documented increase in the number of American children diagnosed and treated for ADHD.

         b. According to the *Diagnostic and Statistical Manual of Mental Disorders, fifth edition,* 2013, symptoms must be present for at least six months for diagnosis and symptoms must be excessive for medicinal treatment.

         c. The drugs Ritalin and Dexedrine are also used to treat ADHD. Adderall, however, remains the most widely prescribed of these drugs (Spiller, Hays, & Aleguas, 2013).

         d. According to the *Journal of the American Academy of Child and Adolescent Psychology,* approximately 6.4 million American children, ages 4 to 17 (up from 4.4 million in 2005) were diagnosed with ADHD in 2001, and over 3.5 million of those patients have been prescribed medicine to treat the condition.

      2. Adderall is also prescribed to treat narcolepsy, which occurs when the brain can't normally regulate cycles of sleep and waking.

         a. Sufferers of narcolepsy experience excessive daytime sleepiness that results in episodes of suddenly falling asleep.

Figure 12.5

(Continued)

Figure 12.5

(Continued)

        b. A chronic sleep disorder, narcolepsy affects between 50,000 and 2.4 million Americans. (National Heart, Lung, and Blood Institute, 2008).

    3. Adderall can also be used to treat clinical depression.

        a. Clinical depression is a disorder characterized by low mood, a loss of interest in normal activities, and low self-esteem.

        b. According to the National Institute of Mental Health, 9.5% of the adult population—that is nearly 1.8 million American adults—suffer from clinical depression.

Transition: Now that we understand the basic properties and medical uses of the drug Adderall, let's assess the increasing level of abuse of the drug by college students.

II. Unfortunately, Adderall has become popular among college students who use it as a study aid and for recreational purposes.

    Listener relevance link: As college students, we need to be aware of what students believe about Adderall and why they are abusing it.

    A. College students who don't suffer from ADHD, narcolepsy, or depression will take it with no prescription because they believe that it will improve their focus and concentration, allowing them to perform better on academic tasks (Teter, McCabe, Crandford, Boyd, & Gunthrie, 2005).

        1. Adderall abuse among college students occurs especially at stressful times of the semester when students get little sleep.

            a. DeSantis, Webb, and Noar (2008) found that 72 percent of the students they surveyed reported using the drug to stay awake so they could study longer when they had many assignments due.

            b. Katherine Stump, a Georgetown University student, reported in the school newspaper: "During finals week here at Georgetown, campus turns into an Adderall drug den. Everyone from a cappella singers to newspaper writers become addicts, while anyone with a prescription and an understanding of the free market becomes an instant pusher (Kent, 2013, October 29).

            c. Collegians report using the drug frequently during stressful times of the semester. One student said, "I use it every time I have a major paper due" (Daley, 2004, April 20).

    B. Students also use Adderall for purposes other than academic ones.

        1. A survey of undergraduate and graduate students revealed that students engage in Adderall abuse for partying at a frequency just slightly less than taking the drug for academic purposes (Prudhomme White, Becker-Blease, & Grace-Bishop, 2006).

        2. DeSantis, Webb, and Noar (2007) report that students take the drug for its energizing effects. Other students report taking the drug to make them more social and outgoing at parties.

        3. Some college students, especially women, report using the drug for its use as an appetite suppressant for dieting purposes.

Transition: Now that we understand that Adderall abuse is prevalent among students on university campuses, it is important to understand the detrimental effects that can accompany the illegal use of Adderall.

Figure 12.5

(Continued)

III. Whether students acknowledge the dangers or not, there are great risks involved in using Adderall illegally.

Listener relevance link: As we have now discussed the pervasiveness of Adderall abuse, statistically, it is likely that several of you have used this substance without a prescription to either enhance your academic performance or your social outings. Thus, it is important that we all recognize the adverse effects that result from taking Adderall without a prescription.

A. Adderall abuse can cause negative health effects for individuals not diagnosed with ADHD (Daley, 2004, April 20).

1. Adderall is reported to cause a heightened risk for heart problems when used inappropriately. Problems include sudden heart attack or stroke, sudden death in individuals with heart conditions, and increased blood pressure and heart rate (FDA, 2010).

2. Adderall abuse also can result in a myriad of mental problems, including manifestation of bipolar disorder, an increase of aggressive thoughts, and a heightened risk for psychosis similar to schizophrenia (FDA, 2010).

B. Adderall is highly addictive.

1. Adderall is an amphetamine, and while amphetamines were once used to treat a variety of ailments including weight loss in the 1950s and '60s, the drugs began to be much more closely regulated once their addictive nature was realized (Daley, 2004, April 20).

2. Adderall has similar properties to cocaine, and, as a result, abuse of the drug can lead to substance dependence (FDA, 2010).

C. Though clear risks are associated with the illegal use of Adderall, unlike other drugs, collegians do not view the inappropriate use of Adderall as harmful or illegal.

1. College students typically view stimulant abuse as morally acceptable and physically harmless. In a 2010 study, DeSantis and Hane found that students were quick to justify their stimulant abuse by claiming its use was fine in moderation.

2. The *Kentucky Kernel*, the student newspaper at the University of Kentucky, published an editorial of a student who flippantly described the use of Adderall among college students. He states, "If you want to abuse ice cream, amphetamines or alcohol, then there are going to be serious problems; however, let's not pretend a person using Adderall twice a semester to help them study is in any way likely to die a horrible death or suffer terrible side effects" (Riley, 2010, May 3).

3. In a study assessing the attitudes of college students toward the inappropriate use of stimulants, the authors found that "the majority of students who reported misuse or abuse were not concerned about the misuse and abuse of prescription stimulants, and a number of students thought that they should be more readily available (Prudhomme White, Becker-Blease, & Grace-Bishop, 2006, p. 265).

Conclusion

I. *Restatement of thesis:* Adderall is a prescription stimulant that is increasingly being abused by college students primarily as a study aid.

Figure 12.5

(Continued)

II.   *Main point review:* We have examined today what the drug Adderall is, its growing popularity among college students especially as a study aid, and the risks associated with using the drug illegally.

III. *Clincher:* The next time you or a friend considers taking Adderall as a study aid, think again. The potential harm that the drug could cause to your body is not worth even a perfect grade point average.

References

American Psychiatric Association. (2013). *Diagnostic and statistical manual of mental disorders (5th ed.).* Arlington, VA: Author.

Centers for Disease Control and Prevention. (2005, September 2). *Morbidity and Mortality Weekly Report (MMWR).* Retrieved from http://www.cdc.gov

DeSantis, A. D., & Hane, A. C. (2010). "Adderall is definitely not a drug": Justifications for the illegal use of ADHD stimulants. *Substance Use & Misuse, 45,* 31–46.

DeSantis, A. D., Webb, E. M., & Noar, S. M. (2008). Illicit use of prescription ADHD medications on a college campus: A multimethodological approach. *Journal of American College Health, 57,* 315–324.

Faraone, S. V., Biederman, J., Weiffenbach, B., Keith, T., Chu, M. P., Weaver, A., ... & Sakai, J. (2014). Dopamine D4 gene 7-repeat allele and attention deficit hyperactivity disorder. *The American Journal of Psychiatry, 156,* 768-770.

Food and Drug Administration. (2010). *Drugs @ FDS: FDA approved drug-products.* Retrieved from http://www.accessdata.fda.gov.

Kent, J. K. (2013, October 29). Adderrall: America's Favorite Amphetamine. *Huffington Post.* Retrieved from: http://www.huffingtonpost.com/high-times/adderall-amphetamine_b_4174297.html

National Heart, Blood, and Lung Insitute (2008). "What is narcolepsy?" *National Heart, Blood, and Lung Institute Diseases and Conditions Index.* Retrieved from http://www.nhlbi.nih.gov/health/dci/Diseases/nar/nar_what.html

McCabe, S. E., Teter, C. J., & Boyd, C. J. (2004). The use, misuse and diversion of prescription stimulants among middle and high school students. *Substance Use and Misuse, 39,* 1095–1116.

Prudhomme White, B., Becker-Blease, K. A., & Grace-Bishop, K. (2006). Stimulant medication use, misuse, and abuse in an undergraduate and graduate student sample. *Journal of American College Health, 54,* 261–268.

Riley, T. (2010, May 3). Prescription drug abuse is a personal choice. *Kentucky Kernel.* Retrieved from http://kykernel.com

Substance Abuse and Mental Health Services Administration, Office of Applied Studies. (April 7, 2009). *The NSDUH Report: Nonmedical Use of Adderall among Full-Time College Students.* Rockville, MD.

Spiller HA, Hays HL, Aleguas A (June 2013). Overdose of drugs for attention-deficit hyperactivity disorder: clinical presentation, mechanisms of toxicity, and management". *CNS Drugs* 27 (7): 531–543. doi:10.1007/s40263-013-0084-8

Teter, J. C., McCabe, S. E., Crandford, J. A., Boyd, C. J., & Gunthrie, S. K. (2005). Prevalence and motives for illicit use of prescription stimulants in an undergraduate student sample. *Journal of American College Health, 53,* 253–262.

Visser, S. N., Danielson, M. L., Bitsko, R. H., Holbrook, J. R., Kogan, M. D., Ghandour, R. M., Perou, R., & Blumber, S. J. (2014). Trends in the parent-report of health care provider-diagnosed and medicated attention-deficit/hyperactivity disorder: United States, 2003-3011. *Journal of the American Academy of Child and Adolescent Psychiatry, 53,* 34–46.

WHAT WOULD YOU DO?

A Question of Ethics

As Marna and Gloria were eating lunch together, Marna happened to ask Gloria, "How are you doing in Woodward's speech class?"

"Not bad," Gloria replied. "I'm working on this speech about product development. I think it will be really informative, but I'm having a little trouble with the opening. I just can't seem to get a good idea for getting started."

"Why not start with a story? That always worked for me in class."

"Thanks, Marna. I'll think on it."

The next day when Marna ran into Gloria again, she asked, "How's that introduction going?"

"Great. I've prepared a great story about Mary Kay—you know, the cosmetics entrepreneur? I'm going to tell about how she was terrible in school and no one thought she'd amount to anything. But she loved dabbling with cosmetics so much that she decided to start her own business—and the rest is history."

"That's a great story. I really like that part about being terrible in school. Was she really that bad?"

"I really don't know—the material I read didn't really focus on that part of her life. But I thought that angle would get people listening right away. And after all, I did it that way because you suggested starting with a story."

"Yes, but . . ."

"Listen, she did start the business. So what if the story isn't quite right? It makes the point I want to make—if people are creative and have a strong work ethic, they can make it big."

Is anyone really hurt by Gloria's opening the speech with this story and, if not, is Gloria's decision to do so ethically ok?

MindTap®

Reflection and Assessment

Organizing is the process of arranging your ideas in a way that will help your audience follow along and remember your speech. To assess how well you've learned what we addressed in these pages, answer the following questions. If you have trouble answering any of them, go back and review that material. Once you can answer each question accurately, you are ready to move ahead to read the next chapter.

1. Why do you want to limit the number of main points to two to four?

2. What are the two key elements of an effective section transition?

3. What are the key components of an introduction?

4. What makes for an effective clincher?

5. Why do you need to include a reference list?

COMMUNICATE!

RESOURCE AND ASSESSMENT CENTER

MindTap

Now that you have read Chapter 12, go to your MindTap for *Communicate!* for quick access to the electronic resources that accompany this text.

Applying What You've Learned

Impromptu Speech Activity

From an assortment of thesis statements provided by your instructor, create two introductions and two conclusions based on the guidelines offered in this chapter. Deliver both versions to the class as though you were giving an actual speech on the topic. Ask for feedback regarding which version the class likes better and why.

Assessment Activities

1. Identifying Structural Elements of the Speech Body Access the American Rhetoric Online Speech Bank (http://www.americanrhetoric.com/speechbank .htm). Select a speech and listen to the audio recording of it following along with its transcript. As you listen, identify and write down what you believe is the thesis statement. If you feel any one of the speeches does not contain an explicit thesis statement, identify its implied thesis. Now try to identify and write down the main points. What organizational pattern is being used?

What types of supporting material does the speaker use? Does the speaker cite the sources for his or her supporting material?

Identify and write down the transitions used in each speech.

Were transitions missing and, if so, did it make following along more difficult? Why or why not?

2. Access the American Rhetoric Online Speech Bank Web Site Select a speech and listen to the audio recording while you follow along with the transcript of it. As you listen, identify what the speaker uses to get attention.

Is it effective? Why or why not? Does the speaker offer listener relevance and speaker credibility? Explain.

What is the thesis statement? Based on the guidelines suggested in this chapter, is it an effective thesis statement?

Why or why not? Does the speaker summarize the main points in his or her conclusion?

How does the speaker clinch? Is it effective? Why or why not?

Skill-Building Activity

Create a thesis statement for each of the following:

    a. General goal: To inform

    b. Specific goal: I want my audience to understand the pros and cons of spanking as a form of discipline.

    c. Thesis statement:

    a. General goal: To persuade

    b. Specific goal: I want my audience to agree with my prediction that (insert name) is the best team in baseball.

    c. Thesis statement:

    a. General goal: To inform

    b. Specific goal: I want my audience to know how to change a flat tire.

    c. Thesis statement:

    a. General goal: To persuade

    b. Specific goal: I want to convince my audience to enroll in an auto mechanics class.

    c. Thesis statement:

Presentational Aids

When you've finished this chapter, you'll be able to:

- Articulate several benefits of using presentation aids in your speeches.

- Identify different types of presentational aids.

- Choose appropriate presentational aids.

- Prepare presentational aids that consider the best visual design layout, size, style, graphics, color, simplicity, and format.

- Display presentational aids using a method that is professional looking, enhances your ethos and your verbal message.

- Plan when and how to use presentational aids effectively in your speeches.

MindTap®

Start with quick warm-up activity.

As Scott and Carrie drove home from the Seattle 6 Ignite Speech event, Carrie exclaimed, "Wow! Dominic's speech was really great. I learned so much about what we can do to develop more sustainable electronics."

"Yeah, I know what you mean," Scott replied. "I've even got some ideas for reducing the e-waste he talked about."

"You know, what's really amazing to me is how much I learned from such a short talk!"

"I know what you mean. When I heard these were going to be PowerPoint presentations, all I could think was 'Oh no! Here we go again! It's going to be Death by PowerPoint: a darkened room and a faceless speaker talking to an oversized screen.'

Thank goodness I was wrong. Dominic's visuals really helped me picture what he was explaining and actually reinforced the important points he was making. My manager could benefit from watching someone like Dominic."

"I know. I can't believe we learned so much in five minutes! Tomorrow when I get into the office, I'm going to check out Dominic's blog."

13

ACTION STEP   4

Identify, Prepare, and Use Appropriate Presentational Aids

This conversation might have occurred between two people who attended the Ignite Seattle 6 event when industrial designer Dominic Muren (2009) gave a 5-minute PowerPoint-aided presentation titled "Humblefacturing a Sustainable Electronic Future." During an Ignite event, speakers give 5-minute presentations, often on technical topics, aided by 20 PowerPoint slides. Unlike the "death by PowerPoint" speeches Scott alluded to (and we've all had to suffer through), the speeches given at these events are adapted to people today—people for whom online social networking, talking or texting on mobile phones, and eating dinner are simultaneous activities. You can read more about this contemporary approach to public speaking in the *Communicating in the World* feature in this chapter.

COMMUNICATING IN THE WORLD

Ignite: The Power(Point) of Extreme Audience Adaptation

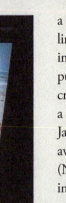

Ignite Baltimore/ Mike Subelsky

The first Ignite event was conceived in 2006 as a way for the tech community in the Seattle area to share their personal and professional passions and innovations. Ignite asks speakers, "If you had five minutes on stage, what would you say? What if you only had 20 slides and they rotated automatically after 15 seconds?" Since its 2006 inception, the events have spread to cities all over the United States and beyond, including Sydney, Australia, and Buenos Aires, Argentina (Guzman, 2009).

Speeches at Ignite events range from "Fighting Dirty in Scrabble" and "Causal Inference Is Hard" to "How I Learned to Appreciate Dance: Being Married to a Ballerina," "Geek Generation," and "How to Buy a Car Without Getting Screwed" ("Ignite Seattle 7," 2009; Guzman, 2009). The emphasis on extreme brevity as

a way to share ideas is reflected in Ignite Seattle's tagline: "Enlighten us, but make it quick," and reveals the importance of well-designed visual aids to successful public speaking (*Ignite Seattle,* n.d.). This condensed yet creative use of visual aids is part of what makes Ignite a great model for public speaking. Event organizer Jason Prothero says, "[Ignite is] a deliberate attempt to avoid what sucks about presentations. They're boring" (Neznanski, 2008). "Ignite's presentation style is a slap in the face to convention" (Weill, 2006).

Tailoring assignments to Ignite's short presentation style helps students develop as speakers by honing their ability to analyze and distill research into its most important points as well becoming comfortable with creating and delivering presentations using digital media.

As Ignite co-creator Brady Forrest (2009) explains, "It's not about slides, it's not even about your words, it's about a performance that marries the two together and lets people walk away with at least one new idea."

Extreme audience adaptation? Perhaps for now—sounds like pretty soon *everybody* will be doing it. If you'd like to see for yourself what Ignite is all about, visit IgniteSeattle.com.

How could you apply Ignite's approach to using presentational aids in your own speeches?

MindTap®

We live in an era when the written, oral, visual, and digital modes of communicating are merging. Whether it is a TV news program, your professor's lecture, or a motivational speech, audiences have come to expect messages to be enhanced with presentational aids. This means that as you prepare your speech, you will need to decide what presentational aids will enhance your verbal message and motivate your audience to both pay attention and remember it. In fact, presentational aids have become so important to public speeches that they are essentially a form of supporting material you should be looking for when conducting your research. Ultimately, you might use them to get attention in the introduction, to support a main point in the body, or to clinch in the conclusion.

A **presentational aid** is any visual, audio, audiovisual, or other sensory material used to enhance a verbal message. **Visual aids** enhance a speech by allowing audience members to see what a speaker is describing or explaining. Examples of visual aids include actual objects, models, photographs, drawings and diagrams, maps, charts, and graphs. **Audio aids** enhance the speaker's verbal message through sound. Some examples include musical clips from CDs and iTunes, recorded clips from conversations, interviews, famous speeches, and recordings of nature sounds like bird calls and whale songs. **Audiovisual aids** enhance the speech using a combination of sight and sound. Examples of audiovisual aids include clips from movies and television, YouTube videos, and podcasts, as well as other events or observations captured on video. **Other sensory aids** include materials that enhance your ideas by appealing to smell, touch, or taste. For example, a speaker can enhance the verbal description of the fragrance of a particular perfume by allowing audience members to smell it and the flavor of a particular entrée by allowing audience members to taste it.

presentational aid
any visual, audio, audiovisual, or other sensory material used to enhance a verbal message

visual aids
enhance a speech by allowing audience members to see what it is you are describing or explaining

audio aids
enhance a verbal message through sound

audiovisual aids
enhance a verbal message through a combination of sight and sound

other sensory aids
enhance a verbal message through smell, touch, or taste

Benefits of Presentational Aids

Research documents several benefits for using presentational aids. First, they get audience attention by dramatizing your verbal message. Second, they help audiences understand and remember information (Garcia-Retamero & Cokely, 2013). Third, they allow you to address the diverse learning styles of your audience members (Rogers, 2013). Fourth, they increase persuasive appeal (Krauss, 2012). Finally, using presentational aids may help you feel more competent and confident (Campbell, 2015).

Today, presentational aids are usually developed into computerized slide shows using presentation software such as PowerPoint, MediaPro, Adobe Acrobat, or Photodex and projected onto a large screen via a computer and projector. These programs allow you to embed audio and audiovisual links from local files and the Internet, which makes it fairly simple to create effective multimedia presentations. Whether creating multimedia presentations or developing simpler presentational aids, your purpose for using them is the same: to enhance your message without overpowering it. Speakers who violate this purpose end up with what Scott called "death by PowerPoint" in the chapter opener. In this chapter, we describe various types of presentational aids, criteria to consider when choosing and preparing them, and how to display and use them during your speech.

Types of Presentational Aids

Presentational aids range from those that are readily available from existing sources to those that are custom produced for a specific speech. As we mentioned earlier, they can come in the form of visual, audio, audiovisual, or other sensory aids.

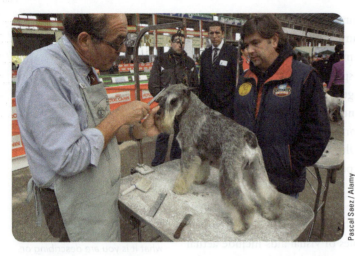

Pascal Saez / Alamy

Photo 13.1 Why might a speaker use an animal as a presentational aid? Would you? Why or why not?

actual objects
inanimate or animate physical samples of the idea being communicated

model
a three-dimensional scaled-down or scaled-up version of an actual object

Photo 13.2 Models can be effective visual aids when actual objects are too small, too large, or too complex to be effective. What are some other examples of models one could use in a speech?

Visual Aids

Visual aids enhance the verbal message by allowing audiences to see what it is you are describing or explaining. They include actual objects and models, photographs, drawings and diagrams, maps, charts, and graphs.

Actual Objects **Actual objects** are inanimate or animate physical samples of the idea you are communicating. Inanimate objects make good visual aids if they are (1) large enough to be seen by all audience members, (2) small enough to transport to the speech site, (3) simple enough to understand visually, and (4) safe. A volleyball or a Muslim prayer rug would be appropriate in size for most classroom audiences. An iPhone or Android might be OK if the goal is to show what a smartphone looks like, but it might be too small if you want to demonstrate how to use any of the phone's specialized functions. A smartboard or Mondopad would work better for this purpose.

On occasion, *you* can be an effective visual aid. For instance, you can demonstrate the motions involved in a golf swing; or you can use your attire to illustrate the native dress of a particular country. Sometimes it can be appropriate to use another person as a visual aid, such as when Jenny used a friend to demonstrate the Heimlich maneuver. Animals can also be effective visual aids (Photo 13.1). For example, Josh used his AKC Obedience Champion dog to demonstrate the basics of dog training. But keep in mind that some animals placed in unfamiliar settings can become difficult to control and then distract from your message.

Models When an actual object is too large or too small for the room where you'll be speaking, too complex to understand visually, or potentially unsafe or uncontrollable, a model of it can be an effective visual aid (Photo 13.2). A **model** is a three-dimensional scaled-down or scaled-up version of an actual object that may also be simplified to aid understanding. In a speech on the physics of wind energy, a scale model of a wind turbine could be an effective visual aid.

Photographs If an exact reproduction of material is needed, enlarged photographs can be excellent visual aids. In a speech on smart weapons, enlarged before-and-after photos of target sites would be effective in helping the audience understand the pinpoint accuracy of these weapons. When choosing photographs, be sure that the image is large enough for the audience to see, that the object of interest in the photo is clearly identified, and ideally, that the object is in the foreground. For example, if you are giving a speech about your grandmother and project a photo of her with her college

Jose Luis Pelaez Inc/Blend Images / Alamy

graduating class, you might circle her image or use an LED pointer to highlight her image among her classmates in the photo.

Simple Drawings and Diagrams Simple drawings and **diagrams** (a type of drawing that shows how the whole relates to its parts) can be effective because you can choose how much detail to include. To make sure they look professional, you can prepare them using a basic computer software program or find them already prepared in a book, an article, or on the Internet. If you do this, however, be sure to credit the source during your speech to enhance your credibility and avoid plagiarism. Andria's diagram of the human body and its pressure points, for example, worked well to clarify her message visually (see Figure 13.1).

Maps Simple maps allow you to orient audiences to landmarks (mountains, rivers, and lakes), states, cities, land routes, weather systems, and so on. As with drawings and diagrams, include only the details that are relevant to your purpose (see Figure 13.2).

Charts A **chart** is a graphic representation that distills a lot of information into an easily interpreted visual format. Flow charts, organizational charts, and pie charts are the most common. A **flow chart** uses symbols and connecting lines to diagram the progression through a complicated process. Tim used a flow chart to help listeners move through the sequence of steps to assess their weight (Figure 13.3) An **organizational chart** shows the structure of an organization in terms of rank and chain of command. The chart in Figure 13.4 illustrates the organization of a student union board. A **pie chart** shows the relationships among parts of a single unit. Ideally, pie charts have two to five "slices," or wedges—more than eight wedges clutter a pie chart. If your chart includes too many wedges, use another kind of chart unless you can consolidate several of the less important wedges into the category of "other," as Kirk did to show the percentage of total calories that should come from the various components of food (see Figure 13.5).

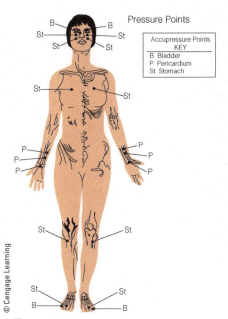

© Cengage Learning

Figure 13.1

Sample diagram

diagram
a type of drawing that shows how the whole relates to its parts

chart
a graphic representation that distills a lot of information into an easily interpreted visual format

flow chart
uses symbols and connecting lines to diagram the progression through a complicated process

organizational chart
shows the structure of an organization in terms of rank and chain of command

pie chart
shows the relationships among parts of a single unit

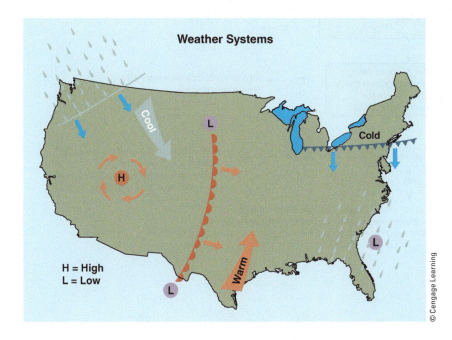

© Cengage Learning

Figure 13.2

Sample map

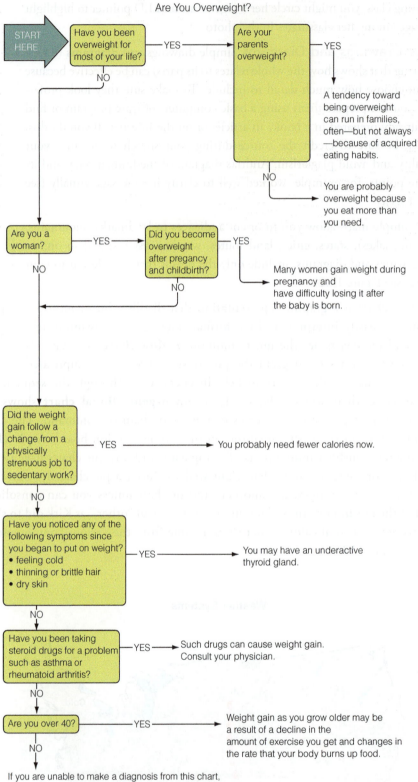

Are You Overweight?

START HERE → Have you been overweight for most of your life? —YES→ Are your parents overweight? —YES→

A tendency toward being overweight can run in families, often—but not always—because of acquired eating habits.

NO↓ (from parents overweight) → You are probably overweight because you eat more than you need.

NO (from "most of your life") ↓

Are you a woman? —YES→ Did you become overweight after pregancy and childbirth? —YES→

Many women gain weight during pregnancy and have difficulty losing it after the baby is born.

NO ↓

Did the weight gain follow a change from a physically strenuous job to sedentary work? —YES→ You probably need fewer calories now.

NO ↓

Have you noticed any of the following symptoms since you began to put on weight?
• feeling cold
• thinning or brittle hair
• dry skin
—YES→ You may have an underactive thyroid gland.

NO ↓

Have you been taking steroid drugs for a problem such as asthma or rheumatoid arthritis? —YES→ Such drugs can cause weight gain. Consult your physician.

NO ↓

Are you over 40? —YES→ Weight gain as you grow older may be a result of a decline in the amount of exercise you get and changes in the rate that your body burns up food.

NO ↓

If you are unable to make a diagnosis from this chart, your excess weight is probably due only to overeating. If, after a month of dieting, you fail to lose weight, consult your physician.

© Cengage Learning

Figure 13.3

Sample flow chart

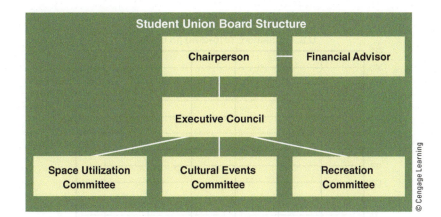

© Cengage Learning

Figure 13.4

Sample organizational chart

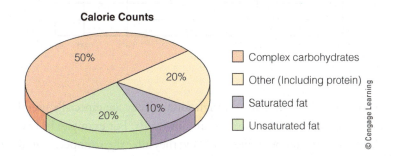

© Cengage Learning

Figure 13.5

Sample pie chart

Graphs A **graph** presents numerical information in visual form. A **bar graph** uses vertical or horizontal bars to show relationships between two or more variables. For instance, Jacqueline used a bar graph to compare the amounts of caffeine found in one serving each of brewed coffee, instant coffee, tea, cocoa, and cola (see Figure 13.6). A **line graph** indicates the changes in one or more variables over time. In a speech on the population of the United States, for example, the line graph in Figure 13.7 helps by showing the population increase, in millions, from 1810 to 2010.

graph
a diagram that presents numerical information

bar graph
uses vertical or horizontal bars to show relationships between two or more variables

line graph
indicates the changes in one or more variables over time

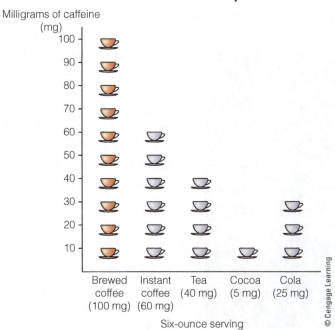

© Cengage Learning

Figure 13.6

Sample bar graph

Figure 13.7

Sample line graph

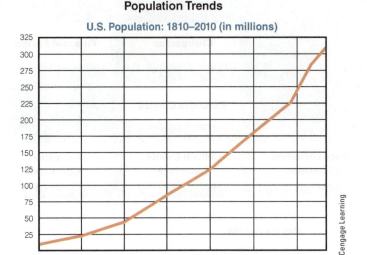

Audio Aids

Audio aids enhance a verbal message through sound. They are especially useful when it is difficult, if not impossible, to describe a sound in words. For example, in David's speech about the three types of trumpet mutes and how they alter the trumpet's sound, he played his trumpet so listeners could hear what he meant. If you can't or don't want to make your own sounds, you can use recorded excerpts from sources such as famous speeches, radio programs, and interviews, as well as music or environmental sounds. Chas wrote a song and used a snippet from it as an attention catcher and clincher in his speech. He later posted a link to it on his Facebook page, which he also referenced in this speech in case anyone would like to hear the song in its entirety later. Before using an audio aid, make sure you have enough time to present it (it should take no more than about 5 percent of your total allotted speaking time) and that you have access to a quality sound system.

Audiovisual Aids

Audiovisual aids enhance a verbal message using a combination of sight and sound. You can use short clips from films and videos that are relatively easy to access on Internet sites such as YouTube and import as hyperlinks in your slides. For example, in his speech about the use of robots in automobile production, Chad, who worked as a technician at the local Ford plant, showed a 20-second video clip of a car being painted in a robotic paint booth. As with audio aids, your audiovisual aid should take no more than 5 percent of your speaking time.

Other Sensory Aids

Depending on your topic, *other sensory aids* that appeal to smell, touch, or taste may effectively enhance your speech (Photo 13.3). For example, a speech about making perfume

Photo 13.3 Celebrity chefs and their guests often sample each other's dishes to confirm that they really taste good. Can you imagine any other way they could confirm the taste of their products?

might benefit from allowing your audience to smell scented swatches as you describe the ingredients used to make the scents. In a speech about Braille, Javier handed out copies of his outline written in Braille for audience members to touch.

Choosing Presentational Aids

With so many different types of presentational aids, you have to decide which ones will best illustrate the content you want to highlight. In our opening scenario, Carrie and Scott were motivated to pay attention to and remember Dominic's Ignite speech in part because his took the time to carefully choose aids that would best illustrate his points. Some simple guidelines can help you make good choices. Choose aids that:

- illustrate the most important ideas to understand and remember.

- clarify complex ideas that are difficult to explain verbally.

- are appropriate for the size of the audience.

- make dull information and details more interesting.

- you will feel comfortable using and transporting to the speech site.

- enhance rather than overwhelm the verbal message.

- you have the time and money to prepare

- demonstrate cultural sensitivity and do not offend members of your audience. (To understand why, read the following *Diverse Voices* feature by Neil Payne.)

DIVERSE VOICES

Public Relations Across Cultures

by Neil Payne

Director, Kwintessential (a cross-cultural communication consultancy)

The public relations (PR) industry is responsible for creating and maintaining relationships between clients and customers. PR practitioners are aware of how best to foster interest, trust and belief in a product or company when dealing within their own nations and cultures, however, when dealing with a foreign audience, analysis is critical. To illustrate the impact cross-cultural awareness can have on the success or failure of a PR campaign, consider these examples: Pepsodent tried to sell its toothpaste in Southeast Asia by emphasizing that it "whitens your teeth." They found out that the local natives chew betel nuts to blacken their teeth because they find it attractive.

Similarly, when Ford launched the Pinto in Brazil they were puzzled as to why sales were dead. They eventually found out that Brazilians did not want to be seen driving a car meaning "small male genitals."

Finally, a company advertised eyeglasses in Thailand by featuring a variety of cute animals wearing glasses. The ad failed, because animals are considered to be a low form of life in Thailand and no self-respecting Thai would wear anything worn by animals. (Payne, n.d.). Clearly, these examples illustrate how critical it is to understand your audience, particularly across cultures.

Payne, N. (n.d.). Public relations across cultures: Building international communication bridges. All About Public Relations with Steven R. Van Hook. Retrieved on April 26, 2012 at: http://www.aboutpublicrelations.net /ucpayne.htm

APPLY IT

Consider a time when a speaker or teacher used visual aids that required you to read a lot of information. How much do you remember about the speech or lecture and why?

MindTap®

Preparing Presentational Aids

However simple your presentational aids, you still need to produce them carefully. You may need to find or create charts, graphs, diagrams, maps, or drawings. You may need to search for and prepare photographs. You may look for audio or audiovisual snippets and then convert them to a format that you can use at your speech site.

The goal is to prepare professional-looking and sounding presentational aids that will enhance your ethos (perceived competence, credibility, and character) in addition to clarifying your message and making it more memorable. To do so, follow these guidelines:

1. **Limit the reading required of the audience.** The audience should be listening to you, not reading the presentational aid. So use key words and short phrases rather than complete sentences.

2. **Customize presentational aids from other sources.** As you conducted research, you probably found potential supporting material already represented in visual, audio, or audiovisual form. In these cases, simplify the aid to include only the relevant information. For example, Jia Li was preparing a speech on alcohol abuse by young adults. During her research, she found a graph called "Current, Binge, and Heavy Alcohol Use among Persons Aged 12 or Older by Age." Since this graph presented information pertaining to drinkers from ages 12 to 65+, she simplified it to include only information on young adults aged 16 to 29.

3. **Use a photo, print, or type size that can be seen easily and a volume and sound quality that can be heard easily by your entire audience.** Check visuals for size by moving as far away from the presentational aid as the farthest person in your audience will be sitting. If you can see the image, read the lettering, and see the details from that distance, your aid is large enough. If not, create another and check it again. Check audio materials for volume and quality in a similar way.

4. **Use a consistent print style that is easy to read.** Avoid fancy print styles and stick to one print style on the aid and throughout the computerized slide show. In addition, use uppercase and lowercase letters rather than ALL CAPS as doing so is actually easier to read.

5. **Make sure information is laid out in a way that is aesthetically pleasing.** Leave sufficient white space around the whole visual so that it's easy to identify each component. Also, use typefaces and indenting to visually represent relationships between ideas.

6. **Use graphic illustrations in visuals.** To truly enhance a verbal message, a presentational aid should consist of something other than or more than just words (Booher, 2003). Even something as simple as a relevant piece of clip art can make the verbal message more memorable. Of course; clip art can be overdone, so don't let your message be overpowered by unnecessary pictures or animations.

7. **Use color strategically.** Although black and white can work well for your visual aids, consider using color strategically to emphasize points. Here are some suggestions for doing so:

   - Use the same background color and theme for all your presentational aids.

   - Use the same color to show similarities, and use opposite colors (on a color wheel) to show differences between ideas.

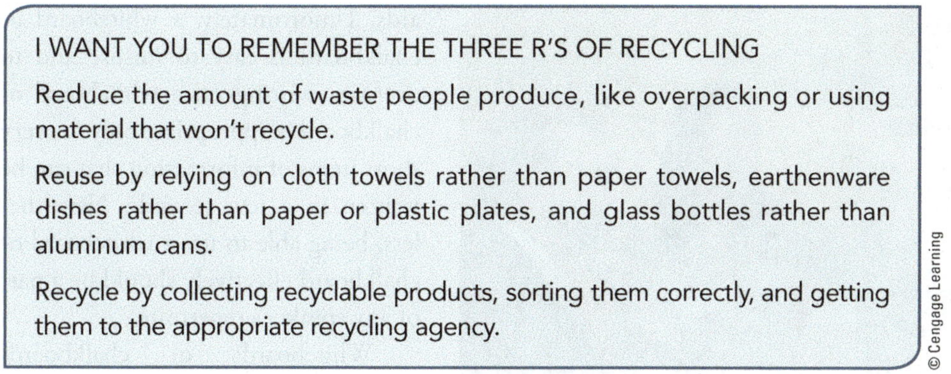

I WANT YOU TO REMEMBER THE THREE R'S OF RECYCLING

Reduce the amount of waste people produce, like overpacking or using material that won't recycle.

Reuse by relying on cloth towels rather than paper towels, earthenware dishes rather than paper or plastic plates, and glass bottles rather than aluminum cans.

Recycle by collecting recyclable products, sorting them correctly, and getting them to the appropriate recycling agency.

© Cengage Learning

Figure 13.8

A cluttered and cumbersome visual aid

- Use bright colors, such as red, to highlight important information. Be sure to avoid using red and green together, however, because audience members who are color blind may not be able to distinguish between them.

- Use dark colors for lettering on a white background and a light color for lettering on black or deep blue backgrounds.

- Use no more than two or three colors on any presentational aid that is not a photograph or video clip.

- Pretend you are your audience. Sit as far away as they will be sitting, and evaluate the colors you have chosen for their readability and appeal.

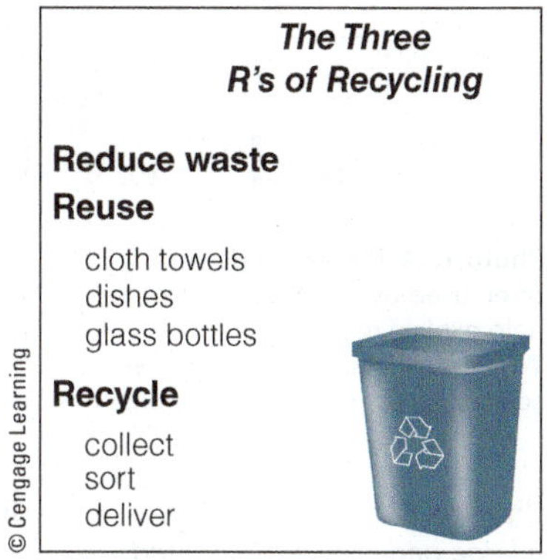

**The Three
R's of Recycling**

Reduce waste
Reuse
   cloth towels
   dishes
   glass bottles
Recycle
   collect
   sort
   deliver

© Cengage Learning

Figure 13.9

A simple but effective visual aid

Let's see if we can put all of these principles to work. Figure 13.8 contains a lot of important information, but notice how unpleasant it is to the eye. As you can see, this visual aid ignores all the principles we've discussed. However, with some thoughtful simplification, this speaker could produce the visual aid shown in Figure 13.9, which sharpens the focus by emphasizing the key words (*reduce, reuse, recycle*), highlighting the major details, and adding clip art for a professional touch.

Displaying Presentational Aids

Once you have decided on the specific presentational aids for your speech, you need to choose a method for displaying them. As with choosing and preparing aids, your goal is to display them using a method that is professional looking and sounding to enhance your ethos, as well as your verbal message. Speakers can choose from the following methods for displaying presentational aids.

Posters

The easiest method for displaying simple drawings, charts, maps, photos, and graphs is on a poster. Because posters tend to be fairly small, use them only with smaller audiences (30 people or fewer). Many professional conference presentations use poster boards to explain complex research studies (Photo 13.4).

Whiteboards or Chalkboards

Because a whiteboard or chalkboard is a staple in every college classroom, many novice (and ill-prepared) speakers rely on this method for displaying their visual

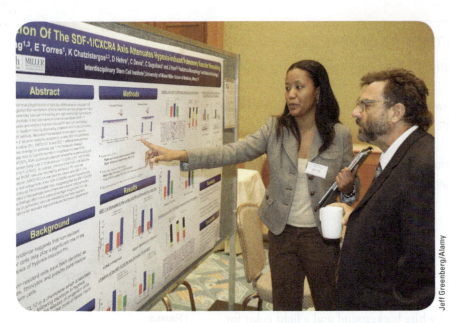

Photo 13.4 Posterboards are often used by professionals to help explain research projects. Why do you think posters remain so popular for such presentations?

flip chart
a large pad of paper mounted on an easel

handout
material printed on sheets of paper

Photo 13.5 Although "chalk talks" are easy to prepare, they are not appropriate for formal presentations. On what occasions do you think a "chalk talk" would be appropriate?

aids. Unfortunately, a whiteboard or chalkboard is easy to misuse and to overuse. Writing on a whiteboard or chalkboard is appropriate only for very short items of information that can be written in a few seconds. Nevertheless, being able to use a whiteboard or chalkboard effectively should be a part of any speaker's repertoire.

Whiteboards or chalkboards should be written on prior to speaking or during a break in speaking. Otherwise, the visual is likely to be either illegible or partly obscured by your body as you write. Or you may end up talking to the board instead of to the audience. Should you need to draw or write on the board while you are talking, you should practice doing it. If you are right-handed, stand to the right of what you are drawing. Try to face at least part of the audience while you work. Although it may seem awkward at first, your effort will allow you to maintain contact with your audience and will allow the audience to see what you are doing while you are doing it.

Such "chalk talks" are easy to prepare, but they are the most likely to result in damage to speaker credibility (Photo 13.5). It is the rare individual who can develop well-crafted visual aids on a whiteboard or chalkboard. More often, they signal a lack of preparation.

Flip Charts

A **flip chart**, a large pad of paper mounted on an easel, can be an effective method for presenting visual aids. Flip charts (and easels) are available in many sizes. For a presentation to four or five people, a small tabletop version works well; for a larger audience, use a larger-size pad (30" × 40").

As with whiteboards and chalkboards, you should prepare them prior to giving the speech. In some situations, you may write down some information before the speech begins and then add information while speaking.

Handouts

At times, it may be useful for each member of the audience to have a personal copy of the visual aid. In these situations, you can prepare a **handout** (material printed on sheets of paper). The benefit is that everyone in the audience can have a copy to refer to and take with them after the speech. The drawback is that distributing handouts can distract audience members from you and your message.

Before you decide to use handouts, carefully consider why they would be better than some other method. Handouts are effective for information you want listeners to refer to after the speech, such as a set of steps to follow later, useful telephone numbers and addresses, or mathematical formulas.

If you do decide on handouts, distribute them at the end of the speech. If you want to refer to information on the handout during the speech, create another visual aid that you can reveal when discussing it during your speech.

Document Cameras

Another simple way to project drawings, charts, photos, and graphs is using a document camera, such as an Elmo. If you choose this method, be sure to transfer drawings, charts, photos, and graphs from original sources onto a sheet of 8½" × 11" piece of paper so you can display them smoothly and professionally.

Computers, CD/DVD Players, and LCD Projectors

Most people today prefer to present audio and audiovisual recordings, as well as computerized slide shows using a computer and an LCD projector. However, you should always prepare back-up aids to use if equipment fails. Also, to ensure that audience members focus their attention on you when you're not talking about one of your slides or clips, insert blank screens between slides, press the "B" key on your keyboard, or use the "mute" key on your projector remote to display blank screens.

Using Presentational Aids

Many speakers think that once they have chosen and prepared good presentational aids, they will have no trouble using them during the speech. However, effective speakers also practice using them in advance. Although we will spend more time explaining how to do so in Chapter 15 (Delivery), we introduce several guidelines here, as well.

1. Plan carefully when to use each presentational aid and make a note of it on your formal outline and in your speaking notes.

2. Position presentational aids and equipment where all audience members can see and/or hear them before beginning your speech.

3. Show and/or play presentational aids only when talking about them so they do not distract audience members from your message.

4. Pass objects and handouts around AFTER rather than during the speech so they do not become a distraction.

5. Talk about the visual aid while showing it, and the audio or audiovisual aid just before and just after playing it.

ACTION STEP 4

Identifying Presentational Aids

The goal of this activity is to help you decide which presentational aids you will use in your speech.

1. Identify the key ideas you could emphasize with a presentational aid to increase audience interest, understanding, or retention.

2. For each idea you have identified, list the type of presentational aid you think would be most appropriate to develop and use.

3. For each idea you plan to enhance with an aid, decide on the method you will use to display it.

4. Write a brief paragraph describing why you chose the types of presentational aids and display methods that you did. Be sure to consider how your choices will affect your preparation time and the audience's perception of your credibility.

MindTap® *Identify your presentational aids with the PREPARE Your Informative Speech Activity in Chapter 16 of the MindTap. Select the Outline tab to find Action Step 4.*

COMMUNICATE ON YOUR FEET

Speech Assignment

Battle of the Visual Aids

The Assignment

Form groups of four or five people. Your instructor will provide you with three sample visual aids that might be used in a speech. Based on the criteria and guidelines you learned in this chapter, evaluate each visual aid and select the best one. At your instructor's request, one member of each team should go to the front of the room and give a 2- to 3-minute speech that makes a case for why the visual aid you selected is the best of the three. After all groups have made their presentations, vote as a class on the best one and discuss why.

WHAT WOULD YOU DO?

A Question of Ethics

As Oscar and Max were finishing dinner, Max asked:

"Have you figured out what you're going to use for presentational aids in your speech next week in Professor Gilman's class? I'm totally stumped."

Oscar replied, "Yeah, I am so ready and actually pretty pumped about mine."

"What are you going to use?" inquired Max.

"Well, you know I'm going to try to persuade the class to agree with me that the death penalty is wrong. Well, I got a hold of an audio clip of someone writhing in pain during an execution. I'm going to play it while I show several photographs of people who have been executed. THAT should really make my speech memorable and my argument convincing!"

"Yikes," exclaimed Max. "Are you sure that's such a good idea?"

"Yeah, why not?"

Is it ethical to use potentially offensive presentational aids if doing so will make your speech more memorable or your argument more convincing? Why or why not?

MindTap®

Reflection and Assessment

Presentational aids are useful when they help audience members understand and remember important information. Today most formal presentations employ computerized slide shows like PowerPoint or Prezi. Unfortunately, however, not all follow the principles of effective presentational aids you've learned in this chapter. To assess how well you've learned what we addressed in this chapter, answer the following questions. If you have trouble answering any of them, go back and review that material. Once you can answer each question accurately, you are ready to move ahead to read the next chapter.

1. Why might you decide to use presentational aids in your speech?

2. What are some different types of presentational aids you might use to complement your speech?

3. What are some questions to consider when choosing presentational aids?

4. What are some guidelines to follow when preparing visual, audio, and audiovisual aids?

5. What should you consider when displaying presentational aids?

6. What should you consider when preparing to use presentational aids in your speeches?

COMMUNICATE!

RESOURCE AND ASSESSMENT CENTER

Now that you have read Chapter 13, go to your MindTap for *Communicate!* for quick access to the electronic resources that accompany this text.

Applying What You've Learned

Impromptu Speech Activity

Locate one magazine advertisement that seems to do a good job of following the guidelines of effective visual aids and one that does not, according to what you've read in this chapter. Prepare a short 2- to 3-minute speech articulating why you think one is effective and the other is not.

Assessment Activity

Locate a visual, audio, and audiovisual aid example that you believe represents an effective and ineffective presentational aid based on the information and guidelines offered in this chapter. Prepare a 2- to 3-page paper explaining why you assessed them as you did.

Skill-Building Activity

Choosing Appropriate Presentational Aids For each of the following, identify what type of presentational aid you would use and why:

(a) the Great Wall of China

(b) how to bake cookies

(c) energy comparison between fluorescent and incandescent light bulbs

(d) college tuition rate trends

(e) time management in one typical day of a college student

(f) members and roles in a campus club

Language and Oral Style

When you have finished this chapter, you will be able to:

- Explain how oral style differs from written style.

- Use appropriate language for the audience and occasion in your speeches by considering four audience variables.

- Choose language that conveys your ideas accurately by using four language and delivery techniques.

- Use vivid language in your speeches.

MindTap®

Start with quick warm-up activity.

Nathan asked his friend Josh to read through his formal speech outline and provide suggestions for improvement. After reading Nathan's outline on the congenital condition known as a Meckel's Diverticulum, Josh asked, "What class are you giving this speech for? Isn't it your public speaking class?"

"Yeah, why?" Nathan responded.

"Well," Josh replied, "Don't take this the wrong way, ok? I actually think it would be great for classmates in your human anatomy and physiology class. But it seems awfully technical for classmates who come from all sorts of majors. I'm afraid it might go over their heads."

Nathan sounded bummed as he responded, "Oh, good point. Darn it! I guess I'll have to go back to the drawing board and pick a different topic."

"Actually," said Josh, "I don't think you have to start over. You just need to adjust some of your language to be appropriate and clear for a more general audience. Here, let me show you. . . ."

14

With your outline in hand and presentational aids prepared, you are ready to move to the next step in the speech preparation process. In other words, you turn your focus from the macrostructure (the overall framework for organizing your speech content) to the microstructure (the specific language and style choices used to verbalize your ideas for a particular audience). Recall from Chapter 11 that **audience adaptation** is the process of tailoring your speech to a specific audience and occasion. This chapter focuses on tailoring your language and oral style. In the vignette, Josh realized that Nathan's speech can be adapted to his pubic speech class audience by choosing appropriate, clear, and vivid language.

In written communication, effective style evolves through a repetitious process of reading and revising. In a speech, effective style develops through a similarly repetitious process of practicing aloud and revising. In this chapter, we help you do so first by clarifying how oral style differs from written style, as well as how the formal oral style we use in public speeches differs from the informal oral style we use in casual conversations. Then, we review several aspects of semantic, pragmatic, and sociolinguistic word meanings we introduced in Chapter 4 as they relate specifically to public speaking.

audience adaptation
the process of tailoring your speech to the specific audience and occasion

---

ACTION STEP 5

Practice Oral Language and Delivery Style

Oral Style

oral style
how one conveys messages through the spoken word

Oral style refers to how we convey messages through the spoken word. An effective oral style differs quite a bit from written style, though when giving a speech your oral style is still more formal than everyday talk. The goal is to adapt your language to the purpose, audience, and occasion. For example, although your language when speaking to a small audience of colleagues at a business meeting will be more formal than when conversing with a friend at dinner, it will not be as formal as when speaking to an audience of 100 or more at a professional conference or workshop. Still, even in a formal public speaking situation, you must *establish a relationship* with your listeners. Although your oral style is slightly more formal than in everyday conversations, it should still reflect a personal tone that encourages listeners to perceive you to be *having a conversation with them*. Four primary characteristics distinguish an effective oral style from an effective written style.

1. **An effective oral style tends toward short sentences and familiar language.** Because listeners expect to grasp your main ideas while they listen, choose words that your audience is likely to understand without looking up definitions. Likewise, opt for short, simple sentences rather than complex ones that require additional time to decipher. We certainly live in a digital age in which live public speeches can be recorded and even posted online to be heard multiple times. But even when watching a recorded public speech, listeners should not be required to press "pause" to look up word meanings or to press "reverse" to replay complex sentences.

2. **An effective oral style features plural personal pronouns.** Using plural personal pronouns such as "we," "us," and "our" creates a sense of relationship with the audience. It demonstrates respect for the audience as participants in the rhetorical situation.

Remember your goal is to create a perception of conversing *with* your audience rather than presenting *to* or *in front of* them. Personal pronouns help foster that perception.

3. **An effective oral style features descriptive words and phrases that appeal to the ear in ways that sustain listener interest and promote retention.** By using colorful adjectives and adverbs that appeal to the senses, as well as rhetorical figures of speech (discussed later in this chapter), you will capture the interest of your audience to pay attention and motivate them to stay focused on it throughout.

4. **An effective oral style incorporates clear macrostructural elements** (e.g., main point preview, section transitions, and signposts as discussed in Chapter 12). Unless your public speech is being recorded and posted for additional viewing, listeners will be afforded the opportunity to hear it only once. Consequently, you need to intentionally articulate a preview of your main points so listeners can conceptualize the framework for your main ideas at the outset. Similarly, you need to provide section transitions that verbally signal when you are moving from one major idea to the next, as well as signposts such as "first," "second," "third," and "fourth" to help listeners follow your train of thought as the speech progresses.

President Obama has been described as someone that uses these characteristics of effective oral style to capture and maintain the attention of his listeners. To learn more about how he does so, read the *Communicating in the World* feature in this chapter.

> **APPLY IT**
>
> Identify a time when you attended a lecture or other public speaking event where the speaker read the manuscript to you using long sentences and unfamiliar vocabulary. How well did the speaker maintain your attention? How well did you end up understanding the main points and why?
>
>

COMMUNICATING IN THE WORLD

The President's Way with Words

In the NPR news story, "The Art of Language, Obama-Style," correspondent Linton Weeks explains that President Barack Obama understands that carefully selected language and oral style are powerful means for reaching the hearts and minds of listeners. How does he do it? He does it by following the guidelines for effective oral style.

First, he relies on simple language. He begins sentences with "look" or "listen" and uses everyday expressions such as "screwed up" and "folks." In other words, "he doesn't use $5 words when nickel ones will suffice" (Weeks, 2009). In fact, according to a study that tracked language patterns of presidential candidates from 1948 to 2012, Obama scored lower than anyone else on both "complexity" (average word size) and "embellishment" (number of words used to make a point) (Hart & Jamieson, 2012). As a result, Obama comes across as a "plain spoken Midwesterner."

Second, according to political science professor John Geer, is the President's unique ability to "reach rhetorical heights" by finding the most descriptive words to make his point.

Third, he draws upon his "rare gift" and "real strength" for sounding conversational and appearing "comfortable whether scripted or extemporaneous" by using personal pronouns like "we" and "our" as he claims, for example, that "we're going to win this struggle" by working together and "our journey is not complete until" (Leith, 2013).

Whether or not you agree with his politics, President Obama capitalizes on his own unique language and oral style to appeal effectively to the "folks" in his audience.

Do you agree that Obama's language and oral style helps him sound conversational and sincere as he speaks? Why or why not?

MindTap®

Now that we've described the nature of oral style as it differs from written style, let's turn our attention to some specific language choices you should consider as you practice and revise your speeches. These include speaking appropriately, clearly, and vividly.

Speaking Appropriately

speaking appropriately
using language that adapts to the needs, interests, knowledge, and attitudes of the audience

verbal immediacy
the psychological distance between speaker and audience

Speaking appropriately means using language that adapts to the needs, interests, knowledge, and attitudes of listeners and avoiding language that might alienate anyone. In the communication field, we use the term **verbal immediacy** to describe language used to reduce the psychological distance between you and your audience (Witt, Wheeless, & Allen, 2004). In other words, speaking appropriately means making language choices that enhance a sense of connection between you and your audience members. Speaking appropriately means highlighting the relevance of your topic, establishing common ground and speaker credibility, demonstrating linguistic sensitivity, and adapting to cultural diversity.

Relevance

timeliness
how the information can be used now

timely
information audience members can use now

proximity
information in relation to listeners' personal space

Photo 14.1 How can you establish relevance in a speech about phoning or texting while driving?

Listeners pay attention to and are interested in ideas they perceive as personally relevant (when they can answer the question, "What does this have to do with me?"). You can help the audience perceive your topic as relevant by highlighting its **timeliness**, proximity, and personal impact (Photo 14.1). Listeners are more likely to be interested in information they perceive as **timely**—they want to know how they can use the information *now*. So whenever possible, use the present tense as you explain your ideas. Your listeners are also more likely to be interested in information that has **proximity**, a relationship to their personal "space." Psychologically, we pay more attention to information that is related to our "territory"—to our family, our neighborhood, or our city, state, or country. You have probably heard speakers say something like this: "Let me bring this closer to home by showing you . . ." and then make their point by using a local example. Finally, your audience members are more likely to be interested when you present information that can have a serious physical, economic, or psychological impact on them. For example, in the opening vignette, Josh could have suggested that Nathan pique listener interest by pointing out that major league pitcher Chan Ho Park was diagnosed with a Meckles Diverticulum in 2006. To include this detail would add relevance, since Park once pitched for the home team of Josh and Nathan's college.

© Solphoto/Shutterstock.com

Common Ground

Common ground is the combination of background, knowledge, attitudes, experiences, and philosophies that you share with your audience. You should use audience analysis to identify areas of similarity; then speak using plural personal pronouns, rhetorical questions, and common experiences to help establish common ground (Photo 14.2).

Use Plural Personal Pronouns As we've already mentioned, one simple way to establish common ground is to use *plural personal pronouns: we, us, and our.* You can easily replace "I" and "you" language in the macrostructural elements of your speech. In your thesis statement, for example, you can say "let's discuss . . ." rather than "I will inform you . . ." and in your section transitions, you can say "Now that we all have a clearer understanding of . . .," rather than, "Now that I've explained . . ." and so on. For his Meckles Diverticulum speech, Josh suggested Nathan introduce his thesis and preview using "we" language this way: "In the next few minutes, let's explore the symptoms, diagnosis, and treatment of a fairly unknown defect in the small intestine known as a Meckel's Diverticulum."

Mark Peterson/Corbis News/Corbis

Photo 14.2 In what ways do you think the speaker in this situation can create common ground with the audience?

common ground
background, knowledge, attitudes, experiences, and philosophies shared by speaker and audience

Ask Rhetorical Questions Recall that a *rhetorical question* is one whose answer is obvious to audience members and to which they are not expected to reply. Rhetorical questions create common ground by alluding to experiences that are shared by audience members and the speaker. They are often used in speech introductions but can also be effective as transitions and in other parts of the speech. For instance, notice how this transition, phrased as a rhetorical question, creates common ground:

> *When watching a particularly violent TV program, have you ever asked yourself, "Did they really need to be this graphic to make the point"?*

Draw from Common Experiences You can also develop common ground by sharing personal experiences, examples, and illustrations that embody what you and the audience have in common. For instance, in a speech about the effects of television violence, you might allude to a common viewing experience:

> *At a key moment when you're watching a really frightening scene in a movie, do you ever quickly shut your eyes? I vividly remember closing my eyes over and over again during the scariest scenes in* The Shining, The Blair Witch Project, *and* Halloween.

Speaker Credibility

Credibility is the confidence an audience places in the truthfulness of what a speaker says. Some people are widely known experts in a particular area and don't have to adapt their remarks to establish their credibility. However, most of us—even if we are given a formal introduction to acquaint the audience with our credentials—will still need to adapt our remarks to demonstrate our knowledge and expertise. In the opening vignette,

credibility
the confidence an audience places in the truthfulness of what a speaker says

Josh could have suggested that Nathan establish credibility by sharing that he is a pre-med student majoring in human anatomy.

Linguistic Sensitivity

To demonstrate *linguistic sensitivity*, choose words that are respectful of others and avoid potentially offensive language. Just as this is crucial to effective interpersonal and group communication, it is also imperative in public speaking situations. To demonstrate linguistic sensitivity, avoid using generic language, nonparallelism, potentially offensive humor, as well as profanity and vulgarity.

Generic Language **Generic language** uses words that apply only to one sex, race, or other group as though they represent everyone. In the past, English speakers used the masculine pronoun *he* to stand for all humans regardless of sex. This example of generic language excludes 50 percent of the audience. The best way to avoid using generic language in public speeches is to use plurals: "When we shop, we should have a clear idea of what we want to buy" (Stewart, Cooper, Stewart, & Friedley, 2003). You can also do so by using terms such as *police officer* rather than *policeman*, *firefighter* instead of *fireman*, *flight attendant* rather than *stewardess*, and *server* instead of *waitress*.

Nonparallel Language **Nonparallel language** is when terms are changed because of the sex, race, or other group characteristics of the individual. Two common forms of nonparallelism are marking and irrelevant association.

Marking is the *addition* of sex, race, age, or other group designations to a description. For instance, a doctor is a person with a medical degree who is licensed to practice medicine. Notice the difference between the following two sentences:

Jones is a good doctor.

Jones is a good black doctor.

In the second sentence, use of the marker "black" has nothing to do with doctoring. Marking is inappropriate because it trivializes the subject's role by introducing an irrelevant characteristic (Treinen & Warren, 2001). The speaker may be intending to praise Jones, but listeners may interpret the sentence as saying that Jones is a good doctor for a black person (or a woman or an aged person).

A second form of nonparallelism is **irrelevant association**, which is when one person's relationship to another is emphasized, even though that relationship is irrelevant to the point. For example, it is inappropriate to introduce a speaker as "Gladys Thompson—whose husband is CEO of Acme, Inc.—is the chairperson for this year's United Way campaign." Mentioning her husband's status implies that Gladys Thompson is chairperson because of her *husband's* accomplishments, not her own.

Offensive Humor Dirty jokes and racist, sexist, or other "-ist" remarks may not be intended to be offensive, but if some listeners are offended, you will have lost verbal immediacy. To be most effective with your formal public speeches, avoid humorous comments or jokes that may be offensive to some listeners. As a general rule, when in doubt, leave it out.

Profanity and Vulgarity Profanity and vulgar expressions are not considered appropriate language. Fifty years ago, a child was punished for saying "hell" or "damn," and adults used profanity and vulgarity only in rare situations to express strong emotions.

---

generic language
words used that apply to one co-cultural group as though they represent everyone

nonparallel language
words that are changed because of the sex, race, or other group characteristics of the individual

---

APPLY IT

Some people think it is excessive to use generic language because everyone knows we mean both males and females when we say "policeman," "fireman," or "mailman." Do you agree? Do you think of both males and females when someone says "stewardess" or "waitress?" Why or why not?

MindTap®

---

marking
the addition of sex, race, age, or other group designation to a description

irrelevant association
emphasizing one person's relationship to another when doing so is not necessary to make the point

Today, "casual swearing"—profanity injected into regular conversation—is an epidemic in some language communities, including college campuses (Lehman & Dufrene, 2008). As a result, some of us have become desensitized to it. However, when giving a public speech, we need to remember that some people in our audience may still be offended by swearing. People who casually pepper their formal speeches with profanity and vulgar expressions are often perceived as abrasive and lacking in character, maturity, intelligence, manners, and emotional control (O'Connor, 2000).

Cultural Diversity

Language rules and expectations vary from culture to culture. When you address an audience comprised of people from cultural and co-cultural groups different from your own, make extra effort to ensure that you are being understood. When the first language spoken by audience members is different from yours, they may not be able to understand what you are saying because you may speak with an accent, mispronounce words, choose inappropriate words, and misuse idioms. Speaking in a second language can make you anxious and self-conscious. But most audience members are more tolerant of mistakes made by a second-language speaker than they are of those made by a native speaker.

Nevertheless, when speaking in a second language, you can help your audience by speaking more slowly and articulating as clearly as you can. By slowing your speaking rate, you give yourself additional time to pronounce difficult sounds and choose words whose meanings you know. This gives your audience members additional time to adjust their ears to more easily process what you are saying. You can also use visual aids to reinforce key terms and concepts as you move through the speech. Doing so assures listeners that they've understood you correctly.

One of the best ways to improve when you are giving a speech in a second language is to practice the speech in front of friends who are native speakers. Ask them to take note of words and phrases you mispronounce or misuse. Then they can work with you to correct the pronunciation or choose other words that better express your idea. Also, keep in mind that the more you practice speaking the language, the more comfortable you will become with it.

In the *Diverse Voices* feature, Ann Neville Miller provides insights into public speaking practices in Kenya and how Kenyans must adapt their speeches to appeal to their audiences' shared experiences and knowledge.

DIVERSE VOICES

Public Speaking Patterns in Kenya

by Ann Neville Miller

Much public speaking in the United States is informative or persuasive in purpose; ceremonial occasions for public speaking are less common. The average Kenyan, in contrast, will give far more ceremonial speeches in life than any other kind of speech. These may be speeches of greeting, introduction, tribute, and thanks, among others. Life

continued

events, both major and minor, are marked by ceremonies, and ceremonies occasion multiple public speeches.

For example, when a Kenyan attends a church service or other event away from home, he or she will often be asked to stand up and give an impromptu word of greeting to the assembly. Weddings and funerals overflow with ceremonial speeches; virtually any relative, friend, or business associate of the newly married or deceased may give advice or pay tribute. Older members of the bride's family, for example, may remind her how important it is to feed her husband well, or warn the groom that in their family men are expected never to abuse their wives, but to settle marital disputes with patience. Even the woman selected to cut the cake expects to give a brief word of exhortation before performing her duty. The free dispensing of advice, a hallmark of Kenyan wedding celebrations, would be out of place at most receptions in the United States, where the focus of speeches is normally more on remembrances and well-wishing.

In fact, when it comes to marriage, speech making begins long before the actual wedding day, at bridal negotiations where up to 40 or 50 people from the two families attempt to settle on a bride price. At these negotiations especially, but also in other ceremonial speeches, "deep" language replete with proverbs and metaphors is expected. The family of the man may explain that their son has seen a beautiful flower, or a lovely she-goat, or some other item in the compound of the family of the young lady and that they would like to obtain it for their son. In a negotiation of this type that I recently attended, the speaker for the bride's relatives explained that the family would require 20 goats as a major portion of the bride price. Because both parties were urban dwellers and would have no space to keep that many animals, the groom's family conferred with each other and determined that the bride's family really wanted cash. They settled on what they considered to be a reasonable price per goat, multiplied it by 20, and presented the total amount through a designated spokesperson to the representative of the bride. The original speaker from the bride's family looked at the money and observed dryly that goats in the groom's area were considerably thinner than those the bride's family were accustomed to! This type of indirect communication, the subtlety of which affords immense satisfaction and sometimes amusement to both speaker and listener, is a form of the high-context communication described by [Edward T.] Hall. A full appreciation of the speech requires extensive knowledge of shared experiences and traditions.

Excerpted from Ann Neville Miller, "Public Speaking Patterns in Kenya." In Larry A. Samovar, Richard E. Porter, & Edwin R. McDaniel, eds., Intercultural Communication: A Reader *(11th ed., pp. 238–245). Belmont, CA: Wadsworth, 2006.*

Speaking Clearly

speaking clearly
using words that convey one's meaning precisely

Speaking clearly means using words that convey your meaning precisely. Remember from our discussion in Chapter 4 that words are arbitrarily chosen symbols to represent our thoughts and feelings (Saeid, 2003). In communication studies, we often simply say the *word* is NOT the *thing*. In their influential book, *The Meaning of Meaning: A Study of the Influence of Language upon Thought and the Science of Symbolism,* I. A. Richards and C. K. Ogden (1923) clarify this idea using the semantic triangle. As depicted in Figure 14.1, a "referent" is the *thing* or object we refer to with a word, which is the "symbol" we use to refer to it. Our audience then attaches meaning to that symbol, which is what Richards and Ogden label the "thought of referent." For example, when you hear the word *dog*, what image forms in your mind? Do you visualize a poodle? A sheepdog? A mutt? There is so much variation in what the word *dog* conjures in our minds because the word *dog* is not the actual animal. The word is a symbol used to represent the animal. So if you use the word *dog* in a speech, each member of your audience may picture something different. Because the *word* is not the *thing,* as a public speaker you should use words that most closely match the thing or idea you want your audience to understand. By doing so, your meaning is more likely to be understood as you intended. Let's review four strategies for improving clarity: use specific language, choose familiar terms, provide details and examples, and limit vocalized pauses.

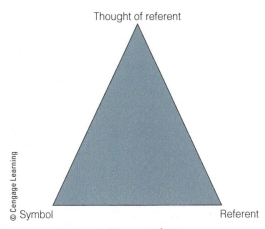

Thought of referent

© Cengage Learning

Symbol   Referent

Figure 14.1

The semantic triangle

specific language
words that narrow what is understood from a general category to a particular item or group within it

Use Specific Language

Specific language refers to using precise words that clarify meaning by narrowing what is understood from a general category to a particular item or group within that category. For instance, if in her speech Nevah refers to a "blue-collar worker," you might picture any number of occupations that fall within this broad category. If, instead, she says he's a "construction worker," the number of possible images you can picture is reduced. Now you select your image from the subcategory of construction worker, and your meaning is likely to be closer to the one she intended. If she is even more specific, she may say "bulldozer operator." Now you are even clearer on the specific occupation.

Choosing specific language is easier when you have a large working vocabulary. As a speaker, the larger your vocabulary, the more choices you have from which to select the word you want. As a listener, the larger your vocabulary, the more likely you are to understand the words used by others. Some speakers think that to be effective they must impress their audience with their extensive vocabularies. As a result, instead of looking for specific and *precise words,* they use words that appear pompous, affected, or stilted to the listener. Speaking precisely and specifically does not mean speaking obscurely. The following story illustrates the problem with pretentious words:

A plumber e-mailed a government agency, saying he found that hydrochloric acid quickly opened drainpipes, but he wasn't sure whether it was a good thing to use.

A scientist at the agency replied, "The efficacy of hydrochloric acid is indisputable, but the corrosive residue is incompatible with metallic permanence."

The plumber wrote back thanking him for the assurance that hydrochloric acid was all right.

Disturbed by this, the scientist showed the e-mail to his boss, another scientist, who then e-mailed the plumber: "We cannot assume responsibility for the production of toxic and noxious residue with hydrochloric acid and suggest you use an alternative procedure."

The plumber e-mailed back that he agreed. Hydrochloric acid worked fine.

Greatly disturbed by this misunderstanding, the scientists took their problem to the top boss. She wrote to the plumber: "Don't use hydrochloric acid. It eats the hell out of pipes."

As a general rule, use a more complex word *only* when you believe that it is the very best word for a specific context. Let's suppose you want to use a more precise or

specific word for *building*. Using the guideline of familiarity, you might select *house*, *apartment*, *high-rise*, or *skyscraper*, but you would avoid *edifice*. Each of the other choices is more precise or more specific, but *edifice* is neither more precise nor more specific, and in addition to being less commonly understood, it will be perceived as affected or stilted.

Choose Familiar Terms

Using familiar terms is just as important as using specific words. Avoid jargon, slang, abbreviations, and acronyms unless (1) you define them clearly the first time they are used and (2) using them is central to your speech goal.

Jargon is the unique technical terminology of a trade or profession that is not generally understood by outsiders. We might forget that people who are not in our same line of work or who do not have the same hobbies may not understand the jargon that seems such a part of our daily communication. In short, limit your use of jargon in formal speeches and always define jargon in simple terms the first time you use it. Josh suggested that Nathan not only say that a technetium-99m scan is the test used to diagnose a Meckel's Diverticulum, but also what that test is. He simply defined it as a nuclear medicine tracing agent injected to take an X-ray of the intestines.

Slang refers to nonstandard vocabulary and definitions assigned to words by a social group or co-culture. For example, today the word *wicked*, which has a standard definition denoting something wrong or immoral, can mean quite the opposite in some social groups and co-cultures (Rader, 2007). You should generally avoid slang in your public speeches not only because you risk being misunderstood but also because slang doesn't sound professional and it can hurt your credibility.

Overusing and misusing abbreviations and acronyms can also hinder clarity. Even if you think the abbreviation or acronym is a common one, always define it the first time you use it in the speech. For example, in a speech about NASCAR, refer to it initially by the organization's full name and then provide the acronym: "National Association for Stock Car Auto Racing, or NASCAR." Providing the full and abbreviated forms of the name will ensure clarity for all listeners.

Provide Details and Examples

Sometimes, the word we use may not have a precise synonym. In these situations, clarity can be achieved by adding details or examples. Saying "He lives in a really

jargon
the unique technical terminology of a trade or profession

slang
informal, nonstandard vocabulary and definitions assigned to words by a social group or co-culture

APPLY IT

Think of a time when a professor or other speaker used a lot of technical jargon, abbreviations, and/or acronyms that were unfamiliar to you. How did that impact your ability to pay attention, understand, and remember the points he or she was trying to make?

big house" can be clarified by adding, "He lives in a fourteen-room mansion on a six-acre estate."

Limit Vocalized Pauses

Vocalized pauses are unnecessary words interjected into sentences to fill moments of silence. Words commonly used for this purpose are "like," "you know," "really," and "basically," as well as "um" and "uh." We sometimes refer to vocalized pauses as "verbal garbage" because they do not serve a meaningful purpose and when used excessively actually distract audience members from the message. Although a few vocalized pauses typically don't hinder clarity, practicing your speech aloud will help you eliminate them.

vocalized pauses *unnecessary words interjected to fill moments of silence*

Speaking Vividly

Speaking vividly is one effective way to maintain your audience's interest and help them remember what you say. **Vivid language** is full of life—vigorous, bright, and intense. For example, a mediocre baseball announcer might say, "Jackson made a great catch," but a better commentator's vivid account might be, "Jackson leapt and made a spectacular one-handed catch just as he crashed into the center field wall." The words *leapt, spectacular, one-handed catch,* and *crashed* paint a vivid verbal picture of the action. You can make your ideas come to life by using sensory language and by using rhetorical figures and structures of speech.

vivid language *words that are full of life*

Use Sensory Language

Sensory language appeals to the senses of seeing, hearing, tasting, smelling, and feeling. Vivid sensory language begins with vivid thought. You are much more likely to express yourself vividly if you can physically or psychologically sense the meanings you are trying to convey (Photo 14.3). If you feel the "bite of the wind" or "the sting of freezing rain," and if you hear and smell "the thick, juicy T-bone steaks sizzling on the grill," you will be able to describe these sensations. Does the cake "taste good"? Or do your taste buds "quiver with the sweet double-chocolate icing and velvety feel of the rich, moist cake"?

sensory language *words that appeal to seeing, hearing, tasting, smelling, and feeling*

To develop vivid sensory language, begin by considering how you can re-create what something, someone, or some place *looks like.* Consider, too, how you can help listeners imagine how something *sounds.* How can you use language to convey the way something *feels* (textures, shapes, temperatures)? How can language recreate a sense of how something *tastes* or *smells*? To achieve this in your speech, use colorful descriptors. They make your ideas more concrete and can arouse emotions. They invite listeners to imagine details. Here's an example about downhill skiing:

Sight: *As you climb the hill, the bright winter sunshine glistening on the snow is blinding.*

Touch and feel: *Just before you take off, you gently slip your goggles over your eyes. They are bitterly cold and sting your nose for a moment.*

Taste: *You start the descent and, as you gradually pick up speed, the taste of air and ice and snow in your mouth invigorates you.*

Photo 14.3 You can help listeners remember by appealing to the senses. How might you use sensory language to describe this image?

rhetorical figures of speech
make striking comparisons between things that are not obviously alike

rhetorical structures of speech
combine ideas in a particular way

simile
a direct comparison of dissimilar things using the word like or as

metaphor
an implied comparison between two unlike things, expressed without using like or as

analogy
an extended metaphor

Sound: *An odd* silence *fills the air. You hear nothing but the swish of your skis against the snow beneath your feet. At last, you arrive at the bottom of the slope. Reality hits as you hear the hustle and bustle of other skiers and instructors directing them to their next session.*

Smell and feel: *You enter the warming house. As your fingers thaw in the warm air, the aroma from the wood stove in the corner comforts you as you ready yourself to drift off into sleep.*

By using colorful descriptors that appeal to the senses, you arouse and maintain listener interest and make your ideas more memorable.

Use Rhetorical Figures and Structures of Speech

Rhetorical figures of speech make striking comparisons between things that are not obviously alike. Doing so helps listeners visualize or internalize what you are saying. **Rhetorical structures of speech** combine ideas in a particular way. Any of these devices can serve to make your speech more memorable as long as they aren't overused. Let's look at some examples.

A **simile** is a direct comparison of dissimilar things using the word *like* or *as.* Clichés such as "He walks like a duck" and "She's as busy as a bee" are similes. If you've seen the movie *Forrest Gump,* you might recall Forrest's use of the simile: "Life is like a box of chocolates. You never know what you're going to get." An elementary school teacher used a simile by saying that being back at school after a long absence "was like trying to hold 35 corks under water at the same time"(Hensley, 1995). Similes can be effective because they make ideas more vivid in listeners' minds. But they should be used sparingly or they lose their appeal. Clichés should be avoided because their predictability reduces their effectiveness.

A **metaphor** is an implied comparison between two unlike things, expressed without using *like* or *as.* Instead of saying that one thing is *like* another, a metaphor says that one thing *is* another. Thus, a problem car is a "lemon," and the leaky roof is a "sieve." Metaphors can be effective because they make an abstract concept more concrete, strengthen an important point, or heighten emotions. Dan used a metaphor to help explain the complex concept of bioluminescence. He described it as "a miniature flashlight that fireflies turn on and off at will."

An **analogy** is an extended metaphor. Sometimes, you can develop a story from a metaphor that makes a concept more vivid. If you were to describe a family member as the "black sheep in the barnyard," that's a metaphor. If you went on to talk about the other members of the family as different animals on the farm and the roles ascribed to them, you would be extending the metaphor into an analogy. Analogies can be effective for holding your speech together in a creative and vivid way. Analogies are particularly useful to highlight the similarities between a complex or unfamiliar concept and a familiar one.

Alliteration is the repetition of consonant sounds at the beginning of words that are near one another. Tongue twisters such as "Sally sells seashells by the seashore" use alliteration. In her speech about the history of jelly beans, Sharla used alliteration when she said, "And today there are more than fifty fabulous fruity flavors from which to choose." Used sparingly, alliteration can catch listeners' attention and make the speech memorable. But overuse can hurt the message because listeners might focus on the technique rather than the speech content.

alliteration
repetition of consonant sounds at the beginning of words that are near one another

Assonance is the repetition of vowel sounds in a phrase or phrases. "How now brown cow" is a common example. Sometimes, the words rhyme, but they don't have to. As with alliteration, assonance can make your speech more memorable as long as it's not overused.

assonance
repetition of vowel sounds in a phrase or phrases

Onomatopoeia is the use of words that sound like the things they stand for, such as "buzz," "hiss," "crack," and "plop." In the speech about skiing, the "swish" of the skis is an example of onomatopoeia.

onomatopoeia
use of words that sound like the things they stand for

Personification attributes human qualities to a concept or an inanimate object. When Madison talked about her truck, "Big Red," as her trusted friend and companion, she used personification. Likewise, when Rick talked about flowers dancing on the front lawn, he used personification.

personification
attributing human qualities to a concept or an inanimate object

Repetition is restating words, phrases, or sentences for emphasis. Martin Luther King Jr.'s "I Have a Dream" speech is a classic example:

repetition
restating words, phrases, or sentences for emphasis

I say to you today, my friends, so even though we face the difficulties of today and tomorrow, I still have a dream. It is a dream deeply rooted in the American dream.

I have a dream that one day this nation will rise up and live out the true meaning of its creed: "We hold these truths to be self-evident: that all men are created equal."

I have a dream that one day on the red hills of Georgia the sons of former slaves and the sons of former slave owners will be able to sit down together at the table of brotherhood.

I have a dream that one day even the state of Mississippi, a state sweltering with the heat of injustice, sweltering with the heat of oppression, will be transformed into the oasis of freedom and justice.

I have a dream that my four little children will one day live in a nation where they will not be judged by the color of their skin but by the content of their character. I have a dream today.

Antithesis is combining contrasting ideas in the same sentence, as when John F. Kennedy said, "My fellow Americans, ask not what your country can do for you. Ask what you can do for your country." Likewise, astronaut Neil Armstrong used antithesis when he first stepped on the moon: "That's one small step for man, one giant leap for mankind." Speeches that offer antithesis in the concluding remarks are often very memorable.

antithesis
combining contrasting ideas in the same sentence

ACTION STEP 5.A

Adapting Oral Language and Style

The goal of this activity is to plan how you will adapt your language and style to the specific audience and occasion.

Write your thesis statement:

_____

Review the audience analysis that you completed in Action Steps 1 through 4. Now, verbally adapt to your audience by answering the following questions:

1. How can I adapt my language to foster verbal immediacy with this audience?

2. How can I adapt my language choices to demonstrate respect for this audience?

3. Where can I adapt my language to be most intelligible for this audience?

4. How can I use sensory language and rhetorical figures of speech to make my ideas more vivid for this audience?

MindTap *Adapt your language with the PREPARE Your Informative Speech Activity in Chapter 16 of the MindTap. Select the Outline tab for Action Step 5.A.*

WHAT WOULD YOU DO?

A Question of Ethics

"Kendra, I heard you telling Jim about the speech you're giving tomorrow. You think it's a winner, huh?"

"You got that right, Omar. I'm going to have Bardston eating out of the palm of my hand."

"You sound confident."

"This time I have reason to be. See, Professor Bardston's been talking about the importance of audience adaptation. These last two weeks that's all we've heard—adaptation, adaptation."

"What does she mean?"

"Talking about something in a way that really relates to people personally."

"OK—so how are you going to do that?"

"Well, you see, I'm giving this speech on abortion. Now here's the kick. Bardston let it slip that she's Pro- Life. So I'm going to give this informative speech on the Right to Life movement.

But I'm going to discuss the major beliefs of the movement in a way that'll get her to think that I'm a supporter. I'm going to mention aspects of the movement that I know she'll like."

"But I've heard you talk about how you're pro-choice."

"I am—all the way. But by keeping the information positive, she'll think I'm a supporter. It isn't as if I'm going to be telling any lies or anything."

In a speech, is it ethical to adapt in a way that resonates with your audience but isn't in keeping with what you really believe? Why or why not?

MindTap

Reflection and Assessment

Audience adaptation is the process of customizing your speech to your specific audience. It begins with topic selection and development and continues throughout the speech-making process. In this chapter, we focused on how to adapt your language and oral style to address the needs and expectations of the audience and occasion. To assess how well you've learned what we addressed in these pages, answer the following questions. If you have trouble answering any of them, go back and review that material. Once you can answer each question accurately, you are ready to move ahead to read the next chapter.

1. What are several ways oral style differs from written style?

2. What is considered appropriate and inappropriate language for formal speeches and why?

3. What are some strategies you can use to ensure your language choices are clear?

4. What are some examples of sensory language and rhetorical figures of speech?

MindTap

RESOURCE AND ASSESSMENT CENTER

Now that you have read Chapter 14, go to your MindTap for *Communicate!* for quick access to the electronic resources that accompany this text.

Applying What You've Learned

Impromptu Speech Activity

Draw a card from a stack provided by your instructor. The card will have a rhetorical figure of speech printed on it. Create a short 2- to 3-minute speech about a local event that uses that particular figure of speech at least twice.

Assessment Activity

Search online for the article "A Question of Real American Black Men," by Bailey B. Baker Jr., *Vital Speeches*, April 15, 2002. Analyze how this speaker uses personal pronouns, rhetorical questions, common experiences, and personalized information to create common ground. Write a short essay describing the conclusions of your analysis.

Skill-Building Activities

1. Practice Using Sensory Language Create a description of each of the following events appealing to each of the five senses: sight, touch/feel, taste, sound, smell.

(a) lawn mowing

(b) tacos

(c) traffic congestion

(d) babysitting

2. Rhetorical Figures of Speech Describe a circus using each of the following figures of speech: simile, metaphor, analogy, alliteration, assonance, onomato-poeia, personification, repetition, and antithesis.

Delivery

When you finish this chapter, you'll be able to

- Employ strategies to effectively manage public speaking apprehension.

- Practice using your voice and body to convey a conversational and animated delivery style.

- Select one of three appropriate delivery methods for your speeches.

- Engage in effective speech rehearsals.

- Adapt appropriately to audience feedback, misspeaks, unexpected events, and questions as you deliver your speech.

- Evaluate speech effectiveness based on content, structure, and delivery.

MindTap®

Start with quick warm-up activity.

When Alyssa and Katie finished watching a recording of Alyssa's first speech practice, Alyssa said:

"Ugh! That was horrible! I bored myself. And I even *look* bored while I'm talking. I just don't get it. I have all this great information and am passionate about the topic. Why is it so hard to stay focused? "

Katie responded, "Don't be so hard on yourself, Alyssa. Your speech is good. The topic is interesting and relevant, you cite great evidence, it's well organized, and you use compelling language. You just need to work a bit more on your delivery to make it sound conversational and dynamic. Let's add some delivery cues to your speaking notes to help you remember to emphasize key points with your voice, facial expressions and gestures, as well as cues to clarify structure with gestures and movement. Then you can practice a few more times until you look and sound spontaneous and convincing."

"Ok," Alyssa replied. "After watching that rehearsal, I'll try anything. . . ."

308

15

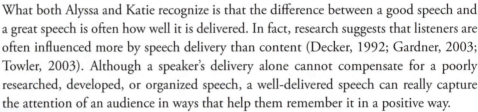

What both Alyssa and Katie recognize is that the difference between a good speech and a great speech is often how well it is delivered. In fact, research suggests that listeners are often influenced more by speech delivery than content (Decker, 1992; Gardner, 2003; Towler, 2003). Although a speaker's delivery alone cannot compensate for a poorly researched, developed, or organized speech, a well-delivered speech can really capture the attention of an audience in ways that help them remember it in a positive way.

In the last chapter, we focused on one aspect of the fifth action step: oral language style. In this chapter, we turn our attention to the other aspect: delivery style. We begin by discussing public speaking anxiety or apprehension and several ways to manage it effectively. Then we explain how to use your voice and body effectively, as well as three common methods for delivering a speech. We then introduce a process designed to make your practice sessions productive and some guidelines to consider while giving the actual speech. Finally, we offer several criteria you can use to evaluate your speeches and apply that criteria to a sample student speech.

Public Speaking Apprehension

Most of us feel some fear about public speaking. In fact, according to the National Institute of Mental Health, as many as 75 percent of us suffer from some public speaking anxiety (Fear of Public Speaking Statistics, 2013). Did you know, for example, that award-winning actors Meryl Streep, Kim Basinger, and Harrison Ford, singer Barbra Streisand, singer/actor Donny Osmond, former professional football player Ricky Williams, and evangelists Billy Graham and Joel Osteen all experience a fear of public speaking? In spite of their fear, they are all effective public speakers.

public speaking apprehension
the level of fear a person experiences when anticipating or actually speaking to an audience

Public speaking apprehension is the level of fear a person experiences when anticipating or actually speaking to an audience (Photo 15.1). Fortunately, we can benefit from the results of a good deal of research about managing public speaking apprehension effectively. We say *manage* because having some fear actually makes us better speakers. Just as an adrenaline boost helps athletes, musicians, and actors perform better, it can also help us deliver better public speeches (Kelly, Duran, & Stewart, 1990; Motley, 1997; Phillips, 1977).

Photo 15.1 Many famous speakers feel some apprehension about public speaking. Did you know Academy Award–winning actresses like Meryl Streep experience public speaking anxiety?

Kevin Winter/Getty Images Entertainment/Getty Images

Symptoms and Causes

The symptoms of public speaking apprehension vary from individual to individual and range from mild to debilitating. Symptoms can be cognitive, physical, or emotional. Cognitive symptoms stem from negative self-talk (e.g., "I'm going to blow it" or "I just know I'll make a fool of myself"), which is also the most common cause of speech apprehension (Richmond & McCroskey, 2000). Physical symptoms may be stomach upset (or butter-flies), flushed skin, sweating, shaking, light-headedness, rapid or pounding heartbeats, stuttering, and vocalized pauses ("like," "you know," "ah," "um," and so on). Emotional symptoms include feeling anxious, worried, or upset.

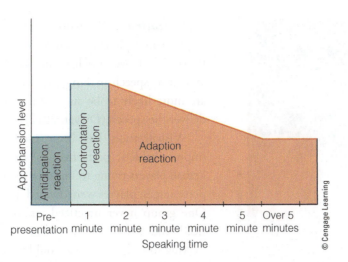

© Cengage Learning

Figure 15.1

Phases of public speaking apprehension

In addition to negative self-talk, previous experience, modeling, and negative reinforcement can also cause public speaking apprehension. Previous experience has to do with being socialized to fear public speaking as a result of modeling and negative reinforcement (Richmond & McCroskey, 2000). Modeling has to do with observing how your friends and family members react to speaking in public. If they tend to be quiet and reserved and avoid public speaking, your fears may stem from modeling. Negative reinforcement concerns how others have responded to your public speaking endeavors. If you experienced negative reactions, you might be more apprehensive about speaking in public than if you had been praised for your efforts (Motley, 1997).

Luckily, apprehension gradually decreases for most of us as we speak. Researchers have identified three phases we proceed through: anticipation, confrontation, and adaptation (Behnke & Carlile, 1971). Figure 15.1 illustrates these phases. The **anticipation phase** is the anxiety we experience before giving the speech, both while preparing it and waiting to speak. The **confrontation phase** is the surge of anxiety we feel as we begin delivering the speech. The **adaptation phase** is the period during which our anxiety level gradually decreases. It typically begins about one minute into the presentation and tends to level off after about five minutes (Beatty & Behnke, 1991). So it's normal to feel nervous before you speak and, when managed effectively, can result in a better speech than having no nervousness at all.

Management Techniques

We propose five techniques to help manage apprehension effectively: communication orientation, visualization, systematic desensitization, cognitive restructuring, and public speaking skills training.

1. ***Communication Orientation Motivation (COM)*** helps reduce anxiety by adopting a *communication* rather than *performance* orientation toward speeches (Motley, 1997). When we have a **performance orientation**, we believe we must *impress* a hypercritical audience with our knowledge and delivery. On the other hand, when we have a **communication orientation**, we focus on talking with our audience about an important topic and *getting a message across to them*—not about how they might be judging our performance.

anticipation phase
anxiety we experience before giving the speech

confrontation phase
the surge of anxiety we experience when beginning to deliver the speech

adaptation phase
the period during which our anxiety gradually decreases

Communication Orientation Motivation (COM)
adopting a communication rather than performance orientation toward speeches

performance orientation
believing we must impress a hypercritical audience with our knowledge and delivery

communication orientation
focusing on talking with others about an important topic and getting the message across to them

Michelle Donahue Hillison/Shutterstock.com

Photo 15.2 Do you use positive self-talk to pump yourself up before you have an important event? Do the same before you speak. If you believe you can perform well, you will.

visualization
developing a mental picture of yourself giving a masterful speech

systematic desensitization
gradually visualizing and then engaging in more frightening speaking events

cognitive restructuring
replacing anxiety-arousing negative self-talk with anxiety-reducing positive self-talk

2. *Visualization* helps reduce anxiety by developing a mental picture of ourselves giving a masterful speech. If we visualize ourselves going through an entire speech-making process successfully, we are more likely to be successful when we actually deliver the speech (Dwyer, 2012).

Visualization has been used extensively to improve athletic performances. In a study of basketball players trying to improve their foul-shooting percentages, players were divided into three groups. One group never practiced, another group practiced, and a third group visualized practicing and making foul shots. As we would expect, those who physically practiced improved far more than those who didn't. What is amazing, however, is that those who simply visualized practicing improved almost as much as those who practiced (Scott, 1997). Imagine what happens when you both visualize yourself giving a great speech *and* practice!

3. *Systematic Desensitization* can help reduce anxiety by gradually visualizing and engaging in increasingly more frightening speaking events while remaining in a relaxed state. The process starts with consciously tensing and then relaxing muscle groups in order to learn how to recognize the difference between the two states. Then, while in a relaxed state, you first imagine yourself and then engage in successively more stressful situations—for example, researching a speech topic in the library, practicing the speech out loud to a roommate, and finally, giving a speech to an audience. The ultimate goal of systematic desensitization is to transfer the calm feelings we attain while visualizing to the actual speaking event. Calmness on command—and it works.

4. *Cognitive Restructuring* helps reduce anxiety by replacing anxiety-arousing negative self-talk with anxiety-reducing positive self-talk through a four-step process.

- **Identify your fears.** Write down all the fears that come to mind when you know you must give a speech.

- **Determine whether or not these fears are rational.** Most are irrational because public speaking is not life threatening.

- **Develop positive coping statements to replace each negative self-talk statement.** There is no list of coping statements that will work for everyone. Psychologist Richard Heimberg of the State University of New York at Albany reminds his clients that most listeners don't notice or even care if the clients do what they're afraid of doing when giving a speech. Ultimately, he asks them, "Can you cope with the one or two people who [notice or criticize or] get upset?"

- **Incorporate positive coping statements into your life so they become second nature (Photo 15.2).** You can do this by writing your statements down and reading them aloud to yourself each day, as well as before you give a speech.

Figure 15.2

Negative self-talk versus positive coping statements

© Cengage Learning

Here are the positive statements Alyssa developed to counter her negative self-talk:

Negative self-talk
1. I'm afraid I'll stumble over my words and look foolish.
2. I'm afraid everyone will be able to tell that I am nervous.
3. I'm afraid my voice will crack.
4. I'm afraid I'll sound boring.

Positive coping statements
1. Even if I stumble, I will have succeeded as long as I get my message across.
2. They probably won't be able to tell I'm nervous, but as long as I focus on getting my message across, that's what matters.
3. Even if my voice cracks, as long as I keep going and focus on getting my message across, I'll succeed at what matters most.
4. I won't sound bored if I focus on how important this message is to me and to my audience. I don't have to do somersaults to keep their attention, because my topic is relevant to them.

The more you repeat your coping statements, the more natural they will become (see Figure 15.2).

5. **_Public Speaking Skills Training_** is systematically practicing the skills involved in preparing and delivering an effective public speech. Skills training is based on the assumption that some public speaking anxiety is caused by not knowing how to be successful. So if we learn the skills associated with effective speech making (e.g., audience analysis, topic selection and development, organization, oral language, and delivery style), then we will be less anxious (Kelly, Phillips, & Keaten, 1995).

public speaking skills training
the systematic teaching of the skills associated with preparing and delivering an effective public speech

Characteristics of Effective Delivery Style

Think about one of the best speakers you have ever heard. What made this person stand out in your mind? In all likelihood, how the speaker delivered the speech had a lot to do with it. **Delivery** is how a message is communicated through the use of voice and body. We achieve effective delivery by adapting the types of nonverbal communication introduced in Chapter 5 to a public speaking situation. Effective public speech delivery style is both conversational and animated.

You have probably heard ineffective speakers whose delivery was overly dramatic and affected or stiff and mechanical. In contrast, an effective delivery uses a **conversational style**. The audience perceives you as _talking with_ them and not performing _in front of_ or _reading to_ them. The hallmark of a conversational style is spontaneity. **Spontaneity** is the ability to sound natural—as though you are really thinking about the ideas _and_ about getting them across to your audience—no matter how many times you've practiced.

Have you ever been bored by a professor reading a well-structured lecture while looking at the lecture notes rather than the students? Even a well-written speech given by an

delivery
how a message is communicated orally and visually through the use of voice and body

conversational style
presenting a speech so that your audience feels you are talking with them

spontaneity
the ability to sound natural when giving a speech

expert can bore an audience unless its delivery is **animated**, that is, lively and dynamic (Photo 15.3).

How can we sound conversational and animated at the same time? The secret is to focus on conveying the passion we feel about the topic through our voice and body. When we are passionate about sharing something with someone, almost all of us become more animated in our delivery. The goal is to duplicate this level of liveliness when delivering our speeches. The next two sections focus more closely on how to use your voice and body to achieve effective conversational and animated delivery.

Use of Voice

Recall from Chapter 5 that your *voice* is the sound you produce using your vocal organs. How your voice sounds depends on its pitch, volume, rate, and quality. As a public speaker, you can achieve a conversational and animated delivery style by varying your pitch, volume, rate, and quality in ways that make you more intelligible and expressive.

Photo 15.3 How does a lack of vocal expression impact what you recall of a speaker's message content?

animated
lively and dynamic

intelligible
understandable

Intelligibility To be **intelligible** means to be understandable. All of us have experienced situations when we couldn't understand what was being said because the speaker was talking too softly or too quickly. If you practice your speech using appropriate pitch, volume, rate, and vocal quality, you can improve the likelihood that you will be intelligible to your audience.

Most of us speak at a pitch that is appropriate for us and intelligible to listeners. However, some people naturally have voices that are higher or lower in register or become accustomed to talking in tones that are either above or below their natural pitch. Speaking at an appropriate pitch is particularly important if your audience includes people who have hearing loss because they may find it difficult to hear a pitch that is too high or too low.

Appropriate volume is key to intelligibility. You must speak loudly enough, with or without a microphone, to be heard easily by the audience members in the back of the room but not so loudly as to cause discomfort to listeners seated in the front. You can also vary your volume to emphasize important information. For example, you may speak louder when you introduce each main point or when imploring listeners to take action. When recording a speech to post online, you want to be heard easily, but not sound as though you are shouting.

The rate at which you speak can also influence intelligibility. Speaking too slowly gives your listeners time to let their minds wander after they've processed an idea. Speaking too quickly, especially when sharing complex ideas and arguments, may not give listeners enough time to process the information completely. Because nervousness may cause you to speak more quickly than normal, monitor your rate and adjust if you are speaking more quickly than normal.

Tomas Rodriguez/AGE Fotostock

Word	Incorrect	Correct
arctic	ar'-tic	arc'-tic
athlete	ath'-a-lete	ath'-lete
family	fam'-ly	fam'-a-ly
February	Feb'-yu-ary	Feb'-ru-ary
get	git	get
hundred	hun'-derd	hun'-dred
larynx	lar'-nix	ler'-inks
library	ly'-ber-y	ly'-brer-y
nuclear	nu'-kyu-ler	nu'-klee-er
particular	par-tik'-ler	par-tik'-yu-ler
picture	pitch'-er	pic'-ture
recognize	rek'-a-nize	rek'-ig-nize
relevant	rev'-e-lant	rel'-e-vant
theater	thee-ay'-ter	thee'-a-ter
truth	truf	truth
with	wit or wid	with

Table 15.1

Commonly Mispronounced Words

© 2017 Cengage Learning

Articulation, pronunciation, and accent can also affect intelligibility. **Articulation** is using the tongue, palate, teeth, jaws, and lips to shape vocalized sounds that combine to produce a word. Many of us suffer from minor articulation and **pronunciation** problems such as adding an extra sound ("athalete" for *athlete*), leaving out a sound ("libary" for *library*), transposing sounds ("revalent" for *relevant*), and distorting sounds ("troof " for *truth*). Table 15.1 lists a number of the most commonly mispronounced words.

Accent is the inflection, tone, and speech habits typical of native speakers of a language. When you misarticulate or speak with a heavy accent during a conversation, your listeners can ask you to repeat yourself until they understand you. But in a speech setting, audience members are unlikely to interrupt to ask you to repeat something.

Accent can be a major concern for second language speakers or even speakers from various regions across the United States. Everyone speaks with some kind of accent, since "accent" means any tone or inflection that differs from the way others speak. Natives of a particular city or region in the United States will speak with inflections they believe are "normal" spoken English—for instance, people from the Northeast who drop the *r* sound (saying "cah" for *car*) or people from the South who elongate their vowels and "drawl," or people from the upper Midwest who elongate certain vowels (e.g., "Min-ne-SOOO-ta"). But when they visit a different city or region, they are perceived as having an accent. If your accent is "thick" or very different from that of most of your audience, practice pronouncing key words so that you are easily understood, speak slowly to allow your audience members more time to process your message, and consider using visual aids to reinforce key terms, concepts, and important points. Alyssa from the opening scenario grew up in Arkansas before moving to Lexington to attend the University of Kentucky.

APPLY IT

Think of someone you know or even a celebrity that has a very distinguishable vocal quality. Do you think they are difficult to understand? Why or why not?

MindTap®

articulation
using the tongue, palate, teeth, jaw movement, and lips to shape vocalized sounds that combine to produce a word

pronunciation
the form and accent of various syllables of a word

accent
the articulation, inflection, tone, and speech habits typical of the native speakers of a language

Although her accent was similar to many of her classmates, she decided to ask Katie to listen to her speech and point out any words she might want to articulate differently or reinforce with visual aids.

vocal expression
variations in pitch, volume, rate, and quality that affect the meaning an audience gets from the sentences you speak

Vocal Expression **Vocal expression** is achieved by changing your pitch, volume, and rate, stressing certain words, and using pauses strategically. Doing so clarifies the emotional intent of your message and helps animate your delivery. Generally, speeding up your rate, raising your pitch, or increasing your volume reinforces emotions such as joy, enthusiasm, excitement, anticipation, and a sense of urgency or fear. Slowing down your rate, lowering your pitch, or decreasing your volume can communicate resolution, peacefulness, remorse, disgust, or sadness.

monotone
a voice in which the pitch, volume, and rate remain constant, with no word, idea, or sentence differing significantly from any other

A total lack of vocal expression produces a **monotone**—a voice in which the pitch, volume, and rate remain constant, with no word, idea, or sentence differing significantly in sound from any other. Although few people speak in a true monotone, many severely limit themselves by using only two or three pitch levels and relatively unchanging volume and rate when giving public speeches. An actual or near monotone not only lulls an audience to sleep but, more important, diminishes the chances of audience understanding. For instance, if the sentence "Congress should pass laws limiting the sale of pornography" is presented in a monotone, listeners will be uncertain whether the speaker is concerned with *who* should be taking action, what Congress should *do*, or *what* the laws should be.

pauses
moments of silence strategically used to enhance meaning

Pauses, moments of silence strategically used to enhance meaning, can also mark important ideas. If you use one or more sentences in your speech to express an important idea, pause before each sentence to signal that something important is coming or pause afterward to allow the idea to sink in. Pausing one or more times within a sentence can also add impact. Nick included several short pauses within and a long pause after his sentence "Our government has no compassion (*pause*), no empathy (*pause*), and no regard for human feeling" (*longer pause*).

Use of Body

Because your audience can see as well as hear you, how you use your body also contributes to how conversational and animated your audience perceives you to be. Body language elements that affect delivery are appearance, posture, poise, eye contact, facial expressions, gestures, and movement (Photo 15.4).

Appearance Some speakers think that what they wear doesn't or shouldn't affect the success of their speech. But unless your audience cannot see you because you are doing a voiced-over slideshow, studies show that a neatly groomed and professional appearance sends important messages about a public speaker's commitment to the topic and occasion, as well as about the speaker's credibility (ethos) (Hammer, 2000; Howlegg, Pine, Chaill, Orakcioglu, & Fletcher, 2015; Morgan, 2013; Sellnow & Treinen, 2004). Three guidelines can help you decide how to dress for your speech.

1. **Consider the audience and occasion.** Dress a bit more formally than you expect members of your audience to dress. If you dress too formally, your audience is likely to perceive you to be untrustworthy and insincere. If you dress too casually, your audience may view you as uncommitted to your topic or disrespectful of them or the occasion.

2. **Consider your topic and purpose.** In general, the more serious your topic, the more formally you should dress. For example, if your topic is AIDS and you are trying to convince your audience to be tested for HIV, you will want to look like someone who is an authority by dressing the part. But if your topic is yoga and you are trying to convince your audience to take a yoga class at the new campus recreation center, you might dress more casually.

3. **Avoid extremes.** Your attire shouldn't detract from your speech. Avoid gaudy jewelry, over- or undersized clothing, and sexually suggestive attire. Remember you want your audience to focus on your message, so your appearance should be neutral.

Jupiterimages CAL

Photo 15.4 Effective speakers handle questions respectfully even when they don't know the answer. What emotional intent do you think this speaker is conveying and why?

Posture Recall from Chapter 5 that *posture* is how you hold your body. When giving a public speech, an upright stance and squared shoulders communicate a sense of confidence. Speakers who slouch may be perceived as lacking self-confidence and not caring about the topic, audience, and occasion.

Poise **Poise** is a graceful and controlled use of the body. Poise gives the impression that you are self-assured, calm, and dignified. Mannerisms that convey nervousness (swaying from side to side, drumming fingers on the lectern, taking off or putting on glasses, jiggling pocket change, smacking the tongue, scratching the nose, hand, or arm) should be noted during practice sessions and avoided during the speech.

poise
graceful and controlled use of the body

Eye Contact When giving a formal presentation, effective *eye contact* involves looking at people in all parts of the room (including the camera if being recorded) throughout the speech. As long as you are looking at someone (i.e., those in front of you, in the left rear of the room, in the right center of the room) and not at your notes or the ceiling, floor, or window, everyone in the audience will perceive you as having good eye contact with them. Generally, you should look at your audience at least 90 percent of the time, glancing at notes (even if they are on your PowerPoint or Prezi slides) only when you need a quick reference point. Maintaining eye contact is important for several reasons.

1. **Maintaining eye contact helps audiences concentrate on the speech.** If you do not look at audience members while you talk, they are unlikely to maintain eye contact with you. This break in mutual eye contact reduces a sense of conversational delivery and often decreases concentration on the message.

2. **Maintaining eye contact bolsters ethos.** Just as you are likely to be skeptical of people who do not look you in the eye as they converse, audiences also will be skeptical of speakers who do not look at them. In the dominant American culture, eye contact is perceived as a sign of sincerity. Speakers who fail to maintain eye contact with audiences are perceived almost always as ill at ease and often as insincere or dishonest (Levine, Asada, & Park, 2006).

3. **Maintaining eye contact helps you gauge the audience's reaction to your ideas.** Because communication is two-way, audience members communicate with you while you are speaking to them. In conversation, the partner's response is likely to be both verbal and nonverbal. In public speaking, the audience's response is likely to only be through nonverbal cues. Bored audience members might yawn, look out the window, slouch in their chairs, and even sleep. Confused audience members might look puzzled by furrowing their brows or shaking their head. Audience members who understand or agree with something might smile and nod their heads. By monitoring your audience's behavior, you can adjust by becoming more animated, offering additional examples, or moving more quickly through a point.

When speaking to large audiences of 100 or more people, you must create a *sense* of looking listeners in the eye even though you actually cannot. This process is called **audience contact**. You can create audience contact by mentally dividing your audience into small groups. Then, tracing the letter Z with your gaze, talk for four to six seconds with each group as you move through your speech.

When speaking virtually via Web conferencing software using a computer screen and camera, be sure to look into the camera as you speak rather than at your image or their image(s) on the screen. When you look into the camera, your audience will perceive you as having eye contact with them.

Facial Expressions Recall from Chapter 5 that *facial expression* is the arrangement of facial muscles to express emotions. For public speakers, effective facial expressions can convey **nonverbal immediacy** by communicating that you are personable and likable. They can also help animate your speech. Speakers who do not vary their facial expressions during the speech and instead wear a deadpan expression, perpetual grin, or permanent scowl tend to be perceived as boring, insincere, or stern. To assess whether you are using effective facial expressions during your speech, practice delivering it to yourself in front of a mirror or record your rehearsal and evaluate your facial expressions as you watch it.

Gestures As we discussed in Chapter 5, *gestures* are the movements of your hands, arms, and fingers. Effective gestures emphasize important points or ideas, refer to presentational aids, or clarify structure. For example, as Aaron began to speak about the advantages of smart phone apps, he said, "on one hand" and lifted his right hand face up. When he got to the disadvantages, he lifted his left hand face up as he said, "on the other hand." Recall from Chapter 5, however, that certain gestures mean different things in different cultures. Gestures may also create confusion between cultures as Bill French illustrates this in the *Diverse Voices* feature in this chapter. Figure 15.3 illustrates some examples of gestures you might use to enhance intelligibility and expressiveness in your speeches.

Some people who are nervous when giving a speech clasp their hands behind their backs, bury them in their pockets, or grip the lectern. Feeling unable to pry their hands free gracefully, they wiggle their elbows or appear stiff, which can distract listeners from the message.

As with facial expressions, effective gestures must appear spontaneous and natural even though they are actually carefully planned and practiced. When you practice and then deliver your speech, leave your hands free so they will be available to gesture as you normally do.

---

audience contact
when speaking to large audiences, create a sense of looking listeners in the eye even though you actually cannot

nonverbal immediacy
communicating through body language that you are personable and likeable

APPLY IT

What distracting behaviors do you engage in when you are nervous? How can you work to eliminate them when you are giving a public speech?

MindTap

- The supine hand with palm upward to express good humor, frankness, and generalization.

- The prone hand with palm downward to show superposition or the resting of one thing upon another.

- The vertical hand with palm outward to indicate warding off, putting from, or a disagreeable thought.

- The clenched hand to reinforce anger or defiance or to emphasize an important point.

- The index finger to specialize or reinforce the first in a sequence of events.

Figure 15.3

Common hand gestures used by speakers

© Cengage Learning

DIVERSE VOICES

"Language Barriers" Are Not Necessarily Verbal

By Bill French
Co-Founder, MyST Technology

I was asked to present a 90-minute database programmer productivity session in many cities in Asia; starting in Singapore and ending in Taipei. All along the route, the conference promoters indicated there were no language translation issues or requirements; English and the programming languages of the products I was speaking about, dBase and Clipper would be enough.

When we arrived in Taipei, as was customary, I presented first. Also as customary, I started my session with a few questions to get to know the general knowledge and programmer demographics of the audience. It went something like this:

"How many of you use Ashton-Tate's dBASE?" (On asking the question, I raised my own hand.) The Taipei audience was almost unanimous in raising their own hands. I continued.

"How many here use Nantucket's Clipper compiler for dBASE development?" (Again, I raised my

hand first.) And once again, nearly 100 percent of the attendees raised their hands.

"How many of you use dBRIEF, the most productive editing system for dBASE programming?" Amazingly, nearly everyone in the audience raised [a] hand! Either I was staring at 700 copyright infringers who unabashedly proclaim their theft in public, or I was simply engaged in a monkey-see, monkey-do early morning exercise program for my right arm and 700 or so other arms. In a blink, I knew exactly what to ask next:

"How many of you want to be a fire engine?" Fearfully, I watched as everyone's hands went up. I might as well have been speaking to an alien society from Alpha Centauri—nearly 100 percent of the audience spoke Chinese, and only Chinese. It was very easy to see who in the auditorium spoke English, since they were the ones practically rolling on the floor laughing.

French, B. (n.d.). Language barriers. Public Speaking International. Retrieved on May 3, 2012 from http://www.publicspeakinginternational .com/funny-stories/

Photo 15.5 Using appropriate facial expressions, gestures, and motivated movement enhances your intelligibility and effectiveness. What do you think this speaker is communicating through her use of her body and why?

Movement Recall that *movement* refers to changing your body position. During your speech, engage only in **motivated movement**, movement with a specific purpose such as emphasizing an important idea, referencing a presentational aid, or clarifying macrostructure (Photo 15.5). To emphasize a particular point, you might move closer to the audience. To create a feeling of intimacy before telling a personal story, you might walk out from behind a lectern and sit down on a chair placed at the edge of the stage. Each time you begin a new main point, you might take a few steps to one side of the stage or the other. To use motivated movement effectively, you must practice when and how you will move until you can do so in a way that appears spontaneous and natural while remaining "open" to the audience (not turning your back to them).

Avoid unmotivated movement such as bobbing, weaving, shifting from foot to foot, or pacing from one side of the room to the other because unplanned movements distract the audience from your message. Because many unplanned movements result from nervousness, you can minimize them by paying mindful attention to your body as you speak. At the beginning of your speech, stand up straight on both feet. If you find yourself fidgeting, readjust and position your body with your weight equally distributed on both feet.

Delivery Methods

Speeches vary in the amount of preparation and practice you do ahead of time. The three most common delivery methods are impromptu, scripted, and extemporaneous.

Impromptu Speeches

An **impromptu speech** is one that is delivered with only seconds or minutes of advance notice for preparation and is usually presented with very few if any notes. Because impromptu speakers must quickly gather their thoughts just before and while they speak, carefully organizing and developing ideas can be challenging. As a result, they may leave out important information or confuse audience members. Delivery can suffer as speakers often use "ahs," "ums," "like," and "you know" to buy time as they scramble to collect their thoughts. That's why the more opportunities you have to organize and deliver your thoughts using an impromptu method, the better you'll become at doing so.

Some of the most common situations that require using the impromptu method are during employment and performance review interviews, at business meetings, in class, at social ceremonies, and to the media. In each situation, having practiced organizing ideas quickly and conveying them intelligibly and expressively will bolster your ethos and help you succeed.

You can improve your impromptu performances by practicing mock impromptu speeches. For example, if you are taking a class where the professor often calls on students at random to answer questions, you can prepare by anticipating the questions that might be asked and practice giving your answers aloud. Over time, you will become more adept at organizing your ideas and thinking on your feet.

Scripted Speeches

At the other extreme, a **scripted speech** is one that is prepared by creating a complete written manuscript and then delivered by reading from or memorizing a written copy. Obviously, effective scripted speeches take a great deal of time to prepare because both an outline and a word-for-word transcript must be prepared, practiced, and delivered in a way that sounds both conversational and animated. When you memorize a scripted speech, you face the increased anxiety of forgetting your lines. When you read a scripted speech from a manuscript or teleprompter, you must become adept at looking at the script with your peripheral vision so that you don't appear to be reading and you must still sound conversational and animated.

Because of the time and skill required to effectively prepare and deliver a scripted speech, they are usually reserved for important occasions that have important consequences. Political speeches, keynote addresses at conventions, commencement addresses, and CEO remarks at annual stockholder meetings are examples of occasions when a scripted speech might be most appropriate and worth the extra effort.

Extemporaneous Speeches

Most speeches, whether in the workplace, in the community, or in class, are delivered extemporaneously. An **extemporaneous speech** is researched and planned ahead of time, but the

motivated movement
movement with a specific purpose

impromptu speech
a speech that is delivered with only seconds or minutes of advance notice

scripted speech
a speech prepared by creating a complete written manuscript and delivered by rote memory or by reading a written copy

extemporaneous speech
a speech that is researched and planned ahead of time, although the exact wording is not scripted and will vary from presentation to presentation

exact wording is not scripted and will vary somewhat from presentation to presentation. When speaking extemporaneously, you refer to speaking notes reminding you of key ideas, structure, and delivery cues as you speak. Some speakers today use their computerized slideshows as speaking notes. If you choose to do so, however, be careful not to include too many words on any given slide, which will ultimately distract listeners from focusing on you as you speak.

Extemporaneous speeches are the easiest to give effectively. Unlike impromptu speeches, when speaking extemporaneously, you are able to prepare your thoughts ahead of time and have notes to prompt you. Unlike scripted speeches, extemporaneous speeches do not require as lengthy a preparation process to be effective.

Choosing the most effective delivery method and style can be particularly challenging for public figures who are attempting to influence public opinion and win elections. Read the *Communicating in the World* feature, "Politics, Politicians, and Public Speech Delivery," to consider what style you find most compelling and why.

COMMUNICATING IN THE WORLD

Politics, Politicians, and Public Speech Delivery

In political speeches, delivery style is as important, and sometimes even more important, than the message itself. In other words, it is not always *what* you say that resonates with audiences, but *how* you say it. Opinions vary, however, about what the most effective delivery style is. For example, President Barack Obama is often held up as an example of a successful public speaker. However, some criticize his use of a teleprompter. Republican politician Rick Santorum once took a swipe at Obama when he suggested it "should be illegal" for political candidates to read from a teleprompter "because all you're doing is reading someone else's words to people" (Cillizza, 2012). However, presidents and candidates, including some of Obama's detractors, have been using teleprompters to deliver speeches since the technology's invention over 50 years ago. Presidential historian Doris Kearns Goodwin argues that many presidents have relied on teleprompters to ensure the clarity of the message. She says, "if a president says something that is not what he meant to say, it could be an international situation" (quoted in Rucker, 2011).

Another politician with a much different delivery style is New Jersey governor Chris Christie. Christie is often celebrated for using a blunt and straightforward speaking style that contrasts with Obama's scripted style. He is well known for routinely using words like "stupid," "crap," and "insane" in news briefings, town hall meetings, and even more formal political speeches (Ibid).

However, not everyone is a fan of Christie's frank and confrontational style. Some critics suggest that his delivery style makes him come off as a bully. For example, while speaking at a town hall meeting on education reform, Christie scolded a teacher who accused him of unfairly criticizing teachers and teachers unions. He said, "If what you want to do is put on a show and giggle every time I talk, well then I have no interest in answering your question" (Shear, 2012). At another town hall meeting, Christie called a Navy veteran an "idiot" after the man questioned Christie's plan to merge two of New Jersey's public universities into a single school (Mandell, 2012). Christie's critics call him a bully, but his supporters say his style is what makes Christie appealing as a politician.

Do you think a scripted or extemporaneous style better serves our politicians and our democracy? Why or why not?

MindTap

Rehearsals

Rehearsing is the iterative process of practicing your speech aloud. A speech that is not practiced out loud is likely to be far less effective than it would have been had you given yourself sufficient time to revise, evaluate, and mull over all aspects of the speech (Anderson, 2013). Figure 15.4 provides a useful timetable for preparing and practicing a classroom speech. In the sections that follow, we describe how to rehearse effectively by preparing speaking notes, handling presentational aids, and recording, analyzing, and refining delivery.

rehearsing
the iterative process of practicing your speech aloud

Preparing Speaking Notes

Prior to your first rehearsal session, prepare a draft of your speaking notes. **Speaking notes** are a key word outline of your speech including hard-to-remember information or quotations and delivery cues. The best notes contain the fewest words possible written in lettering large enough to be seen instantly at a distance.

speaking notes
a key word outline of your speech

To develop your notes, begin by reducing your speech outline to an abbreviated outline of key words and phrases. Then, if there are details you must cite exactly accurately—such as a specific example, a quotation, or a set of statistics—add these in the appropriate spots. You might also put these on a separate card as a "Quotation Card" to refer to when delivering direct quotations during the speech, which is what Alyssa did (see Figure 15.5). Next, indicate exactly where you plan to share presentational aids. Finally, incorporate delivery cues indicating where you want to make use of your voice and body to enhance intelligibility or expressiveness. For example, indicate where you want to pause, gesture, or make a motivated movement. Capitalize or underline words you want to stress. Use slash marks (//) to remind yourself to pause. Use an upward-pointing arrow to remind yourself to increase rate or volume.

For a 3- to 5-minute speech, you should need no more than three 3-by-5-inch note cards for your speaking notes. For longer speeches, you might need one card for the introduction, one for each main point, and one for the conclusion. Speakers using computerized slideshows may also use the "notes" feature on the program for their speaking notes.

Use your notes during practice sessions as you will when you actually give the speech. If you will use a lectern, set the notes on the stand or, alternatively, hold them in

8 days before	Select topic; begin research
7 days before	Continue research
6 days before	Outline body of speech
5 days before	Work on introduction and conclusion
4 days before	Finish outline; find additional material if needed; have all presentational aids completed
3 days before	First rehearsal session
2 days before	Second rehearsal session
1 day before	Third rehearsal session
Due date	Deliver speech

Figure 15.4

Timetable for preparing a speech

© Cengage Learning

Figure 15.5

Alyssa's speaking notes

---

a. NOTE CARD 1: Introduction

PLANT FEET. . . . DIRECT EYE CONTACT. . . . POISE/ETHOS!

I. Famous Indian peace activist Mahatma Gandhi: "We must become the change we seek in the world."
Tall order. . . . We can make a difference right here in Lexington, KY

II. Think for a moment. . . . child/homework, neighbor/leaves, stranger/groceries. . . . It's easy for college students like us to get involved.

III. I volunteer at LRM and reaped benefits (Slide 1)

IV. Benefits volunteering. . . .
   a. get acquainted
   b. responsibility & privilege
   c. resumé-building skills

BLANK SLIDE, WALK RIGHT, EYE C.: Let's begin by explaining the ways volunteering can help us connect to our local community.

---

b. NOTE CARD 2: Body

I. GREAT WAY to become acquainted
LR: Comforts of home. . . . unfamiliar city. . . . volunteering. . . . easy and quick way. . . .
Natalie Cunningham—May 2nd (Q. CARD #1)
Social issues and conditions
Acc. to a 1991 article published in the *J. of Prevention and Intervention in the Community* by Cohen, Mowbray, Gillette, and Thompson raise awareness. . . .
My experience at LRM (SLIDES 2 & 3)

BLANK SLIDE, WALK LEFT, EYE C.: Not only is volunteering important. . . . familiar and social issues. . . . FRANKLY. . . . dem society. . . .

II. Civic responsibility AND privilege. . . . LR: We benefit college. . . . give back.
I agree with Wilson and Musick who said in their 1997 article in *Social Forces* active participation or deprived. (SLIDES 4 & 5)

Also a privilege. . . . make a difference. . . . feel good. . . . self-actualization (SLIDE #6)

---

c. NOTE CARD 3: Body & Conclusion

BLANK SLIDE, WALK RIGHT, EYE C: privilege & responsibility. . . . resume building . . .

III. Life skills
Article "Employability Credentials: A Key to Successful Youth Transition to Work" by I. Charner—1988 issue of the Journal of Career Development. . . . (Q. CARD #2)
Laura Hatfield. . . . leadership, teamwork, and listening skills
Andrea Stockelman, volunteer (SLIDE #7) (Q. CARD #3)
MY RESUMÉ (SLIDE #8)
BLANK SLIDE, WALK TO CENTER, EYE C: Today, we've discussed. . . . get acquainted, responsibility & privilege, resumé-building life skills help after grad.
CL: So, I'm hoping the next time you recall. . . . not distant past. Instead, I hope you'll be thinking bout how you **ARE** being the change you seek in the world by **volunteering right here / in Lexington /// right now!**

PAUSE, EYE CONTACT, POISE, NOD

Figure 15.5

(Continued)

d.Quotation Card

#1: "My first group of students needed rides to all the various volunteer sites b/c they had no idea where things were in the city. It was really easy for the students who lived on campus to remain ignorant of their city, but while volunteering they become acquainted with Lexington and the important issues going on here."

#2: "Employers rely on credentials to certify that a young person will become a valuable employee. Credentials that document the experiences and employ-ability skills, knowledge, and attitude."

#3: "I learned that there was a lot more that went into preparing food for the homeless than I ever thought possible. It was neat to be a part of that process."

one hand and refer to them only when needed. How important is it to construct good speaking notes? Speakers often find that the act of making the notes is so effective in helping cement ideas in the mind that during practice, or later during the speech itself, they rarely refer to them at all.

Handling Presentational Aids

Some speakers think that once they have prepared good presentational aids, they will have no trouble using them during the presentation. However, many speeches with good aids have become shambles because the aids were not well handled. You can avoid problems by following these guidelines:

1. **Carefully plan when to use presentational aids.** Indicate in your speaking notes exactly when you will reveal and conceal each aid. Practice introducing and using your aids until you can use them comfortably and smoothly.

2. **Consider audience needs carefully.** As you practice, eliminate any presentational aid that does not contribute directly to the audience's attention to, understanding of, or retention of the key ideas in your speech.

3. **Position presentational aids and equipment before beginning your speech.** Make sure your aids and equipment are where you want them and that everything is ready and in working order. Test electronic equipment to make sure everything from visual displays to sound to hyperlinks work and are cued correctly.

4. **Share a presentational aid only when talking about it.** Because presentational aids will draw audience attention, practice sharing them only when you are talking about them, and then concealing them when they are no longer the focus of attention.

   Because a single presentational aid may contain several bits of information, practice revealing only the portion you are currently discussing. On computerized slideshows, you can do so by using the "custom animation" feature to allow only one item to appear at a time. You can also strike the "B" key for a black screen when you aren't directly referencing the aid and insert blank slides where ideas in your speech are not being supplemented with something on the slideshow.

5. **Display presentational aids so that everyone in the audience can see and hear them.** The inability to see or hear an aid is frustrating. If possible, practice in the space where you will give your speech so you can adjust equipment accordingly. If you cannot practice in the space ahead of time, then arrive early enough on the

Photo 15.6 Effective speakers use gestures to reference their visual aids while discussing them. How will you practice referencing aids in your speeches?

day of the presentation to practice quickly with the equipment you will use.

6. **Reference the presentational aid during the speech.** Because you already know what you want your audience to see in a visual aid, tell your audience what to look for, explain the various elements in it, and interpret figures, symbols, and percentages. For an audio or audiovisual aid, point out what you want your audience to listen for before you play the excerpt. Also, when showing a visual or audiovisual aid, use the "turn-touch-talk" technique.

• When you display the visual, walk to the screen—that's where everyone will look anyway. Slightly turn to the visual and touch it—that is, point to it with an arm gesture or a pointer. Then, with your back to the screen and your body still facing the audience at a slight forty-five-degree angle, talk to your audience about it.

• When you finish making your comments, conceal the aid and return to the lectern or your speaking position.

7. **Talk to your audience, not to the presentational aid.** Although you will want to acknowledge the presentational aid by looking at it occasionally, it is important to maintain eye contact with your audience as much as possible (Photo 15.6). As you practice, resist the urge to stare at or read from your presentational aid.

8. **Resist the temptation to pass objects through the audience.** People look at, read, handle, and think about whatever they hold in their hands. While they are so occupied, they are not likely to be listening to you. If you have handouts or objects to distribute, do so after the speech rather than during it.

Practice Rounds

As with any other activity, effective speech delivery requires practice. Each practice round should consist of: (a) practicing aloud, (b) analyzing and making adjustments, an (c) practicing aloud again. The more of these practice rounds you have, the better your speech will be. During each practice round, evaluate your language choices, as well as your use of voice, body, and presentational aids. Do so until your speech delivery appears spontaneous and is both conversational and animated. Let's look at how you can proceed through several practice rounds.

First Practice Round Record (audio and video) your practice session so you can analyze the delivery and make improvements. You may also want to have a friend sit in on it and offer suggestions afterward.

1. Read through your complete sentence outline once or twice to refresh your memory. Then put the outline out of sight and practice the speech using only your speaking notes.

2. Make the practice as similar to the speech situation as possible, including using the presentational aids you've prepared. Stand up and face your imaginary audience. Pretend that the chairs, lamps, books, and other objects in your practice room are people.

3. Write down the time that you begin or use the stopwatch feature on your smart phone if you have one.

4. Begin speaking. Regardless of what happens, keep going until you have presented your entire speech. If you goof, make a repair as you would have to do if you were actually delivering the speech to an audience.

5. Write down the time you finish or stop the stopwatch. Compute the length of the speech for this first rehearsal.

Analysis Watch and listen to the recorded performance while reviewing your complete outline. How did it go? Did you leave out any key ideas? Did you talk too long on any one point and not long enough on another? Did you clarify each of your points? Did you adapt to your anticipated audience? (If you had a friend or relative watch and listen to your practice, have him or her help with your analysis.) Were your speaking notes effective? How well did you do with your presentational aids? Make any necessary changes before your second practice.

Second Practice Repeat the six steps outlined for the first practice. By practicing a second time right after your analysis, you are more likely to make the kind of adjustments that begin to improve the speech.

Additional Practice Rounds After you have completed one full practice round—consisting of two practices and the analysis in between them—put the speech away until that night or the next day. Although you should rehearse the speech at least a couple more times, you will not benefit if you cram all the practices into one long rehearsal time. You may find that a final practice right before you go to bed will be very helpful; while you are sleeping, your subconscious will continue to work on the speech. As a result, you are likely to find significant improvement in delivery when you practice again the next day.

Adapting While Delivering the Speech

Even when you've practiced your speech to the point that you know it inside and out, you must be prepared to adapt to your audience and possibly change course a bit as you give your speech. Remember that your primary goal is to generate shared understanding, so pay attention to the audience's feedback as you speak and adjust accordingly. Here are six tips to guide you.

1. **Be aware of and respond to audience feedback.** As you make eye contact with members of your audience, notice how they react to what you say. For instance, if you see quizzical looks on the faces of several listeners, you may need to explain a particular point in a different way. On the other hand, if you see listeners nodding impatiently, recognize that you don't need to belabor your point and can move on. If you notice that many audience members look bored, try to rekindle their interest by showing emotional expression in your delivery.

2. **Be prepared to use alternative developmental material.** Your ability to adjust to your audience's needs depends on how much additional alternative information you have to share. If you prepared only one example to make a particular point, you won't be ready if your audience is confused and needs another. If you have prepared only one definition for a term, you may be unable to rephrase with an additional definition if needed.

Photo 15.7 Effective speakers handle questions respectfully even when they don't know the answer. What would you say if you didn't know the answer to an audience member's question and why?

3. **Correct yourself when you misspeak.** Every speaker makes mistakes. They stumble over words, mispronounce terms, forget information, and mishandle presentational aids. Doing so is normal. If you stumble over a phrase or mispronounce a word, correct yourself and move on. Don't make a big deal of it by laughing, rolling your eyes, or in other ways drawing unnecessary attention to it. If you suddenly remember that you forgot to provide some information, consider how important it is for your audience to have that information. If what you forgot to say will make it difficult for your audience to understand a point that comes later, figure out how and when to provide the information later in your speech. Usually, however, information we forget to share is not critical to the audience's understanding and its better to leave it out and move on.

4. **Adapt to unexpected events.** Maintain your composure if something unexpected happens, such as a cell phone ringing or someone entering the room while you're speaking. Simply pause until the disruption ceases and then move on. If the disruption causes you to lose your train of thought or has distracted the audience, take a deep breath, look at your speaking notes, and continue your speech at a point slightly before the the point at which interruption occurred. This will allow both you and your audience to refocus on your speech. You might acknowledge that you are backtracking by saying something like, "Let's back up a bit and remember where we were. . . ."

5. **Adapt to unexpected audience reactions.** Sometimes, you'll encounter listeners who disagree strongly with your message. They might show their disagreement by being inattentive or rolling their eyes when you try to make eye contact with them. If these behaviors are limited to one or only a few members of your audience, ignore them and focus on the rest of your audience. If, however, you find that a majority of your audience is hostile to what you are saying, you might acknowledge their feedback and then ask them to suspend judgment while they listen. For example, you could say something like, "I can see that most of you don't agree with my first point. But let me ask you to put aside your initial reaction and think along with me on this next point. Even if we end up disagreeing, at least you will understand my position."

6. **Handle questions respectfully.** It is rare for audience members to interrupt speakers with questions during a speech. But if you are interrupted, be prepared to deal respectfully with the question (Photo 15.7). If the question is directly related to understanding the point you are making, answer it immediately. If it is not, acknowledge the question, indicate that you will answer it later during the question and answer period, and then remember to do so.

In most professional settings, you will be expected to answer questions when you've finished your speech. Some people will ask you to clarify information. Some will ask you for an opinion or to draw conclusions beyond what you have said. Whenever you answer a question, be honest about what you know and don't know. If an audience member asks a question you don't know the answer to, admit it by saying something like, "That's an excellent question. I'm not sure of the answer, but I would be happy to follow up on it later if you're interested." Then move on to the next question. If someone asks you to state an opinion about a matter you haven't thought much about, it's okay to say, "You know, I don't think I have given that enough thought to have a valid opinion."

Be sure to monitor how much time you have to answer questions. When the time is nearly up, mention that you'll entertain one more question to warn listeners that the question-and-answer period is almost over. You might also suggest that you'll be happy to talk more with individuals one on one later—this provides your more reserved listeners an opportunity to follow up with you.

Adapting Your Speech for Virtual Audiences

When Plato, Aristotle, and Cicero engaged in public speaking thousands of years ago, the communication event always occurred in real time with both the speaker and the audience physically present. Thanks to technology, however, public speeches today may be delivered in both face-to-face and virtual environments. In the opening scenario, for example, Alyssa and Katie would be delivering their speeches in a classroom with some audience members present while simultaneously streaming to several classmates who would be watching online via their computers. Their speeches would also be recorded and uploaded to the class Web site so they could watch, critique, and prepare reflective written assessments of themselves later.

With the proliferation of Internet accessibility comes both additional opportunities and challenges. For example, because speeches today may be easily uploaded to Web sites like YouTube with or without our permission and then quickly go viral, we also must always be cognizant of possible audiences we never intended to target. Thus, we offer here some guidelines to consider when adaption your speeches for virtual audiences.

1. Adapt your speech to address multiple audiences. Assume that any speech you give ay be recorded and made available to those who are not in your immediate audience. Always consider how your delivery (as well as content and structure) will respectfully address uninformed, apathetic, and oppositional audience who may view your speech virtually.

2. Choose presentational aids carefully. Make sure the visuals and audiovisuals you use can be easily viewed and heard in an online format. Also, be sure to explain them so that those who only have audio access or who view them on a small smart phone screen can understand the information on them.

3. Become proficient with the technology in advance. Technological proficiency is no longer considered a value-added skill. Make it a regular practice to consult with technology experts to learn how to use the most up-to-date programs and equipment effectively.

4. Employ the fundamentals of public speaking. Although it might seem to go without saying, be sure to adhere to the strategies of effective public speaking even when delivering your speech online. The action steps regarding topic selection and development, organization, presentational aids, language, and delivery remain fundamental to effective formal presentations in both face-to-face and virtual settings. Treat the camera as a person. As you do so, use your voice and body in ways that are intelligible, conversational, animated, and poised just as you would if the camera were someone sitting in the room with you.

Evaluating Speeches

In addition to learning to prepare and present speeches, you are learning to evaluate (critically analyze) the speeches you hear. An effective and ethical speech critique provides the speaker with an analysis of where the speech went well and what could be done to improve the next time. It also gives the critic insight into methods to incorporate or avoid in their own speeches. In this section, we look at some general criteria for evaluating public speeches.

If a speech has good content that is adapted to the audience, is clearly organized, and is delivered well, it is likely to achieve its goal. Thus, you can evaluate any speech by answering questions that relate to the basics of content, structure, and delivery. Figure 15.6 is a speech critique checklist. You can use this checklist to analyze your own speeches as you practice, to critique sample student speeches at the end of this chapter, and to critique speeches delivered by your classmates and others.

Thinking Critically About Speeches
Check all items that were accomplished effectively.

Content
_____ 1. Was the goal of the speech clear?
_____ 2. Did the speaker offer breadth and depth to support each main point?
_____ 3. Did the speaker use high-quality information and sources?
_____ 4. Did the speaker provide appropriate listener relevance links?
_____ 5. Were presentational aids appropriate?

Structure
_____ 6. Did the introduction gain attention, establish relevance and listener relevance, and lead into the speech using a thesis with main point preview?
_____ 7. Were the main points clear, parallel, and in meaningful complete sentences?
_____ 8. Did section transitions lead smoothly from one point to another?
_____ 9. Was the language appropriate, accurate, clear, and vivid?
_____ 10. Did the conclusion tie the speech together by summarizing the goal and main points and providing a clincher?

Delivery
_____ 11. Did the speaker appear and sound conversational?
_____ 12. Did the speaker appear and sound animated?
_____ 13. Was the speaker intelligible?
_____ 14. Was the speaker vocally expressive?
_____ 15. Was the speaker's appearance appropriate?
_____ 16. Did the speaker have good posture and poise?
_____ 17. Did the speaker look directly at and throughout the audience at least 90% of the time?
_____ 18. Did the speaker have good facial expressions?
_____ 19. Were the speaker's gestures and movement appropriate?
_____ 20. Did the speaker handle the presentational aids effectively?

Based on these criteria, evaluate the speech as (check one):
_____ excellent _____ good _____ satisfactory _____ fair _____ poor

Figure 15.6

Speech critique checklist

© Cengage Learning

ACTION STEP 5

Rehearsing Your Speech

The goal of this activity is to practice your speech, analyze it, and practice it again. One complete practice round includes a practice, an analysis, and a second practice.

1. Find a place where you can be alone to practice your speech. Follow the steps for the first practice explained earlier.

2. Review your outline as you watch and listen to the recording and then answer the following questions.

Are you satisfied with how well

The introduction got attention and led into the speech? ___

Main points were clearly stated? ___ And well developed? ___

Material adapted to the audience? ___

Section transitions were used? ___

The conclusion summarized the main points? ___
Left the speech on a high note?___

Presentational aids were used? ___

Ideas were expressed vividly? ___ And clearly? ___

Sounded conversational throughout? _____

Sounded animated? ___ Sounded intelligible? ____

Used natural gestures and movement? ___ Used effective eye contact? _____Facial expression? ___ Posture? ___ Appearance? ___

List the three most important changes you will make in your next practice session:

One: _____

Two: _____

Three: _____

3. Go through the steps outlined for the first practice again.

Then assess: Did you achieve the goals you set for the second practice?

_____

Reevaluate the speech using the checklist and continue to practice until you are satisfied with all parts of your presentation.

MindTap® *PREPARE Your Informative Speech Activity in Chapter 15 of the MindTap. Select the Outline tab for Action Step 5.A.*

COMMUNICATE ON YOUR FEET

Speech Assignment

Presenting Your First Speech

The Assignment

1. Follow the Action Steps to prepare an informative or persuasive speech. Your instructor will provide you with specific parameters for this assignment.

2. Criteria for evaluation include all the essentials of topic and purpose, content, organization, and presentation, but special emphasis will be placed on clarity of goal, clarity and appropriateness of main points, and delivery (items that are grouped under the boldface headings in the Speech Critique

Checklist in Figure 15.6). As you practice, you can use the checklist to ensure that you are meeting all of the basic criteria. In addition, you may want to refer to the sample student outline and speech that follow this assignment box.

3. Prior to presenting your speech, prepare a complete sentence outline and a written plan for adapting your speech to the audience.

If you completed the Action Step activities in Chapter 13, you can use them for the basis of your written adaptation plan.

SAMPLE SPEECH PLAN AND OUTLINE

Informative Speech with Presentational Aids

This section presents a sample informative speech given by a student, including an adaptation plan, an outline, and a transcript.

College Student Volunteering and Civic Engagement[1]

By Alyssa Grace Millner

MindTap® Read the speech adaptation plan, outline, and transcript of a speech by Alyssa Grace Millner. You can access a video of Alyssa's speech through the Chapter 15 resources of your Mindtap for *Communicate!* You can also use your MindTap to analyze this speech in terms of concepts covered in this chapter.

Adaptation Plan

1. **Key aspects of audience.** The majority of listeners know what volunteering is in a general sense, but they probably don't know the ways it can benefit them as college students.

2. **Establishing and maintaining common ground.** I'll use personal pronouns throughout the speech, as well as specific examples about volunteering from volunteers right here in Lexington.

3. **Building and maintaining interest.** I'll insert listener relevance links in the introduction and for each main point that point out how volunteering is directly related to improving the lives of college students in some way.

4. **Building credibility.** I will point out right away that I volunteer and that I've done a good deal of research on it. I'll insert examples of my own experiences throughout the speech, as well as cite credible research to support my claims.

5. **Audience attitudes.** Some may be indifferent, but according to the research I've found, most will probably be open to the idea of volunteering. They might not know how easy it can be to get started though.

6. **Adapting to audiences from different cultures and language communities.** Although most of my classmates are U.S. citizens, there are a couple of international students in the class. So, when I talk about volunteering being a civic responsibility, I'll make sure to talk about how all of us are reaping the benefits of a U.S. education; that's why we are all responsible for giving back in some way. I'll talk about it as an ethical responsibility.

7. **Use presentational aids.** I will show photographs of people engaged in volunteer work throughout the speech. I think this will make my ideas very concrete for the audience and will enhance pathos (emotional appeal). I'll also show some graphs about homelessness in Lexington and the percentage of college students who believe in volunteering. I think these will bolster my ethos as the audience will see I've done research. Finally, I'll show my résumé

with elements highlighted that I've been able to include because I've volunteered. I think this will drive home my point about the future benefits for college students who volunteer while still in school.

Formal Speech Outline

General goal: I want to inform my audience.

Specific goal: I want my audience to realize the benefits of volunteering in Lexington while we are still students at the University of Kentucky.

Introduction

I. The famous Indian peace activist and spiritual leader Mahatma Gandhi is known for saying "We must become the change we seek in the world." That sounds at first like an awfully tall order, but today I'd like to show you how each of us can do just that and make a difference right here in Lexington, Kentucky.

Attention getter

II. Think for a moment of a time in your life when you did something kind for someone else. Maybe you helped a child do homework, or a neighbor rake leaves, or even a stranger get groceries from the store to the car. Do you remember how that made you feel? Well, that feeling can be a normal part of your week when you choose to be a volunteer. And for college students like us, it's easy to get involved as volunteers in our local community.

Listener relevance link

III. Personally, I volunteer at the Lexington Rescue Mission and have reaped many benefits by doing so. *(Show slide 1: picture of me volunteering at the Mission)* I've also done extensive research on volunteering and civic engagement.

Speaker credibility

IV. So, let's spend the next few minutes discussing the benefits volunteering can have for us as college students by focusing on how volunteering helps us get acquainted with the local community, why civic engagement is the responsibility of every one of us, and what volunteering can do to teach us new skills and build our résumés.

Thesis statement with main point preview

Let's begin by explaining the ways volunteering can connect each of us to our local community.

Transition

Body

I. Volunteering is a great way to become acquainted with a community beyond the university campus.

Some college students move away from the comforts of home to a new and unfamiliar city. Not knowing what there is to do or even how to get around can be overwhelming and isolating. Volunteering is an easy way to quickly become familiar with and begin to feel a part of this new place in addition to the campus community.

Listener relevance link

A. Volunteering allows you to learn your way around town.

   1. In an interview I had with Natalie Cunningham, the volunteer coordinator of the Lexington Rescue Mission, she said, "I've been working with students for several years now. While every group is different, one lingering trend is each group's unawareness of their city. It is easy for the students who live on campus to stay in their 'on-campus bubble.' Volunteering allows students to become acquainted with Lexington and the important issues facing their new home" (personal communication, January 2, 2013).

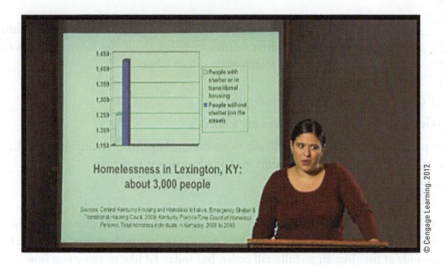

© Cengage Learning, 2012

2. It seems like a silly thing, but knowing your way around town starts to make any city feel like home. Volunteering gets you out into the local area and helps you begin to get acquainted with new people and places.

B. Volunteering can also open your eyes to local social issues and conditions.

1. Many nonprofit organizations strive to raise awareness of important social issues, things like hunger and homelessness, (Norris Center, 2013).

2. The second time I showed up to volunteer at the Lexington Rescue Mission, I served food to the homeless. *(Show slide 2: group of volunteers in the kitchen)*

a. I served soup and hung out with other volunteers and local homeless people. One of the "veteran" volunteers explained to me that Lexington has approximately 3,000 homeless people. *(Show slide 3: homelessness statistics in Lexington)*

b. I was shocked to learn that we had such a large number of men, women, and children without a regular place to sleep. I wouldn't have known about this problem or the organizations working to end homelessness if I hadn't been a volunteer.

Transition

Not only is volunteering important because it helps us become familiar with a town and its social issues; frankly, as members of a democratic society, volunteering is our civic responsibility.

II. Giving back to the community through volunteer work is our civic responsibility and a privilege.

Listener relevance link

Each of us in this room—whether as U.S. citizens or international students—are reaping the benefits of earning college degrees in this democratic society. With that benefit comes the responsibility and privilege of giving back.

A. Volunteering is our civic responsibility.

1. Grant (2012) explains that, without active participation in the local community, civil society becomes deprived.

2. I agree. Giving back by volunteering helps the community in so many ways. *(Show slides 4 and 5: volunteers sorting clothes at the mission and then volunteers playing cards with people served at the shelter)*

B. Volunteering is also a privilege. Making a difference by volunteering ends up making us feel better about ourselves and our role in the world we live in.

   1. In fact, according to the Bureau of Labor Statistics, about 25% of the U.S. population volunteered in 2014. What is troubling, however, is that on 18.7% of people aged 20 to 24 volunteered that year (Volunteering in the United States, 2014). *(Show slide 6: bar graph of demographic comparisons)*

   2. This seems odd in light of the study of first-year college students done by the Higher Education Research Institute published in January 2009 revealed that 69.7 percent of students believe it is *essential or very important* to volunteer in order to help people in need (Pryor et al., 2009).

Certainly, the privilege of giving back as volunteers is our civic responsibility and helps our local community, but we can also reap valuable résumé-building life skills by volunteering. Transition

III. Volunteering helps teach us new skills. Listener relevance link

These new skills and talents can actually make us more marketable for better jobs once we graduate.

A. Being a consistent volunteer at a nonprofit organization while attending college can strengthen your résumé.

   1. Educational credentials are not enough to ensure college graduates are ready for the workforce. They also need credentials that document their experiences and employability skills (Tomlinson, 2008). They can be a pathway to getting a job (Spera, Ghertner, Nerino, & DiTommaso, 2013).

   2. Laura Hatfield, director of the Center for Community Outreach at the University of Kentucky, points out that volunteers can include leadership, teamwork, and listening skills on their résumés because they can document the experiences where they had to use them effectively in the real world.

   3. Andrea Stockelman, another volunteer at the Lexington Rescue Mission, explained some of the new skills she picked up with volunteering. She said, "I learned that there was a lot more that went into preparing food for the homeless than I ever thought possible. It was neat to be a part of that process" (personal communication, April 28, 2010). *(Show slide 7: photo of Andrea preparing food)*

B. Volunteering at the Lexington Rescue Mission taught me new skills that bolstered my résumé. *(Show slide 8: résumé with skills highlighted)*

   1. I learned to coordinate the schedules of other volunteers.

   2. I also practiced important people skills such as teamwork, empathy, conflict management, and listening.

Conclusion

I. Today we've discussed why volunteering is beneficial to college students by focusing on how volunteering can connect us quickly and easily to our local community, why it's both our responsibility and a privilege to do so, and how volunteering will benefit us after we graduate. Thesis restatement with main point summary

II. So, I'm hoping the next time you recall a time you really enjoyed making a difference by helping someone, that memory won't come from the distant past. Instead, I hope you'll be thinking about how you are being the change you seek in the world by volunteering right here in Lexington right now. Clincher

References

Corporation for National and Community Service. (2006). *College students helping America.* Washington, DC: Author.

Grant, A. (2012). Giving time, time after time: Work design and sustained employee participation in corporate volunteering. *Academy of Management Review,* amr-2010.

Norris Center (2013, January 2). Center for student involvement: Volunteer opportunities. Northwestern University. Retrieved from: http://norris.northwestern.edu/csi/community/volunteer-opportunities/

Pryor, J. H., Hurtado, S., DeAngelo, L., Sharkness, J., Romero, L., Korn, W. S., & Tran, S. (2009). *The American freshman: National norms for fall 2008.* Los Angeles, CA: Higher Education Research Institute.

Spera, C., Ghertner, R., Nerion, A., & DiTommaso, A. (2013). *Volunteering as a Pathway to Employment: Does Volunteering Increase Odds of Finding a Job for the Out of Work?* Washington, DC: Corporation for National and Community Service.

Tomlinson, M. (2008). The degree is not enough: Students' perceptions of the role of higher education for graduate work and employability. British Journal of Sociology of Education, 29(1), 49–61. Doi: 10.1080/01425690701737457

United States Bureau of Labor Statistics. (2015, February 25). Economic News Release: Volunteering in the United States, 2014. Retrieved from: http://www.bls.gov/news.release/volun.nr0.htm

SPEECH AND ANALYSIS

Speech

Analysis

The famous Indian peace activist and spiritual leader Mahatma Gandhi is known for saying "We must become the change we seek in the world." That sounds at first like an awfully tall order, but today I'd like to show you how each of us can do just that and make a difference right here in Lexington, Kentucky. Think for a moment of a time in your life when you did something kind for someone else. Maybe you helped a child do homework, or a neighbor rake leaves, or even a stranger get groceries from the store to the car. Do you remember how that made you feel? Well, that feeling can be a normal part of your week when you choose to be a volunteer. And for college students like us, it's easy to get involved as volunteers in our local community. Personally, I volunteer at the Lexington Rescue Mission and have reaped many benefits by doing so. *(Show slide 1: picture of me volunteering at the Mission)* I've also done extensive research on volunteering and civic engagement. So, let's spend the next few minutes discussing the benefits volunteering can have for us as college students by focusing on how volunteering helps us get acquainted with the local community, why civic engagement is the responsibility of every citizen, and what volunteering can do to teach us new skills and build our résumés. Let's begin by explaining the ways volunteering can connect each of us to our local community.

Notice how Alyssa uses a famous quotation to get the attention of her audience in a way that also piques interest about the topic.

Here, Alyssa establishes listener relevance by pointing out that helping others makes us feel good and volunteering can be easy.

Alyssa mentions that she volunteers, which bolsters ethos and establishes her credibility to speak on the topic.

Notice how Alyssa's thesis with main point preview gives us a sense of the organizational framework for her ideas.

Volunteering is a great way to become acquainted with a community beyond the university campus. Most college students move away from the comforts of home to a new and unfamiliar city. Not knowing what there is to do or even how to get around can be overwhelming and isolating. Volunteering is an easy way to quickly become familiar with and begin to feel a part of this new city in addition to the campus community.

Volunteering allows you to learn your way around town. In an interview I had with Natalie Cunningham, the volunteer coordinator of the Lexington Rescue Mission, she said, "I've been working with students for several years now. While every group is different, one lingering trend is each group's unawareness of their city. It is easy for the students who live on campus to stay in their 'on-campus bubble.' Volunteering allows students to become acquainted with Lexington and the important issues facing their new home." It seems like a silly thing, but knowing your way around town starts to make any city feel like home. Volunteering gets you out into the local area and helps you begin to get acquainted with new people and places.

Volunteering can also open your eyes to local social issues and conditions. Many nonprofit organizations strive to raise awareness of important social issues, things like hunger and homelessness. The second time I showed up to volunteer at the Lexington Rescue Mission, I served food to the homeless. *(Show slide 2: group of volunteers in the kitchen)* I served soup and hung out with other volunteers and local homeless people. One of the "veteran" volunteers explained to me that Lexington has approximately 3,000 homeless people. *(Show slide 3: homelessness statistics in Lexington)* I was shocked to learn that we had such a large number of men, women, and children without a regular place to sleep. I wouldn't have known about this problem or the organizations working to end homelessness if I hadn't been a volunteer. Not only is volunteering important because it helps us become familiar with a town and its social issues; frankly, as members of a democratic society, volunteering is our civic responsibility.

Giving back to the community through volunteer work is our civic responsibility and a privilege. Each of us in this room—whether as U.S. citizens or international students—are reaping the benefits of earning college degrees in this democratic society. With that benefit comes the responsibility and privilege of giving back. Volunteering is our civic responsibility. In a 2012 article published in *the Academy of Management Review*, Grant explains that, without active participation in the local community, civil society becomes deprived. I agree. Giving back by volunteering helps the community in so many ways. *(Show slides 4 and 5: volunteers sorting clothes at the mission and then volunteers playing cards with people served at the shelter)*

Again, as Alyssa introduces the first main point, she gets us to tune in because we all know how overwhelming and isolating we can feel when we move to a new place.

Quoting the volunteer coordinator is a great piece of developmental material that encourages us to trust that Alyssa's message is trustworthy. (Note that interviews are not included in the reference section but are cited in the text of the outline.)

Alyssa intersperses actual photos of her and others volunteering throughout the speech. Doing so enhances her verbal message but doesn't replace it. The photos also provide pathos, making her ideas more emotionally compelling.

Here and throughout the speech, notice how Alyssa uses effective section transitions to verbally tie the point she is wrapping up with an introduction of the point to come. This makes her speech flow smoothly so listeners can follow her train of thought and bolsters her ethos because she sounds prepared.

Alyssa's careful audience analysis reveals itself here as she reminds her audience that even those who are not American citizens are benefiting as students in our educational system and, thus, have a responsibility to give back in some way.

Volunteering is also a privilege. Making a difference by volunteering ends up making us feel better about ourselves and our role in the world around us. In fact, In fact, according to the Bureau of Labor Statistics, about 25% of the U.S. population volunteered in 2014. What is troubling, however, is that on 18.7% of people aged 20 to 24 volunteered that year. I say this because volunteering, according to a 2013 article published by the Corporation for National and Community Service, can be a pathway to getting a job after graduating. (Spera, Ghertner, Nerino, & DeTommaso, 2013). *(Show slide 6: bar graph of demographic comparisons)*. This seems odd in light of a study done by the Higher Education Research Institute published in January of 2009 shows that a whopping 69.7 percent of first-year college students believe it is essential or very important to volunteer to help people in need. Certainly, the privilege of giving back as volunteers is our civic responsibility and helps our local community, but we can also reap valuable résumé-building life skills by volunteering.

Alyssa's choice to include national statistics of college student volunteers bolsters her credibility and provides listener relevance by reinforcing that college students are doing this, want to do this, and feel good about doing this kind of work.

Volunteering helps teach us new skills. These new skills and talents can actually make us more marketable for better jobs once we graduate. Being a consistent volunteer at a nonprofit organization while attending college can strengthen your résumé. According to Tomlinson, in the *British Journal of Sociology of Education* Academic degrees are not enough to prepare students adequately for the workforce. Credentials that document the experiences and employability skills, knowledge, and attitude." Laura Hatfield, director of the Center for Community Outreach at the University of Kentucky, points out that volunteers can include leadership, teamwork, and listening skills on their résumés because they can document the experiences where they had to use them effectively in the real world. Andrea Stockelman, another volunteer at the Lexington Rescue Mission, explained some of the new skills she picked up with volunteering. She said, "I learned that there was a lot more that went into preparing food for the homeless than I ever thought possible. It was neat to be a part of that process." *(Show slide 7: photo of Andrea preparing food)*

Students want to know how to market themselves to get good jobs. So this main point will help maintain listener interest at a point when minds might tend to wander.

By including a quotation from another volunteer, we don't have to take Alyssa's word alone.

Volunteering at the Lexington Rescue Mission taught me new skills that bolstered my résumé. *(Show slide 8: résumé with skills highlighted)* I learned to coordinate the schedules of other volunteers. I also practiced important people skills such as teamwork, empathy, conflict management, and listening.

Today we've discussed why volunteering is beneficial to college students by focusing on how volunteering can connect us quickly and easily to our local community, why it's both our responsibility and privilege to do so, and how volunteering will benefit us after we graduate. So, I'm hoping the next time you recall a time you really enjoyed making a difference by helping someone, that memory won't come from the distant past. Instead, I hope you'll be thinking about how you are being the change you seek in the world by volunteering right here in Lexington right now.

This very clear thesis restatement with main point summary signals a sense of closure.

Notice how Alyssa ties back to her opening quotation in her clincher. This provides a sense of wrapping up without saying thank you that helps listeners feel like the speech is complete in a memorable way.

WHAT WOULD YOU DO?

A Question of Ethics

Nalini sighed loudly as the club members of Toastmasters International took their seats. It was her first time meeting with the public speaking group, and she didn't want to be there, but her mom had insisted that she join the club in the hopes that it would help Nalini transfer from her community college to the university. It wasn't that the idea of public speaking scared Nalini. She had already spent time in front of an audience as the lead singer of the defunct emo band Deathstar. To Nalini's mind, public speaking was just another type of performance—like singing or acting—albeit a stuffy one, better suited to middle-aged men and women than people her age, a sentiment that explained why she wanted to be elsewhere at the moment.

After the club leader called the meeting to order, he asked each of the new members to stand, introduce themselves, and give a brief speech describing their background, aspirations, and reasons for joining the club. "Spare me," Nalini muttered loud enough for those next to her to hear. The club leader then called on a young woman to Nalini's left, who rose and began to speak about her dream of becoming a lawyer and doing public advocacy work for the poor. After the young woman sat down, the club members applauded politely. Nalini whistled and clapped loudly and kept on clapping after the others had stopped.

The club leader, somewhat taken aback, called on Nalini next. She rose from her seat and introduced herself as the secret love child of a former president and a famous actress. Nalini then strung together a series of other fantastic lies about her past and her ambitions. She concluded her speech by saying that she had joined the club in the hopes that she could learn how to hypnotize audiences into obeying her commands. After Nalini sat, a few of the club members applauded quietly, while others cast glances at each other and the club leader.

What ethical obligations does an audience member have to a speaker and a speaker to his or her audience?

MindTap

Reflection and Assessment

Effective speeches must not only provide strong and relevant content that is clearly organized, they must also be presented using an effective delivery that is both conversational and animated. The major elements of speech delivery are embedded within your use of voice (pitch, volume, rate, quality, articulation, and pronunciation) and use of body (appearance, poise, posture, eye contact, facial expression, gestures, and movement) and requires rehearsals. To assess how well you've learned what we addressed in these pages, answer the following questions. If you have trouble answering any of them, go back and review that material. Once you can answer each question accurately, you are ready to move ahead to read the next chapter.

1. Why do we offer tips to manage speech anxiety effectively rather than to eliminate it altogether?

2. How do you use your voice and body to convey effective delivery?

3. What are the advantages and disadvantages of the different delivery methods?

4. What does an effective speech practice round consist of?

5. How might you adapt while you're delivering your speech considering both face-to-face and virtual settings?

6. How do you construct an ethical speech critique?

COMMUNICATE!

RESOURCE AND ASSESSMENT CENTER

MindTap®

Now that you have read Chapter 15, go to your MindTap for *Communicate!* for quick access to the electronic resources that accompany this text.

Applying What You've Learned

Impromptu Speech Activity

Pick a slip of paper from a container provided by your instructor. The slip of paper will identify an element we've discussed about effective speech preparation (identifying a topic and writing a speech goal, audience analysis and adaptation, locating and evaluating secondary research sources, types of developmental material, conducting primary research, elements of an effective macrostructure, elements of effective microstructure, constructing presentational aids, effective delivery, use of voice, use of body, delivery methods, rehearsal sessions, etc.). Prepare and present a 2- to 3-minute impromptu speech explaining the element with specific examples.

Assessment Activities

1. Controlling Nervousness Interview one or two people who give frequent speeches (such as a minister, a politician, a lawyer, a businessperson, or a teacher). Ask what is likely to make them more or less nervous about giving the speech. Find out how they cope with their nervousness. Write a short paragraph summarizing what you have learned from the interviews. Then identify the behaviors used by those people that you believe might work for you.

2. Evaluating Speaker's Vocal and Body Action Behaviors Attend a public speech event on campus or in your community. Watch and evaluate the speaker's use of vocal characteristics (voice and articulation), body action (facial expressions, gestures, movement, poise, and posture), animation, spontaneity, and eye contact. Which vocal or body action behaviors stood out and why? How did the speaker's use of voice, body actions, animation, spontaneity, and eye contact contribute to or detract from the speaker's message? What three things could the speaker have done to improve the delivery of the speech?

Skill-Building Activities

1. Articulation Practice The goal of this activity is to practice articulating difficult word combinations. To find a list of sentences that are difficult to articulate, go to the Jim Powell Communications Web site, click on "Directing Tips," and then on "Articulation Exercises." Practice saying each of these sentences until you can do so without error.

2. Cognitive Restructuring Prepare and practice your personal cognitive restructuring by following the process outlined in this chapter.

Informative Speaking

When you finish this chapter, you'll be able to:

- Describe five distinguishing characteristics of informative speaking.

- Describe five major methods of informing in your speeches.

- Create informative process speeches, which carefully delineate the steps and order of a process.

- Create informative expository speeches with a clear organizational pattern that use a variety of research and information methods.

MindTap®

Start with quick warm-up activity.

As Logan finished his informative speech, the class burst into spontaneous applause. Anna turned to her friend, Ryan, and whispered, "Wow, when Logan introduced his speech about online social networks, I thought it would be boring. We all use Facebook, Twitter, and YouTube all the time. What could he possibly teach us that we don't already know? Was I ever wrong!"

"I know what you mean," Ryan responded. "I guess Professor Chung was right. You really *can* make a familiar topic interesting if you can share new and relevant insight about it."

"Yeah," Anna continued. "Now I'm really glad I don't have to speak today. I'm going to take another look at my speech tonight to make sure I'm sharing new and relevant insight about online identity theft."

16

After listening to Logan, Anna and Ryan discovered firsthand what makes informative speeches effective. Effective informative speeches don't just share information. They share information that is both new and relevant for a particular audience. Not only that, Ryan and Anna also learned that even familiar topics can be intellectually stimulating when speakers share new and relevant insight about them.

An **informative speech** is one whose goal is to explain or describe facts, truths, and principles in a way that stimulates interest, facilitates understanding, and increases the likelihood of remembering. In short, informative speeches are designed to educate audiences. Informative speeches answer questions about a topic, such as those beginning with who, when, what, where, why, how to, and how does. For example, your informative speech might describe who popular singer-songwriter Adele is, define Scientology, compare and contrast the similarities and differences between Twitter and Facebook, tell the story of golf professional Rory McIlroy's rise to fame, or demonstrate how to create and post a video on a Web site like YouTube. Informative speaking differs from other speech forms (such as speaking to persuade, to entertain, or to celebrate) in that your goal is simply to achieve mutual understanding about an object, person, place, process, event, idea, concept, or issue.

In this chapter, we discuss five distinguishing characteristics of informative speeches and five methods of informing. Then, we discuss two common types of informative speeches (process and expository speeches) and provide an example of an informative speech.

Characteristics of Effective Informative Speaking

We face some unique challenges to gain and sustain listener attention when giving informative speeches. We can address these challenges effectively by attending to five key characteristics of informative speeches.

Intellectually Stimulating

Your audience will perceive information to be **intellectually stimulating** when it is new to them and when it is explained in a way that piques their curiosity and interest. By *new*, we mean information that most of your audience is unfamiliar with or fresh insights into a topic with which they are already familiar.

If your audience is unfamiliar with your topic, you should consider how you might tap their natural curiosity. Imagine you are an anthropology major who is interested in prehistoric humans, which is not an interest shared by most members of your audience. You know that in 1991, the 5,300-year-old remains of a man, now called Ötzi, were found surprisingly well preserved in an ice field in the mountains between Austria and Italy. Even though the discovery was big news at the time, your audience today probably doesn't know much about it. You can draw on their natural curiosity, however, as you present "Unraveling the Mystery of the Iceman," describing scientists' efforts to understand who Ötzi was and what happened to him ("Ötzi, the Ice Man," n.d.).

If your audience is familiar with your topic, you will need to identify new insight about it. Begin by asking yourself, "What things about my topic do listeners probably not know?" Answer the question by considering depth and breadth. *Depth* has to do with going into more detail than people's general knowledge of the topic. Logan did so by sharing details

---

informative speech
explains facts, truths, and principles in a way that increases understanding

intellectually stimulating
information that is new to audience members and piques interest

about the history of online social networks, something his audience of young users probably never thought about before. If you've ever watched programs on the Food Network, that's what they do. Most people know basic recipes, but these programs show new ways to cook the same foods (Photo 16.1). *Breadth* has to do with looking at how your topic relates to associated topics. Trace considered breadth when he informed his audience about Type 1 diabetes. He discussed not only the physical and emotional effects of the disease on a diabetic person, but also the emotional and relational effects on family and friends, as well as financial implications for society.

Relevant

A general rule to remember when preparing your informative speeches is this: Don't assume your listeners will recognize how the information is relevant to them. Remember to incorporate *listener relevance links* throughout the speech. As you prepare each main point, ask and answer the question: How would knowing this information make my listeners happier, healthier, wealthier, wiser, and so forth?

Creative

Your audience will perceive your information to be **creative** when it yields innovative ideas and insights. You may not ordinarily consider yourself to be creative, but that may be because you have never recognized or fully developed your own innovative ideas. Creativity comes from doing good research, taking time, and practicing productive thinking.

Creative informative speeches begin with *good research*. The more you learn about a topic, the more you will have to work with in order to develop it creatively.

The creative process also requires *time* to mull over ideas. Rarely do creative insights come when we are in a time crunch. Instead, they come when we least expect it—when we're driving our car, preparing for bed, or daydreaming.

For the creative process to work, you also have to *think productively*. **Productive thinking** occurs when we contemplate something from a variety of perspectives. Then, with numerous ideas to choose from, we can select the ones that are best suited to our particular audience. In the article "A Theory about Genius," Michael Michalko (1998) describes several tactics we can use to become better at productive thinking. They include:

1. Rethink a problem, issue, or topic from many perspectives. Albert Einstein actually came up with the theory of relativity this way. As you brainstorm, try to think about a possible topic as it might be perceived by many different groups and co-cultural groups. Then as you conduct research, try to find sources that represent a variety of viewpoints and perspectives, as well.

2. Make your thoughts visible by sketching drawings, diagrams, and graphs. Galileo revolutionized science by doing this. Try concept mapping as you generate topics and approaches to them.

3. Set regular goals to *produce something*. The great NHL hockey player, Wayne Gretzky, put it this way: "You miss every shot you don't take." So take some shots!

AP Images/J. Pat Carter

Photo 16.1 You can make familiar topics intellectually stimulating by sharing fresh insight focused on depth and breadth. What would make a speech about a recipe for a familiar dish new and relevant for you?

creative
using information in a way that yields innovative ideas and insights

productive thinking
contemplating something from a variety of perspectives

AP Images/Chris O'Meara

Photo 16.2 If you take a shot and write something down, even if it's not very good, you have something to revise. If you don't take a shot, you most assuredly have nothing to work with. Why don't you try it right now?

Thomas Edison actually set a goal to produce an invention every 10 days. J. S. Bach wrote one cantata per week. And T. S. Eliot's many drafts of *The Waste Land* eventually became a masterpiece. Don't let writer's block keep you from drafting an initial outline. You need to start somewhere. Getting ideas out of your head and onto paper or a computer screen gives you something to work with and revise (Photo 16.2). After all, you can't edit air.

4. Combine and recombine ideas, images, and thoughts in different ways. The Austrian monk Gregor Mendel combined mathematics and biology to come up with the laws of heredity, which still ground the modern science of genetics today. Jennifer's list of possible speech topics included gardening, something she loved to do, and the issue of rising college tuition costs. She put the two ideas together and came up with the idea of doing an informative speech about how to use gardening (services, produce, and products) to raise money to help pay for college.

To nurture creative thinking about transnational celebrity activism in global politics, Anne Marie not only conducted an extensive library search on several databases, but she also researched the topic by reading celebrity gossip magazines and visiting the Web sites of celebrities known for practicing it. After learning about what people like Angelina Jolie, Matt Damon, George Clooney, Madonna, and others were doing, she gave herself time to let what she had discovered percolate in her mind for a few days and even sketched a concept map to visualize links among her material. Ultimately, she was able to make the topic more interesting for her audience.

Memorable

If your speech is really informative, your audience will hear a lot of new information but will need help remembering what is most important. Emphasizing your specific goal, main points, and key facts are good starting points. Figure 16.1 summarizes several memory-enhancing techniques you might use.

Learning Styles

Because audience members differ in how they prefer to learn, you will be most successful when you address four diverse learning styles: feeling, watching, thinking, and doing. You can appeal to people who prefer to learn through the feeling dimension by providing concrete, vivid images, examples, stories, and testimonials. Address the watching dimension by using visual aids. Address the thinking dimension by including definitions, explanations, and statistics. Address the doing dimension by encouraging your listeners to do something during the speech or afterward. In his speech about what it is like to do a tour of duty as a soldier in Iraq, Zach addressed diverse learning styles by sharing stories of his own experiences (feeling), showing visual aids of the places he had been and the equipment he used (watching), explaining why the days were structured as they were (thinking), and asking his audience to respond silently to four questions every soldier must answer "yes" to (doing).

Technique	Use	Example
Presentational aids	To provide audience members with a visual, audio, or audiovisual conceptualization of important information	A diagram of the process of making ethanol
Repetition	To give the audience a second or third chance to retain important information by repeating or paraphrasing it	"The first dimension of romantic love is passion; that is, it can't really be romantic love if there is no sexual attraction."
Transitions	To help the audience understand the relationship between the ideas, including primary and supporting information	"So the three characteristics of romantic love are passion, intimacy, and commitment. Now let's consider five ways to keep love alive."
Humor and other emotional anecdotes	To create an emotional memory link to important ideas	"True love is like a pair of socks, you have to have two, and they've got to match. So you and your partner need to be mutually committed and compatible."
Mnemonics and acronyms	To provide an easily remembered memory prompt for a series or a list	"You can remember the four criteria for evaluating a diamond as the four Cs: carat, clarity, cut, and color." "As you can see, useful goals are SMART: S for specific, M for measurable, A for action-oriented, R for reasonable, and T for time-bound. That's SMART."

© Cengage Learning

Figure 16.1

Techniques for making informative speeches memorable

Methods of Informing

We can inform through description, definition, comparison and contrast, narration, and demonstration. Let's look at each of these methods more closely.

Description

Description is a method used to create an accurate, vivid, verbal picture of an object, geographic feature, setting, person, event, or image. This method usually answers an overarching "who," "what," or "where" question. Descriptions are most effective when accompanied by a presentational aid, but vivid verbal descriptions can also create informative mental pictures. To describe something effectively, you can explain its size, shape, weight, color, composition, age, condition, and spatial organization.

You can describe size subjectively as large or small and objectively by noting specific numerical measurements. For example, you can describe New York City subjectively as the largest city in the United States or more objectively as home to more than 8 million people

description
method used to create an accurate, vivid, verbal picture of an object, geographic feature, setting, person, event, or image

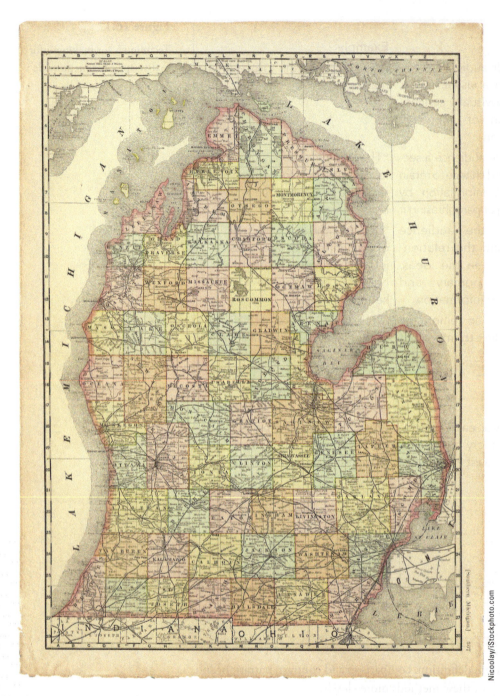

Photo 16.3 Can you see why Michigan is sometimes described as looking like the left hand of a mitten?

Nicoolay/iStockphoto.com

with more than 26,000 people per square mile.

You can describe shape by reference to common geometric forms like round, triangular, oblong, spherical, conical, cylindrical, or rectangular, or by reference to common objects such as a book or a milk carton. For example, the Lower Peninsula of Michigan is often described as being shaped like a left-hand mitten (Photo 16.3). Shape is made more vivid by using adjectives, such as *smooth* or *jagged*.

You can describe weight subjectively as heavy or light and objectively by pounds and ounces or kilograms, grams, and milligrams. As with size, you can clarify weight with comparisons. For example, you can describe a Humvee (Hummer) objectively as weighing about 7,600 pounds, or subjectively about as much as three Honda Civics.

You can describe color by coupling a basic color (such as black, white, red, or yellow) with a common object. For instance, instead of describing something as puce or ochre, you might describe the object as "eggplant purple" or "lime green."

You can describe the composition of something by indicating what it is made of, such as a building made of brick, concrete, or wood. Sometimes, you might describe what it looks like rather than what it is. For example, you might say something looks metallic, even if it is made of plastic rather than metal.

You can also describe something by its age and by condition. For example, describing a city as ancient, historic, and well kept produces different mental pictures than does describing a city as old and war torn.

Finally, you can describe spatial organization going from top to bottom, left to right, outer to inner, and so on. A description of the Sistine Chapel, for example, might go from the floor to the ceiling; and a description of a NASCAR automobile might go from the body to the engine to the interior (Photo 16.4).

Definition

Definition is a method that explains the meaning of something. There are four ways to define something. First, you can define a word or idea by classifying it and differentiating it from similar words or ideas. For example, in a speech on vegetarianism, you might use information from the Vegan Society's Web site (www .vegansociety.com): "A vegan is a vegetarian who is seeking a lifestyle free from animal products for the benefit of people, animals, and the environment. Vegans eat a plant-based diet free from all animal products including milk, eggs, and honey. Vegans also don't wear leather, wool, or silk and avoid other animal-based products."

Photo 16.4 How might you describe a NASCAR automobile?

Second, you can define a word by explaining its derivation or history. For instance, the word *vegan* is made from the beginning and ending of the word *vegetarian* and was coined in the United Kingdom in 1944, when the Vegan Society was founded.

Third, you can define a word by explaining its use or function. For example, in vegan recipes, you can use tofu or tempeh to replace meat and use almond milk or soy milk to replace cow's milk (Photo 16.5).

The fourth, and perhaps the quickest way to define something, is by using a familiar synonym or antonym. A **synonym** is a word that has the same or a similar meaning; an **antonym** is a word that has the opposite meaning. So you could define a *vegan* by comparing it to the word *vegetarian*, which is a synonym with a similar although not identical meaning, or to the word *carnivore*, which is an antonym.

definition
method that explains the meaning of something

synonym
word that has the same or similar meaning

antonym
word that has the opposite meaning

comparison and contrast
method that explains something by focusing on how it is similar and different from other things

narration
method that explains something by recounting events or stories

Photo 16.5 How might a presentational aid help enhance your informative speech about veganism?

Comparison and Contrast

Comparison and contrast is a method that focuses on how something is similar to and different from other things. For example, in a speech on veganism, you might tell your audience how vegans are similar and different from other types of vegetarians. You can point out that like vegetarians, vegans don't eat meat. In contrast, semi-vegetarians eat fish or poultry. Like lacto vegetarians, vegans don't eat eggs, but unlike this group and lacto-ovo vegetarians, vegans don't use dairy products. So of all vegetarians, vegans have the most specific diet. Because comparisons and contrasts can be figurative or literal, you can use metaphors and analogies as well as make direct comparisons.

Narration

Narration is a method that recounts an autobiographical or biographical event, myth, or other story. Narratives usually have four parts. First, the narrative orients listeners by describing when and where the event took place and introducing important characters. Second, the narrative explains the sequence of events that led to a complication or problem. Third, the narrative discusses how the complication or problem affected key characters. Finally, the narrative recounts how the complication or problem was solved. The characteristics of a good narrative

Photo 16.6 The first-person narrative method used in the TV program *How I Met Your Mother* is an example of informing. How does this technique capture and maintain audience interest?

include a strong story line; use of descriptive language and detail that enhance the plot, people, setting, and events; effective use of dialogue; pacing that builds suspense; and a strong voice (Baerwald, n.d.).

Narratives can be presented in a first-, second-, or third-person voice (Photo 16.6). A first person narrative reports what you experienced or observed personally, using the pronouns *I, me,* and *my*: "Let me tell you about the first time I tried to water-ski." In a second person narrative, you place your audience at the scene by using pronouns *you* and *your*: "Imagine that you just got off the plane in Hong Kong and cannot read Cantonese. You look at the signs, but can't read a thing. Which way is the terminal?" Finally, in a third person narrative, you describe what has happened, is happening, or will happen to other people by using pronouns like *he, she, his, her,* and *they*: "When the students arrived in Venice for their study-abroad experience, the first thing they saw was the Rialto bridge. "

Demonstration

demonstration

method that explains something by showing how it is done, by displaying the stages of a process, or by depicting how something works

Demonstration is a method that shows how something is done, displays the stages of a process, or depicts how something works. Demonstrations range from very simple with a few easy-to-follow steps (how to craft a cover letter) to very complex (how a nuclear reactor works).

In a demonstration, your experience with what you are demonstrating is critical. Expertise gives you the necessary background to supplement bare-bones instructions with personally lived experience. Why are TV cooking shows so popular? Because the chef doesn't just read the recipe and do what it says. Rather, while performing each step, the chef shares tips that aren't mentioned in any cookbook. It is the chef's experience that allows him or her to say that one egg will work as well as two, or how to tell if the cake is really done.

In a demonstration, organize the steps from first to last to help your audience remember the sequence of actions accurately. If there are many steps, grouping them will also help audiences remember. Suppose you want to demonstrate the steps in using a touch-screen voting machine. If, rather than presenting 14 separate steps, you group them under three headings—(1) Get ready to vote; (2) Review your choices; and (3) Cast your ballot—chances are much higher that your audience will be able to remember them.

Most demonstrations actually show the audience the process or parts of the process. That's in part why the how-to shows on HGTV are so popular. If what you are explaining is relatively simple, you can demonstrate the entire process from start to finish. However, if the process is lengthy or complex, you may choose to pre-prepare material for some of the steps. Although you will show all stages in the process, you will not have to take the time for every single step as the audience watches. For example, many of the ingredients used by TV chefs are already cut up, measured, and separated into small bowls.

Effective demonstrations require practice. Remember that under the pressure of speaking to an audience, even the simplest task can become difficult. (Have you ever tried to thread a needle with 25 people watching you?) As you practice, also consider the size of your audience and the configuration of the room. Be sure that everyone in the audience will be able see what you are doing.

Speech Assignment

A Process Speech

1. Follow the speech plan Action Steps in Chapters 11–15 to prepare a process speech. Your instructor will announce the time limit and other parameters for this assignment.

2. Criteria for evaluation include the general criteria of topic and purpose, content, organization, and presentation, but special emphasis will be placed on how intellectually stimulating the topic is made for the audience, how creatively ideas are presented, and how clearly the important information is emphasized.

3. Prior to presenting your speech, prepare a complete sentence outline and reference list (bibliography), as well as a written plan for adapting your speech to the audience.

Informative Process Speeches

The goal of a **process speech** is to explain and show how something is done, is made, or works. Effective process speeches require you to carefully delineate the steps and the order in which they occur. These steps typically become the main points and explanations of each step become the subpoints. Most process speeches rely heavily on the demonstration method of informing.

Although most process speeches require you to demonstrate, others are not suited to demonstrations. For these, you can use visual or audiovisual aids to help the audience see the steps in the process. In a speech on remodeling a kitchen, it would not be practical to demonstrate the process; however, you could greatly enhance the verbal description by showing visuals before and after the remodeling, as well as short audiovisual clips while the remodeling was being done. Figure 16.2 illustrates some topic examples for process speeches.

process speech
an informative speech that explains and shows how something is done or made, or how it works

APPLY IT

Identify several hobbies you enjoy. Which of them could you develop a process speech on? What steps would you use for your main points?

MindTap®

Process Speech Topics		
How to do it	**How to Make it**	**How it works**
select running shoes	*compost bin*	*3-D movies*
apply for a loan	*rope knots*	*stem cell reproduction*
bouldering	*lefse*	*solar energy*

© 2017 Cengage Learning

Figure 16.2
Process Speech Topics

Informative Expository Speeches

The goal of an **expository speech** is to provide carefully researched, in-depth knowledge about a complex topic. For example, "understanding the gun control debate," "the origins and classification of nursery rhymes," "the sociobiological theory of child abuse," and "rap as poetry" are all topics on which you could give an interesting expository speech.

All expository speeches require speakers to draw from an extensive research base, choose an organizational pattern best suited to topic and goal, and use a variety of informative methods (e.g., descriptions, definitions, comparisons and contrasts,

expository speech
an informative speech that provides carefully researched, in-depth knowledge about a complex topic

narratives, short demonstrations) to sustain the audience's attention and help them understand the material.

Expository speeches include those that explain a political, economic, social, religious, or ethical issue; forces of history; a theory, principle, or law; and a creative work.

Exposition of Political, Economic, Social, Religious, or Ethical Issues

In an expository speech, you have the opportunity to help the audience understand the context of an issue, including the forces that gave rise to and continue to affect it. You may also present the various positions held about the issue and the reasoning behind these positions. Finally, you may discuss various attempts made for resolving the issue.

Since the general goal of your speech is to inform (not to persuade), be sure to present different sides of controversial issues without advocating which side is better. Also, make a concerted effort to present complex issues in ways that help your audience understand them without oversimplifying them. Finally, be sure to carefully evaluate sources for bias. For example, while researching a speech on fracking—the controversial method for extracting natural gas deposits—be sure to consult articles and experts on all sides of this issue and fairly represent those views in your outline. You should discuss not only the technology that is used, but also the controversies that surround its use. If time is limited, you might discuss all sides of just one or two of these issues, but you should at least mention the others, as well. Figure 16.3 provides examples of topic ideas for an expository speech about a political, economic, social, religious, or ethical issue. We once considered broadcast news programs as unbiased. As you read the *Communicating in the World* feature, reflect on whether that assumption still holds true today.

Exposition of Historical Events and Forces It has been said that those who don't understand history may be doomed to repeat it. So an expositional speech about historical events and forces can be fascinating for its own sake, but it can also be relevant for what is happening today. Unfortunately, some people think history is boring. So, you have an obligation to seek out stories and narratives that can enliven your speech. And you will want to analyze the event and its impact at the time it occurred, as well as the meaning it has for us today. For example, most schoolchildren learn about Paul Revere's famous midnight ride warning Americans that the British army was coming. Few know, however, about others who did similar heroic things. In 1777, for instance, 16-year-old Sybil Ludington rode 40 miles through the enemy-infested woods in the dark of night waking men to prepare for an attack. She succeeded in her mission, returned home safely, and was considered a local heroine (Dacquino, 2000). Today, anyone can visit Putnam County New York where she lived, hike the trail she rode that night, and view a statue erected in her

Figure 16.3

Topic ideas for expository speeches about political, economic, social, religious, or ethical issues

gay marriage	cyber bullying	fracking
climate change	home schooling	digital remixing
media bias	stem cell reserach	celebrity culture
gun control	biotechnology	crowdsourcing

© Cengage Learning

COMMUNICATING IN THE WORLD

Coloring the News: Is the Media Biased?

Featureflash/Shutterstock.com

When you watch a newscast or read an online news article, do you expect the information to be reported objectively? Or do you assume that the news media is biased in some way? If you do think the news media is biased, you are not alone. The Pew Research Center for the People and the Press (2011) found that 77 percent of Americans across political affiliations think news organizations "tend to favor one side" and 66 percent believe news organizations are politically biased in their reporting.

In fact, news media were once considered reporters of the truth. One journalist who personified a professional, unbiased delivery—even almost thirty years after his final broadcast as a news anchor—was Walter Cronkite. Cronkite anchored and reported for the *CBS Evening News* from 1962 to 1981 and was so admired and respected that he was named "the most trusted man in America" in a 1972 poll. One communication strategy he employed consistently was to make it very clear when he was veering from reporting the news to expressing an opinion. A tireless advocate of objective journalism, he once said, "[The journalist's] job is only to hold up the mirror—to tell and show the public what has happened" (Leopold, 2009).

Today, however, most Americans agree that media bias is a problem, In fact, recent PEW research polls (2014) report "public polarization of media habits" and the "striking differences between liberals and conservatives" in terms of the stations they turn to for the news. Thus, to be an informed consumer

of news today, it is crucial to learn how to evaluate news bias critically. Fairness and Accuracy in Reporting (FAIR) provides a helpful list of factors that can contribute to bias in news reporting ("What's Wrong with the News?," n.d.):

- Corporate ownership
- Advertiser influence
- Official agendas
- Telecommunications policy
- The public relations industry
- Pressure groups
- The narrow range of debate
- Censorship
- Sensationalism

FAIR also recommends asking the following critical questions when evaluating news information ("How to Detect Bias," n.d.):

- Who are the sources?
- Is there a lack of diversity?
- From whose point of view is the news reported?
- Are there double standards?
- What are the unchallenged assumptions?
- Is the language loaded?
- Is there a lack of context?
- Do the headlines and stories match?
- Are stories on important issues featured prominently?

Perhaps the days of Walter Cronkite and unbiased news reporting are gone for good. What that means for us as consumers then is to take the time to critically evaluate the information we hear and see, as well as the sources from which the "fact" is being drawn.

Do you think biased news reporting is a problem? Explain your answer.

MindTap®

Figure 16.4

Topic ideas for expository speeches about historical events and forces

genocide	the colonization of Africa	Irish immigration
women's suffrage	Ghandi and his movement	the War on Terror
the Olympics Pakistan	the Spanish Flu Epidemic	the Ming Dynasty
the New Madrid Earthquake	the Industrial Revolution	the Balfour Declaration
the papacy	the Vietnam War	the Space Shuttle *Challenger* explosion

© Cengage Learning

honor. Figure 16.4 offers some topic ideas for an expository speech about historical events and forces.

Exposition of a Theory, Principle, or Law The way we live is affected by natural and human laws and principles and is explained by various theories. Yet there are many theories, principles, and laws that we do not completely understand. An expository speech can inform us by explaining these important phenomena. The main challenge is to explain the theory, law, or principle in language that is understandable to the audience. You will want to search for or create examples and illustrations that demystify complicated concepts and terminology. You can also compare unfamiliar ideas with those about which the audience is already familiar. In a speech on the psychological principles of operant conditioning, for instance, a speaker could help the audience understand the difference between continuous reinforcement and intermittent reinforcement in this way:

> When a behavior is reinforced continuously, a reward is given each time the person performs the behavior. When a behavior is reinforced intermittently, however, the reward is not always given when the behavior is performed. Behavior learned via continuous reinforcement stops when the reward no longer is provided. On the contrary, behavior learned via intermittent reinforcement continues for a long time, even when not reinforced with a reward. To clarify, consider the behavior of putting a coin into a machine. If it is a vending machine, we expect to be rewarded every time we "play." If the machine doesn't dispense the item, we might wonder if it is out of order and probably won't put in more coins. But suppose the machine is a slot machine. Who knows how many coins might we "play" before we stop, right? Why the difference? Because we were conditioned to a vending machine on a continuous schedule, but a slot machine "rewards" us on an intermittent schedule.

Figure 16.5 provides some examples of topic ideas for an expository speech about a theory, principle, or law.

natural selection	Boyle's law	Maslow's hierarchy of needs
gravity	number theory	
Murphy's Law	the Law of Diminishing Returns	intelligent design
the Peter Principle		social cognitive theory
feminist theory	color theory	
diminishing returns	psychoanalytic theory	

Figure 16.5

Topic ideas for expository speeches about theories, principles, or laws

© Cengage Learning

Exposition of a Creative Work Courses in art, theatre, music, literature, and film appreciation give students tools by which to recognize the style, historical period, and quality of a particular piece or group of pieces. Yet most of us know very little about how to understand a creative work, so presentations designed to explain creative works like poems, novels, songs, or even famous speeches can be very instructive.

When developing a speech that explains a creative work, you will want to find information on the work and the artist who created it. You will also want to find sources that help you understand the period in which the work was created, as well as learn about the criteria that critics use to evaluate works of this type. For example, if you wanted to give an expository speech on Fredrick Douglass's Fourth of July Oration given in Rochester, New York in 1852, you might need to orient your audience by first reminding them of who Douglass was. Then you might explain the traditional expectations for Fourth of July speakers at this point in history. After this, you might want to summarize the speech and perhaps share a few memorable quotations from it. Finally, you would want to discuss how speech critics view the speech and why the speech is considered "great" still today. Figure 16.6 presents examples of topics for expository speeches about creative works. Figure 16.7 is a checklist you can use to analyze any informative speech you rehearse or to critique the speeches of others.

hip-hop music	the love sonnets of Shakespeare	the *Hunger Games* trilogy
Impressionist painting	Kabuki theater	iconography
salsa dancing	graphic novels	Spike Lee's *Mo' Better Blues*
women in cinema	the Martin Luther King National Memorial	*Boyhood*, the film
the films of Alfred Hitchcock		

Figure 16.6

Topic ideas for expository speeches about creative works

© Cengage Learning

COMMUNICATE ON YOUR FEET

Speech Assignment

An Expository Speech

1. Follow the speech plan Action Steps in Chapters 11–15 to prepare a 5- to 8-minute informative speech in which you present carefully researched, in-depth information about a complex topic. Your instructor will announce other parameters for this assignment.

2. Criteria for evaluation include all the general criteria of topic and purpose, content, organization, and presentation, but special emphasis will be placed on how intellectually stimulating the topic is made for the audience, how creatively ideas are presented, and how clearly the important information is emphasized. Use the informative speech evaluation checklist in Figure 16.7 to critique yourself as you practice your speech.

3. Prior to presenting your speech, prepare a complete-sentence outline, a reference list (bibliography), and a written plan for adapting your speech to the audience.

You can use this form to critique informative speeches you hear in class. As you listen, outline the speech and identify which informative speech framework the speaker is using. Then answer the questions that follow.

Informative Speech Critique

Process Speech:
___ How something is done
___ How something is made
___ How something works

Expository Speech:
___ Exposition of political, economic, social, religious, or ethical issue
___ Exposition of historical events or forces
___ Exposition of a theory, principle, or law
___ Exposition of creative work

General Criteria
___ 1. Was the specific goal clear?
___ 2. Were the main points developed with breadth and depth of appropriate supporting material?
___ 3. Was the introduction effective in creating interest and introducing the main points?
___ 4. Was the speech organized and easy to follow?
___ 5. Was the language appropriate, clear, and vivid?
___ 6. Was the conclusion effective in summarizing the main points and providing closure?
___ 7. Was the vocal delivery intelligible, conversational, and expressive?
___ 8. Did the body actions appear poised, natural, spontaneous, and appropriate?

Specific Criteria for Process Speeches
___ 1. Was the introduction clear in previewing the process to be explained?
___ 2. Was the speech easy to follow and organized in a time order?
___ 3. Were presentational aids used effectively to clarify the process?
___ 4. Did the process use a demonstration method effectively?

Specific Criteria for Expository Speeches
___ 1. Was the specific goal of the speech to provide well-researched information on a complex topic?
___ 2. Did the speaker effectively use a variety of methods to convey the information?
___ 3. Did the speaker emphasize the main ideas and important supporting material?
___ 4. Did the speaker present in-depth, high-quality, appropriately cited information?

Figure 16.7

Informative speech evaluation checklist

© Cengage Learning

SAMPLE SPEECH PLAN AND OUTLINE

Sample Informative Speech

This section presents a sample informative speech given by a student, including an adaptation plan, an outline, and a transcript.

Internet Identity Theft: Self-Protection Steps

Anna Rankin

MindTap Read the speech adaptation plan, outline, and transcript of a speech by Anna Rankin. You can access a video of Anna's speech through the Chapter 16 resources of your MindTap for *Communicate*! You can also use your MindTap to analyze this speech in terms of concepts covered in this chapter.

Adaptation Plan

1. **Key aspects of audience.** Most people in my audience are probably aware of identity theft but probably don't know all the steps they can take to protect themselves from becoming victims of it.

2. **Establishing and maintaining common ground.** I will begin my speech by using a hypothetical example placing them as victims of Internet identity theft. Throughout the speech, I will refer to the audience's previous knowledge and experience.

3. **Building and maintaining interest.** I will try to gain interest in the introduction by relating the problem of Internet identity theft to college students. Throughout the speech, I will use common analogies and metaphors to explain the self-protection steps. Finally, I will use a well-designed PowerPoint presentation to capture and maintain attention.

4. **Audience knowledge and sophistication.** Because most of the class is probably not familiar with the actual self-protection steps regarding Internet identity theft, I will focus specifically on them throughout my speech.

5. **Building credibility.** Early in the speech, I will tell the audience how I got interested in Internet identity theft and the research I did to learn about it as a pre-law student.

6. **Audience attitudes.** I will try to address audience apathy by using interesting examples and compelling stories they can easily relate to.

7. **Adapting to audiences from different cultures and language-communities.** I will use visual and audiovisual aids in my PowerPoint presentation to help those listeners from different cultures understand what I'm talking about even though English is not their native language.

8. **Using presentational aids to enhance understanding and memory.** Throughout the speech, I will use color-coded PowerPoint slides with headers to reinforce the steps being discussed.

Formal Outline

General goal: To inform

Specific goal: I want my audience to understand the steps to protect themselves from online identity theft.

Introduction

Attention getter

I. Imagine this: you are filing your income tax return after starting your first real job after college. After completing the tedious online forms, you hit the "calculate" button. You are ecstatic when the online filing system says you are due a return of a whopping $2,800! Then, imagine hitting "file" to submit your tax return. Then you get the error message "*Your tax return has already been processed.*" Someone has stolen your identity and pocketed your return.

Listener relevance

II. If you think this cannot happen to you, think again! According to the U.S. Government Accountability Office (White, 2012), approximately 642,000 cases of tax-related identity theft were reported in the first nine months of 2012 alone.

Speaker credibility and listener relevance

III. Through my research, I discovered that 8.3 million Americans were victims of identity theft in 2005 (FTC, 2007). Identity theft can happen when someone simply digs through your trash for bank statements and most of us now shred such items before discarding them. Recently, however, Internet identity theft is becoming far more prevalent (U.S. Department of Justice, n.d.). An identity thief who accesses your information online can apply for jobs, loans, and credit cards, can receive medical care or prescription drugs, and can make large purchases all under your name (FTC, 2012).

Thesis statement with main point preview

IV. Today, let's discuss several simple steps we can all take to prevent Internet identity theft (*Show Slide 1: Four Steps to Prevent Identity Theft*). These three steps are designed to help prevent phishing, hacking, and pharming.

Body

First main point

I. The first step in preventing online identity theft is to protect yourself from phishing (*Show Slide 2: Email Phishing [Photo]*).

Listener relevance

A. Most likely, everyone in this room receives hundreds of email messages every week. Whether it is an update from our college professor or coupons from our favorite retail stores, we are bombarded with emails that we do not hesitate to open or reply to.

B. Phishing is a process through which identity thieves persuade Internet users to provide personal information by posing as legitimate organizations (NCPC, 2013).

   1. Identity thieves might send you an email that appears to be from a legitimate organization.

   2. In it, they will ask you to provide personal information such as your bank account numbers, social security number, or personal passwords.

C. One way to prevent phishing is by never providing personal information online without verifying the legitimacy of the sender.

   1. Always contact the organization's customer service number provided to verify the legitimacy of the email.

   2. And make it a standard practices to always provide such information over the phone rather than via email (FTC, 2012).

D. Another way to avoid becoming a victim of identity theft through phishing is never to click on links in emails from unknown sources (NCPC, 2013).

   1. Clicking on these links can automatically install software on your computer that re-routes your personal information to the identity thief's personal data collection website.

   2. Once the thief or thieves have this information, they can basically "become you" all over the Internet.

Now that we all know what we can do to keep our identity safe through good email practices, let's consider how we can prevent identity theft by surfing the Internet wisely.

II. The second step we can take to protect ourselves from identity theft is to prevent hacking (*Show Slide 3: Computer Hacking [Photo]*).

A. Take a moment to think about all the personal and financial information you have stored on your electronic devices. If someone were to gain open access to your computer, or even to your smart phone for that matter, he or she would be able to steal your identity in a few swipes of the keys.

B. Hacking refers to a process through which an identity thief gains access to your personal computer to view documents, files, and personal information (NCPC, 2013).

C. Here are a few simple steps you can take to protect yourself from becoming a victim of hacking.

1. The first step is to password-protect all of your accounts and devices, and to get creative with your passwords (FTC, 2012).

   a. Avoid using personal information such as your name, date of birth, address, or other personal information that is easily discovered by others (NCPC, 2013).

   b. Never use words that are found in the dictionary—some hacking programs can quickly attempt every word found in the dictionary to access your information.

   c. Try creating acronyms that you will always remember. For example, the phrase "I graduate from college in 2017" could turn into the password IgFcI2k16—a strong and unique password that you can easily remember (*Show Slide 4: Unique Password Examples*)!

   d. Finally, avoid sharing too much information on social networking sites. If an identity thief finds out enough about your personal life, they can easily answer those "challenge" questions you use to keep your accounts and devices protected.

2. The second step to protect identity theft from hacking is to be sure you wipe clean any of your electronic devices before selling them or disposing of them (FTC, 2012).

   a. Before you dispose of your laptop or smart phone, eliminate any personal information including saved passwords, photos, web search histories, and contact information.

   b. There are several programs you can use to wipe your hard drive clean. However, the National Crime Protection Council (2005) suggests removing and destroying your computer's hard drive altogether before selling or disposing of your laptop.

So now that we know how to protect our email accounts from phishing and our computers from hacking, let's focus on what we need to do to protect ourselves from the most advanced method of online identity theft.

III. The third step in protecting ourselves from identity theft is to prevent pharming (*Show Slide 5: Pharming Website Dangers [Photo]*).

A. Virtually every day, we engage in online transactions. We may log on to our online banking to make sure we have enough money for dinner with friends, we may purchase a gift for someone using Amazon.com, or we may pay tuition using the online payment system.

B. Pharming, one of the toughest methods of online identity theft to detect, is a process through which criminals hack established websites, such as Amazon.com, and re-route the website to a "poser" website that looks very similar and allows them to gather our personal information during a transaction (NCPC, 2005).

C. Although pharming is the most difficult method of identity theft to detect, there are a few steps we can take to protect ourselves when making online transactions.

1. First, look for the "lock" icon on your Internet browser's status bar. This lock indicates that the website you are on is safe (*Show Slide 6: Internet Browser Safety Features*).

2. Next, verify that the website is secure by inspecting the URL. A safe website URL will begin with https:// instead of http://

3. Finally, you can purchase encryption software that makes sure any information you send over the Internet is jumbled and unreadable to others.

Conclusion

Thesis restatement

I. As you can see, the Internet is literally a gold mine for identity thieves when our personal information is not protected.

Main point summary

II. Fortunately, we can take steps to protect ourselves from phishing, hacking, and pharming (*Show Slide 7 [same as slide 1]*).

Clincher

III. According to a 2011 article in the *New York Times* (Perlroth, 2011), it is extremely difficult to prosecute online identity thieves even though they deserve it. One thing we can do, however, is to put a padlock on our goldmines so these criminals can't access them in the first place!

References

Federal Trade Commission. (2007). FTC releases survey of identity theft in the U.S. study shows 8.3 million victims in 2005. Retrieved from http://www.ftc.gov/opa/2007/11/idtheft.shtm

Federal Trade Commission. (2012). Identity theft. Retrieved from http://www.consumer.ftc.gov/features/feature-0014-identity-theft

Koster, C. (n.d.) Identity theft. Retrieved from the Missouri Attorney General Web site: http://ago.mo.gov/publications/idtheft.htm#header3

National Crime Prevention Council. (2013). Evolving with technology: A comprehensive introduction to cybercrime with links to resources. Retrieved from: http://www.ncpc.org/topics/fraud-and-identity-theft/evolving-with-technology

Perlroth, N. (2011, December 19). A unit to fight cybercrimes. The New York Times. Retrieved from http://query.nytimes.com/

U.S. Department of Justice. (n.d.). Identity theft and fraud. Retrieved from http://www.justice.gov/criminal/fraud/websites/idtheft.html

White, J. R. (2012). Identity theft: Total extent of refund fraud using stolen identities is unknown (GAO Publication No. GAO-13-132T). Washington, DC: U.S. Government Accountability Office. Retrieved from http://www.gao.gov/assets/660/650365.pdf

SPEECH AND ANALYSIS

Speech	Analysis

Online Identity Theft (Process Speech)
Anna Rankin

Imagine this: you are filing your income tax return after starting your first real job after college. After completing the tedious online forms, you hit the "calculate" button. You are ecstatic when the online filing system says you are due a return of a whopping $2,800! Then, imagine hitting "file" to submit your tax return and you get the error message "*Your tax return has already been processed.*" Someone has stolen your identity and pocketed your return.

If you think this cannot happen to you, think again! According to a U.S. Government Accountability Office report published in 2012, approximately 642,000 cases of tax-related identity theft were reported in the first nine months of 2012 alone. Through my research, I discovered that 8.3 million Americans were victims of identity theft in 2005. Of course, identity theft can happen when someone simply digs through your trash for bank statements and most of us now shred such items before discarding them. Recently, however, according the U.S. Department of Justice, Internet identity theft is becoming far more prevalent. According to the Federal Trade Commission, an identity thief who accesses your information online can apply for jobs, loans, and credit cards, can receive medical care or prescription drugs, and can make large purchases all under your name.

Today, let's discuss several simple steps we can all take to prevent Internet identity theft (*Show Slide 1: Four Steps to Prevent Identity Theft*). These three steps are designed to help prevent phishing, hacking, and pharming.

The first step in preventing online identity theft is to protect ourselves from phishing (*Show Slide 2: Email Phishing [Photo]*). Most likely, everyone in this room receives hundreds of email messages every week. Whether it is an update from our college professor or coupons from our favorite retail stores, we are bombarded with emails that we do not hesitate to open or reply to.

According to the National Crime Protection Council, phishing is a process through which identity thieves persuade Internet users to provide personal information by posing as legitimate organizations. Identity thieves might send you an email that appears to be from a legitimate organization. In it, they will ask you to provide personal information such as your bank account numbers, social security number, or personal passwords.

One way to prevent phishing is by never providing personal information online without verifying the legitimacy of the sender. Always contact the organization's customer service number provided to verify the legitimacy of the email. And make it a standard practice to always provide your information over the phone rather than via email.

Another way to avoid becoming a victim of identity theft through phishing is never to click on links in emails from unknown sources. Clicking on these links can automatically install software on your computer that re-routes your personal information to the identity thief's personal data collection website. Once the thief or thieves have this information, they can basically "become you" all over the Internet.

Notice how Anna uses a hypothetical example to draw her audience into her speech with this attention getter. Not only that, she also offers listener relevance by using a dollar amount that most college students would find enticing.

This paragraph is chock full of listener relevant statements supported with evidence from reputable sources, which serve to establish Anna's credibility very well.

Anna very succinctly offers her thesis and main point preview using personal pronouns and "we" language that foster a sense of immediacy with her audience.

As Anna presents her first main point, she also incorporates a listener relevance link that piques audience member interest.

Anna appeals to the thinking dimension of the learning cycle here with a clear definition and explanation of what phishing is.

Here Anna appeals to the doing dimension of the learning cycle by offering specific things listeners can do to protect themselves from online identity theft.

Although this is another great action step, Anna could have improved by offering a narrative from someone who experienced this or referencing the 2013 feature film focused on this topic.

Now that we all know what we can do to keep our identity safe through good email practices, let's consider how we can prevent identity theft by surfing the Internet wisely.

The second step we can take to protect ourselves from identity theft is to prevent hacking (*Show Slide 3: Computer Hacking [Photo]*).

Take a moment to think about all the personal and financial information you have stored on your electronic devices. If someone were to gain open access to your computer, or even to your smart phone for that matter, he or she would be able to steal your identity in a few swipes of the keys.

Hacking refers to a process through which an identity thief gains access to our personal computers to view documents, files, and personal information. Fortunately, the Federal Trade Commission and the National Crime Protection Council outline several things we can do to protect ourselves from becoming a victim of hacking. The first step is to password-protect all of our accounts and devices, and to get creative with our passwords. We can avoid using personal information such as name, date of birth, address, or other personal information that is easily discovered by others. We can also avoid using words that are found in the dictionary—some hacking programs can quickly attempt every word found in the dictionary to access our information. And we can create acronyms that we will always remember. For example, the phrase "I graduate from college in 2017" could turn into the password IgFcI2k16—a strong and unique password that you can easily remember if you are graduating in 2016 (*Show Slide 4: Unique Password Examples*)! Finally, we can avoid sharing too much information on social networking sites. If an identity thief finds out enough about our personal life, they can easily answer those "challenge" questions we use to keep our accounts and devices protected.

Another way to protect identity theft from hacking is to be sure you wipe clean any of your electronic devices before selling them or disposing of them. Before you dispose of your laptop or smart phone, eliminate any personal information including saved passwords, photos, web search histories, and contact information. There are several programs you can use to wipe your hard drive clean. However, the National Crime Protection Council suggests removing and destroying your computer's hard drive altogether before selling or disposing of your laptop.

So now that we know how to protect our email accounts from phishing and our computers from hacking, let's focus on what we need to do to protect ourselves from the most advanced method of online identity theft.

The third step in protecting ourselves from identity theft is to prevent pharming (*Show Slide 5: Pharming Website Dangers [Photo]*).

Virtually every day, we engage in online transactions. We may log on to our online banking to make sure we have enough money for dinner with friends, we may purchase a gift for someone using Amazon.com, or we may pay our tuition using the online payment system.

Pharming, according to the National Crime Protection Council, is one of the toughest methods of online identity theft to detect. It is essentially a process through which criminals hack established websites, such as Amazon.com, and re-route the website to a "poser" website that looks very similar and allows them to gather our personal information during a transaction. Although pharming is the most difficult method of identity theft to detect, there are a few steps we can take to protect ourselves when making online transactions.

Anna does a great job here of tying the two points together using "we" language that fosters immediacy.

Here again Anna does a great job establishing personal relevance for her second main point.

Although this is great information, it might be clearly for the listener if Anna would break it into two points: (1) password protection and (2) creative passwords.

Again, this is interesting and helpful information that could be more compelling with oral footnotes to reputable sources and a narrative account from someone who experienced it.

Notice how Anna again provides a transition that verbally ties the two main points together creating a fluent sense of forward motion into her next main point.

Here Anna provides great examples that should help her classmates see the relevance of what she is discussing and, thus, motivate them to stay tuned in.

Here and throughout the speech Anna provides excellent information. What is missing, however, are personal quotations, stories, and testimonials that would appeal to the feeling dimension of the learning cycle.

First, we can look for the "lock" icon on the Internet browser's status bar. This lock indicates that the website we are on is safe (*Show Slide 6: Internet Browser Safety Features*). And we can verify that the website is secure by inspecting the URL. A safe website URL will begin with https:// instead of http:// Finally, we can purchase encryption software that makes sure any information we send over the Internet is jumbled and unreadable to others.

As you can see, the Internet is literally a gold mine for identity thieves when our personal information is not protected. Fortunately, we can take steps to protect ourselves from phishing, hacking, and pharming (*Show Slide 7 [same as slide 1]*). According to a 2011 article in the *New York Times*, it is extremely difficult to prosecute online identity thieves even though they deserve it. One thing we can do, however, is to put a padlock on our goldmines so these criminals can't access them in the first place!

Anna makes her conclusion more memorable by using the analogy of a "goldmine" to refer to our identities and identity thieves as "criminals."

WHAT WOULD YOU DO?

A Question of Ethics

After class, Gina and Paul were discussing what they intended to talk about in their process speeches. Paul said, "I think I'm going to talk about how to make a synthetic diamond."

Gina was impressed. "That sounds interesting. I didn't know you had expertise with that."

"I don't. But the way I see it, Professor Henderson will really be impressed with my speech because my topic will be so novel."

"Well, yeah," Gina replied, "but didn't he stress that for this speech we should choose a topic that was important to us and that we knew a lot about?"

"Sure," Paul said sarcastically, "he's going to be impressed if I talk about how to maintain a blog? Forget it. Just watch—everyone's going to think I make diamonds in my basement, and I'm going to get a good grade."

What would you say to Paul if you were Gina and why?

MindTap®

Reflection and Assessment

Informative speeches explain facts, truths, and principles in ways that stimulate interest, facilitate understanding, and increase the likelihood that audiences will remember. In short, informative speeches are designed to educate. To assess how well you've learned what we addressed in this chapter, answer the following questions. If you have trouble answering any of them, go back and review that material. Once you can answer each question accurately, you are ready to move ahead to read the next chapter.

1. What are the primary characteristics of informative speeches?

2. What informative speaking methods can you employ to develop your speeches?

3. What are some topics you could explore for an informative process speech?

4. What are some topic areas you might consider for an informative expository speech?

COMMUNICATE!

RESOURCE AND ASSESSMENT CENTER

MindTap®

Now that you have read Chapter 16, go to your MindTap for *Communicate!* for quick access to the electronic resources that accompany this text.

Applying What You've Learned

Impromptu Speech Activity

Pick three slips of paper from a container offered by your instructor. Each slip will identify a historical event or historical figure on it. Select one event you'd like to experience or one figure you'd like to meet if you could travel back in time. Do a 2- to 3-minute impromptu speech about why you'd like to experience that historical event or meet that historical figure if you could travel back in time.

Assessment Activities

1. Evaluating Demonstrations Watch an informative speech involving a demonstration, and evaluate how effectively the speaker performs the demonstration. (Do-it-yourself and home improvement TV programs, like those on the cable channels DIY and HGTV, often feature demonstrations, as do programs on the Food Network.) Did the speaker perform a complete or modified demonstration? Did the speaker use only the tools and equipment needed to perform the demonstrated task, or did he or she also use other items, such as visual aids? How effective was the demonstration overall? Were there any areas of the demonstration the speaker could have improved?

2. Evaluating Descriptions Identify a contemporary celebrity (e.g., television or movie actor, sports star, or musician). Learn more about that person by visiting his or her personal Web site or blog, a social networking site devoted to him or her, and an entertainment magazine. How does the information differ in each source? Why might he or she be an appropriate person to do an expository speech on (or not)? How trustworthy do you think the information you have discovered is and why? What might you do to verify the truth of your information and credibility of your sources?

Skill-Building Activity

Creating Process and Expository Informative Speech Goals For each subject area listed below, create a process an expository informative speech goal statement.

    a. hip hop music

    b. U.S. Presidents

    c. murder mysteries

    d. earthquakes

Persuasive Speaking

○ **When you've finished this chapter, you'll be able to:**

- Explain how people listen to and process persuasive messages.
- Write your persuasive speech goal as a proposition tailored to your target audience.
- Apply logos in your persuasive messages.
- Apply ethos in your persuasive messages.
- Apply pathos in your persuasive messages.
- Organize your persuasive speeches using an appropriate persuasive speech pattern.

MindTap®

Start with quick warm-up activity.

Rick loves his golden retriever, Trini. He lives in an apartment downtown and enjoys taking Trini for walks twice a day, but he wishes there was a place nearby where he could let Trini off her leash to run. He decides to try to convince the city council to fence off an area of a large inner-city park and turn it into a dog park where owners can let their dogs run free. He needs to circulate a petition about the idea, get at least 500 others to sign it, and collect $1000 in donations to help pay for the fence. Rick easily gathers more than enough signatures. However, after a few weeks of knocking on doors, he hasn't even raised half of the $1,000 he needs. He wonders what he can do to convince more people to actually donate money for the cause.

This scenario is not unusual. As is the case with Rick and the downtown dog park, whenever we attempt convince others to agree with our position or behave a certain way, we actually construct and present persuasive messages. How successful we are, however, actually depends on how effectively we employ persuasive strategies in doing so. **Persuasion** is the word we use to label this process of influencing people's attitudes, beliefs, values, or behaviors. **Persuasive speaking** is the process of doing so in a public speech.

Persuasive messages are pervasive. Whether we are attempting to convince others or others are attempting to convince us, we are constantly involved in influencing or being influenced. Friends convince us to go to a particular movie or eat at a certain restaurant, salespeople persuade us to buy a certain sweater or pair of shoes, and advertisements bombard us whenever we turn on the radio or television, or log onto the Internet. It is critical to understand persuasion so we can critically examine and evaluate the persuasive messages we receive and can create effective and ethical peruasive messages of our own.

In this chapter, we begin by describing the nature of persuasive messages and how people process them. Then, we explain how to form an effective persuasive speech goal and develop it with logos, ethos, and pathos. Finally, we discuss several persuasive speech patterns you can use to organize your speech.

The Nature of Persuasion

Persuasive messages are fundamentally different from informative ones. Whereas the goal of an informative message is to teach, the goal of a persuasive message is to lead. Persuasive speakers are only successful when their audience members are convinced to agree, change their behavior, or take action. In the opening scenario, Rick was successful in convincing others to agree with him, but unsuccessful in getting them to take action.

Persuasive speaking can actually be traced to its roots in ancient Greece, where men used it to debate public issues and make important decisions. Thinkers like Aristotle and Plato used the word **rhetoric** to mean using any and all "available means of persuasion" (Solmsen, 1954, p. 24). Persuasive speakers do so by developing solid arguments. An argument, in this context, is not synonymous with "quarrel" as we sometimes define it today. Rather, **argument** means articulating a position with the support of logos, ethos, and pathos (Perloff, 2010). **Logos** is a persuasive strategy of constructing logical arguments that uses evidence and reasoning to support a position. **Ethos** is a persuasive strategy of highlighting your competence, credibility, and good character as a means to convince others to support your position (Kennedy, 1980). And **pathos** is a persuasive strategy of appealing to emotions in order to convince others to support your position. We make our decisions about whether to accept the arguments being presented to us in one of two general ways.

Processing Persuasive Messages

Recall our discussion in Chapter 2 about the Elaboration Likelihood Model (ELM). According to this dual processing model, we process persuasive messages in one of two ways. Sometimes we use the "central route" and listen carefully, reflect thoughtfully, and maybe even mentally elaborate on the message before making a decision. In doing so, we base our decision primarily on appeals to logic and reasoning (logos). The second way, called the "peripheral route," is a shortcut that relies on simple cues, such as a quick evaluation of the speaker's competence, credibility, and character (ethos), or a gut check about what we feel (pathos) about the message (Photo 17.1).

We choose a route based on how important we perceive the issue to be for us. When we believe the issue is important, we will expend the energy necessary to process it using the central route. When we don't, we take the peripheral route. For example, if you have a serious chronic illness that is expensive to treat, you are more likely to pay attention to and evaluate carefully any proposals to change health care benefits. If you are healthy, you are more likely to quickly agree with suggestions from someone you perceive to be credible or with a proposal that seems compassionate. The ELM also suggests that when we form attitudes as a result of central processing, we are less likely to change our minds than when we base our decisions on peripheral cues.

When you prepare a persuasive speech, use strategies that address both the central and peripheral routes. In other words, be sure to integrate rhetorical strategies that appeal to logos (logic and reasoning), which will appeal best to audience members using the central processing route and rhetorical strategies that appeal to both ethos (competence, credibility, and good character) and pathos (emotions) to appeal to audience members using the peripheral processing route. Ultimately, the most compelling persuasive messages offer appeals to all three: logos, ethos, and pathos. Before doing so, however, you need to form your speech goal as a proposition.

Photo 17.1 Many Hollywood celebrities are also activists for social equality across the globe. How does the fact that Angelina Jolie is a Hollywood celebrity and activist influence your perception of her ethos?

Persuasive Speech Goals

Persuasive speech goals are stated as propositions. A **proposition** is a declarative sentence that clearly indicates the position you advocate. For example, "I want to convince my audience that pirating (downloading from the Internet) copyrighted media without paying for it is wrong." Notice how a persuasive proposition differs from an information speech goal on the same subject: "I want to inform my audience about the practice of pirating copyrighted media." In the informative speech, you will achieve your goal if the audience understands and remembers what you talk about. In the persuasive speech, however, they must not only understand and remember, but also agree with your position and possibly even take action. The three types of propositions are fact, value, and policy.

Types of Propositions

A **proposition of fact** is a statement designed to convince your audience that something: (1) did, probably did, probably did not, or did not exist or occur; (2) is, probably is, probably is not, or is not true; or (3) will, probably will, probably will not, or will not occur. Although propositions of fact may or may not be true—both positions are arguable—they are stated as though they are, in fact, true. For example, whether or not Princess Diana's death was an unfortunate car accident or an assassination is debatable. So you could argue a proposition of fact in two ways: "Princess Diana's death was nothing more than a tragic car accident" or "Princess Diana's death was, in fact, a successful

---

APPLY IT

Think of a time when you were persuaded because you perceived the speaker as "really smart." Which processing route would you say you used and why?

MindTap®

---

proposition
a declarative sentence that clearly indicates the speaker's position on the topic

proposition of fact
a statement designed to convince the audience that something did or did not occur, is or is not true, or will or will not occur

assassination attempt." Examples of propositions of fact concerning the present include "God exists" or "There is no God"; and "Mobile phone use causes brain cancer" or "Mobile phone use does not cause brain cancer." Propositions of fact concerning the future are predictions. For example, "Thanks to the Internet, iPads, and Kindles, paper-bound books will eventually cease to exist," and "The New York Yankees will surely win the World Series next year" are propositions of fact concerning the future.

A **proposition of value** is a statement designed to convince your audience that something is good, bad, desirable, undesirable, fair, unfair, moral, immoral, sound, unsound, beneficial, harmful, important, or unimportant (van Eemeren, Garssen, Krabbe, Henkemans, Verheij, & Wagemans, 2014). You can attempt to convince your audience that something has more value than something else, or you can attempt to convince them that something meets valued standards. "Running is a better form of exercise than bicycling" is an example of the former, and "The real value of a college education is that it creates an informed citizenry" is an example of the latter.

A **proposition of policy** is a statement designed to convince your audience that a particular rule, plan, or course of action should be taken. Propositions of policy implore listeners by using phrases such as *do it/don't do it*, *should/shouldn't*, and *must/must not*. "All college students *should* be required to take an oral communication skills course in order to graduate," "The U.S. *must* stop deep-sea oil drilling," "Water packaged in plastic bottles *should* be taxed to pay for the cost of recycling," and "*Don't* text while driving" are propositions of policy. Figure 17.1 provides several examples of how propositions of fact, value, and policy can be developed from the same topic idea.

proposition of value
a statement designed to convince the audience that something is good, fair, moral, sound, etc., or its opposite

proposition of policy
a statement designed to convince the audience that a specific course of action should or should not be taken

Propositions of fact	Propositions of value	Propositions of policy
Mahatma Gandhi was the father of passive resistance.	Mahatma Gandhi was a moral leader.	Mahatma Gandhi should be given a special award for his views on and practices of passive resistance.
Pharmaceutical advertising to consumers increases prescription drug prices.	Advertising of new prescription drugs on TV is better than marketing new drugs directly to doctors.	Pharmaceutical companies should be prohibited from advertising prescription drugs on TV.
Using paper ballots is a reliable method for voting in U.S. elections.	Paper ballots are better than electronic voting machines.	Using paper ballots should be required for U.S. elections.

© Cengage Learning

Figure 17.1

Examples of persuasive speech propositions

Tailoring Propositions to Your Target Audience

Because it is very difficult to convince people to change their minds, what you can hope to accomplish in one speech depends on where your audience stands on your topic. So you'll want to analyze your audience and tailor your proposition based on their initial attitude toward the topic.

Audience members' attitudes can range from highly favorable to strongly opposed and can be visualized on a continuum like the one in Figure 17.2. Even though an

Highly opposed	Opposed	Mildly opposed	Neither in favor nor opposed	Mildly in favor	In favor	Highly in favor
2	2	(11)	1	2	2	0

© Cengage Learning

Figure 17.2

Sample speech continuum

audience will include individuals with opinions at nearly every point along the continuum, generally audience members' opinions tend to cluster in one area of it. For instance, most of the audience members represented in Figure 17.2 are "mildly opposed," even though a few people are more highly opposed and a few have favorable opinions. This cluster point represents your **target audience**, the group of people you most want to persuade. Based on your target audience, you can classify your audience's initial attitude toward your topic as "in favor" (already supportive), "no opinion" (uninformed, neutral, or apathetic), or "opposed" (holding an opposite point of view).

Opposed It is unrealistic to believe that you will change your target audience's attitude from "opposed" to "in favor" in only one short speech. Instead, seek **incremental change**, that is, attempt to move them only a small degree in your direction, hoping for additional movement later. For example, if your target audience is opposed to the goal "I want to convince my audience that gay marriage should be legalized," you might rephrase it to "I want to convince my audience that committed gay couples should be afforded the same legal protection as committed heterosexual couples through state-recognized civil unions." Then brainstorm potential objections, questions, and criticisms that might arise and shape your speech to address them.

No Opinion If your target audience has no opinion for or against your topic, consider whether they are uninformed, neutral, or apathetic (Photo 17.2). If they are **uninformed**, that is, they do not know enough about the topic to have formed an opinion, provide the basic arguments and information needed for them to become informed. For example, if your target audience is uninformed about the topic of gay marriage, you might need to begin by highlighting the legal benefits of marriage in general. If your target audience is **neutral**, that is, they know the basics about your topic but not enough to have formed an opinion, provide evidence and reasoning illustrating why your position is superior to others. Perhaps your audience knows the legal benefits of marriage in general but needs to understand how committed gay couples who do not have these benefits are disadvantaged. When target audience members have no opinion because they are **apathetic**, find ways to show how it relates to them or their needs. In other words, provide answers to a question such as, "I'm not gay, so why should I care?" You can do this by including strong listener relevance links for each main point.

In Favor If your target audience is only mildly in favor of your proposal, your task is to reinforce and strengthen their beliefs. Audience members who favor your topic may become further committed to the belief

target audience
the group of people a speaker most wants to persuade

incremental change
attempt to move audience only a small degree in the speaker's direction

uninformed
not knowing enough about a topic to have formed an opinion

neutral
knowing the basics about a topic but still having no opinion about it

apathetic
having no opinion because one is uninterested, unconcerned, or indifferent to a topic

Photo 17.2 When trying to convince people to give money to a cause, is it more challenging when your audience is apathetic, or when they are neutral?

BRUCE ACKERMAN/Landov

Photo 17.3 Logos is making an argument by drawing inferences from factual information to support your conclusion. What inferences might you draw based on this photo?

by hearing new reasons and more recent evidence that support it. When your target audience strongly agrees with your position, then you can consider a proposition that moves them to act on it. For example, if the topic is gay marriage and your target audience is in favor of the idea, then your goal may be "I want my audience members to e-mail or write letters to their state representatives urging them to support legislation extending the right to marry to same sex couples." Jeff did so in his speech about exorbitant course fees for college classes. Since he knew his classmates agreed, he tailored his goal as a proposition of policy to lobby the state legislature, the university's Board of Trustees, and the campus president to stop raising them for two full years. Once you have identified your topic and tailored your proposition to your target audience, you are ready to develop content by using rhetorical strategies appealing to logos, ethos, and pathos.

Rhetorical Appeals to Logos

Logos strategies are built on logic and reasoning. Stephen Toulmin (1958) developed a three-part model to describe logos arguments that has stood the test of time. A sound argument consists of a claim, support, and warrant (Photo 17.3).

claim
the conclusion the speaker wants the audience to agree with

The **claim (C)** is the conclusion the speaker wants the audience to agree with. For example, you might *claim:* "Jim's car needs a tune-up." The **support (S)** is the evidence offered as grounds for accepting/agreeing with the claim. You can support a claim with facts, opinions, experiences, and observations. In the car example, we might support our claim with observations that the engine is "missing at slow speeds" and "stalling at stop-lights." The **warrant (W)** is the reasoning process that connects the support to the claim. Sometimes the warrant is verbalized and sometimes it is implied. In the car example, you might offer a warrant such as "Missing at slow speeds and stalling at lights *are common indications* that a car needs a tune-up." Or you might assume that others see these as signs that a car needs a tune-up. Not knowing whether audience members will make these connections, however, the most effective public speakers verbalize their reasoning warrants.

support
evidence offered as grounds to accept the claim

warrant
reasoning process that connects the support to the claim

You can connect your supporting evidence to the claim using an inductive or deductive reasoning warrant. **Inductive reasoning** is arriving at a general conclusion based on several pieces of specific evidence. When we reason inductively, how much our audience agrees with our conclusion depends on the number, quality, and typicality of each piece of evidence you offer. For Jim's car, an inductive reasoning argument might look like this:

inductive reasoning
arriving at a general conclusion based on several pieces of evidence

S: Jim's car is missing at slow speeds.
S: Jim's car is stalling at stoplights.
W: These are common indicators that a car needs a tune-up.
C: Jim's car needs a tune-up.

deductive reasoning
arguing that if something is true for everything in a certain class, then it is true for a given item in that class

Deductive reasoning is arguing that if something is true for everything that belongs to a certain class (major premise) and a specific instance is part of that class (minor premise), then we must conclude that what is true for all members of the class must be true in the specific instance (claim). This three-part form of deductive reasoning is called a **syllogism**. For Jim's car, a deductive syllogism might look like this:

> Major Premise: Cars need a tune-up when the engine misses consistently at slow speeds.
> Minor Premise: Jim's car is missing at slow speeds.
> Claim: Jim's car needs a tune-up.

With this introduction in mind, let's look at some different types of logical arguments.

Types of Logical Arguments

Although a logical argument *always* includes a claim and support, different types of reasoning warrants can be used to illustrate the relationship between the claim and the support. Four common types of such reasoning are sign, example, analogy, and causation.

Arguing from Sign You **argue from sign** when you support a claim by providing evidence that certain events that signal the claim have occurred. The general warrant for reasoning from sign is: When phenomena that usually or always accompany a specific situation occur, then we can expect that specific situation is occurring (or will occur). For example: "Hives and a slight fever are indicators (signs) of an allergic reaction."

Signs should not be confused with causes; signs accompany a phenomenon but do not bring about, lead to, or create the claim. In fact, signs may actually be the effects of the phenomenon. In the allergy example, a rash and fever don't *cause* an allergic reaction; however, they are indications of a reaction.

When arguing from sign, make sure that your reasoning is valid by answering the following questions:

1. Do these signs always or usually accompany the conclusion drawn?

2. Are a sufficient number of signs present?

3. Are contradictory signs present?

If your answer to either of the first two questions is "no" or your answer to the third is "yes," then your reasoning is flawed.

Arguing from Example You **argue from example** when the evidence you use as support are examples of the claim you are making. The warrant for reasoning from example is: "What is true in the examples provided is (or will be) true in general or in other instances."

Suppose you support Juanita Martinez for president of the local neighborhood council. One of your reasons is that "Juanita is electable." You provide several examples of her previous victories to support your claim. She was elected treasurer of her high school junior class, chairperson of her church youth group, and president of her college sorority.

When arguing from example, make sure your reasoning is valid by answering the following questions:

1. Are enough examples cited?

2. Are the examples typical?

3. Are negative examples accounted for?

If the answer to any of these questions is "no," then your reasoning is flawed.

syllogism
the three-part form of deductive reasoning

arguing from sign
supports a claim by citing information that signals the claim

arguing from example
supports a claim by providing one or more individual examples

APPLY IT

Do cats or dogs make better pets? Provide as many examples as you can think of to support your claim. Do you think your reasoning is valid? Why or why not?

MindTap

Arguing from Analogy

You **argue from analogy** when you support a claim with a single comparable example that is so significantly similar to the claim as to be strong proof. The general warrant is: "What is true for situation A will also be true in situation B, which is similar to situation A" or "What is true for situation A will be true in all similar situations."

Suppose you want to argue that the Cherry Fork Volunteer Fire Department should conduct a raffle to raise money for three portable defibrillator units (claim). You could support the claim with an analogy to a single comparable example like this: The Jefferson City Fire Department, which is very similar to that of Cherry Fork, conducted a raffle and raised enough money to purchase four units.

When arguing from analogy, make sure that your reasoning is valid by answering the following questions:

1. Are the subjects being compared similar in every important way? If they are not, then your reasoning is flawed.

2. Are any of the ways in which the subjects are dissimilar important to the conclusion? If so, then your reasoning is flawed.

Arguing from Causation

You **argue from causation** when you support a claim by citing events always (or almost always) bring about or lead to a predictable effect or set of effects (Photo 17.4). The general warrant for arguments from cause is: "If A, which is known to bring about B, has been observed, then we can expect B to occur." Let's return to Juanita's election campaign for an example.

In researching Juanita's election campaign, you might discover that (1) she has campaigned intelligently (S) and (2) she has won the endorsement of key community leaders (S). In the past, these two events have usually been associated with victory (W), thus Juanita is electable (C).

When arguing from causation, make sure that your reasoning is valid by answering the following questions.

1. Are the events alone sufficient to cause the stated effect?

2. Do other events accompanying the cited events actually cause the effect?

3. Is the relationship between the causal events and the effect consistent?

If the answer to any of these questions is "no," then your reasoning is flawed.

Photo 17.4 How would you evaluate the causal claim made on this billboard?

Reasoning Fallacies

As you develop your arguments, be sure to avoid **fallacies**, or errors in reasoning. Five common fallacies are hasty generalization, false cause, either/or, straw man, and ad hominem arguments.

1. A **hasty generalization** occurs when a claim is either not supported with evidence or is supported with only one weak example. Enough supporting material must be cited to satisfy the audience that the instances are not isolated or handpicked. For example, someone who argued, "All Akitas are vicious dogs," whose sole piece of evidence was,

"My neighbor had an Akita and it bit my best friend's sister," would be guilty of a hasty generalization. It is hasty to generalize about the temperament of a whole breed of dogs based on a single action of one dog. Josh knew a lot of classmates who used or abused drugs like marijuana, Adderall, and anabolic steroids. To make sure he didn't make a hasty generalization that a growing percentage of young adults are doing so throughout the United States, he did an online search for statistics from credible sources such as the National Institute on Drug Abuse (NIDA), National Institute of Health (NIH), and the U.S. Department of Health and Human Services.

2. A **false cause** occurs when the alleged cause fails to produce the effect. The Latin term for this fallacy is *post hoc, ergo propter hoc*, meaning "after this, therefore because of this." Just because two things happen one after the other does not mean that the first necessarily caused the second. An example of a false cause fallacy is when a speaker claims that school violence is caused only by television violence, the Internet, a certain song or musical group, or lack of parental involvement. When one event follows another, there may be no connection at all, or the first event might be just one of many causes that contribute to the second.

3. An **either/or** fallacy occurs by suggesting there are only two alternatives when, in fact, others exist. Many such cases are oversimplifications of a complex issue. For example, when Robert argued that "we'll either have to raise taxes or close the library," he committed an either/or fallacy. He reduced a complex issue to one oversimplified solution when there were many other possible solutions.

4. A **straw man** fallacy occurs when a speaker weakens the opposing position by misrepresenting it in some way and then attacks that weaker (straw man) position. For example, in her speech advocating a seven-day waiting period to purchase handguns, Colleen favored regulation, not prohibition, of gun ownership. Bob argued against that by claiming "It is our constitutional right to bear arms." However, Colleen did not advocate abolishing the right to bear arms. Hence, Bob distorted Colleen's position, making it easier for him to refute.

5. An **ad hominem** fallacy attacks or praises the person making the argument rather than addressing the argument itself. *Ad hominem* literally means "to the man." For example, if Jamal claims that everyone should buy a Mac because Steve Jobs, the founder and former president of Apple Computer, was a genius, he is making an ad hominem argument. Jobs's intelligence isn't really a reason to buy a particular brand of computer. Unfortunately, politicians sometimes resort to ad hominem arguments when they attack their opponent's character rather than their platforms. Bullying in person, over the Internet, and via text messaging is another example of ad hominem attacks that can have dire consequences. TV commercials that feature celebrities using a particular product are often guilty of ad hominem reasoning. For example, Jerry Seinfeld appeared in American Express commercials, Jennifer Aniston has been in SmartWater ads, and Brad Pitt has done ads for Chanel. What makes any of these celebrities experts about the products they are endorsing (Photo 17.5)?

false cause
occurs when the alleged cause fails to be related to, or to produce, the effect

either/or
occurs when a speaker supports a claim by suggesting there are only two alternatives when, in fact, others exist

straw man
occurs when a speaker weakens the opposing position by misrepresenting it in some way and then attacks that weaker (straw person) position

ad hominem
occurs when one attacks the person making the argument, rather than the argument itself

Photo 17.5 Celebrities are often used to endorse products, even though they aren't experts regarding the product. These are examples of ad hominem arguments. What celebrities can you think of that are used to endorse products in this way?

WENN US/Alamy

Have you ever watched an infomercial and been convinced to purchase the product? Although the arguments posed in infomercials may seem compelling, a student of persuasion will quickly identify common reasoning fallacies in them. You can read more about the history of infomercials, how they've changed over time, and what we can expect of them in the future in the *Communicating in the World!* feature, "You Too Can Have Six-Pack Abs in Only Three Weeks!"

COMMUNICATING IN THE WORLD

You Too Can Have Six-Pack Abs in Only Three Weeks!

AP Images/Chris O'Meara

Body by Jake, Body Dome, Bun & Thigh Max, and Smart Abs all promise that you can trim and tone your way to a better body in just minutes a day. Besides promising to be the most effective exercise equipment ever, what do all these products have in common? They're the subject of infomercials. Infomercials are television and online programs designed to look like 30- or 60-minute talk shows, but they're actually extended advertisements that focus on a product's extraordinary features and offer testimonials of its effectiveness.

Until 1984, the Federal Communications Commission banned program-length commercials on TV in the USA, and the ban is still in effect for products that are marketed to children. Although some view infomercials with skepticism and derision, others view them as "an example of capitalism at its best" ("Billy Mays," 2009). Infomercials have even become sources of entertainment. In 2008 and 2009, the Snuggie—"A blanket with sleeves!"—and a similar product, the Slanket, have been featured in You Tube parodies ("The Cult of Snuggie") and *30 Rock* TV storylines (with Liz Lemon asserting, "It's not product placement; I just like it!"). When "infomercial king" Billy Mays passed away unexpectedly in June 2009, a "Billy Mays Gangsta Remix" grew to quick popularity

on YouTube (Mastamokei, 2008), and a Facebook page "RIP Billy Mays" gained 175,000 fans. Despite the fun we like to have with infomercials, they have come under criticism in recent years. Many Americans claim that such advertising often causes people to buy things they don't need and can't afford (Crain, 2009). But consumer suspicion of the ability of infomercials in particular to deceive is nothing new. For example, in 2002 Guthy-Renker, the largest producer of television infomercials, whose products include the popular Proactiv Solution acne treatment, became the subject of a class-action lawsuit, which claimed Guthy-Renker made exaggerated claims of profitability and promoted an Internet "shopping mall" that was simply a scam ("Timothy D. Naegele & Associates," 2002). The case is ongoing, but the online consumer complaint sites like complaints.com and pissedcustomer.com are full of testimonials from disgruntled customers who believe the products did not deliver what they promised.

If you suspect that an infomercial is making questionable claims, be careful before you buy. A good strategy is to first contact a reputable consumer watchdog group such as the Better Business Bureau to see if there have been any complaints lodged about the company advertising the product. If so, buyer beware!

Do you think calling these advertisements "info"-mercials is ethical? Why or and why not?

MindTap

Rhetorical Appeals to Ethos

Not everyone will choose the central processing route to make a decision regarding a persuasive proposition. One important cue people use when they process information by the peripheral route is ethos. So, you will also want to demonstrate good character, as well as say and do things to convey competence and credibility.

Conveying Good Character

We turn again to the ancient Greek philosopher Aristotle (384–322 B.C.E.) who first observed that perceived credibility depends on the audience's perception of the speaker's goodwill. Today, we define **goodwill** as a perception the audience forms of a speaker who they believe (1) understands them, (2) empathizes with them, and (3) is responsive to them. When audience members believe in the speaker's goodwill, they are more willing to believe what the speaker says.

You can demonstrate that you understand your audience is by personalizing your information. Use examples that are directly related to them and their experiences. You can also empathize with your audience. **Empathy** is the ability to see the world through the eyes of someone else. Empathizing with the views of the audience doesn't necessarily mean that you accept their views as your own. It does mean that you acknowledge them as valid. For example, consider what spokespersons lead with when responding to a national emergency or crisis event. They begin with "our hearts go out to the victims and their loved ones." In short, they demonstrate empathy (Photo 17.6). Finally, you can demonstrate goodwill by being responsive. Speakers who are **responsive** show that they care about the audience by acknowledging feedback, especially subtle negative cues. This feedback may occur during the presentation, but it also may have occurred prior to the speech.

Conveying Competence and Credibility

Not surprisingly, we are more likely to be persuaded when we perceive a speaker to be competent and credible. We propose the following strategies so that your **terminal credibility**, the audience's perception of your expertise at the end of your speech, is greater than your **initial credibility**, their perception of your expertise at the beginning of your speech.

1. **Explain your competence.** Unless someone has formally introduced you and your qualifications to your audience, your initial credibility will be low, and as you speak, you will need to tell your audience about your expertise. Sending these types of messages during the speech results in your achieving a level of **derived credibility** with your audience. You can interweave comments about your expertise into introductory comments and at appropriate places within the body of the speech.

2. **Use evidence from respected sources.** You can also increase your derived credibility by using supporting material from well-recognized and respected sources. If you have a choice between using a statistic from a known partisan organization or from a dispassionate professional association, choose the professional association. Likewise, if you can quote a local expert who

goodwill
the audience perception that the speaker understands, empathizes with, and is responsive to them

empathy
the ability to see the world through the eyes of someone else

responsive
show that you care about the audience by acknowledging feedback

terminal credibility
perception of a speaker's expertise at the end of the speech

initial credibility
perception of a speaker's expertise at the beginning of the speech

derived credibility
perception of a speaker's expertise during the speech

Photo 17.6 You can demonstrate goodwill by empathizing with your audience. Why might demonstrating care enhance goodwill?

Jessica McGowan/Getty Images News/Getty Images

is well known and respected by your audience or an international scholar with limited name recognition with your audience, use the local expert's opinion.

3. **Use nonverbal delivery to enhance your credibility.** Your audience assesses your credibility not only from what it hears about you before you begin speaking but also from what it observes by looking at you. Although professional attire enhances credibility in any speaking situation, it is particularly important for persuasive speeches. Persuasive speakers dressed more formally are perceived as more credible than those dressed casually or sloppily (Sellnow & Treinen, 2004).

   The audience will also notice how confident you appear as you prepare to address them. From the moment you rise to speak, you will want to convey through your nonverbal behavior that you are competent. Plant your feet firmly, glance at your notes, then make eye contact or audience contact with one person or group before taking a breath and beginning to speak. Likewise, pause and establish eye contact upon finishing the speech. Just as pausing and establishing eye contact or audience contact before the speech enhance credibility, doing so upon delivering the closing lines has the same result.

4. **Use vocal expression to enhance your credibility.** Research shows that credibility is strongly influenced by how you sound. Speaking fluently, using a moderately fast rate, and expressing yourself with conviction makes you appear more intelligent and competent.

Rhetorical Appeals to Pathos

We are more likely to be involved with a topic when we have an emotional stake in it. **Emotions** are the buildup of action-specific energy (Petri & Govern, 2012). You can increase audience involvement by evoking negative or positive emotions during your speech (Nabi, 2002).

emotions
buildup of action-specific energy

Evoking Negative Emotions

Negative emotions are disquieting, so when people experience them, they look for ways to eliminate them. Although you can tap numerous negative emotions, we describe five of the most common and how you might use them in a persuasive speech.

Fear We experience *fear* when we perceive ourselves to have no control over a situation that threatens us. We may fear physical harm or psychological harm. If you use examples, stories, and statistics that evoke fear in your audience, they will be more motivated to hear how your proposal can eliminate the source of their fear or allow them to escape from it. For example, in a speech whose goal was to convince the audience that they are at risk of developing high blood pressure, the speaker might use a fear appeal in this way:

> *One of every three Americans aged 18 and older has high blood pressure. It is a primary cause of stroke, heart disease, heart failure, kidney disease, and blindness. It triples a person's chance of developing heart disease, boosts the chance of stroke seven times, and the chance of congestive heart failure six times. Look at the person on your right; look at the person on your left. If they don't get it, chances are, you will. Today, I'd like to convince you that you are at risk for developing high blood pressure.*

Guilt We feel *guilt* when we personally violate a moral, ethical, or religious code that we hold dear. We experience guilt as a gnawing sensation that we have done something wrong. When we feel guilty, we are motivated to "make things right" or to atone for our transgression. For example, in a speech designed to motivate the audience to take their turn as designated drivers, a speaker might evoke guilt like this:

> *Have you ever promised your mom that you wouldn't ride in a car driven by someone who had been drinking and then turned around and got in the car with your buddy even though you both had had a few? You know that wasn't right. Lying to your mother, putting yourself and your buddy at risk . . . (pause) but what can you do? Well, today I'm going to show you how to avoid all that guilt, live up to your promises to Mom, and keep both you and your buddy safe.*

Shame We feel *shame* when a moral code we violate is revealed to someone we think highly of. The more egregious our behavior or the more we admire the person who finds out, the more shame we experience. When we feel shame, we are motivated to "redeem" ourselves in the eyes of that person. If in your speech you can evoke feelings of shame and then demonstrate how your proposal can either redeem someone after a violation has occurred or prevent feelings of shame, then you can motivate the audience to carefully consider your arguments. For example, in a speech advocating thankfulness, the speaker might use a shame-based approach by quoting the old saying, "I cried because I had no shoes until I met a man who had no feet."

Anger When we are faced with an obstacle that stands in the way of something we want, we experience *anger*. We may also experience anger when someone demeans us or someone we love. Speakers who choose to evoke anger must be careful not to incite so much anger that reasoning processes are short-circuited.

If you can rouse your audience's anger and then show how your proposal will help them achieve their goals or stop or prevent the demeaning that has occurred, you can motivate them to listen to and really consider your arguments. For example, suppose you want to convince the audience to support a law requiring community notification when a convicted sex offender moves into the neighborhood. You might arouse the audience's anger to get their attention by personalizing the story of Megan Kanka.

> *She was your little girl, just seven years old, and the light of your world. She had a smile that could bring you to your knees. And she loved puppies. So when that nice man who had moved in down the street invited her in to see his new puppy, she didn't hesitate. But she didn't get to see the puppy, and you didn't ever see her alive again. He beat her, he raped her, and then he strangled her. He packaged her body in an old toy chest and dumped it in a park. Your seven-year-old princess would never dig in a toy chest again or slip down the slide in that park. And that hurts. But what makes you really angry is that she wasn't his first. But you didn't know that. Because no one bothered to tell you that the guy down the street was likely to kill little girls. The cops knew it. But they couldn't tell you. You, the one who was supposed to keep her safe, didn't know. Angry? You bet. Yeah, he's behind bars again, but you still don't know who's living down the street from you. But you can. There is a law before Congress right now that will require active notification of the community when a known sex offender takes up residence, and today I'm going to tell how you can help to get this passed. ("Megan's Law," n.d.)*

Sadness When we fail to achieve a goal or experience a loss, we feel *sadness*. Unlike other negative emotions, we tend to withdraw and become isolated when we feel sad. Because sadness is an unpleasant feeling, we look for ways to end it. Speeches that help us understand and find answers for what has happened can comfort us and help relieve this unpleasant feeling. For example, after 9/11, many Americans were sad. Yes, they were also afraid and angry, but overlaying it all was profound sadness for those who had been lost and what had been lost. The questions "Why? Why did they do this? Why do they hate us so?" capture the national melancholy. So, when politicians suggest that they understand the answers to these questions and can repair the relationships that led to 9/11, Americans tend to listen to and think about what they say.

Evoking Positive Emotions

Just as evoking negative emotions can cause audience members to internalize your arguments, so too can you tap *positive emotions*, which are feelings that people enjoy experiencing. We discuss five of them here.

Happiness or Joy *Happiness* or *joy* is the buildup of positive energy we experience when we accomplish something, when we have a satisfying interaction or relationship, or when we see or possess objects that appeal to us. As a speaker, if you can show how your proposal will lead your audience members to be happy or joyful, then they are likely to listen and to think about your proposal. For example, suppose you want to motivate your audience to attend a couples encounter weekend where they will learn how to "rekindle" their relationship with a partner. If you can remind them about how they felt early in their relationship and then prove that they can reignite those feelings, they may be more motivated to listen.

Pride When we experience satisfaction about something we or someone we care about accomplishes, we feel *pride*. "We're number one! We're number one!" is the chant of the crowd feeling pride in the accomplishment of "their" team. Whereas happiness is related to feelings of pleasure, pride is related to feelings of self-worth. If you can demonstrate how your proposal will help audience members to feel good about themselves, they will be more motivated to support your proposition. For example, suppose you want to convince your audience to volunteer to work on the newest Habitat for Humanity house being constructed in your community. You might allude to the pride they will feel when they see people moving into the house they helped to build. As Rick revised his persuasive speech campaign to raise money for a dog park, he decided to appeal to pride by focusing on how helping build the park would provide a beautiful green space in the heart of the city and, at the same time, provide a welcome place for our family friends to run and play.

Relief When a threatening situation has been alleviated, we feel the positive emotion of *relief*. We relax and put down our guard. As a speaker, you use relief to motivate audience members by combining it with the negative emotion of fear. For example, suppose your goal is to convince the audience that they are not at risk for high blood pressure. You might use the same personalization of statistics that was described in the example of fear appeals, but instead of stopping at convincing the audience that they are at risk, you could also promise relief if they hear you out and do what you advocate.

Hope The emotional energy that stems from believing something desirable is likely to happen is called *hope*. Whereas relief causes us to relax and let down our guard, hope energizes us to take action to overcome the situation. Hope empowers. As with relief, hope appeals are usually accompanied by fear appeals. So you can motivate audience members to listen by showing them how your proposal provides a plan for overcoming a difficult situation. For example, if you propose adopting a low-fat diet to reduce the risk of high blood pressure, you can use the same personalization of statistics cited in the example of fear but change the ending to state: "Today, I'm going to convince you to beat the odds by adopting a low-fat diet."

Compassion When we feel selfless concern for the suffering of another person and that concern energizes us to try to relieve that suffering, we feel *compassion* (Photo 17.7). Speakers can evoke audience members' feelings of compassion by vividly describing the suffering endured by someone. The audience will then be motivated to listen to see how the speaker's proposal can end that suffering. For example, when a speaker whose goal is to gather donations to Project Peanut Butter displays a slide of an emaciated child, claims that 13 percent of all Malawi children die of malnutrition, and states that for $10 you can save a child, he or she is appealing to compassion.

You can evoke negative emotions, positive emotions, or both as a way to encourage listeners to internalize your message. You can do so by telling vivid stories and testimonials, offering startling statistics, using striking presentational aids and provocative language, as well as through an animated and expressive delivery style.

Photo 17.7 Speakers appeal to compassion by showing how someone is suffering and how we can help. What advertisements can you recall that appeal to compassion in this way?

Persuasive Speech Patterns

Persuasive speeches are organized as speeches to convince (to reinforce or change an audience's belief or attitude) or speeches to actuate (to take action). The most common patterns for organizing persuasive speeches include statement of reasons, comparative advantages, criteria satisfaction, refutative, problem–solution, problem–cause–solution, and motivated sequence (Photo 17.8). In this section, we describe and illustrate each pattern by examining the same topic with slightly different propositions.

Statement of Reasons

The **statement of reasons pattern** is used to confirm propositions of fact by presenting the best-supported reasons in a meaningful order. For a speech with three reasons or more, place the strongest reason last because this is the reason you believe the audience will find most persuasive. Place the second strongest reason first because you want to start with a significant point. Place the other reasons in between.

statement of reasons pattern
confirms propositions of fact by presenting best-supported reasons in a meaningful order

Photo 17.8 How would you apply each of the organizational patterns described in this chapter to a speech about rebuilding after Superstorm Sandy?

> **Proposition of Fact:** *The proposed school tax levy is necessary.*
>
> I. *The income is needed to restore vital programs.* [second strongest]
>
> II. *The income is needed to give teachers cost of living raises.*
>
> III. *The income is needed to maintain local control.* [strongest]

Comparative Advantages

comparative advantages
pattern
*attempts to convince that
something is of more value
than something else*

The **comparative advantages pattern** attempts to convince others that something has more value than something else. A comparative advantages approach to a school tax proposition might look like this:

Proposition of Value: *Passing the school tax levy is better than not passing it.* [compares the value of change to the status quo]

    I. *With new income from a tax levy, schools will be able to reintroduce important programs that had been cut.* [advantage 1]

    II. *New income from a tax levy will provide salaries for teachers and avert a strike.* [advantage 2]

    III. *Income from a tax levy will make it possible to retain local control of our schools, which will be lost to the state if additional local funding is not provided.* [advantage 3]

Criteria Satisfaction

criteria satisfaction pattern
*seeks audience agreement
on criteria that should be
considered when they evaluate
a particular proposition and
then shows how the proposition
satisfies those criteria*

The **criteria satisfaction pattern** seeks agreement on the criteria that should be considered when evaluating a particular proposition and then shows how the proposition satisfies the criteria. A criteria satisfaction pattern is especially useful when your audience is opposed to your proposition, because it approaches the proposition indirectly by first focusing on the criteria that the audience should agree with before introducing the specific solution. A criteria satisfaction organization for the school levy would look like this:

Proposition of Value: *Passing a school levy is a good way to fund our schools.*

    I. *We all agree that the funding method we select must meet three criteria:*

        A. *The funding method must provide resources needed to reinstate important programs.*

        B. *The funding method must provide funds to pay teachers.*

        C. *The funding method must generate enough income to maintain local control.*

    II. *Passing a local school tax levy will satisfy each of these criteria.*

        A. *A local levy will allow us to fund important programs again.*

        B. *A local levy will provide revenue for teacher raises.*

        C. *A local levy will generate enough income to maintain local control.*

Refutative

refutative pattern
*arranges main points according
to opposing arguments and
then both challenges them
and bolsters your own*

The **refutative pattern** arranges main points according to opposing arguments and then both challenges them and bolsters your own. This pattern is particularly useful when the target audience opposes your position. Begin by acknowledging the merit of opposing arguments and then showing their flaws. Once listeners understand the flaws, they will be more receptive to the arguments you present to support your proposition. A refutative pattern for the school tax proposition might look like this:

Proposition of Value: *A school levy is the best way to fund our schools.*

    I. *Opponents of the tax levy argue that the tax increase will fall only on property owners.*

        A. *Landlords will recoup property taxes in the form of higher rents.*

        B. *Thus, all people will be affected.*

II. *Opponents of the tax levy argue that there are fewer students in the school district, so schools should be able to function on the same amount of revenue.*

   A. *Although there are fewer pupils, costs continue to rise.*

      1. *Salary costs are increasing.*

      2. *Energy costs are increasing.*

      3. *Maintenance costs are increasing.*

      4. *Costs from unfunded federal and state government mandates are increasing.*

   B. *Although there are fewer pupils, there are many aging school buildings that need replacing or renovating.*

III. *Opponents of the tax levy argue that parents should be responsible for the excessive cost of educating their children.*

   A. *Historically, our nation has flourished under a publicly funded educational system.*

   B. *Parents today are already paying more than previous generations did.*

      1. *Activity fees*

      2. *Lab fees*

      3. *Book fees*

      4. *Transportation fees*

   B. *Of school-age children today in this district, 42 percent live in families that are below the poverty line and have limited resources.*

Problem–Solution

The **problem–solution pattern** explains the nature of a problem and proposes a solution. This organization is particularly effective when the audience is neutral or agrees only that there is a problem but has no opinion about a particular solution. A problem–solution organization for the school tax proposition might look like this:

> **problem–solution pattern**
> *explains the nature of a particular problem and then proposes a solution*

   Proposition of Policy: *We must solve the current fiscal crisis in the school district.*

   I. *The current funding is insufficient* [statement of problem]

     A. *The schools have had to cut important programs.*

     B. *The teachers have not had a cost of living raise in five years.*

     C. *The state could take over control.*

   II. *The proposed local tax levy will solve these problems.* [solution]

     A. *The schools will be able ot reinstate important programs.*

     B. *Teachers will be afforded raises.*

     The district will be able to maintain control.

   III. *We must each do our part to make this happen* [call to action]

     A. *Vote "yes"*

     B. *Encourage your friends and neighbors to vote "yes"*

Problem–Cause–Solution

The **problem–cause–solution pattern** is similar to the problem–solution pattern, but differs from it by adding a main point that reveals the causes of the problem and a

> **problem–cause–solution pattern**
> *demonstrates that there is a problem caused by specific things that can be alleviated with the proposed solution that addresses the causes*

solution designed to alleviate those causes. This pattern is particularly useful for addressing seemingly intractable problems that have been dealt with unsuccessfully in the past as a result of treating symptoms rather than underlying causes. A problem–cause–solution organization for the school tax proposition might look like this:

Proposition of Policy: *We must solve the current fiscal crisis in the school district.*

I. *The current funding is insufficient.* [statement of problem]

    A. *The schools have had to cut programs.*

    B. *Teachers have not had a cost of living raise in five years.*

    C. *The state could take over control.*

II. *We can trace these problems to several key things.* [causes]

    A. *Government support continues to dwindle.*

    B. *Operating expenses continue to rise.*

III. *The proposed local tax levy will address these issues.* [solution]

    A. *The levy will supplement inadequate government support.*

    B. *The levy will fill the gap in operating expense needs.*

IV. *Each one of us is responsible for making sure the tax levy passes* [call to action]

    A. *Vote "yes."*

    B. *Encourage your friends and neighbors to vote "yes."*

Motivated Sequence

motivated sequence pattern
combines the problem–solution pattern with explicit appeals designed to motivate the audience to act

The **motivated sequence pattern** combines a problem–solution pattern with explicit appeals designed to motivate the audience to act. The motivated sequence pattern is a five-point sequence that replaces the normal introduction–body–conclusion model with (1) an attention step, (2) a need step that fully explains the nature of the problem, (3) a satisfaction step that explains how the proposal solves the problem in a satisfactory manner, (4) a visualization step that provides a personal application of the proposal, and (5) an action appeal step that emphasizes the direction that audience action should take. A motivated pattern for the school tax levy proposition might look like this:

Proposition of Policy: *We must solve the current fiscal crisis in the school district.*

I. *Attention Step: Introduction to the problem.*

    A. *Comparisons of worldwide test scores in math and sciences show the United States continues to lose ground.*

    B. *I've done extensive research on this problem and today I'm going to convince you to join with me to take actions to stop it.*

    C. *To do so, we'll start by describing the problem, then explain what we can do to stop it, and finally show you what the future will look like after doing so.*

II. *Need Step: The local schools are underfunded.*

    A. *The current funding is insufficient and has resulted in major program cuts.*

    B. *Excellent teachers are leaving because of stagnant wages.*

    C. *A threatened state takeover of local schools would lead to more bureaucracy and less learning.*

III. Satisfaction Step: The proposed tax levy is large enough to solve these problems.

    A. Programs will be restored.

    B. Qualified teachers will get the needed raises to stay.

    C. We will retain local control.

    D. We can retain pride in our community.

IV. Visualization Step: Imaging the best and the worst.

    A. What it will be like if we pass the levy.

    B. What it will be like if we don't pass the levy.

V. Action Appeal Step: Vote "yes."

    A. If you want to see our schools improve, vote "yes."

    B. Come join me. I'm registered and voting for the levy.

    C. They say it takes a village. Now is our chance. Together we can make a difference for our schools, our kids, and our community.

Figure 17.3 is a checklist that you can use to analyze your persuasive speeches or the persuasive speeches of others.

You can use this form to critique a persuasive speech you hear in class. As you listen to the speaker, outline the speech, paying close attention to the reasoning process the speaker uses. Also note the claims and support used in the arguments and identify the types of warrants being used. Then answer the questions that follow.

General Criteria

_____ 1. Was the proposition clear? Could you tell the speaker's position on the issue?

_____ 2. Was the introduction effective in creating interest and involving the audience in the speech?

_____ 3. Was the speech organized using an appropriate persuasive pattern?

_____ 4. Was the language clear, vivid, inclusive, and appropriate?

_____ 5. Was the conclusion effective in summarizing what had been said and mobilizing the audience to act?

_____ 6. Was the speech delivered conversationally and expressively?

       7. Did the speaker establish credibility by demonstrating:

        _____ expertise?

        _____ personableness?

        _____ trustworthiness?

Primary Criteria

_____ 1. Was the specific goal phrased as a proposition (were you clear about the speaker's position on the issue)?

_____ 2. Did the proposition appear to be adapted to the initial attitude of the target audience?

_____ 3. Were emotional appeals used to involve the audience with the topic?

Figure 17.3

Persuasive speech evaluation checklist

Figure 17.3

(Continued)

4. Were the reasons used in the speech
   _____ directly related to the proposition?
   _____ supported by strong evidence?
   _____ persuasive for the particular audience?

5. Was the evidence [*support*] used to back the reasons [*claims*]
   _____ from well-respected sources?
   _____ recent and/or still valid?
   _____ persuasive for this audience?
   _____ typical of all evidence that might have been used?
   _____ sufficient [*enough evidence cited*]?

6. Could you identify the types of arguments that were used?
   _____ Did the speaker argue from example?   _____ If so, was it valid?
   _____ Did the speaker argue from analogy?   _____ If so, was it valid?
   _____ Did the speaker argue from causation?   _____ If so, was it valid?
   _____ Did the speaker argue from sign?   _____ If so, was it valid?

7. Could you identify any fallacies of reasoning in the speech?
   _____ hasty generalizations
   _____ arguing from false cause
   _____ ad hominem attacks
   _____ straw person
   _____ either-or

_____ 8. Did the speaker demonstrate goodwill?

9. If the speech called for the audience to take action,
   _____ did the speaker describe incentives and relate them to audience needs?
   _____ did the speaker acknowledge any costs associated with the action?

10. Did the speaker use an appropriate persuasive organizational pattern?
    _____ statement of reasons
    _____ comparative advantages
    _____ criteria satisfaction
    _____ refutative
    _____ problem-solution
    _____ problem-cause-solution
    _____ motivated sequence

Overall evaluation of the speech (check one):
_____ excellent _____ good _____ average _____ fair _____ poor
Use the information from this checklist to support your evaluation.

COMMUNICATE ON YOUR FEET

Speech Assignment

A Persuasive Speech

1. Follow the speech plan Action Steps to prepare a persuasive speech. Your instructor will announce the time limit and other parameters for this assignment.

2. Criteria for evaluation include all the general criteria of topic and purpose, content, organization, and presentation, but special emphasis will be placed on the primary persuasive criteria of how well the speech's specific goal was adapted to the audience's initial attitude toward the topic, the soundness of the reasons, the evidence cited in support of them, and the credibility of the arguments.

3. Use the persuasive speech evaluation checklist in Figure 17.3 to critique yourself as you practice your speech.

4. Prior to presenting your speech, prepare a complete sentence outline and reference list (bibliography).

SAMPLE SPEECH PLAN AND OUTLINE

Sample Actuation Persuasive Speech

This section presents a sample speech to actuate given by a student, including an adaptation plan, an outline, and a transcript.

Together, We Can Stop Cyber-Bullying[1]
By Adam Parrish

MindTap® Read the speech adaptation plan, outline, and transcript of a speech by Adam Parrish. You can access a video of Adam's speech through the Chapter 17 resources of your MindTap for *Communicate!* You can also use your MindTap to analyze this speech in terms of concepts covered in this chapter.

© Cengage Learning

Adaptation Plan

1. **Target audience initial attitude and background knowledge:** My audience is composed of traditional-aged college students with varying majors and classes. Most are from middle-class backgrounds. The initial attitude about bullying for most will be to agree with me already that it's a bad thing. So I will try to get them to take action. My perception is that my audience knows about cyber-bullying but not the nuances of it.

2. **Organizational framework:** I will organize my speech using a problem–cause–solution framework because my audience already agrees that bullying is bad but may not know what they can and should do to help stop it.

3. **Arguments (logos):** I will demonstrate what widespread (breadth) and harmful (depth of effects) cyber-bullying is and why it persists (causes). Once I've convinced my audience, I will propose solutions that must be taken and cite specifically what we must do to help stop this horrible practice.

4. **Building competence, credibility, and good character (ethos):** I will use credible sources to support my claims and cite them using oral footnotes. I will also offer personal stories to create goodwill.

5. **Creating and maintaining interest (pathos):** I will involve my audience by appealing to several emotions, including guilt, sadness, relief, hope, and compassion.

Outline

General goal: To persuade

Specific goal: To convince my audience to take action to help stop cyber-bullying.

Introduction

Attention catcher

I. "I'll miss just being around her." "I didn't want to believe it." "It's such a sad thing." These quotes are from the friends and family of 15-year-old Phoebe Prince, who, on January 14, 2010, committed suicide by hanging herself. Why did this senseless act occur? The answer is simple: Phoebe Prince was bullied to death.

Listener relevance

II. Many of us know someone who has been bullied in school. Perhaps they were teased in the parking lot or in the locker room. In the past, bullying occurred primarily in and around schools. However, with the advent of new communication technologies such as cell phones with text messaging capability, instant messaging, e-mails, blogs, and social networking sites, bullies can now follow their victims anywhere, even into their own bedrooms. Using electronic communications to tease, harass, threaten, and intimidate another person is called cyber-bullying.

Speaker credibility

III. As a tutor and mentor to young students, I have witnessed cyber-bullying firsthand, and by examining current research, I believe I understand the problem, its causes, and how we can help end cyber-bullying.

Thesis statement (stated as a proposition)

IV. Cyber-bullying is a devastating form of abuse that must be confronted and stopped.

Preview

V. Today, we will examine the widespread and harmful nature of cyber-bullying, discover how and why it persists, and propose some simple solutions that we must engage in to thwart cyber-bullies and comfort their victims.

Transition

Let's begin by tackling the problem head-on.

Body

The problem

I. Cyber-bullying is a pervasive and dangerous behavior.

Listener relevance

Many of us have read rude, insensitive, or nasty statements posted about us or someone we care about on social networking sites like Twitter and Facebook. Whether or not those comments were actually intended to hurt another person's feelings, they are perfect examples of cyber-bullying.

A. Cyber-bullying takes place all over the world through a wide array of electronic media.

1. According to *Statisticbrain.com*, as of 2012, 52 percent of American middle-school students had experienced instances of cyber-bullying ranging

from hurtful comments to threats of physical violence (Statisticbrain .com, 2012).

2. According to recent statistics reported by the National Crime Prevention Council, females are just as likely as males to engage in cyber-bullying, although women are twice as likely to be victimized.

3. A 2011 study reported in the journal of *Pediatrics* noted that instances of bullying via text messages have risen significantly since 2006 (Ybarra, Mitchell, & Korchmaros, 2011). And according to an article in the June 2011 issue of *Consumer Reports,* one million young people experienced cyber-bullying on Facebook in 2011 alone.

4. Internet and cell-phone are most commonly used by bullies to harass, torment, and threaten young people in North America, Europe, and Asia (National Crime Prevention Council).

5. A particularly disturbing incident occurred in Dallas, Texas, where an overweight student with multiple sclerosis was targeted on a school's social networking page. One message read, "I guess I'll have to wait until you kill yourself, which I hope is not long from now, or I'll have to wait until your disease kills you" (Keith & Martin, 2005, p. 226).

Clearly, cyber-bullying is a widespread problem. What is most disturbing about cyber-bullying, however, is its effects upon victims, bystanders, and perhaps even upon the bullies themselves.　　　　　　　　　　　　　　　　　　　　　　　　Transition

B. Cyber-bullying can lead to traumatic physical psychological injuries upon its victims.

1. According to a 2012 article in the *Children and Youth Services Review,* 50 percent of the victims of cyber-bullies are also harassed by their attackers in school (Mishna, Khoury-Kassabri, Gadalla, & Daciuk, 2012).

2. For example, the Dallas student with MS had eggs thrown at her car and a bottle of acid thrown at her house (Keith & Martin, 2005).

3. Victims of cyber-bullying experience such severe emotional distress that they often exhibit behavioral problems such as poor grades, skipping school, and receiving detentions and suspensions (Wang, Nansel, Iannotti, 2011).

4. Smith et al. (2008) suggested that even a few instances of cyber-bullying can have these long-lasting and heartbreaking results.

5. What is even more alarming is that victims of cyber-bullying are significantly more likely to carry weapons to school as a result of feeling threatened (Ybarra et al., 2007). Obviously, this could lead to violent, and perhaps even deadly, outcomes for bullies, victims, and even bystanders.

Now that we realize the devastating nature, scope, and effects of cyber-bullying, let's look at its causes.　　　　　　　　　　　　　　　　　　　　　　　　Transition

II. Cyber-bullying is perpetuated because victims and bystanders do not report their abusers to authorities.　　　　　　　　　　　　　　　　　　　　The cause

Think back to a time when you may have seen a friend or loved one being harassed online. Did you report the bully to the network administrator or other authorities? Did you console the victim? I know I didn't. If you are like me, we may unknowingly be enabling future instances of cyber-bullying.　　　　　Listener relevance

A. Cyber-bullies are cowards who attack their victims anonymously.

   1. Ybarra et al. (2007) discovered that 13 percent of cyber-bullying victims did not know who was tormenting them.

   2. This is an important statistic because, as Keith and Martin (2005) point out, traditional bullying takes place face to face and often ends when students leave school. However, today, students are subjected to bullying in their own homes.

   3. Perhaps the anonymous nature of cyber-attacks partially explains why Li (2007) found that nearly 76 percent of victims of cyber-bullying and 75 percent of bystanders never reported instances of bullying to adults.

B. Victims and bystanders who do not report attacks from cyber-bullies can unintentionally enable bullies.

   1. According to De Nies, Donaldson, and Netter of *ABCNews.com* (2010) several of Phoebe Prince's classmates were aware that she was being harassed but did not inform the school's administration.

   2. Li (2007) suggested that victims and bystanders often do not believe that adults will actually intervene to stop cyber-bullying.

   3. However, *ABCNews.com* (2010) reports that 41 states have laws against bullying in schools, and 23 of those states target cyber-bullying specifically.

Transition

Now that we realize that victims of cyber-bullies desperately need the help of witnesses and bystanders to report their attacks, we should arm ourselves with the information necessary to provide that assistance.

The solution

III. Cyber-bullying must be confronted on national, local, and personal levels.

Listener relevance

Think about the next time you see a friend or loved one being tormented or harassed online. What would you be willing to do to help?

A. There should be a comprehensive national law confronting cyber-bullying in schools. According to Soptbullying.gov, at present, there is no federal law that directly addresses bullying. This is simply unacceptable. However, certain statutes currently in state laws could and should be amalgamated to create the strongest protections for victims and the most effective punishments for bullies as possible.

   1. According to Limber and Small's (2003) article titled *State Laws and Policies to Address Bullying in Schools,* Georgia law requires faculty and staff to be trained on the nature of bullying and what actions to take if they see students being bullied.

   2. Furthermore, Connecticut law *requires* school employees to report bullying as part their hiring contract (Limber & Small, 2003). Washington takes this a step further by protecting employees from any legal action if a reported bully is proven to be innocent (Limber & Small, 2003).

   3. When it comes to protecting victims, West Virginia law demands that schools must ensure that a bullied student does not receive additional abuse at the hands of his or her bully (Limber & Small, 2003).

   4. Legislating punishment for bullies is difficult. Zero-tolerance polices often perpetuate violence because at-risk youth (bullies) are removed from all of the benefits of school, which might help make them less abusive.

5. A comprehensive anti-cyber-bullying law should incorporate the best aspects of these state laws and find a way to punish bullies that is both punitive and has the ability to rehabilitate abusers.

B. Local communities must organize and mobilize to attack the problem of cyber-bullying.

   1. According to Greene (2006), communities need to support bullying prevention programs by conducting a school-based bullying survey for individual school districts. We can't know how to best protect victims in our community without knowing how they are affected by the problem.

   2. It is critical to know this information. As Greene noted, only 3 percent of teachers in the United States perceive bullying to be a problem in their schools (Greene, 2006).

   3. Local school districts should create a Coordinating Committee made up of "administrators, teachers, students, parents, school staff, and community partners" to gather bullying data and rally support to confront the problem (Greene, 2006, p. 73).

   4. Even if your local school district is unable or unwilling to mobilize behind this dire cause, there are some important actions you can take personally to safeguard those you love against cyber-bullying.

C. Take note of these warning signs that might indicate a friend or loved one is a victim of a cyber-bully (Keith & Martin, 2005).

   1. Victims of cyber-bullies often use electronic communication more frequently than do people who are not being bullied.

   2. Victims of cyber-bullies have mood swings and difficulty sleeping.

   3. Victims of cyber-bullies seem depressed and/or become anxious.

   4. Victims of cyber-bullies become withdrawn from social activities and fall behind in scholastic responsibilities.

D. If you see a friend or loved one exhibiting any of these signs, I implore you not to ignore them. Rather, take action. Get involved. Do something to stop it.

   1. According to Raskauskas and Stoltz (2007), witnesses of cyber-bullying should inform victims to take the attacks seriously, especially if the bullies threaten violence.

   2. Tell victims to report their attacks to police or other authority figures (Raskauskas & Stoltz, 2007).

   3. Tell victims to block harmful messages by blocking e-mail accounts and cell phone numbers.

   4. Tell victims to save copies of attacks and provide them to authorities.

   5. If you personally know the bully and feel safe confronting him or her, do so! As Raskauskas and Stoltz (2007) noted, bullies will often back down when confronted by peers.

   6. By being a good friend and by giving good advice, you can help a victim report his or her attacks from cyber-bullies and take a major step toward eliminating this horrendous problem.

Transition

So, you see, we are not helpless to stop the cyber-bulling problem as long as we make the choice NOT to ignore it.

Conclusion

Thesis restatement

I. Cyber-bullying is a devastating form of abuse that must be reported to authorities.

Main point summary

II. Cyber-bullying is a worldwide problem perpetuated by the silence of both victims and bystanders. By paying attention to certain warning signs, we can empower ourselves to console victims and report their abusers.

Call to action and clincher

III. Today, I implore you to do your part to help stop cyber-bullying. I know that you agree that stopping cyber-bullying must be a priority. First, although other states have cyber-bullying laws in place, ours does not. So I'm asking you to sign this petition that I will forward to our district's state legislators. We need to make our voices heard that we want specific laws passed to stop this horrific practice and to punish those caught doing it. Second, I'm also asking you to be vigilant in noticing signs of cyber-bullying and then taking action. Look for signs that your friend, brother, sister, cousin, boyfriend, girlfriend, or loved one might be a victim of cyber-bullying and then get involved to help stop it! Phoebe Prince showed the warning signs, and she did not deserve to die so senselessly. None of us would ever want to say, "I'll miss just being around her," "I didn't want to believe it," "It's such a sad thing" about our own friends or family members. We must work to ensure that victims are supported and bullies are confronted nationally, locally, and personally. I know that, if we stand together and refuse to be silent, we can and will stop cyber-bullying.

References

Bullying. (2015). National Crime Prevention Council. Retrieved from: http://www.ncpc.org/resources/files/pdf/bullying

Cyber-Bullying Statistics. (2012). Retrieved from http://www.statisticbrain.com/cyber-bullying-statistics/

De Nies, Y., Donaldson, S., & Netter, S. (2010, January 28). Mean girls: Cyberbullying blamed for teen suicides. ABCNews.com. *Retrieved from http://abcnews.go.com/GMA/Parenting/girls-teen-suicide-calls-attention-cyberbullying/story?id=9685026*

Greene, M. B. (2006). Bullying in schools: A plea for measure of human rights. Journal of Social Issues, 62(1), *63–79.*

Keith, S., & Martin, M. (2005). Cyber-bullying: Creating a culture of respect in the cyber world. Reclaiming Children and Youth, 13(4), *224–228.*

Li, Q. (2007). New bottle of old wine: A research of cyberbullying in schools. Computers in Human Behavior, *23, 1777–1791.*

Limber, S. P., & Small, M. A. (2003). State laws and policies to address bullying in schools. School Psychology Review, 32(3), *445–455.*

Mishna, F., Khoury-Kassabri, M., Gadalla, T., & Daciuk, J. (2012). Risk factors for involvement in cyber bullying: Victims, bullies and bully–victims. Children and Youth Services Review, 34(1), *63-70.*

Raskauskas, J., & Stoltz, A. D. (2007). Involvement in traditional and electronic bullying among adolescents. Developmental Psychology, 43(3), *564–575.*

Smith, P. K., Mahdavi, J., Carvalho, M., Fisher, S. Russel, S., & Tippett, N. (2008). *Cyberbullying: Its nature and impact in secondary school pupils. Journal of Child Psychology and Psychiatry, 49(4), 374–385.*

Stopbullying.gov. (2015). *U.S. Department of Health and Human Services.* Retrieved from: http://www.stopbullying.gov/laws/federal/index.html

That Facebook Friend might be 10 years old, and other troubling News. (June 2011). *Consumer Reports Online.* Retrieved from: http://www.consumerreports.org/cro /magazine-archive/2011/june/electronics-computers/state-of-the-net/facebook -concerns/index.htm

Wang, J., Nansel, T. Rl, & Iannotti, R. J. (2011). *Cyber and traditional bullying: Differential association with depression.* Journal of Adolescent Health, 48(4) 415–417.

Ybarra, M. L., Diener-West, M., & Leaf, P. J. (2007). *Examining the overlap in internet harassment and school bullying: Implications for school intervention.* Journal of Adolescent Health, 41, S42–S50.

Ybarra, M. L., Mitchell, K. J., Wolak, J., & Finkelhor, D. (2006). *Examining characteristics and associated distress related to Internet harassment: Findings from the second Youth Internet Safety Survey.* Pediatrics, 118, *1169–1177.*

Ybarra, M. L., Mitchell, K. M., & Korchmaros, J. D. (2011). *National trends in exposure to and experiences of violence on the Internet among children. Pediatrics.* Retrieved from http://pediatrics.aappulications.org/content/early/2011/11/16 /peds.2011-0118.full.pdf+html

SPEECH AND ANALYSIS

Speech

"I'll miss just being around her." "I didn't want to believe it." "It's such a sad thing." These quotes are from the friends and family of 15-year-old Phoebe Prince, who, on January 14, 2010, committed suicide by hanging herself. Why did this senseless act occur? The answer is simple. . . . Phoebe Prince was bullied to death.

Many of us know someone who has been bullied in school. Perhaps they were teased in the parking lot or in the locker room. In the past, bullying occurred primarily in school. However, with the advent of new communication technologies such as cell phones, text messaging, instant messaging, blogs, and social networking sites, bullies can now follow and terrorize their victims anywhere, even into their own bedrooms. Using electronic communications to tease, harass, threaten, and intimidate another person is called cyber-bullying.

As a tutor and mentor to young students, I have witnessed cyber-bullying firsthand, and by examining current research, I believe I understand the problem, its causes, and how we can help end cyber-bullying. What I know for sure is that cyber-bullying is a devastating form of abuse that must be confronted on national, local, and personal levels.

Analysis

Adam uses quotes from family and friends of cyber-bullying victim Phoebe Prince to get attention and lead into his proposition.

Here Adam further entices his listeners to pay attention by offering listener relevance that we all can relate to.

Using the vivid term "terrorize," Adam appeals to negative emotions (pathos).

Adam begins to establish ethos by mentioning why he has credibility about this topic. Mentioning that he is a tutor and mentor also conveys goodwill. Listeners are likely to think he must have good character if he volunteers as a tutor and mentor.

Today, we will examine the widespread and harmful nature of cyber-bulling, uncover how and why it persists, and pinpoint some simple solutions we must begin to enact in order to thwart cyber-bullies and comfort their victims. Let's begin by tackling the problem head on.

Many of us have read rude, insensitive, or nasty statements posted about us or someone we care about on social networking sites like Twitter and Facebook. Well, whether or not those comments were actually intended to hurt another person's feelings, if they did hurt their feelings, then they are perfect examples of cyber-bullying.

Cyber-bullying is a pervasive and dangerous behavior. It takes place all over the world and through a wide array of electronic media. According to *Statisticbrain.com, as of 2012, 52 percent of American middle-school students had experienced instances of cyber-bullying ranging from hurtful comments to treats of physical violence.* Moreover, recent statistics reported by the National Crime Prevention Council reveal that females are just as likely as males to engage in cyber-bullying, but are twice as likely to be victimized.

A 2011 study reported in the journal *Pediatrics* noted that instances of bullying via text messages have risen significantly since 2006. And according to an article in Consumer Reports, one million young people experienced cyberbullying on Facebook in 2011 alone. The problem does not exist in the United States alone.

Li noted that Internet and cell-phone technologies have been used by bullies to harass, torment, and threaten young people in North America, Europe, and Asia. However, some of the most horrific attacks happen right here at home.

According to Keith and Martin, a particularly disturbing incident occurred in Dallas, Texas, where an overweight student with multiple sclerosis was targeted on a school's social networking page. One message read, "I guess I'll have to wait until you kill yourself which I hope is not long from now, or I'll have to wait until your disease kills you." Clearly, cyber-bullying is a worldwide and perverse phenomenon. What is most disturbing about cyber-bullying is its effects upon victims, bystanders, and perhaps even upon bullies themselves.

Cyber-bullying can lead to physical and psychological injuries upon its victims. According to a 2012 article in the *Children and Youth Services Review, 50* percent of the victims of cyber-bullies are also harassed by their attackers in school. For example, the Dallas student with MS had eggs thrown at her car and a bottle of acid thrown at her house.

According to a 2011 article published in *the Journal of Adolescent Health, Wang and colleagues* reported that victims of cyber-bullying experience such severe emotional distress that they often exhibit behavioral problems such as poor grades, skipping school, and receiving detentions and suspensions.

What is even more alarming is that, victims of cyber-bullying are significantly more likely to carry weapons to school as a result of feeling threatened. Obviously, this could lead to violent outcomes for bullies, victims, and even bystanders (Bullying, 2015, National Crime Prevention Council).

Now that we have heard about the nature, scope, and effects of cyber-bullying, let's see if we can discover its causes. Let's think back to a time when we may have seen a friend or loved one being harassed online. Did we report the bully to the network administrator or other authorities? Did we console the victim? I know I didn't. If you are like me, we may unknowingly be enabling future instances of cyber-bullying.

Adam does a nice job of previewing his problem–cause–solution organizational framework, but his thesis statement phrased as a proposition is somewhat lost and could be made more overtly here.

Again, Adam's use of a listener relevance helps keep listeners tuned in and interested in hearing more.

Here Adam bolsters his ethos (and avoids plagiarism) by citing an oral footnote for his statistics.

Notice Adam's word choices (harass, torment, threaten, horrific) to enhance pathos.

This example provides an emotional appeal by offering a real example of a real victim in Dallas, Texas.

This vivid example enhances pathos.

Now that Adam has established the breadth of the problem as widespread, he moves into a discussion about the depth of the effects it can have on victims.

Here Adam helps pique listener interest by pointing out how bystanders could also be hurt if we don't do something to stop this form of terrorism.

Notice how Adam's transition verbally ties the point he is finishing (problem) to the next point (causes) clearly using inclusive "we" language. This, too, bolsters a sense of goodwill and uses a conversational style that keeps listeners engaged.

Cyber-bullying occurs because of the anonymity offered to bullies by cell phone and Internet technologies, as well as the failure of victims and bystanders to report incidents of cyber-bullying. You see, unlike schoolyard bullies, cyber-bullies can attack their victims anonymously.

Ybarra and colleagues discovered that 13 percent of cyber-bullying victims did not know who was tormenting them. This devastating statistic is important because, as Keith and Martin noted, traditional bullying takes place face to face and often ends when students leave school. However, today, students are subjected to nonstop bullying, even when they are alone in their own homes.

Perhaps the anonymous nature of cyber-attacks partially explains why Li found that nearly 76 percent of victims of cyber-bullying and 75 percent of bystanders never reported instances of bullying to adults. Victims and bystanders who do not report attacks from cyber-bullies can unintentionally enable bullies.

According to De Nies, Donaldson, and Netter of *ABCNews.com* (2010), several of Phoebe Prince's classmates were aware that she was being harassed but did not inform the school's administration. Li suggested that victims and bystanders often do not believe that adults will actually intervene to stop cyber-bullying. However, *ABCNews.com* reports that 41 states have laws against bullying in schools, and 23 of those states target cyber-bullying specifically.

Now that we know that victims of cyber-bullies desperately need the help of witnesses and bystanders to report their attacks, we should arm ourselves with the information necessary to provide that assistance. Think about the next time you see a friend or loved one being tormented or harassed online. What would you be willing to do to help?

Again, Adam does a nice job with his transition.

Cyber-bullying must be confronted on national, local, and personal levels. According to Soptbullying.gov., as of 2015, there is no federal law that directly addresses bullying. This is simply unacceptable. There should be a comprehensive national law confronting cyber-bullying in schools. Certain statutes currently in state laws should be amalgamated to create the strongest protections for victims and the most effective punishments for bullies as possible.

Notice how Adam gets right to the point about needing to take action on a variety of levels to stop this practice.

According to Limber and Small's article titled State *Laws and Policies to Address Bullying in Schools,* Georgia law requires faculty and staff to be trained on the nature of bullying and what actions to take if they see students being bullied.

Adam gives credence to his policy statement by pointing to several states that have already succeeded in creating such laws.

Furthermore, Connecticut law *requires* school employees to report bullying as part of their hiring contract. Washington takes this a step further by protecting employees from any legal action if a reported bully is proven to be innocent. When it comes to protecting victims, West Virginia law demands that schools must ensure that a bullied student does not receive additional abuse at the hands of his or her bully.

Legislating punishment for bullies is difficult. As Limber and Small noted, zero-tolerance polices often perpetuate violence because at-risk youth, i.e., bullies, are removed from all of the benefits of school, which might help make them less abusive. A comprehensive anti-cyber-bullying law should incorporate the best aspects of these state laws and find a way to punish bullies that is both punitive and has the ability to rehabilitate abusers. However, for national laws to be effective, local communities need to be supportive.

Here Adam points to the need for consequences for bullying behavior when it is caught.

Local communities must organize and mobilize to attack the problem of cyber-bullying. Communities need to support bullying prevention programs by conducting a school-based bullying survey for individual school districts. We can't know how to best protect victims in our community without knowing how they are affected by the problem.

Adam offers specific action steps that communities ought to do to help stop cyber-bullying.

Local school districts should create a Coordinating Committee made up of administrators, teachers, students, parents, school staff, and community partners to gather bullying data and rally support to confront the problem. Even if your local school district is unable or unwilling to mobilize behind this dire cause, there are some important actions you can take personally to safeguard those you love against cyber-bullying.

There are several warning signs that might indicate a friend or loved one is a victim of a cyber-bully. If you see a friend or loved one exhibiting these signs, the decision to get involved can be the difference between life and death.

According to Keith and Martin's article *Cyber-Bullying: Creating a Culture of Respect in a Cyber World,* victims of cyber-bullies often use electronic communication more frequently than do people who are not being bullied. Victims of cyber-bullies have mood swings and difficulty sleeping. They seem depressed and/or become anxious. Victims can also become withdrawn from social activities and fall behind in scholastic responsibilities. If you witness your friends or family members exhibiting these symptoms, there are several ways you can help.

According to Raskauskas and Stoltz's 2007 article in *Developmental Psychology,* witnesses of cyber-bullying should inform victims to take the attacks seriously, especially if the bullies threaten violence. You should tell victims to report their attacks to police or other authorities, to block harmful messages by blocking e-mail accounts and cell phone numbers, and to save copies of attacks and provide them to authorities.

If you personally know the bully and feel safe confronting him or her, do so! As Raskauskas and Stoltz noted, bullies will often back down when confronted by peers. By being a good friend and by giving good advice, you can help a victim report his or her attacks from cyber-bullies and take a major step toward eliminating this horrendous problem. So, you see, we are not helpless to stop the cyber-bulling problem as long as we make the choice NOT to ignore it.

To conclude, cyber-bullying is a devastating form of abuse that must be reported to authorities. Cyber-bullying is a worldwide problem perpetuated by the silence of both victims and bystanders. By paying attention to certain warning signs, we can empower ourselves to console victims and report their abusers.

Today, I'm imploring you to do your part to help stop cyber-bullying. I know that you agree that stopping cyber-bullying must be a priority. First, although other states have cyber-bullying laws in place, ours does not. So I'm asking you to sign this petition that I will forward to our district's state legislators. We need to make our voices heard that we want specific laws passed to stop this horrific practice and to punish those caught doing it.

Second, I'm also asking you to be vigilant in noticing signs of cyber-bullying and then taking action. Look for signs that your friend, brother, sister, cousin, boyfriend, girlfriend, or loved one might be a victim of cyber-bullying, and then get involved to help stop it! Phoebe Prince showed the warning signs, and she did not deserve to die so senselessly. None of us would ever want to say, "I'll miss just being around her," "I didn't want to believe it," "It's such a sad thing" about our own friends or family members. We must work to ensure that victims are supported and bullies are confronted nationally, locally, and personally.

I know that, if we stand together and refuse to be silent, we can and will stop cyber-bullying.

Here Adam gets personal, pointing out that each person in the room has an ethical responsibility to help stop cyber-bullying.

Adam could make this statement more compelling by offering a specific example of what one might tell the police, as well as how to install blockers on e-mail and mobile phones.

Here Adam restates his proposition, but it actually could be more comprehensive (beyond just our need to report bullying to authorities).

Adam reminds us of his specific call to action and even asks listeners to sign a petition today. His approach encourages listeners to follow through with his goal, that is, to actuate.

Adam does a nice job with his clincher in terms of tying back to the Phoebe story in his attention catcher. Doing so also appeals to emotions (pathos) in a way that should make his speech very memorable.

Reflection and Assessment

Persuasive speeches are designed to influence the attitudes, beliefs, values, and/or behavior of audience members. They do so by developing strong arguments using logos, ethos, and pathos. To assess how well you've learned what we addressed in these pages, answer the following questions. If you have trouble answering any of them, go back and review that material. Once you can answer each question accurately, you are ready to move ahead to read the appendix on interviewing.

1. What are the two ways people process persuasive messages?

2. In what ways might you tailor your persuasive speech propositions based on your target audience?

3. What types of logical appeals might you use in your persuasive speeches?

4. How can you incorporate rhetorical strategies of ethos into your persuasive speeches?

5. What are some examples of positive and negative pathos?

6. What persuasive patterns might you choose when attempting your audience to agree with you or to take action?

RESOURCE AND ASSESSMENT CENTER

MindTap

Now that you have read Chapter 17, go to your MindTap for *Communicate!* for quick access to the electronic resources that accompany this text.

Applying What You've Learned

Impromptu Speech Activities

1. Identifying Strategies of Logos, Ethos, and Pathos Draw a common household product from a box of products your instructor provides. Some products in the box might be nonperishable foods (soup, cereal, snacks, etc.), cleaning supplies (window wash, hand soap, dishwashing liquid), and paper products (toilet paper, paper towels, napkins). Prepare a 2- to 3-minute speech identifying how the product you selected appeals to logos, ethos, and pathos.

2. Point/Counterpoint Propositions of Value You and a partner will draw a slip of paper from a container provided by your instructor. The paper will identify competing topics (e.g., superman versus batman, butter versus margarine, eggs versus egg substitutes, flying versus driving, running versus biking). Each of you will prepare a 1- to 2-minute persuasive impromptu speech advocating opposing positions (point/counterpoint).

Assessment Activities

1. Assessing the Persuasive Success of a TV Commercial on its Target Audience Watch a television commercial for a similar product that airs on a cable news network, sports network, and family channel. Who is the target audience for each and why?

Identify similar and different rhetorical appeals used in them. Would you rate them as effective for the target audience?

Why or why not?

Prepare a 1- to 2-page reflection paper describing what you discovered and the assessment you drew from it.

2. Assessing Effects of Rhetorical Appeals in Daily Life Consider an interaction you had in the last week with a friend or family member who convinced you (a) *to do something* you hadn't planned on doing (e.g., go to a movie, attend an event)

or (b) *not to do something* you had intended to do (e.g., a household chore, homework).

What rhetorical strategies can you identify that influenced your decision?

Prepare a 1- to 2-page paper documenting examples of logos, ethos, and pathos that persuaded you.

Skill-Building Activities

1. Forming Propositions Create a proposition of fact, value, and policy for each of the following topics.

(a) TV violence

(b) Obesity

(c) Illiteracy

(d) Civility

(e) Sexuality

2. Practicing Pathos Identify a negative and positive emotional appeal statement for each of the propositions of fact, value, and policy you created in Skill Builder #1.

Appendix: Interviewing

- Develop a clear interview protocol.

- Employ best practices when conducting information-gathering interviews.

- Prepare for and conduct an effective employment interview using best practices.

- Prepare for and conduct a media interview following the four provided strategies.

Rosalita, the manager at *Qwik In and Out*, a convenience store and gas station, needed a new night cashier and was interviewing applicants. Her first candidate arrived on time, and after taking a tour around the store, they retired to Rosalita's office for the interview.

Rosalita began, "Take a seat. What did you say your name was again?"

"Bobby. And, um. . . . I'm not sure where you want me to sit."

"Oh, well, just sit on that box over there. Sorry for the mess, but, you know, I've had a lot to do. So, Bobby, you want to work here at *Qwik In and Out*?"

"Yeah."

"Well, you understand that you will be working alone at night, right?"

"Yeah."

"So, it says on your application that you went to Highlands High School. Is that right?"

"Uh-huh."

"And now you're a student at CSCTU?"

"Yeah."

"Will school interfere with your work schedule?"

"Nope."

"Is there anything else I should know?"

"No."

"Well, I've got several other people to talk to, and I'll let you know by Monday what I decide."

"Okay."

After Bobby left the store, Rosalita turned to Mary, the day cashier, and said, "Boy, that guy was sure a loser. He just wasn't at all prepared for the interview. I sure hope the next one's better."

interview
a highly structured conversation in which one person asks questions and another person answers them

What do you think about how Rosalita conducted the interview? What do you think about Bobby's answers? What do you think about Rosalita's assessment of Bobby? Unfortunately, this type of interview scenario happens all too often. An **interview** is a highly structured conversation where one person asks questions and another person answers them. By *highly structured*, we mean that the questions to be asked are determined ahead of time. Throughout the course of our lives, we end up participating and many kinds of interviews. Sometimes we interview to get a job and other times to hire an employee. We also conduct interviews to gather information and even to share our stories with the media. Rarely, however, do we get any training to conduct ourselves effectively in them. This chapter is focused on providing these important skills for both interviewers and interviewees. We begin by describing how to develop good questions for an interview protocol. Then we propose some guidelines to follow when engaged in information-gathering, employment, and media interviews.

The Interview Protocol

interview protocol
the list of questions used to elicit desired information from the interviewee

The **interview protocol** is the list of questions used to elicit desired information from the interviewee. An effective interviewer always prepares a protocol in advance. How many questions you plan to ask depends on how much time you will have for the interview. Figure A.1 presents a list of topics for an interview with a music producer when the goal is to learn about how producers find and sign new talent.

Just as the topics in a well-developed speech are structured in an outline with main points, subpoints, and supporting material, an effective interview protocol is structured into primary and secondary questions. The questions should be a mix of open-ended and closed questions, as well as neutral and leading questions. Let's briefly examine each type.

Figure A.1

Music producer interview topics

Music producer interview topics
- Finding artists
- Decision process
- Criteria
- Stories of success and failure

© Cengage Learning

Primary and Secondary Questions

Primary questions are introductory questions about each major interview topic. Figure A.2 illustrates what the primary questions might be for the music producer interview.

Secondary questions are follow-up questions that probe the interviewee to expand on the answers given to primary questions. The interviewee may not realize how much detail you want or may be purposely evasive. Some follow-up questions probe by simply encouraging the interviewee to continue ("And then?" or "Is there more?"); some probe into a specific detail the person mentioned or failed to mention ("What does 'regionally popular' mean?" and "You didn't mention genre. What role might that play in your decision to offer a contract?"); and some probe into their feelings ("How did it feel when her first record went platinum?").

Open and Closed Questions

Open questions are broad-based queries that allow freedom about how to respond to the specific information, opinions, or feelings. Open questions encourage the interviewee to talk and allow the interviewer an opportunity to listen and observe. For example, in a job interview you might be asked, "What one accomplishment has best prepared you for this job?" In a customer service interview, a representative might ask, "What seems to be the problem?" or "Can you tell me the steps you took when you first set up this product?"

By contrast, **closed questions** are narrowly focused and require very brief (1- or 2-word) answers. Closed questions range from those that can be answered yes or no, such as "Have you had a course in marketing?" to those that require only a short answer, such as "Which of the artists that you have signed have won Grammys?" By asking closed questions, interviewers can control the interview and obtain specific information quickly. But the answers to closed questions cannot reveal the nuances behind responses, nor are they likely to capture the complexity of the story.

Neutral and Leading Questions

Open and closed questions may also be either neutral or leading. **Neutral questions** do not direct a person's answer. "What can you tell me about your work with Habitat for Humanity?" and "What criteria do you use in deciding whether to offer an artist a contract?" are neutral questions. The neutral question gives the respondent free rein to answer the question without any knowledge of what the interviewer thinks or believes.

primary questions
introductory questions about each major interview topic

secondary questions
follow-up questions that probe the interviewee to expand on the answers given to primary questions

open questions
broad-based queries that allow freedom about what specific information, opinions, or feelings to divulge

closed questions
narrowly focused questions that require very brief (one- or two-word) answers

neutral questions
questions that do not direct a person's answer

---

(1) How do you find artists to consider for contract?
(2) Once an artist has been brought to your attention, what course of action do you follow?
(3) What criteria do you use when deciding to offer a contract?
(4) Can you tell me the story of how you came to sign one of your most successful artists and then one about an unsuccessful artist?

Figure A.2

Music producer primary questions

© Cengage Learning

leading questions
questions that guide respondents toward providing certain types of information and imply that the interviewer prefers one answer over another

By contrast, **leading questions** guide respondents toward providing certain types of information and imply that the interviewer prefers one answer over another. "What do you like about working for Habitat for Humanity?" steers respondents to describe only the positive aspects of their volunteer work. "Having a 'commercial sound' is an important criteria, isn't it?" directs the answer by providing the standard for comparison. In most types of interviews, neutral questions are preferable because they are less likely to create defensiveness in the interviewee. In the opening interview, which of Rosalita's questions were neutral and which were leading?

A good interview protocol will use a combination of open, closed, neutral, and leading questions. With this in mind, look again at the opening interview. What kinds of questions did Rosalita ask Bobby? How did this affect what happened? Figure A.3 provides a sample interview protocol for the music producer interview.

Information-Gathering Interviews

Interviewing is a valuable method for obtaining information on nearly any topic. Lawyers and police officers interview witnesses to establish facts; health care providers interview patients to obtain medical histories before making diagnoses; reporters interview sources for their stories; managers interview employees to receive updates on projects; and students interview experts to obtain information for research projects. Once you have prepared a good interview protocol, you need to choose an appropriate person to interview, conduct the interview effectively, and follow up respectfully.

Choosing the Interviewee

Sometimes the choice is obvious, but other times, you must do research to identify the right person to interview. Suppose your purpose is to learn about how to get a recording contract. You might begin by asking a professor in the music department for the name of a music production agency in the area. Or you could find the name of an agency by searching online. Once you find a Web site, you can usually find an "About Us" or "Contact Us" link on it, which will offer names, titles, e-mail addresses, and phone numbers. You should be able to identify someone appropriate to your purpose from this list. Once you have identified the person or people to be interviewed, you should contact them to make an appointment. Today, it is generally best to do so by both e-mail and telephone if possible. When you contact them, be sure to clearly state the purpose of the interview, how the interview information will be used, and how long you expect the interview to take. When setting a date and time, suggest several dates and time ranges and ask which would be best for them. As you conclude, thank the person for agreeing to be interviewed and confirm the date, time, and location you have agreed to for the interview. If you make the appointment more than a few days in advance, call or e-mail the day before the interview to confirm the appointment.

You don't want to bother your interviewee with information you can get elsewhere. So to prepare appropriate protocol questions, do some research on the topic in advance. This includes learning about what the interviewee may have written about the topic and his or her credentials. Interviewees will be more responsive if you appear informed and being informed will ensure that you ask good questions. For instance, if you are going to interview a music producer, you will want to do preliminary research about what

Rapport-Building Opener

How did you get interested in becoming a music producer?

Major Topic Questions

Primary Question #1: How do you find artists to consider for contract?
   Secondary Question: Is this different from the methods used by other producers?
   Secondary Question: Do artists ever come to you in other ways?
Primary Question #2: Once an artist has been brought to your attention, what course of action follows?
   Secondary Question: Do you ever just see an artist or band and immediately sign them?
   Secondary Question: What's the longest period of time you "auditioned" an artist or band before signing them?
Primary Question #3: What criteria do you use in deciding to offer a contract?
   Secondary Question: How important are the artist's age, sex, or ethnicity?
Primary Question #4: Can you tell me the story of how you came to sign one of your most successful artists?
   Secondary Question: What do you think made the artist so successful?
Primary Question #5: Can you tell me the story of an artist you signed that was not successful?
   Secondary Question: Why do you think this artist failed?
   Secondary Question: Do you think it was a mistake to sign this artist?
   Secondary Question: In retrospect, what could you or the artist have done differently that might have helped him or her succeed?

© Cengage Learning

Figure A.3

Sample music producer interview protocol

a music producer is and does, whether any general "best practices" exist for signing artists, and whether this particular producer has published any criteria. You can usually do so by carefully reading the information posted on their Web site. Then, during the interview, you can ask about additional criteria, different criteria, or to expand on how the criteria is used in making judgments.

Conducting the Interview

To guide you in the process of conducting effective and ethical interviews, we offer this list of best practices.

1. **Dress professionally.** Doing so sends a message that you *respect the interviewee* and the time they are giving you and that you take the interview seriously.

2. **Be prompt.** You also *demonstrate respect* by showing up prepared to begin at the time you have agreed to. Remember to allow enough time for potential traffic and parking problems.

3. **Be courteous.** Begin by introducing yourself and the purpose of the interview and by thanking the person for taking the time to talk to you. Remember, although interviewees may enjoy talking about the subject, may be flattered, and may wish to share knowledge, they most likely have nothing to gain from the interview.

4. **Ask permission to record.** If the interviewee says no, *respect* his or her wishes and take careful notes instead.

5. **Keep the interview moving.** You do not want to rush the person, but you do want to behave *responsibly* by getting your questions answered during the allotted time.

6. **Monitor your nonverbal reactions.** Maintain good eye contact with the person. Nod to show understanding, and smile occasionally to maintain the friendliness of the interview. How you look and act is likely to determine whether the person will warm up to you and give you an informative interview.

7. **Get permission to quote.** Be sure to get permission for exact quotes. Doing so demonstrates that you *respect* the interviewee and want to report his or her ideas *honestly* and *fairly.* Doing so also communicates that you have *integrity* and strive to act *responsibly.* You might even offer to let the person see a copy of what you prepare before you share it with others. That way, he or she can double-check the accuracy of direct quotations.

8. **Confirm credentials.** Before you leave, be sure to confirm your interviewee's professional title and the company or organization he or she represents. To do so is to act *responsibly* because you will need these details when explaining why you chose to interview this person.

9. **End on time.** As with arriving promptly, ending the interview when you said you would demonstrates *respect* for the interviewee and that you act *responsibly* and with *integrity.*

10. **Thank the interviewee.** Thanking the interviewee leads to positive rapport, should you need to follow up later, and demonstrates that you appreciate his or her valuable time. You may even follow up with a short thank-you note after you leave.

Following Up

Because your interview notes were probably taken in outline or shorthand form, the longer you wait to translate them, the more difficult doing so will be. So you'll need to sit down with your notes as soon as possible after the interview to make more extensive notes of the information you may want to use later. If you recorded the interview, take some time to **transcribe** the responses by translating them word for word into written form. If at any point you are not sure whether you have accurately transcribed what the person said or meant, telephone or e-mail them to double-check. When you have completed a draft of your paper, project, or speech outline, you can demonstrate *respect* for the person and *integrity* as a reporter by providing him or her with a copy of the product if it is a written paper or report, a link to it if it is an online document, or an invitation to attend if it is a public speech or performance.

transcribe
translate oral interview responses word for word into written form

Employment Interviews

Believe it or not, in the past 50 years, the average amount of time an employee stays with one company or organization has gone from over 23 years to about 4 years (Employee Tenure, 2010). What this means is that we spend more time doing employment interviews both as interviewers and interviewees than ever before. Employment interviews help interviewers assess which applicants have the knowledge, experience, and skills that best fit the responsibilities of the position and culture of the organization—characteristics and skills that cannot be judged from a résumé. And employment interviews help employment-seekers make an educated guess about whether the organization is one they would enjoy working in. So let's look at some best practices for both employment interviewers and employment seekers.

Employment Interviewers

Historically, human resource professionals have conducted most employment interviews on behalf of a firm, but today more and more workplaces rely on coworkers as interviewers. You may have already helped conduct employment interviews, or you may be asked to do so in the near future. As with any interview, you will need to follow some guidelines as you both prepare for and conduct the interview.

Preparing for the Interview As with information interviews, begin by doing research. In the case of employment interviewing, this means becoming familiar with the knowledge, skills, and aptitudes someone must have to be successful in the job. It also means studying the résumés, reference letters, and other application materials to narrow the applicant pool to the short list of applicants you will interview. Before interviewing each candidate on the short list, prepare by reviewing their materials again, making notes about topics to address with probing secondary questions.

In most employment interviewing situations, you will see several candidates. It's important to make an interview protocol to ensure that all applicants are asked the same (or very similar) questions about characteristics and skills. Be sure to identify primary questions and secondary questions that will probe knowledge, skills, characteristics, and experiences relevant to the position and the culture of your organization. Using a protocol will also help you avoid questions that violate fair employment practice legislation. The Equal Opportunity Commission has detailed guidelines that spell out what questions are unlawful.

Conducting the Interview As with information-gathering interviews, begin with introductions and a question or two designed to establish rapport and to help the interviewee relax. What follows are some best-practice tips to follow when conducting employment interviews.

1. **Greet the applicant.** Warmly greet the applicant by name, shake hands, and introduce yourself. Ask a couple of rapport-building "warm-up" questions to put the applicant at ease. For example, you might ask how the traffic was, whether it was difficult to find parking, or something about the weather.

2. **Ask a series of prepared protocol questions.** Here is where you ask your well-planned questions to determine whether the applicant's knowledge, skills, experiences, personal characteristics, and interpersonal style fit the demands of the job and the organizational culture. You want to give the applicant sufficient time to answer your questions, but don't waste time by allowing the applicant to over-answer questions.

3. **Consider your verbal and nonverbal cues.** As you ask questions, strive to sound spontaneous and to speak in a voice that is easily heard. Be sensitive to the nonverbal messages you send. Be careful that you are not leading applicants to answer in certain ways through your nonverbal cues.

4. **Use secondary follow-up questions.** Probe the applicant to expand on answers that are vague or too brief. Remember, your goal is to understand the applicant, which includes his or her strengths, weaknesses, and potential fit with the position and your organization.

5. **Conclude with a clarification of next steps.** As the interview comes to an end, tell the applicant what will happen next. Explain how and approximately when the hiring decision will be made, as well as how the applicant will be notified. Unless you are the person with hiring authority, remain neutral about the applicant. You don't want to mislead the applicant with false hope or discouragement.

Following Up Once you have hired one of the interviewees, be sure to follow up with a short e-mail or letter informing each of the other candidates that the position has been filled. You can do so *respectfully* by thanking them for their interest in the position and taking the time to participate in the interview, reminding them that they were a strong candidate in a strong applicant pool, and wishing them well in their future employment-seeking endeavors.

Employment Seekers

employment seeker
anyone who is looking for a job or considering a job change

An **employment seeker** is anyone looking for a job or considering a job change. Some may be unemployed and dedicating 100 percent of their time to finding a job. Others may be happily employed and recruited to apply for another position. Still others could be employed, but seeking a more rewarding position. As many employment experts will tell you, "As a rule, the best jobs do *not* go to the best-qualified individuals—they go to the best job seekers" (Graber, 2000, p. 29). Successful employment seekers are obviously the ones who get the job. To be successful, you need to follow guidelines searching for job openings, as well as when applying and interviewing.

Locating Job Openings At this point in your life, you have probably been through the hiring process at least once and perhaps many times. So you know how stressful it can be. You also probably know that sometimes the most difficult part is finding out about job openings. Sometimes openings are easily accessible by searching the Internet, newspaper, career fairs, and career centers. We call this the **visible job market**. Other times, however, job openings are not readily apparent and require you to use other methods to locate and apply for them. We call this the **hidden job market** (Yena, 2011). We focus here on locating jobs in both visible and hidden job markets by searching published resources (in print and online), using referral services, and networking.

visible job market
easily accessible job opening announcements

hidden job market
job openings that are not readily apparent and require alternative methods to locate

Published Resources When employers want to cast a wide net for applicants, they publish in a variety of outlets that are read widely by employment seekers. These range from Web sites such as CareerBuilder, Monster Worldwide, the Federal Government's USAJOBS, CollegeJobBank, as well as classified sections of online and print newspapers and newsletters. Some sites allow you to post your résumé online and will forward it to potential employers when your credentials fit their needs. Although employers often use these sites, they also very often publish openings on their own Web sites. So, even if you find an announcement posted on another site, you can improve your chances of landing an interview if you actually apply through the company's own Web site (Light, 2011).

Referral Services Some employers like to use referral services to do the initial screening of applicants. Most colleges and universities have an on-site career center that serves this purpose. Your tuition dollars pay for this service, so it's one of the first places you should look. They post and publish local, regional, national, and international openings in a variety of for-profit, nonprofit, and government organizations. In addition to doing initial screenings for employers, career service officers also provide applicants helpful advice about writing cover letters, preparing résumés, selecting references, and doing interviews. Finally, they often facilitate on-campus **career fairs** to help bring potential employers and applicants together to learn about the company and make contacts.

Some employers also have in-house **employee referral programs** that reward current employees for referring strong candidates to the company. If you are interested in working for a particular company, you might seek an opportunity to ask a current employee to recommend you.

Networking **Networking** is the process of using developing or established relationships to make contacts with people who can help you discover positions that may or may not be accessible through the *visible job market*. In fact, some research suggests that the majority of jobs are filled this way (Betty, 2010). Your **network** consists of the people you know, people you meet, and the people who are known to the people you know. These people may include teachers, counselors, your friends, family friends, relatives, service club members, mentors, classmates, colleagues, and even people you meet at sporting events, country clubs, and health clubs. We offer two guidelines to help make networking work for you.

1. **Reach out to people you know and tell them you are in the job market.** Speak up and tell the people you know that you are looking for a job. Bring it up during a conversation you may be having with them or intentionally seek them out to let them know. Prepare business cards with your contact information on them and give them to the people you talk to. Similarly, don't assume they know your résumé. In addition to business cards, be prepared to provide them with an **elevator speech**—a 60-second oral summary of the type of job you're seeking and your qualifications for it. Ask them if they know of (1) any job opportunities that might be appropriate, and (2) anyone you might contact to help you find such opportunities. Finally, (3) ask them to keep their eyes and ears open about anything that might be of interest to you.

2. **Grow your network.** Attend networking events in your area that may be hosted by your college or university career center, the local chamber of commerce, and alumni association. Join professional and civic organizations. Volunteer. The more people you know, the more people you will have to ask about potential opportunities on the *hidden job market*. You should also join online networking groups such as *LinkedIn, Facebook,* and *Twitter.* Remember the key here is to develop and nurture relationships. People will make a special effort to help you if they believe you are a friend and a good person.

career fairs
events that bring potential employers and applicants together to foster networking and create awareness about opportunities

employee referral programs
in-house reward programs for employees who refer strong candidates to the company

networking
the process of using developing or established relationships to make contacts regarding job openings

network
the people you know, people you meet, and people who are known to the people you know

elevator speech
a 60-second oral summary of the type of job you are seeking and your qualifications for it

Preparing Application Materials

Because interviewing is time consuming, most organizations do not interview all the people who apply for a job. Rather, they use a variety of screening devices to eliminate people who don't meet their qualifications. Chief among them are evaluating the qualifications you highlight on your résumé and in your cover letter (Kaplan, 2002). A **résumé** is a summary sheet highlighting your related experience, educational background, skills, and accomplishments. A **cover letter** is a short well-written letter or e-mail expressing your interest in the position and piquing curiosity about why your application materials deserve a closer look. The goal of your cover letter and résumé is to land an interview (Farr, 2009). Whether you send your application materials electronically or through regular postal mail, the guidelines for preparing them effectively are the same. Before you can even begin, you need to know something about the company and about the job requirements so you can tailor your resume and cover letter in ways that highlight how and why you are the best candidate. Today you can learn a lot about an organization by visiting its Web site and reading online material thoroughly. You can also talk to people you know who work or worked there, or acquaintances of employees. Let's look at three guidelines to follow when tailoring your résumé and cover letter.

Tailoring Your Résumé Tailor your résumé to highlight your skills and experiences related to the position and its responsibilities. There are two types of résumés. In both, begin by supplying basic contact information (name, address, e-mail, phone number), educational degrees or certificates earned, and career objective. In a **chronological résumé**, list your job positions and accomplishments in reverse chronological order. Chronological résumés are most appropriate if you have held jobs in the past that are clearly related to the position you are applying for. In a **functional résumé**, focus on highlighting the skills and experiences you have that qualify you for the position. You may find a functional résumé best for highlighting your skills and accomplishments if you are changing careers, have a gap in your work history, or have limited formal job experience, but have acquired job-related skills in other ways (courses you have taken, clubs you have belonged to, service-learning, internships, and volunteer work, etc.). Figures A.4 and A.5 are examples of a chronological and functional résumé for the same college student.

Tailoring Your Cover Letter Tailor your cover letter to the position. Be sure to highlight your qualifications for *a specific job and its responsibilities*. You can learn some of this information in the job description, but you may also need to make inferences about it by visiting the company's Web site and talking to people associated with the organization or familiar with the type of position described in the advertisement.

Your cover letter should be short, no more than four or five paragraphs. If you prepare your cover letter in the body of an e-mail message, it should be even shorter. These paragraphs should highlight your job-related skills and experiences *using key words that appeared in the posting*. Many employers use software programs that scan e-mails and résumés for job-relevant key words. Using them in your cover letter will increase the likelihood that someone will actually look at your application materials. Use a spell-checker and carefully proofread for errors such programs don't catch. Your cover letter

---

résumé
a summary sheet highlighting your related experience, educational background, skills, and accomplishments

cover letter
a short, well-written letter or e-mail expressing your interest in a particular job and piquing curiosity about you as an applicant

chronological résumé
listing your job positions and accomplishments in reverse chronological order

functional résumé
focuses on highlighting the skills and experiences that qualify you for the position

Elisa C. Vardin

2326 Tower Place
Cincinnati, OH 45220
(513) 861-2497
ECVardin@yahoo.com

Professional Objective:

An entry-level marketing research position where I can use my quantitative training to create and analyze marketing data and use my organizing, writing and public speaking skills to communicate technical findings to decision makers.

Educational Background:

University of Cincinnati, Cincinnati, OH, B.A. June 2001.

Major: Applied Mathematics, Minor: Marketing.

GPA 3.36. Dean's List.

Work and Other Relevant Experience:

Marketing Solutions, Inc., Cincinnati, OH. Summer 2011.

Intern at marketing research firm. Provided administrative support to marketing research team. Created a new method for tracking internal project workflow. Analyzed Survant generated data with Mentor. Helped prepare client reports.

McMicken College of Arts and Sciences, U.C. Student Ambassador. 2008–2011. Chair, Activities Committee 2010–2011. Responsible for planning social events and scheduling over 6,000 student visits. Over 45 presentations to groups.

Strategic Planning Committee, Summit Country Day School, Cincinnati, OH. Fall 2006–2007. One of two student members. Worked with the board of directors developing the first strategic plan for a 1,000-student independent school (pre-K through 12).

AYF National Leadership Conference, Miniwanca Conference Center, Shelby, MI. Summer 2005–2006. Participant in conference sponsored by American Youth Foundation.

Technical Skills and Training:

MINITAB, SAS, SPSS, MatLab, MATHSTAT, MicroSoft Office, Survant, Mentor. Coursework in statistics, regression analysis, math stats, nonparametric stats, applied complex analysis, marketing research.

© Cengage Learning

Figure A.4

Sample chronological résumé

must be 100% error free to serve as a catalyst for getting an interview. Figures A.6 and A.7 provide a sample cover letter and sample cover e-mail.

Tailoring Materials for Online Submissions Tailor your application materials for a variety of online submission programs. Because you will apply for most jobs online, make sure your materials can be submitted in several formats. Some of them are illustrated in Figure A.8 along with their advantages and disadvantages.

Figure A.5

Sample functional résumé

Elisa C. Vardin

2326 Tower Place
Cincinnati, OH 45220
(513) 861-2497
ECVardin@yahoo.com

Professional Objective:

Entry-level marketing research position allowing me to use my quantitative train-ing to create and analyze marketing data and use my organizing, writing and public speaking skills to communicate technical findings to decision makers.

Educational Background:

University of Cincinnati, Cincinnati, OH, B.A. June 2015.

Major: Applied Mathematics, Minor: Marketing.

GPA 3.36. Dean's List.

Relevant Coursework: Multivariate Stats, Regression Analysis, Math Stats, Nonparametric Stats, Applied Complex Analysis, Marketing Research.

Technical Skills: MINITAB, SPSS, SAS, MatLab, MATHSTAT, MicroSoft Office

Professional Skills:

Statistical and Analytical

- Proficient with various statistical software packages used to analyze mar-keting research data.
- Hands-on experience cleaning marketing research data sets.
- Analyzed complex statistical output from a multisite marketing research study under extreme time pressure.

Organizing/Leadership Skills

- Created and coordinated a schedule for over 6,000 client visits.
- Participated in strategic planning process for an independent private school.
- Graduated from two-year national leadership development program.

Communication Skills

- Presented over 45 10- to 30-minute presentations using PowerPoint.
- Drafted marketing research report and PowerPoint presentation for client.
- Public speaking, persuasion, and technical writing coursework.

Experience:

Marketing Solutions, Inc., Cincinnati, OH. Summer 2015. Intern.

McMicken College of Arts and Sciences, U.C. Student Ambassador. 2011–2015. Chair, Activities Committee 2014–2015.

Strategic Planning Committee, Summit Country Day School, Cincinnati, OH. Fall 2010. Student Representative. Strategic Planning Committee.

National Leadership Conference, American Youth Foundation. Summer 2009.

Figure A.6

Sample cover letter

2326 Tower Place
Cincinnati, OH 45220
April 8, 2016

Mr. Kyle Jones
Acme Marketing Research Associates
P.O. Box 482
Cincinnati, OH 45201

Dear Mr. Jones:

I am applying for the position of first-year associate at Acme Marketing Research Associates, which I learned about through the Office of Career Counseling at the University of Cincinnati. I am a senior mathematics major at the University of Cincinnati who is interested in a career in marketing research. I am highly motivated, eager to learn, and I enjoy working with all types of people. I am excited by the prospect of working for a firm like Acme Marketing Research Associates, where I can apply my leadership and problem-solving skills in a professional setting.

As a mathematics major, I have developed the analytical proficiency that is necessary for working through complex problems. My courses in statistics have especially prepared me for data analysis, and my more theoretical courses have taught me how to construct an effective argument. My leadership training and experiences have given me the ability to work effectively in groups and have taught me the benefits of both individual and group problem solving. My work on the Strategic Planning Committee has given me an introduction to market analysis by teaching me skills associated with strategic planning. Finally, from my theatrical experience, I have gained the poise to make presentations in front of small and large groups alike. I believe these experiences and others have shaped who I am and have helped me to develop many of the skills necessary to be successful. I am interested in learning more and continuing to grow.

I look forward to having the opportunity to interview with you. I have enclosed my résumé with my school address and phone number. Thank you for your consideration. I hope to hear from you soon.

Sincerely,
Elisa C. Vardin

Conducting the Employment Interview

An **employment interview** is a conversation or set of conversations between a job candidate and a representative or representatives of a hiring organization. Your goal is to convince the interviewer(s) that you are the best qualified candidate and the best fit for the position and company. Successful interviewing begins with thorough preparation, then with the actual interview, and finally with appropriate follow up.

employment interview
a conversation or set of conversations between a job candidate and a representative or representatives of a hiring organization

Figure A.7

Sample cover e-mail

Dear Mr. Jones:

I am applying for the position of research assistant at Acme Marketing Research Associates. Professor Robert Carl at the University of Cincinnati suggested that I might be a good fit for your company.

As an applied mathematics major at the University of Cincinnati with a minor in marketing, I have prepared myself for a career in marketing research. I have worked hard to develop a comprehensive background in statistics and am equipped with the skills to use the major statistical packages required to analyze market research data. In addition to these technical qualifications I have also developed my organizational, leadership, and communication skills though a variety of paid and volunteer positions.

I am excited by the prospect of a career at AMRA because your company is known for its cutting-edge marketing research programs as well as high ethical standards. I look forward to having the opportunity to speak with you. I have attached both a .txt and a .rtf formatted copy of my résumé for your consideration. I look forward to hearing from you about the next steps I can take to become a member of your marketing research team.

Sincerely,
Elisa C. Vardin

© Cengage Learning

Preparing Once you submit your application materials, you need to prepare for the interview you hope to get. In this section, we offer four suggestions to prepare for a job interview.

1. **Do your homework.** Although you should have already done extensive research on the position and the organization to prepare your application materials, you should review what you've learned before going to the interview. Be sure you know the organization's products and services, areas of operation, ownership, and financial health. Nothing puts off interviewers more than applicants who arrive at an interview knowing little about the organization. Be sure to look beyond the "Work for Us" or "Frequently Asked Questions" links on the company's Web site. Find more specific information such as pages that target potential investors, report company stock performance, and describe the organization's mission (Slayter, 2006). Likewise, pictures can suggest the type of organizational culture you can expect—formal or informal dress, collaborative or individual work spaces, diversity, and so on. Researching these details will help you decide whether the organization is right for you, as well as help you form questions to ask during the interview.

2. **Prepare a self-summary.** You should not have to hesitate when an interviewer asks you why you are interested in the job. You should also be prepared to describe your previous accomplishments. Form these statements as personal stories with specific examples that people will remember (Beshara, 2006). Robin Ryan (2000), one of the nation's foremost career authorities, advises job seekers to prepare a 60-second general statement they can share with a potential employer. She advises job seekers

TYPE	USE	FILE EXTENTION	ADVANTAGES	DISADVANTAGES
Formatted	For print résumé or e-mail attachments	.doc .wpd .wps	• Visually attractive	• Vulnerable to viruses • Inconsistencies in formatting from computer to computer
Text	• Posting to job boards • Conversion to scannable résumé	.txt	• Key word searchable • Consistent formatting computer to computer • Not vulnerable to viruses	• Not visually appealing
Rich Text	• When sending résumé as an attachment • When you don't know employer's format preference	.rft	• Good for résumé attachment because it is compatible with all platforms and word processing programs • Formatting of original résumé holds up pretty well • Less vulnerable to viruses	None
Portable Document	• When you want to retain the exact identical formatting and pagination • When employers request it	.pdf	• Invulnerable to viruses • Compatible across computer systems	• Hard to do key word search • If prepared by others, can not make revisions without expensive software
Web Based	• For passive job searching • To post resume to your Web site or a hosted	.html .htm	• Employer can find your résumé • Available 24/7	• Need a host site

Adapted from: Hansen, K. Your e-résumé's file format aligns with its delivery method. Accessed at Quintessential Careers.com: http://www.quintcareers.com/e-resume_format.html.

Figure A.8

Online application submission variations

to identify which aspects of their training and experience would be most valued by a potential employer. She suggests making a five-point agenda that can (a) summarize your most relevant experience and (b) "build a solid picture emphasizing how you *can* do the job" (p. 10). Once you have your points identified, practice communicating them fluently in 60 seconds or less.

3. **Prepare a list of questions about the organization and the job.** The employment interview should be a two-way street, where you size up the company as they are sizing you up. So you will probably have a number of specific questions to ask the interviewer. For example, "Can you describe a typical workday for the person in this position?" or "What is the biggest challenge in this job?"

Make a list of your questions and take it with you to the interview. It can be difficult to come up with good questions on the spur of the moment, so you should prepare several questions in advance. One question we do not advise asking during the interview, however, is "How much money will I make?" Save salary, benefits, and vacation-time negotiations until after you have been offered the job.

4. **Rehearse the interview.** Several days before the interview, spend time outlining the job requirements and how your knowledge, skills, and experiences meet those requirements. Practice answering questions commonly asked in interviews, such as those listed in Figure A.9.

Interviewing The actual interview is your opportunity to sell yourself to the organization. Although interviews can be stressful, your preparation should give you the confidence you need to relax and communicate effectively. Believe it or not, the job interview is somewhat stressful for the interviewer as well. Most companies do not interview potential employees every day. Moreover, the majority of interviewers have little or no formal training in the interview process. Your goal is to make the interview a comfortable conversation for both of you. Use these guidelines to help you have a successful interview.

1. **Dress appropriately.** You want to make a good first impression, so it is important to be well groomed and neatly dressed. Although "casual" or "business casual" is common in many workplaces, some organizations still expect employees to be more formally dressed. If you don't know the dress code for the organization, call the human resources department and ask.

2. **Arrive on time.** The interview is the organization's first exposure to your work behavior, so you don't want to be late. Find out how long it will take you to travel by making a dry run at least a day before. Plan to arrive 10 or 15 minutes before your appointment.

3. **Bring supplies.** Bring extra copies of your résumé, cover letter, business cards, and references, as well as the list of questions you plan to ask. You might also bring a portfolio of previous work you have done. You also want to have paper and a pen so that you can make notes.

Figure A.9

Frequently asked interview questions

- In what ways does your transcript reflect your ability?
- Can you give an example of how you work under pressure?
- What are your major strengths? Weaknesses?
- Can you give an example of when you were a leader and what happened?
- Tell me about a time when you tried something at work that failed. How did you respond to the failure?
- Tell me about a time you had a serious conflict with a co-worker. How did you deal with the conflict?
- What have you done that shows your creativity?
- What kind of position are you looking for?

© Cengage Learning

4. **Use active listening.** When we are anxious, we sometimes have trouble listening well. Work on paying attention to, understanding, and remembering what is asked. Remember that the interviewer will be aware of your nonverbal behavior, so be sure to make and keep eye contact as you listen.

5. **Think before answering.** If you have prepared for the interview, make sure that as you answer the interviewer's questions, you also tell your story. Take a moment to consider how your answers portray your skills and experiences.

6. **Be enthusiastic.** If you come across as bored or disinterested, the interviewer is likely to conclude that you would be an unmotivated employee.

7. **Ask questions.** As the interview is winding down, be sure to ask any questions you prepared that have not already been answered. You may also want to ask how well the interviewer believes your qualifications match the position, and what your strengths are.

8. **Thank the interviewer and restate your interest in the position.** As the interview comes to a close, shake the interviewer's hand and thank him or her for the opportunity. Finally, restate your interest in the position and desire to work on the company team.

Following Up

Once the interview is over, you can set yourself apart from the other applicants by following these important steps:

1. **Send a thank-you note.** It is appropriate to write a short note thanking the interviewer for the experience and again expressing your interest in the job.

2. **Self-assess your performance.** Take time to critique your performance. How well did you do? What can you do better next time?

3. **Contact the interviewer for feedback.** If you don't get the job, you might call the interviewer and ask for feedback. Be polite and indicate that you are only calling to get some help on your interviewing skills. Actively listen to the feedback, using questions and paraphrases to clarify what is being said. Be sure to thank the interviewer for helping you.

Media Interviews

Today we live in a media-saturated environment where any individual may be approached by a newsperson and asked to participate in an on-air interview. For example, the authors have a friend who became the object of media interest when the city council refused to grant him a zoning variance to complete building a new home on his property. In the course of three days, his story became front-page news, and reports about his situation made the local radio and TV news shows. You might be asked for an interview at public meetings, at the mall, or within the context of your work or community service. For example, you may be asked to share your knowledge of your organization's programs, events, or activities. Because media interviews are likely to be edited in some way before they are aired and because they reach a wide audience, there are specific strategies you should use to prepare for and participate in them.

Before the Interview

The members of the media work under very tight deadlines, so it is crucial that you respond immediately to media requests for an interview. When people are insensitive to media deadlines, they can end up looking like they have purposefully evaded the interview and have something to hide. When you speak with the media representative, clarify what the focus of the interview will be and how the information will be presented. At times, the entire interview will be presented; however, it is more likely that the interview will be edited or paraphrased and not all of your comments will be reported.

As you prepare for the interview, identify three or four **talking points**, that is, the central ideas you want to present as you answer questions during a media interview. For example, before our friend was interviewed by the local TV news anchor, he knew that he wanted to emphasize that he was a victim of others' mistakes: (1) he had hired a licensed architect to draw the plans; (2) the city inspectors had repeatedly approved earlier stages of the building process; (3) the city planning commission had voted unanimously to grant him the variance; and (4) he would be out half the cost of the house if he were forced to tear it down and rebuild. Consider how you will tailor your information to the specific audience in terms they can understand. Consider how you will respond to tough or hostile questions.

> **talking points**
> *the three or four central ideas you will present as you answer the questions asked during a media interview*

During the Interview

Media interviews call for a combination of interviewing, nonverbal communication, and public speaking skills. Follow these strategies during a media interview:

1. **Present appropriate nonverbal cues.** Inexperienced interviewees can often look or sound tense or stiff. By standing up during a phone interview, your voice will sound more energetic and authoritative. With on-camera interviews, when checking your notes, move your eyes but not your head. Keep a small smile when listening. Look at the interviewer, not into the camera.

2. **Make clear and concise statements.** It is important to speak slowly, to articulate clearly, and to avoid technical terms or jargon. Remember that the audience is not familiar with your area of expertise.

3. **Realize that you are always "on the record."** Say nothing as an aside or confidentially to a reporter. Do not say anything that you would not want quoted. If you do not know an answer, do not speculate, but instead indicate that the question is outside of your area of expertise. Do not ramble during the interviewer's periods of silence. Do not allow yourself to be rushed into an answer.

> **bridge**
> *the transition you create in a media interview in order to move from the interviewer's subject to the message you want to communicate*

4. **Learn how to bridge.** Media consultant Joanna Krotz (2006) defines a **bridge** as a transition you create to move from the interviewer's subject to the message you want to communicate. To do this, you first answer the direct question and then use a phrase such as "What's important to remember, however … ," "Let me put that in perspective … ," or "It's also important to know. …" With careful preparation, specific communication strategies during the interview, and practice, one can skillfully deliver a message in any media interview format.

WHAT WOULD YOU DO?

A Question of Ethics

Ken shifted in his chair as Ms. Goldsmith, his interviewer, looked over his résumé.

"I have to tell you that you have considerably more experience than the average applicant we usually get coming straight out of college," Ms. Goldsmith said. "Let's see, you've managed a hardware store, been a bookkeeper for a chain of three restaurants, and were the number-one sales-man for six straight months at a cell phone store."

"That's right," Ken said. "My family has al-ways stressed the value of hard work, so I have worked a full-time job every summer since I en-tered junior high school, right through my last year of college."

"Very impressive," Ms. Goldsmith said. "And still you managed to get excellent grades and do a considerable amount of volunteer work in your spare time. What's your secret?"

"Secret?" said Ken nervously. "There's no secret—just a lot of hard work."

"Yes, I see that," said Ms. Goldsmith. "What I mean is that there are only 24 hours in a day and you obviously had a lot on your plate each day,

especially for someone so young. How did you manage to do it?"

Ken thought for a moment before answering. "I only need five hours of sleep a day." He could feel Ms. Goldsmith's eyes scrutinizing his face. He hadn't exactly lied on his résumé—just exaggerated a little bit. He had, in fact, helped his father run the family hardware store for a number of years. He had helped his aunt, from time to time, keep track of her restaurant's re-ceipts. He had also spent one summer selling cell phones for his cousin.

"And you can provide references for these jobs?" Ms. Goldsmith asked.

"I have them with me right here," said Ken, pulling a typed page from his briefcase and handing it across the desk.

Are the exaggerated claims Ken made in his résumé ethical? Do the ethics of his ac-tions change at all if he has references (family members) who will vouch for his claims?

MindTap®

Reflection and Assessment

Interviewing can be a productive way to obtain information from an expert for a paper, an article, or a speech. The key to effective interviewing begins with a highly structured interview protocol identifying a series of good questions. To assess how well you've learned what we addressed in these pages, answer the following questions. If you have trouble answering any of them, go back and review that material until you can do so.

1. What kinds of questions need to go into a good interview protocol?

2. What guidelines should inform your information-gathering interviews?

3. What should you do to ensure an effective employment interview?

4. What are some tips to follow when you find yourself doing a media interview?

MindTap®

Note:

Activities for this chapter can be found on the Speech Communication MindTap at cengagebrain.com.

References

CHAPTER 1

Beebe, S., & Masterson, J. (2006). *Communicating in groups: Principles and practices* (8th ed.). Boston: Pearson.

Berger, C. (1997). *Planning strategic interaction: Attaining goals through communicative action.* Mahwah, NJ: Lawrence Erlbaum.

Burgoon, J. K., Bonito, J. A., Ramirez, Artemio, Dunbar, N. E., Kam, K., & Fisher, J. (1998). The interactivity principle: Effects of mediation, propinquity, and verbal and nonverbal modalities in interpersonal interaction. *Journal of Communication, 48,* 657–677.

Burleson, B. R. (2009). Understanding the outcomes of supportive communication: A dual-processing approach. *Journal of Social and Personal Relationships, 26,* 21–38.

College learning for the new global century. (2007). *A Report from the National Leadership Council for Liberal Education and America's Promise.* Washington, DC: Association of American Colleges and Universities.

Darling, A. L., & Dannels, D. P. (2003). Practicing engineers talk about the importance of talk: A report on the role of oral communication in the workplace. *Communication Education, 52,* 1–16.

Hansen, R. S., & Hansen, K. (2007). What do employers really want? Top skills and values employers seek from job-seekers. Retrieved November 14, 2014 from Quintessential Careers Web site: http://www.quintcareers.com /job_skills_values.html

Hart Research Associates. (2010, January 10). Raising the bar: Employers' views on college learning in the wake of the economic downturn. Washington, DC: Association of American Colleges and Universities.

Hart Research Associates. (2006, December 28). How should colleges prepare students to succeed in today's global economy? Washington, DC: Association of American Colleges and Universities.

Hirokawa, R., Cathcart, R., Samovar, L., & Henman, L. (Eds.). (2003). *Small group communication theory and practice* (8th ed.). Los Angeles: Roxbury.

Robert M. Hutchins (n.d.). *FinestQuotes.com.* Retrieved November 25, 2014, from FinestQuotes.com Web site: http://www.finestquotes.com/author_quotes-author- Robert M. Hutchins-page-0.htm.

Kellerman, K. (1992). Communication: Inherently strategic and primarily automatic. *Communication Monographs, 59,* 288–300.

Knapp, M., & Daly, J. (2002). *Handbook of interpersonal communication.* Thousand Oaks, CA: Sage.

Littlejohn, S. W., & Foss, K. A. (2008). *Theories of human communication* (9th ed.). Belmont, CA: Thomson Wadsworth.

Littlejohn, S. W., & Foss, K. A. (2011). *Theories of human communication* (10th ed). Long Grove, IL: Waveland Press.

McCroskey, J. C. (1977). Oral communication apprehension: A review of recent theory and research. *Human Communication Research, 4,* 78–96.

Millar, F. E. & Rogers, L. E. (1987). Relational dimensions of interpersonal dynamics. In M. E. Roloff & G. E. Miller (Eds.), *Interpersonal processes: New directions in communication research* (pp. 117–139). Newbury Park, CA: Sage.

Pajares, F., Prestin, A., Chen, J., & Nabi, R. L. (2009). Social cognitive theory and media effects. In R. L. Nabi and M. B. Oliver (Eds.), *The SAGE handbook of media processes and effects* (pp. 283–297). Los Angeles, CA: Sage.

Samovar, L. A., Porter, R. E., & McDaniel, E. R. (2007). *Communication between cultures* (6th ed.). Belmont, CA: Thomson Wadsworth.

Spitzberg, B. H. & Cupach, W. R. (Eds.). (2011). *The dark side of close relationships II.* New York: Routledge.

Spitzberg, B. H. (2000). A model of intercultural communication competence. In L. A. Samovar & R. E. Porter (Eds.), *Intercultural communication: A reader* (9th ed., pp. 375–387). Belmont, CA: Wadsworth.

Terkel, S. N., & Duval, R. S. (Eds.). (1999). *Encyclopedia of ethics.* New York: Facts on File.

Richmond, V. P., & McCroskey, J. C. (2000). *Communication: Apprehension, avoidance, and effectiveness* (5th ed.). Scottsdale, AZ: Gorsuch Scarisbrick.

Young, M. (2003). Integrating communication skills into the marketing curriculum: A case study. *Journal of Marketing Education, 25,* 57–70.

CHAPTER 2

Aron, A., Mashek, D., & Aron, E. (2004). Closeness as including other in the self. In D. Mashek & A. Aron (Eds.), *Handbook of closeness and intimacy* (pp. 27–41). Mahwah, NJ: Lawrence Erlbaum.

Bandura, A. (1977). Self-efficacy: Toward a unifying theory of behavioral change. *Psychological Review, 84,* 191–215.

Baron, R. A., Byrne, D., & Branscombe, N. R. (2006). *Social psychology* (11th ed.). Boston: Allyn & Bacon.

Benet-Martinez, V., & Haritatos, J. (2005). Bi-cultural identity integration: Components and socio-personality antecedents. *Journal of Personality, 73,* 1015–1049.

Berger, C.R., & Bradac, J.J. (1982). *Language and social knowledge.* London: Edward Arnold Publishers Ltd.

Centi, P. J. (1981). *Up with the positive—out with the negative.* Upper Saddle River, NJ: Prentice Hall.

Chen, G., & Starosta, W. (1998). *Foundations of intercultural communication.* Boston: Allyn & Bacon.

Demo, D. H. (1987). Family relations and the self-esteem of adolescents and their parents. *Journal of Marriage and the Family, 49,* 705–715.

Downey, G., Freitas, A. L., Michaelis, B., & Khouri, H. (2004). The self-fulfilling prophecy in close relationships: Rejection sensitivity and rejection by romantic partners. In H. T. Reis & C. E. Rusbult (Eds.), *Close relationships* (pp. 153–174). New York: Psychology Press.

Engel, B. (2005). *Breaking the cycle of abuse: How to move beyond your past to create an abuse-free future.* Hoboken, NJ: John Wiley and Sons.

Gangestad, S. W., & Snyder, M. (2000). Self-monitoring: Appraisal and reappraisal. *Psychological Bulletin, 126,* 530–555.

Gibson, J. J. (1966). *The senses considered as perceptual systems.* Boston: Houghton Mifflin.

Guerrero, L., Anderson, P., Afifi, W. (2007). *Close encounters: Communication in relationships* (2nd ed.). Los Angeles: Sage Publications.

Hinduja, S., & Patchin, J. W. (2010). Bullying, cyberbullying, and suicide. *Archives of Suicide Research, 14,* 206–221.

Jones, M. (2002*). Social psychology of prejudice.* Upper Saddle River, NJ: Prentice Hall.

"Lady Gaga discusses her struggles and connections to fans in *Rolling Stone* cover story" (2011, May 25). Retrieved from http://www.rollingstone.com/music/news/lady-gaga-discusses -her-struggles-and-connection-to-fans-in-rolling-stone -cover-story-20110525

Leary, M. R. (2002). When selves collide: The nature of the self and the dynamics of interpersonal relationships. In A. Tesser, D. A. Stapel, & J. V. Wood (Eds.), *Self and motivation: Emerging psychological perspectives* (pp. 119–145). Washington, DC: American Psychological Association.

Littlejohn, S. W., & Foss, K. A. (2011). *Theories of human communication* (10th ed). Long Grove, IL: Waveland Press.

Markus, H., & Kitayama, S. (*1991*). Culture and the self: Implications for cognition, emotion, and motivation. *Psychological Review, 98,* 224–253.

Merton, R. K. (1968). *Social theory and social structure.* New York: Free Press.

Mruk, C. J. (2006). *Self-esteem research, theory, and practice: Toward a positive psychology of self-esteem.* New York: Springer.

Mruk, C. (1999). *Self-esteem: Research, theory, and practice* (2nd ed.). New York: Springer.

Rayner, S. G. (2001). Aspects of the self as learner: Perception, concept, and esteem. In R. J. Riding & S. G. Rayner (Eds.), *Self-perception: International perspectives on individual differences* (Vol. 2). Westport, CN: Ablex.

Sampson, E. E. (1999). *Dealing with differences: An introduction to the social psychology of prejudice.* Fort Worth, TX: Harcourt Brace.

Schillaci, S. (2011, Feb 14). Lady Gaga on *60 Minutes*: "I'm a master of the art of fame." Zap2It. Retrieved from http://blog.zap2it.com/pop2it/2011/02/lady-gaga-on -60-minutes-im-a-master-of-the-art-of-fame.html

Weiten, W. (1998). *Psychology: Themes and variations* (4th ed.). Pacific Grove, CA: Brooks/Cole.

Willis, J. and Todorov, A (2006). First impressions: making up your mind after a 100-ms exposure to a face. *Psychological Science, 17,* 592–598.

Wood, J. T. (2007). *Gendered lives: Communication, gender, and culture* (7th ed.). Belmont, CA: Wadsworth.

CHAPTER 3

Andersen, P. A., Hecht, M. L., Hoobler, G. D., & Smallwood, M. (2003). Nonverbal communication across cultures. In W. B. Gudykunst (Ed.), *Cross-cultural and intercultural communication.* Thousand Oaks, CA: Sage.

A Ruby Films, Gerson Saines Production in association with HBO Films Leo Trombetta, A.C.E., *Editor.*

Association of Black Women Historians. (2011, Aug 7). *An open statement to the fans of* The Help. Retrieved from http://www.abwh.org

Bornstein, M. H., & Bradley, R. H. (Eds.). (2003). *Socioeconomic status, parenting, and child development.* Mahwah, NJ: Lawrence Erlbaum Associates.

Brown, S. E. (2002). What is disability culture? *Disabilty Studies Quarterly, 22* (2), 34–50.

Chen, G., & Starosta, W. (1998). *Foundations of intercultural communication.* Boston: Allyn and Bacon.

Desilver, D. (2013, June 7). World's Muslim population more widespread than you might think. *Pew Research Center.* Retrieved on September 25, 2014 from http://www.pewresearch.org/fact-tank/2013/06/07/worlds-muslim-population-more-widespread-than-you-might-think/

Ellis, R. (1999). *Learning a second language through interaction.* Amsterdam: John Benjamins.

Gleiberman, O. (2011, Aug 14). Is 'The Help' a condescending movie for white liberals? Actually, the real condescension is calling it that. *EW.com.* Retrieved from http://insidemovies.ew.com/2011/08/14/is-the-help-a-movie-for-white-liberals/

Hall, E. T. (1976). *Beyond culture.* New York: Random House.

Haviland, W. A. (1993). *Cultural anthropology.* Fort Worth, TX: Harcourt, Brace, Jovanovich.

Hofstede, G. (2000). Masculine and feminine cultures. In A. E. Kazdin (Ed.), *Encyclopedia of psychology, vol. 5.* Washington, DC: American Psychological Association.

Hofstede, G. (1998). *Masculinity and femininity: The taboo.* Thousand Oaks, CA: Sage.

Jackson, M. (Director). (2010). *Temple Grandin* [Motion picture]. USA: Home Box Office.

Jackson, R. L., II (Ed.). (2004). *African American communication and identities.* Thousand Oaks, CA: Sage.

Kim, Y. Y. (2001). *Becoming intercultural: An integrative theory of communication and cross-cultural adaptation.* Thousand Oaks, CA: Sage.

Kim, M. (2005). Culture-based conversational constraints theory: Individual- and culture-level analyses. In W. B. Gudykunst (Ed.), *Theorizing about intercultural communication*, (pp. 93–117). Thousand Oaks, CA: Sage.

Klyukanov, I. E. (2005). *Principles of intercultural communication.* New York: Pearson.

Kraus, M. W., & Keltner, D. (2009). Signs of socioeconomic status: A thin-slicing approach. *Psychological Science, 20,* 99–106.

Luckmann, J. (1999). *Transcultural communication in nursing.* New York: Delmar.

MacSwan, J. (2013). Code-switching and grammatical theory. In T. Bhatia and W. Ritchie *Handbook of multilingualism* (2nd ed.). Cambridge, Blackwell.

Lynch, D. J. (2013, December 11). Americans say dream fading as income gap shows unequal chances. *Bloomberg.* Retrieved on September 26, 2014 at: http://www.bloomberg.com/news/2013-12-11/americans-say-dream-fading-as-income-gap-hurts-chances.html

Neuliep, J. W. (2006). *Intercultural communication: A contextual approach* (3rd ed.). Thousand Oaks, CA: Sage.

Pew Research Center. (2007). *A portrait of "Generation Next": How young people view their lives, futures, and politics* (survey report). Retrieved from http://people-press.org/report/300/a-portrait-of-generation-next

Pierce, W. (2011, Aug 15). The movie *The Help* was painful to watch. This passive segregation lite was hurtful. I kept thinking of my grandmother who was The Help [Twitter post]. Retrieved from http://twitter.com/#!/WendellPierce/status/103257666805170176

Pierce, W. (2011, Aug 16). Watching the film in Uptown New Orleans to the sniffles of elderly white people while my 80-year-old mother was seething, made clear distinction [Twitter post]. Retrieved from http://twitter.com/#!/WendellPierce/status/103351421965041665

Prensky, M. (2001). Digital natives, digital immigrants. From *On the Horizon* (MCB University Press, Vol. 9 No. 5, October 2001).

Turner, P. A. (2011, Aug 28). Dangerous white stereotypes. *The New York Times.* Retrieved from http://www.nytimes.com/2011/08/29/opinion/dangerous-white-stereotypes.html

Renard, J. (2011). *Islam and Christianity: Theological themes in comparative perspective.* Berkeley, CA: University of California Press.

Samovar, L. A., Porter, R. E., & McDaniel, E. R. (2012). *Communication between cultures* (8th ed.). Boston: Wadsworth Cengage.

Samovar, L., Porter, R. E., & McDaniel, E. R. (2009). *Communication between cultures* (7th ed.). Boston: Wadsworth Cengage.

Schein, E. H. (2010*). Organizational culture and leadership* (4th ed.). San Francisco, CA: John Wiley and Sons.

Ting-Toomey, S., & Chung, L. C. (2012). *Understanding intercultural communication* (2nd ed.). New York: Oxford University Press

Ting-Toomey, S., Yee-Jung, K., Shapiro, R., Garcia, W., Wright, T., & Oetzel, J. G. (2000). Cultural/ethnic identity salience and conflict styles. *International Journal of Intercultural Relations, 23*, 47–81.

2010 Census: State Population Profile Maps. Retrieved December 10, 2014 At: www.census.gov/2010census/

Turner, P. A. (2011, Aug 28). Dangerous white stereotypes. *The New York Times.* Retrieved from http://www.nytimes .com/2011/08/29/opinion/dangerous-white-stereotypes.html

Wallis, C. (2006), "The multitasking generation", *Time*, Vol. 167 No. 13, pp. 48–55.

Waples, R. S., & Gaggiotti, O. (2006). What is a population? An empirical evaluation of

some genetic methods for identifying the number of gene pools and their degree of connectivity. *Molecular Ecology 15*(6): 1419-1439. DOI: 10.1111/j.1365-294X.2006.02890.x

Wood, J. T. (2010). *Gendered lives: Communciation, gender and culture* (9th ed.). Boston: Wadsworth Cengage.

Wood, J. T. (2007). *Gendered lives: Communication, gender, and culture* (7th ed.). Belmont, CA: Wadsworth.

Zemke, R., Raines, C., & Filipczak (2000). *Generations at work.* New York: AMACOM Books.

CHAPTER 4

Aronoff, M. & Rees-Miller, J (Eds.). 2001. *The handbook of linguistics.* Blackwell Handbooks in Linguistics. Oxford: Blackwell.

Chaika, E. (2008). *Language: The social mirror (4th ed.).* Boston: Heinle ELT/Cengage.

Cvetkovic, L. (February 21, 2009) *Serbian, Croatian, Bosnian, or Montanegrin, or "Just our language."* Radio Free Europe/Radio Liberty Web site. Retrieved from http://www.rferl.org /content/Serbian_Croatian_Bosnian_or_Montenegrin_Many _In_Balkans_Just_Call_It_Our_Language_/1497105.html

Grice, H. P. (1975). Logic and conversation. In P. Cole & J. L. Morgan (Eds.) *Syntax and Semantics (Vol. 3, Speech Acts).* New York, NY: Academic Press.

Higginbotham, J. (2006). Languages and idiolects: Their language and ours. In E. Lepore & B.C. Smith (Eds.), *The Oxford handbook of philosophy of language.* Oxford, UK: Oxford University Press.

Kabat-Ainn, J. (2009). *Letting everything become your teacher: 100 lessons in mindfulness.* New York: Dell Publishing Company.

Korta, K. and Perry, J. (2008). Pragmatics. In Edward N Zalta (Ed.), *The Stanford Encyclopedia of Philosophy (Fall 2008 Edition).* Retrieved from http://plato.stanford.edu/archives /fall2008/entries/pragmatics/

Langer, E. J. & Moldoveanu, M. (2000). The construct of mindfulness. *Journal of Social Issues, 56*(1), 1–9.

Lewis, M. P. (Ed.). (2009). *Ethnologue: Languages of the world* (16th ed.). Dallas: SIL International.

Maresca, R. (2012, Jan 18). Jennifer Aniston's pregnancy rumors through the years. [Blog post]. Retrieved from http://www.celebuzz.com/2012-01-18/jennifer -anistons -pregnancy-rumors-through-the-years-photos/

O'Grady, W., Archibald, J., Aronoff, M., & Rees-Miller, J. (2001). *Contemporary linguistics* (4th ed.). Boston: Bedford/St. Martin's.

Slattery, K., Doremus, M., & Marcus, L. (2001). Shifts in public affairs reporting on the network evening news: A move toward the sensational. *Journal of Broadcasting & Electronic Media 45*(2), 295–298.

Ting-Toomey, S., & Chung, L. C. (2005). *Understanding Intercultural Communication.* Los Angeles: Roxbury Publishing.

Wright, R. (2010). Chinese language facts. Retrieved from http://www.languagehelpers.com/languagefacts/chinese.html

CHAPTER 5

American Museum of Natural History. (1999). Exhibition highlights. *Body art: Marks of identity.* Retrieved from http://www.amnh.org/exhibitions/bodyart/exhibition _highlights.html

Australian Museum. (2009). Shaping. *Body art.* Retrieved from http://amonline.net.au/bodyart/shaping/

Axtell, R. E. (1998). *Gestures: The Do's and Taboos of body language around the world.* Hoboken, NJ: John Wiley and Sons.

Birdwhistell, R. (1970). *Kinesics and context.* Philadelphia: University of Pennsylvania Press.

Burgoon, J. K., & Bacue, A. E. (2003). Nonverbal communication skills. In J. O. Greene & B. R. Burleson (Eds.), *Handbook of communication and social interaction skills* (pp. 179–220). Mahwah, NJ: Erlbaum.

Burgoon, J. K., Blair, J. P., & Strom, R. E. (2008). Cognitive biases and nonverbal cue availability in detecting deception. *Human Communication Research, 34*, 572–599.

Gudykunst, W. B., & Kim, Y. Y. (1997). *Communicating with strangers: An approach to intercultural communication.* New York: McGraw-Hill.

Hall, E. T. (1968). Proxemics. *Current Anthropology, 9,* 83–108.

Knapp, M. L., Hall, J. A., & Horgan, T. G. (2014). *Nonverbal communication in human interaction.* (8th ed.). Boston: Wadsworth Cengage.

Lakin, J. L. (2006). Automatic cognitive processes and nonverbal communication. In V. Manusov & M. L. Patterson (Eds.), *The SAGE Handbook of Nonverbal Communication* (pp. 59–77). Thousand Oaks, CA: Sage Publications.

Littlejohn, S. W., & Foss, K. A. (Eds.). (2009). *Encyclopedia of communication theory.* (Vols. 1–2). Thousand Oaks, CA: SAGE Publications, Inc. DOI: http://dx.doi .org/10.4135/9781412959384

Martin, J. N., & Nakayama, T. K. (2000). *Intercultural communication in contexts* (2nd ed.). Mountain View, CA: Mayfield.

Mehrabian, A. (1972). *Nonverbal communication.* Chicago: Aldine.

Neuliep, J. W. (2006). *Intercultural communication: A contextual approach* (3rd ed.). Thousand Oaks, CA: Sage.

Samovar, L. A., Porter, R. E., McDaniel, E. R., & Roy, C. S. (2012). *Intercultural communication: A reader* (14th ed.). Boston: Cengage Learning.

Santilli, V., & Miller, A. N. (2011). The effects of gender and power distance on nonverbal immediacy in symmetrical and asymmetrical power conditions: A cross-cultural study of classrooms and friendships. *Journal of International and Intercultural Communication, 4*(1), 3–22. DOI: 10.1080/17513057.2010.533787

Yuasa, M., Saito, K., & Mukawa, N. (2011). Brain activity when reading sentences and emoticons: An fMRI study of verbal and nonverbal communication. *Electronics and Communication in Japan, 94*(5), 17–24.

Walther, J. B., & Parks, M. R. (2002). Cues filtered out, cues filtered in: Computer-mediated communication and relationships. In M. C. Knapp & J. A. Daly (Eds.), *Handbook of interpersonal communication* (3rd ed.; pp. 529–563). Thousand Oaks, CA: Sage.

Watzlawick, P., Bavelas, J. B., & Jackson, D. D. (1967). *Pragmatics of human communication.* New York: Norton.

Wood, J. T. (2007). *Gendered lives: Communication, gender, and culture* (7th ed.). Belmont, CA: Wadsworth.

CHAPTER 6

Bodie, G. D., Cyr, K. S., Pence, M., Rold, M., & Honeycutt, J. (2012). Listening competence in initial interactions I: Distinguishing between what listening is and what listeners do. *International Journal of Listening, 26*(1), 1–28.

Brownell, J. (2006). *Listening: Attitudes, principles, and skills* (3rd ed.). Boston: Allyn & Bacon.

Burleson, B. R. (2010). Explaining recipient responses to supportive messages: Development and test of a dual-process theory. In S. W. Smith and S. R. Wilson (Eds). *New Directions in Interpersonal Research.* (pp. 159–180). Thousand oaks, CA: Sage. DOI: http://dx.doi.org/10.4135 /9781483349619.n8

Carbaugh, D., Nuciforo, E. V., Salto, M., & Shin, D. (2011). "Dialogue" in cross-cultural perspective: Japanese, Korean, and Russian Discourses. *Journal of International and Intercultural Communication, 4*(2), 87–108. DOI: 10.1080/17513057.2011.557500

Carnegie, D. (1936). *How to win friends and influence people.* New York: Simon and Schuster. Dale Carnegie Training. [Web site] Retrieved on June 20, 2013 at www.dalecarnegie.com

Donoghue, P. J., & Siegel, M. E. (2005). *Are you really listening?: Keys to successful communication.* Notre Dame, IN: Sorin Books.

Dunkel, P., & Pialorsi, F. (2005). *Advanced listening comprehension: Developing aural and notetaking skills.* Boston: Thomson Heinle.

Galagan, P. (2013). ASTD Research: Leadership Development for Millennials. Retrieved from http://www.astd.org/Publications /Newsletters/LX-Briefing/LXB-Archives/2013/03/ASTD -Research-Leadership-Development-For-Millennials

Gearhart, C. C., Denham, J. P., & Bodie, G. D. (2014). Listening as a goal-directed activity. *Western Journal of Communication, 78*(5), 668–684. DOI: 10.1080/10570314.2014.910888.

Gonzalez, A., Houston, M., & Chen, V. (2011). *Our voices: Essays in culture, ethnicity, and communication.* Oxford, England: Oxford University Press

Harris, J. A. (2003). Learning to listen across cultural divides. *Listening Professional, 2,* 4–21.

Imhof, M. (2010). The cognitive psychology of listening. In A. S. Wolvin (Ed.), *Listening and Human Communication in the 21st Century* (pp. 97–126). Boston: Blackwell.

International Listening Association (2003). *Listening factoid.* Retrieved from http://www.listen.org/pages/factoids/html

Janusik, L. A., & Wolvin, A. D. (2009). 24 hours in a day: A listening update to the time studies. *International Journal of Listening, 23,* 104–120. DOI: 10.1080/ 10904010903014442.

Janusik, L. A., & Wolvin, A. D. (2006). *24 hours in a day: A listening update to the time studies.* Paper presented at the meeting of the International Listening Association, Salem, OR.

Kobayashi, K. (2006). Combined effects of note-taking/reviewing on learning and the enhancement through interventions: A meta-analytic review. *Educational Psychology: An International Journal for Experiemenal Educational Psychology, 26*(3) 459-477. DOI: 10.1080/014434105000342070

Leadership skill requirements across organizational levels. *The Leadership Quarterly, 18*(2), 154–166. DOI:10.1016/j.leaqua.2007.01.005

Listening factoid. (2003). International Listening Association. Retrieved from http://www.listen.org/pages/factoids.html

Mumford, T.V., Campion, M.A., & Morgeson, F.P. (2007). The leadership skills strataplex: Leadership skill requirements across organizational levels. *The Leadership Quarterly, 18*(2), 154–166.

National Association of Colleges and Employers. (2012, November 8). Employers look for communication skills, ability to work in a team in new college grads [Press release]. Retrieved from http://www.naceweb.org/Press/Releases/Employers_Look_for_Communication_Skills,_Ability_to_Work_in_a_Team_in_New_College_Grads.aspx

O'Shaughnessey, B. (2003). Active attending or a theory of mental action. *Consciousness and the world, 29*: 379–407.

Pomeroy, A. (2007). CEOs emphasize listening to employees. *HR Magazine, 52*(1), 14. Retrieved from http://www.shrm.org/Publications/hrmagazine/EditorialContent/Pages/0107execbrief.aspx

Salisbury, J. R. & Chen, G. M. (2007). An examination of the relationship between conversational sensitivity and listening styles. *Intercultural Communication Studies, XVI*(1) 251–262.

Titsworth, S. B. (2004). Students' notetaking: The effects of teacher immediacy and clarity. *Communication Education, 53*(4), 305–320.

Watson, K. W., Barker, L. L., & Weaver, J. B., III (1995). The listening styles profile (LSP-16): Development and validation of an instrument to assess four listening styles. *International Journal of Listening, 9,* 1–13.

Weaver, J. B. III, & Kirtley, M. D. (1995). Listening styles and empathy. *The Southern Communication Journal, 60*(2): 131–140.

Weger Jr., H., Bell, G. C., Minel, E. M., & Robinson, M. C. (2014). The relative effectiveness of active listening in initial interactions. *International Journal of Listening, 28*(1), 13–31. DOI: 10.1080/10904018.2013.813234

Wolvin, A. D., & Coakley, C. G. (1996). *Listening.* Dubuque, IA: Wm. C. Brown.

CHAPTER 7

Alsever, J. (2007, March 11). In the computer dating game, room for a coach. *The New York Times.* Retrieved from http://www.nytimes.com/2007/03/11/business/yourmoney/11dating.html

Altman, I., & Taylor, D. (1973). *Social penetration: The development of interpersonal relationships.* New York: Holt.

Baxter, L. A. (2011). *Voicing relationships: A dialogic perspective.* Thousand Oaks, CA: Sage.

Baxter, L. A., & Braithwaite, D. O. (2009). Relational dialectics theory, applied. In S. W. Smith & S. R. Wilson (Eds.), *New directions in interpersonal communication.* Sage.

Baxter, L. (1982). Strategies for ending relationships: Two studies. *Western Journal of Speech Communication, 46,* 223–241.

Baxter, L. A., & Montgomery, B. M. (1996). *Relating: Dialogues and dialectics.* New York: Guilford.

Baxter, L. A., & West, L. (2003). Couple perceptions of their similarities and differences: A dialectical perspective. *Journal of Social and Personal Relationships, 20,* 491–514.

Beebe, S. A., Beebe, S. J., & Ivy, D. K. (2013). *Communication: Principles for a lifetime* (5th ed.). Upper Saddle River, NJ: Pearson.

Berger, C. (1987). Communicating under uncertainty. In M. Roloff & G. Miller (Eds.), *Interpersonal processes: New directions in communication research* (pp. 39–62). Newbury Park, CA: Sage.

Brooks, M. (2011, February 14). How has internet dating changed society? An insider's look. *Courtland Brooks.* Retrieved from http://internetdating.typepad.com/courtland_brooks/2011/02/how-has-internet-dating-changed-society.html

Bryner, J. (2011, November 4). You gotta have friends? Most have just 2 true pals. *Live Science.* Retrieved from http://vitals.msnbc.msn.com/_news/2011/11/04/8637894-you-gotta-have-friends-most-have-just-2-true-pals?lite

Burleson, B. R. (2009). Understanding the outcomes of supportive communication: A dual-process approach. *Journal of Social and Personal Relationships, 26*(1), 21–38.

Canary, D. J., Cody, M. J., & Manusov, V. L. (2008). *Interpersonal communication: A goals-based approach.* Boston: Bedford St. Martins.

Carnegie, D. (1936). *How to win friends and influence people.* New York: Simon and Schuster.

Dindia, K. (2009). Sex differences in personal relationships. In H. Reis & S. Sprecher, (Eds.), *Encyclopedia of Human Relationships*. Thousand Oaks, CA: Sage.

Dindia, K. & Canary, D.J. (2006). (Eds.), *Sex Differences and Similarities in Communication* (2nd ed.). Mahwah, NJ: Erlbaum.

Dindia, K. (2003). Definitions and perspectives on relational maintenance communication. In D. J. Canary and M. Dainton (Eds.), *Maintaining relationships through communication*. Mahwah, NJ: Erlbaum.

Dindia, K., & Timmerman, L. (2003). Accomplishing romantic relationships. In J. O. Greene & B. R. Burleson (Eds.), *Handbook of communication and social interaction* (pp. 685–722). Mahwah, NJ: Erlbaum.

Duck, S. W., & McMahan, D. T. (2012). *The basics of communication: A relational perspective*. Thousand Oaks, CA: Sage.

Duck, S. (1999). *Relating to others*. Philadelphia: Open University Press.

Duck, S. (2007). *Human relationships* (4th ed.). Thousand Oaks, CA: Sage.

Gibbs, J.L., Ellison, N.B., & Lai, C. (2011). First comes love, then comes Google: An investigation of uncertainty reduction strategies and self-disclosure in online dating. *Communication Research, 38*(1), 70–100.

Hatfield, E., & Rapson, R. L. (2006). Passionate love, sexual desire, and mate selection: Cross-cultural and historical perspectives. In P. Noller & J. A. Feeney (Eds.). *Close relationships: Functions, forms and processes* (pp. 227–243). Hove, UK: Psychology Press/Taylor & Francis.

Ianotti, L. (2010, Sept 13). Do you need a professional to write your online dating profile? *Marie Claire*. Retrieved from http://www.marieclaire.com/sex-love/relationship-issues/online-dating-profile-ghostwriters?click=main_sr

Knapp, M. L., & Daly, J. A. (2011). *The SAGE handbook of interpersonal communication* (4th ed.). Thousand Oaks, CA: Sage.

Knapp, M. L., & Miller, G. R. (1985). *Handbook of interpersonal communication*. Beverly Hills, CA: Sage.

Knapp, M. L., & Vangelisti, A. L. (2000). *Interpersonal communication and human relationships* (4th ed.). Boston: Allyn & Bacon.

Littlejohn, S. W., & Foss, K. A. (2011). *Theories of human communication* (10th ed). Long Grove, IL: Waveland Press.

Luft, J. (1969). *Of human interaction*. Palo Alto, CA: National Press.

Lustig, M. W., & Koester, J. (2013). Intercultural competence (7th ed.). Upper Saddle River, NJ: Pearson.

McPherson, M., Smith-Lovin, L., & Brashears, M. E. (2006). Social isolation in America: Changes in core discussion networks over two decades. *American Sociological Review, 71*(3): 353–375.

Moore, D. W. (2003, January 3). Family, health most important aspects of life. *Gallup*. Retrieved from http://www.gallup.com/poll/7504/family-health-most-important-aspects-life.aspx

Parks, M. R. (2006). *Personal relationships and personal networks*. Mahwah, NJ: Erlbaum.

Peterson, C. (2006). *A primer in positive psychology*. New York: Oxford.

Petronio, S. (2002). *Boundaries of privacy: Dialectics of disclosure*. Albany: State University of New York Press.

Saramaki, J., Leicht, E. Al., Lopez, E., Roberts, S. G. B., Reed-Tsochas, R., & Dunbar, R. I. M. (2014). Persistence of social signatures in human communication. *PNAS 2014. 111* (3), 942–947. DOI: 10.1073/pnas.1308540110.

Taylor, D., & Altman, I. (1987). Communication in interpersonal relationships: Social penetration processes. In Roloff, M. E., and Miller, G. R. *Interpersonal processes: New directions in communication research* (pp. 257–277). Newbury Park, CA: Sage.

Ting-Toomey, S. (2005) The matrix of face: An updated face-negotiation theory. In W.B. Gudykunst (Ed.), *Theorizing About Intercultural Communication* (pp. 71–92). Thousand Oaks, CA: Sage.

Ting-Toomey, S. (2004). The matrix of face: An updated face-negotiation theory. In W. Gudykunst (Ed.), *Theorizing about intercultural communication* (pp. 71–92). Thousand Oaks, CA: Sage.

Walther, J. B. (2011). Theories of computer-mediated communication and interpersonal relationships. In M. L. Knapp & J. A. Daly (Eds.). *The Sage Handbook of Interpersonal Communication* (pp. 443–479). Thousand Oaks, CA: Sage.

Wang, J. (2011, January 25). A marketer coaches online daters on personal branding. *Entrepreneur*. Retrieved from http://www.entrepreneur.com/article/217911

Ward, C. C., & Tracy, T. J. G. (2004). Relation of shyness with aspects of online relationship involvement. *Journal of Social and Personal Relationships, 21*, 611–623.

Wazlawick, P., Bavelas, J., & Jackson, D. (1967). *Pragmatics of human communication: A study of interactional patterns, pathologies, and paradoxes*. New York: Norton.

Wood, J.T. (2000). *Relational communication: Continuity and change in personal relationships* (2nd ed.). Belmont, CA: Wadsworth.

CHAPTER 8

Alberti, R. E., & Emmons, M. L. (2008). *Your perfect right: Assertiveness and equality in your life and relationships* (9th ed.). Atascadero, CA: Impact Publishers.

Altman I. (1993). Dialectics, physical environments, and personal relationships. *Communication Monographs, 60*, 26–34.

Bilton. N. (2012, February 28). Apple loophole gives developers access to photos. *The New York Times.* Retrieved from http://bits.blogs.nytimes.com/2012/02/28/tk-ios-gives -developers-access-to-photos-videos-location/

Burleson, B. R. (2003). Emotional support skills. In J. O. Greene & B. R. Burleson (Eds.), *Handbook of communication and social interaction skills* (pp. 551–594). Mahwah, NJ: Erlbaum.

Chen, A. (2011, November 10). Facebook is the final frontier in amateur porn. *Gawker* [Blog post]. Retrieved from http://gawker.com/5858485/facebook-is-the-final-frontier -in-amateur-porn

Cissna, D. (2011). Studying communication, confirmation, and dialogue: In dialogue with Maurice Freedman In K. P. Kramer (Ed.), *Dialogically Speaking: Maurice Friedman's Interdisciplinary Humanism* (pp. 262–276). Eugene, OR: Pickwick Publications.

Dindia, K. (2000b). Sex differences in self-disclosure, reciprocity of self-disclosure, and self-disclosure and liking: Three metaanalyses reviewed. In S. Petronio (Ed.), *Balancing the secrets of private disclosures* (pp. 21–36). Mahwah, NJ: Erlbaum.

Gold, D. (2011, November 10). The man who makes money publishing your nude pics. *The Awl* [Blog post]. Retrieved from http://www.theawl.com/2011/11/the-man-who-makes -money-publishing-your-nude-pics

Hample. D. (2003). Arguing skill. In J. O. Greene & B. R. Burleson (Eds.) *Handbook of communication and social interaction skills.* Mahwah, NJ: Lawrence Erlbaum.

Hendrick, S. S. (1981). Self-disclosure and marital satisfaction. *Journal of Personality and Social Psychology, 40*, 1150–1159.

Hess, N. H., & Hagen, E. H. (2006). Psychological adaptations for assessing gossip veracity. *Human Nature, 17*, 337–354.

Holt, J. L., & DeVore, C. J. (2005). Culture, gender, organizational role, and styles of conflict resolution: A meta-analysis. *International Journal of Intercultural Relations, 29*, 165–196.

Kleinman, S. (2007). *Displacing place: Mobile communication in the twenty-first century.* New York, NY: Peter Lang Publishing.

Maul, K. (2009, February 25). Rihanna aftermath rouses ethics debate. *PR Week.* Retrieved from http://www .prweekus.com/Rihanna-aftermath-rouses-ethics-debate /article/127824

McCartney, A. (2009, February 20). Rihanna won't discuss Chris Brown, but thanks fans [Television story]. Retrieved from http://abcnews.go.com/Entertainment /wireStory?id=6918527

Petronio, S. (2013). Brief status report on communication privacy management theory. *Journal of Family Communication, 13*(1), 6–14.

Petronio, S. (2002). *Boundaries of privacy: Dialectics of disclosure.* Albany: State University of New York Press.

Rancer, A. S., & Avtgis, T. A. (2006). *Argumentative and aggressive communication: Theory, research, and application.* Thousand Oaks, CA: Sage.

Roloff, M. E., & Ifert, D. E. (2000). Conflict management through avoidance: Withholding complaints, suppressing arguments, and declaring topics taboo. In S. Petronio (Ed.), *Balancing the secrets of private disclosures* (pp. 151–163). Mahwah, NJ: LEA.

Samovar, L. A., Porter, R. E., & McDaniel, E. R. (Eds.). (2012). *Intercultural communication: A reader* (13th ed.). Belmont, CA: Cengage. Tate, R. (2009, February 20). Battered Rihanna picture a media ethics lightning rod. *Gawker* [Blog post]. Retrieved from http://gawker .com/5157078/battered-rihanna-picture-a-media-ethics -lightning-rod

Thomas, K. W., & Kilmann, R. H. (1978). Comparison of four instruments measuring conflict behavior. *Psychological Reports, 42*, 1139–1145.

Thomas, K. W. (1992). Conflict and conflict management: Reflections and update. *Journal of Organizational Behavior, 13*, 265–274.

Ting-Toomey, S., & Chung, L.C. (2012). *Understanding intercultural communication,* (2nd ed). New York: Oxford University Press.

TMZ responds to LAPD internal investigation on battered Rihanna photo [Television story]. (2009, February 22). In *On the Record.* Retrieved from http://www.foxnews .com/story/0,2933,498157,00.html

Wilmot, W., & Hocker, J. L. (2010). *Interpersonal conflict* (8th ed.). New York: McGraw-Hill.

CHAPTER 9

Beebe, S. A., & Masterson, J. T. (2014). *Communicating in small groups: Principles and practices* (11th ed.). Upper Saddle River, NJ: Pearson.

Belbin, R. M. (2010). *Team roles at work* (2nd ed.). Burlington, MA: Elsevier.

Berry, G. R. (2011). Enhancing effectiveness on virtual teams: Understanding why traditional team skills are insufficient. *International Journal of Business Communication, 48*(2), 186-206. DOI: 10.1177/0021943610397270

Bradley, B. H., Postlethwaite, B. E., Klotz, A. C., Hamdani, M. R., & Brown, K. G. (2012). Reaping the benefits of task conflict in teams: The critical role of team psychological safety climate. *Journal of Applied Psychology, 97*(1), 151–158. http://dx.doi.org/10.1037/a0024200

Cartwright, D., & Zander, A. (1968). *Group dynamics: Research and theory.* New York: Harper and Row.

Croucher, M. (2008, February 29.) I just want to be thin. If it takes dying to get there—so be it. *The Epoch Times.* Retrieved from http://en.epochtimes.com/news/8-2-29/66794.html

Eisenberg, J. (2007). Group cohesiveness. In R. F. Baumeister & K. D. Vohs (Eds.), *Encyclopaedia of social psychology* (pp. 386–388). Thousand Oaks, CA: Sage.

Forsyth, D. R. & Burnette, J. L. (2005). The history of group research. In S. A. Wheelen (Ed.), *The handbook of group research and practice.* Thousand Oaks, CA: Sage.

Galvin, K. M., Braithwaite, D. O., & Bylund, C. L. (2015). *Family communication: Cohesion and change* (9th ed.). Upper Saddle River, NJ: Pearson.

Giles, D. (2006). Constructing identities in cyberspace: The case of eating disorders. *British Journal of Social Psychology 45*(3): 463–477. Retrieved from http://www.brown.uk.com/eatingdisorders/giles2.pdf

Goffee,R., & Jones, G. (May 2013). Creating the best workplace on the earth. *Harvard Business Review,* pp. 99–106.

Janis, I. L. (1982). *Groupthink: Psychological studies of policy decisions and fiascoes.* Boston: Houghton Mifflin.

Jiang, L., Bazarova, N. N., & Hancock, J. T. (2011). The disclosure-intimacy link in computer-mediated communication: An attributional extension of the hyperpersonal model. *Human Communication Research, 371*(1), 58–77.

Katzenbach, J. R., & Smith, D. K. (2003). *The wisdom of teams: Creating the high-performance organization.* New York: Harper Business Essentials.

Kimble, C. (2011). Building effective virtual teams: How to overcome the problems of trust and identity in virtual teams. *Global Business and Organizational Excellence, 30,* 6–15. DOI: 10.1002/joe.20364

Koerner, A. F., & Fitzpatrick, M. A. (2006). Family communication patterns theory: A social cognitive approach. In D. O Braithwaite & L. A. Baxter (Eds.). *Engaging theories in family communication: Multiple perspectives* (pp. 50–66). Thousand Oaks, CA: SAGE. DOI: http://dx.doi.org/10.4135/9781452204420.n4

Levine, J. M. (Ed.). (2013). *Group processes.* New York: Taylor and Francis.

Li, J., & Hambrick, D. C. (2005). Factional groups: A new vantage on demographic faultlines, conflict, and disintegration in work teams. *Academy of Management Journal, 48,* 794–813.

Mead, M. (n.d.). "Never doubt…" Retrieved from http://www.quoteland.com/author/Margaret-Mead-Quotes/390/

Midura, D. W., & Glover, D. R. (2005). *Essentials of team-building.* Champaign, IL: Human Kinetics.

Myers, S., & Anderson, C. A. (2008). *The fundamentals of small group communication.* Thousand Oaks, CA: Sage.

Pascoe, C. J. (2008, January 22). Interview in Growing up online [Television series episode]. In D. Fanning. (Executive producer) *Frontline.* Boston: WGBH. Retrieved from http://www.pbs.org/wgbh/pages/frontline/kidsonline/interviews/pascoe.html

Platow, M. J., Grace, D. M. & Smithson, M. J. (2011). Examining the preconditions for psychological group membership: Perceived social interdependence as the outcome of self-categorization. *Social Psychological and Personality Science, 3*(1), 5–13.

Segrin, C., & Flora, J. (2011). *Family communication* (2nd ed.). New York: Routledge.

Sell, J., Lovaglia, M. J., Mannix, E. A., Samuelson, C. D., & Wilson, R. K. (2004). Investigating conflict, power, and status within and among groups. *Small Group Research, 35,* 44–72.

Settles, B. H., & Steinmetz, S. (2013). *Concepts and Definitions of Family for the 21st Century.* New York: Routledge

Stokes, P. (2008, November 26). Perfectionist school girl hanged herself while worried about appearance. *Telegraph.co.uk.* Retrieved from http://www.telegraph.co.uk/news/uknews/3525738/Perfectionist-schoolgirl-hanged-herself-while-worried-about-appearance.html

Timmerman, C. E., & Scott, C. R. (2006). Virtually working: Communicative and structural predictors of media use and key outcomes in virtual work teams. *Communication Monographs, 73,* 108–136.

Ting-Toomey, S., & Chung, L.C. (2012). *Understanding Intercultural Communication*, (2nd ed.). New York: Oxford University Press.

Tuckman, B. W. (1965). Developmental sequence in small groups. *Psychological Bulletin, 6393*, 384–399.

Walther, J. B. (2013). Groups and computer-mediation. In Amichai-Hamburger, Y. (Ed.), *The social net* (2nd ed., pp. 165–179). Oxford, England: Oxford University Press

Wang, Z., Walther, J. B., & Hancock, J. T. (2009). Social identification and interpersonal communication in computer mediated communication: What you do versus who you are in virtual groups. *Human Communication Research, 35*(1), 59–85.

"What Is the It Gets Better Project?" Retrieved from http://www.itgetsbetter.org/pages/about-it-gets-better-project/

White, A. (2009). *From comfort zone to performance management.* Baisy-Thy, Belgium: White and MacLean.

Wilmot, W. W., & Hocker, J. L. (2007). *Interpersonal conflict.* New York: McGraw-Hill.

CHAPTER 10

Bailey, S. (2013, August 8). Just say no: How your meeting habit is harming you. *Forbes.* Retrieved on December 28, 2014 at: http://www.forbes.com/sites/sebastianbailey/2013/08/08/just-say-no-how-your-meeting-habit-is-harming-you/

de Wit, F. R. C., Greer, L. L., & Jehn, K. A. (2012). The paradox of intragroup conflict: A meta-analysis. *Journal of Applied Psychology, 97*(2), 360–390.

Drummond, D. (2004). *Miracle meetings* [e-book]. Retrieved from http://www.superteams.com.

Duch, B. J., Groh, S. E., & Allen, D. E. (Eds.). (2001). *The power of problem-based learning.* Sterling, VA: Stylus.

Ebeling, R. (2008, March 6). So long, Dungeon Master. *Newsweek.* Retrieved from http://www.newsweek.com/id/119782

Fairhurst, G. T. (2011). *The power of framing: Creating the language of leadership.* San Francisco, CA: John Wiley & Sons.

Frey, L., & Sunwulf. (2005). The communication perspective on group life. In S. A. Wheelen (Ed.)., *The handbook of group research and practice* (pp. 159–186). Thousand Oaks, CA: Sage.

Gardner, H. (2011). *Leading minds: An anatomy of leadership.* Basic Books.

Huling, R. (2008, May 27). "Dungeons & Dragons" owns the future. *The Escapist.* Retrieved from http://www.escapistmagazine.com/articles/view/issues/issue_151/4931-Dungeons-Dragons-Owns-the-Future.2

Jackson, S. E., & Joshi, A. (2011). Work team diversity. In S. Zedeck (Ed.). *APA handvook of industrial and organizational psychology, Vol. 1: Building and developing the organization.* (pp. 681–686). Washington, DC: American Psychological Association.

Kippenberger, T. (2002). *Leadership styles.* New York: John Wiley and Sons.

Levi, D. (2014). *Group dynamics for teams* (4th ed.). Thousand Oaks, CA: Sage.

Levin, B. B. (Ed.). (2001). *Energizing teacher education and professional development with problem-based learning.* Alexandria, MN: Association for Supervision and Curriculum Development.

"MIT's Education Arcade uses online gaming to teach science." (2012, Jan 17). [Press release]. Retrieved from http://education.mit.edu/blogs/louisa/2012/pressrelease

Newman, H. (2007). "World of Warcraft" players: Let's slay together. *Detroit Free Press.* Retrieved from InfoTrac.

Northouse, P. G. (2013). *Leadership: Theory and practice* (6th ed.). Thousand Oaks, CA: Sage.

Schiesel, S. (2008, March 5). Gary Gygax, game pioneer, dies at 69. *The New York Times.* Retrieved from http://www.nytimes.com/2008/03/05/arts/05gygax.html

Seely Brown, J., & Hagel, J. (2009). How "World of Warcraft" promotes innovation. *Business Week Online.* Retrieved from Infotrac.

Sultanoff, S. (1993). Tickling our funny bone: Humor matters in health. *International Journal of Humor Research, 6*, 89–104.

Teams that succeed (2004). *Harvard Business Review.* Boston: Harvard Business School Press.

Weiten, W., Dunn, D. S., & Hammer, E. Y. (2011). *Psychology applied to modern life: Adjustment in the 21st century.* Boston: Cengage.

Williams, C. (2013). *Management* (7th ed.). Mason, OH: South-Western/Cengage Learning.

Williams, J. P., Hendricks, S. Q., & Winkler, W. K. (Eds.). (2006). *Gaming as culture: Essays on reality, identity and experience in fantasy games.* Jefferson, NC: McFarland.

Young, K. S., Wood, J. T., Phillips, G. M., & Pedersen, D. J. (2007). *Group discussion: A practical guide to participation and leadership* (4th ed.). Long Grove, IL: Waveland Press.

CHAPTER 11

Berger, C. R., & Calabrese, R. J. (1975). Some exploration in initial interaction and beyond: Toward a developmental theory of communication. *Human Communication Research, 1,* 99–112.

Bitzer, L. F. (1995). The rhetorical situation. In W. A. Covino and D. A. Joliffe (Eds)., *Rhetoric: Concepts definitions boundaries.* Boston: Allyn & Bacon.

Bitzer, L. F. (1968). The rhetorical situation. *Philosophy and Rhetoric, 1*(1) 1–14.

Cohen N. (2009, August 24). Wikipedia to limit changes to articles on people. *The New York Times.* Retrieved from http://www.nytimes.com/2009/08/25/technology/internet/25wikipedia.html?_r=1

Cohen, N. (2011, May 23) Wikipedia. *The New York Times.* Retrieved from http://topics.nytimes.com/top/news/business/companies/wikipedia/index.html

Crovitz, D., & Smoot, W. S. (2009, January). Wikipedia: Friend, not foe. *English Journal, 98*(3), 91–97. Retrieved from http://www.nytimes.com/learning/teachers/archival/EnglishJournalArticle2.pdf

Durst, G. M. (1989, March 1). The manager as a developer. *Vital Speeches of the Day* (pp. 309–314).

Exigence. (2009). In *Microsoft Encarta world English dictionary.* Retrieved from:http://encarta.msn.com/dictionary_1861609760/exigency.html

Gallagher, M. P. (2009, April 27). Wikipedia held too malleable to be reliable as evidence. *New Jersey Law Journal.* n.p. Retrieved from Infotrac.

Gregoire, S. W. (2009, December 8). Considering cultural differences when speaking. *Becoming a Christian women's speaker: With author and speaker Sheila Wray Gregoire.* Retrieved from http://christianwomensspeaker.wordpress.com/2009/12/08/considering-cultural-differences-when-speaking/

Helm, B. (2005, December 14). Wikipedia: "A work in progress." *Business Week.* Retrieved from http://www.businessweek.com/technology/content/dec2005/tc20051214_441708.htm?chan=db

Jaschik, S (2007, January 26). A stand against Wikipedia. *Inside Higher Ed.* Retrieved from http://www.insidehighered.com/news/2007/01/26/wiki

Kirkpatrick, M. (2011, November 2). Wikipedia is a mess, wikipedians say: 1 in 20 articles bare of references. *ReadWiteWeb.* Retrieved from http://www.readwriteweb.com/archives/wikipedia_is_a_mess_wikipedians_say_1_in_20_articl.php

Knobloch, L. K., & McAninch, K. G. (2014). 13 Uncertainty management. In C. A. Berger (Ed.). *Interpersonal Communication,* (pp. 297–319). Boston: Walter de Gruyter.

Manguard, S. (2011, October 31). The monster under the rug. *The Signpost.* Retrieved from http://en.wikipedia.org/wiki/Wikipedia:Wikipedia_Signpost/2011-10-31/Opinion_essay

Mesgari, M., Okoli, C., Mehdi, M., Nielsen, F. Å., & Lanamäki, A. (2015). "The sum of all human knowledge": A systematic review of scholarly research on the content of Wikipedia. *Journal of the American Society for Information Science and Technology 66*(2), 219–245.

Moon, B., Hoffman, R. R., Novak, J., & Canas, A. (2011). *Applied concept mapping: Capturing, analyzing, and organizing knowledge.* London, England: CRC Press.

Nelson J. C. (2006). *Leadership.* Utah School Boards Association 83rd Annual Conference, Salt Lake City, Utah. Retrieved from http://www.ama-assn.org/ama/pub/category/15860.html

Seigenthaler J. (2005, November 29). A false Wikipedia "biography." *USA Today.* Retrieved from http://www.usatoday.com/news/opinion/editorials/2005-11-29-wikipedia-edit_x.htm

Wikimedia Foundation (2015). *Report Card.* Retrieved on January 18, 2015 at: http://en.wikipedia.org/wiki/Wikipedia:About

CHAPTER 12

Aristotle. (1954). *Rhetoric* (W. Rhys Roberts, Trans.). New York: Modern Library.

Calloway, N. (n.d.) Tips for the Best Man on writing a wedding toast. *About.com Weddings.* Retrieved from http://weddings.about.com/od/theweddingparty/a/toastwriting.htm

Cossolotto, M. (2009, December). An urgent call to action for study abroad alumni to help reduce our global awareness deficit. *Vital Speeches,* pp. 564–568.

Fisher, W. (1987). *Human communication as narration: Toward a philosophy of reason, value, and action.* Columbia, SC: University of South Carolina Press.

Gupta, Y. (February 2010). Beyond wisdom: Business dimensions of an aging America. *Vital Speeches,* pp. 69–75.

Humes, J. C. (1988). *Standing ovation: How to be an effective speaker and communicator.* New York: Harper and Row.

Jobs, S. (2005, June 15). You've got to find what you love. *Stanford University News.* Retrieved from http://news.stanford.edu/news/2005/june15/jobs-061505.html

Mackay, H. (July 2009). Changing the world: Your future is a work in progress. *Vital Speeches of the Day,* pp. 319–323.

Mariano, C. (January 2010). Unity, quality, responsibility: The real meaning of the words. *Vital Speeches of the Day,* pp. 20–22.

Marshall, L. B., & Armstrong, T. (2010, July 16). How to make a wedding toast. *The Public Speaker: Quick and Dirty Tips.* Retrieved from http://publicspeaker.quickanddirtytips.com/Making-Wedding-Toast.aspx

Mason, S. (2007, April). Equality will someday come. *Vital Speeches of the Day,* pp. 159–163.

Osteen, J. (2012). Best jokes of Joel Osteen. *Better Days TV.* Retrieved on April 6, 2012 from http://www.betterdaystv.net/play.php?vid=247

Patterson, T. (2010, June 20). How to give a wedding toast. *Slate.* Retrieved from http://www.slate.com/articles/news_and_politics/weddings/2011/06/how_to_give_a_wedding_toast.html

Post, A. (2010). Vermont vows: The toast!. *Emily Post Etipedia.* Retrieved from http://www.emilypost.com/weddings/your-day/719-toasts

CHAPTER 13

Ayers, J. (1991). Using visual aids to reduce speech anxiety. *Communication Research Reports,* 73–79.

Booher, D. D. (2003). *Speak with confidence [electronic resources]: Powerful presentations that inform, inspire, and persuade.* New York, NY: McGraw-Hill.

Brandt, J. R. (2007, January). Missing the (Power)point: When bullet points fly, attention spans die. *Industry Week.* Retrieved from http://www.industryweek.com

Campbell, S. (2015). Presentation anxiety analysis: Comparing face-to-face presentations and webinars. *Journal of Case Studies in Education, 7,* 1-13.

"Digital Media Assignments: Ignite Presentations for the Information Society (Comm-B course)" (n.d.). Retrieved from http://engage.wisc.edu/dma/awards/downey/index.html

Forrest, B. (2009). Speaker confessions. True tales from a veteran public speaker. O"Reilly Media, Inc. Retrieved from http://www.speakerconfessions.com/press/

Garcia-Retamero, R., & Cokely, E. T. (2013). Communiciating health risks with visual aids. *Current Directions in Psychological Science, 22*(5), 392-399. DOI: 10.1177/0963721413491570

Guzman, M. (2009, April 16). A Seattle geek fest spreads its wings. *Seattle PI.* Retrieved from http://www.seattlepi.com/business/405192_IGNITE16.html

Ignite Seattle. (n.d.). Retrieved from http://www.igniteseattle.com/

Ignite Seattle 7 is happening on 8/3. (2009). *Ignite.* Retrieved from http://ignite.oreilly.com/2009/07/ignite-seattle-7-is-happening-on-83.html

Kolb, D. (1984). *Experiential learning: Experience as the source of learning and development.* Englewood Cliffs, NJ: Prentice Hall; Gallo, C. (2006, December 5). Presentations with something for everyone. *Business Week Online.* Retrieved from http://www.businessweek.com/smallbiz/content/dec2006/sb20061205_454055.htm

Krauss, J. (2012). Infographics: More than words can say. *Learning and Leading with Technology, 39*(5), 10–14.

Muren, D. (2009). *Humblefacturing a sustainable electronic future.* Presentation at Ignite Seattle 6. Retrieved from http://www.youtube.com/watch?v=FIoU1pemi18

Neznanski, M. (2008, November 14). Sharing ideas quickly. *Gazette Times.* Retrieved from http://www.gazettetimes.com/articles/2008/11/14/news/community/3loc01_tech.txt

Payne, N. (n.d.). Public relations across cultures: Building international communication bridges. *All About Public Relations with Steven R. Van Hook.* Retrieved from http://www.aboutpublicrelations.net/ucpayne.htm

Rogers, L. (2013). *Visual supports for visual thinkers: Practical ideas for students with autism spectrum disorders and other special education needs.* London: Jessica Kingsley Publishers.

"Tips—Special instructions for presenters" (n.d.) Retrieved from http://ignitephoenix.com/tips/

Weill, J. (2006, December 18). All presentations should be five minutes long. *Jason Weill Web Productions.* Retrieved from http://weill.org/2006/12/08/all-presentations-should-be-five-minutes-long/

CHAPTER 14

DuFrene, D. D., & Lehman, C. M. (2002). Persuasive appeal for clean language. *Business Communication Quarterly, 65* (March), 48–56.

Hart, R., & Jamieson, K. H. (2012). Campaign mapping project. The Annette Strauss Institute for Civic Life at the University of Austin Texas. [Funding support from the Ford Foundation and Carnegie Foundation of New York]. Retrieved from http://communication.utexas.edu/strauss/campaign-mapping-project

Hensley, C. W. (1995, September 1). Speak with style and watch the impact. *Vital Speeches of the Day,* p. 703.

Leith, S. (2013, January 21). Barack Obama inauguration speech. A greatest hits of rhetorical tricks. *The Guardian.*

Retrieved from http://www.guardian.co.uk/world/2013/jan/21/barack-obama-speech-greatest-hits-rhetoric

Rader, W. (2007). The online slang dictionary. Retrieved from http://www.ocf.berkeley.edu/~wrader/slang/b.html

Richards, I. A., & Ogden, C. K. (1923). *The meaning of meaning: A study of the influence of language upon thought and the science of symbolism.* Orlando, FL: Harcourt.

Saeid, J.I. (2003). *Semantics* (2nd ed.). Malden, MA: Blackwell Publishing Ltd.

Stewart, L. P., Cooper, P. J., Stewart, A. D., & Friedley, S. A. (2002). *Communication and gender* (4th ed.). Boston: Allyn & Bacon.

Treinen, K. P., & Warren, J. T. (2001). Anti-Racist Pedagogy in the Basic Course: Teaching Cultural Communication as if Whiteness Matters. *Basic Communication Course Annual 13,* 46–75.

Weeks, L. (2009, February 11). The art of language, Obama style? National Public Radio. Retrieved from http://www.npr.org/templates/story/story.php?storyId=100525275

Witt, P., Wheeless, L., & Allen, M. (2004). A meta-analytical review of the relationship between teacher immediacy and student learning. *Communication Monographs, 71*(2), 184–207.

CHAPTER 15

Anderson, C. (2013). How to give a killer presentation. Harvard Business Review, 91(6), 121–125.

Beatty, M. J., & Behnke, R. R. (1991). Effects of public speaking trait anxiety and intensity of speaking task on heart rate during performance. *Human Communication Research, 18,* 147–176.

Cizillia, C. (2012, March 12). Republicans war on the TelePrompter—and its limits. *The Washington Post.* [Blog post] Retrieved from http://www.washingtonpost.com/blogs/the-fix/post/republicans-war-on-the-teleprompter--and-its-limits/2012/03/12/gIQAjuMV7R_blog.html

Corporation for National and Community Service. (2006). *College students helping America.* Washington, DC: Author

Decker, B. (1992). *You've got to be believed to be heard.* New York: St. Martin's Press.

Dilliplane, S. (2012). Race, rhetoric, and running for President: Unpacking the significance of Barack Obama's "A More Perfect Union" speech. *Rhetoric & Public Affairs, 15*(1), 127–152.

Dwyer, K. K. (2012). *iConquer speech anxiety: A workbook to help you overcome your nervousness about public speaking.* Omaha, NE: KLD Publications.

Fear of Public Speaking Statistics-Statistics Brain. (2013, November 23). 2014 Statistic Brain Research Institute, publishing as Statistics Brain. Retrieved from http://statisticbrain.com/fear-of-public-speaking-statistics/

French, B. (n.d.). Language barriers. *Public Speaking International.* Retrieved from http://www.publicspeakinginternational.com/funny-stories/

Gardner, W. L. (2003). Perceptions of leader charisma, effectiveness, and integrity: Effects of exemplification, delivery, and ethical reputation. *Management Communication Quarterly, 16*(4), 502–527.

Grant, A. (2012). Giving time, time after time: Work design and sustained employee participation in corporate volunteering. *Academy of Management Review,* amr-2010.

Haberman, M. (2010, August 16). Chris Christie warns GOP on mosque. *Politico* [Blog post]. Retrieved from http://www.politico.com/news/stories/0810/41141.html#ixzz1pHr4SS14

Hammer, D. P. (2000). Professional attitudes and behaviors: The "As" and "Bs" of professionalism. *American Journal of Pharmaceutical Education, 64,* 455–464.

Howlett, N., Pine, K. J., Cahill, N., Orakçıoğlu, İ., & Fletcher, B. C. (2015). Unbuttoned: The Interaction Between Provocativeness of Female Work Attire and Occupational Status. *Sex Roles, 72*(3–4), 105–116.

Frenkel, D. (2011, November 16). Public speaking 101: A lesson in leadership from Barack Obama. *The Drum* [Blog post]. Retrieved from http://www.abc.net.au/unleashed/3674660.html

Kelly, L., Duran, R. L., & Stewart, J. (1990). Rhetoritherapy revisited: A test of its effectiveness as a treatment for communication problems. *Communication Education, 39,* 207–226.

Kelly, L., Phillips, G. M., & Keaten, J. A. (1995). *Teaching people to speak well: Training and remediation of communication reticence.* Cresskill, NJ: Hampton.

Levine, T., Asada, K. J. K., & Park, H. S. (2006). The lying chicken and the gaze avoidant egg: Eye contact, deception, and causal order. *Southern Communication Journal, 71,* 401–411.

Mandell, N. (2012, March 9). New Jersey Governor Chris Christie calls Navy veteran an "idiot." *New York Daily News.* Retrieved from http://articles.nydailynews.com/2012-03-09/news/31141625_1_chris-christie-town-hall-meeting-law-school

Morgan, N. (2013, December 5). How to avoid disaster: Six rules for what to wear when giving a speech. *Forbes.* Retrieved from http://www.forbes.com/sites/nickmorgan/2013/12/05/how-to-avoid-disaster-six-rules-for-what-to-wear-when-giving-a-speech/

Motley, M. (1997). COM therapy. In J. A. Daly, J. C. McCroskey, J. Ayres, T. Hopf, & D. M. Ayres (Eds.) *Avoiding communication: Shyness reticence, and communication apprehension* (2nd ed.). Cresskill, NJ: Hampton Press.

Norris Center (2013, January 2). Center for student involvement: Volunteer opportunities. Northwestern University. Retrieved from http://norris.northwestern.edu/csi /community/volunteer-opportunities/

Phillips, G. M. (1977). Rhetoritherapy versus the medical model: Dealing with reticence. *Communication Education, 26*, 34–43.

Pryor, J. H., Hurtado, S., DeAngelo, L., Sharkness, J., Romero, L., Korn, W. S., & Tran, S. (2009). *The American freshman: National norms for fall 2008.* Los Angeles, CA: Higher Education Research Institute.

Richmond, V. P., & McCroskey, J. C. (2000). *Communication: Apprehension, avoidance, and effectiveness* (5th ed.). Scottsdale, AZ: Gorsuch Scarisbrick.

Rucker, P. (October 20, 2011). Republicans mock Obama's teleprompters. *The Washington Post.* Retrieved from http:// www.thehawkeye.com/story/WPBLOOM-101811--bc -teleprompter

Scott, P. (1997, January–February). Mind of a champion. *Natural Health, 27*, 99.

Sellnow , D. D., & Treinen, K. P. (2004). The role of gender in perceived speaker competence: An analysis of student peer critiques. *Communication Education, 53*(3), 286–296.

Shear, M. D. (2011, September 30). Imagining a Christie campaign for president. *The New York Times.* Retrieved from http://www.nytimes.com/2011/10/01/us/politics/imagining -a-christie-campaign-for-president.html?pagewanted=all

Spera, C., Ghertner, R., Nerion, A., & DiTommaso, A. (2013). *Volunteering as a pathway to employment: Does volunteering increase odds of finding a job for the out of work?* Washington, DC: Corporation for National and Community Service.

Tomlinson, M. (2008). The degree is not enough: Students' perceptions of the role of higher education for graduate work and employability. *British Journal of Sociology of Education, 29*(1), 49–61. DOI: 10.1080/01425690701737457

Towler, A. J. (2003). Effects of charismatic influence training on attitudes, behavior, and performance. *Personnel Psychology, 56*, 363–381.

United States Bureau of Labor Statistics. (2015, February 25). Economic News Release: Volunteering in the United States, 2014. Retrieved from http://www.bls.gov/news .release/volun.nr0.htm

CHAPTER 16

Baerwald, D. (n.d.). Narrative. Retrieved from Northshore School District Web site: http://ccweb.norshore.wednet .edu/writingcorner/narrative.html.

Dacquino, V. T. (2000). *Sybil Ludington: The call to arms (New Yorkers and the Revolution.* Fleischmanns, NY: Purple Mountain Press.

Federal Trade Commission. (2007). *FTC releases survey of identity theft in the U.S. study shows 8.3 million victims in 2005.* Retrieved from http://www.ftc.gov/opa/2007/11 /idtheft.shtm

Federal Trade Commission. (2012). *Identity theft.* Retrieved from http://www.consumer.ftc.gov/features/feature-0014 -identity-theft

Goldberg, B. (2011, March 14). No liberal bias at NPR— just ask NPR. [Blog post] Retrieved from http://www .bernardgoldberg.com/no-liberal-bias-at-npr-just-ask-npr/

Hinckley, D. (2009, July 18). Walter Cronkite remains gold standard for journalists. *NYDailyNews.com.* Retrieved from http://www.nydailynews.com/entertainment/tv /2009/07/18/2009-07-18_he_remains_the_gold _standard_among_all.html

How to detect bias in news media. (n.d.) Retrieved from FAIR (Fairness and Accuracy in Reporting) Web site: http://www.fair.org/index.php?page=121

Howell, D. (2008, August 17). Obama's edge in the coverage race. *Washington Post.* Retrieved from http://www .washingtonpost.com/wp-dyn/content/article/2008/08 /15/AR2008081503100.html?sub=AR

Koster, C. (n.d.) Identity theft. Retrieved from the Missouri Attorney General Web site: http://ago.mo.gov/publications /idtheft.htm#header3

Leopold, T. (2009, July 18). Former CBS anchor '"Uncle Walter" Cronkite dead at 92. *CNN.com.* Retrieved from http://www.cnn.com/2009/US/07/17/walter.cronkite .dead/index.html

Moyers, B., & Winship M. (2011, March 25). What the right means when it calls NPR "liberal." *Salon.* Retrieved from http://www.salon.com/2011/03/25/moyers_winship_npr/

National Crime Prevention Council. (2013). *Evolving with technology: A comprehensive introduction to cybercrime with links to resources.* Retrieved from http://www.ncpc.org /topics/fraud-and-identity-theft/evolving-with-technology

Perlroth, N. (2011, December 19). A unit to fight cyber-crimes. *The New York Times.* Retrieved from http:// query.nytimes.com/

Pew Research Center for the People & the Press. (2014, October 20). *Striking differences between liberals and conservatives, but they also share common ground.* Retrieved on January 12, 2015 at: http://www.journalism.org/2014/10/21/political-polarization-media-habits/10-20-2014-2-31-55-pm/

Pew Research Center for the People & The Press. (2011, September 22*). Press widely criticized, but trusted more than other information sources.* [Press Release] Retrieved from http://www.people-press.org/2011/09/22/press-widely-criticized-but-trusted-more-than-other-institutions/

Ötzi, the ice man. (n.d.). *Dig: The archaeology magazine for kids.* Retrieved from http://www.digonsite.com/drdig/mummy/22.html

U.S. Department of Justice. (n.d.). *Identity theft and fraud.* Retrieved from http://www.justice.gov/criminal/fraud/websites/idtheft.html

What's wrong with the news? (n.d.). Retrieved from FAIR (Fairness and Accuracy in the News) Web site: http://www.fair.org/index.php?page=101

White, J. R. (2012). *Identity theft: Total extent of refund fraud using stolen identities is unknown* (GAO Publication No. GAO-13-132T). Washington, DC: U.S. Government Accountability Office. Retrieved from http://www.gao.gov/assets/660/650365.pdf

CHAPTER 17

Billy Mays, the infomercial king; Death of a great American salesman; Want to know the secret of America's innovation edge? Call now! (2009, July 1). *Global Agenda.* Retrieved from InfoTrac College Edition.

Bullying. (2015). National Crime Prevention Council. Retrieved from: http://www.ncpc.org/resources/files/pdf/bullying

Camia, C. (2011, October 31). Rick Perry's speech video goes viral. *USA Today.* Retrieved from http://content.usatoday.com/communities/onpolitics/post/2011/10/rick-perry-viral-video-new-hampshire-/1#.T7jPKY57ipI

Carter, B. (2008, October 31). Infomercial for Obama is big success in ratings. *The New York Times, 158*(54480), A19. Retrieved from InfoTrac College Edition.

Crain, R. (2009, May 4). Deceitful financial infomercial tars entire advertising industry. *Advertising Age, 80*(16), 17. Retrieved from InfoTrac College Edition.

Cummings, J. (2008, October 29). Obama infomercial: Smart or overkill? *Politico.* Retrieved from http://www.politico.com/news/stories/1008/15056_Page2.html

Cyber-Bullying Statistics. (2012). Retrieved from http:/www.statisticbrain.com/cyber-bullying-statistics/

Kennedy, G. A. (1999). *Classical rhetoric and its Christian and secular tradition from ancient to modern times* (2nd ed). Chapel Hill, NC: University of North Carolina Press.

Mastamokei. (2008, April 30). Billy Mays gangsta remix [Video file]. Retrieved from www.youtube.com/watch?v=_tyct9l-fD8

Megan's Law. (n.d.). *Parents for Megan's Law.* Retrieved from http://www.parentsformmeganslaw.com/html/questions.lasso.

Nabi, R. L. (2002). Discrete emotions and persuasion. In James P. Dillard and Michael Pfau (Eds.), *The persuasion handbook: Developments in theory and practice* (pp. 291–299). Thousand Oaks, CA: Sage.

Obama, B. (n.d.). Your weekly address. *The White House.* Retrieved from http://www.whitehouse.gov/briefing-room/weekly-address/

Presentation Revolution. Retrieved from http://info.sliderocket.com/rs/sliderocket/images/Death-By-PowerPoint-Infographic.jpg

Perloff, R. M. (2010). *The dynamics of persuasion: Communication and attitudes in the 21st century* (4th ed.). New York: Taylor & Francis.

Petri, H. L., & Govern, J. M. (2012). *Motivation: Theory, research, and application* (6th ed.). Belmont, CA: Wadsworth.

Petty, R. E., & Cacioppo, J. (1996). *Attitudes and persuasion: Classic and contemporary approaches.* Boulder, CO: Westview.

Schneider, M. (2008, November 23). Longform ads replace kids fare on Fox. *Variety.* Retrieved from http://www.variety.com/article/VR1117996360?refCatId=14

Sellnow, D., & Treinen, K. (2004). The role of gender and physical attractiveness in perceived speaker competence: An analysis of student peer critiques. *Communication Education, 53*(3) 286–296.

Solmsen, F. (Ed). (1954). *The rhetoric and the poetics of Aristotle.* New York: The Modern Library.

Timothy D. Naegele & Associates announces class action lawsuit against Guthy-Renker. (2002, June 26). *All Business.* Retrieved from http://www.allbusiness.com/crime-law/criminal-offenses-cybercrime/5968871-1.html

Toulmin, S. (1958). *The uses of argument.* Cambridge, England: Cambridge University Press.

Van Eemeren, F. H., Garssen, B., Krabbe, E. C. W., Henkemans, A. F. S., Verheij, B., & Wagemans, J. H. M. (2014). *Handbook of argumentation theory.* New York: Springer.

APPENDIX

Beshara, T. (2006). *The Job Search Solution*. New York: AMACOM.

Betty, K. (2010, July 1). *The math behind the networking claim*. Retrieved from http://blog.jobfully.com/2010/07/the-math-behind-the-networking-claim/

Boyd, A. (1999). *How to handle media interviews*. London: Mercury.

Employee Tenure in 2010. (2012, September 14). *Bureau of labor statistics economic news release*. U.S. Department of Labor: Washington, DC. Retrieved from http://www.bls.gov/news.release/tenure.nr0.htm

Farr, J. M. (2009). *Top 100 careers without a four-year degree: Your complete guidebook to major jobs in many fields*. Indianapolis, IN: JIST.

Graber, S. (2000). *The everything get-a-job book: From resume writing to interviewing to finding tons of job openings*. Avon, MA: Adams Media.

Hansen, K. (n.d.). Your e-résumé's file format aligns with its delivery method. *Quintessential Careers.com*. Retrieved from http://www.quintcareers.com/e-resume_format.html

Kaplan, R. M. (2002). *How to say it in your job search: Choice words, phrases, sentences and paragraphs for résumés, cover letters and interviews*. Paramus, NJ: Prentice Hall.

Krotz, J. (2006). *6 tips for taking control in media interviews*. Retrieved from http://www.microsoft.com/smallbusiness/resources/management/leadership-training/6-tips-for-taking-control-in-media-interviews.aspx#tipsfortakingcontrolinmediainterviews

Light, J. (2011, April, 4). For job seekers, company sites beat online job boards, social media. *Wall Street Journal*. Retrieved from http://online.wsj.com/article/SB10001424052748703806304576236731318345282.html?KEYWORDS=JOE+LIGH

Ryan, R. (2000). *60 seconds & you're hired*. New York: Penguin Books.

Slayter, M. E. (2006, January 14). Rehearse, rehearse, repeat: Have a rock-solid plan when preparing for an interview. *The Forum*, p. E3.

Taylor, J., & Hardy D. (2004). *Monster careers: How to land the job of your life*. New York: Penguin Books.

Tengler, C. D., & Jablin, F. M. (1983). Effects of question type, orientation, and sequencing in the employment screening interview. *Communication Monographs, 50*, 261.

Yena, D. J. (2011). *Career directions: The path to your ideal career*. New York: McGraw-Hill.

Index

Page numbers in italics indicate figures